The Philosophy of Money

The Philosophy of Money

Georg Simmel

Translated by
Tom Bottomore and David Frisby

Routledge & Kegan Paul
London, Henley and Boston

First published in 1978
by Routledge & Kegan Paul Ltd
39 Store Street,
London WC1E 7DD,
Broadway House,
Newtown Road,
Henley-on-Thames,
Oxon RG9 1EN and
9 Park Street,
Boston, Mass. 02108, USA
Set in 10 on 12pt Ehrhardt by
HBM Typesetting Ltd,
Chorley, Lancs
and printed in Great Britain by
Lowe & Brydone Ltd
Translation © Routledge & Kegan Paul 1978

British Library Cataloguing in Publication Data

Simmel, Georg
Philosophy of Money.
1. Money
I. Title
332.4'01   HG221   77-30759

ISBN 0 7100 8874 4

Contents

Contents

Contents

Acknowledgments

The first two chapters and part of the third chapter were translated by Tom Bottomore and the remainder by David Frisby. I would like to thank Glyn Adey for supplying me with a draft translation of some sections of the present volume. Our greatest debt must be to the late Kaethe Mengelberg who originally provided a draft of the whole volume. Without the assistance of this earlier work, it is doubtful whether the present translation could have been completed. This translation is therefore dedicated to her memory.

I would also like to thank Pru Larsen for the onerous task of typing the manuscript in its final version. I am grateful to the Leverhulme Trust for awarding me a Faculty Fellowship in European Studies which enabled me to undertake the research for the introduction to this translation at the University of Konstanz, and to Professor Horst Baier for his assistance in its preparation.

David Frisby
Glasgow

Note on the Translation

The translation contained in this volume is of the second, enlarged edition of *Philosophie des Geldes*, published in Berlin in 1907, and is identical to later editions (3rd ed. 1920; 4th ed. 1922; 5th ed. 1930; 6th ed. 1958). The first edition of the work appeared in 1900 and was somewhat shorter (pp. xvi+554). As Simmel explains in the preface to the second edition, the substance of the work was not substantially altered and in fact the major additions occur in the early chapters on value.

The German original appears without sub-headings in the text and without an index. Since almost no writers are cited in the text, and since Simmel provided an annotated table of contents, it was decided to insert these annotations, wherever possible, into the body of the text both in order to break down the somewhat monolithic nature of Simmel's prose and to act as a substitute for an index. Occasionally, too, Simmel's paragraphs have been broken down into smaller units.

D.F.

Introduction to the Translation

'She's got an indiscreet voice', I remarked.
'It's full of –' I hesitated.
'Her voice is full of money', he said suddenly.
That was it. I'd never understood before.
It was full of money – that was the
inexhaustible charm that rose and fell in it,
the jingle of it, the cymbals' song of it.
                    F. Scott Fitzgerald, *The Great Gatsby*

I

Gustav Schmoller, probably the most important of the younger members of the Historical School of political economy in Germany, relates that 'on the 20th May 1889, Dr. Simmel delivered a paper on the "Psychology of Money" in my political science seminar. . . . It was the germ of the important book which now appears before us as *The Philosophy of Money*.'[1] This paper was subsequently published in the same year in Schmoller's *Jahrbuch*[2] and was followed by a series of articles between 1896 and 1899 which formed sketches for parts of *The Philosophy of Money* when the whole work was published in 1900.[3] In this original essay on the psychology of money, Simmel already raised in a very schematic manner many of the issues that were subsequently to preoccupy him in his more detailed work later: money's relationship to the ends–means dichotomy; its effect upon the teleological sequences of human purposive action; its colourless and seemingly neutral character; and the problems of establishing a satisfactory theory of value. Here, too, Simmel already briefly referred to some of the examples of the workings of money, such as its relationship to the blasé attitude and to the sale of women. In the intervening eleven years between the appearance of Simmel's first article in this area in 1889 and the publication of the first edition of the present work in 1900, the 'psychology' of money was transformed into the 'philosophy' of money. His more common essay style gained an architectonic structure in *The Philosophy of Money* which few of his later works possessed. Simmel's views on the relationship between money and the division of labour had taken on a more substantive focus with the publication of his own work in this area, *Über sociale Differenzierung*, in 1890.[4] His philosophical concerns had been deepened both by his work on the philosophy of history – *Die Probleme der Geschichtsphilosophie* – in 1892[5] and on moral philosophy with his *Einleitung in die Moralphilosophie*, published in two volumes in 1892 and 1893.[6] Yet though the psychological dimensions of Simmel's interest in money did not completely disappear and though his philosophical interests were broadening and coming increasingly to the fore, there was another dimension of his thought that was clearly apparent to his contemporaries when they read *The Philosophy of Money*. It is indeed in this intervening period that most of the essays that make up his *Soziologie* were published in article form.[7] When Max Weber commenced a critical review of Simmel's sociological work – probably in 1908 – which he never completed, he concerned himself not merely with his *Soziologie*, published in 1908, but also with *The Philosophy of Money*.[8] Weber sought to review Simmel's work as a 'sociologist and theorist of the money economy'. Weber subsequently acknowledged some of his debt to Simmel in his published work, though most often this acknowledgment was tempered by severe criticism. Yet like many of Simmel's contemporaries, Weber clearly found it difficult to locate Simmel's work within some readily recognized discipline and tradition.

One contemporary, writing a long obituary review of Simmel's works, argues that *The Philosophy of Money* is a transitional work in the sequence of Simmel's writings from a concern to establish an empirical sociology to the attempt to establish a philosophy of culture and ultimately, in his last works, a metaphysics of life.[9] Frischeisen-Köhler argues that:[10]

> the aim of the young thinker was certainly not to establish and develop a philosophical standpoint as such. . . . In his youth he strove towards a sociology whose distinguishing feature he saw not so much in the uncovering of a new reality as in the development of a method which would permit a new total view of the historical–social world.

Yet this goal was not the only one present in *The Philosophy of Money*. Though it did concern itself with psychological and sociological dimensions of the emergence and development of the money economy:[11]

> its ultimate aim lay yet further beyond them; it was, as Simmel himself formulated it, to extract from the surface of economic events a way into the ultimate values and importance of all that is human. An economic element, such as money, should . . . reveal itself as a timelessly valid symbol of the essential forms of motion themselves.

In this important respect, then, Simmel's *Philosophy of Money* not only embraces a sociological concern for the effects of a money economy upon social and cultural life but also reveals Simmel's attempt to establish a philosophy of culture and, ultimately, a metaphysics of life.

It is perhaps this diversity of intentions in Simmel's work that made it difficult for his contemporaries to gain an overall view of *The Philosophy of*

Money and this may have contributed to the relative neglect of this work compared with Simmel's other studies. Karl Joël expressed this difficulty when he suggested that Simmel's *Philosophy of Money* 'will be ill understood because money meant more to him than money, because it became for him a symbol of the world, an image of exchange as a whole, of the infinite interrelationship which ultimately extended itself into the dominant principle of a world view'.[12] This diversity of intention also accounts for the hostility that Simmel's work excited among some of his contemporaries, since it could not easily be compartmentalized into existing academic disciplines. Max Weber saw this as one of the major reasons why Simmel's work had not received the full academic recognition that it justly deserved and he argued that:[13]

> there exists not only a great number of specialists in *philosophy* who clearly abhor him – the typical sectarian character of the philosophical 'schools' of the time, to *none* of which Simmel belongs, makes this only too intelligible (quite apart from other motives that may be involved) – but there are also scholars who are to be taken very seriously in disciplines that border on Simmel's sociological field of work who are inclined . . . to acknowledge Simmel's scholarship on certain details but to reject his work as a whole. Among economists, for example, one can experience outright explosions of rage over him . . . and from that same circle of specialists has come the statement that Simmel's art is ultimately a matter of 'dividing the air and then uniting it again'.

This account of the lack of full academic recognition of Simmel's work – the year after the publication of *The Philosophy of Money*, Simmel was awarded the title of *Ausserordentlicher Professor* at the University of Berlin, but this honorary title excluded him from participation in academic affairs – must be supplemented with the pervasive anti-Semitism in German academic life in this period. Max Weber, for example, attempted several times to secure a professorial chair for Simmel but was confronted each time with hostility not only from state authorities but also from eminent academics whose ultimate reason for rejecting Simmel may well have been the anti-Semitism that prevailed at the time.[14] Baumgarten argues that in later years it was certain that 'Weber had never forgiven Dilthey, Rickert and Windelband for concertedly blocking the call to a full professorship for Georg Simmel – who in his eyes was the most significant of contemporary German philosophers – because he was a Jew.'[15] At the time of the publication of *The Philosophy of Money* after fifteen years at Berlin University and with many other works to his credit, Simmel was merely a *Privatdozent* which meant, in this period, that he was an unpaid lecturer who relied upon students' fees as remuneration. Only in 1914 did Simmel receive an academic chair at Strasbourg University where he remained until his death in 1918. In this double sense, then, Simmel remained, as Coser puts it, a 'stranger in the academy'.

Yet if we survey the contemporary response to *The Philosophy of Money* by those writers who made a genuine attempt to understand the importance of Simmel's work and who were not so hide-bound by the restrictiveness of a purely academic standpoint then it is apparent that many saw it as a work of major significance. It is all the more surprising then that this work, with a few exceptions, failed to make a lasting impact upon a whole range of writers, disciplines and interests in Germany. Elsewhere, since the whole work was almost never translated, its impact was even less. It is probably true to say that Simmel founded no school or group of followers in Germany, though Litt, Vierkandt and von Wiese, in particular, were clearly influenced by his work.[16] In the spirit of *The Philosophy of Money*, Simmel himself saw that his own position was a marginal one:[17]

> I know that I shall die without spiritual heirs (and this is good). The estate I leave is like cash distributed among many heirs, each of whom puts his share to use in some trade that is compatible with *his* nature but which can no longer be recognized as coming from that estate.

Such a view is a remarkably accurate judgment, for example, of many of those theorists of conflict and exchange who claim to have drawn upon Simmel's work but whose own work is, perhaps necessarily, very much distanced from Simmel's original contribution.[18] A more faithful overview of Simmel's impact may therefore be derived, at least at the outset, not from latter-day judgments of sociologists and others remote from Simmel's concerns but from his contemporaries. A genuine understanding of any work does not derive from treating that work like a vast rubbish heap of latent hypotheses which may be instrumentally extracted from their context and incorporated into the service of contemporary interests, but from an immanent understanding of a work and its own context. The constant quarrying into Simmel's works for illuminating insights that can be operationalized in an empirical setting may certainly advance the boundaries of empirical knowledge, but it hardly aids our understanding of Simmel's work as a whole.[19] In turn, however, this should not be taken to imply that Simmel's work can be confined to some mausoleum status in the history of sociology. Rather, his importance for our contemporary concerns must be reconstructed out of a fuller understanding of his own particular interests and their reception by his contemporaries. This is all the more important since there exists no satisfactory full-length examination of Simmel's work in English, least of all one that deals adequately with his *Philosophy of Money*.[20] The last attempt to provide an overview of Simmel's work by Spykman, published in 1925, concludes negatively and blatantly inadequately that 'Simmel's *Philosophy of Money* is best suited to illustrate his conception of the function of a social metaphysics as distinct from the function of a social science or a philosophic enquiry into the presuppositions of the social sciences.'[21]

II

Of all his major works, Simmel's *Philosophy of Money* possesses a structure that is absent from most others. Even his *Soziologie*, published in 1908 and certainly more influential than *The Philosophy of Money*, is actually a collection of essays assembled together. Simmel was certainly, as Frischeisen-Köhler suggested, 'the master of the philosophical essay', and we can clearly add to this that he was a master of the sociological essay; but this very mastery probably prevented him from conceiving of a major structured piece of work. Frischeisen-Köhler argues that 'in the last resort, all his writings, even those of the first period, are either actual essays or collections of them'.[22] Furthermore *The Philosophy of Money* was not written in the style of an academic treatise, but in a freer style of presentation that Simmel had already established in his dissertation, much to the annoyance of his examiners. Simmel's writing, like poetry, requires no footnotes. None are provided in *The Philosophy of Money* and almost no works are cited in the text (an interesting exception is Marx's *Capital*). If, at times, *The Philosophy of Money* is difficult to follow in terms of its sequence of argument – and not merely because of Simmel's over-extensive use of argument by analogy – then this reflects the strain that Simmel no doubt felt in constructing and holding together such a large work. This strain is all the more apparent since, especially in the later chapters of the work, Simmel, in a characteristic fashion, is concerned to exploit his analysis of the meaning of the apparently most insignificant details of life of the purposes of his more general intentions.

These intentions are clearly expressed in the preface to the work. Simmel's attempt to construct a philosophy of money, as distinct from an economics or psychology of money, is the constant aim throughout this work. It is present in the analytical part of the book, which comprises the first three chapters. This philosophy of money:[23]

> can only lie on either side of the economic science of money. On the one hand, it can present the preconditions which . . . give money its meaning and its practical position. . . . The first part of this book, therefore, relates money to the conditions which determine its essence and the meaning of its existence.

This philosophical intention is also present in the synthetic part of the book, which comprises the last three chapters. Here it is the 'historical phenomenon of money' that is investigated and 'its effects upon the inner world – upon the vitality of individuals, upon the linking of their fates with culture in general'. But since such connections have not yet been fully studied 'they can only be dealt with in a philosophical manner, namely, by a general estimation, by representing individual occurrences through connections between abstract concepts'. Thus, taking the work as a whole, we can see that the first part 'seeks to make the essence of money intelligible from the conditions and connections of life in general; the other part seeks to make the essence and organisation of the latter intelligible from the effectiveness of money'.[24]

A further implication of this philosophical intention is that it does not aim at a specific content of knowledge. Least of all does it aim at economic knowledge, for 'not a single line of these investigations is meant to be a statement about economics'. Karl Joël, reviewing the book, suggested that it 'wanders from economics to philosophy; it inserts itself into the spot at which economics ceases; it operates behind economics' back'.[25] Thus, however much the work makes use of economic material, Simmel did not see it as a contribution to economics. Rather, 'money is simply a means, a material or an example for the presentation of relations which exist between the most superficial, "realistic", and fortuitous phenomena and the most idealised powers of existence, the most profound currents of individual life and history.' What gives the work its peculiar unity does not reside in some 'assertion about a particular content of knowledge . . . but rather in *the possibility* – which must be demonstrated – *of finding in each of life's details the totality of its meaning*'.[26] Not for nothing do we find Simmel making continual reference to art and aesthetics. Nor is it surprising that Georg Lukács – one of Simmel's favourite pupils – called him 'the true philosopher of impressionism', 'a philosophical Monet'.[27]

Yet however general and abstract Simmel's philosophical intention in *The Philosophy of Money* may have been, it was expressed methodologically in a more specific direction. Through his particular type of analysis of money and economic life, Simmel sought[28]

> to construct a new storey beneath historical materialism such that the explanatory value of the incorporation of economic life into the causes of intellectual culture is preserved, whilst these economic forms themselves are recognised as the result of more profound valuations and currents of psychological, even metaphysical preconditions.

This ceaseless mutual interaction between the economic and intellectual realms, this preservation of the relative autonomy of the intellectual realm, this reduction of the economic realm to 'psychological' or 'even metaphysical preconditions' represented Simmel's methodological attempt to come to terms with the historical materialism of contemporary Marxists. At a more concrete level, this intention becomes most apparent in Simmel's critical discussion of the labour theory of value later in the book.

If Simmel's intentions in writing *The Philosophy of Money* were quite clearly stated, were they responded to by his contemporaries when they read that work? Simmel's attempt to demonstrate 'the possibility . . . of finding in each of life's details the totality of its meaning' was facilitated by his concentration upon that social entity which itself functions as the mediator par excellence, as the mysterious thing that brings together and connects seemingly unlikely individuals, groups and situations. Siegfried Kracauer thought that Simmel came closer to capturing the totality of modern life in *The Philosophy of Money* than in any of his other works. He suggested that:[29]

> Simmel placed one cross section after the other through the social and individual life of men in the age of the developed money economy. His observations, however, result neither from an economic nor from a historical standpoint but grow out of the purely philosophical intention to reveal the interwoven nature of the assembled parts of the diversity of the world. In none of his other works does the author outline such a comprehensive picture of the interconnectedness and entanglement of phenomena. He clearly extracts their essence in order to melt it down once more into a multitude of connections . . . and reveals the many common meanings that reside within them. Amongst these phenomena belong, for instance, exchange, ownership, greed, extravagance, cynicism, individual freedom, the style of life, culture, the value of the personality etc.

This interconnectedness of phenomena and effects and the multitude of analogies that Simmel draws between phenomena are not arbitrary. Kracauer argues that:[30]

> the inexhaustible multitude of interspersed analogies refer back time and time again to the unifying core conception of the whole work which may be briefly expressed as follows: from any point of the totality one can arrive at any other, each phenomenon bears and supports the other, there exists nothing absolute that exists unconnected to other phenomena and that possesses validity in and for itself.

Kracauer refers to this position as 'not merely a practically operating but also a theoretically grounded relativism'. Similarly, each individual phenomenon can serve Simmel as the starting point for his philosophical reflections. But this very multiplicity of starting points and this interconnectedness of all things made it difficult for readers to discover in his procedures anything approaching a systematic method: 'This wandering from relationship to relationship, this extension into the far and near, this intermeshing secures for the mind which seeks to grasp a totality no resting place; it loses itself in infinity.'[31] Indeed, Simmel himself saw the preoccupation with methodology as a kind of fetishism and took method to be somewhat akin to style in art. As he later expressed his views, 'Method has much in common with style in the artistic realm.'[32] Simmel's approach to his subject is indeed so distinctive that it will be examined in detail later.

Another much closer contemporary of Simmel's also indicated that Simmel had extracted the totality of the spirit of the age from his analysis of money.

Karl Joël, a philosopher and friend of Simmel's, saw his *Philosophy of Money* as 'a philosophy of the times'. Joël presents us with a sense of the contemporary importance of this work when he states that:[33]

> this book could only be written in these times and in Berlin. . . . This work, with the most sensitive ear, has overheard the innermost tone of modern life from the babble of the vast market place, the tone which one does not hear, like the Pythagoreans in relation to the harmony of the spheres, because it is always audible.

That Simmel was able to view the effects of the rapid development of a mature money economy and the consequences of equally rapid urbanization in a metropolitan context as a problem may in part be due to his experiences in Berlin in a more specific sense than Joël was aware. Berlin experienced not only a rapid urbanization and development as a metropolis after German unification in 1870 but also the major wave of financial speculation in the *Gründerjahre*. Perhaps for both these reasons Walter Rathenau later described Berlin as 'Chicago on the Spree'.[34]

Yet Joël goes on to argue that Simmel's work is not merely a description of the 'innermost nerve' of a particular period – that of the developed money economy – but also an analysis of it that is deeply critical of the consequence of a money economy for the development of culture. Similarly, Joël suggests that the book transcends a merely economic interpretation of money and places it on a philosophical universal level; in fact, that it is the opposite of the materialistic interpretation of money in so far as it translates and deepens the economic element into the philosophical.

Whereas Joël's review concentrates upon the general philosophical aspects of Simmel's book, other reviewers were concerned with the substantive aspects of Simmel's analysis of money. Schmoller, for example, saw the real purpose of the book 'to ascertain what the money economy, particularly the modern economy of the nineteenth century, has made of men and society, of their relationships and arrangements. Money appears, as it were, as the focal point, the key, the quintessence of modern economic life and pursuits.'[35] Yet Schmoller sees that Simmel's approach is not that of the historical political economist; rather 'he takes what we know of money historically and economically as it were as the raw material in order to make use of it sociologically and philosophically, in order to extract psychological, social, scientific, cultural conclusions from it.'[36] In so doing, Simmel throws up much that is relevant to economics even though this is not his primary intention. None the less, 'Simmel has certain predecessors in economists who have dealt with the money economy, the division of labour, credit and their consequences' such as Knies, but he extends their relevance to the 'sociological, psychological and philosophical realm'.[37]

Simmel's broad-ranging reflections, the product of 'a thinker schooled in philosophy and dialectics', on the effects of the developed money economy are often seen by Schmoller to exhibit 'a strong strain of pessimism', whereas Schmoller himself assumes that the shadowy side of money can be corrected by morality and legal measures. Yet on balance Schmoller was very favourably impressed with Simmel's *Philosophy of Money*, in which 'he prefers to provide more caviar than black bread, to illuminate with a firework rather than a study lamp'. Indeed, Schmoller equates *The Philosophy of Money* in terms of its significance with Durkheim's *Division of Labour in Society* when he suggests that:[38]

> just as Durkheim provides a sociological–philosophical treatment of the division of labour, so Simmel seeks to provide a similar treatment of money or, one could almost say, of modern economic forms as a whole; for he extends far beyond money, he assembles everything that he has to say about the modern economy around money as the centre of these phenomena.

This applies to his examination of the effects of the modern economy upon the individual no less than to its effects upon culture as a whole.

Yet for all Schmoller's praise, he has some reservations concerning the reception of Simmel's work. In part, Schmoller argues that many untrained in philosophy and a knowledge of economic relations will find it difficult 'to follow the course of observations and investigations without considerable strain' and 'to gain an overview of the connections clearly'. Many readers will have difficulty not merely with the style and presentation but with the content:[39]

> the more immature, the more uneducated the reader is, the more easily and more often will he put the book aside, shaking his head, and say that he does not understand it, that it is too refined for me, too artificial, that he does not know what to do with it. The philistines amongst the economists too will do the same. The conventional socialists will scent an aristocrat in him.

The only other detailed review of the first edition of *The Philosophy of Money* by an economist is that of Altmann which appeared in German and in the *American Journal of Sociology* in 1903,[40] no doubt encouraged by its editor Albion Small who had himself studied in Berlin and was enthusiastic about Simmel's work.[41] For Altmann, *The Philosophy of Money* is 'the keystone of his social psychological investigations', and 'in many ways excels his former works'; it provides 'an infinitely deep psychological interpretation of life'. Its central perspective is that of:[42]

> the world as the great market-place, seen from a bird's eye view, from which everything is seen in relation to everything else. . . . Only an economic

phenomenon like money . . . could in its totality give an image of the world in which everything is part of the whole.

As an economist Altmann concentrates upon Simmel's economic theory of value, which he views as 'an eclectic combination of the theories of the Austrian School' (Altmann astonishingly includes Marx here), and concludes that Simmel presents us with 'a highly developed theory of sacrifice' and is 'the first who undertakes to interpret the idea of valuation purely deductively'.[43] He shows how some of these general aspects of a theory of value and of money have their origin not merely in Knies but also, and more significantly, in Tönnies's *Gemeinschaft und Gesellschaft*. Altmann also suggests that:[44]

> Simmel has learned a great deal from Marx, but neither in his theory of value, nor in psychological and ethical questions has he stopped there. For that reason the attacks of one of the most talented of our younger socialists made against his book, which does not at all intend to give anything but a theory of value, seems to me one-sided and unjust.

The young socialist referred to here is probably Conrad Schmidt, author of a critique of *The Philosophy of Money* published in 1901.[45] Just as Schmoller had seen a pervasive pessimism, so Altmann concludes that in this major work there exists 'a tragic strain [which] means burdening every thought with the fate of the eternal Jew, if the author treats every thought as if it was the one hope before the last'.[46] This tragic strain and this restlessness are perhaps what, for Altmann, give the work its distinctive quality. In this respect, he sees Simmel as sharing many other qualities in common with Nietzsche. A much more orthodox economist, and a specialist in monetary theory, Knapp referred to *The Philosophy of Money* as 'weavings of gold in the carpet of life'.[47]

There were, in fact, two reviews of *The Philosophy of Money* that appeared in socialist journals, the more significant of which was that by Conrad Schmidt referred to above. Schmidt, a socialist economist who had already written on Marx's theory of value, evaluates Simmel's book largely in comparison with Marx's work. Schmidt argues that, despite Simmel's capacity for abstraction – a capacity seldom found among professional economists – his mode of procedure, his 'proliferate intertwining of analogies', makes the reader increasingly lose sight of the book's aims. Specifically, Schmidt suggests that Simmel's philosophy of money fails to take up the diverse functions of money. In particular, he argues that Simmel ignores its function as capital and that consequently since he 'does not at all systematically enter into the inner *concrete structure of the money economy*, the psychology of the money economy which extends into an infinite breadth remains necessarily trapped at the superficial level'.[48] For this reason, Simmel remains enamoured and captivated by money's symbolism and 'concerns himself not with the question of the *emergence* of money, which in any case does not belong to philosophy but to history, but rather with the question of the meaning and significance of money'.[49] Schmidt objects that this latter question, which Simmel seeks to reserve as 'the cardinal point for his philosophical observations', has in fact been dealt with in economic theory, especially by Marx.

This extension of theoretical economics on to a philosophical plane is seen by Schmidt to have an insufficiently concrete basis, especially in Simmel's incapacity to deal adequately with the problem of the value of money, with the fact that 'money must not only historically be a measure of value of commodities but must also in its very essence itself be an object of value'. Ultimately, Schmidt concludes, despite Simmel's refinement in producing such an 'arabesque work', its actual fruits are few. In contrast, the review by Koigen[50] ostensibly views Simmel as an apologist for money and attempts to relate money to religious notions and its representation as 'the ideal concept of the times'. Yet in the end it is difficult to say whether Koigen in fact succeeds in showing why Simmel is an apologist for money.

It is Simmel's relationship to Marx – which must be examined in detail later – that is taken up at the very start of a review by Goldscheid[51] for whom *The Philosophy of Money*:[52]

> forms a very interesting correlate to Marx's *Capital*. Marx could very well have said in the foreword to *Capital* that not a single line of his investigations were intended psychologically. And in fact some passages of *The Philosophy of Money* read like a translation of Marx's economic discussions into the language of psychology. Yet one would do Simmel's book a great disservice if one merely treated it as such a translation. Just as *The Philosophy of Money* could undoubtedly not have been written if it had not been preceded by Marx's *Capital*, so it is equally important to emphasize that Simmel's book contains a supplementation of Marx's life work such as has hitherto not existed in social science or in its extensions. In any case, *The Philosophy of Money* is written too much in the spirit of philosophical meditations.

Goldscheid argues that Simmel should have spent more time confronting Marx's theory and suggests that where he takes up the labour theory of value Simmel's standard of argument is weaker than elsewhere in the book. None the less, Goldscheid is convinced that there exists 'a multitude of very interesting parallels between Marx's theory of capitalism and Simmel's theories concerning the relativism of money. . . . In my opinion it is an error of Simmel's book that it confronts Marx too little.'[53]

But there exists another major feature of Simmel's work which Goldscheid sees as a weakness. In a remarkably perceptive passage he anticipates the critiques of Simmel's perspective which locates it within a tragic consciousness. He asserts that:[54]

behind Simmel's whole work there stands not the ethical but the aesthetic ideal. And it is this aesthetic ideal that determines his whole interpretation of life and thus his whole scientific life activity. . . . Out of this pure aestheticization of their nature springs this excessive cobweb-like nature of his presentation of real circumstances.

It is this 'purely aesthetic ideal' that 'entices him into a false pathos of distance from all practical life'. Out of this 'pathos of distance' there emerges 'a powerless hyper-objectivity' which confronts 'the highest aesthetic ideal of the individual'. Yet like all the other reviewers of *The Philosophy of Money*, Goldscheid is unsparing in his overall praise of the book, which he holds to be 'one of the most important phenomena of the last decade just as, without a doubt, Simmel . . . is one of the sharpest philosophical minds of our times'.[55]

Aside from Altmann's review, there remains only one foreign review of *The Philosophy of Money* to be considered, that published by Durkheim in *L'Année Sociologique* in 1901.[56] Durkheim saw it as 'a treatise on social philosophy which is offered to us', a treatise upon money as a 'pure symbol, an abstract expression of abstract relationships'. Durkheim's interest lay in the manner in which Simmel demonstrated the influence of money and monetary relationships upon 'moral life'. Precisely because of 'its formal and symbolic character, money affects our moral judgments'.[57] Since it is associated with such a variety of objects both high and low it produces 'a kind of moral depreciation' of all of them. The money economy when fully developed results in 'a kind of de-colouring of existence'.[58]

Yet despite the 'number of ingenious ideas' and 'curious relationships' that are presented in *The Philosophy of Money*, Durkheim found the mode of presentation somewhat '*laborieuse*'. At a substantive level, Durkheim questioned some aspects of Simmel's analysis of types of money and (in the second part of the book) the nature of Simmel's argument, which he found quite beyond the bounds of logic. Aside from the illuminating insights found in the book, Durkheim seems to conclude that it belongs to 'a kind of illegitimate speculation' ('*speculation bâtard*').[59]

On balance, however, the reviews of *The Philosophy of Money* were almost universally favourable. Yet despite this, and despite the claims made for the volume at the time, it did not at first sight have a major impact upon German social theory. The much more fragmentary *Soziologie* published the year after the second enlarged edition of *The Philosophy of Money* had a significantly greater influence upon German sociology. Why was it that this book on 'the spirit of capitalism' was so neglected? Was it merely because Simmel's work as a whole suffered from a relative neglect, partly because the institutional constraints in Berlin prevented him from taking on doctoral candidates, and thus building up a following, because his work was so unacademic, almost anti-academic, or because he was, as Honigsheim puts it, 'completely different from the typical German university professor'?[60] Of course, such reasons only account for the reception of Simmel's work as a whole and not for *The Philosophy of Money* in particular. Perhaps, however, the dominant perspectives on sociology today have so shifted that we are unable to see the part played by Simmel's study in the work of earlier writers. Perhaps we have too easily dismissed it, as did Spykman in the only substantial American account of Simmel's work before the late 1950s, as an illustration of Simmel's 'conception of the function of a social metaphysics'.[61] In the 'sh rt-sleeved world picture of many a positivist' today, there can certainly be no place for such a work except as a source of promising hypotheses cleansed of their contamination with unverifiable notions. Fortunately some writers did take up Simmel's *Philosophy of Money* and attempt to develop some of the analyses of money, individualism and rationality presented in it. Some of these connections will now be examined.

III

In his evaluation of Simmel's work, Frischeisen-Köhler says of *The Philosophy of Money* that:[62]

> in its statement of the problem the work belongs alongside the group of those fundamental attempts which almost simultaneously economists such as Sombart and Max Weber, students of religion such as Troeltsch and others have undertaken to interpret the 'spirit of capitalism' in a common rejection of historical materialism. . . . However, Simmel differs from them in that he does not confine himself to the investigation of a specific historical epoch but rather strives, as it were, towards a greater generality, towards the most comprehensive constellation of meaning in which the significance of the money economy is ultimately illuminated.

Of the three writers mentioned here, only Troeltsch subsequently discussed Simmel's work in any detail, and then only in the context of his philosophy of history.[63] Reference has already been made to the fragment of Weber's incomplete assessment of Georg Simmel as 'sociologist and theorist of the money economy'.[64] It is clear even from this fragment that Weber was both highly impressed by much of Simmel's work and, at the same time, deeply critical of many aspects of it. This fragment was intended to be 'a critique of Simmel's scientific style in his two major sociological writings' – *Philosophie des Geldes* and *Soziologie* – but it does not extend far enough to examine *The Philosophy of Money*. Weber does have praise for Simmel's mode of exposition, which is 'simply brilliant and, what is more important, attains results that are intrinsic to it and not to be attained by any imitator', and for the content of his works, in which almost every one 'abounds in important new theoretical ideas and the most subtle observations'.[65] However, what do we know specifically of the relation between Simmel's *Philosophy of Money* and Weber's work?

In his introduction to a selection of Simmel's writings, Levine writes: 'In *Philosophie des Geldes* Weber found a model for sociological analysis that was both penetrating and restrained, and a provocative interpretation of the all-pervasive effects of rationalization in modern society and culture.'[66] Unfortunately, Levine does not go on to substantiate this claim, however true it may be. We do know from the fragment quoted above that Weber was deeply impressed by this work, and we also know that after his first serious breakdown in 1899–1900 one of the first books that he took up and studied was Simmel's *The Philosophy of Money*.[67] What still does not exist is a thorough examination of the relationship between Simmel's work as a whole and that of Max Weber.

Where Weber does explicitly mention Simmel it is usually, though not always, accompanied by critical comment. Simmel's attempt to 'find in each of life's details the totality of its meaning' was regarded by Weber as being based on an inadequately refined conceptualization. In his *Economy and Society*, Weber suggests that this work 'departs from Simmel's method (in his *Soziologie* and his *Philosophie des Geldes*) in drawing a sharp distinction between subjectively intended and objectively valid "meanings"; two different things which Simmel not only fails to distinguish but often deliberately treats as belonging together'.[68] However, Simmel's emphasis on the form and interrelatedness of social relationships did not clearly require him to develop such a distinction. In a different direction, though still at the level of methodology, it has been suggested that Weber's notion of ideal type may be traced back to, among other notions, Simmel's concept of form, though the evidence for this view is by no means unambiguous.[69] In his incomplete evaluation of Simmel's work, Weber makes clear that he is in agreement with many, though not all, of the criticisms made by Spann, and it is clear from the context that, had he completed this assessment, he would certainly have developed these criticisms.

Spann's criticisms centred round Simmel's notions of sociology and society.[70] Spann suggested that Simmel adhered to a 'psychologistic concept of society' which rested upon 'the definition of *societal* interaction as the interaction of *psychic* entities'. For example, Spann argues that Simmel:[71]

> interprets the economy as interaction in the basic form of the act of exchange. This means that the act of exchange, this primitive aspect of the economy, is for him a process of interrelationship between the individual psychic forces of the individual.

Spann maintains that from such definitions we can never derive social concepts. This leads Simmel, Spann continues, into a position in which he is unable fully to establish the basic premises for sociology since its basic problematic – that of society – is defined 'more in the sense of a collective name' for a whole diversity of interactional forms and relationships. Spann therefore concludes that 'Simmel is . . . the sole and first epistemologist of psychologistic sociology'.[72] Weber suggests that he was critical of Spann's attack on Simmel's notions of society and sociology and did not accept all its points, but it is probably true that, had Weber completed his assessment of Simmel, he would have gone on to criticize the psychological elements of Simmel's attempt to ground sociology in a notion of society based on the interaction of psychic entities.

At the substantive level there are few references to Simmel's work. This is surprising because Weber placed considerable emphasis upon the development of a money economy for the development of capitalism, upon the ensuing calculability of means in an ends–means rationality and upon the process of rationalization in general – and all of these are themes that are dealt with at length and in interesting detail by Simmel's *Philosophy of Money*. Aside from *Economy and Society*, this can be seen in Weber's study of the Protestant ethic. There Weber is critical of Simmel's *Philosophy of Money* since 'the money economy and capitalism are too closely identified to the detriment of his concrete analysis'.[73] Certainly it is difficult to find much discussion of money as capital in that work and there is certainly a tendency, in view of Simmel's level of generalization, 'to move from a discussion of the money economy to the effects of capitalism without realising that there is a distinction between the two'.[74] However, with reference to his analysis of the spirit of capitalism, Weber refers to Simmel's 'brilliant analysis' in *The Philosophy of Money*. But any reader will soon be aware that Simmel's analysis moves in quite a different direction to that of Weber.

None the less, Simmel's account of the nature of that economic rationality brought about by a money economy and the extent to which this new rationality pervades many aspects of social life probably had a deep impact upon Weber's own account of the increasing rationalization of industrial society. Simmel's detailed investigation of ends–means rationality within the context of purposive action is intended to show, among other things, that money is the most obvious instance of a means becoming an end.[75] His pessimistic portrayal of the pervasive levelling effects of intellectuality and rationalization and the functionalization of human relationships anticipates Weber's own philosophy of history that permeates his later works.[76]

We thus know very little of the precise relationship between Simmel's *Philosophy of Money* and Weber's major works. This is much less true of Simmel's influence upon his younger contemporary, Georg Lukács, for whom Simmel was 'the most important and interesting transitional phenomenon in the whole of modern philosophy'.[77] Lukács attended Simmel's lectures in 1909–10, though he had already begun a serious study of his writings in 1904. He rapidly became one of Simmel's favourite pupils and regularly attended private seminars at

Simmel's home. Simmel and, one might add, Weber exerted a powerful influence upon the work of the young Lukács, an influence of which he was subsequently highly critical but probably never regretted.[78] This is true not merely of Lukács's early appreciation of Simmel's work as a whole but also, more specifically, of his *Philosophy of Money*.

In his assessment of Simmel's work written in 1918, Lukács saw *The Philosophy of Money* as being his major contribution to sociology. Lukács writes,[79]

> Simmel's importance for sociology – I am thinking here primarily of his *Philosophy of Money* – lies in the fact that he drives the analysis of determinations so far and crowns it with such sensitivity as has never been carried out before him and yet, at the same time, he makes evident with inimitable precision the sudden changes in the determinations, their autonomous limitation, their halting before that which they cannot determine. A sociology of culture, such as has been undertaken by Max Weber, Troeltsch, Sombart and others – however much they might all also wish to distance themselves from him methodologically – has surely only been made possible on the foundation created by him.

Yet this is not the first time that Lukács had singled out *The Philosophy of Money* as a crucial instance of Simmel's sociological work. In a review article published in 1915 on the nature and methods of the sociology of culture, Lukács referred to two works which he considered decisive for 'the clarification of a sociology of culture' – Tönnies's *Gemeinschaft und Gesellschaft* and Simmel's *Philosophie des Geldes*.[80] Furthermore, Lukács's statement of the problems of the fundamental grounding of a sociology of culture in part echoes Simmel's own standpoint. Lukács argues that[81]

> if a sociology of culture as an independent discipline is to exist . . . then its basic question can only be: what new viewpoints emerge if we treat cultural objectivations as social phenomena? Expressed in terms of transcendental logic: what is changed in the meaning, content and structure of cultural objectivations if they are changed out of the systematic–sociological form in which they appear as social products and thus as objects of sociology? Sociology is, like every method, like every science a form and not a realm of study or content. Whether or not this form is viewed as an abstract-constructive science of the 'forms of sociation' [*Formen der Vergesellschaftung*] or is sought as an 'interpretative' or even 'descriptive' sociology this problem remains always the same: to search for the interest of the purely social in cultural objectivations.

Lukács here clearly recognizes Simmel's notion of sociology as being a significant one for the development of the sociology of culture and seems to accept his concept of sociology as a form. Yet even earlier, Lukács's adherence to Simmel's social theory was manifested specifically with reference to the theory of alienation which Simmel expounds in the last chapter of *The Philosophy of Money*. In his work on the development of modern drama, completed in the winter of 1908–9 and published in 1911 in Budapest, Lukács refers in several places to Simmel's work and, more importantly, produces an analysis of modern society that is heavily indebted to Simmel's *Philosophy of Money*.[82]

This is apparent not only from several explicit references to Simmel but also from the manner in which Lukács takes up aspects of Simmel's analysis in *The Philosophy of Money*. Lukács takes modern drama to be a 'symbol of the whole of bourgeois culture'. Its crisis lies in the powerlessness of the individual – despite the emphasis upon individualism – against the facticity of what exists. This crisis, this 'problem of life', arises out of the relationship between the individual and his culture and the social consequences of a capitalist economy. Modern life reaches its apogee in metropolitan life in which 'the anarchistic tendencies to tear everything asunder, to dissolve everything into spiritual atoms' are most readily manifested.[83] This crisis is also manifested in the pervasive intellectualism that emerges out of an increased rationalization:[84]

> Rationalisation, the desire to reduce everything to signs and formulae, progressively increases however not only in the pure natural sciences but also in the more historical sciences (sociology) . . . the development leads from the immediate sensual type of apperception to the mediated intellectual type: the category of the qualitative is superseded by that of the quantitative, or – expressed in the language of art – the symbol is displaced by the definition, by analysis.

This intellectualism 'as the form of the mental process certainly has the strongest tendency to dissolve every community, to isolate human beings from one another and to emphasize their incomparability'. All these processes are examined in greater or lesser detail in Simmel's *Philosophy of Money*, to which reference is explicitly made in Lukács's study.

The objectification of the phenomena of life and the individual's powerlessness in the face of his own creations is referred to more explicitly by Lukács in a manner that is similar, though not identical, to Simmel's treatment of objectification and reification. With reference to the power of 'the existent, of naked existence', Lukács argues that it is 'not only that every idea and every theory is powerless when confronted with its power: rather they immediately come under the domination of this unformulable law . . . from the moment they are expressed'.[85] At a more concrete level, Lukács argues that individualism as a value has become problematic in the face of forms of alienation in which 'this new life' of modern capitalism has made everything 'uniform' – clothing, transport, 'the diverse forms of activity [have become] increasingly similar (bureaucracy, industrial machine labour); education, the experiences of childhood become

increasingly similar (the influence and ever-increasing importance of the metropolis) etc.'[86] Lukács, like Simmel, also refers to the uniformity of the soldier's
occupation compared with earlier times. Alongside this uniformity and parallel
to it is the 'objectification of life' ['*Versachlichung des Lebens*']:[87]

> From the standpoint of the individual, the essence of the modern division of
> labour is perhaps that it makes work independent of the always irrational
> and thus only qualitatively determinable capacities of the worker and places
> it under objective, goal-oriented criteria that lie outside his personality and
> have no relationship to it. The major economic tendency of capitalism is this
> same objectification of production, its separation from the personality of the
> producers. By means of the capitalist economy, an objective abstraction –
> capital – becomes the real producer even though it hardly stands in an
> organic connection to the personality of those who happen to own it; indeed
> it becomes increasingly superfluous whether the owners are persons or not
> (joint stock companies).

Scientific method too loses its 'close relationship with the personality' and
becomes 'increasingly objective and impersonal'. This applies to work in general,
which 'takes on a specific, objective life over against the individual character of
the human being, so that he is forced to express himself in something other than
in what he does'.[88] Lukács, like Simmel, takes up the effects of modern economic
activity upon human relationships. Bonds between human beings become 'increasingly looser' and relate only to concrete, one-sided aspects of the human
personality:[89]

> The number of these bonds, however, constantly increase, their interactions
> become more developed and their total effects achieve an increasingly incal-
> culable intensity: 'Thus we might well express as the major scheme of the
> modern period' writes Simmel 'that it makes human beings increasingly
> dependent upon totalities and universalities and increasingly independent of
> particularities.'

Lukács, too, examines the most significant 'antinomies of individualism',
namely 'that the assertion of the personality is unthinkable without the suppression of the personality of others'.[90] Lukács draws the same conclusion as Simmel
and again makes explicit reference to him:[91]

> Through the objectification of life, individuality is increasingly ousted from
> its realities and actions and the manifestation of the personality is left with
> increasingly less room for manouver in this sphere. On the other hand, it
> makes possible, and even contributes to, the fact that the real innermost life
> of the soul becomes completely independent of these facts and consequently
> becomes exclusively inward. Simmel points out at the same time with regard

to this statement that this development of the introversion of the life of the soul is necessary to the same extent that it runs counter to every aesthetic ideal of life.

What is remarkable in Lukács's study is the extent to which he relies upon Simmel's work and especially upon *The Philosophy of Money*, since every theme that has been illustrated here in Lukács's study is taken up in a similar manner there. This is not to deny that important differences already emerge in Lukács's account of alienation and objectification. The crisis of modern life to which both Simmel and Lukács refer is given a specifically historical dimension; that is, the crisis is seen as that of the bourgeoisie in a modern capitalist society. In other words, unlike Simmel, Lukács is concerned with the social class structure of capitalist societies in a somewhat more concrete manner. Secondly, Lukács begins to place this whole discussion of individualism and objectification within the context of a critique of ideology – a framework missing from Simmel's work.

It has already been suggested that there is a major aesthetic dimension to Simmel's *Philosophy of Money*, one that will be examined in more detail later. For the moment, it is sufficient to point out the extent to which this dimension is also central to Lukács's early work and, even though perhaps within different contexts, to his whole life's work too. It is well known that Simmel elevated the category of form to the very centre of his analysis of human society. It is also central to Lukács's early writings on culture. For example, in his essay, 'The Metaphysics of Tragedy', Lukács views life as[92]

> an anarchy of light and dark: nothing is ever completely fulfilled in life, nothing ever quite ends; new confusing voices always mingle with the chorus of those that have been heard before. Everything flows, everything merges into another thing, and the mixture is uncontrolled and impure; everything is destroyed, everything is smashed, nothing ever flowers into real life.

The problem here is how 'true life' and structures of meaning can emerge out of this chaos. Lukács's answer is in terms of form as 'the highest judge of life. Form-giving is a judging force, an ethic; there is a value-judgment in every-thing that has been given form. Every kind of form-giving, every literary form, is a step in the hierarchy of life-possibilities.'[93] Again, like Simmel, Lukács conceives of this metaphysic of forms as lying quite outside historical social reality and in fact its basis lies in a Kantianism remoulded by *Lebensphilosophie*. In *The Theory of the Novel*, completed in 1914, Lukács is still referring to 'philosophy as a form of life'.[94]

Yet Lukács's treatment of cultural phenomena soon took on a more Hegelian and eventually a Marxist dimension, even though elements of Simmel's influence persist in some of the shorter articles written after Lukács had joined the Hungarian Communist Party in December 1918. In an article on old and new culture published in *Kommunismus* in 1920, for example, Lukács takes fashion as his example of the revolutionary character of capitalist production.[95] Cultural renewal is still seen as the crucial aim just as in the previous year Lukács had stated that 'politics is merely a means, culture is the goal'.[96] Culture in capitalist society is seen to suffer from the contradiction between 'the forms and contents of cultural expressions'. The persistence of Simmel's formulations in Lukács's work should not be surprising to anyone who does not wish to establish a radical break in his work that is based on a change in his political allegiance.

It is, however, Lukács's *History and Class Consciousness*, which stands as the most decisive reception and reinterpretation of Marx's work in the 1920s, that is also significant for following up Simmel's influence in Lukács's work.[97] In *History and Class Consciousness* and also in some of his earlier works, particularly his study of modern drama, many commentators have pointed to the striking 'links between Lukács' standpoint here and the theory of alienation developed by Marx'.[98] What is perhaps more striking is that some of the relevant passages can be drawn from sections of Simmel's *Philosophy of Money*, a book that is ostensibly deeply critical of Marxism and one that owed its political economy not to Marx but perhaps to Schmoller, Sombart, Tönnies and others. In *The Philosophy of Money* Simmel outlines a theory of alienation based on the process of objectification, though one that is largely directed towards showing the alienation of culture and the inevitability of that process. Simmel frequently employs the concept of reification (*'Verdinglichung'*), a concept also employed by Nietzsche as well as Marx. It is the concept of reification that is elevated by Lukács to a crucial position in his critique of bourgeois interpretations of capitalist society as a whole. In the course of that central analysis Lukács criticizes Simmel's *Philosophy of Money* for failing to recognize the historical nature of the process of reification. Lukács, with obvious reference to Simmel though with equal relevance to Lukács's own earlier works, argues that even those writers who[99]

> have no desire to deny or obscure its existence and who are more or less clear in their own minds about its humanly destructive consequences remain on the surface and make no attempt to advance beyond its objectively most derivative forms, the forms furthest from the real life-process of capitalism, i.e. the most external and vacuous forms, to the basic phenomenon of reification itself.

Such writers detach the manifestations from capitalism itself and 'make them independent and permanent by regarding them as the timeless model of human relations in general. (This can be seen most clearly in Simmel's book, *The Philosophy of Money*, a very interesting and perceptive work in matters of detail).'[100] This does not prevent Lukács from using Simmel's analysis (or Weber's for that matter)[101] for an account of the phenomenology of capitalist society. Even the manner of presentation of the tragedy of the bourgeoisie may retain vestiges of Simmel's own tragic vision.

Lukács is the one writer in the Marxist tradition who is most clearly influenced by Simmel's *Philosophy of Money* as well as by his other writings. The importance of this work for other writers within the Marxist tradition is much less easy to determine. Ernst Bloch, who persuaded Lukács to study in Berlin, was certainly close to Simmel when he studied under him, but his judgment of Simmel was ultimately a negative one:[102]

> Simmel has the finest mind among all contemporaries. But beyond this, he is wholly empty and aimless, desiring everything except the truth. He is a collector of standpoints which he assembles all around truth without ever wanting or being able to possess it. [On the other hand,] Simmel has given to thought nuances and a heightened temperature which, if only taken out of the hands of a man born without a hard core, can indeed be of great service to philosophy.

Yet it is unlikely that *The Philosophy of Money* had the same importance for Bloch as it did for Lukács.[103] Of greater interest perhaps is Walter Benjamin's comment on Simmel whose work he had used for his study of Baudelaire and Paris in the nineteenth century. Benjamin, a member of the Frankfurt School, wrote to Adorno in 1939 that he had earlier taken up Simmel's *Philosophy of Money* and said that the work[104]

> is certainly not dedicated to Reinhold and Sabine Lepsius for nothing; not without reason does it emerge out of the period in which Simmel sought to 'approach' the George circle. However, one can find much that is interesting in the book if one is resolved to disregard its basic thoughts. I was struck by the critique of Marx's theory of value.

Adorno, however, was highly critical of Simmel's work even though he was impressed by Simmel's use of the essay form. Despite his critical response to Simmel, we can see in much of Adorno's work that preoccupation with the manner in which works of art are enmeshed in the division of labour and that search for the totality of meaning in the individual details of life that also characterizes much of Simmel's work.[105] Associated with the Frankfurt School and a close friend of Adorno's was Siegfried Kracauer, whose essay on Simmel has already been referred to. Kracauer wrote a full-length study of Simmel's work but only the introductory chapter was published in 1920.[106] However, Kracauer's work moved in the direction of a kind of critical phenomenology, though his studies of the detective novel, white-collar employees and other shorter pieces in the 1920s exhibited that attempt to capture the totality of meaning of social phenomena through working through the nuances of meaning residing in single elements that is reminiscent of Simmel's approach.[107] Such a procedure must be predicated upon the assumption of the delicate interrelatedness of phenomena. Kracauer was clearly more impressed by Simmel's attempt to demonstrate the fundamental interrelatedness (*Wesenszusammengehörigkeit*) of the most diverse phenomena than by his persistent use of argument by analogy which represents relations between objects as opposed to metaphorical connections which present the relationship between a subject and an object.

Yet aside from these somewhat diverse strands of continuity, Simmel's *Philosophy of Money* does not seem to have been treated with the same acclaim as his *Soziologie*. Simmel's 'impressionistic pluralism' (Landmann) may have appealed to the young Lukács and Bloch as well as to Kracauer, but it did not earn him a consistent following. It has been suggested that Simmel's value perspectivism permeates Mannheim's sociology of knowledge, but this may be part of the more general influence of value-relativism found not merely in Simmel but in Dilthey, Nietzsche and Weber.[108] Of greater importance in this context is probably the influence of Simmel's cultural theory of alienation and reification upon the sociology of knowledge. Even writers like von Wiese, whose monumental attempt to develop a formal sociology in the post-First World War period ostensibly provides the most direct example of Simmel's influence, did not single out Simmel's *Philosophy of Money* for special emphasis.[109] However, one consequence of Simmel's attracting large numbers of students to his lectures from 'the eastern countries' (as a hostile referee of Simmel's work termed them) may have been that his work, including *The Philosophy of Money*, was translated into several languages. Three articles that were later reworked and incorporated into *The Philosophy of Money* were translated into Russian between 1899 and 1900 while the whole of *The Philosophy of Money* was translated into Polish and published in 1904.[110] Nor does this take account of writers like Kistiakowski, whose work was heavily indebted to Simmel[111] and influential in eastern Europe.

However, it remains true to say that Simmel's *Philosophy of Money* exerted its greater effect upon Weber's examination of rationality and the emergence and consequences of a money economy and upon Lukács's early writings. What is perhaps most surprising is that the book was so significant to writers in the Marxist tradition. This can be understood only if we now examine Simmel's relationship to Marx and the Marxism of the Second International.

IV

It is worth while investigating Simmel's relationship to Marx for a number of reasons. First, his *Philosophy of Money* was probably the most important work on the consequences of a money economy to be published since Marx's *Capital*.

Second, writers like Goldscheid saw Simmel's *Philosophy of Money* as an extension of Marx's *Capital*. We need to examine in what sense this was true. Third, we need to ask how it is that writers like Lukács could approach Marx through the eyes of Simmel. This is apparently all the more surprising in view of Simmel's avowed intention in the preface to *The Philosophy of Money* 'to construct a new storey beneath historical materialism' and his critique of the labour theory of value in the last section of the fifth chapter of that work. Finally, it is important to investigate the use of such concepts as reification and objectification, the analysis of the consequences of the division of labour in society in order to examine whether Goldscheid is correct in arguing that *The Philosophy of Money* 'could undoubtedly not have been written if it had not been preceded by Marx's *Capital*'.

In his preface to the new edition of *History and Class Consciousness* in 1967, Lukács suggested that his study of Marx commenced around 1908 and that 'it was Marx the "sociologist" that attracted me – and I saw him *through spectacles tinged by Simmel and Max Weber*'.[112] More explicitly, Lukács later argued that[113]

> a properly scholarly use of my knowledge of Marx was greatly influenced by the philosophy and sociology of Simmel[114] [and that] when I looked for the perspectives, foundations and methods of application of philosophic generalisation, I found a theoretical guide in the German philosopher Simmel, not the least of reasons being that this approach brought me closer to Marx, though in a distorted way.

Certainly Lukács's own attraction to Simmel's work may have been partly due to his own deep concern for cultural renewal and for the preservation of the authenticity of the individual's modes of expression. In this respect, Simmel's own concern for the inevitable clash between subjective and objective culture and his analysis of the myriad connections between cultural phenomena must have been attractive to the young Lukács. This is not to suggest that Lukács was not subsequently deeply critical of Simmel, as has already been shown. This critique reached its most negative depths in *Die Zerstörung der Vernunft*, where Lukács, referring to Simmel's attempt to 'deepen historical materialism' in *The Philosophy of Money*, argues that such a[115]

> deepening of historical materialism in fact exists in the subsumption of its results under a *Lebensphilosophie* framework, that in this case appears as the insoluble opposition between subjectivity and cultural forms, between soul and mind. This opposition is, according to Simmel, the peculiar tragedy of culture.

What Lukács suggests here is that where elements of historical materialism do exist in *The Philosophy of Money* – such as the notion of reification – then they are embedded in an idealist metaphysics of culture.

However true this may be, it hardly illuminates Simmel's own knowledge of Marx's work though it does again highlight the fact that many writers saw Simmel's work as containing at least elements of Marx's work. But what do we know of Simmel's knowledge of Marx's writings? It is not clear from Simmel's published works themselves or his correspondence how fully Simmel had studied Marx's work and especially *Capital*. Despite the occasional affinities between passages in *The Philosophy of Money* and Marx's work it is probably true that, as one commentator suggests, 'his knowledge is certainly not as profound as that of Tönnies who has written a volume on Marx'.[116] Even the two sections of *The Philosophy of Money* that bear directly upon Marx's *Capital* – Simmel's critique of the labour theory of value and his discussion of the consequences of the division of labour – do not directly take up the kind of problems that Marx examines in the relevant contexts. Rather, it seems more likely that Simmel's knowledge of Marx is mediated by that of other contemporary writers such as Schmoller on the division of labour and Tönnies on rationality.[117] Certainly in the decade preceding the publication of *The Philosophy of Money* there were numerous discussions and critiques of Marx's work, especially of *Capital*, some of which, at least, Simmel was probably acquainted with.[118]

We also know that Simmel found the development of his own subjective theory of value extremely difficult to formulate. While working on *The Philosophy of Money* in 1898 Simmel wrote to Rickert explaining the difficulties he was having in advancing a theory of value. Simmel here suggests that[119]

> the concept of value seems to me to not only contain the same kind of *regressus in infinitum* as does that of causality but also contains a *circulus vitiosus* because, if one follows through the connections far enough, one always finds that the value of A is based on that of B or that of B is only based on that of A. . . . I see no end to the difficulties since, in any case, I am convinced of the fact that I can only maintain my relativism if it is capable, as it were, of solving all the problems which are presented by theories of absolutism.

In fact Simmel's own theory of value, with its subjective and relativist assumptions, has much in common with the subjectivist theory of value advanced by marginal utility theorists such as Menger and Böhm-Bawerk and very little in common with Marx's theory of value. Neither Simmel's nor, for that matter, Weber's often-remarked-upon similarities with some aspects of Marx's theory extend to the very marked differences in the political economy of these writers. However 'interesting' Simmel found the labour theory of value, he did not accept its basic premises and his own subjective theory of value ran directly contrary to it. This is perhaps the major reason why his critique of the labour theory of value appears somewhat uneasily when set against the context of

Simmel's own formulation of a subjective theory of value in the early chapters of *The Philosophy of Money*.

It has indeed been suggested that Simmel's concern with money as a phenomenon is, in fact, a diversionary theme in order to arrive at that of value.[120] That is, money is seen as mediating between value and life in such a manner that money and exchange not only enable an objective comparison of subjective values but permit Simmel to take up the problem of value itself. However, Simmel's own theory of value was beset by the problem of avoiding a totally relativist standpoint. Simmel himself saw that his introduction of the concept of interaction of elements and their interconnectedness within the sociological sphere led him to take up this mutual interaction as a 'comprehensive metaphysical principle'. Yet in doing so this presented Simmel with the relativist problematic since[121]

> the contemporary historical dissolution of all that is substantial, absolute and eternal in the flux of things, in historical mutability, in a merely psychological reality seems to me to be then only preserved against an unceasing subjectivism and scepticism if one substitutes for every substantial secure value the living interaction of elements which ultimately underlies, in turn, the same dissolution into infinity. The central concepts of truth, value, objectivity etc., revealed themselves to me as changing effective phenomena (*Wechselwirksamkeiten*), as the contents of a relativism which no longer implies the sceptical loosening of all determinations but rather means securing against this by means of a new concept of determination ('Philosophie des Geldes').

It is in this work then that, as Margaret Susman says, 'Simmel's relativism and thus, at the same time his relation to the absolute finds its most complete expression'.[122] Certainly, this relativism is expressed not merely in a general metaphysical standpoint but, more specifically, in a subjectivist theory of value to be counterposed, presumably, to an objectivist theory of value provided by historical materialism.

This intention is most apparent in Simmel's critique of the labour theory of value. In earlier chapters Simmel outlined his theory of exchange as a basis for examining the role of money in this process. But Simmel's delineation of an exchange economy was one far removed from that of Marx since, as Blumenberg points out, 'Simmel still postulated the concept of exchange for a "solipsistic economy, as it were", that is, one in which the isolated person does not confront other persons but immediately confronts nature'.[123] It would not be possible at this point to develop all the differences between the value theories of Simmel and Marx. It must suffice here to suggest that one of the key aspects of Simmel's critique of the labour theory fails to come to terms with Marx's theory at all. Simmel's argument on value obfuscates the distinction between use and exchange value with respect to labour power and hence any possibility of discussing commodity exchange rather than the exchange of goods. Secondly, Simmel's critique centres around a number of examples of concrete labour without again confronting Marx's distinction between concrete labour and labour power, between concrete and abstract labour. The discussion of money seldom takes up the relationship between money and capital that is symptomatic of Simmel's lack of interest in the sphere of production as opposed to that of distribution and circulation. This can lead Simmel to argue that the sphere of exchange is just as productive and value-creating as that of production itself and to view exchange exclusively from the standpoint of the consumption of use values.[124]

The origin of these differences between Simmel and Marx lies in the fundamentally divergent economic theories of the two writers. Simmel wrongly describes Marx's theory of money as a theory of labour money – a theory that he expressly rejects both in *Capital* and, in more detail, in *A Contribution to the Critique of Political Economy*.[125] In his critique of Marx's theory, Simmel correctly points to the importance of the separation of intellectual and manual labour, but in the course of the discussion intended to preserve the freedom of the intellect and to assert that intellectual labour is free he confuses two notions of value. As Brinkmann argues,[126]

> Simmel uses two concepts of value in an undifferentiated manner: on the one hand, his concept of value which . . . is orientated towards that of each individual valuation of an object . . . on the other, however, Marx's concept of value which commences from abstract labour.

Brinkmann goes on to show that Simmel's notion of an economic crisis too differs markedly from that of Marx. Simmel views an economic crisis not in terms of over-production but rather as a distorted relationship between the means of payment and the supply of goods. This is the result of a more basic difference between Simmel's and Marx's views on a capitalist economy since 'whereas Simmel seeks to analyse the economy from the side of demand and thus from the side of consumption and distribution, thereby allowing supply to be more or less a function of demand, Marx starts out from supply, from production'.[127] Of course, in this Simmel's views do not differ markedly from those of many of his contemporary sociologists or, for that matter, from many writers today on social stratification.

It is however in Simmel's analysis of the consequences of the money economy and of the division of labour that the affinities between his work and that of Marx appear to be greatest. It is at this level rather than in terms of Simmel's theory of value that we must examine Goldscheid's claim that *The Philosophy of Money* is an extension of Marx's *Capital* or Lukács's claim to have come to Marx's work via Simmel. One recent commentator suggests that[128] in the *Philosophie des Geldes* at least, the power of the analysis lies precisely in the constant return of the argument to the process of industrial production. In this context, Simmel rediscovered major moments of Marx's theory of alienation that most interpreters (except Lukács in 1923) associated with Marx only after the discovery of the 1844 *Paris Manuscripts*.

In what sense is this true?

It must again be pointed out that any affinity between Simmel's analysis and that of Marx need not rest upon Simmel's reading of Marx. Without in any way detracting from Simmel's originality, many strands of Simmel's analysis may be traced back to other writers. Arato has rightly suggested that Simmel's discussion of rationality and, one might add, possibly his account of its relation to science, has its roots in Tönnies's earlier work.[129] It would be surprising if Simmel had not been impressed by the work of his colleague Schmoller on the division of labour.[130] Similarly, many of the historical examples that illuminate Simmel's analysis of the emergence of the money economy are probably drawn from such works as those of Knapp on agricultural workers.[131] Yet having pointed to all these influences – and they are by no means exhaustive – it remains to examine what affinities do exist between Simmel's and Marx's analysis of the division of labour and alienation.

In the last chapter of the present work, Simmel draws a remarkable picture of the alienation of man from his products and from the culture that he has himself produced. This is accompanied by a divergence of what Simmel views as subjective and objective culture and is attributed to the division of labour 'in terms of its importance within production as well as consumption'.[132] In the production process the division of labour develops increasingly refined skills that form a 'one-sided activity' while at the same time these skills and activities become ever more detached from the total personality and often lead to the stunting of the human subject as a whole. The increased fragmentation of the production process results in the meaning of the product for its producer lying not in that person but in other products. This increased fragmentation of production and of human beings results in their progressive standardization and the destruction of their individuality. In this last sense, human subjects become alienated from their species' being.

It is not possible or necessary to develop at this point Simmel's analysis of the consequences of the division of labour. That account is presented by Simmel himself in the middle section of the last chapter of *The Philosophy of Money*. Suffice it to say that he does present us with a remarkable account of the processes of fragmentation, atomization, objectification, reification and standardization brought about by the division of labour. An analysis of these processes is, of course, to be found in Marx's work too. But there are crucial differences in the two accounts.

In terms of Simmel's analysis of the money economy as a whole, one significant difference was highlighted by Karl Mannheim, who argued that[133]

> Simmel in particular had characterised in many ways the experientially changing objects of the world which are associated with money forms . . . yet in so doing he had abstracted, in a completely unhistorical manner, the capitalistic money form from its capitalistic background and imputed the characteristic structural change to 'money as such'.

Similarly, like Weber and Sombart, Simmel had also spoken of the progressive rationalization of the world yet had overlooked 'that money calculation also existed earlier but that it is precisely in modern capitalism and only here that the category of commodity becomes a universal category which structures the whole world view'.[134] That is, Simmel's analysis lacks that level of historical concretion that locates the consequences of a *specific* mode of the division of labour as resulting from the nature of capitalist society. In this way, for example, 'Simmel makes the development of alienation independent of social relations: the victims of alienation confront only an objective process';[135] they do not confront a social class that stands in opposition to them. Unlike, for instance, Schmoller's neglected account of the consequences of the division of labour for social class formation, Simmel's analysis moves in a different direction. The location of the consequences of the division of labour in a capitalist society, all of which are specific to that society, becomes increasingly part of a universal human predicament.

Though Simmel's description of these consequences is presented with 'seismographic accuracy' (Gadamer), the location of their origin is increasingly lost, at least as far as their historically specific origin is concerned. This can only give to society and to objective culture a natural character which effectively destroys any basis for a critique of society. Marx's analysis is predicated upon a critique of capitalist society as a whole. Simmel is certainly acutely aware of some of the consequences of that society's operation, but his analysis leads him ultimately into a 'metaphysical pathos'. Whereas *The Philosophy of Money* does provide a high level of concretion in its analysis of the effects of a money economy, it also contains within itself the basis for that universal tragedy of culture that is symptomatic of Simmel's later work. In an essay on the tragedy of culture published in 1911, Simmel argues that the ' "fetishism" which Marx assigned to economic commodities represents only a special case of this general fate of contents of culture'.[136] In the same vein, the 'extreme and total specialisation' produced by the division of labour 'is only a special form of this very general cultural predicament',[137] namely the alienation of objective from subjective culture. Similarly, the process of fragmentation that Simmel analyses in detail in *The Philosophy of Money* was later destined to become absorbed into a metaphysic of human existence in which life itself was viewed as composed of fragments whose relation to totality was increasingly obscured.[138]

Ultimately, then, Simmel's analysis of the capitalist social order has little in common with that of a socialist critique. As Margaret Susman correctly argues, with reference to Simmel's *Philosophy of Money*, it is the case that[139]

> in place of the word socialism there stands here, and with the same though contrary justification, the word individualism to which he confessed throughout. And here he has finally developed the increasingly solitary ego, the deeply lonely soul out of the industrial world which was later to become the agent of the individual law.

V

We have already seen that many contemporary commentators on Simmel's *Philosophy of Money* and on his work as a whole detected a strong aesthetic dimension in his approach to his subject. Goldscheid, for example, observed a 'pure aesthetic ideal' which 'enticed him into a false pathos of distance in relation to all practical life', a 'pathos of distance' which led him into 'a powerless hyper-objectivity'. Lukács, as we have seen, characterized him as 'the true philosopher of impressionism', as 'a philosophical Monet'. Leopold von Wiese saw Simmel's sociology as 'possessing great aesthetic attractiveness. From a certain aspect I would even call his sociology the sociology of an aesthete, a sociology for the literary salon.'[140] Certainly, it is this aestheticization of reality and this distancing from the material world that has led some recent commentators to see in Simmel's work a distinctive version of the tragic vision, to see him as 'the philosopher of the tragic'.[141] We need to examine in what ways this aesthetic dimension manifests itself in Simmel's work, especially in *The Philosophy of Money*, and to investigate its consequences for Simmel's own world view.

This aesthetic dimension in Simmel's work is not at all surprising or problematical at one level. In *The Philosophy of Money* many aesthetic analogies are drawn. Elsewhere, Simmel's notion of method is clearly one that often refers to the author's individual style rather than to any systematic methodological precepts. At the substantive level, Simmel produced studies of Goethe, Michelangelo, Rodin and Rembrandt which, according to Lukács, 'displayed the pathbreaking element of his way of looking at things'[142] more than any of his other works. Simmel's concern for artistic forms is further manifested at a personal level in terms of his association with poets such as Stefan George and Rilke and with dramatists such as Paul Ernst, as well as visits to Rodin in Paris.

Of particular interest here is the fact that the publication of *The Philosophy of Money* probably coincides with the height of Simmel's affinity with the George Circle, although he was never formally a member of it.[143] It was in this period that Simmel wrote two appreciative articles on Stephen George's poetry.[144] It is not clear at this time, however, whether Simmel also subscribed to George's conception of a renewal of culture through an intellectual élite, though elements of such a view do surface from time to time in *The Philosophy of Money*.[145] In one of the studies on George published in 1901 Simmel refers to the work of art as 'a completely self-sufficient, perfectly autonomous cosmos'[146] and thus to an aesthetic dimension that can be abstracted from a social and historical context. Perhaps what specifically appealed to Simmel in George's poetry was what Lukács termed 'the impressionism of the typical. All his poems are symbolic snapshots.'[147] Again it is clear that this impressionist stance is also present in Simmel's own work, as indeed Lukács himself pointed out.

However, there is a more far-reaching aspect of this aesthetic dimension in Simmel's work, one which may be termed the aestheticization of reality. This aestheticism is manifested in the convergence of a distancing from reality and a particular version of the tragic vision which often gives his work its peculiar pathos. These two elements were recognized, as we have seen, by some of Simmel's contemporaries as being present in *The Philosophy of Money* and have received attention from recent commentators on his work.[148] Of course, both elements of aestheticism were accentuated in Simmel's later writings, especially when he was preoccupied with the tragedy of culture and the development of a metaphysical *Lebensphilosophie*. Yet as his contemporaries saw, in important respects this aestheticism is central to *The Philosophy of Money* both in terms of Simmel's approach to his subject matter and in the light of his preoccupation with the tragedy of culture – a concern that was already present in Simmel's 'sociological' phase.

Simmel's approach is usually seen as a preoccupation with the *form* that social interactions and relationships take. But this can only be understood as a problem of the relationship between form and content. In Simmel's case this is most often presented as the problem of extracting the supra- or ahistorical essence or nature of social phenomena from their historical concrete existence. Thus, for example, Simmel maintained that the task of sociology was to extract from the complex phenomena of social and historical concretions what was 'really only society, i.e., sociation [*Vergesellschaftung*]'.[149] What this implies is not merely the abstraction of form out of the historical dimension but also the presentation of historical knowledge within an artistic model. Form, like art itself, is to be a 'perfectly autonomous cosmos'. In concrete terms, this results in *The Philosophy of Money* in a problematic 'which is orientated towards the polarity of ahistorical essential form and historically specific appearances'.[150] The combination of this way of seeing the task of sociology and the substantive treatment of money in *The Philosophy of Money* has important consequences. As Lieber argues,[151]

> If, in *The Philosophy of Money*, the methodological distinction between an essential form removed from history and a historically located phenomenon is given and offered as the index for the continued validity of philosophy as opposed to any individual social science, if precisely such a grasp establishes the inalienable justification for philosophy and if, on the other hand, according to Simmel the same methodical grasp is the basis for the independent foundation of sociology then it is to be expected that a sociology of this type does not extend beyond the dimension of essential determination. Thus it remains in this sense an ahistorical social philosophy or social ontology, it remains what Hans Freyer has quite legitimately characterised it as – the philosophical theory of a binding world of forms of the spirit.

Such a justification of both philosophy and sociology had already been established by Simmel and was to be elaborated in his later works.

This same distinctive extraction of timeless form from historical content that we find in Simmel's work perhaps accounts for Lukács's characterization of Simmel as 'a philosophical Monet', as 'the true philosopher of impressionism'. For, according to Lukács, Simmel possesses 'the capacity to see the smallest and most inessential phenomenon of everyday life so strongly *sub specie philosophiae* that it becomes transparent and behind its transparency reveals an eternal constellation [*Formzusammenhang*] of philosophical meaning'.[152] Simmel's attempt to reveal 'the eternal forms in their perfection' testifies to the fact that his work is 'a conceptual formulation of the impressionist world view'. But this grasping after the eternal forms, however removed from life it may be, must connect once more with that life in order that the particular work may be 'a true work, a self-sufficient world, a microcosm'. Lukács perceptively draws out the aestheticism that lies both in the nature of impressionism and in Simmel's work which has so many affinities with that movement in this period. Lukács suggests that[153]

> Impressionism experiences and evaluates the major, hard and eternal forms as the violation of life, its wealth and its multi-colouredness, its richness and its polyphony; it is always a glorifier of life and places every form in its service. In so doing, however, the nature of form becomes problematic. . . . Every great impressionistic movement is nothing other than the protest of life against the forms which solidify too much in it and which become too weak in this paralysis to be able to incorporate its richness in forms. However, because they remain contained in this elevation of the apperception of life they are, in their very nature, transitional phenomena: the preliminary of a new classical period which makes eternal the richness of life, that becomes revealed through its sensibility, in new, hard and strict but all-encompassing forms.

One could perhaps go further than Lukács and suggest other affinities with impressionism. The rejection of a historical dimension produced a composition crisis which in Simmel is reflected in his preference for the essay form and his rejection of systematic analyses. The fragments of human interaction are to represent the lost totality. But these fragments, however symptomatic, are those of sociability, of sociation, increasingly removed from the cares of everyday life.

A similar view of Simmel's work was later provided by Karl Mannheim who had attended his lectures in Berlin in 1912. Much later, in an article assessing the important features of German sociology, Mannheim argued that Simmel applied[154]

> the same method for the description of everyday life that was previously used to describe pictures or to characterize works of literature. He had an aptitude for describing the simplest everyday experiences with the same precision as is characteristic of a contemporary impressionistic painting which has learned to reflect the previously unobserved shades and values of the atmosphere. He might well be called the 'impressionist' in sociology, because his was not an ability to take a constructive view of the whole of society but to analyse the significance of minor social forces that were previously unobserved. When he describes the social significance of the senses, for instance the human glance or the psychic position of the poor, or the various forms of sociability, the thousand hidden relationships which go to make up social life are suddenly revealed.

Here Mannheim not merely confirms the centrality of the aesthetic dimension in Simmel's work and his impressionistic approach but he also points to the absence of 'a constructive view of the whole of society'.

This is not to suggest that Simmel himself was unaware of this distancing from the present and from reality. In *The Philosophy of Money* he consciously presents the constellation of feelings that constitutes this distancing from reality and which, in its pathological form, is the extended version of agoraphobia, of 'hyper-aestheticism'. The forms of life 'place us at a distance from the substance of things, they speak to us "as from afar"; reality is not touched with direct confidence but with fingertips that are immediately withdrawn.'[155] The basic intention of 'the subjectivism of modern times' is therefore 'to gain a more intimate and truer relationship to objects by dissociating ourselves from them and retreating into ourselves, or by consciously accepting the inevitable distance between ourselves and the objects'.[156] It is thus both the interior retreat from, and the increased intellectualization of, reality. In this way it has affinities with a mode of distancing from reality that is specific to a whole tradition of aestheticism in the nineteenth century. The flight from reification is one that comes to rest in an inward retreat. In another context, Adorno has attempted to examine 'the bourgeois intérieur of the nineteenth century'.[157] Its paradoxicality is only apparent, since,[158] in order to explain the image of the intérieur historically, a sociology of inwardness would be necessary. The notion of intérieur is only apparently paradoxical. Inwardness exists as the confinement of human existence in a private sphere, which should be able to transcend the power of reification. However, as a private sphere it does itself belong, even though polemically, to the social structure.

It is clear that, at least in *The Philosophy of Money*, Simmel is aware of this paradox as the connection between interiority and society. Indeed, with a remarkable degree of self-reflection, Simmel not only portrays this pervasive aestheticism but also indicates the direction in which his own metaphysics ultimately takes him. The real world later becomes 'one of many possible worlds'. Its human dimension is revealed not only in the analyses in *The Philosophy of Money* referred to above but also in Musil's *Man without Qualities*, for whom 'the present is nothing other than a hypothesis from which one has still not extracted oneself'.[159] The world of almost infinite possibilities is the world without human decisions, or praxis. All this is to suggest that in *The Philosophy of Money* and elsewhere 'Simmel not only *consciously* concerned himself with art but also *transposed* its specific structural qualities onto social phenomena'.[160]

This far-reaching aestheticism is an essential element of Simmel's methodology and of his tragic world view. We find his ability to illuminate aspects of the social totality through an examination of one moment's relationship with many others aesthetically satisfying, but, as Lukács points out, 'this web of interrelationships must remain a labyrinth and cannot be a system'.[161] Simmel argues that all the expressions of cultural life stand in innumerable relationships to each other and that none can be extracted from the context in which they are found. This interconnectedness is revealed either through examining the actual basic interrelationship of the most diverse phenomena or through demonstrating the analogous structure possessed by different social phenomena. This web or network of relationships is itself located within a social process that has been dehistoricized. It is one that excludes levels of contradiction and therefore moves towards a view of society as a natural harmonious whole.

In *The Philosophy of Money* the interconnections of phenomena are removed from the level of their historical concretion. The 'false pathos of distance' transposes the phenomena studied on to a more abstract level. As Lieber argues, Simmel's critique is to be understood as a critique of culture rather than its economic social and political context. Where a historical dimension is absent, the effects of money and the money economy become the fate of all culture. Simmel's analysis of money 'must be conceived of as extending beyond its economic concretion as the symbol or index for a much more fundamental . . . process, one of the objectivation of the subjective, the quantification of the qualitative, the equalisation of what is not equal'.[162] This much was apparent to some of Simmel's contemporaries. Frischeisen-Köhler, for example, argues that he sought 'to conceive of the money economy as the expression of intellectualism',[163] to extend his analysis beyond the divisions of the 'work culture' to the sphere of their transcendence, to the 'intellectual culture'. Simmel himself saw *The Philosophy of Money* as an attempt 'to derive from the surface level of economic affairs a guideline which leads to the ultimate values and things of importance in all that is human'.[164] It is in this context that we may understand Simmel's view that capitalism itself is only one historically specific instance of the tragedy that is inherent in culture – the irreconcilable contradiction between subjective and objective culture, between the subjective spirit and objective formations. It is this problematic that lies behind Simmel's account of reification rather than the origins of commodity fetishism as in Marx's analysis.

Simmel himself later defined this tragic consciousness as one in which 'the destructive forces directed against some being spring forth from the deepest levels of this very being; or when its destruction has been initiated in itself, and forms the logical development of the very structure by which a being has built its own positive form'.[165] In *The Philosophy of Money* this tragedy springs from the objectification of the human subject but not, as in Hegel, as a necessary externalization of the human subject in the process of self-consciousness. Rather, Simmel presents us with a radicalized subject–object dualism; a dualism of life and form, of subjective and objective culture. Lieber argues that Simmel is[166]

> aware of and recognizes the contradictions and also injustices of the society of his time. . . . Since, however, he does not, or at least does not sufficiently, subject them to a concrete, historical and social analysis and as a result is hardly in a position to reveal the tendencies pointing towards their transcendence in society . . . , the concrete history and society congeals into a purely exemplary instance of an all-encompassing essential tension between subjectivity and objectivity, and this means, finally, between the individual and society, a tension which is interpreted as being fundamentally tragic.

The humanistic impulse must then be forced back into an inner subjectivity, into the *intérieur*, and society must remain as it is.

This tragic vision is not, however, one that is peculiar to Simmel though the specific form which it takes is clearly Simmel's own. Rather, recent commentators such as Lieber and Lenk have argued that some version of this tragic vision characterizes the whole of *Lebensphilosophie*.[167] Furthermore, Lenk suggests that it lies at the roots of the sociology of knowledge developed by Max Scheler and Karl Mannheim in Weimar Germany. We have already seen the extent to which elements of this vision predominate in Lukács's early work. It might even be suggested that, when Lucien Goldmann traces back his own version of the tragic consciousness to the young Lukács, what he is in fact doing is developing elements of Simmel's tragic vision.[168] Thus, neither the aestheticization of reality nor the tragic vision have disappeared from some theoretical traditions in the social sciences.

VI

One need not accept the extravagant claims that have been made in the past for Simmel's *Philosophy of Money* in order to argue that it is an important work in the development of social theory. Nisbet, for example, engages in misplaced comparison when he suggests that[169]

> only Spengler's *Decline of the West* presents us with as detailed and imaginative a picture of money and credit as the alembic within which the Western mind became transposed from preoccupation with metaphysical and social essence to quantity and variations of quantity.

Similarly, Albert Salomon suggests that Simmel's study of money[170]

> is the sociological pendant to Jacob Burckhardt's *Civilization of the Renaissance in Italy*. It presents under the sociological aspect the problematic character of the modern independence and of the modern individualism after the disintegration of the social system of the feudal societies.

In a different vein, Lawrence makes even more dubious claims for Simmel's *Philosophy of Money* when he states that it[171]

> anticipated many of the ideas later developed by thinkers such as Ivan Illich, Alvin Gouldner and Charles Reich. All the ideas of admass, means–ends disjunction, anomie, personal inauthenticity, ambiguous freedom and technological determinism are to be found here.

In all these cases, the judgment of Simmel's work is based upon an abstract comparison, one that extracts Simmel's study from a specific concrete historical context and then goes on to suggest connections that often cannot be substantiated. In short, such comparisons suffer from the same failing as Simmel's own abstract excessive use of argument by analogy.

This is in no way intended to suggest that one cannot make significant claims for the importance of Simmel's *Philosophy of Money* both in its own right and in terms of the extent to which it extends our understanding of a distinctive but widespread response to certain problems faced by German society at the turn of the century. Further, it has been possible to trace the specific relationship between Simmel's work and that of other central figures in European social theory and philosophy.

We have already seen that most of Simmel's contemporary reviewers, even where they were not entirely in agreement with his approach or conclusions, were impressed with *The Philosophy of Money* as a major contribution to sociology and philosophy. In terms of the direct significance of this work for contemporaries and later writers it has been shown that, with the exception of Weber (and much more work is necessary on his connections with Simmel), Lukács and a few other writers largely in Weimar Germany, the work has not received the attention which it deserves. It stands with Tönnies's *Gemeinschaft und Gesellschaft* and some of Tönnies's other contemporary writings as an attempt to conceptualize the transition to a capitalist society and its attendant effects upon human relationships. Within the context of this transition to capitalism, Salomon quite rightly suggests that 'Simmel's work remains highly relevant for the critical re-examination of Max Weber's thesis on inner worldly asceticism and on the Puritan spirit. Simmel has made suggestions which point to a quite different solution.'[172]

At a different level, it has also been argued that *The Philosophy of Money* represents an important rediscovery or anticipation of many of the ideas contained in Marx's early writings, especially with regard to alienation. Certainly there do exist many surprising affinities but they should not obscure the significantly different context within which they are presented, namely, within the framework of an aesthetic and cultural critique of the money economy that is far removed from Marx's own intentions. On the other hand, the development of the concept of reification, first systematically developed by Lukács in *History and Class Consciousness*, can be understood only in the light of Lukács's attempt to grasp the diverse insights of Hegel, Marx and, as has been argued, Simmel.

However, quite apart from these and other diverse strands and connections which specifically link Simmel's work to his contemporaries, it is the case that the publication of his *Philosophy of Money* should seriously challenge many accepted assumptions about and interpretations of his work as a whole. It is not merely that Simmel here presents a more comprehensive discussion of such issues as social exchange, the effects of the division of labour, reification and the consequences of metropolitan life than is found in many of his other writings, but also that these discussions exist within a much wider and more far-reaching context, which enables us to grasp more readily his philosophical and social world view. Furthermore, *The Philosophy of Money* contains an examination of many areas of social life, such as the account of social action in terms of an end–means teleology, that are hardly dealt with elsewhere in his work. All this should lead to a reassessment of Simmel's work as a whole and, necessarily, that of many of his contemporaries and successors.

NOTES

1 G. Schmoller, 'Simmels Philosophie des Geldes', *Jahrbuch für Gesetzgebung, Verwaltung und Volkswirtschaft*, vol. 25, no. 3, 1901, p. 799. Strangely, this review is not listed in the otherwise quite comprehensive bibliography of reviews of Simmel's work in K. Gassen and M. Landmann (eds), *Buch des Dankes an Georg Simmel*, Berlin, 1958, pp. 314–15.

2 G. Simmel, 'Zur Psychologie des Geldes', *Jahrbuch für Gesetzgebung, Verwaltung und Volkswirtschaft*, vol. 13, no. 4, 1889, pp. 1251–64.

3 See the following articles by Simmel: 'Das Geld in der modernen Kultur', *Neue Freie Presse*, Vienna, 1896, reprinted in *Zeitschrift des Oberschlesischen Berg-und-Huttenmannischen Vereins*, vol. 35, 1896, pp. 319–24; 'Die Bedeutung des Geldes für das Tempo des Lebens', *Neue Deutsche Rundschau*, vol. 8, 1897, pp. 111–22; 'Fragmente aus einer "Philosophie des Geldes"', *Zeitschrift für immanente Philosophie*, vol. 3, 1898; 'Die Rolle des Geldes in den Beziehungen der Geschlechter. Fragment aus einer "Philosophie des Geldes"', *Die Zeit*, Vienna, vol. 14 (15, 22, 29 January), 1898; 'Fragmente aus einer "Philosophie des Geldes"', *Jahrbuch für Gesetzgebung, Verwaltung und Volkswirtschaft*, vol. 23, 1899; 'Zur Philosophie der Arbeit', *Neue Deutsche Rundschau*, vol. 10, 1899, pp. 449–63; 'Sozialismus und Pessimismus', *Die Zeit*, vol. 22, Vienna (3 February), 1900.

4 G. Simmel, *Über sociale Differenzierung. Sociologische und psychologische Untersuchungen*, Leipzig, 1890. Some extracts from this work have recently been translated. See P. Lawrence, *Georg Simmel: Sociologist and European*, London, 1976, pp. 95–138.

5 G. Simmel, *Die Probleme der Geschichtsphilosophie. Eine erkenntnistheoretische Studie*, Leipzig, 1892. This volume was revised by Simmel several times: see 5th ed., 1923.

6 G. Simmel, *Einleitung in die Moralwissenschaft. Eine Kritik der ethischen Grundbegiffe*, Berlin, vol. 1, 1892; vol. 2, 1893.

7 G. Simmel, *Soziologie. Untersuchungen über die Formen der Vergesellschaftung*, Leipzig, 1908. See the bibliography in K. Gassen and M. Landmann (eds), *Buch des Dankes an Georg Simmel*, op. cit. A translation of many sections of Simmel's work is to be found in K. H. Wolff (trans. and introd.), *The Sociology of Georg Simmel*, New York, 1950.

8 This fragment has now been translated. See D. Levine's translation and introduction to Max Weber, 'Georg Simmel as Sociologist', *Social Research*, vol. 39, 1972, pp. 155–63.

9 Such a periodization of Simmel's work is to be found in M. Frischeisen-Köhler, 'Georg Simmel', *Kantstudien*, vol. 24, 1920, pp. 1–53. The reader of *The Philosophy of Money* will no doubt see elements of all three phases of Simmel's work in this volume.

10 M. Frischeisen-Köhler, 'Georg Simmel', op. cit., pp. 12–13.

11 ibid., pp. 19–20.

12 K. Joël, 'G. Simmel', *Neue Züricher Zeitung*, 17 October 1918, Abendblatt, reprinted in K. Gassen and M. Landmann (eds), *Buch des Dankes an Georg Simmel*, op. cit., p. 167. In a similar vein, Max Adler argued that Simmel took up the theme of money in order to show 'how living connections exist in individual life and history between the most external, realistic phenomena and the most ideal potentialities of human existence. This work discloses, first, from which emotional presuppositions a phenomenon such as money is possible and then it shows how the fact of money, once it has emerged, may itself be traced back to the individual's emotions, to the interlinkings of his fortunes and to the structure of his social relationships.' Cf. M. Adler, *Georg Simmels Bedeutung für die Geistesgeschichte*, Vienna, 1919, p. 41.

13 Max Weber, 'Georg Simmel as Sociologist', op. cit., p. 159.

14 See the negative report on Simmel when he was being considered for a chair of philosophy in Heidelberg. The translation is to be found in L. Coser, 'The Stranger in the Academy' in L. A. Coser (ed.), *Georg Simmel*, Englewood Cliffs, New Jersey, 1965, pp. 37–9. For the German original and several other interesting reports on Simmel at various points of his career see M. Landmann, 'Bausteine zur Biographie', in K. Gassen and M. Landmann (eds), *Buch des Dankes an Georg Simmel*, op. cit., pp. 11–33.

15 E. Baumgarten, *Max Weber. Werk und Person*, Tübingen, 1964, p. 611. This view should be compared with the letters of recommendation for Simmel at various stages of his career signed by, among others, Dilthey and Windelband. See M. Landmann, 'Bausteine zur Biographie', op. cit., pp. 22ff.

16 For a brief discussion of Simmel's influence on other writers see M. Landmann, 'Einleitung des Herausgebers' in M. Landmann (ed.), *Georg Simmel, Das individuelle Gesetz*, Frankfurt, 1968, pp. 24ff. See also below, pp. 13f.

17 M. Steinhoff, 'Die Form als soziologische Grundkategorie bei Georg Simmel', *Kölner Vierteljahrshefte für Soziologie*, vol. 4, 1924–5, p. 259; translated in H. Maus, 'Simmel in German Sociology', in K. H. Wolff (ed.), *Essays on Sociology, Philosophy and Aesthetics*, Columbus, Ohio, 1959, p. 195.

18 The work which is most apparently based upon Simmel's analysis is L. A. Coser, *The Functions of Social Conflict*, London, 1956, though it is very doubtful whether Simmel was quite the functionalist that Coser makes him out to be.

19 Lawrence, for instance, in his introduction to *Georg Simmel*, op. cit., indeed suggests that even in Simmel's more difficult works it is possible to extract 'clear propositions . . . without any violation of the writer's intentions'

(p. 33). Later, he states that 'it is not difficult to derive straightforward relationship-between-phenomena propositions from Simmel's writings, and . . . such propositions may well be candidates for operationalization in the fuller sense' (p. 34). How this can possibly be performed without violating 'the writer's intentions' is difficult to imagine. Simmel's critique of science would suggest that Lawrence advocates precisely what Simmel objects to so strongly. Furthermore, it has often been suggested that Simmel's notion of sociology is hardly intelligible without reference to his deeply critical relationship not just to Marxism but also to positivism.

20 The collection edited by Wolff, *Essays on Sociology, Philosophy and Aesthetics*, op. cit., contains many interesting essays and a brief essay by Howard Becker 'On Simmel's *Philosophy of Money*', pp. 216–32. See also the collection translated and edited by K. H. Wolff, *The Sociology of Georg Simmel*, op. cit., and the useful bibliography; D. N. Levine (ed.), *Georg Simmel. On Individuality and Social Forms*, Chicago/London, 1971; P. Lawrence, *Georg Simmel: Sociologist and European*, op. cit. For German sources see K. Gassen and M. Landmann (eds), *Buch des Dankes an Georg Simmel*, op. cit., which contains an indispensable bibliography; H. Böhringer and K. Gründer (eds), *Aesthetik und Soziologie um die Jahrhundertwende: Georg Simmel*, Frankfurt, 1976, which contains a number of valuable essays and discussions. These works also make reference to many other briefer studies of Simmel's work. See also the examination of Simmel's sociology in P. E. Schnabel, *Die soziologische Gesamtkonzeption Georg Simmels*, Stuttgart, 1974, as well as the same author's brief 'Georg Simmel' in D. Kasler (ed.), *Klassiker des soziologischen Denkens*, vol. 1, Munich, 1976, pp. 267–311; further, H. J. Becher, *Georg Simmel. Die Grundlagen seiner Soziologie*, Stuttgart, 1971. On some aspects of *The Philosophy of Money* see also H. Brinkmann, *Methode und Geschichte. Die Analyse der Entfremdung in Georg Simmel's 'Philosophie des Geldes'*, Giessen, 1974.

21 N. J. Spykman, *The Social Theory of Georg Simmel*, Chicago, 1925, p. 218. With reference to Simmel's work as a whole, though in a similar vein, Abel had already argued for the need to remove the metaphysical and philosophical ballast from Simmel's work in order to render it more scientific. See T. Abel, *Systematic Sociology in Germany*, New York, 1925.

22 M. Frischeisen-Köhler, 'Georg Simmel', op. cit., p. 7.

23 p. 54 below. For an interesting discussion of the notion of a *philosophy* of money in relation to Simmel, see B. Liebrucks, 'Über den logischen Ort des Geldes' in his *Erkenntnis und Dialektik*, Hague, 1972, pp. 265–301.

24 p. 54 below.

25 K. Joël, 'Eine Zeitphilosophie', *Neue deutsche Rundschau*, vol. 12, 1901, p. 814.

26 p. 55 below. My emphasis.

27 See Georg Lukács, 'Georg Simmel', *Pester Lloyd*, 2 October 1918, reprinted in K. Gassen and M. Landmann (eds), *Buch des Dankes an Georg Simmel*, op. cit., pp. 171–6, esp. 172–3.

28 p. 56 below.

29 S. Kracauer, 'Georg Simmel', *Logos*, vol. 9, 1920; reprinted in S. Kracauer *Das Ornament der Masse*, Frankfurt, 1963, pp. 238–9. Kracauer's much neglected essay captures the flavour of Simmel's work. It was originally intended as an introductory chapter to a whole book on Simmel which, unfortunately, was never published. A much briefer discussion is to be found in S. Kracauer, *Soziologie als Wissenschaft*, Dresden, 1922; now reprinted in S. Kracauer, *Schriften I*, Frankfurt, 1971, see esp. pp. 65f.

30 S. Kracauer, 'Georg Simmel', op. cit., p. 239.

31 ibid., p. 241.

32 G. Simmel, *Probleme der Geschichtsphilosophie*, 3rd ed., Leipzig, 1907, p. 123n.

33 K. Joël, 'Eine Zeitphilosophie', op. cit., p. 813.

34 For an introductory account of Berlin in this period see G. Masur, *Imperial Berlin*, New York, 1970/London, 1971, esp. Chs 3ff.

35 G. Schmoller, 'Simmels Philosophie des Geldes', op. cit., p. 800.

36 ibid., p. 799.

37 ibid., p. 813.

38 ibid., p. 814.

39 ibid., p. 816.

40 S. P. Altmann, 'Simmel's Philosophy of Money', *American Journal of Sociology*, vol. 9, 1903, pp. 46–68.

41 For a brief examination of Small's relationship to Simmel see D. N. Levine, 'Introduction', *Georg Simmel. On Individuality and Social Forms*, op. cit., p. xlviii. Levine relates that 'shortly after Small founded the *American Journal of Sociology* in 1895 he began a program of publishing papers by Simmel – a total of fifteen entries between volumes 2 and 16, most translated by Small himself.' One of these translations, though the translator is not indicated, was in fact a section from *The Philosophy of Money*. See 'A Chapter in the Philosophy of Value', *American Journal of Sociology*, vol. 5, 1900, pp. 577–603. As Levine goes on to show, however, the reception of Simmel in American sociology in fact owes more to Robert Park, who attended Simmel's lectures in Berlin in the winter semester of 1899–1900. See D. Levine, 'Introduction', op. cit., pp. xlix–lvi.

42 S. P. Altmann, 'Simmel's Philosophy of Money', op. cit., p. 48.

43 ibid., p. 53.

44 ibid., p. 57.

45 C. Schmidt, 'Eine Philosophie des Geldes', *Sozialistische Monatshefte*, vol. 5, 1901, pp. 180–85. See also later D. Koigen, 'Georg Simmel als Geldapologet', *Dokumente des Sozialismus*, vol. 5, 1905, pp. 317–23.

46 S. P. Altmann, 'Simmel's Philosophy of Money', op. cit., p. 67.

47 Cited in M. Landmann, 'Bausteine zur Biographie', op. cit., p. 33. For other positive evaluations of later editions of *The Philosophy of Money* see, for example, W. Lexis, 'Neuere Schriften über das Geldwesen', *Jahrbücher für Nationalökonomie und Statistik*, vol. 41, 1911, esp. pp. 547–50; K. Elster, 'Philosophie des Geldes', *Jahrbücher für Nationalökonomie und Statistik*, vol. 61, 1921, pp. 353–63.

48 C. Schmidt, 'Eine Philosophie des Geldes', op. cit., p. 182.

49 ibid., p. 183.

50 D. Koigen, 'Georg Simmel als Geldapologet', op. cit., pp. 317–23. Although not a review of *Philosophie des Geldes*, it is worth while mentioning in this context the discussion of Simmel by August Koppel in his 'Für oder Wider Karl Marx. Prolegomena zu einer Biographie', *Volkswirtschaftliche Abhandlungen der Badischen Hochschulen*, vol. xiii, 1905. Besides arguing that *The Philosophy of Money* was one of the most important studies responsible for emancipating German sociology from both philosophy and economics, Koppel also emphasized the importance of Simmel's treatment of alienation.

51 R. Goldscheid, 'Jahresbericht über Erscheinungen der Soziologie in den Jahren 1899–1904', *Archiv für systematische Philosophie*, vol. 10, 1904, pp. 397–413.

52 ibid., pp. 397–8.

53 ibid., p. 411.

54 ibid., p. 412.

55 ibid., p. 413.

56 E. Durkheim, 'Philosophie des Geldes', *L'Année Sociologique*, vol. 5, 1900–01, pp. 140–5.

57 ibid., p. 142.

58 ibid., p. 143.

59 ibid., p. 145.

60 P. Honigsheim, 'Erinnerungen an Max Weber' in R. König and J. Winckelmann (eds), *Max Weber zum Gedächtnis* (*Kölner Zeitschrift für Soziologie. Sonderheft*, no. 7), 1966, p. 239.

61 N. J. Spykman, *The Social Theory of Georg Simmel*, op. cit., p. 218. It is instructive to note here that one of the major influences upon a whole generation of American sociologists, Talcott Parsons, confines Simmel to a marginal status in his *Structure of Social Action*, Glencoe, Illinois, 1937. This is surprising since there are affinities between some aspects of Parsons's work and Simmel's study of social differentiation. More difficult to understand is why Parsons should have considered Simmel's work insignificant for the development of a theory of social action and for an account of the capitalist economic order, especially in *The Philosophy of Money*.

62 M. Frischeisen-Köhler, 'Georg Simmel', op. cit., p. 20.

63 See E. Troeltsch, *Der Historismus und seine Probleme*, Tübingen, 1922, esp. pp. 572–95. Here Troeltsch describes Simmel as 'a child and favourite of modernity with all its terrible sicknesses and weaknesses', cf. p. 593. In the case of Sombart, his major work on modern capitalism makes few references to Simmel but reviewers like Altmann saw some echoes of Simmel's work in W. Sombart, *Der moderne Kapitalismus*, Berlin, 1902.

64 M. Weber, 'Georg Simmel as Sociologist', op. cit.

65 ibid., p. 158.

66 D. Levine, 'Introduction', *Georg Simmel. On Individuality and Social Forms*, op. cit., p. xlv.

67 See H. Gerth and C. Wright Mills, 'Introduction. The Man and His Work', in H. Gerth and C. Wright Mills, *From Max Weber*, London, 1947, pp. 12–14, esp. p. 14.

68 M. Weber, *Economy and Society* (ed. G. Roth and C. Wittich), New York, 1968, p. 4.

69 A number of important connections between Simmel and Weber at the methodological level are made in F. H. Tenbruck, 'Formal Sociology', in K. H. Wolff (ed.), *Essays on Sociology, Philosophy and Aesthetics*, op. cit. pp. 61–99. On the origins of Weber's methodology see earlier F. H. Tenbruck, 'Die Genesis der Methodologie Max Webers', *Kölner Zeitschrift für Soziologie*, vol. 11, 1959. It has been suggested that, in part, Weber's concept of ideal type may be traced back to Simmel's use of the notion of form but the evidence for this view is not compelling. On this see H. Baier, *Von der Erkenntnistheorie zur Wirklichkeitswissenschaft. Eine Studie über die Begründung der Soziologie bei Max Weber*, unpublished Habilitationsschrift, Münster, 1969, esp. pp. 194ff.

70 Weber speaks of 'the perceptive criticism which Dr O. Spann has made on some essential points concerning Simmel's concepts of "society" and "sociology" '; cf. M. Weber, 'Georg Simmel as Sociologist', p. 162. The work referred to is O. Spann, *Wirtschaft und Gesellschaft*, Dresden, 1907, reprinted in O. Spann. *Frühe Schriften in Auswahl*, Graz, 1974, esp. pp. 223–60.

71 O. Spann, *Frühe Schriften*, op. cit., p. 245.

72 ibid., p. 259.

73 M. Weber, *The Protestant Ethic and the Spirit of Capitalism* (trans. T. Parsons), London, 1930, p. 185.

74 ibid., p. 193. Schnabel argues that 'In Simmel's "Philosophy of Money" . . . Weber found those methods outlined and in part carried out which he made use of in his later analysis of capitalism, "The Protestant Ethic and the Spirit of Capitalism". He found a mode of procedure described there . . . which did not remain content with the derivation and application of mere ideal types but rather extended them into embodiments of whole complexes

of meaning which grasped the distinctiveness of levels of historical development and thereby first developed them as a useful instrument for a cultural and social science'. See P. Schnabel, 'Georg Simmel', op cit., pp. 288–9.

75 This is true not merely of Simmel's analysis of the teleological series and ends–means rationality in *The Philosophy of Money* but was also evident in his early article 'Zur Psychologie des Geldes', op. cit., p. 1254.

76 See, for example, the discussion in W. Mommsen, 'Max Weber's Political Sociology and his Philosophy of World History', *International Social Science Journal*, vol. 17, 1965; W. Mommsen, *The Age of Bureaucracy*, Oxford, 1974; W. Mommsen, *Max Weber: Gesellschaft, Politik und Geschichte*, Frankfurt, 1974.

77 G. Lukács, 'Georg Simmel', op. cit., p. 171. In the context of Simmel's influence upon Lukács, it has been argued that Lukács's central notion of totality was greatly indebted to Simmel's work. See S. Rücker, 'Totalität als ethisches und ästhetisches Problem', *Text und Kritik* 39/40, pp. 52–64.

78 See T. Pinkus (ed.), *Conversations with Lukács*, London, 1974, where Lukács says that 'I do not at all regret today that I took my first lessons in social science from Simmel and Max Weber and not from Kautsky. I don't know whether one cannot even say today that this was a fortunate circumstance for my own development.' Passim, p. 100.

79 G. Lukács, 'Georg Simmel', op. cit., p. 175. It is interesting that Max Adler, the Austro-Marxist, should also single out *The Philosophy of Money* as the most significant of Simmel's sociological works. See M. Adler, *Georg Simmels Bedeutung für die Geistesgeschichte*, Vienna/Leipzig, 1919, pp. 41f.

80 See G. Lukács, 'Zum Wesen und zur Methode der Kultursoziologie', *Archiv für Sozialwissenschaft und Sozialpolitik*, vol. 39, 1915, p. 216. The extent to which the major themes of these two works by Tönnies and Simmel remained central to Lukács's later work is instructive. Lukács's preference for the organic community, the *Gemeinschaft*, as a model of human society is, in many ways, intensely conservative, yet it is one which permeates his historical outline of the development of culture. It is also a view which, in another context, was heavily criticized by Brecht. See B. Brecht, 'Against Lukács', *New Left Review*, 84, 1974.

81 G. Lukács, 'Zum Wesen und zur Methode der Kultursoziologie', op. cit., p. 218. The manner in which Lukács outlines the alternative methods in a sociology of culture and his notion of sociology as a form suggests his adherence to Simmel's position.

82 G. Lukács, *A modern dráma fejlödésének története*, Budapest, 1911; German version of the early sections of this book as G. Lukács, 'Zur Soziologie des modernen Dramas', *Archiv für Sozialwissenschaft und Sozialpolitik*, vol. 38, nos 283, pp. 303–45, 662–706. All references are to the German version.

83 G. Lukács, 'Zur Soziologie des modernen Dramas', op. cit., p. 311.

84 ibid., p. 314.

85 ibid., p. 322.

86 ibid., p. 665.

87 ibid., pp. 665-6.

88 ibid., p. 666.

89 ibid., p. 667.

90 ibid., p. 674.

91 ibid., p. 684.

92 G. Lukács, 'The Metaphysics of Tragedy', in G. Lukács, *Soul and Form* (trans. A. Bostock), London, 1973, pp. 152-3.

93 ibid., p. 173.

94 G. Lukács, *The Theory of the Novel* (trans. A. Bostock), London, 1971, p. 29.

95 G. Lukács, 'Alte Kultur und neue Kultur', *Kommunismus*, vol. 1, no. 43, 1920, pp. 1538-49.

96 Quoted in D. Kettler, *Marxismus und Kultur. Mannheim und Lukács in den ungarischen Revolutionen 1918/19*, Neuwied/Berlin, 1967, p. 5.

97 In recent years there has been a renewed interest in Lukács's early works and in his development down to the publication of *Geschichte und Klassenbewusstsein*. See the articles by Breines and Arato referred to below. See also, J. Kammler, *Politische Theorie von Georg Lukács. Struktur und historischer Praxisbezug bis 1929*, Darmstadt/Neuwied, 1974; T. Hanak, *Lukács war anders*, Meisenheim, 1973; D. Kettler, *Marxismus und Kultur*, Neuwied/Berlin, 1967; A. Grunenberg, *Bürger und Revolutionär: Georg Lukács 1918-28*, Cologne/Frankfurt, 1976; A. Heller, et. al., *Die Seele und das Leben*, Frankfurt, 1977.

98 P. Breines, 'Lukács, Revolution and Marxism, 1885-1918: Notes on Lukács's "Road to Marx" ', *The Philosophical Forum*, vol. 3, 1972, p. 414. See also A. Arato, 'Lukács's Path to Marxism (1910-1923)', *Telos*, no. 7, 1971, pp. 128-36; A. Arato, 'The Neo-Idealist Defense of Subjectivity', *Telos*, no. 21, 1974, pp. 108-61.

99 G. Lukács, *History and Class Consciousness* (trans. R. Livingstone), London, 1971, p. 94.

100 ibid., p. 95. It is interesting to note here that Lukács immediately follows this critique of Simmel with a quotation from Marx's *Capital* that comes from a passage in which Marx's only reference to reification (*Verdinglichung*) is made. See K. Marx and F. Engels, *Werke*, vol. 25 (*Das Kapital*, vol. 3), Berlin, 1972, pp. 838-9. The concept appears in relation to Marx's critique of vulgar economy in the section on the trinity formula and then only once as *Verdinglichung* ('die Mystifikation der kapitalistischen Produktionsweise, die Verdinglichung der gesellschaftlichen Verhältnisse', op. cit., p. 828). It appears as *Versachlichung* on p. 839. Unfortunately, the reference

is obscured in the English translation as 'the complete mystification of the capitalist mode of production, the conversion of social relations into things' in K. Marx, *Capital*, vol. 3, Moscow, 1962, p. 809. For a discussion of the term see L. Goldmann, 'la Réification', in *Recherches dialectiques*, Paris, 1959, pp. 64–106; also Y. Ishaghpour, 'Avant-Propos' to L. Goldmann, *Lukács et Heidegger*, Paris, 1973, esp. pp. 12ff. For a further reference to Lukács's critique of Simmel see G. Lukács, *History and Class Consciousness*, op. cit., pp. 156–7.

101 For a brief discussion of Lukács's debt to Weber see K. Maretsky, 'Industrialisierung und Kapitalismus – Probleme der Marxrezeption in Georg Lukács' Geschichte und Glassenbewusstsein', *Das Argument*, no. 65, 1971, pp. 289–312.

102 E. Bloch, *Geist der Utopie*, Munich, 1918. pp. 246–7. Quoted and translated in H. Maus, 'Simmel in German Sociology', op. cit., pp. 194–5.

103 This is not to suggest that Simmel's influence as a whole was insignificant. See, for example, M. Landmann, 'Ernst Bloch im Gespräch', in S. Unseld (ed.), *Ernst Bloch zu Ehren*, Frankfurt, 1965, esp. pp. 347f.

104 See W. Benjamin, *Briefe* (ed. G. Scholem and T. W. Adorno), vol. 2, Frankfurt, 1966, pp. 824f. Benjamin too sought to encapsulate the spirit of the age, albeit in a critical manner, in his examination of apparently insignificant details of social existence.

105 One of Adorno's highly critical attacks on Simmel is to be found in T. W. Adorno, 'Henkel, Krug und frühe Erfahrung', in S. Unseld (ed.), *Ernst Bloch zu Ehren*, op. cit., pp. 9–20. For a critique of Adorno's reception to Simmel here see M. Landmann, 'Georg Simmel als Prugelknabe', *Philosophische Rundschau*, vol. 14, 1967, pp. 258–74, esp. 267–74.

106 See S. Kracauer, 'Georg Simmel', op. cit.

107 See S. Kracauer, 'Der Detektiv-Roman', in *Schriften I*, op. cit., pp. 105–204; S. Kracauer, *Die Angestellten. Aus dem neuesten Deutschland*, Frankfurt, 1930, reprinted in *Schriften I*, op. cit., pp. 207–304. It is possible to trace other direct links between Simmel and phenomenology – not least his influence on Husserl and Schutz – but such connections hardly arise primarily out of *The Philosophy of Money*.

108 For the argument that relates Simmel's work to the sociology of knowledge in Germany see K. Lenk, *Marx in der Wissenssoziologie*, Neuwied/Berlin, 1972.

109 L. v. Wiese, *Allgemeine Soziologie als Lehre von den Beziehungen und Beziehungsgebilden der Menschen*, Munich/Leipzig, 1924.

110 For the relevant translations see the bibliography in K. Gassen and M. Landmann (eds), *Buch des Dankes an Georg Simmel*, op. cit., pp. 338–9.

111 See esp. T. Kistiakowski, *Gesellschaft und Einzelwesen. Eine methodologische Studie*, Berlin, 1899.

`112` G. Lukács, *History and Class Consciousness*, op. cit., p. ix.

`113` Quoted in F. Tökei, 'Lukács and Hungarian Culture', *New Hungarian Quarterly*, vol. xiii, no. 47, 1972, p. 110.

`114` G. Lukács, 'Art and Society', *New Hungarian Quarterly*, vol. 13, no. 47, 1972, pp. 44–5.

`115` G. Lukács, *Die Zerstörung der Vernunft*, Berlin, 1954, p. 397.

`116` See H. J. Lieber in H. Böhringer and K. Gründer (eds), *Aesthetik und Soziologie um die Jahrhundertwende: Georg Simmel*, op. cit., p. 13.

`117` See, for example, F. Tönnies, 'Historismus und Rationalismus', *Archiv für systematische Philosophie*, vol. 1, 1895, pp. 227–52; translated as F. Tönnies, 'Historicism, Rationalism and the Industrial System', in W. J. Cahnman and R. Heberle (eds), *Ferdinand Tönnies on Sociology: Pure, Applied and Empirical*, Chicago/London, 1971, pp. 266–87. It is possible too that Simmel was acquainted with the preparation of the work by W. Sombart, *Der Moderne Kapitalismus*, Berlin, 1902.

`118` See, for example, F. W. Gärtner, 'Ein Beitrag zur Widerlegung der Marxschen Lehre von Mehrwert', *Zeitschrift für Staatswissenschaft*, vol. 49, 1893; W. Sombart, 'Zur Kritik des ökonomischen Systems von Karl Marx', *Archiv für soziale Gesetzgebung und Statistik*, vol. 7, no. 4, 1894; E. Böhm-Bawerk, 'Zum Abschluss des Marxschen Systems', in O. v. Boenigk (ed.), *Staatswissenschaftliche Arbeiten: Festgaben für Karl Knies*, Berlin, 1896; C. Schmidt, 'Grenznutzenpsychologie und Marxsche Wertlehre', *Sozialistische Monatshefte*, vol. 1, 1897.

`119` Quoted in K. Gassen and M. Landmann (eds), *Buch des Dankes an Georg Simmel*, op. cit., p. 94.

`120` See H. Blumenberg, 'Geld oder Leben', in H. Böhringer and K. Gründer (eds), *Aesthetik und Soziologie um die Jahrhundertwende: Georg Simmel*, op. cit., pp. 121–34.

`121` G. Simmel, 'Anfang einer unvollendeten Selbstdarstellung', in K. Gassen and M. Landmann (eds), *Buch des Dankes an Georg Simmel*, op. cit., p. 9.

`122` M. Susman, *Die geistige Gestalt Georg Simmels*, Tübingen, 1959, p. 9.

`123` H. Blumenberg, 'Geld oder Leben', op. cit., p. 125.

`124` See below, p. 84.

`125` See K. Marx, *Capital* (trans. B. Fowkes), vol. 1, London, 1976, p. 188, n. 1; K. Marx, *A Contribution to the Critique of Political Economy*, London, 1971, pp. 83ff.

`126` H. Brinkmann, *Methode und Geschichte. Die Analyse der Entfremdung in Georg Simmels 'Philosophie des Geldes'*, Giessen, 1974, p. 82.

`127` ibid., p. 87.

`128` See A. Arato, 'The Neo-Idealist Defense of Subjectivity', op. cit., p. 153.

`129` ibid., p. 152.

130 See G. Schmoller, 'Die Thatsache der Arbeitsteilung', *Jahrbuch für Gesetzgebung, Verwaltung und Volkswirtschaft*, vol. 13, 1889; G. Schmoller, 'Arbeitsteilung und sociale Klassenbildung', *Jahrbuch für Gesetzgebung, Verwaltung und Volkswirtschaft*, vol. 14, 1890. It is interesting to note with regard to the latter article that Simmel, unlike Schmoller, does not deal with the relationship between the division of labour and the formation of social classes.

131 G. F. Knapp, *Die Landarbeiter in Knechtschaft und Freiheit*.

132 See below, pp. 453–4.

133 K. Mannheim, 'Eine soziologische Theorie der Kultur und ihrer Erkennbarkeit', unpublished MS. (*c.* 1926), p. 9.

134 ibid.

135 A. Arato, 'The Neo-Idealist Defense of Subjectivity', op. cit., p. 154.

136 G. Simmel, 'Der Begriff und die Tragödie der Kultur', in G. Simmel, *Philosophie der Kultur*, Leipzig, 1911; English version as 'On the Concept and the Tragedy of Culture', in G. Simmel, *The Conflict in Modern Culture and other Essays* (trans. P. Etzkorn), New York, 1968, p. 42.

137 ibid., p. 43.

138 See, for example, G. Simmel, 'Der Fragmentarcharakter des Lebens', *Logos*, vo. 6, 1917, pp. 29–40. For a general discussion of Simmel's philosophy of culture see R. Weingartner, *Experience and Culture: The Philosophy of Georg Simmel*, Middletown, Conn., 1960; and a brief account of Simmel's theory of alienation see J. Israel, *Alienation*, Boston, 1971, pp. 121–34.

139 M. Susman, *Die geistige Gestalt Georg Simmels*, op. cit., p. 16.

140 L. v. Wiese, 'Neuere soziologische Literatur', *Archiv für Sozialwissenschaft und Sozialpolitik*, vol. 31, 1910, p. 300. Extract translated in L. A. Coser (ed.), *Georg Simmel*, op. cit., pp. 53–7, esp. p. 56.

141 See K. Lenk, *Marx in der Wissenssoziologie*, op. cit., esp. ch. 1; S. Hübner-Funk, 'Aesthetizismus und Soziologie bei Georg Simmel', in H. Böhringer and K. Gründer (eds), *Ästhetik und Soziologie um die Jahrhundertswende: Georg Simmel*, op. cit., pp. 44–58 and the subsequent discussion, pp. 59–70; H. J. Lieber, *Kulturkritik und Lebensphilosophie*, Darmstadt, 1974; more briefly, M. Landmann, 'Einleitung', op. cit.

142 G. Lukács, 'Georg Simmel', op. cit., p. 175.

143 For a recent sociological study of the George Circle see M. Nutz, *Werte und Wertungen im Georg-Kreis*, Bonn, 1976.

144 G. Simmel, 'Stefan George. Eine kunstphilosophische Betrachtung', *Die Zukunft*, vol. 6, 1898, pp. 386–96; G. Simmel, 'Stefan George. Eine kunstphilosophische Studie', *Neue Deutsche Rundschau*, vol. 12, 1901, pp. 207–15.

145 Discussing the subjectivization of aesthetics, Gadamer speaks of 'the protest against modern industrial society which at the beginning of our century

caused the words Erlebnis and Erleben to become almost sacred clarion calls. The rebellion of the Jugend Bewegung (Youth Movement) against bourgeois culture and its forms was inspired by these ideas, the influence of Friedrich Nietzsche and Henry Bergson played its part, but also a "spiritual movement" like that around Stefan George and, not least, the seismographic accuracy with which the philosophy of Georg Simmel reacted to these events are all part of the same thing.' See H. G. Gadamer, *Truth and Method*, London, 1975, p. 57.

146 G. Simmel, 'Stefan George', *Neue Deutsche Rundschau*, vol. 12, 1901, p. 212.

147 G. Lukács, *Soul and Form*, op. cit., p. 83.

148 See the works by Hubner-Funk and Lieber, op. cit.

149 G. Simmel, *Soziologie*, 1908, Leipzig, p. 31.

150 H. J. Lieber, *Kulturkritik und Lebensphilosophie*, op. cit., p. 78.

151 ibid., p. 78.

152 G. Lukács, 'Georg Simmel', op. cit., p. 172. Bloch also argues that 'Simmel was fundamentally impressionistic'. Cf. S. Unseld (ed.), *Ernst Bloch im Gespräch*, op. cit., p. 350.

153 G. Lukács, 'Georg Simmel', op. cit., p. 173.

154 K. Mannheim, 'German Sociology (1918–1933)', in K. Mannheim, *Essays on Sociology and Social Psychology*, London, 1953, p. 217.

155 See below, p. 474.

156 See p. 475 below.

157 T. W. Adorno, *Kierkegaard*, 3rd ed., Frankfurt, 1966, esp. pp. 75f. For an interesting discussion of pathos and melancholy see also W. Lepenies, *Melancholie und Gesellschaft*, Frankfurt, 1969.

158 T. W. Adorno, *Kierkegaard*, op. cit., p. 87.

159 See E. Heintel, 'Der Mann ohne Eigenschaften und die Tradition', *Wissenschaft und Weltbild*, vol. 13, 1960, pp. 179–94, esp. p. 189.

160 S. Hübner-Funk, 'Aesthetizismus und Soziologie bei Georg Simmel', op. cit., pp. 68–9.

161 G. Lukács, 'Georg Simmel', op. cit., p. 175.

162 H. J. Lieber, *Kulturkritik und Lebensphilosophie*, op. cit., p. 17.

163 M. Frischeisen-Köhler, 'Georg Simmel', op. cit., p. 21.

164 See below, p. 55.

165 G. Simmel, 'On the Concept and the Tragedy of Culture', op. cit., p. 43. For a discussion of his concept of tragedy see I. Bauer, *Die Tragik in der Existenz des Modernen Menschen bei G. Simmel*, Berlin, 1962.

166 H. J. Lieber, *Kulturkritik und Lebensphilosophie*, op. cit., p. 77.

167 ibid.; K. Lenk, *Marx in der Wissenssoziologie*, op. cit. Another central figure in the *Lebensphilosophie* tradition, and also a Berlin philosopher, was Wilhelm Dilthey. For a useful comparison of Simmel and Dilthey which makes reference to *The Philosophy of Money* see U. Gerhardt, 'Immanenz und

Widerspruch. Die philosophischen Grundlagen der Soziologie Georg Simmels und ihr Verhältnis zur Lebensphilosophie Wilhelm Diltheys', *Zeitschrift für philosophische Forschung*, no. 25, 1971, pp. 276–92.

168 L. Goldmann, 'Introduction aux premiers écrits de Georges Lukács', *Les Temps Modernes*, 1962, pp. 254–80; see also L. Goldmann, *Lukács et Heidegger*, op. cit.

169 R. A. Nisbet, *The Sociological Tradition*, New York, 1966/London, 1967, p. 100.

170 A. Salomon, 'German Sociology', in G. Gurvitch and W. F. Moore (eds), *Twentieth Century Sociology*, New York, 1945; extract reprinted in L. A. Coser, *Georg Simmel*, op. cit., p. 137.

171 P. Lawrence, *Georg Simmel*, op. cit., p. 48.

172 A. Solomon, op. cit., p. 137. For a fuller appraisal see my *Georg Simmel: A Reassessment*, London, 1979 (forthcoming).

The Philosophy of Money

Preface

Every area of research has two boundaries marking the point at which the process of reflection ceases to be exact and takes on a philosophical character. The pre-conditions for cognition in general, like the axioms of every specific domain, cannot be presented and tested within the latter domain, but rather they call for a science of a more fundamental nature. The goal of this science, which is located in infinity, is to think without pre-conditions – a goal which the individual sciences deny themselves since they do not take any step without proof, that is, without pre-conditions of a substantive and methodological nature. Philosophy, too, cannot completely transcend such pre-conditions with regard to its own activity when it presents and tests them. But in this case, it is always the last point of cognition at which an authoritative decision and the appeal to the unprovable arises within us, and yet in view of the advances made in terms of what can be proved this point is never definitively fixed. If the start of the philosophical domain marks, as it were, the lower boundary of the exact domain, then its upper boundary lies at the point where the ever-fragmentary contents of positive knowledge seek to be augmented by definitive concepts into a world picture and to be related to the totality of life. If the history of the sciences really does reveal that the philosophical mode of cognition is the primitive mode, is a mere estimate of the phenomena in general concepts, then this provisional procedure is nevertheless indispensable when confronted with certain questions, namely those questions – especially those related to valuations and the most general relations of intellectual life – that we have so far been unable either to answer or to dismiss. Moreover, even the empirical in its perfected state might no more replace philosophy as an interpretation, a colouring and an individually selective emphasis of what is real than would the perfection of the mechanical reproduction of phenomena make the visual arts superfluous.

53

Out of this general appraisal of philosophy's position there emerge the rights that it possesses with regard to individual objects. If there is to be a philosophy of money, then it can only lie on either side of the economic science of money. On the one hand, it can present the pre-conditions that, situated in mental states, in social relations and in the logical structure of reality and values, give money its meaning and its practical position. This is not the question of the origin of money, for such a question belongs to history and not to philosophy. Moreover, no matter how much we appreciate the gain in the understanding of a phenomenon that is derived from a study of its historical development, its substantive meaning and importance often rest upon connections of a conceptual, psychological or ethical nature that are not temporal but rather are purely material. Such connections have, of course, been realized by historical forces, but are not exhausted by the fortuitousness of the latter. The significance, the dignity and the substance of justice, religion or knowledge lie completely beyond the question concerning the manner in which they were historically realized. The first part of this book, therefore, relates money to the conditions that determine its essence and the meaning of its existence.

The historical phenomenon of money, the idea and structure of which I shall attempt to develop out of feelings of value, out of praxis in relation to things and the reciprocal relationships between people as its presupposition, is studied in the second part of the book in its effects upon the inner world – upon the vitality of individuals, upon the linking of their fates, upon culture in general. Here, then, it is a question, on the one hand, of connections that are basically open to exact and detailed investigation but that, given the present state of knowledge, are not studied. They can only be dealt with in a philosophical manner, namely by a general estimation, by representing individual occurrences through connections between abstract concepts. On the other hand, it is a question of mental causes that will always be a matter of hypothetical interpretation and artistic reconstruction which can never be completely free from individual colouring. This combination of the money principle with the developments and valuations of inner life stands just as far behind the economic science of money as the problem area of the first part of the book stood before it. The one part seeks to make the essence of money intelligible from the conditions and connections of life in general; conversely, the other part seeks to make the essence and organization of the latter intelligible from the effectiveness of money.

Not a single line of these investigations is meant to be a statement about economics. That is to say, the phenomena of valuation and purchase, of exchange and the means of exchange, of the forms of production and the values of possession, which economics views from *one* standpoint, are here viewed from another. It is merely the fact that the aspect of these phenomena closest to economics is the most interesting in practical terms, is the most thoroughly investigated and can be represented in the most exact manner which has given rise to the

54

apparent justification for regarding them simply as 'economic facts'. But just as the appearance of a founder of a religion is by no means simply a religious phenomenon, and can also be studied by using the categories of psychology, perhaps even of pathology, general history and sociology; or just as a poem is not simply a fact of literary history, but also an aesthetic, a philological and a biographical fact; or just as the very standpoint of a single science, which is also based on the division of labour, never exhausts the totality of reality – so the fact that two people exchange their products is by no means simply an economic fact. Such a fact – that is, one whose content would be exhausted in the image that economics presents of it – does not exist. Moreover, and just as legitimately, such an exchange can be treated as a psychological fact, or as one that derives from the history of morals or even as an aesthetic fact. Even when it is considered to be an economic fact, it does not reach the end of a cul-de-sac; rather, in this guise it becomes the object of philosophical study, which examines its pre-conditions in non-economic concepts and facts and its consequences for non-economic values and relationships.

In this problem-complex, money is simply a means, a material or an example for the presentation of relations that exist between the most superficial, 'realistic' and fortuitous phenomena and the most idealized powers of existence, the most profound currents of individual life and history. The significance and purpose of the whole undertaking is simply to derive from the surface level of economic affairs a guideline that leads to the ultimate values and things of importance in all that is human. The abstract philosophical construction of a system maintains such a distance from the individual phenomena, especially from practical existence, that actually, at first sight, it only *postulates* their salvation from isolation and lack of spirituality, even from repulsiveness. Here the achievement of such salvation will be *exemplified* in only a single instance, but in one which, like money, not merely reveals the indifference of purely economic techniques but rather is, as it were, indifference itself, in that its entire significance does not lie in itself but rather in its transformation into other values. But since the opposition between what is apparently most superficial and insubstantial and the inner substance of life reaches a peak here, there must be the most effective reconciliation if this particular fact not only permeates, actively and passively, the entire range of the intellectual world but also manifests itself as the symbol of the essential forms of movement within this world. The unity of these investigations does not lie, therefore, in an assertion about a particular content of knowledge and its gradually accumulating proofs but rather in the possibility – which must be demonstrated – of finding in each of life's details the totality of its meaning. The great advantage of art over philosophy is that it sets itself a single, narrowly defined problem every time: a person, a landscape, a mood. Every extension of one of these to the general, every addition of bold touches of feeling for the world is made to appear as an enrichment, a gift, an undeserved benefit. On the other hand, philosophy, whose problem is nothing less than the totality of being, tends to reduce the magnitude of the latter when compared with itself and offers less than it seems obliged to offer. Here, conversely, the attempt is made to regard the problem as restricted and small in order to do justice to it by extending it to the totality and the highest level of generality.

Methodologically, this basic intention can be expressed in the following manner. The attempt is made to construct a new storey beneath historical materialism such that the explanatory value of the incorporation of economic life into the causes of intellectual culture is preserved, while these economic forms themselves are recognized as the result of more profound valuations and currents of psychological or even metaphysical pre-conditions. For the practice of cognition this must develop in infinite reciprocity. Every interpretation of an ideal structure by means of an economic structure must lead to the demand that the latter in turn be understood from more ideal depths, while for these depths themselves the general economic base has to be sought, and so on indefinitely. In such an alternation and entanglement of the conceptually opposed principles of cognition, the unity of things, which seems intangible to our cognition but none the less establishes its coherence, becomes practical and vital for us.

The intentions and methods referred to here could not lay claim to any justification in principle if they were not able to serve a substantive diversity of basic philosophical convictions. It is possible to relate the details and superficialities of life to its most profound and essential movements, and their interpretation in accordance with the total meaning of life can be performed on the basis of idealism just as much as of realism, of a rational as much as a volitional or an absolutist as much as a relativistic interpretation of being. The fact that the following investigations are founded on one of these world pictures, which I consider to be the most appropriate expression of the contemporary contents of science and emotional currents and decisively exclude the opposing world picture, might secure for them at worst the role of a mere typical example which, even if it is factually incorrect, reveals its methodological significance as the form of future truths.

At no point do the amendments to the second impression affect the essential motifs. However, through new examples and discussions and, above all, through an extension of the foundations, I have attempted to increase the likelihood of these motifs being intelligible and acceptable.

Analytical Part

CHAPTER 1

Value and Money

I

Reality and value as mutually independent categories through which our conceptions become images of the world

The order in which things are placed as natural entities is based on the proposition that the whole variety of their qualities rests upon a uniform law of existence. Their equality before the law of nature, the constant sum of matter and energy, the convertibility of the most diverse phenomena into one another, transform the differences that are apparent at first sight into a general affinity, a universal equality. Yet on a closer view this means only that the products of the natural order are beyond any question of a law. Their absolute determinateness does not allow any emphasis that might provide confirmation or doubt of their particular quality of being. But we are not satisfied with this indifferent necessity that natural science assigns to objects. Instead, disregarding their place in that series we arrange them in another order – an order of value – in which equality is completely eliminated, in which the highest level of one point is adjacent to the lowest level of another; in this series the fundamental quality is not uniformity but difference. The value of objects, thoughts and events can never be inferred from their mere natural existence and content, and their ranking according to value diverges widely from their natural ordering. Nature, on many occasions, destroys objects that, in terms of their value, might claim to be preserved, and keeps in existence worthless objects which occupy the place of the more valuable ones. This is not to say that there is a fundamental opposition between the two series, or that they are mutually exclusive. Such a view would imply a relation between the two series; it would establish, indeed, a diabolical world, determined by values, but with the signs reversed. The case is, rather,

59

that the relation between these series is completely accidental. With the same indifference, nature at one time offers us objects that we value highly, at another time withholds them. The occasional harmony between the series, the realization through the reality series of demands derived from the value series, shows the absence of any logical relationship between them just as strikingly as does the opposite case. We may be aware of the same life experience as both real and valuable, but the experience has quite a different meaning in the two cases. The series of natural phenomena could be described in their entirety without mentioning the value of things; and our scale of valuation remains meaningful, whether or not any of its objects appear frequently or at all in reality. Value is an addition to the completely determined objective being, like light and shade, which are not inherent in it but come from a different source. However, we should avoid one misinterpretation; namely, that the formation of value concepts, as a psychological fact, is quite distinct from the natural process. A superhuman mind, which could understand by means of natural laws everything that happens in the world, would also comprehend the fact that people have concepts of values. But these would have no meaning or validity for a being that conceived them purely theoretically, beyond their psychological existence. The meaning of value concepts is denied to nature as a mechanical causal system, while at the same time the psychic experiences that make values a part of our consciousness themselves belong to the natural world. Valuation as a real psychological occurrence is part of the natural world; but what we mean by valuation, its conceptual meaning, is something independent of this world; is not part of it, but is rather the whole world viewed from a particular vantage point. We are rarely aware of the fact that our whole life, from the point of view of consciousness, consists in experiencing and judging values, and that it acquires meaning and significance only from the fact that the mechanically unfolding elements of reality possess an infinite variety of values beyond their objective substance. At any moment when our mind is not simply a passive mirror or reality – which perhaps never happens, since even objective perception can arise only from valuation – we live in a world of values which arranges the contents of reality in an autonomous order.

Thus, value is in a sense the counterpart to being, and is comparable to being as a comprehensive form and category of the world view. As Kant pointed out, being is not a quality of objects; for if I state that an object, which so far existed only in my thoughts, exists, it does not acquire a new quality, because otherwise it would not be the same object that I thought of, but another one. In the same way, an object does not gain a new quality if I call it valuable; it is valued because of the qualities that it has. It is precisely its whole already determined being that is raised to the sphere of value. This is supported by a thorough analysis of our thinking. We are able to conceive the contents of our world view without regard for their real existence or non-existence. We can conceive the aggregates of qualities that we call objects, including all the laws of their interrelation and development, in their objective and logical significance, and we can ask – quite independently of this – whether, where and how often all these concepts or inner notions are realized. The conceptual meaning and determinateness of the objects is not affected by the question as to whether they do exist, nor by the question whether and where they are placed in the scale of values. However, if we want to establish either a theory or a practical rule, we cannot escape the necessity to answer these two questions. We must be able to say of each object that it exists or does not exist, and each object must have a definite place for us in the scale of values, from the highest through indifference to negative values. Indifference is a rejection of positive value; the *possibility* of interest remains inactive but is always in the background. The significance of this requirement, which determines the constitution of our world view, is not altered by the fact that our powers of comprehension are often insufficient to decide upon the reality of concepts, or by the fact that the range and certainty of our feelings are often inadequate to rank things according to their value, especially in any permanently and universal fashion. Over against the world of mere concepts, of objective qualities and determinations, stand the great categories of being and value, inclusive forms that take their material from the world of pure contents. Both categories have the quality of being fundamental, that is irreducible to each other or to other simpler elements. Consequently, the being of objects can never be inferred logically; being is rather a primary form of our perception, which can be sensed, experienced and believed, but cannot be deduced for somebody who does not yet know it. When this form of perception has once grasped a specific content – by a non-logical act – it can then be interpreted in its logical context and developed as far as this logical context reaches. As a rule, we are able to state why we assume the reality of a particular phenomenon; namely, because we have already assumed another phenomenon with which this one is connected by its specific characteristics. The reality of the first one, however, can be shown only by tracing it in similar fashion to a more fundamental one. This regression requires a final member whose existence depends only upon a sense of conviction, affirmation and acceptance, a sense that is directly given. Valuation has exactly the same relation to objects. All proofs of the value of an object are nothing more than the necessity of recognizing for that object the same value as has been assumed, and for the time being accepted, as indubitable for another object. We will later analyse the motives of this action. Here it will suffice to say that what we consider a proof of value is only the transference of an existing value to a new object. It does not reveal the essence of value, or the reason why value was originally attached to the object from which it is transferred to others.

If we accept the existence of a value, then the process of its realization, its evolution, can be comprehended rationally, because in general it follows the structure of the contents of reality. That there is a value at all, however, is a primary phenomenon. Value inferences only make known the conditions under which values are realized, yet without being produced by these conditions, just as theoretical proofs only prepare the conditions that favour the sense of affirmation or of existence. The question as to what value really is, like the question as to what being is, is unanswerable. And precisely because they have the same formal relation to objects, they are as alien to each other as are thought and extension for Spinoza. Since both express the same absolute substance, each in its own way and perfect in itself, the one can never encroach upon the other. They never impinge upon each other because they question the concepts of objects from completely different points of view. But this disjunctive parallelism of reality and value does not divide the world into a sterile duality, which the mind with its need for unity could never accept – even though its destiny and the method of its quest may be to move incessantly from diversity to unity and from unity to diversity. What is common to value and reality stands above them: namely the contents, which Plato called 'ideas', the qualitative, that which can be signified and expressed in our concepts of reality and value, and which can enter into either one or the other series. Below these two categories lies what is common to both: the soul, which absorbs the one or produces the other in its mysterious unity. Reality and value are, as it were, two different languages by which the logically related contents of the world, valid in their ideal unity, are made comprehensible to the unitary soul, or the languages in which the soul can express the pure image of these contents which lies beyond their differentiation and opposition. These two compilations made by the soul, through perceiving and through valuing, may perhaps once more be brought together in a metaphysical unity, for which there is no linguistic term unless it be in religious symbols. There is perhaps a cosmic ground where the heterogeneity and divergencies that we experience between reality and value no longer exist, where both series are revealed as one; this unity either being unaffected by the two categories, and standing beyond them in majestic indifference, or signifying a harmonious interweaving of both, which is shattered and distorted into fragments and contrasts only by our way of regarding it, as if we had an imperfect visual faculty.

The psychological fact of objective value

The characteristic feature of value, as it appears in contrast to reality, is usually called its subjectivity. Since one and the same object can have the highest degree of value for one soul and the lowest for another, and vice versa, and since on the other hand the most extensive and extreme differences between objects are compatible with equality of value, there appears to remain only the subject with his customary or exceptional, permanent or changing, moods and responses as the ground for valuation. This subjectivity, needless to say, has nothing to do with the subjectivity that refers to 'my perception' of the totality of the world. For the subjectivity of value contrasts value with the given objects, regardless of the way they are conceived. In other words, the subject who comprehends all objects is different from the subject who is confronted with the objects; the subjectivity that value shares with all other objects does not play any role here. Nor is his subjectivity merely caprice; independence from reality does not mean that value can be bestowed here and there with unrestrained and capricious freedom. Value exists in our consciousness as a fact that can no more be altered than can reality itself. The subjectivity of value, therefore, is first of all only negative, in the sense that value is not attached to objects in the same way as is colour or temperature. The latter, although determined by our senses, are accompanied by a feeling of their direct dependence upon the object; but in the case of value we soon learn to disregard this feeling because the two series constituted by reality and by value are quite independent of each other. The only cases more interesting than this general characterization are those in which psychological facts appear to lead to an opposite view.

In whatever empirical or transcendental sense the difference between objects and subjects is conceived, value is never a 'quality' of the objects, but a judgment upon them which remains inherent in the subject. And yet, neither the deeper meaning and content of the concept of value, nor its significance for the mental life of the individual, nor the practical social events and arrangements based upon it, can be sufficiently understood by referring value to the 'subject'. The way to a comprehension of value lies in a region in which that subjectivity is only provisional and actually not very essential.

The distinction between subject and object is not as radical as the accepted separation of these categories in practical life and in the scientific world would have us believe. Mental life begins with an undifferentiated state in which the Ego and its objects are not yet distinguished; consciousness is filled with impressions and perceptions while the bearer of these contents has still not detached himself from them. It is as a result of a second-stage awareness, a later analysis, that a subject in particular real conditions comes to be distinguished from the content of his consciousness in those conditions. This development obviously leads to a situation where a man speaks of himself as 'I' and recognizes the existence of other objects external to this 'I'. Metaphysics sometimes claims that the transcendent essence of being is completely unified, beyond the opposition of subject–object, and this has a psychological counterpart in the simple, primitive condition of being possessed by the content of a perception, like a child who does not yet speak of himself as 'I', or as may perhaps be observed in a rudimentary form at all stages of life. This unity from which the categories of subject and object develop in relation to each other – in a process to be examined later – appears to us as a subjective unity because we approach it with the concept of objectivity developed later; and because we do not have a proper term for such unities, but name them usually after one of the partial elements that appear in the subsequent analysis. Thus, it has been asserted that all actions are essentially egoistic, whereas egoism has a meaning only within a system of action and by contrast with its correlate, altruism. Similarly, pantheism has described the universality of being as God, although a positive concept of God depends on its contrast with everything empirical. This evolutionary relation between subject and object is repeated finally on a large scale: the intellectual world of classical antiquity differs from that of modern times chiefly in the fact that only the latter has, on the one hand, developed a comprehensive and clear concept of the Ego, as shown by the significance of the problem of liberty which was unknown in ancient times; and on the other, expressed the independence and force of the concept of the object through the idea of unalterable laws of nature. Antiquity was much closer than were later periods to the stage of indifference in which the contents of the world were conceived as such, without being apportioned between subject and object.

Objectivity in practice as standardization or as a guarantee for the totality of subjective values

This development which separates subject and object appears to be sustained on both sides by the same theme, but operating at different levels. Thus, the awareness of being a subject is already an objectification. This is a basic feature of the mind in its form as personality. The fundamental activity of our mind, which determines its form as a whole, is that we can observe, know and judge ourselves just like any other 'object'; that we dissect the Ego, experienced as a unity, into a perceiving subject and a perceived object, without its losing its unity, but on the contrary with its becoming aware of its unity through this inner antagonism. The mutual dependence of subject and object is here drawn together in a single point; it has affected the subject itself, which otherwise stands confronting the world as object. Thus man has realized the basic form of his relation to the world, of his acceptance of the world, as soon as he becomes aware of himself and calls himself 'I'. But before that happens there exists – in respect of meaning as well as of mental growth – a simple perception of content which does not distinguish between subject and object and is not yet divided between them. Regarded from the other side, this content itself, as a logical and conceptual entity, likewise lies beyond the distinction between subjective and objective reality. We can think of any object simply in terms of its qualities and their interconnection without asking whether or not this ideal complex of qualities has an objective existence. To be sure, so far as such a pure objective content is thought, it becomes a conception and to that extent a subjective structure. But the subjective is here only the dynamic act of conception, the function that apprehends the content; in itself this content is thought of as being independent of the act of conceiving. Our mind has a remarkable ability to think of contents as being independent of the act of thinking; this is one of its primary qualities, which cannot be reduced any further. The contents have their conceptual or objective qualities and relationships which can be apprehended but which are not thereby completely absorbed; they exist whether or not they are part of my representation and whether or not they are part of objective reality. The content of a representation does not coincide with the representation of contents. The simple undifferentiated conception that consists only in becoming aware of a content cannot be characterized as subjective, because it does not yet know the contrast between subject and object. Similarly, the pure content of objects or conceptions is not objective, but escapes equally this differential form and its opposite, while being ready to present itself in one or the other. Subject and object are born in the same act: logically, by presenting the conceptual ideal content first as a content of representation, and then as a content of objective reality; psychologically, when the still ego-less representation, in which person and object are undifferentiated, becomes divided and gives rise to a distance between the self and its object, through which each of them becomes a separate entity.

Economic value as the objectification of subjective values

This process, which finally produces our intellectual world view, also occurs in the sphere of our volitional practical activity. Here also the distinction between the desiring, consuming, valuing subject and the valued object does not comprehend all aspects of mental life, nor all the objective circumstances of practical activity. Human enjoyment of an object is a completely undivided act. At such moments we have an experience that does not include an awareness of an object confronting us or an awareness of the self as distinct from its present condition. Phenomena of the basest and the highest kind meet here. The crude impulse, particularly an impulse of an impersonal, general nature, wants to release itself towards an object and to be satisfied, no matter how; consciousness is exclusively concerned with satisfaction and pays no attention to its bearer on one side or its object on the other. On the other hand, intense aesthetic enjoyment displays the same form. Here too 'we forget ourselves', but at the same time we no longer experience the work of art as something with which we are confronted, because our mind is completely submerged in it, has absorbed it by surrendering to it. In this case, as in the other, our psychological condition is not yet, or is no longer, affected by the contrast between subject and object.

65

Only a new process of awareness releases those categories from their undisturbed unity; and only then is the pure enjoyment of the content seen as being on the one hand a state of the subject confronting an object, and on the other the effect produced by an object that is independent of the subject. This tension, which disrupts the naive-practical unity of subject and object and makes us conscious of each in relation to the other, is brought about originally through the mere fact of desire. In desiring what we do not yet own or enjoy, we place the content of our desire outside ourselves. In empirical life, I admit, the finished object stands before us and is only then desired – if only because, in addition to our will, many other theoretical and emotional events contribute to the objectification of mental contents. Within the practical world, however, in relation to its inner order and intelligibility, the origin of the object itself, and its being desired by the subject, are correlative terms – the two aspects of this process of differentiation which splits the immediate unity of the process of enjoyment. It has been asserted that our conception of objective reality originates in the resistance that objects present to us, especially through our sense of touch. We can apply this at once to the practical problem. We desire objects only if they are not immediately given to us for our use and enjoyment; that is, to the extent that they resist our desire. The content of our desire becomes an object as soon as it is opposed to us, not only in the sense of being impervious to us, but also in terms of its distance as something not-yet-enjoyed, the subjective aspect of this condition being desire. As Kant has said: the possibility of experience is the possibility of the objects of experience – because to have experiences means that our consciousness creates objects from sense impressions. In the same way, the possibility of desire is the possibility of the objects of desire. The object thus formed, which is characterized by its separation from the subject, who at the same time establishes it and seeks to overcome it by his desire, is for us a value. The moment of enjoyment itself, when the opposition between subject and object is effaced, consumes the value. Value is only reinstated as contrast, as an object separated from the subject. Such trivial experiences as that we appreciate the value of our possessions only after we have lost them, that the mere withholding of a desired object often endows it with a value quite disproportionate to any possible enjoyment that it could yield, that the remoteness, either literal or figurative, of the objects of our enjoyment shows them in a transfigured light and with heightened attractions – all these are derivatives, modifications and hybrids of the basic fact that value does not originate from the unbroken unity of the moment of enjoyment, but from the separation between the subject and the content of enjoyment as an object that stands opposed to the subject as something desired and only to be attained by the conquest of distance, obstacles and difficulties. To reiterate the earlier analogy: in the final analysis perhaps, reality does not press upon our consciousness through the resistance that phenomena exert, but we register those representations which have feelings of resistance and inhibition associated with them, as being objectively real, independent and external to us. Objects are not difficult to acquire because they are valuable, but we call those objects valuable that resist our desire to possess them. Since the desire encounters resistance and frustration, the objects gain a significance that would never have been attributed to them by an unchecked will.

Value, which appears at the same time and in the same process of differentiation as the desiring Ego and as its correlate, is subordinate to yet another category. It is the same category as applies to the object that is conceived in theoretical representations. We concluded, in that case, that the contents that are realized in the objective world and also exist in us as subjective representations have, in addition, a peculiar ideal dignity. The concepts of the triangle or of the organism, causality or the law of gravitation have a logical sense, an inner structural validity which indeed determines their realization in space and in consciousness; but even if they were never realized, they would still belong to the ultimate unanalysable category of the valid and significant, and would differ entirely from fantastic and contradictory conceptual notions to which they might be akin in their reference to physical and mental non-reality. The value that is attributed to the objects of subjective desire is analogous to this, with the qualifications required by its different sphere. Just as we represent certain statements as true while recognizing that their truth is independent of our representation, so we sense that objects, people and events are not only appreciated as valuable by us, but would still be valuable if no one appreciated them. The most striking example is the value that we assign to people's dispositions or characters, as being moral, dignified, strong or beautiful. Whether or not such inner qualities ever show themselves in deeds that make possible or demand recognition, and whether their bearer himself reflects upon them with a sense of his own value, appears to us irrelevant to their real value; still more, this unconcern for recognition endows these values with their characteristic colouring. Furthermore, intellectual energy and the fact that it brings the most secret forces and arrangements of nature into the light of consciousness; the power and the rhythm of emotions that, in the limited sphere of the individual soul, are yet much more significant than the external world, even if the pessimistic view of the predominance of suffering in the world is true; the fact that, regardless of man, nature moves according to reliable fixed norms, that the manifold natural forms are not incompatible with a more profound unity of the whole, that nature's mechanism can be interpreted through ideas and also produces beauty and grace – all this leads us to conceive that the world is valuable no matter whether these values are experienced consciously or not. This extends all the way down to the economic value that we assign to any object of exchange, even though nobody is willing to pay the price, and even though the object is not in demand at all and remains unsaleable. Here too a basic capacity of the

mind becomes apparent: that of separating itself from the ideas that it conceives and representing these ideas as if they were independent of its own
representation. It is true that every value that we experience is a sentiment; but
what we mean by this sentiment is a significant content which is realized
psychologically through the sentiment yet is neither identical with it nor
exhausted by it. Obviously this category lies beyond the controversy about the
subjectivity or objectivity of value, because it denies the relation to a subject
that is indispensable for the existence of an 'object'. It is rather a third term, an
ideal concept which enters into the duality but is not exhausted by it. In conformity with the practical sphere to which it belongs, it has a particular form of
relationship to the subject which does not exist for the merely abstract content
of our theoretical concepts. This form may be described as a claim or demand.
The value that attaches to any object, person, relationship or happening
demands recognition. This demand exists, as an event, only within ourselves as
subjects; but in accepting it we sense that we are not merely satisfying a claim
imposed by ourselves upon ourselves, or merely acknowledging a quality of the
object. The ability of a tangible symbol to awaken in us religious feelings; the
moral challenge to revolutionize particular conditions of life or to leave them
alone, to develop or retard them; the feeling of obligation not to remain indifferent to great events, but to respond to them; the right of what is perceived
to be interpreted in an aesthetic context – all of these are claims that are experienced or realized exclusively within the Ego and have no counterpart or objective point of departure in the objects themselves, but which, as claims, cannot
be traced either to the Ego or to the objects to which they refer. Regarded from
a naturalistic point of view such a claim may appear subjective, while from the
subject's point of view it appears to be objective; in fact, it is a third category,
which cannot be derived from either subject or object, but which stands, so to
speak, between us and the objects. I have observed that the value of things
belongs among those mental contents that, while we conceive them, we experience at the same time as something independent within our representation, and
as detached from the function by which it exists in us. This representation,
when its content is a value, appears upon closer scrutiny as a sense that a claim
is being made. The 'function' is a demand which does not exist as such outside
ourselves, but which originates in an ideal realm which does not lie within us.
It is not a particular quality of the objects of valuation, but consists rather in
the significance that the objects have for us as subjects through their position in
the order of that ideal realm. This value, which we conceive as being independent
of its recognition, is a metaphysical category, and as such it stands as far beyond
the dualism of subject and object as immediate enjoyment stands below it. The
latter is a concrete unity to which the differentiating categories have not yet
been applied; the former is an abstract or ideal unity, in whose self-subsistent
meaning the dualism has again disappeared, just as the contrast between the

empirical Ego and the empirical Non-Ego disappears in the all-comprehending system of consciousness that Fichte calls the Ego. At the moment of complete fusion of the function and its content, enjoyment cannot be called subjective, because there is no counterposed object that would justify the concept of a subject. Likewise, this independent, self-justifying value is not objective simply because it is conceived as independent by the subject who conceives it; although it becomes manifest within the subject as a claim for recognition, it will not forfeit anything of its reality if this claim is not fulfilled.

This metaphysical sublimation of value does not play any role in the valuations of daily life, which are concerned only with values in the consciousness of the subject and with the objectivity that emerges as a counterposed object in this psychological process of valuation. I showed earlier that this process of the formation of values develops with the increase in distance between the consumer and the cause of his enjoyment. The differences in valuation which have to be distinguished as subjective and objective, originate from such variations in distance, measured not in terms of enjoyment, in which the distance disappears, but in terms of desire, which is engendered by the distance and seeks to overcome it. At least in the case of those objects whose valuation forms the basis of the economy, value is the correlate of demand. Just as the world of being is my representation, so the world of value is my demand. However, in spite of the logical–physical necessity that every demand expects to be satisfied by an object, the psychological structure of demand is such that in most cases it is focused upon the satisfaction itself, and the object becomes a matter of indifference so long as it satisfies the need. When a man is satisfied with any woman whatsoever, without exercising an individual choice, when he eats anything at all that he can chew and digest, when he sleeps at any resting place, when his cultural needs can be satisfied by the simplest materials offered by nature, then his practical consciousness is completely subjective, he is inspired exclusively by the agitations and satisfactions of his own subjective condition and his interest in objects is limited to their being the causes of these effects. This fact is observed in the naive need for projection by primitive man, who directs his life towards the outside world and takes his inner life for granted. But the conscious wish cannot always be taken as a sufficient index of the really effective valuation. Often enough it is some expediency in the direction of our practical activities that leads us to regard an object as valuable, and it is not in fact the significance of the object but the possible subjective satisfaction that excites us. From this condition – which is not always temporally prior but is, so to speak, the simplest and most fundamental and thus in a systematic sense prior – consciousness is led to the object along two roads which finally merge. When an identical need rejects a number of possible satisfactions, perhaps all but one, and when, therefore, it is not satisfaction as such but satisfaction by a specific object that is desired, there begins a fundamental reorientation from the subject to the object.

It may be said that this is still only a question of the subjective satisfaction of need, but that in this second case the need is differentiated to such an extent that only a specific object can satisfy it. In this case also the object is only the cause of sensation and is not valued in itself. Such an objection would indeed nullify the difference, if it were the case that the differentiation of the impulse directed it exclusively upon a single satisfying object and ruled out the possibility of satisfaction through any other object. However, this is a very rare and exceptional case. The broader basis from which even the most highly differentiated impulses evolve, and the original diffuseness of need which includes only a drive but not yet a definite single goal, remain as a substratum upon which a consciousness of the individual character of more specific desires for satisfaction develops. The circle of objects that can satisfy the subject's needs is diminished as he becomes more refined, and the objects desired are set in a sharper contrast with all the others that might satisfy the need but are no longer acceptable. It is well known from psychological investigations that this difference between objects is largely responsible for directing consciousness towards them and endowing them with particular significance. At this stage the need seems to be determined by the object; feeling is guided increasingly by its *terminus ad quem* instead of its *terminus a quo*, in the measure that impulse no longer rushes upon every possible satisfaction. Consequently, the place that the object occupies in our consciousness becomes larger. There is also another reason for this. So long as man is dominated by his impulses the world appears to him as an undifferentiated substance. Since it represents for him only an irrelevant means for the satisfaction of his drives – and this effect may arise from all kinds of causes – he has no interest in the nature of the objects themselves. It is the fact that we need a particular single object that makes us acutely aware that we need an object at all. But such awareness is, so to speak, more theoretical – and it diminishes the blind energy of the impulse which is directed only to its own extinction.

Since the differentiation of need goes hand in hand with the reduction of its elemental power, consciousness becomes more able to accommodate the object. Or regarded from the other aspect: because consciousness is constrained by the refinement and specialization of need to take a greater interest in the object, a certain amount of force is removed from the solipsistic need. Everywhere the weakening of the emotions, that is to say of the absolute surrender of the Ego to his momentary feelings, is correlated with the objectification of representations, with their appearance in a form of existence that stands over against us. Thus, for instance, talking things over is one of the most powerful means for subduing emotions. The inner process is, as it were, projected by the word into the external world; it now stands over against the individual like a tangible structure, and the intensity of the emotions is diverted. The tranquillization of the passions, and the representation of the objective world as existing and significant, are two sides of one and the same basic process. The diversion of inner interest from mere need and its satisfaction to the object itself, as a result of diminishing the possibility of satisfying the need, can obviously be brought about and strengthened just as well from the side of the object, if the latter makes satisfaction difficult, rare, and to be attained only indirectly or by exceptional effort. Even if we assume a highly differentiated desire concentrated upon selected objects, satisfaction might still be regarded as more or less a matter of course so long as there is no difficulty or resistance. What really matters, in order to conceive the independent significance of objects, is the distance between them and our impression of them. It is one of the numerous cases in which one has to stand back from the objects, to establish a distance between them and oneself, in order to get an objective picture of them. This is certainly no less subjective a view than the unclear or distorted picture that is obtained when the distance is too great or too small; but inner expediential reasons of our cognition lay a special emphasis upon subjectivity in the case of these extremes. At first, the object exists only in our relationship to it and is completely absorbed in this relationship; it becomes something external and opposed to us only in the degree that it escapes from this connection. Even the desire for objects, which recognizes their autonomy while seeking to overcome it, develops only when want and satisfaction do not coincide. The possibility of enjoyment must be separated, as an image of the future, from our present condition in order for us to desire things that now stand at a distance from us. Just as in the intellectual sphere the original oneness of perception, which we can observe in children, is only gradually divided into awareness of the self and of the object, so the naive enjoyment of objects only gives way to an awareness of the significance of things, and respect for them, when the objects are somewhat withdrawn. Here, too, the relationship between the weakening of desire and the beginning of an objectification of values is apparent, since the decline of the elemental strength of volition and feeling favours the growing awareness of the self. So long as a person surrenders unreservedly to a momentary feeling and is completely possessed by it, the Ego cannot develop. The awareness of a self that exists beyond its various emotions can emerge only when it appears as an enduring entity amid all these changes, and when the emotions do not absorb the whole self. The emotions must leave a part of the self untouched, as a neutral point for their contrasts, so that a certain reduction and limitation of the emotions allows the self to develop as the unchanging bearer of diverse contents. In all areas of our life Ego and object are related concepts, which are not yet separated in the initial forms of representation and only become differentiated through each other; and in just the same way, the independent value of objects develops only by contrast with an Ego that has become independent. Only the repulsions that we experience, the difficulties of attaining an object, the waiting and the labour that stand between a wish and its fulfilment, drive the Ego and the object apart; otherwise they remain undeveloped and undifferentiated in the propinquity of need and satisfaction. Whether the effective definition of the object arises from its scarcity, in relation to demand, or from the positive effort to acquire it, there is no doubt that only in this way is distance established between the object and ourselves which enables us to accord it a value beyond that of being merely enjoyed.

It may be said, therefore, that the value of an object does indeed depend upon the demand for it, but upon a demand that is no longer purely instinctive. On the other hand, if the object is to remain an economic value, its value must not be raised so greatly that it becomes an absolute. The distance between the self and the object of demand could become so large – through the difficulties of procuring it, through its exorbitant price, through moral or other misgivings that counter the striving after it – that the act of volition does not develop, and the desire is extinguished or becomes only a vague wish. The distance between subject and object that establishes value, at least in the economic sense, has a lower and an upper limit; the formula that the amount of value equals the degree of resistance to the acquisition of objects, in relation to natural, productive and social opportunities, is not correct. Certainly, iron would not be an economic value if its acquisition encountered no greater difficulty than the acquisition of air for breathing; but these difficulties had to remain within certain limits if the tools were to be manufactured which made iron valuable. To take another example: it has been suggested that the pictures of a very productive painter would be less valuable than those of one who was less productive, assuming equal artistic talent. But this is true only above a certain quantitative level. A painter, in order to acquire the fame that raises the price of his pictures, is obliged to produce a certain number of works. Again, the scarcity of gold in some countries with a paper currency has created a situation in which ordinary people will not accept gold even when it is offered to them. In the particular case of precious metals, whose suitability as the material of money is usually attributed to their scarcity, it should be noted that scarcity can only become significant above a considerable volume, without which these metals could not serve the practical demand for money and consequently could not acquire the value they possess as money. It is, perhaps, only the avaricious desire for an unlimited quantity of goods, in terms of which all values are scarce, that leads us to overlook that a certain proportion between scarcity and non-scarcity, and not scarcity itself, is the condition of value. The factor of scarcity has to be related to the significance of the sense for differences; the factor of abundance to the significance of habituation. Life in general is determined by the proportion of these two facts: that we need variety and change of content just as we need familiarity; and this general need appears here in the specific form that the value of objects requires, on the one hand, scarcity – that is to say, differentiation and particularity – while on the other hand it needs a certain comprehensiveness, frequency and permanence in order that objects may enter the realm of values.

An analogy with aesthetic value

I would like to show the universal significance of distance for supposedly objective valuation by an example that has nothing to do with economic values and which therefore illustrates the general principle, namely aesthetic valuation. What we call the enjoyment of the beauty of things developed relatively late. For no matter how much immediate sensual enjoyment may exist even today in the individual case, the specific quality of aesthetic enjoyment is the ability to appreciate and enjoy the object, not simply an experience of sensual or supra-sensual stimulation. Every cultivated person is able to make a clear distinction in principle between the aesthetic and the sensual enjoyment of female beauty, even though he may not be able to draw the line between these components of his impression on a particular occasion. In the one case we surrender to the object, while in the other case the object surrenders to us. Even though aesthetic value, like any other value, is not an integral part of the object but is rather a projection of our feelings, it has the peculiarity that the projection is complete. In other words, the content of the feeling is, as it were, absorbed by the object and confronts the subject as something which has autonomous significance, which is inherent in the object. What was the historical psychological process in which this objective aesthetic pleasure in things emerged, given that primitive enjoyment which was the basis for any more refined appreciation must have been tied to direct subjective satisfaction and utility? Perhaps we can find a clue in a very simple observation. If an object of any kind provides us with great pleasure or advantage we experience a feeling of joy at every later viewing of this object, even if any use or enjoyment is now out of the question. This joy, which resembles an echo, has a unique psychological character determined by the fact that we no longer want anything from the object. In place of the former concrete relationship with the object, it is now mere contemplation that is the source of enjoyable sensation; we leave the being of the object untouched, and our sentiment is attached only to its appearance, not to that which in any sense may be consumed. In short, whereas formerly the object was valuable as a means for our practical and eudaemonistic ends, it has now become an object of contemplation from which we derive pleasure by confronting it with reserve and remoteness, without touching it. It seems to me that the essential features of aesthetic enjoyment are foreshadowed here, but they can be shown more plainly if we follow the changes in sensation from the sphere of individual psychology to that of the species as a whole. The attempt has often been made to derive beauty from utility, but as a rule this has led only to a

philistine coarsening of beauty. This might be avoided if the practical expediency and sensual eudaemonistic immediacy were placed far enough back in the
history of the species, as a result of which an instinctive, reflex-like sense of
enjoyment in our organism were attached to the appearance of objects; the
physico-psychic connection would then be genetic and would become effective
in the individual without any consciousness on his part of the utility of the
object. There is no need to enter into the controversy about the inheritance of
such acquired associations; it suffices here that the events occur as if such
qualities were inheritable. Consequently, the beautiful would be for us what
once proved useful for the species, and its contemplation would give us pleasure
without our having any practical interest in the object as individuals. This
would not of course imply uniformity or the reduction of individual taste to an
average or collective level. These echoes of an earlier general utility are absorbed
into the diversity of individual minds and transformed into new unique qualities, so that one might say that the detachment of the pleasurable sensation from
the reality of its original cause has finally become a form of our consciousness,
quite independent of the contents that first gave rise to it, and ready to absorb
any other content that the psychic constellation permits. In those cases that
offer realistic pleasure, our appreciation of the object is not specifically aesthetic,
but practical; it becomes aesthetic only as a result of increasing distance,
abstraction and sublimation. What happens here is the common phenomenon
that, once a certain connection has been established, the connecting link itself
disappears because it is no longer required. The connection between certain
useful objects and the sense of pleasure has become so well established for the
species through inheritance or some other mechanism, that the mere sight of
these objects becomes pleasurable even in the absence of any utility. This
explains what Kant calls 'aesthetic indifference', the lack of concern about the
real existence of an object so long as its 'form', i.e. its visibility, is given. Hence
also the radiance and transcendence of the beautiful, which arises from the
temporal remoteness of the real motives in which we now discover the aesthetic.
Hence the idea that the beautiful is something typical, supra-individual, and
universally valid; for the evolution of the species has long ago eliminated from
these inner states of mind anything specific and individual in the motives and
experiences. In consequence it is often impossible to justify on rational grounds
aesthetic judgments or the opposition that they sometimes present to what is
useful and agreeable to the individual. The whole development of objects from
utility value to aesthetic value is a process of objectification. When I call an
object beautiful, its quality and significance become much more independent of
the arrangements and the needs of the subject than if it is merely useful. So
long as objects are merely useful they are interchangeable and everything can be
replaced by anything else that performs the same service. But when they are
beautiful they have a unique individual existence and the value of one cannot be

replaced by another even though it may be just as beautiful in its own way. We need not pursue these brief remarks on the origin of aesthetic value into a discussion of all the ramifications of the subject in order to recognize that the objectification of value originates in the relative distance that emerges between the direct subjective origin of the valuation of the object and our momentary feeling concerning the object. The more remote for the species is the utility of the object that first created an interest and a value and is now forgotten, the purer is the aesthetic satisfaction derived from the mere form and appearance of the object. The more it stands before us in its own dignity, the more we attribute to it a significance that is not exhausted by haphazard subjective enjoyment, and the more the relationship of valuing the objects merely as means is replaced by a feeling of their independent value.

Economic activity establishes distances and overcomes them

I have chosen the above example because the objectifying effect of what I have called 'distance' is particularly clear when it is a question of distance in time. The process is, of course, intensive and qualitative, so that any quantitative designation in terms of distance is more or less symbolic. The same effect can be brought about by a number of other factors, as I have already mentioned: for example, by the scarcity of an object, by the difficulties of acquisition, by the necessity of renunciation. Even though in these economically important instances the significance of the objects remains a significance *for us* and so dependent upon our appreciation, the decisive change is that the objects confront us after these developments as independent powers, as a world of substances and forces that determine by their own qualities whether and to what extent they will satisfy our needs, and which demand effort and hardship before they will surrender to us. Only if the question of renunciation arises – renunciation of a feeling that really matters – is it necessary to direct attention upon the object itself. The situation, which is represented in stylized form by the concept of Paradise, in which subject and object, desire and satisfaction are not yet divided from each other – a situation that is not restricted to a specific historical epoch, but which appears everywhere in varying degrees – is destined to disintegrate, but also to attain a new reconciliation. The purpose of establishing a distance is that it should be overcome. The longing, effort and sacrifice that separate us from objects are also supposed to lead us towards them. Withdrawal and approach are in practice complementary notions, each of which presupposes the other; they are two sides of our relationship to objects, which we call subjectively our desire and objectively their value. We have to make the object enjoyed more remote from us in order to desire it again, and in relation to the distant object this desire is the first stage of approaching it, the first ideal relation to it. This dual significance of desire – that it can arise only at a distance from objects, a distance that it attempts to overcome, and yet that it presupposes a closeness between the objects and ourselves in order that the distance should be experienced at all – has been beautifully expressed by Plato in the statement that love is an intermediate state between possession and deprivation. The necessity of sacrifice, the experience that the satisfaction of desire has a price, is only the accentuation or intensification of this relationship. It makes us more distinctly aware of the distance between our present self and the enjoyment of things, but only by leading along the road towards overcoming it. This inner development towards the simultaneous growth of distance and approach also appears as a historical process of differentiation. Culture produces a widening circle of interests; that is, the periphery within which the objects of interest are located becomes farther and farther removed from the centre, the Ego. This increase in distance, however, depends upon a simultaneous drawing closer. If objects, persons and events hundreds or thousands of miles away acquire a vital importance for modern man, they must have been brought much closer to him than to primitive man, for whom they simply do not exist because the positive distinction between close and far has not yet been made. These two notions develop in a reciprocal relation from the original undifferentiated state. Modern man has to work in a different way, to apply a much greater effort than primitive man; the distance between him and the objects of his endeavours is much greater and much more difficult obstacles stand in his way, but on the other hand he acquires a greater quantity of objects, ideally through his desire and in practice through his work. The cultural process – which transposes the subjective condition of impulse and enjoyment into the valuation of objects – separates more distinctly the elements of our dual relationship of closeness and distance.

The subjective events of impulse and enjoyment become objectified in value; that is to say, there develop from the objective conditions obstacles, deprivations, demands for some kind of 'price' through which the cause or content of impulse and enjoyment is first separated from us and becomes, by this very act, an object and a value. The fundamental conceptual question as to the subjectivity or objectivity of value is misconceived. The subjectivity of value is quite erroneously based upon the fact that no object can ever acquire universal value, but that value changes from place to place, from person to person, and even from one hour to the next. This is a case of confusing subjectivity with the individuality of value. The fact that I want to enjoy, or do enjoy, something is indeed subjective in so far as there is no awareness of or interest in the object as such. But then an altogether new process begins: the process of valuation. The content of volition and feeling assumes the form of the object. This object now confronts the subject with a certain degree of independence, surrendering or refusing itself, presenting conditions for its acquisition, placed by his original capricious choice in a law-governed realm of necessary occurrences and restrictions. It is completely irrelevant here that the contents of these forms of objectivity are not the same for all subjects. If we assumed that all human beings evaluated objects in exactly the same way, this would not increase the degree of objectivity beyond that which exists in an individual case; for if any object is valued rather than simply satisfying desire it stands at an objective distance from us that is established by real obstacles and necessary struggles, by gain and loss, by considerations of advantage and by prices. The reason why the misleading question about the objectivity or subjectivity of value is raised again and again is that we find empirically an infinite number of objects that are entirely the products of representations. But if an object in its finished form arises first in our consciousness, its value seems to reside entirely in the subject; the aspect from which I began – the classification of objects in the two series of being and value – seems to be identical with the division between objectivity and subjectivity. But this fails to take into account that the object of volition is different from the object of representation. Even though both may occupy the same place in the series of space, time and quality, the desired object confronts us in a different way and has quite a different significance from the represented object. Consider the analogy of love. The person we love is not the same being as our reason represents. I am not referring here to the distortions or falsifications that emotions may produce in the object of cognition; for these remain within the sphere of representation and of intellectual categories, even though the content is modified. It is in a completely different way from that of intellectual representations that the beloved person is an object to us. Despite the logical identity it has a different meaning for us, just as the marble of the Venus de Milo means different things for a crystallographer and an art critic. A single element of being, although recognized as one and the same, can become an object for us in quite different ways: as an object of representation, and as an object of desire. Within each of these categories the confrontation between subject and object has other causes and other effects, so that it leads only to confusion if the practical relation between man and his object is equated with the alternative between subjectivity and objectivity which is valid only in the realm of intellectual representation. For even though the value of an object is not objective in the same manner as colour or weight, it is also not at all subjective in the sense of corresponding with this kind of objectivity; such subjectivity would apply rather to a perception of colour resulting from a deception of the senses, or of any other quality of the object based on a mistaken conclusion, or of a quality suggested by superstition. The practical relation to objects, however, produces a completely different kind of objectivity, because the conditions of reality withdraw the object of desire and enjoyment from the subjective realm and thus produce the specific category that we call value.

Within the economic sphere, this process develops in such a way that the content of the sacrifice or renunciation that is interposed between man and the object of his demand is, at the same time, the object of someone else's demand. The one has to give up the possession or enjoyment that the other wants in order to persuade the latter to give up what he owns and what the former wants. I shall show that the subsistence economy of an isolated producer can be reduced to the same formula. Two value formations are interwoven; a value has to be offered in order to acquire a value. Thus it appears that there is a *reciprocal* determination of value by the objects. By being exchanged, each object acquires a practical realization and measure of its value through the other object. This is the most important consequence and expression of the distance established between the objects and the subject. So long as objects are close to the subjects, so long as the differentiation of demand, scarcity, difficulties and resistance to acquisition have not yet removed the objects to a distance from the subject, they are, so to speak, desire and enjoyment, but not yet objects of desire and enjoyment. The process that I have outlined through which they become objects is brought to completion when the object, which is at the same time remote and yet overcomes the distance, is produced specifically for this purpose. Thus, pure economic objectivity, the detachment of the object from any subjective relationship to the subject, is established; and since production is carried out for the purpose of exchange with another object, which has a corresponding role, the two objects enter into a reciprocal objective relationship. The form taken by value in exchange places value in a category beyond the strict meaning of subjectivity and objectivity. In exchange, value becomes supra-subjective, supra-individual, yet without becoming an objective quality and reality of the things themselves. Value appears as the demand of the object, transcending its immanent reality, to be exchanged and acquired only for another corresponding value. The Ego, even though it is the universal source of values, becomes so far removed from the objects that they can measure their significance by each other without referring in each case to the Ego. But this real relationship between values, which is executed and supported by exchange, evidently has its purpose in eventual subjective enjoyment, that is, in the fact that we receive a greater quantity and intensity of values than would be possible without exchange transactions. It has been said that the divine principle, after having created the elements of the world, withdrew and left them to the free play of their own powers, so that we can now speak of an objective cosmos, subject to its own relations and laws; and further, that the divine power chose this independence of the cosmic process as the most expedient means of accomplishing its own purposes for the world. In the same way, we invest economic objects with a quantity of value as if it were an inherent quality, and then hand them over to the process of exchange, to a mechanism determined by those quantities, to an impersonal confrontation between values, from which they return multiplied and more enjoyable to the final purpose, which was also their point of origin: subjective experience. This is the basis and source of that valuation which finds its expression in economic life and whose consequences represent the meaning of money. We turn now to their investigation.

II

Exchange as a means of overcoming the purely subjective value significance of an object

The technical form of economic transactions produces a realm of values that is more or less completely detached from the subjective–personal substructure. Although the individual buys because *he* values and wants to consume an object, his demand is expressed effectively only by an object in exchange. Thus the subjective process, in which differentiation and the growing tension between function and content create the object as a 'value', changes to an objective, supra-personal relationship between objects. The individuals who are incited by their wants and valuations to make now this, now that exchange are conscious only of establishing value relationships, the content of which forms part of the objects. The quantity of one object corresponds in value with a given quantity of another object, and this proportion exists as something objectively appropriate and law-determined – from which it commences and in which it terminates – in just the same way as we conceive the objective values of the moral and other spheres. The phenomenon of a completely developed economy, at least, would appear in this light. Here the objects circulate according to norms and measures that are fixed at any one moment, through which they confront the individual as an objective realm. The individual may or may not participate in this realm, but if he wants to participate he can do so only as a representative or executor of these determinants which lie outside himself. The economy tends toward a stage of development – never completely unreal and never completely realized – in which the values of objects are determined by an automatic mechanism, regardless of how much subjective feeling has been incorporated as a pre-condition or as content in this mechanism. The value of an object acquires such visibility and tangibility as it possesses through the fact that one object is offered for another. This reciprocal balancing, through which each economic object expresses its value in another object, removes both objects from the sphere of merely subjective significance. The relativity of valuation signifies its objectification. The basic relationship to man, in whose emotional life all the processes of valuation admittedly take place, is here presupposed; it has been absorbed, so to speak, by the objects, and thus equipped they enter the arena of mutual balancing, which is not the result of their economic value but its representative or content.

In exchange, objects express their value reciprocally

The fact of economic exchange, therefore, frees the objects from their bondage to the mere subjectivity of the subjects and allows them to determine themselves reciprocally, by investing the economic function in them. The object acquires its practical value not only by being in demand itself but through the demand for another object. Value is determined not by the relation to the demanding subject, but by the fact that this relation depends on the cost of a sacrifice which, for the other party, appears as a value to be enjoyed while the object itself appears as a sacrifice. Thus objects balance each other and value appears in a very specific way as an objective, inherent quality. While bargaining over the object is going on – in other words, while the sacrifice that it represents is being determined – its significance for both parties seems to be something external to them, as if each individual experienced the object only in relation to himself. Later on we shall see that an isolated economy also imposes the same necessity of sacrifice for the acquisition of the object, since it confronts economic man with the demands of nature; so that in this case, too, the same relationship endows the object with the same objectively conditioned significance even though there is only one participant in the exchange. The desire and sentiment of the subject is the driving force in the background, but it could not by itself bring about the value-form, which is the result of balancing objects against each other. The economy transmits all valuations through the form of exchange, creating an intermediate realm between the desires that are the source of all human activity and the satisfaction of needs in which they culminate. The specific characteristic of the economy as a particular form of behaviour and communication consists not only in exchanging *values* but in the *exchange* of values. Of course, the significance that objects attain in exchange is not wholly independent of their directly subjective significance which originally determines the relationship. The two are inseparably related, as are form and content. But the objective process, which very often also dominates the individual's consciousness, disregards the fact that values are its material; its specific character is to deal with the equality of values. In much the same way, geometry has as its aim the determination of the relationship between the size of objects without referring to the substances for which these relationships are valid. As soon as one realizes the extent to which human action in every sphere of mental activity operates with abstractions, it is not as strange as it may seem at first glance that not only the study of the economy but the economy itself is constituted by a real abstraction from the comprehensive reality of valuations. The forces, relations and qualities of things – including our own nature – objectively form a unified whole which has to be broken down by our interests into a multitude of independent series or motives to enable us to deal with it. Every science investigates phenomena that are homogeneous and clearly distinguished from the problems of other sciences, whereas reality ignores boundaries and every section of the world presents an aggregate of tasks for all the sciences. Our practice excludes unilateral series from the outer and inner complexity of things and so constructs the great systems of cultural interests. The same is true for our sentiments. When we experience religious or social sentiments, when we are melancholy or joyful, it is always abstractions from total reality that are the objects of our feeling – whether because we react only to those impressions that can be brought within the scope of some common cultural interest, or because we endow every object with a certain colouring which derives its validity from its interweaving with other colourings to form an objective unity. Thus, the following formula is one way in which the relationship of man to the world may be expressed: our practice as well as our theory continually abstracts single elements from the absolute unity and intermingling of objects, in which each object supports the other and all have equal rights, and forms these elements into relative entities and wholes. We have no relationship to the totality of existence, except in very general sentiments; we attain a definite relation to the world only by continually abstracting from phenomena, in accordance with our needs of thought and action and investing these abstractions with the relative independence of a purely inner connection which the unbroken stream of world processes denies to objective reality. The economic system is indeed based on an abstraction, on the mutuality of exchange, the balance between sacrifice and gain; and in the real process of its development it is inseparably merged with its basis and results, desire and need. But this form of existence does not differentiate it from the other spheres into which we divide the totality of phenomena for the sake of our interests.

The value of an object becomes objectified by exchanging it for another object

The decisive fact in the objectivity of economic value, which makes economics a special area of investigation, is that its validity transcends the individual subject. The fact that the object has to be exchanged against another object illustrates that it is not only valuable for me, but also valuable independently of me; that is to say, for another person. The equation, objectivity = validity for subjects in general, finds its clearest justification in economic value. The equivalence of which we become aware, and in which we develop an interest through exchange, imparts to value its specific objectivity. For even though each of the elements in exchange may be personal or only subjectively valuable, the fact that they are equal to each other is an objective factor which is not contained within any one of these elements and yet does not lie outside of them either. Exchange presupposes an objective measurement of subjective valuations, not in the sense of being chronologically prior, but in the sense that both phenomena arise from the same act.

Exchange as a form of life

It should be recognized that most relationships between people can be interpreted as forms of exchange. Exchange is the purest and most developed kind of interaction, which shapes human life when it seeks to acquire substance and content. It is often overlooked how much what appears at first a one-sided activity is actually based upon reciprocity: the orator appears as the leader and inspirer to the assembly, the teacher to his class, the journalist to his public; but, in fact, everyone in such a situation feels the decisive and determining reaction of the apparently passive mass. In the case of political parties the saying is current that: 'I am the leader, therefore I must follow them'; and an outstanding hypnotist has recently emphasized that in hypnotic suggestion – obviously the clearest case of activity on one side and absolute dependence on the other – there is an influence, that is difficult to describe, of the person hypnotized upon the hypnotist, without which the experiment could not be carried out. Every interaction has to be regarded as an exchange: every conversation, every affection (even if it is rejected), every game, every glance at another person. The difference that seems to exist, that in interaction a person offers what he does not possess whereas in exchange he offers only what he does possess, cannot be sustained. For in the first place, it is always personal energy, the surrender of personal substance, that is involved in interaction; and conversely, exchange is not conducted for the sake of the object that the other person possesses, but to gratify one's personal feelings which he does not possess. It is the object of exchange to increase the sum of value; each party offers to the other more than he possessed before. It is true that interaction is the more comprehensive concept and exchange the narrower one; however, in human relationships the former appears predominantly in forms that may be Interpreted as exchange. Every day of our lives comprises a process of gain and loss, of accretion and diminution of life's content, which is intellectualized in exchange since the substitution of one object for another becomes conscious there. The same synthesizing mental process that turns the mere co-existence of things into a systematic relationship, the same Ego that imposes its own unity upon the material world, has seized upon the natural rhythm of our existence and through exchange has organized its elements in a meaningful interconnection. It is above all the exchange of economic values that involves the notion of sacrifice. When we exchange love for love, we have no other use for its inner energy and, leaving aside any later consequences, we do not sacrifice any good. When we share our intellectual resources in a discussion, they are not thereby reduced; when we display the image of our personality, and take in those of other people, our possession of ourselves is not at all reduced by this exchange. In all these cases of exchange the increase of value does not involve a balancing of gain and loss; either the contribution of each party lies beyond this antithesis, or it is already a gain to be able to make it, and we accept the response as a gift which is made independently of our own offering. But economic exchange – whether it is of objects of labour or labour power invested in objects – always signifies the sacrifice of an otherwise useful good, however much eudaemonistic gain is involved.

The interpretation of economic life as interaction in the specific sense of an exchange of sacrifices meets with an objection raised against the equation of economic value with exchange value. It has been argued that even the completely isolated producer, who neither buys nor sells, has to value his products and his means of production, and to form a concept of value independent of exchange if his costs and output are to be properly related. But this fact proves exactly what it is supposed to disprove. The evaluation of whether a particular product justifies the expenditure of a given quantity of work or other goods is exactly the same as the evaluation of what is offered against what is received in exchange. The concept of exchange is often misconceived, as though it were a relationship existing outside the elements to which it refers. But it signifies only a condition or a change within the related subjects, not something that exists between them in the sense in which an object might be spatially located between two other objects. By subsuming the two events or changes of condition that are going on in reality under the concept of 'exchange', one is tempted to assume that something else has occurred beyond what is experienced by the contracting parties; just as the concept of a 'kiss', which is also 'exchanged', might tempt us to regard the kiss as something beyond the movement and experiences of two pairs of lips. So far as its immediate content is concerned, exchange is only the causally connected double event in which one subject now possesses something he did not have before and has given away something he did possess before. Thus, the isolated individual who sacrifices something in order to produce certain products, acts in exactly the same way as the subject who exchanges, the only difference being that his partner is not another subject but the natural order and regularity of things which, just like another human being, does not satisfy our desires without a sacrifice. The valuations that determine his action are generally exactly the same as those involved in exchange. It is of no concern to the economic subject whether he invests his property or labour power in the land or transfers them to another person, if the result for him is the same. This subjective process of sacrifice and gain in the individual mind is in no way secondary to, or imitated from, exchange between individuals; on the contrary, the interchange between sacrifice and acquisition within the individual is the basic presupposition and, as it were, the essential substance of exchange between two people. Exchange is only a sub-variety in which the sacrifice is brought about by the demand of another individual; but it can be brought about with the same result for the subject by the technical–natural condition of things. It is of great importance to reduce the economic process to what really happens in the mind of each economic subject. One should not be deceived by the fact that the process of exchange is mutual; the natural or self-sufficient economy can be traced back to the same basic form as the exchange between two persons – to the practice of weighing against each other two subjective processes within the individual. This activity is not affected by the secondary question as to whether the stimulus comes from the nature of things or the nature of man, whether it operates in a subsistence or a market economy. Every enjoyment of values by means of attainable objects can be secured only by forgoing other values, which may take the form not only of working indirectly for ourselves by working for others, but often enough of working directly for our own ends. This also clarifies the point that exchange is just as productive and value-creating as is production itself. In both cases one is concerned with receiving goods for the price of other goods in exchange, in such a way that the final situation shows a surplus of satisfaction as compared with the situation before the action. We are unable to create either matter or force; we can only transfer those that are given in such a way that as many as possible rise from the realm of reality into the realm of values. This formal shift within the given material is accomplished by exchange between people as well as by the exchange with nature which we call production. Both belong to the same concept of value; in both cases the empty place of what we gave away is filled by an object of higher value, and only through this movement does the object that was previously merged with the Ego detach itself and become a value. The profound connection between value and exchange, as a result of which they are mutually conditioning, is illustrated by the fact that they are in equal measure the basis of practical life. Even though our life seems to be determined by the mechanism and objectivity of things, we cannot in fact take any step or conceive any thought without endowing the objects with values that direct our activities. These activities are carried out in accordance with the schema of exchange; from the lowest level of satisfaction of wants to the attainment of the highest intellectual and religious goods, every value has to be acquired by the sacrifice of some other value. It is perhaps impossible to determine exactly what is the starting point and what is the consequence. For the two elements cannot be separated in the basic processes, which make up the unity of practical life; a unity that we cannot grasp as a whole and that we differentiate into these two elements. Or, alternatively, a never-ending process occurs between the two, in which every exchange refers back to a value, and each value refers back to an exchange. For our purposes it is more enlightening to trace value to exchange, since the opposite seems better known and more obvious. To recognize value as the result of a sacrifice discloses the infinite wealth that our life derives from this basic form. Our painful experience of sacrifice and our effort to diminish it leads us to believe that its total elimination would raise life to perfection. But here we overlook that sacrifice is by no means always an external obstacle, but is the inner condition of the goal

84

itself and the road by which it may be reached. We divide the enigmatic unity of our practical relation to things into sacrifice and gain, obstruction and attainment, and since the different stages are often separated in time we forget that the goal would not be the same without impediments to overcome. The resistance that we have to overcome enables us to prove our strength; only the conquest of sin secures for the soul the 'joy of heaven' that the righteous man cannot enjoy. Every synthesis needs the analytical principle which it nevertheless negates, for without this principle it would not be a synthesis of different elements but an absolute unity; conversely, every analysis requires a synthesis which it dissolves, for analysis still needs a certain interconnectedness, without which it would be mere unrelatedness: even the most violent animosity is a stronger relationship than mere indifference, and indifference stronger than simple unawareness. In brief, the inhibiting counter-motion, to eliminate which a sacrifice is required, is often, perhaps even always, the positive pre-condition of the goal. The sacrifice does not in the least belong in the category of what ought not to be, as superficiality and avarice would have us believe. Sacrifice is not only the condition of specific values, but the condition of value as such; with reference to economic behaviour, which concerns us here, it is not only the price to be paid for particular established values, but the price through which alone values can be established.

Exchange is accomplished in two forms, which I propose to illustrate here with reference to the value of labour. In so far as there is a desire for leisure, or for the use of energy for its own sake in recreation, or for the avoidance of painful effort, all labour is undeniably a sacrifice. However, there is also a certain amount of latent work-energy which either we do not know how to employ or which manifests itself in an impulse to voluntary labour which is not incited by need or by ethical motives. A number of demands compete for this quantity of labour power, the use of which is not in itself a sacrifice, but not all of them can be satisfied. For every use of energy, one or more other possible and desirable uses have to be sacrificed. Unless we could utilize the energy to perform labour A also for labour B, there would not be any sacrifice in doing labour A; the same is true for B if we execute it instead of A. What is sacrificed eudaemonistically is not labour, but rather non-labour; we pay for A not by sacrificing labour – since, as we presuppose, here labour does not involve any disutility – but by renouncing B. The sacrifice that we give in exchange by our labour may be, so to speak, either absolute or relative: the disutility is either directly connected with labour, where this is experienced as toil and pain, or it is indirect in the case where labour is eudaemonistically irrelevant or even of a positive value, but we can acquire one object only by renouncing another. Thus the instance of enjoyable labour can also be related to the form of exchange as sacrifice which characterizes the economy.

85

Value and Money

The idea that objects have a specific value before they enter into an economic relationship – in which each of the two objects of the transaction signifies for one contracting party the desired gain and for the other the sacrifice – is valid only for a developed economy, but not for the basic processes on which the economy rests. The logical difficulty, that two things can only be of equal value if each of them has a value of its own, seems to be illustrated by the analogy that two lines can be equally long only if each of them has a definite length. But strictly speaking, a line gains the quality of length only by comparison with others. For its length is determined not by itself – since it is not simply 'long' – but by another line against which it is measured: and the same service is performed for the other line, although the result of the measurement does not depend upon this act of comparison but upon each line as it exists independently of the other. Let us recall the category that embraces the objective value judgment, which I termed metaphysical; from the relationship between us and objects develops the imperative to pass a certain judgment, the content of which, however, does not reside in the things themselves. The same is true in judging length; the objects themselves require that we judge them, but the quality of length is not given by the objects and can only be realized by an act within ourselves. We are not aware of the fact that length is established only by the process of comparison and is not inherent in the individual object on which length depends, because we have abstracted from particular relative lengths the general concept of length – which excludes the definiteness without which specific length does not exist. In projecting this concept onto objects we assume that things must have length before it can be determined individually by comparison. Moreover, definite standards have grown out of the innumerable comparisons of length, and they form the basis for determining the length of all tangible objects. These standards embody as it were the abstract concept of length; they seem no longer to be relative because everything is measured by them, while they themselves are no longer measured. The error is the same as if one believes that the falling apple is attracted by the earth, while the earth is not attracted by the falling apple. Finally, we delude ourselves as to the inherent quality of length by the fact that the multiplicity of elements, the relationship of which determines substance, already exists in the individual parts. If we were to assume that there is only a single line in the whole world, it would not have any specific length since it lacks any relation to others. It is impossible to measure the world as a whole, because there is nothing outside the world in relation to which it could have a specific size. This is true of a line so long as it is considered without being compared with others, or without its own parts being compared with each other; it is neither short nor long, but lies outside the whole category. This analogy makes clear the relativity of economic value rather than disproving it.

86

If we regard the economy as a special case of the general form of exchange –
a surrender of something in order to gain something – then we shall at once
suspect that the value of what is acquired is not ready made, but rather accrues
to the desired object wholly or in part from the extent of the sacrifice required.
These frequent and theoretically important instances seem indeed to contain an
inner contradiction: would the sacrifice of a value be required for valueless
objects? No reasonable person would give away a value without receiving an
equal value in return, and it would be a perverted world in which the desired
object attained its value only as a result of the price that had to be paid for it.
This is an important point so far as our immediate consciousness is concerned,
more important than the popular viewpoint will admit. In fact, the value that a
subject sacrifices can never be greater, in the particular circumstances of the
moment, than the value that he receives in return. All appearance to the contrary rests on a confusion of the value experienced by the subject and the value
which the object in exchange has according to other apparently objective forms
of appraisal. Thus, during a famine somebody will give away a jewel for a piece
of bread because under the given conditions the latter is more valuable to him
than the former. It always depends upon circumstances whether sentiments of
value are attached to an object, since every valuation is supported by an elaborate complex of feelings which are always in a process of flux, adjustment and
change. It is of no significance in principle whether the circumstances are
momentary or relatively enduring. If the starving person gives the jewel away he
demonstrates unambiguously that the piece of bread is more valuable to him.
There is no doubt that, at the moment of exchange, of offering the sacrifice, the
value of the object received sets a limit up to which the value of the object
offered in exchange can rise. Quite independent of this is the question as to
where the object received derives its value; whether it is perhaps the result of
the sacrifice offered, so that the balance between gain and cost is established *a
posteriori* by the sacrifice. We shall see in a moment that value often originates
psychologically in this seemingly illogical manner. Once the value has been
established – no matter how – there is a psychological necessity to regard it as
being of equal value with the sacrifice.

Even superficial psychological observation discloses instances in which the
sacrifice not only increases the value of the desired object but actually brings it
about. This process reveals the desire to prove one's strength, to overcome
difficulties, or even simply to be contrary. The necessity of proceeding in a
roundabout way in order to acquire certain things is often the occasion, and
often also the reason, for considering them valuable. In human relations, and
most frequently and clearly in erotic relations, it is apparent that reserve, indifference or rejection incite the most passionate desire to overcome these
barriers, and are the cause of efforts and sacrifices that, in many cases, the goal
would not have seemed to deserve were it not for such opposition. The aesthetic

enjoyment of mountain climbing would no longer be highly regarded by many people if it did not exact the price of extraordinary effort and danger, which constitute its charm, appeal and inspiration. The attraction of antiques and curiosities is often of the same kind. If there is no aesthetic or historical interest attached to them, this is replaced by the mere difficulty of acquiring them; they are worth as much as they cost, which leads to the conclusion that they cost as much as they are worth. Furthermore, moral merit always signifies that opposing impulses and desires had to be conquered and sacrificed in favour of the morally desirable act. If such an act is carried out without any difficulty as a result of natural impulse, it will not be considered to have a subjective moral value, no matter how desirable its objective content. Moral merit is attained only by the sacrifice of lower and yet very tempting goods, and it is the greater the more inviting the temptations and the more comprehensive and difficult the sacrifice. Of all human achievements the highest honour and appreciation is given to those that indicate, or at least seem to indicate, a maximum of commitment, energy and persistent concentration of the whole being, and along with this, renunciation, sacrifice of everything else, and devotion to the objective idea. Even in those cases where, by contrast, aesthetic performance, and the ease and charm that originate from a natural impulse, exercise a supreme attraction, this is also due to the resonance of the efforts and sacrifices that are usually required for such accomplishments. The significance of a connection is often transferred to its opposite by the mobility and inexhaustible power of association in our mental life; as, for example, the association between two representations may take place as a result of the fact that they affirm each other or deny each other. We realize the specific value of what we gain without difficulty and through good fortune only in terms of the significance of that which is hard to achieve and involves sacrifices; the latter has the same value, but with a negative sign, and it is the primary source from which the former value is derived.

Of course, these may be exaggerated or exceptional cases. In order to discover their general type in the economic sphere, it is necessary first of all to distinguish the economic aspect, as a special characteristic or form, from the fact of value as a universal quality of substance. If we accept value as being given, it follows from what has been said previously that economic value is not an inherent quality of an object, but is established by the expenditure of another object which is given in exchange for it. Wild grain, which can be harvested without effort and immediately consumed without any exchange, is an economic good only if its consumption saves some other expenditure. But if all the necessities of life could be obtained in this way without any sacrifice there would be no economic system, any more than in the case of birds or fish or the inhabitants of the land of milk and honey. No matter how the two objects A and B have become values, A becomes an *economic* value only because I have to exchange it for B, and B only because I can acquire A in exchange for it. It makes no difference whether the sacrifice is accomplished by transferring a value to another person through inter-individual exchange, or by balancing the efforts and gains within the individual's own sphere of interest. Economic objects have no significance except directly or indirectly in our consumption and in the exchange that occurs between them. The former alone is not sufficient to make the object an economic one; only the latter can give it the specific characteristic that we call economic. Yet this distinction between value and its economic form is artificial. In the first place, although the economy may seem to be a mere form in the sense that it presupposes value as its content in order to make the balancing of sacrifice and gain possible, in reality this process through which an economic system is constructed from the presupposed values may be interpreted as the originator of economic values.

The economic form of value lies between two limits: on the one side is the desire for the object, arising from the anticipated satisfaction of possession and enjoyment; on the other side is the enjoyment itself, which is not strictly speaking an economic act. If the previous argument is accepted, namely that the direct consumption of wild grain is not an economic act (except to the extent that it economizes on the production of economic values), then the consumption of real economic values is itself no longer an economic act, for these two acts of consumption are totally indistinguishable. Whether somebody has found, stolen, cultivated or bought the grain does not make the slightest difference for the act of consumption and its direct consequences. The object, as we have seen, is not yet a value so long as it is only the direct stimulant and a natural part of our sentiments inseparable from the subjective process. The object has to be detached from this in order to gain the specific significance that we call value. Desire by itself cannot bring about value unless it encounters obstacles; if every desire could be satisfied completely without a struggle, the economic exchange of values would never have developed, and the desire itself would never have reached a high level. Only the deferment of satisfaction through obstacles, the fear of never attaining the object, the tension of struggling for it, brings together the various elements of desire; the intense striving and continuous acquisition. But even if the strongest element of desire came only from within the individual, the object that satisfies it would still have no value if it were abundantly available. The whole genus of things that guarantee the satisfaction of our wishes would be important to us, but not the limited portion that we acquire because this could be replaced without effort by any other portion. Our awareness of the value of the whole genus would arise from the idea of its being absent altogether. In this case, our consciousness would be simply determined by the rhythm of the subjective wishes and satisfactions without paying any attention to the mediating object. Need and enjoyment alone do not comprehend either value or economic life, which are realized simultaneously through the exchange between two subjects each of whom requires a sacrifice by the other (or its equivalent in the self-sufficient economy) in order to be satisfied. Exchange, i.e. the economy, is the source of economic values, because exchange is the representative of the distance between subject and object which transforms subjective feelings into objective valuation. I mentioned earlier Kant's summary of his epistemology: the conditions of experience are at the same time the conditions of the objects of experience – by which he meant that the process that we call experience and the representations that form its contents and objects are subject to the same laws of the understanding. Objects can be experienced because they are representations within us, and the same power that determines experience determines also the formation of representations. In the same manner we can state: the possibility of the economy is at the same time the possibility of the objects of the economy. The process between two owners of objects (of substances, labour power or rights of any kind) that establishes the relationship called 'economy' – i.e. a reciprocal surrender – raises these objects at the same time into the category of value. The logical difficulty, that values had to exist as values in order to enter the form and movement of the economy, is now eliminated by the significance of the psychic relation which we designated as the distance between us and the object. This psychic relationship differentiates the original subjective condition of feeling into the desiring subject and the opposed object which possesses value. In the economy, this distance is brought about through exchange, through the two-sided influence of barriers, obstacles and renunciation. Economic values are produced by the same reciprocity and relativity that determine the economic character of values.

Exchange is not the mere addition of two processes of giving and receiving, but a new third phenomenon, in which each of the two processes is simultaneously cause and effect. The value that the object gains through renunciation thereby becomes an economic value. In general, value develops in the interval that obstacles, renunciation and sacrifice interpose between the will and its satisfaction. The process of exchange consists in the mutual determination of taking and giving, and it does not depend upon a particular object having previously acquired a value for a particular subject. All that is needed is accomplished in the act of exchange itself. Of course, in an actual economic system the value of objects is usually indicated when they enter into exchange. I am referring here only to the inner, systematic meaning of the concept of value and exchange, which exists only in rudimentary form, or as an ideal significance in the historical phenomena or as their ideal meaning. I refer not to their real form, in the historical genetic sense, but to their objective–logical form.

Theories of utility and scarcity

This transposition of the concept of economic value from the abstract sphere to that of vital relationships may be further elucidated with the aid of the concepts of utility and scarcity which are generally regarded as constituent elements of value. The first requirement for an economic object to exist, based upon the disposition of the economic subject, is utility. To this, scarcity must be added as a second determining factor if the object is to acquire a specific value. If economic values are regarded as being determined by supply and demand, supply would correspond with scarcity and demand with utility. Utility would decide whether the object is in demand at all and scarcity the price that we are obliged to pay. Utility appears as the absolute part of economic values, and its degree has to be known so that the objects can enter into economic exchange. Scarcity is only a relative factor, since it signifies only the quantitative relationship of the object in question to the total available amount. The qualitative nature of the object does not play any role here. Utility, however, seems to exist prior to any economic system, to any comparison or relationship with other objects; it is the substantial factor determining the movement of the economy.

However, this situation is not correctly described by the concept of utility. What is really meant is the desire for the object. Utility as such is never able to bring about economic processes unless it leads to demand, and it does not always do so. Some kind of 'wish' may accompany the perception of useful objects, but real demand, which has practical significance and affects our activity, fails to appear if protracted poverty, constitutional lethargy, diversion to other fields of interest, indifference to the theoretically known advantage, awareness of the impossibility of acquisition or other positive and negative factors counteract such a development. On the other hand, we desire, and therefore value economically, all kinds of things that cannot be called useful or serviceable without arbitrarily straining ordinary linguistic usage. If the concept of usefulness is to encompass everything that is in demand, it is logically necessary to accept the demand for the object as the decisive factor for economic activity, since otherwise not everything useful is in demand. Even with this modification, it is not an absolute factor and does not eliminate the relativity of values. In the first place, as we have seen, demand is not distinctly conscious unless there are barriers, difficulties and sacrifices between the object and the subject. In reality we exert a demand only when the enjoyment of the object is measured by intermediate stages; when the price of patience, the renunciation of other efforts or enjoyments, set the object in perspective, and desire is equated with the exertion to overcome the distance. Secondly, the economic value of the object based upon the demand for it may be interpreted as a heightening or sublimation of the relativity embedded in the demand. For the object in demand becomes a value of practical importance to the economy only when the demand for it is compared with the demand for other things; only this comparison establishes a measure of demand. Only if there is a second object which I am willing to give away for the first, or vice-versa, does each of them have a measurable economic value. There is originally in the world of practice no single value, any more than there is originally in the world of consciousness a number 'one'. It has often been asserted that the concept of 'two' exists prior to the concept of 'one'. The pieces of a broken cane require a term for plurality; the whole cane is a cane and there is no reason to call it one cane unless two canes with some relationship to each other are considered. Thus, the mere demand for an object does not yet create an economic value, because it does not include the required measure; only a comparison of demands, i.e. the exchangeability of its objects, assigns a definite economic value to each of them. Without the category of equality – one of those fundamental concepts that shape the world view out of particulars, yet only gradually acquire a psychological reality – no 'utility' and no 'scarcity', however great, would bring about economic transactions. Whether two objects are equally in demand and equally valuable can only be ascertained – owing to the lack of an external measure – by exchanging them against each other in idea or in reality, while experiencing no variation in value sentiments. In fact, it may be that originally the exchangeability did not indicate equality of value as an objective quality of things, but that equality was simply the term used for exchangeability. The intensity of demand by itself does not necessarily increase the economic value of objects; since value is expressed only through exchange, demand can affect the value only to the extent that it modifies exchange. Even though I crave an object this does not determine its equivalent in exchange. Either I do not yet possess the object, in which case my desire for the object, unless I express it, will not exert any influence upon the demand of the present owner and he will ask a price in accordance with his own or the average interest in the object; or I do possess the object, and in that case my price may be so high that the object cannot be exchanged at all (i.e. it is no longer an economic value), or else I shall have to reduce the price to correspond with the degree of interest shown by a prospective buyer. The decisive fact is that practical economic value is never just value in general, but is by its very nature a definite sum of value; that this sum results from the measurement of two intensities of demand; that the form that this measurement takes within the economy is the exchange of sacrifice and gain; and that, consequently, the economic object does not have – as seems at first sight – an absolute value as a result of the demand for it, but the demand, as the basis of a real or imagined exchange, endows the object with value.

The relativity of value – as a result of which objects in demand become values only through the process of mutual exchange – seems to suggest that value is nothing more than the price, and that no differences in their level can exist; in which case, the frequent discrepancy between price and value would refute the theory. But the theory claims that value would never have been established without the general phenomenon that we call price. That an object is economically valuable means that it is of value to me, that I am willing to give something for it. A value can become practically effective only by being equivalent to other values, i.e. by being exchangeable. Equivalence and exchangeability are reciprocal notions, which express the same state of affairs in two different forms, in a condition of rest and in motion, so to speak. What could possibly motivate us to endow objects, beyond the naive subjective enjoyment that they afford, with the peculiar significance that we call value? It cannot be due simply to their scarcity. For if scarcity existed simply as a fact that we could not alter – as in reality we do not only by productive work but also by changes of ownership – we should accept it as a natural quality of the external world, of which we might not even be aware and which would leave objects without any emphasis beyond their factual qualities. This emphasis arises from the fact that objects have to be paid for by the patience of waiting, the effort of searching, the exertion of labour, the renunciation of other things in demand. Without a price – in the most general meaning of the word – there is no value. A belief of some South Sea Islanders expresses this feeling in a naive way: the cure prescribed by a doctor will not take effect unless he is paid. The fact that one of two objects is more valuable than the other is represented only by the fact that a person is willing to exchange one for the other but not vice-versa. Where practical relationships are still simple and limited in scale, a higher or lower value can only be the consequence or expression of the direct practical will to exchange. And when we say that we have exchanged things because they are of equal value, that is only an example of a frequent conceptual–linguistic reversal, as in the case where we believe that we love somebody because he has certain qualities, whereas we have granted him these qualities because we love him; or where we derive moral imperatives from religious dogmas, whereas we actually believe in the dogmas because the moral imperatives vitally concern us.

In conceptual terms, price coincides with the economically objective value; without price it would be impossible to draw the dividing line between objective value and the subjective enjoyment of goods. From the standpoint of the contracting subjects, the statement that exchange presupposes equality of values is not correct. A and B may exchange their possessions α and β because they are of equal value. But A would not have any reason to give away α if he received only an equal value by acquiring β. β must be a greater value for him than α which he owned before; similarly B must gain more than he loses by the exchange. If, therefore, β is more valuable than α for A and α is more valuable than β for B, the differences objectively balance each other as far as an observer is concerned. But this equailty of values does not exist for the contracting party who receives more than he gives away. If, nevertheless, he is convinced that he has made a fair deal and has exchanged equal values, this should be stated, in respect of A, as follows: objectively, he has given an equivalent to B, the price (α) for the object (β), but subjectively the value of β is greater for him than the value of α. But the sense of value that A attaches to β is a unit, and the dividing line between the objective value and the subjective surplus is no longer

93

perceptible. Only the fact that the object is exchanged, that it is a price and costs a price, draws this line and determines the quantum of subjective value with which the object enters the process of exchange as an objective value.

Another observation also demonstrates that exchange is in no way conditioned by a preceding representation of the objective equality of values. If one watches how children, impulsive individuals and apparently also primitive peoples, carry out exchange, it is apparent that they will give away any treasured property for an object that they strongly desire to own at a given moment, regardless of whether the price is much too high in the general estimation or even for themselves when they have had an opportunity to think the matter over calmly. This contradicts the notion that every exchange must be consciously advantageous to the subject. This is not the case, because the whole action lies subjectively beyond the question of equality or inequality of the objects exchanged. The idea that a balancing of sacrifice and gain precedes the exchange and must have resulted in an equilibrium between them is one of those rationalistic platitudes that are entirely unpsychological. This would require an objectivity towards one's own desires of which the people I have just discussed are incapable. The uneducated or prejudiced person cannot detach himself sufficiently from his momentary interests to make a comparison; at the particular moment he just wants that one object, and the sacrifice of the other object does not strike him as a reduction of the desired gratification, i.e. as a price. In view of the thoughtlessness with which naive, inexperienced and impulsive people appropriate the desired object 'at any price', it seems much more probable that the idea of equality is a product of the experience of many exchanges carried out without any proper balancing of gain and loss. The exclusive desire obsessing the mind has first to be pacified by successful acquisition of the object before a comparison with other objects is possible. The tremendous difference in emphasis between momentary interests and all other ideas and valuations which prevails in the untrained and unbridled mind allows exchange to take place before any judgment of value, i.e. of the relation between various desired objects, has been made. When value concepts are highly developed and a reasonable self-control prevails, a judgment as to the equality of values may precede exchange, but this should not be allowed to obscure the probability that the rational relation – as is so often the case – has evolved from a psychologically opposite relation, and that the exchange of possessions originating from purely subjective impulses has only later taught us the relative value of things. (In the realm of the mind too πρός ἡμᾶς is at first φύσει.)

Value and price

Value is, so to speak, the epigone of price, and the statement that they must be identical is a tautology. I base this view upon the earlier statement that in any individual case no contracting party pays a price that seems to be too high under the given circumstances. If – as in the poem by Chamisso – the robber forces someone at pistol point to sell his watch and rings for three pennies, what he receives under these conditions is worth the price, since it is the only way to save his life. Nobody would work for starvation wages if he were not in a situation in which he preferred such wages to not working at all. The apparent paradox of the assertion that value and price are equivalent in every individual case results from the fact that certain ideas concerning other equivalents of value and price are introduced into it. The relative stability of the conditions that determine the majority of exchanges, and also the analogies that fix the value relationship according to traditional norms, contribute to the notion that the value of a particular object requires as its exchange equivalent another specific object; that these two objects (or categories of objects) have equal value, and that, if abnormal circumstances allow us to exchange an object at a lower or higher value, then value and price would diverge, even though they always coincide in relation to the specific circumstances. One should not forget that the objective and just equivalence of value and price, which we regard as the norm for actual particular cases, is valid only under specific historical and technical conditions and collapses immediately with a change in these conditions. There is no general distinction but only a numerical difference between the norm and the individual cases which are recognized as deviating from or conforming with the norm. One might say of an extraordinarily superior or inferior individual that he is really not a human being, but this concept of a human being is no more than an average which would lose its normative status as soon as a majority of people rose or fell to the level of one of these exceptional types, which would then be accepted as the truly 'human'. In order to realize this fact, however, we have to free ourselves from deeply rooted and practically justified notions of value. Under advanced conditions, these notions encompass two superimposed layers: one of which is formed by social traditions, by habitual experiences, by apparently logical necessities, the other by individual situations, by momentary needs, and by the force of circumstances. The rapid changes within this latter sphere conceal from our perception the slow evolution of the former sphere and its formation by the sublimation of the latter. The second sphere then appears to be empirically valid as the expression of an objective proportion. The discrepancy between value and price is cited whenever the values of sacrifice and gain exchanged in given circumstances are at least equal – for otherwise nobody who compares at all would make the exchange – but are discrepant when measured in more general terms. This is most obvious under two conditions, which are usually found together: first, that a single value-characteristic is accepted as the economic value and that two objects are acknowledged as equal values only to the extent that they represent the same amount of that value; and second, that a definite proportion between two values is seen as proper, in moral as well as in objective terms. The idea, for instance, that the essential feature of value is the socially necessary labour time objectified in it has been used in both these senses to provide a measure of the deviation of value from price. But the concept of this uniform standard of value does not answer the question of how labour power itself became a value. This could not have happened unless the activity of labour in producing all kinds of goods had given rise to the possibility of exchange, and the exertion of labour had been experienced as a sacrifice offered in return for its products. Labour power, too, enters the category of value only through the possibility and reality of exchange, regardless of the fact that subsequently it may provide a standard for measuring other values within this category. Even if labour power is the content of every value, it receives its form as value only by entering into a relation of sacrifice and gain or price and value (here in the narrower sense). According to this theory, if price and value diverge, one contracting party exchanges a quantity of objectified labour power against a smaller quantity; but this exchange is affected by other circumstances which do not involve labour power, such as the need to satisfy urgent wants, whims, fraud, monopoly, etc. In a broader and subjective sense, the equivalence of the values exchanged is maintained here, whereas the uniform norm of labour power, which makes possible the discrepancy, does not originate in exchange.

The qualitative distinctness of objects, which means, subjectively, that they are in demand, cannot claim to bring about an absolute value quantity; it is always the interrelation of demands, realized in exchange, that gives economic value to objects. This relativity is more clearly illustrated by the other constitutive element of value – relative scarcity. Exchange is only the inter-individual attempt to improve the conditions that result from the scarcity of goods; that is, the attempt to reduce subjective needs by changes in the distribution of the given supply. This already indicates a general correlation between what is called scarcity value (which has been legitimately criticized) and what is called exchange value. But here it is more important to see the opposite relationship. I have already emphasized that the scarcity of goods would hardly bring about valuation unless it were alterable by human effort. This is possible only in two ways; either by the application of labour power, which increases the supply of goods, or by the offer of goods already possessed, which would eliminate the scarcity of the object in demand. It may be stated, therefore, that the scarcity of goods conditions exchange objectively in relation to the demand for those goods, and that only exchange makes scarcity an element in value. It is a mistake in many theories of value that, on the basis of utility and scarcity, they conceive economic value – the exchange transactions – as something obvious, as the conceptually necessary consequence of these premises. This is not at all correct. If these premises resulted in ascetic renunciation or in fighting and robbery – as, in fact, is often the case – no economic value or economic life would develop.

Ethnology reveals the astounding arbitrariness, instability and inadequacy of value concepts in primitive culture as soon as anything other than the most urgent present needs is in question. There is no doubt that this comes about as a consequence of, or at least in association with, the primitive man's distaste for exchange. Various reasons have been advanced for this: that he is always afraid of being cheated in exchange, in the absence of any objective and general standard of value; or that he may surrender a part of his personality and give evil powers dominion over him, because the product of labour is always created by and for himself. Perhaps the primitive man's distaste for work originates from the same source. Here, too, a reliable standard for exchange between effort and result is lacking; he is afraid that he will be cheated by nature, the objectivity of which confronts him as an unpredictable and frightening fact until such time as he can establish his own activity as objective, in a regular and verified exchange with nature. Being submerged in the subjectivity of his relationship to the object, exchange – with nature or with other individuals – which coincides with the objectification of things and their value, appears inopportune to him. It is as though the first awareness of the object as such produced a feeling of anxiety, as if a part of the self had become detached. This also explains the mythological and fetishistic interpretation of the object, an interpretation that, on the one hand, hypostatizes this anxiety and makes it comprehensible to primitive man, and on the other hand assuages it by humanizing the object and thus reconciling it with man's subjectivity. This situation explains a series of other phenomena. First, the general acceptance and approval of robbery, as the subjective and normatively unregulated seizure of what is immediately desired. Long after the time of Homer, piracy continued to be regarded, in the backward agricultural areas of Greece, as legitimate business, and some primitive people consider violent robbery more noble than honest payment. This is also understandable; for in exchanging and paying one is subordinated to an objective norm, and the strong and autonomous personality has to efface himself, which is disagreeable. This also accounts for the disdain of trade by self-willed aristocratic individuals. On the other hand, exchange favours peaceful relations between men because they then accept a supra-personal and normative regulation.

There are, as one might expect, a number of intermediate phenomena between pure subjectivity in the change of ownership, exemplified by robbery or gifts, and objectivity in the form of exchange where things are exchanged according to the equal value they contain. This is exemplified by the traditional reciprocity in making gifts. The idea exists among many people that a gift should be accepted only if it can be reciprocated, that is, so to speak, subsequently acquired. This leads on directly to regular exchange when, as often occurs in the Orient, the seller gives the object to the buyer as a 'present', but woe to him if he does not make a corresponding present in exchange. Work given freely in case of urgent need, the co-operation of neighbours or friends without payment, such as is found everywhere in the world, also has its place here. But usually these workers are lavishly entertained and, whenever possible, given a feast; and it is reported of the Serbs, for instance, that only well-to-do people could afford to call upon such voluntary workers. It is true that even now in the Orient, and even in Italy, the concept of a fair price which imposes limits to the subjective advantages of either buyer or seller does not exist. Everyone sells as dearly and buys as cheaply as he can; exchange is simply a subjective action between two persons, the result of which depends only upon the shrewdness, the eagerness and the persistence of the two parties, not upon the object and its supra-individually determined relation to the price. A Roman antique dealer explained to me once that a deal is successfully transacted when the seller who is asking too much and the buyer who is offering too little eventually meet each other at a point acceptable to both. Here one sees clearly how an objectively appropriate price emerges from the bargaining between subjects, the whole process being a vestige of pre-exchange conditions in a predominantly, but not yet completely, exchange economy. Exchange already exists as an objective action between values, but its execution is still subjective and its mode and quantities depend exclusively upon a relation between personal qualities. Here, probably, we find the ultimate reason for the sacred forms, the legal regulation and the protection by publicity and tradition which accompanied mercantile transactions in early cultures. It was a way of transcending subjectivity to meet the demands of exchange, which could not yet be established by real relations between the objects. So long as exchange, and the idea of value-equality between things, were quite novel, it was impossible to reach an agreement when two individuals had to make the decision themselves. Consequently, we find well into the Middle Ages not only public exchange transactions, but more specifically a precise regulation of the rates of exchange of customary goods which none of the contractors could disregard. It is true that this objectivity is mechanical and external, based upon reasons and forces that lie outside the particular exchange transaction. A really adequate objectivity discards such *a priori* determination, and includes in the calculation of exchange all those particular circumstances that, in this case, are disregarded. But the intention and the principle are the same: the supra-subjective determination of value in exchange, which is later established by more objective and immanent means. The exchange carried on by free and independent individuals presupposes a judgment by objective standards, but in an earlier historical stage exchange had to be fixed and guaranteed by society, because otherwise the individual would lack any clue as to the value of the objects. Similar reasons may have been influential in the social regulation of primitive labour, which demonstrates the equality between exchange and labour or, more accurately, the subordination of labour to exchange. The multiple relations between what is objectively valid – both practically and theoretically – and its social significance and acceptance often appear historically

in the following manner. Social interaction, diffusion and standardization provide the individual with the dignity and reliability of a style of life which is later
confirmed as being objectively just. Thus, the child does not accept an explanation on the basis of inner reasons, but because he trusts the person who explains
the situation; he believes not in something but in somebody. In matters of taste
we depend upon fashion, that is upon a socially accepted way of doing and
appreciating things, until such time, late enough, as we learn to judge the
object itself aesthetically. Thus the need for the individual to transcend the self
and so gain a more than personal support and stability becomes the power of
tradition in law, in knowledge and in morality. This indispensable standardization, which transcends the individual subject but not yet subjects in general, is
slowly replaced by a standardization that evolves from the knowledge of reality
and from the acceptance of ideal norms. That which is outside ourselves, which
we need for our orientation, takes the more easily acceptable form of social
universality before we are confronted with it as the objective certainty of reality
and of ideas. In this sense, which applies to cultural development as a whole,
exchange is originally determined by society, until such time as individuals
know the object and their own valuations well enough to decide upon rates of
exchange from case to case. This suggests that the socially and legally established prices that control transactions in all primitive cultures are themselves
only the outcome of many single-exchange transactions which previously
occurred in an unregulated way between individuals. But this objection has no
greater validity in this case than in the case of language, mores, law, religion; in
short, all the basic forms of life that emerge and dominate within the group, and
that for a long time appeared to be explicable only as the invention of individuals. In fact it is certain that, from the outset, they evolved as inter-individual
structures, in the interaction between the individual and the multitude, so that
their origin cannot be attributed to any single individual. I consider it quite
possible that the precursor of socially regulated exchange was not individual
exchange but a change in ownership, which was not exchange at all but was, for
instance, robbery. In that case inter-individual exchange would have been
simply a peace treaty and both exchange and regulated exchange would have
originated together. An analogous case would be that of the capture of women
by force preceding the exogamic peace treaty with neighbours which regulates
the purchase and exchange of women. This newly introduced form of marriage
is immediately established in a form that constrains the individual. It is quite
unnecessary that particular free contracts of the same kind should precede it;
on the contrary, social regulation emerges together with the type. It is a prejudice to assume that every socially regulated relationship has developed historically out of a similar form which is individually and not socially regulated. What
preceded it may have been a similar content in a totally different form of
relationship. Exchange transcends the subjective forms of appropriation such as

robbery and gifts – just as presents to the chief and the fines that he imposes are the first steps towards taxation – and so exchange is socially regulated in the first possible form of supra-subjectivity which then leads to real objectivity. Social standardization is the first step towards that objectivity in the free exchange of property between individuals which is the essence of exchange.

It follows from all this that exchange is a sociological phenomenon *sui generis*, an original form and function of social life. It is in no way a logical consequence of those qualitative and quantitative aspects of things that are called utility and scarcity which acquire their significance for the process of valuation only when exchange is presupposed. If exchange, that is the willingness to sacrifice one thing in order to acquire another, is precluded, then no degree of scarcity of the desired object can produce an economic value. The significance of the object for the individual is always determined by the desire for it, and its utility depends upon the qualities that it has; if we already possess the object, then its significance is not affected at all by whether there exist many or few or no other specimens of its kind. (I leave aside here those cases in which scarcity itself becomes a quality of the object, thus making it desirable, as for example postage stamps, curios and antiques which have no aesthetic or historical value.) The sense of difference that is necessary for enjoyment may, of course, depend upon the scarcity of the object, that is upon the fact that it cannot be enjoyed everywhere and at any time. However, this inner psychological condition of enjoyment does not have any practical effects since, if it had, it would result in the perpetuation or increase of scarcity, which, as experience shows, does not occur. What concerns us here, aside from the direct enjoyment of the quality of objects, is the means by which it is accomplished. If the process is long and complicated, requiring sacrifices in the shape of deferment, disappointment, work, inconvenience and renunciations, we call the object 'scarce'. One might formulate it in this way: objects are not hard to get because they are scarce, rather they are scarce because they are hard to get. The inflexible external fact that the supply of some goods is too small to satisfy the desires of all of us is by itself insignificant. There are many things that are actually scarce, which are not scarce in the economic sense. Whether they are scarce in the latter sense is determined by the degree of strength, patience and sacrifice that is necessary to acquire them by exchange – and such sacrifice presupposes a demand for the object. The difficulty of acquisition, the sacrifice offered in exchange, is the unique constitutive element of value, of which scarcity is only the external manifestation, its objectification in the form of quantity. It is often overlooked that scarcity is only a negative condition, which characterizes being through non-being. Non-being, however, cannot have any effect; every positive result must be initiated by a positive quality and force, of which the negative is only the shadow. These positive forces are obviously those that are involved in exchange. Their positive character should be regarded as being dissociated from the fact that it is not attached to the individual. The relativity of things has the singular characteristic of going beyond individual cases, and subsisting only in multiplicity, yet being something other than a mere conceptual generalization and abstraction.

The profound relationship between relativity and socialization, which is a direct demonstration of relativity for which mankind presents the material, is illustrated here: society is a structure that transcends the individual, but that is not abstract. Historical life thus escapes the alternative of taking place either in individuals or in abstract generalities. Society is the universal which, at the same time, is concretely alive. From this arises the unique significance that exchange, as the economic–historical realization of the relativity of things, has for society; exchange raises the specific object and its significance for the individual above its singularity, not into the sphere of abstraction, but into that of lively inter-action which is the substance of economic value. No matter how closely the inner nature of an object is investigated, it will not reveal economic value which resides exclusively in the reciprocal relationship arising between several objects on the basis of their nature. Each of these relations conditions the other and reciprocates the significance which it receives from the other.

III

Before developing the concept of money as the incarnation and purest expression of the concept of economic value, it is necessary to show the latter as part of a theoretical world view, in terms of which the philosophical significance of money can be understood. Only if the formula of economic value corresponds to a world formula can its highest stage of realization – beyond its direct appearance or rather through this very appearance – claim to contribute to the interpretation of existence.

Economic value and a relativistic world view

We usually systematize our disorderly, fragmentary and confused first perceptions of an object by distinguishing a stable and essential substance from the flux of movements, colours and accidents that leave the essence unchanged. This articulation of the world as a stable core within fleeting appearances, and the accidental manifestations of enduring bearers of such appearances, grows into a contrast between the absolute and the relative. Just as we think that we can find within ourselves a being whose existence and character is centred in ourselves, a final authority which is independent of the outside world; and just as we distinguish this being from the existence and character of our thoughts, experiences and development which are real and confirmable only through relations with others – so we seek in the world substances, entities and forces whose being and significance rest exclusively within them. We distinguish them from all relative existences and occurrences – from all those that are what they are only through comparison, contact or the reactions of others. Our physical–psychological inclination and our relationship to the world determines the direction in which this opposition develops. Even though motion and quiescence, external activity and inner contemplation may be interconnected so that they gain importance and significance only through each other, we nevertheless consider one of this pair of opposites – quiescence, substance, the inner stability of our life's content – as the essentially valuable and definitive in contrast with what is changing, restless, external. Consequently, the goal of our thoughts is to find what is steadfast and reliable behind ephemeral appearances and the flux of events; and to advance from mutual dependence to self-sufficiency and independence. In this way we attain the fixed points that can guide us through the maze of phenomena, and that represent the counterpart of what we conceive in ourselves as valuable and definitive. To begin with an obvious example of this tendency: light is regarded as a fine substance emanating from bodies, heat as a substance, physical life as the activity of material living spirits, psychological processes as being supported by a specific substance of the soul. The mythologies that posit a thunderer behind the thunder, a solid substructure below the earth to keep it from falling or spirits in the stars to conduct them in their celestial course – all these are searching for a substance, not only as the embodiment of the perceived qualities and motions, but as the initial active force. An absolute is sought beyond the mere relationships between objects, beyond their accidental and temporal existence. Early modes of thought are unable to reconcile themselves to change, to the coming and going of all terrestrial forms of physical and mental life. Every kind of living creature represents to them a unique act of creation; institutions, forms of living, valuations have existed eternally and absolutely as they exist today; the phenomena of the world have validity not only for man and his organized life, but are in themselves as we perceive them. In short, the first tendency of thought, by which we seek to direct the disorderly flow of impressions into a regular channel and to discover a fixed structure amidst their fluctuations, is focused upon the substance and the absolute, in contrast with which all particular happenings and relations are relegated to a preliminary stage which the understanding has to transcend.

The epistemology of a relativistic world view

The examples given indicate that this trend has been reversed. Whereas almost all cultures originally took such an approach, the basic tendency of modern science is no longer to comprehend phenomena through or as specific sub-stances, but as motions, the bearers of which are increasingly divested of any specific qualities; and it expresses the qualities of things in quantitative, i.e. relative, terms. Science posits, instead of the absolute stability of organic, psychic, ethical and social forms, a ceaseless development in which each element has a restricted place determined by the relationship to its own past and future. It has abandoned the search for the essence of things and is reconciled to stating the relationships that exist between objects and the human mind from the view-point of the human mind. That the apparent stability of the earth is not only a complicated movement, but that its position in the universe is established by a mutual relationship to other masses of matter, is a very simple but striking case of the transition from the stability and absoluteness of the world's contents to their dissolution into motions and relations.

But all this, even if carried to its conclusion, would still allow, or even require, a fixed point, an absolute truth. Cognition itself, which accomplishes that dis-solution, seems to elude the flux of eternal change and the merely relative determination of its content. The dissolution of the absolute objectivity of what is cognized into modes of apprehension that are valid only for the human mind, presupposes an ultimate point somewhere that cannot be derived from anything else. The flux and the relativity of psychic processes cannot affect those pre-suppositions and norms according to which we decide whether our cognitions have this or that character. The merely psychological derivation, to which all absolutely objective knowledge is supposed to be reduced, depends nevertheless upon certain axioms which cannot have a merely psychological significance if we are to avoid moving in a vicious circle. This is not only a point of the greatest importance for the general view of things on which the following discussion is based, but also provides a model for many particular aspects, and it deserves closer scrutiny.

There is no doubt that the truth of any statement can be known only on the basis of criteria that are completely certain and general. Such criteria may be limited to specific areas and may be legitimated by higher-level criteria, in such fashion that a hierarchical series of cognitions is constructed, the validity of each one depending upon the preceding one. However, if this series is not to be suspended in the air – and indeed, for it to be possible at all – it must have somewhere an ultimate basis, a supreme authority, which provides legitimation to other members of the series without needing legitimation itself. This is the scheme into which our empirical knowledge has to be integrated, and which relates all limited and relative knowledge to knowledge that is no longer condi-tional. Yet we shall never know what this absolute knowledge is. Its real content can never be established with the same certainty as can its general, so to say, formal existence, because the process of incorporation within a higher-level principle, the attempt to find an antecedent for what appeared to be the ultimate principle, is endless. No matter what proposition we have discovered as the ultimate one, standing above the relativity of all other propositions, it remains possible that we shall recognize this one too as being merely relative and conditioned by a superior one. This possibility is a positive challenge, which the history of thought has illustrated many times. Somewhere knowledge may have an absolute basis, but we can never state irrevocably where this basis is; consequently, in order to avoid dogmatic thought, we have to treat each position at which we arrive as if it were the penultimate one.

The sum of knowledge does not thereby become tainted with scepticism. It is just as great a mistake to confuse relativism with scepticism as it was to accuse Kant of scepticism because he treated time and space as conditions of our experience. Both standpoints lend themselves to such a judgment if their opposite is accepted outright as the absolutely correct picture of reality, so that every theory that negates this then appears as a perturbation of 'reality'. If the concept of relativity is constructed in such a way that it requires an absolute, it is impossible to eliminate the absolute without self-contradiction. However, the course of our investigation will show that an absolute is not required as a conceptual counterpart to the relativity of things. Such a postulate involves a transfer from the sphere of empirical circumstances – where, indeed a 'relation' between elements which stand outside any such a relation and in that sense are 'absolute' – to a sphere that concerns the basis of all empiricism. If we admit that our knowledge may have somewhere an absolute norm, a supreme authority that is self-justifying, but that its content remains in constant flux because knowledge progresses and every content attained suggests another which would be more profound and more appropriate for the task, this is not scepticism; any more than it is scepticism when we admit, as is generally done, that while natural phenomena are subject to universal laws, these laws have to be corrected continually as our knowledge increases, that their content is always historically conditioned, and that they lack the absolute character that the concept implies. Equally, the ultimate presuppositions of perfected knowledge cannot be regarded as merely conditioned, and only subjectively or relatively true, but every single presupposition that is available at any particular moment should and must be so regarded.

The construction of proofs in infinite series

The fact that every conception is true only in relation to another one – even though the ideal body of knowledge, infinitely remote from us, may include an unconditioned truth – indicates a relativism in our behaviour that also extends to other areas. It is possible that norms of practical activity exist for human sociation which, recognized by a superhuman mind, might be called the absolute and eternal right. This would have to be a *causa sui* in law, i.e. it would have to be self-legitimating, for if its legitimacy were derived from a superior norm the latter would be the absolute determining factor of the law as valid under any circumstances. There is, in fact, no single legal rule that could claim to be absolutely unalterable; each has only the temporary validity that changing historical circumstances allow. If the legal content is legitimate and not arbitrary, its validity derives from a previously existing legal norm which justifies the setting aside of the former legal content in the same manner as it previously upheld it. Every judicial system contains in itself forces – ideal as well as external – that make for its own alteration, extension or abolition. Thus, for example, the law that assigns legislative power to parliament not only provides the legitimate basis of law A, which abolishes law B enacted by the same parliament, but also makes it a legal act for the parliament to delegate legislative power to another body. This means, regarded from the other side, that the worth of every law depends upon its relation to another law; no law has worth by itself. Just as new and even revolutionary knowledge can be demonstrated only by means of the content, axioms and methods of previous knowledge – though an original truth, which cannot be demonstrated and the self-sufficient certainty of which we shall never be able to attain, has to be assumed – so we lack a self-subsistent right, although the conception of it hovers above the series of relative legal rules, each dependent upon legitimation by another rule. To be sure, our knowledge rests upon first principles which cannot be proved at any given time, because without these we should not arrive at the relative series of derived proofs; but they do not possess the logical dignity of being demonstrated. They are not true in the same sense as that which has been proved, and our thinking accepts them as ultimate points only until it reaches a higher stage at which that which was accepted as axiomatic can be demonstrated. Correspondingly, there are, of course, absolutely and relatively pre-legal conditions, in which an empirical right is established by force or other means. This right, however, is not established legally; it is accepted as law as soon as it exists, but its existence is not a legal fact. It lacks entirely the dignity of that which is based upon law. In fact, every power that establishes such a non-legal right strives for its legitimation or for the fiction of legitimacy, as if in homage to that absolute right, which lies beyond all relativity and is unaffected by it, but which is symbolized for us only by deducing every existing legal rule from a preceding one.

But even if this infinite regress did not still establish our knowledge as conditioned, it would be accomplished perhaps in another fashion. If the proof of a statement is traced to its foundations and these again to theirs, etc., it becomes evident, often enough, that the proof is only possible, i.e. itself provable, if the original statement itself is assumed to be demonstrated. In any individual case, this renders the deduction illusory since it involves circular reasoning, but it is not inconceivable that our knowledge, taken as a whole, is imprisoned within this pattern. If one considers the vast number of hierarchically ordered presuppositions, stretching into infinity, upon which all particular knowledge depends, it seems actually possible that the statement A is proved by the statement B, and the statement B through the truth of C, D, E, etc., until finally it can only be proved by the truth of A. The chain of reasoning C, D, E needs only to be sufficiently long so that the return to the starting point cannot be imagined, just as the size of the earth conceals its global form and gives us the illusion of being able to advance straight into the infinite. The interrelationship that we assume in our knowledge of the world – that from every point we can attain by demonstration every other point – seems to make this plausible. If we do not want to remain dogmatically once and for all with a single truth that needs no proof, it is easy to assume that this reciprocity of proofs is the basic form of knowledge, conceived in its perfect state. Cognition is thus a free-floating process, whose elements determine their position reciprocally, in the same way as masses of matter do by means of weight. Truth is then a relative concept like weight. It is then perfectly acceptable that our image of the world 'floats in the air', since the world itself does so. This is not an accidental coincidence of words but an allusion to a basic connection. The inherent necessity for our minds to know the truth by proofs either removes the discovery of truth to infinity, or leads it into a circle, so that one statement is true only in relation to another one; this other one, however, eventually only in relation to the first. The totality of our knowledge would then be as little 'true' as would the totality of matter be 'heavy'. The qualities that could be asserted validly about the interrelationship of the parts would lead to contradictions if asserted about the whole.

This reciprocity, in which the inner elements of cognition authenticate the meaning of truth for each other, appears to be upheld by another form of relativity, that between the theoretical and the practical interests of our life. We are convinced that all representations of what exists are functions of a specific physical and psychological organization which do not mirror the outside world in any mechanical way. The images of the world of an insect with its mosaic eyes, of an eagle with its almost inconceivably keen sight, of an olm with its buried, functionless eyes, of ourselves and of innumerable other species, must be profoundly different from each other; and we must conclude that none of them reproduces the content of the external world in its inherent objectivity. Nevertheless these representations, which have been characterized at least negatively, form the presuppositions, the material and the directives for our practical activity, through which we establish a relationship with the world as it exists in relative independence of our subjectively determined representation. We expect certain reactions to our actions, and these usually occur in an appropriate way, i.e. one that is useful to us. The same is true of nature's reaction to animal behaviour, which is determined by totally different pictures of the very same world. It seems to me to be a very striking fact that actions carried out on the basis of representations that are not at all identical with objective being nevertheless secure results of a reliability, expediency and accuracy that could hardly be greater if we knew the objective conditions as they are in themselves, whereas other activities based on 'false' representations tend to injure us. We can also see that animals too are subject to deceptions and to corrigible misconceptions. What, then, does 'truth' mean, when it is totally different for animals and for ourselves, does not correspond with objective reality and yet leads to the expected consequences with as much certainty as if it did so correspond? This seems to me explicable only by the following assumption. The difference in organization requires that each species, in order to survive and to attain its essential aims in life, must behave in a way that is distinctive and different from that of other species. Whether an action guided by a representation will have useful consequences cannot be determined by the content of this representation, even though it might correspond with absolute objectivity. The result will depend entirely upon what this representation can accomplish as a real process within the organism, allied with other physical and psychological forces and with reference to the specific needs of life. If we assert that man sustains and supports life only on the basis of true representations, and destroys it by false ones, what does this 'truth' – the content of which is different for each species and which never reflects the true object – mean except that some representation associated with a particular organization and its powers and needs leads to useful results? Initially, truth is not useful because it is true, but vice-versa. We dignify with the name of 'truth' those representations that, active within us as real forces or motions, incite us to useful behaviour. Thus there are as many basically different truths as there are different organizations and conditions of life. The sense perception that is true for the insect would obviously not be true for the eagle; this is because this perception, on the basis of which the insect acts properly in relation to inner and outer constellations, would move the eagle, in relation to his conditions, to unreasonable and destructive action. These perceptions do not lack normative stability; indeed, every perceiving being possesses a generally established 'truth', which his representation may grasp or miss. The law of gravitation remains 'true' whether or not we recognize it, in spite of the fact that it would not be true for beings with a different conception of space, different categories of thought and a different system of numbers. The content that is 'true' for us has the peculiar structure of being totally dependent on our mode of existence – since this is not shared by other beings – but its truth-value is completely independent of its physical realization. On one side a being with its constitution and its needs, on the other side an objective existence is given; thus it is ideally established what is the truth for this being. Since truth for this being means the most favourable representations, a selection takes place among its psychological processes: those that are useful become fixed by the ordinary methods of selection and constitute as a whole the 'true' world of representations. In fact, we do not have any other definitive criterion for the truth of a representation except that the actions based upon it lead to the desired consequences. Once these modes of representation have been finally established as expedient through selection and cultivation, they form among themselves a realm of theory that determines, according to inner criteria, the inclusion or exclusion of every new representation; just as the rules of geometry are built upon each other according to a strict inner autonomy, whereas the axioms and the methodological norms that make this whole structure possible cannot themselves be proved geometrically. The whole system of geometry is not valid at all in the same sense as are its single propositions. The latter can be proved by each other, whereas the whole is valid only in relation to something external, such as the nature of space, our mode of perception and the strength of our ways of thinking. Individual judgments may support each other, since the norms and facts already established substantiate others, but the totality of these norms and facts has validity only in relation to specific physio-psychological organizations, their conditions of life and the furthering of their activity.

The objectivity of truth as well as of value viewed as a relation between subjective elements

The concept of truth as a relation of representations to each other, and not as an absolute quality of any one of them, is also confirmed in respect of a particular object. Kant asserts that to recognize an object means to bring unity into the multiplicity of perceptions. Out of the chaotic material of our images of the world and the continuous flux of impressions, we distinguish some as belonging together and group them in units, which we then designate as 'objects'. An object has been perceived as soon as we have grouped into an entity the multitude of impressions that belong together. What else can this entity signify but the functional interdependence of those single impressions and materials of perception? The unity of these elements is nothing extraneous to the elements themselves; it is the persistent form of their relationship that they represent. When I recognize the object 'sugar' by forming the impressions that pass through my consciousness – white, hard, sweet, crystalline – into a unity, this means that I conceive these contents of perception as bound together; that under the given conditions a connection or mutual interaction exists, that one quality exists at this point and in this relation because the other exists, and so on reciprocally. In the same way as the unity of the social organism, or the social organism as a unit, signifies only the forces of attraction and cohesion among its individual members, so the unity of the single object, the perception of which is its intellectual realization, is only an interaction between the elements that enter into the perception of it. In what is called the 'truth' of a work of art, the mutual relationship of its elements as against its relationship to the object that it depicts is also probably much more significant than is usually acknowledged. If we disregard the portrait, where the problem is more complicated owing to the purely individual theme, single elements in works of fine art or of literature will not convey an impression of either truth or falsehood; in isolation they stand outside these categories. Or looking at the matter from the other side: the artist is free as regards initial elements from which the work of art emerges; only after he has chosen a character, a style, an element of colour and form, an atmosphere, do the other parts become predetermined. They have now to meet the expectations aroused by the first step, which may be fantastic, arbitrary and unreal. So long as the elaboration is harmonious and consistent, the whole will produce an impression of 'inner truth', whether or not an individual part corresponds to outward reality and satisfies the claim to 'truth' in the ordinary and substantial sense. Truth in a work of art means that as a whole it keeps the promise which one part has, as it were, voluntarily offered us. It may be any one part, since the mutual correspondence of the parts gives the quality of truth to each of them. Truth is therefore also a relative concept in the particular context of art. It is realized as a relationship between the elements of a work of art, and not as an exact correspondence between the elements and an external object which constitutes the absolute norm. If the apprehension of an object means to apprehend it as a 'unity', it also means to apprehend it in its 'necessity'. There is a profound relationship between these two things. Necessity is a relation through which the heterogeneity of two elements becomes a unity. The formula of necessity is: if A exists, so does B. This necessary relation states that A and B are the elements of a particular unit of being or occurrence, and 'necessary relation' signifies a completely coherent relation, which is only decomposed and reconstituted by language. The unity of a work of art is obviously exactly the same as this necessity since it develops by the mutual conditioning of the different elements, one of which follows necessarily if another is given, and vice-versa. Necessity is a phenomenon of relations not only with reference to inter-related things, but in itself and according to its concept. Neither of the two most general categories that are the basis of our knowledge of the world, being and laws, contains necessity. The existence of real life is not necessary in terms of any law; it would not contradict any logical or natural law if nothing existed. It is also not 'necessary' that natural laws exist; they are mere facts, just as being is a mere fact, and only so far as they exist are the events subjected to them 'necessary'. There can be no natural law that natural laws must exist. What we call necessity exists only as a relation between being and laws; it is the form of their relation. Both are realities that are strictly independent of each other; for being is conceivable without being subject to laws, and the system of laws would be just as valid even if there were no corresponding being. Only if both exist do the forms of being become subject to necessity; being and laws are the elements of unity which we cannot apprehend directly but only through the relation of necessity. This unity binds together being and laws; it is inherent in neither one separately, but rules exist only because laws exist, and give meaning and significance to the laws only because being exists.

From another aspect bearing upon the same question, relativism with reference to the principles of perception may be formulated in the following way: the constitutive principles that claim to express, once and for all, the essence of objects are transposed into regulative principles which are only points of view in the progress of knowledge. The final, highest abstractions, simplifications and syntheses of thought have to renounce the dogmatic claim to be the ultimate judgments in the realm of knowledge. The assertion that things behave in a determinate way has to be replaced, in the context of the most developed and general views, by the notion that our understanding must proceed as if things behave in such and such a way. This makes it possible to express adequately the manner and method of our understanding in its real relation to the world. There corresponds with and originates in the many-sidedness of our being and the onesidedness of any conceptual expression regarding our relation to things the fact that no such expression is universally and permanently satisfactory, but is usually complemented historically by an opposite assertion. This produces, in many instances, an undetermined wavering, a contradictory mixture, or a disinclination to adopt any comprehensive principles. If the constitutive assertions that aim to establish the essence of things are changed into heuristic assertions that seek only to determine our methods of attaining knowledge by formulating ideal ends, this makes possible the simultaneous validity of opposing principles. If their significance is only methodological, they may be used alternatively without contradiction; there is no contradiction in changing from the inductive to the deductive method. The true unity of apprehension is secured only by such a dissolution of dogmatic rigidity into the living and moving process. Its ultimate principles become realized not in the form of mutual exclusion, but in the form of mutual dependence, mutual evocation and mutual complementation. Thus, for example, the development of the metaphysical world view moves between the unity and the multiplicity of the absolute reality in which all particular perceptions are based. The nature of our thinking is such that we strive for each of them as a definite conclusion without being able to settle upon either. Only when all the differences and variety of things are reconciled in a single aggregate is the intellectual and emotional striving for unity satisfied. However, as soon as this unity is attained, as in the concept of substance by Spinoza, it becomes clear that there is nothing one can do with it in understanding the world, and that a second principle at least is necessary in order to make it fruitful. Monism leads on to dualism or to pluralism, but they again create a desire for unity; and so the development of philosophy, and of individual thinking, moves from multiplicity to unity and from unity to multiplicity. The history of thought shows that it is vain to consider any one of these viewpoints as definitive. The structure of our reason in relation to the object demands equal validity for both principles, and attains it by formulating the monistic principle of seeking to bring unity out of multiplicity so far as possible – i.e. as if we ought to end with absolute monism – and by formulating the pluralistic principle of not resting content with any unity, but always searching for yet simpler elements and creative forces, i.e. as if the final result should be pluralism. The same is the case if one explores pluralism in its qualitative significance: the individual differentiation of things and destinies, their separation according to quality and value. Our innermost vital consciousness oscillates between this separateness and the solidarity among the elements of our existence. Sometimes life only seems bearable by enjoying happiness and bliss in complete separation from suffering and depression, and by keeping these rare moments free from any remembrance of less exalted and contradictory experiences. Then again it seems more admirable, and indeed the very challenge of life, to experience joy and sorrow, strength and weakness, virtue and sin as a living unity, each one being a condition of the other, each sacred and consecrating the other. We may seldom be aware of the general principle in these opposing tendencies, but they determine our attitude towards life in our endeavours, our aims and our fragmentary activities. Even when a person's character seems to be completely oriented in one of these directions, it is constantly thwarted by the other tendency, as diversion, background and temptation. People are not divided into categories by the contrast between differentiation and unification of their life experiences. This contrast exists in every individual, although his inner-personal form evolves in interaction with his social form, which moves between individualization and socialization. The essential point is not that these two trends constitute life, but that they are interdependent in a heuristic form. It seems as if our life employs or consists of a unified basic function which we are unable to grasp in its unity. We have to dissect it by analysis and synthesis, which constitutes the most general form of that contradistinction, and whose co-operation then restores the unity of life. But the singular entity in its separateness makes an absolute claim on us and the unity that comprehends everything singular makes the same demand, so that a contradiction emerges from which life often suffers. This contradiction becomes a logical contradiction since both elements presuppose each other in their existence: neither would have any objective meaning or intellectual interest if the other did not stand in opposition to it. Thus the peculiar difficulty arises – as with many other contrasted pairs – that something unconditioned is conditioned by another unconditioned item which in turn depends on the former. The fact that what we perceive as absolute is nevertheless relative can only be resolved by admitting that the absolute signifies a road stretching to infinity whose direction is still marked out no matter how great the distance we cover. The movement in each segment, so long as it continues, takes a course that appears to lead to a terminal point; this sense of direction remains unchanged even if at some point the movement assumes another direction which is subject to the same norm.

All general and particular systems of knowledge meet in this form of the mutual interdependence of thought processes. If one attempts to understand the political, social, religious or any other cultural aspects of the present time, this can be achieved only through history, i.e. by knowing and understanding the past. But this past, which comes down to us only in fragments, through silent witnesses and more or less unreliable reports and traditions, can come to life and be interpreted only through the experiences of the immediate present. No matter how many transformations and quantitative changes are required, the present, which is the indispensable key to the past, can itself be understood only through the past; and the past, which alone can help us to understand the present, is accessible only through the perceptions and sensibilities of the present. All historical images are the result of this mutuality of interpretative elements, none of which allows the others to come to rest. Ultimate comprehension is transferred to infinity, since every point in one series refers to the other series for its understanding. Psychological knowledge is a similar case. Every human being who confronts us is only a sound-producing and gesticulating automaton for our direct experience. We can only infer that there is a mind behind this appearance, and what processes are going on in it, by analogy with our own mind, which is the only mental entity directly known to us. On the other hand, self-knowledge develops only through the knowledge of others; and the fundamental cleavage of the self into an observed and an observing part comes about only through the analogy of the relation between the self and other persons. Knowledge of ourselves has therefore to find its way through other beings, whose lives we are able to interpret, however, only from self-knowledge. Thus, the knowledge of mental phenomena is an interplay between the I and the You. Each refers to the other, in a constant interchange and exchange of elements against each other, through which truth, no less than economic value, is produced.

And finally, to take a more comprehensive view: modern idealism produces the world from the Ego. The mind creates the world – the only world that we can discuss and that is real for us – according to its receptivity and its ability to construct forms. But on the other hand, this world is also the original source of the mind. From the glowing ball of matter, which we may conceive as the condition of the earth before there was any life, a gradual development has resulted in the possibility of life; and these living beings, at first purely material and without mind, have finally, in ways still unknown, produced the mind. Considered historically, the mind with all its forms and contents is a product of the world – of the same world which is in turn a product of the mind because it is a world of representations. If these two genetic possibilities are rigidly conceptualized they result in a disturbing contradiction. This does not come about, however, if they are regarded as heuristic principles which stand in a relationship of alternation and interaction. Nothing prevents us from attempting to trace any existing state of the world to the mental conditions that have produced it as a content of representations; just as nothing stands in the way of tracing these conditions to cosmic, historical or social facts which could give rise to a mind equipped with these powers and forms. The image of these facts, external to the mind, may again be derived from the subjective presuppositions of scientific and historical knowledge, and these again from the objective conditions of their origin, and so on *ad infinitum*. Of course, this knowledge is never realized in a clear-cut scheme; the two tendencies commingle in a fragmentary, interrupted and accidental way. But the principal contradiction is dissolved by an interpretation of both as heuristic principles; this transforms their opposition into an interaction and their mutual negation into an endless process of interaction.

I will introduce here two other examples – one very specific and the other very general – in which relativity, i.e. the reciprocal character of the significance of criteria of knowledge, appears in the form of succession or alternation. The substantial interdependence of concepts and basic elements in images of the world is frequently represented by such a rhythm of reciprocal alternation in time. The relationship between the historical and the scientific method in economics can be interpreted in this fashion. It is certainly true that every economic process can be understood only in the context of a specific historical-psychological constellation. But such an insight is always based upon the presupposition of definite rule-following relationships. If we did not assume general conditions, universal drives and regular series of effects as a basis for specific cases, there would not be any historical explanation at all; the whole would disintegrate into a chaos of atomized events. One may admit, nevertheless, that the universal regularities, which make the connection between the specific state or event and its conditions possible, depend in turn upon higher laws, so that they themselves are valid only as historical combinations; other events and forces at an earlier stage have shaped things in us and around us which now appear as universally valid and which give the causal elements of a later period their particular form. Thus, while these two methods, dogmatically stated and each claiming objective truth for itself, enter into irreconcilable conflict and mutual negation, they may assume an organic relationship in the form of alternation. Each becomes a heuristic principle, i.e. each has to be substantiated at every point of its application by an appeal to the other. The same is true for the most universal opposition in the process of cognition: between the *a priori* and experience. Ever since Kant we know that all experience, except for mere sense impressions, requires definite forms, inherent in the mind, by which the given is shaped into cognition. This *a priori*, which is brought by us to experience, must therefore be absolutely valid for all cognition and immune to any changes or to any possibility of correction by accidental sense experience. But the certainty that there are such norms is not matched by an equal certainty as to what these norms are. Much that was once considered *a priori* has later been recognized as an empirical and historical construct. On the one hand, we have the task of seeking in every phenomenon, beyond the content provided by sense impressions, the permanent *a priori* norms by which it is formed; but on the other, the maxim applies that we should attempt to trace every single *a priori* (but not the *a priori* as such) back to its source in experience.

This mutual correspondence and dependence of methods is something totally different from the cheap compromise attained by combining methods, where the loss on one side is usually much greater than the gain on the other. Here we are concerned with the possibility of giving unlimited effectiveness to each part of the contrasted pair. And though each of these methods remains to some extent, subjective, yet together, through the relativity of their application, they seem to express adequately the objective significance of things. Thus they correspond to the general principle in our investigation of value: elements, each of which is subjective in its content, can attain their present objectivity through the form of their mutual relations. As we have seen above, mere sensory perceptions, by being connected with each other, can indicate or establish the object. The personality – a structure so solid that a specific spiritual substance was made its foundation – originates, at least for empirical psychology, through reciprocal associations and apperceptions that occur among the individual conceptions. These occurrences, subjective and fleeting, produce by their interactions what exists independently in none of them; namely, the personality as an objective element of the theoretical and practical world. So objective law develops by balancing the subjective interests and forces of individuals, by determining their place and dimensions, and by attaining the objective form of equity and justice through the exchange of claims and restrictions. In this way, objective economic value also crystallized out of subjective individual demands because the form of equality and of exchange was available, and because these relationships had an impartiality transcending subjectivity which the single elements lacked. Those methods of cognition may well be subjective and heuristic; but they approach – even though by an infinite process of evoking each other – the ideal of objective truth by the fact that each finds its supplement and therewith its legitimation through the other.

Truth means the relationship between representations, which may be realized as an infinite construction, since, even if our knowledge is based upon truths that are no longer relative, we can never know whether we have reached the really final stage, or whether we are again on the road to a more general and profound conception; or it may consist in a reciprocal relation within these systems of representations and its demonstration is also reciprocal. But these two processes of thought are related by a peculiar division of functions. It is necessary to consider our mental existence under two categories that complement each other: in terms of its content and in terms of the process that, as an event of consciousness, carries or realizes this content. The structure of these categories is extremely different. We must conceive the mental process as a continuous flux, in which there are no distinct breaks, so that one mental state passes into the next uninterruptedly, in the manner of organic growth. The contents, abstracted from this process and existing in an ideal independence, appear under a totally different aspect: as an aggregate, a graduated scheme, a system of single concepts or propositions clearly distinguished from one another. The logical connection between any two concepts reduces the distance between them but not the discontinuity, like the steps of a ladder that are sharply separated from each other but yet provide the means for a continuous movement of the body. The relation among the contents of thought is characterized by the fact that the foundations of thought, considered as a whole, seem to move in circles, because thought has to support itself 'by being suspended' and has no ποῦ στῶ which supports it from outside. The contents of thought provide a background to each other so that each gets its meaning and colour from the other; they are pairs of mutually exclusive opposites and yet postulate each other for the creation of a possible world view. Every particular content becomes the ground of proof for the other through the whole chain of what is knowable. The process of thinking, however, by which this relation is psychologically accomplished, follows a direct and continuous chronological course; it continues according to its own inner meaning, although the death of the individual brings it to an end. The two categories of our reflection are divided into these two forms, which make knowledge illusory in particular cases but possible in general. Knowledge follows a course of infinite regress, of infinite continuity, of boundlessness, which yet is limited at any particular moment – whereas the contents exhibit the other form of infinity, that of the circle, in which every point is a beginning and an end, and all the parts condition each other mutually.

The process of reciprocal verification is usually hidden from our view for the same reason that we do not notice the reciprocal character of weight. The great majority of our representations are taken for granted and the question of truth is usually applied only to a particular case. A judgment is then made in terms of the consonance or otherwise of this instance with the aggregate of those representations that are assumed to be already established. On another occasion, any representation in the whole complex may become questionable, and the one to be investigated may belong to the determinant majority. The tremendous quantitative disproportion between the number of representations that are questionable and those that are established also helps to conceal the reciprocal relation. In this way, the disproportion of weights caused us, for a long time, to notice the gravitational attraction of the earth upon the apple but not that of the apple upon the earth. Consequently, a body appeared to have weight as an independent quality, because only one side of the relationship was observed. Thus, truth may come to be regarded as a specific quality of an individual representation, because the reciprocal relation between the elements, in which the truth resides, is lost to view on account of the infinitesimal size of the single element in relation to the sum of representations, which are not, for the moment, in question.

The 'relativity of truth', in the sense that all our knowledge is partial and corrigible, is often stated with an emphasis that is strangely disproportionate to the obviousness of this incontrovertible fact. What we understand here by this concept of the relativity of truth is evidently quite different: relativity is not a qualification of an otherwise independent notion of truth but is the essential feature of truth. Relativity is the mode in which representations become truth, just as it is the mode in which objects of demand become values. Relativity does not mean – as in common usage – a diminution of truth, from which something more might have been expected; on the contrary, it is the positive fulfilment and validation of the concept of truth. Truth is valid, not in spite of its relativity but precisely on account of it.

The great epistemological principles suffer from the difficulty they have – since they also are a form of knowledge – in subjecting their own content to the judgment that they pronounce upon knowledge in general. Thus either they are empty or they negate themselves. Dogmatism may base the certainty of knowledge upon some criterion as upon a rock – but what supports the rock? It must be assumed that certain knowledge is possible if the possibility of certain knowledge is to be derived from that criterion. The assertion of the certainty of knowledge presupposes the certainty of knowledge. Similarly, scepticism may assert as uncontrovertible the uncertainty and unreliability of all knowledge or may even assert the impossibility of any truth – the inner contradiction in the concept of truth; but it must then subject scepticism itself to the findings of this thinking about thought. Here, indeed, is a vicious circle: if all knowledge is fallacious, then so is scepticism itself, and it negates itself.

Finally, critical philosophy may derive all objectivity, all the basic forms of the content of knowledge from the conditions of experience, but it cannot prove that experience itself is valid. The criticism that is levelled at everything transcendental is based upon a presupposition, which cannot be examined in the same critical fashion without having the ground cut away beneath it. Epistemology here encounters a typical hazard. In analysing itself, it judges its own case. It needs a vantage point outside itself, and is confronted with a choice between excepting itself from the test or rule imposed on all other knowledge, thus leaving itself open to attack from behind; or else subjecting itself to the laws and the process which it has discovered and thereby committing an act of circular reasoning, as is clearly illustrated by the self-negation of scepticism. Only a relativistic epistemology does not claim exemption from its own principle; it is not destroyed by the fact that its validity is only relative. For even if it is valid – historically, factually, psychologically – only in alternation and harmony with other absolute or substantial principles, its relation to its own opposite is itself only relative. Heuristics, which is only the consequence or the application of the relativistic principle to the categories of knowledge, can accept without contradiction that it is itself a heuristic principle. The question as to the grounding of this principle, which is not incorporated in the principle itself, constitutes no difficulty for relativism, because the ground is removed to infinity. Relativism strives to dissolve into a relation every absolute that presents itself, and proceeds in the same way with the absolute that offers itself as the ground for this new relation. This is a never-ending process whose heuristic eliminates the alternative: either to deny or to accept the absolute. It makes no difference how one expresses it: either that there is an absolute but it can be grasped only by an infinite process, or that there are only relations but that they can only replace the absolute in an infinite process. Relativism is able to make the radical concession that it is possible for the mind to place itself outside itself. The epistemological principles that remained content with one concept and thus excluded the continuing fruitful development of relations ended in self-contradiction: that the mind is supposed to judge itself, that it is either subject to its own definitive statements or exempt from them, and that equally each alternative destroys its validity. But relativism fully accepts the fact that for every proposition there is a higher one that determines whether this proposition is correct. But this second proposition, the logical authority that we ourselves establish, requires – considered as a psychological process – further legitimation by a higher proposition for which the same process repeats itself *ad infinitum*, either by an alternation of the validation between two judgments, or by treating the same content on one occasion as psychological reality, and on another as a logical principle. This view also removes the hazard that other epistemological principles faced, of ending in self-negation by subjecting themselves to their own statements. It is not correct to argue that scepticism, by denying the possibility of truth, must itself by untrue, any more than the pessimistic view of the wickedness of all that exists makes pessimism itself a wicked theory. For it is, in fact, the fundamental ability of our mind to judge itself and to establish its own law over itself. This is nothing but the expression or expansion of the basic fact of self-awareness. Our mind has no substantial unity, but only the unity that results from the interaction between the subject and object into which the mind divides itself. This is not an accidental form of the mind, which could be different without changing our essential qualities. It is rather the decisive form of the mind. To have a mind means nothing more than to execute this inner separation, to make the self an object, to be able to know oneself. That there is 'no subject without an object, no object without a subject' is realized first within the mind, which raises itself as the knowing subject above itself, as the object known; and by knowing this knowledge of itself, the life of the mind proceeds necessarily in the *progressus ad infinitum*. Its actual form, its cross-section, as it were, is a circular movement. The subject knows itself as an object and knows the object as a subject. Relativism as an epistemological principle proves itself by its subordination to its own principle, a process that proves fatal to many absolute principles. Thus relativism expresses most clearly what it is also able to perform for those other principles: the legitimation of the mind's capacity to judge itself, without making the process illusory no matter what the result of this judgment may be. For this setting oneself outside oneself appears now as the basis of the mind; the mind is subject and object at the same time. Only if this infinite process of knowing itself and judging itself is cut at any one link, which then confronts all the others as an absolute, does it become self-contradictory, in the sense that knowledge judging itself claims exemption for itself from the content of this judgment in order to pass judgment on it.

The relativistic view has often been considered as a degradation of the value, reliability and significance of things, regardless of the fact that only the naive adherence to something absolute, which is here questioned, could put relativism in such a position. In reality, however, it is the contrary that is true; only through the continuous dissolution of any rigid separateness into interaction do we approach the functional unity of all elements of the universe, in which the significance of each element affects everything else. Consequently, relativism is closer than one is inclined to think to its extreme opposite – Spinoza's philosophy – with its all-embracing *substantia sive Deus*. This absolute, which has no other content than the universal concept of being, includes in its unity everything that exists. Individual things no longer have any existence by themselves, since all being is in reality unified in the divine substance, just as the abstract concept of being forms a unity. All particular continuities and substantialities, all second-order absolutes, are so completely merged in that single absolute that one might say: all the contents of the world view have become relativities in a monism such as Spinoza's. The all-embracing substance, the only absolute that remains, can now be disregarded without thereby affecting the content of reality – the expropriator will be expropriated, as Marx says of a process that is similar in form – and nothing remains but the relativistic dissolution of things into relations and processes. The interdependence of things, which relativism establishes as their essence, excludes the notion of infinity only on a superficial view, or if relativism is not conceived in a sufficiently radical way. The contrary is indeed true: a concrete infinity seems to me conceivable only in two ways. First, as a rising or falling series, where every link depends upon another, and a third one is dependent upon it – as may be the case with spatial distribution, causal transmission of energy, chronological sequences or logical derivation. Secondly, what this series presents in an extended form is provided in a succinct circular form by interaction. If the effect that one element produces upon another then becomes a cause that reflects back as an effect upon the former, which in turn repeats the process by becoming a cause of retroaction, then we have a model of genuine infinity in activity. Here is an immanent infinity comparable to that of the circle; for the latter also develops only in complete mutuality, by which each part of the circle determines the position of other parts – in contrast with other lines, which also return to their starting point but in which every point is not determined by the interplay of all parts. If infinity is regarded as a substance, or as the measure of an absolute, it always remains something finite though very large. The finiteness of existence is only transcended through the conditioning of every content of being by another content, which in turn is equally conditioned – either by a third factor which undergoes the same process or by an interaction of the two.

This may suffice by way of allusion to a philosophical standpoint which makes possible a final uniformity of interpretation with reference to the variety of things, and which provides a general context for the interpretation of economic value. Since the basic characteristic of all knowable existence, the interdependence and interaction of everything, also refers to economic value and conveys this principle of life to economic material, the essential quality of money now becomes comprehensible. For the value of things, interpreted as their economic interaction, has its purest expression and embodiment in money.

Money as the autonomous manifestation of the exchange relation

Whatever may be the historical origin of money – and this is far from being clearly established – one fact at least is certain, that money did not suddenly appear in the economy as a finished element corresponding to its pure concept. Money can have developed only out of previously existing values in such a way that the quality of money, which forms part of every exchangeable object, was realized to a great extent in one particular object; the function of money was at first still exercised, as it were, in intimate association with its previous value significance. In the next chapter we shall examine whether this genetic connection of money with a non-monetary value has been or can ever be dissolved. At all events, there have been innumerable errors owing to the fact that the essence and significance of money was not conceptually distinguished from the qualities of those values that money evolved by enhancing one of these qualities. We shall first consider money without reference to the material that represents it in substantial form; for the particular qualities that the material adds to money lead to its being subsumed under those goods to which, as money, it stands in contrast. It can be seen at first glance that money constitutes one party, as it were, and the totality of goods bought by money constitutes the other party; so far as its pure essence is concerned, it must be interpreted simply as money, quite apart from all the secondary qualities that connect it with the contrasting party.

In this sense, money has been defined as 'abstract value'. As a visible object, money is the substance that embodies abstract economic value, in a similar fashion to the sound of words which is an acoustic–physiological occurrence but has significance for us only through the representation that it bears or symbolizes. If the economic value of objects is constituted by their mutual relationship of exchangeability, then money is the autonomous expression of this relationship. Money is the representative of abstract value. From the economic relationship, i.e. the exchangeability of objects, the fact of this relationship is extracted and acquires, in contrast to those objects, a conceptual existence bound to a visible symbol. Money is a specific realization of what is common to economic objects – in the language of the scholastics one might call it *universale ante rem*, or *in re* or *post rem* – and the general misery of human life is most fully reflected by this symbol, namely by the constant shortage of money under which most people suffer.

The money price of a commodity indicates the degree of exchangeability between this commodity and the aggregate of all other commodities. If one conceives of money in the abstract sense, independently of all the consequences of its concrete representation, then a change in money price signifies that the exchange relationship between the particular commodity and the aggregate of all other commodities has changed. If the price of a quantity of A rises from 1 to 2 marks, while the prices of the commodities of B, C, D and E remain stable, this signifies a change in the relationship between A and B, C, D and E which also could be expressed by stating that the price of the latter had fallen, while that of A remained constant. We prefer the first version because of its greater simplicity, just as we say, if a body changes its position, that it has moved – for example, from east to west – whereas the actual change could be described equally well as a change of the environment (including the observer) from west to east, while the particular body remains still. The position of a body is not a quality of the body itself, but is a relationship to other bodies; and in every change of position, these others, as well as the body itself, may be regarded as the active or passive subject. In the same way, since the value of A consists of its relation to the economic cosmos, it would be equally justified and only less convenient to interpret any change in the value of A as a change in B, C, D and E. This relativity, as practised for example in barter, becomes crystallized in money as the expression of value. How this can happen, will be examined later. The statement that the value of A is 1 mark has purified A of everything that is not economic, i.e. not an exchange relationship to B, C, D and E. This mark, considered as value, is the function of A detached from its carrier, in relation to the other objects of the economy. Everything else that A may be, in itself and independent of this relation, is irrelevant here. Every A_1 or A_2 which differs in quality is equal to A inasmuch as its value is also 1 mark, and because it has the same relation to quantitative exchange to B, C, D and E. Money is simply 'that which is valuable', and economic value means 'to be exchangeable for something else'. All other objects have a specific content from which they derive their value. Money derives its content from its value; it is value turned into a substance, the value of things without the things themselves. By sublimating the relativity of things, money seems to avoid relativity, just as the norms of reality are not subject to the same relativity that dominates reality, not in spite of but because the relations between things, in their independent life, significance and consistency, are the content of these norms. Everything that exists is subject to laws, but the governing laws themselves are not subject to law. It would be to move in a circle to assume that there is a natural law that entails natural laws. I leave it open, however, as to whether this circle is nevertheless legitimate because it is part of the fundamental processes of thought to return to their origin or to aim at an end that lies in infinity. Norms are the types and forms of relativity that develop among, and give form to, the specific phenomena of reality – whether they are termed ideas, as with Plato and Schopenhauer, *logoi* as with the Stoics, the *a priori* as with Kant or stages in the development of reason as with Hegel. These norms are not relative in the same sense as the objects subjected to them, because they themselves present the relativity of the objects. Thus it becomes comprehensible that money as abstract value expresses nothing but the relativity of things that constitute value; and, at the same time, that money, as the stable pole, contrasts with the eternal movements, fluctuations and equations of the objects. In so far as money does not accomplish this, it does not function according to its pure concept but as a specific object co-ordinated with all others. It would be erroneous to object that, in the business of money-lending and foreign exchange, money is bought for money; and that therefore money, although preserving the purity of its concept, acquires the relativity of individual objects of value, which it was supposed not to have but merely to represent. The fact that money expresses the value relation of valuable objects exempts it from this relation and places it in a different order. By representing the relationship in question and its practical consequences money itself acquires a value by which it not only establishes a relationship to all kinds of concrete values, but can also indicate relations among value quantities within its own domain which excludes tangible objects. One quantum is offered as present money, another as a future promise; one quantum is accepted in one region, the other in another – these are modifications that produce value relationships, unaffected by the fact that the object with whose quanta they deal represents as a whole the relation between objects whose value significance is quite different.

Analysis of the nature of money with reference to its value stability, its development and its objectivity

From this dual role – outside and within the series of concrete values – there result, as I have said, innumerable difficulties in the practical and theoretical treatment of money. To the extent that money expresses the value relationship between goods, measures them and facilitates their exchange, it enters the world of useful goods as a power of entirely different origin; either as an abstract system of measurement or as a means of exchange which moves between tangible objects as does ether between objects possessing weight. In order to perform these services, which depend upon its position outside all other goods, money has to be a concrete or specific value itself; and by performing these services it becomes such a value. In this manner, it becomes one of the links and conditions in the series with which it is, at the same time, contrasted: its value becomes dependent upon supply and demand; its costs of production exert an influence, however slight, upon its value; it appears in qualitatively different values; etc. The payment of interest is a manifestation of this value which results from the functions of money. Or from another aspect: the dual role of money consists, on the one hand, in measuring the value relations of goods exchanged and, on the other, in being exchanged with these goods and thus itself becoming a quantity subject to measurement. Money is measured by the goods against which it is exchanged and also by money itself. For not only is money paid for by money, as the money market and interest-bearing loans show, but the money of one country becomes the measure of value for the money of another country, as is illustrated by foreign exchange transactions. Money is therefore one of those normative ideas that obey the norms that they themselves represent. All such cases result in first-order complications and circular movements of thought, although these can be resolved: the Cretan who declares that all Cretans are liars, and falling under his own axiom condemns his own statement as a lie; the pessimist who brands the whole world as evil, so that his own theory must be so too; the sceptic who cannot maintain the truth of scepticism because he denies all truth, etc. Thus money stands as the measure and means of exchange above valuable objects; and because its services initially require a valuable representative and give value to their representative, money is ranked with those objects and is subsumed under the norms that are themselves derived from money.

What is eventually measured as value is not money, which is merely the expression of value, but the objects; and changes in price signify a change in their relations to each other. Money, viewed in terms of its pure function, has not changed its value; but a greater or lesser quantity of money reflects that change itself, abstracted from its representatives and assuming an independent form of expression. This condition of money is obviously the same as what is called its lack of qualities and lack of individuality. Since it stands between individual objects and in an equal relation to each of them, it has to be completely neutral. Here too, money represents the highest stage of development in a continuous series; this series is logically difficult but of great significance for our world view, in which each link, although formed according to the formula of the series and an expression of its inner forces, at the same time differs from the series as a complementing, controlling or opposing power. The starting point of the series is formed by the irreplaceable values whose specific qualities are easily obscured by the analogy with money equivalents. There is a substitute for most things that we own, at least in the widest sense of the word, so that the total value of our existence would remain the same if we were to lose one thing and gain another instead. The sum of happiness can be kept at the same level by a variety of elements. However, in relation to certain objects this exchangeability fails, not only because other possessions cannot give us the same degree of happiness, but because the sense of value is tied to this individual object, and not to happiness, the provision of which the object shares with other objects. It is a mistaken conceptual realism – regarding the general concept as a completely adequate representation of the particular reality – that makes us believe that we experience the value of things by their reduction to a general denominator of value, by reference to a centre of value where values present themselves as quantitatively different, but basically of the same kind. We often value the individual thing because we want exactly this and nothing else, even though something else would perhaps give us the same or even a greater amount of satisfaction. A high degree of sensitivity distinguishes very precisely between the amount of satisfaction that a certain possession provides, through which it becomes comparable and exchangeable with other possessions, and those specific qualities beyond its eudaemonistic effects which may make it just as valuable to us and in that respect completely irreplaceable. This is very well illustrated, with slight modifications, in those cases where personal affections and experiences make a standard and interchangeable object irreplaceable for us. An identical specimen of the same kind does not, under any circumstances, make good the loss. This could better be accomplished by an object belonging to a totally different category of qualities and sentiments, which would not remind us at all of the former object or suggest any comparison! This individual form of value is negated to the extent that objects become interchangeable, so that money – the representative and expression of exchangeability – is the least individual creation of our practical world. To the extent that things are exchanged for money – but not when they are bartered – they share this lack of

123

individuality. The absence of any inherent worth in an object cannot be more distinctly expressed than by substituting for it, without any sense of inadequacy, a money equivalent. Money is not only the absolutely interchangeable object, each quantity of which can be replaced without distinction by any other; it is, so to speak, interchangeability personified. The two poles between which *all* values stand are: at one extreme, the absolute individual value whose significance does not lie in any general quantity of value that could also be represented by another object, and whose position in our value system could not be filled by any other object; at the other extreme, that which is clearly interchangeable. Between these two poles things are arranged according to the degree of their replaceability, their position being determined by the extent to which they are replaceable and by the variety of objects that can take their place. This can also be represented by distinguishing in each object the irreplaceable and the replaceable part. Most things participate in both qualities, although we are frequently deceived about this, on the one hand, by the volatility of our transactions, and on the opposite side by narrow-mindedness and stubbornness. Even those things that are purchasable and replaceable by money probably possess, upon closer scrutiny, qualities whose value cannot be completely replaced by other possessions. The boundaries of our practical world are shown in those cases where one of these qualities is infinitely small: on the one hand, those very few values upon which the individual integrity of our Ego depends, where exchangeability is out of the question; on the other, money – the distilled exchangeability of objects – whose absolute lack of individuality results from the fact that it expresses the *relation* between things, a relation that persists in spite of changes in the things themselves.

This ability of money to replace every specific economic value – because it is not connected with any of these values but only with the relation into which they may enter – assures the continuity of the series of economic events. This series exists in both the production and the consumption of goods. But this is only the material of the series and still leaves the question of continuity and discontinuity open. Every act of consumption initially breaches the continuity of the economic process, and its relation to production is too unorganized, too much a matter of chance, to preserve the continuity of the line of development. One may conceive this line as an ideal which makes its path through the concrete objects in a manner comparable to the direction of a light beam through the oscillating parts of the ether. Into this stream, which pervades the strictly separated objects and controls their value significance, money now enters in order to compensate for the threatened interruption. By giving money for an object that I want to consume, I fill the gap in the value movement that results, or would result, from my consumption. The primitive forms of exchange of possessions – robbery and gifts – do not allow for such a complement of continuity; in their case, the logical connection in the ideal line of the economic process is, so to speak, interrupted. This connection is established in principle only through the exchange of equivalents, and in fact only through money. Money can compensate for the unevenness that exists in any system of barter, and can fill the gap that results from the removal of the object to be consumed. Obviously, money can attain this practical position within the economic series only through its ideal position outside the series. If money itself were a specific object, it could never balance every single object or be the bridge between disparate objects. Money can enter adequately into the relations that form the continuity of the economy only because, as a concrete value, it is nothing but the relation between economic values themselves, embodied in a tangible substance.

This significance of money shows itself further, in an empirical way, as stability of value, resulting from its interchangeability and lack of specific qualities. This is regarded as one of the outstanding and most useful characteristics of money. The length of the series of economic activities, which is a pre-condition for the continuity, the integration, and the productivity of the economy, depends upon the stability of the value of money without which long-range calculations, large-scale enterprises and long-term credits would be impossible. So long as one considers only the price fluctuations of a single object, one cannot determine whether the value of the object changes and the value of money remains stable or vice-versa. Stability of money value becomes an objective fact only when price decreases of a commodity or group of commodities are accompanied by price increases elsewhere. A general rise in prices would indicate a decrease in the value of money, and when that occurs the stability of money value is destroyed. This is only possible because money has certain qualities beyond its function as the indicator of the value relations of specific objects; these distinguishing qualities render money an object of the market and subject it to business cycles, quantitative changes and autonomous movements. They deprive money of its absolute position as an expression of relations and force it into a relative position, so that it no longer reflects a relation, but has relations. Only to the extent that money, true to its essence, is isolated from such influences does it have a stable value; from which it follows that price fluctuations do not signify a change in the relations of money to objects, but only changing relations among objects themselves. This implies that an increase in the price of one object corresponds to a fall in the price of another. In so far as money really has the essential quality of value stability, this results from its function of expressing the economic relations between objects – or the relations that render things economically valuable – in abstract quantitative terms, without itself entering into these relations. Thus, the function of money is all the more important, the livelier and more extensive are the changes in economic values. Wherever the values of goods are definitely and permanently fixed, exchange in kind is easily carried on. Money corresponds to the condition of change in mutual value relations because it offers an exact and flexible equivalent for every change of value. The variability of these relations illustrates most clearly that the economic value of an object consists in the exchange relationship to all other objects; every partial shift requires other balancing movements and makes us aware of the relativity within the whole. Money is nothing but the symbol of this relativity, and thus we can understand the fact mentioned earlier, that the need for money is connected with the fluctuation of prices, whereas barter presupposes fixed prices.

The distinctive significance of money emerges theoretically as well as practically only with a fully developed monetary economy. The symbol that represents money in the first stage of its gradual development keeps it at the same time among those objects whose mere relation to each other it is meant to symbolize. Medieval theory regarded value as something objective. It required the seller to ask the 'just price' for his commodity and occasionally attempted to fix this price by regulation. Value was considered to inhere in the object as a quality of its isolated existence, with which it entered the act of exchange, regardless of the relations between buyer and seller. This concept of value – which corresponds with the substantial–absolutistic world view of the age – is particularly appropriate to a barter economy. A piece of land in exchange for services rendered, a goat for a pair of shoes, a jewel for twenty masses for the dead; these were things with which certain value sentiments were so closely connected that their values might well appear as objectively corresponding to each other. The more direct the exchange and the simpler the circumstances – so that the position of the object is not determined by a multitude of comparable relations – the more does the value appear as a quality of the object. The straightforward assurance with which such an exchange was carried out was reflected in the idea that it was brought about by an objective quality of the things themselves. Only the incorporation of the single object in diversified production and in many-sided exchange movements suggests that its economic significance lies in its relation to other objects and is reciprocal; and this coincides with the growth of a money economy. That the meaning of the economic object is constituted by this relativity, and that the significance of money is to become the clear expression of this relativity, are facts that come to be realized by their reciprocal influence. In the Middle Ages, it was assumed that there was a direct relation between object and money-price i.e. a relation based upon the independent value of each, which could and should find a 'just' expression. The error of this substantialist interpretation is the same as that which asserts a direct connection between an individual and the content of any right; as though the nature of the person as such, regardless of any external conditions, would have a 'just' claim to this competency. The individualistic conception of the rights of man provides an example. In reality, right is only a relation between men and is consummated only in relation to the interests, objects and absolute powers which we call a content of law, 'a right' in the narrower sense. Such rights do not have any predictable relation to an individual which might be interpreted as 'just' or 'unjust'. Only when such a relationship develops and has established itself in norms is it possible for the norms – referring to a single person in a specific matter – to characterize that person's power of disposal over something as just. Thus there may be, indeed, a just price for a commodity, but only as the expression of a definite, well-adjusted exchange relationship between this commodity and all others, and not as a consequence of the nature of the commodity itself or the amount of money itself, which stand in no relation to each other and have no reference to the just or the unjust.

The significance of money in representing the economic relativity of objects – which is the source of its practical functions – is not a ready-made reality; like all historical phenomena, it discloses its pure concept – its function and place in the realm of ideas – only gradually. This has its counterpart in the fact that all commodities could be regarded as money in a certain sense. Every object A that is exchanged for B, and in turn for C, plays the role of money independently of its tangible qualities. It expresses the fact that B, A and C are exchangeable with each other and it expresses the rate at which they can be exchanged. This happens with innumerable objects; in fact, the further back we trace cultural development, the larger the number of very different objects we discover that perform the function of money in a more or less rudimentary fashion. So long as objects are measured against each other or exchanged with each other *in natura*, their subjective and their economic, objective qualities, their absolute and their relative significance are as yet unseparated; they cease to be money or to be capable of being money to the extent that money ceases to be an object of use. Money becomes more and more a symbol of economic value, because economic value is nothing but the relativity of exchangeable objects. This relativity, in turn, increasingly dominates the other qualities of the objects that evolve as money, until finally these objects are nothing more than embodied relativity.

If money has its origin in barter, it begins to develop only when a single object is exchanged not against another single object but against several others. If a cow is exchanged for a slave, a garment for a talisman, a boat for a weapon, the process of valuation is not yet separated into its elements; it is not carried out by the reduction of the objects to a common denominator as a basis for calculating the value of each unit of several things. If, however, a herd of cattle is taken in exchange for a house, or ten cut beams against a piece of jewelry, or three drinks for a service of labour, then the unit of these multiples – one cow, one beam or one drink – is the measure, the multiple of which is identical with the other object of exchange. In the case of objects that are indivisible, the psychological sense of value does not easily abandon the unity of the single object. But as soon as bargaining begins – is the value of the piece of jewelry twelve or perhaps only eight beams? – then the value of the jewelry is measured, despite its indivisibility, by the value unit of a beam, and it appears possible to compose it out of the eightfold, the twelvefold and finally the tenfold of our beam. The value of both objects of exchange thus becomes more easily commensurable if one object is divisible; and the value of both objects need not be expressed in terms of one and the same unit. The most developed form of divisibility is attained with exchange against money. Money is that divisible object of exchange, the unit of which is commensurable with the value of every indivisible object; thus it facilitates, or even presupposes, the detachment of the abstract value from its particular concrete content. The relativity of economic objects, which can be recognized only with difficulty in the exchange of indivisible objects – because each of the parties possesses, so to speak, an autonomous value – is brought into relief through the reduction to a common denominator of value, of which money is the most distinctive form.

I have shown earlier that relativity creates the value of objects in an objective sense, because only through relativity are things placed at a distance from the subject. Money is the quintessence and zenith of these two qualities and thus illustrates again their interrelationship. Money can never be enjoyed directly – the exceptions to be treated later negate its specific character! – and it is therefore excluded from any subjective relation. Money objectifies the external activities of the subject which are represented in general by economic transactions, and money has therefore developed as its content the most objective practices, the most logical, purely mathematical norms, the absolute freedom from everything personal. Because money is simply the means to acquire objects, it stands by its very nature at an insurmountable distance from the Ego which craves and enjoys; and in so far as it is the indispensable means between the Ego and the objects, it places the objects, too, at a distance. To be sure, money abolishes this distance again; but by doing so, by transferring the objects to subjective use, it removes them from the objective economic cosmos. The division that has appeared in the original unity of the subjective and the objective is, as it were, embodied in money; but on the other hand, it is the function of money – in accordance with the above-mentioned correlation of distance and proximity – to move the otherwise unattainable closer to us. Exchangeability is the prerequisite of economic values, through which the latter attain their objective mutual relation. It unites in one act the distance and the proximity of what is to be exchanged. It has acquired in money not only its technically perfect means, but also a separate, concrete existence which embraces all its various aspects.

Money as a reification of the general form of existence according to which things derive their significance from their relationship to each other

The philosophical significance of money is that it represents within the practical world the most certain image and the clearest embodiment of the formula of all being, according to which things receive their meaning through each other, and have their being determined by their mutual relations. It is a basic fact of mental life that we symbolize the relations among various elements of our existence by particular objects; these are themselves substantial entities, but their significance for us is only as the visible representatives of a relationship that is more or less closely associated with them. Thus, a wedding ring, but also every letter, every pledge, every official uniform, is a symbol or representative of a moral or intellectual, a legal or political, relationship between men. Every sacramental object embodies in a substantial form the relation between man and his God. The telegraph wires that connect different countries, no less than the military weapons that express their dissension, are such substances; they have almost no significance for the single individual, but only with reference to the relations between men and between human groups that are crystallized in them. Of course, the representation of these relations and connections can itself be regarded as an abstraction, inasmuch as only those elements in it are real whose mutually determined conditions we incorporate in specific concepts. Only metaphysical inquiry, which pursues cognition beyond the limits of empiricism, can possibly eliminate this dualism, by dissolving all substantial elements into interaction and processes, the bearer of which becomes subject to the same fate. But practical consciousness has discovered a form by which the processes of relationship and interaction, in which reality is enacted, can be united with the substantial existence, the necessary form of abstract relations in practice.

The projection of mere relations into particular objects is one of the great accomplishments of the mind; when the mind is embodied in objects, these become a vehicle for the mind and endow it with a livelier and more comprehensive activity. The ability to construct such symbolic objects attains its greatest triumph in money. For money represents pure interaction in its purest form; it makes comprehensible the most abstract concept; it is an individual thing whose essential significance is to reach beyond individualities. Thus, money is the adequate expression of the relationship of man to the world, which can only be grasped in single and concrete instances, yet only really conceived when the singular becomes the embodiment of the living mental process which interweaves all singularities and, in this fashion, creates reality. This significance of money would remain even if the value relativity of economic objects were not an initial fact but a final stage of development. The concept with which we define a phenomenon is often not derived from the phenomenon itself but from a more developed and purer form. We cannot infer the nature of language from the first stammerings of the child; and in defining animal life, it will not disconcert us to find that it is only imperfectly represented at the stage of transition from plant life. Similarly, it is only in the highest phenomena of our mental life that we can sometimes discover the meaning of the lower phenomena; although we may perhaps be unable to trace it in these at all. The pure concept of a series of phenomena is often an ideal that is never completely realized, the approach towards which, however, makes possible a valid interpretation of the concept.

The significance of money, that it expresses the relativity of objects of demand through which they become economic values, is not negated by the fact that money also has other qualities that diminish and obscure this significance. In so far as these qualities are effective, it is not money proper. Economic value consists in the exchange relationship of objects according to our subjective reaction to them, but the economic relativity of objects develops only gradually from their other meanings and it can never dominate these meanings entirely in the total representation or the total value of an object. The value that objects acquire by their exchangeability, i.e. the metamorphosis through which their value becomes an economic value, emerges more clearly and strongly with the extensive and intensive growth of the economy – a fact that Marx formulates as the elimination of use-value in favour of exchange value in a society based upon commodity production – but this development seems unable to reach its consummation. Only money, in terms of its pure concept, has attained this final stage; it is nothing but the pure form of exchangeability. It embodies that element or function of things, by virtue of which they are economic. It does not comprehend their totality, but it does comprehend the totality of money. In the following chapter I shall examine how far money in its historical manifestations does represent this idea of money, and whether money in operation does not tend, in some degree, towards another point of reference.

CHAPTER 2

The Value of Money as a Substance

I

The intrinsic value of money and the measurement of value

Through all the discussions of the nature of money there runs the question as to whether money, in order to carry out its services of measurement, exchange and representation of values, is or ought to be a value itself; or whether it is enough if money is simply a token and symbol without intrinsic value, like an accounting sum which stands for a value without being one. The whole technical and historical discussion of this question, which involves the most profound issues in the theory of money and value, would be superfluous if it could be decided by a frequently quoted logical argument. A measuring instrument, it is said, has to have the same quality as the object to be measured: a measure of length has to be long, a measure of weight has to be heavy, a measure of space has to have dimensions; consequently, a measure of value has to be valuable. No matter how unrelated two things may be in all other respects, when I measure them against each other they must both have the quality that I am comparing. Any quantitative and numerical equality or inequality that I assert would be meaningless if it did not refer to relative quantities of one and the same quality. Indeed, this identity of qualities must not be of too general a nature; for instance, it is impossible to compare the beauty of a piece of architecture with the beauty of a person, even though both have the quality of beauty. Only the particular architectural or the particular human qualities of beauty make a comparison possible. But even if a common quality is lacking, one might still consider the reaction of the contemplating subject as a basis for comparability. If the beauty of a building and the beauty of a person are comparable in the amount of enjoyment that the contemplation of either one of them affords us, then an identity of qualities might be asserted in spite of the apparent variation. (The equal effect upon the same subject reflects the equality of the objects with reference to the relation in question.) Two completely different phenomena that give the same pleasure to the same subject have, over and above all their differences, an equal force or an equal relation to the subject; just as when a gust of wind and a human hand break a branch of a tree demonstrate, in spite of the incomparability of their qualities, an equal amount of energy. Thus the substance of money, and everything that is measured by it, may be completely different, but they would have to coincide in the one point that they both have value; and even if value is nothing but a subjective response to the impressions received from things, at least the quality by which they affect the sense of value in men has to be the same in both – even though it cannot be isolated. Thus, it is claimed that money has to have the quality of value because it is compared with values and enters into a quantitative equation with values.

I will contrast this line of argument with another which produces different results. It is true that, in the example given, we can compare the force of the wind that breaks the branch of a tree with that of the human hand doing the same thing, only so far as this force exists as a quantity in both. But we can measure the force of the wind also by the thickness of the branch that it has broken. I admit that the broken branch does not yet express the amount of energy of the wind in the same sense as the energy of the hand may express it; but the comparative force of two gusts of wind, and thus the relative force of each, can be measured by the fact that one has broken a branch which the other was unable to harm. The following example seems to me to be conclusive. The most heterogeneous objects we know, the two poles of the world view which neither metaphysics nor science has succeeded in reducing to each other, are the motions of matter and the states of consciousness. The pure extension of the one and the pure internality of the other have not so far allowed any point to be discovered that could plausibly be regarded as their meeting ground. Nevertheless, the physiological psychologist can measure the relative changes in the strength of conscious sensations by the changes in the external motions that affect our sense organs. Since there is a constant quantitative relation between the two factors, the size of one determines the relative size of the other, without any qualitative relationship or identity having to exist between them. The logical principle that appeared to make the ability of money to measure value dependent upon its own value is thus breached. It is indeed correct that the quantities of different objects can be compared only if they are of the same quality; wherever measurement is done by direct comparison of two quantities it presupposes identical qualities. But wherever a change, a difference or the relation between two quantities is to be measured, it is sufficient for their determination that the proportions of the measuring objects are reflected by the proportions of those measured; and there need be no qualitative identity of the

objects. Two objects with different qualities cannot be equalized, but two proportions between qualitatively different things may be. The two objects *m* and *n*
may have some relationship that has nothing to do with qualitative identity, so
that neither one can serve directly as a measure for the other. The relation may
be one of cause and effect, of symbolism, of common relationship to a third
factor or anything else. Let us assume as given that an object *a* is known to be
a quarter of *m*, and an object *b* is known to be some quantitative part of *n*. If a
relation exists between *a* and *b*, corresponding to the relation *m* and *n*, it follows
that *b* equals a quarter of *n*. In spite of a qualitative difference and the impossibility of any direct comparison between *a* and *b*, it is nevertheless possible to
determine the quantity of one by the quantity of the other. For instance, there
is no relation of identity between a certain quantity of food and the acute need
for food that might be satisfied by it; but if so much food is available that half of
the need is filled, I can accordingly determine that the available quantity of food
equals half of the need. Under these circumstances it is sufficient that an overall
relationship exists in order to measure the quantities of its parts. If one can now
interpret the measurement of objects by money in this fashion, then the idea of
their direct comparability and consequently the logical requirement that money
itself should possess value becomes untenable.

In order to proceed from this logical possibility to reality, we need only
assume a very general relationship between the quantity of goods and the
quantity of money, which is illustrated by the connection – often obscured or
disrupted – between an increasing supply of money and rising prices, an increasing supply of goods and falling prices. Thus we can form, with qualifications as
to their exact scope, the concepts of a total supply of commodities, a total supply
of money and a relationship of mutual dependence between them.

Every single commodity is now a definite part of the available sum of commodities; if we call the latter *a*, the commodity is *1/m a*. Its price is the corresponding part of the total quantity of money; if we call the latter *b*, then the
price equals *1/m b*. If we knew the quantity of *a* and *b*, and the proportion of all
saleable goods which a specific object represents, then we should also know its
price in terms of money, and vice-versa. A definite amount of money can thus
determine or measure the value of an object, regardless of whether money and
the valuable object possess any identical quality, and so regardless of whether
money itself is valuable.

Problems of measurement

It is always necessary to keep in mind the complete relativity of measurement.
Absolute quantities that are equivalent measure each other in a quite different
sense from the partial quantities which are in question here. If it is assumed –

133

with certain qualifications – that the total amount of money equals the value of the total amount of commodities for sale, then this equation need not be taken as a measure of one quantity by the other. They are set in a relation of equivalence only through the relationship that both have to the valuing person and his practical purposes. The following quite common cases show how strong is the tendency to treat money and commodities generally as simply corresponding to each other. If a primitive tribe, who use a commodity as a unit of exchange, trade with a more developed neighbour who uses money, then the two units are frequently treated as equal in value. Thus the ancient Irish, when they entered into relations with the Romans, made their own value-unit, the cow, equivalent to an ounce of silver. The wild mountain tribes in Annam, who trade only in kind, use the buffalo as a basic value-unit; in their transactions with the more cultivated inhabitants of the plains the value-unit of the latter – a bar of silver of a particular size – is regarded as equivalent to one buffalo. The same basic approach can be found in a wild tribe of Laos, who live by trade. Their unit of value is the iron hoe, but they also produce gold which they sell to neighbouring tribes and which is the only object they weigh. For the purpose of weighing it they have no other measure than corn, and so they sell one corn measure of gold for one hoe. One against one is the naive expression of an equivalence between these dubious totalities; since the single commodity in barter exemplifies the value of all commodities just as the single monetary unit represents the idea of the total amount of money, it may be assumed that the relation between single units is, at least symbolically, interpreted as a relation between the totalities.

If the equivalence of these total amounts exists as an effective, though unconscious *a priori*, there emerges an objective proportion between the partial quantities apart from that of their subjective fortuitousness. For now there really exists something that is exactly the same on both sides; namely, the division between each of the two partial quantities and the total quantity to which it belongs. If we assume complete equilibrium of prices, then each commodity would be related to its price, within the area of exchange, in the same way as all available commodities were related to the total amount of spendable money. It is totally irrelevant whether money has a conceptual, qualitative relationship to commodities. If a commodity costs 20 m, this represents $1/n$ of the total money supply, i.e. its value is $1/n$ of the total supply of commodities. By this means, 20 m are able to measure the value of the commodities even though they are generically completely different from them. We have to keep in mind, however, that the assumption of a simple relationship between all commodities and all money is only a preliminary, crude and schematic step. If a single commodity had to be directly equated with a money value, it would be reasonable to insist that the commodity and its measure must have some quality in common. But for the purposes of exchange and valuation it is only necessary to determine the relation of different (or all) commodities to each other (that is, result of the division of the single commodity by all the others), and to equate this with the corresponding fraction of the available supply of money. This requires only that there shall be a numerically determinable quantity. If the commodity n relates to the sum A of all saleable goods, as the money unit a relates to the sum B of all available money units, then the economic value of n is expressed by a/B. The matter is not usually perceived in this way because A as well as B are taken for granted. Their changes are not easily observed and we are not conscious of their function as denominators; we are exclusively interested in the numerators n and a for each individual case. Thus, the idea could emerge that n and a correspond to each other in some absolute and direct way; and if this were so they would indeed have to have some identical quality. If that general element upon which the relationship is based were forgotten, if it operated only practically but not consciously, then it would reveal a profound characteristic of human nature. The limited receptiveness of human consciousness and the economical and expedient manner of its use means that only a small number of the innumerable qualities and aspects of an object that interests us are taken into consideration. It is enough for the different viewpoints that determine the selection and ordering of the factors that attract our attention that the latter can be arranged as a systematic series. This series begins with a succession of phenomena in which only what is common to all is taken into account, only the basis that all the phenomena share, is considered. At the other end of the scale, only the distinctive features of each phenomenon, the absolute individuality, enter our consciousness, while the general and fundamental elements remain unconscious. Between these two extremes, there exists at various levels those points or aspects of the total phenomenon upon whihc the greatest attention is focused. In general, it may be said that theoretical interests direct awareness more to generalities, practical interests more to the specific features of things. For the thinker who is interested in metaphysics, the individual differences between things are often regarded as inessential, and he is concerned with such general conceptions as 'being' and 'becoming' which are common to all things. Practical life, on the other hand, requires us to be attentive to the differences, peculiarities and nuances of people and circumstances with which we are concerned; while the general human qualities and the basis that is common to all the problematic conditions seem obvious and not in need of special attention. Indeed, even such attention can only clarify them with great difficulty. For instance, the relations between members of a family develop on the basis of experience of those personal qualities by which each member is distinguished from any other; the general character of these family relations is usually not a subject for particular observation by the members of that family. Only outsiders seem to be able to describe it. However, this does not mean that the general unconscious basis is not psychologically effective. The individual qualities of the members of each family will, in fact, bring about very different conditions according to the general character and the atmosphere that prevail in the family as a whole. This atmosphere provides the basis, often unremarked, upon which the qualities of the individuals develop in their own specific way. The same holds for larger groups. Even though all relationships among men depend upon the particular contribution of each individual, they are actually established in a specific form only because there are universal human phenomena and conditions which form the denominator to which individual differences are added as the numerators to produce the totality of the relationship. Exactly the same psychological relationship may prevail with respect to money prices. The equation between the value of a commodity and the value of a definite amount of money does not signify an equation between simple factors but a proportion, that is an equation between two fractions, the denominator of which, within a given economic area, is on one side the sum total of all commodities and on the other the total amount of money. These two quantities, of course, have to be more strictly determined. The equation is established by the fact that, for practical reasons, these two sums are posed *a priori* as equivalents; or, to state the matter more precisely, the practical circumstances in which we handle both categories are reflected in our theoretical consciousness as an equation. However, since this is the general basis of all equations between specific commodities and specific prices, it does not enter our consciousness, but provides the unconsciously operating factor without which the individual instances, which alone are interesting and thus enter into consciousness, could not possibly form a relationship. The tremendous importance of that absolute and fundamental equation would make the fact of its remaining unconscious just as probable as in the analogous cases that I have described.

If we were to assume that money has no substantial value, then the single money price would have no relation to the commodity whose value it was supposed to express, if our observation were restricted to these two factors. One would not know why one object is higher or lower in price, by a definite amount, than another. But if we establish as an absolute presupposition that the sum total of everything saleable is equivalent to the total amount of money – the meaning of 'total amount' to be investigated later – then the price of every single commodity becomes simply the proportion between its value and the total value of commodities, a proportion that is repeated in respect of price and total amount of money. I have to emphasize again that this is not a case of circular reasoning, in the sense that the ability of a definite amount of money to measure the value of a specific commodity is based upon an equation between all money and all commodities which already assumes the measurability of one by the other. The question as to whether every measurement requires the existence of some identical qualities in the object and in that which measures it would then not be relevant to the specific case, but would be absorbed unresolved into the assumptions. A measurement of relative quantities is, however, possible if there is some relation between the absolute quantities, which need not be that of measurability or identity. There is certainly no identity or possibility of measurement between the size of an iron pipe and a given water pressure; but if both are integrated parts of a mechanical system with a specific power output, then it is possible, under known conditions of change in the water pressure, to calculate from changes in the output of power what is the diameter of the pipes in the system. In the same way, commodities and money may not be measurable by each other in general. It is sufficient that both play a part in human life, within the system of men's practical ends, for the quantitative modification of one to become an index of the other. It is not without relevance to this reduction of the significance of every money quantity to a fraction – even if it remains undecided what is the absolute quantity of which it is a part – that the Romans marked their coins (with some well-founded exceptions) according to their relative and not their absolute weight. Thus *as* signifies only a whole consisting of twelve parts; it may refer to an inheritance just as well as to quantities and weights, to the pound as well as to any part of a pound. The fact that only the relativity of the measure enters consciousness and is effective is not affected by the hypothesis that suggests that in ancient times the *as* signified a bar of copper of a specific absolute weight.

The quantity of effective money

We now have to deal more specifically with the qualifications to the concept of the total quantity of money. It is not because of the immeasurable quantitative difference between all available commodities and all available money that it is impossible to assert that there is as much money to spend as there are commodities for sale. There exists no direct relation of less and more between the two, because there is no common measure for them as there would be for objects that have identical qualities. No quantity of commodities is related to a definite quantity of money, since all the purposes of money could, in principle, be attained by a quantity of money reduced as much as desired. The extent to which this can be achieved in practice without bringing transactions to a stop is illustrated by the following recorded fact. Some centuries ago, silver coins existed in Russia of such minute size that it was impossible to take them by hand from the table; they were tipped out of the purse, the amount payable was separated out and both parties proceeded to pick up their share with their tongues and spit it back into their purses. One might say that, whatever the absolute amount of money available, it always remains a lot of 'money' so long as it performs the services of money. All that varies is the quantity of these tokens or pieces in a different respect, namely as material of some kind; their quantity as money need not be affected. Thus, a direct comparison between all commodities and all money does not allow any conclusion. The lack of relationship between the total amounts of money and of commodities – as denominators of the fractions that express value – results from the fact that the total supply of money is turned over much more quickly than is the total amount of commodities. Nobody will leave large sums of money unused if it can be avoided, and usually it can be avoided. But no merchant can avoid keeping a considerable part of his stock for some time before it can be sold. The difference in the velocity of turnover becomes greater still if one includes those objects that are not offered for sale, but are occasionally saleable if there is a tempting offer. If the amount of money required for the sale of the total supply of goods were calculated on the basis of the prices actually paid for these goods, the estimate would vastly exceed the actual supply of money. From this point of view, it can be stated that there is much less money than commodities and that the proportion between the commodity and its price is not at all equal to the proportion between all commodities and all money, but is considerably smaller than this. However, there are two ways in which we can save our basic proposition. First, we might regard as the total quantity of commodities, that quantity that is actually in the process of being sold. To use an Aristotelian concept: the unsold commodity is merely a possible commodity, which becomes a real commodity only at the moment of sale. Just as money is real money only at the moment when it buys something, i.e. when it exercises the function of money, so the commodity becomes a commodity only when it is sold; until that time, it is only a possible object for sale, an ideal anticipation. From this standpoint, it is an obvious and analytical statement that there is as much money as there are objects to be sold – including as money, of course, all those money substitutes provided by the banking and credit system. To be sure, the commodities temporarily excluded from the selling process are not without economic effect, and economic life would be changed tremendously if the total supply of commodities were put completely into circulation as is the supply of money. Upon closer scrutiny, the commodity supply in reserve seems to me to have an influence on actual sales only in three ways: on the rate of circulation of money, on the production of the material of money and money equivalents, and on the relation between money expenditure and the reserves. But these factors have already exercised their influence on the actual turnover; the empirical relation between commodity and price has been formed under their influence and they do not exclude an interpretation of the total quantity of commodities as the actual sales of commodities at a given moment.

Secondly, this can also be regarded as a consequence of the fact that the same amount of money – since money is not consumed as commodities are – can effect an unlimited number of transactions; and that its insignificant quantity at any given moment, when compared with the quantity of commodities, is compensated for by the velocity of its circulation. The higher levels of finance illustrate clearly that the substance of money plays only a very minor role in value transactions. In 1890 the Bank of France had a turnover on current accounts which was 135 times the amount of the money actually deposited (54 billion as against 400 million francs), while at the German Reichsbank the ratio was 190. Within the total sum of money in use, which determines the money price of commodities, the actual amount of money is negligible in relation to the total available as a result of its circulation. Thus it is possible to assert, with reference to a specific period but not to a single moment, that the total quantity of money in circulation corresponds with the total amount of objects saleable during this period.

The individual also makes his expenditures and accepts the prices for larger purchases not in relation to his momentary disposal of money, but in relation to his total income over a prolonged period. In our equation, the money fraction may attain equality with the commodity fraction through the fact that its denominator is not the quantity of money available as a substance, but is a multiple of this amount determined by the circulation of money during a given period. From this point of view, the antinomy between the stock of available commodities and those commodities that are the value counterparts of money can be solved; and the assertion that no basic disproportion can arise between the total amount of commodities and of money in an autonomous economic area may be upheld. This is true in spite of disagreements about the proper relation between a particular commodity and its price, in spite of the fluctuations and discrepancies that may develop if some definite size of the fractions concerned has become psychologically established while a different one has become more appropriate by reason of objective changes, and in spite of temporary shortages in the means of exchange resulting from a rapid increase in the number of transactions. Imports and exports of metal which are the result of a shortage or excess of money in relation to commodity values in a given country are nothing but adjustments within a larger economic area in which particular countries are the provinces; they indicate that a proper relation between two provinces has been restored after changes have occurred in one of them. Under these circumstances, an answer to the question whether a given price is appropriate or not can be derived directly from the two previous questions: first, what is the amount of money and the sum total of objects for sale at the present time; and, second, what proportion does the object under consideration form of the total quantity of commodities available? The second question is the decisive one. The equation between the commodity fraction and the money fraction can be objectively and quantitatively true or false; whereas the equation between objects in general and money in general is only a matter of expediency, not one of truth in the sense that it can be logically established. The relationship between the totalities has, as it were, the significance of an axiom, which is not true in the same sense as are the statements based upon it;

only the latter can be proven, whereas the axiom cannot refer to anything from which it could be logically derived. A very important methodological rule is established here, which I will illustrate from a completely different category of values. The basic assertion of pessimism is that there is in life a considerable excess of suffering over happiness, that living beings, considered as a whole or on the average, experience much more pain than pleasure. It is quite impossible to make such an assertion, which presupposes that pleasure and pain can be directly balanced and set off against each other as two qualitatively equal magnitudes with opposite signs. In reality this is impossible because there is no common measure. When we suffer we cannot experience what amount of pleasure would be necessary to compensate for the suffering. How then can we explain that such comparisons are always being made; that in everyday affairs, in a coherent destiny, in the sum of an individual life, we judge that the quantity of enjoyment has fallen below or has exceeded the amount of pain? It is possible only because the experience of life has taught us, more or less strictly, how fortune and misfortune are actually distributed, how much suffering has to be accepted in order to attain a certain amount of pleasure, and how much of each is man's usual portion. Only when we have formed some notion of this kind, no matter how unconscious and vague, is it possible to say that in a particular case a pleasure has been paid for too dearly – i.e. with too large an amount of suffering – or that in one individual life the pain exceeded the happiness. The average itself cannot be 'disproportionate' because it is the standard by which we determine whether the relation between feelings in an individual case is fair or not. In the same way, it is impossible to say that people on the average are tall or small, since the average provides the standard by which the individual is measured; and it is misleading to say that 'time' passes quickly or slowly, since the passage of time – i.e. the average experienced pace of events – is the measuring rod by which the quickness or slowness of the passage of single events is measured, while the average itself is neither quick nor slow. Thus, the pessimistic assertion that the average human life contains more suffering than enjoyment is methodologically just as impossible as the optimistic assertion of the contrary. The sensation of the total quantities of pleasure and pain (or, differently expressed, the average of them for an individual or for a period of time) is the original phenomenon, whose components cannot be compared with each other because this would require a measure independent of both and yet comprehending both equally.

This should suffice to characterize the type of knowledge with which we are dealing here. In the areas mentioned, and also in many others, the primary elements are not comparable because they are of different qualities and cannot be measured by each other or by a third factor. But the fact that a certain amount of one element, and a certain amount of the other element, is present provides a measure to be applied to individual cases, events and problems, where both elements are involved. In so far as, in individual cases, the elements repeat the proportions that occur in the total quantities, then the elements have a 'correct', i.e. normal, average or typical relation, and deviations appear as a 'preponderance' or 'disproportion' of one element. In themselves, the elements in individual cases have no more a right or wrong, an equal or unequal, relation than have the totalities; they acquire such a relation only through the total quantities being established as an absolute, in terms of which the singular, the relative, is calculated. The absolute is not subject to the rules of comparison that it makes possible for the relative.

The relation between the object of sale and its money price could belong to this type. Perhaps they have nothing in common as regards content and perhaps they are qualitatively so unequal that they are quantitatively incomparable. But since everything saleable and the total amount of money together form an economic cosmos, the price of one commodity could be the 'appropriate price' if it constitutes the same part of the total effective amount of money as does the commodity of the total amount of goods. The mutual proportionality need not depend upon the equal 'value' of the object and the specific amount of money. The money price does not have to represent a value at all, or at least not a value in the same sense; it has only to constitute the same fraction of all money as the commodity constitutes of all commodity values. Individual economic transactions illustrate how dependent the money price of a commodity is upon its relation to a total quantity of commodities. We say that we are willing to sacrifice this money – which is rather inconvenient for us – only if we obtain a reasonable equivalent. Every reduction of that sacrifice is counted as a positive profit. But it is a profit only so far as the money can be spent on another occasion. If I had nothing else to do with the money, I would spend all the money I own un-hesitatingly on the one object for which it is demanded. The appropriateness of the price means only that I, as an average person, have enough money left to buy the other things that I want. The expenditure on every single object has to be adjusted to the fact that I want to buy other objects besides. If everybody regulates his private expenditures in such a way that the payment for every type of commodity is proportionate to his total income, this means that his expenditure for the single object is related to his total expenses just as the importance of the single object is related to the totality of desired and available objects. This scheme of the private economy of an individual is obviously not only an analogy of the general economy; its general application determines the average prices. The continuous subjective balancing precipitates the objective relation between commodity and price; this relationship depends not only upon the proportion between the total effective supply of goods and the total amount of money, but also – subject to all kinds of modifications – on the proportion between the total wants of the individual and his total available money income.

The Value of Money as a Substance

Does money possess an intrinsic value?

The preceding argument has not yet touched upon the question as to whether in reality money has value or not. It was only meant to show that the function of money in measuring values does not impose upon it the character of being itself a valuable object. However, the mere possibility that it does have value opens the road to understanding not only the historical development of money but, above all, its essential nature. In the primitive stages of the economy, use-values appear as money: cattle, salt, slaves, tobacco, hides, etc. Whatever the way in which money has evolved, in the beginning it must have been a value experienced as such. It is possible to exchange the most valuable things against a printed form only when the chain of purposes is very extensive and reliable and provides us with a guarantee that what is immediately valueless will help us to acquire other values. It is in this manner that one can carry out a series of logical deductions, through impossible or contradictory stages, to a valid and binding conclusion, but only when the process of thought is assured of its direction and its correctness. Primitive and still vacillating thinking would immediately lose its direction at one of the intermediate stages; and it has, therefore, to exercise its functions in statements each of which has to be concrete and obviously correct – at the cost of being less versatile and less comprehensive in its goals. Similarly, the extension of the succession of values by valueless things enormously increases their range and usefulness, yet is possible only with a growing intellectuality of individuals and with the continued organization of the group. Nobody will be stupid enough to exchange a value against something that is valueless, unless he is sure of being able to convert the latter into values again. Exchange was at first necessarily exchange in kind, an exchange between direct values. One assumes that objects that were frequently exchanged and circulated because of their general desirability, and the value of which in relation to other objects was therefore frequently measured, were psychologically most suited to become general standards of value. Apparently in direct contrast with the earlier result, according to which money as such does not have to be of value, we discover here that the most needed and the most valuable object is apt to become money. I do not mean needed in the physiological sense; for instance, the desire for adornment can play a dominant role among the experienced 'necessities'. Indeed, we are told that for primitive people the adornment of their bodies, and the objects used for it, are more valuable than all the things that we consider so much more urgent. The necessity of things is for us only an emphasis that our sentiments attribute to objects that are in themselves equivalent or 'neutral' and depends entirely upon our purposes. Thus, we cannot calculate theoretically what are the values that are immediately urgent and fit to play the function of money. The only indispensable assumption seems to me that the money character is originally attached to those objects that show a particular frequency of exchange against a variety of other things as a result of experienced necessity. Money could not have developed as a means of exchange or as a measure of value unless its material substance had been experienced as immediately valuable.

At the present time, by comparison, money is no longer valuable because its substance is regarded as a necessity, an indispensable value. No European today regards a coin as valuable because it can be changed into a piece of jewelry. The present-day value of money cannot be traced to its value as metal, precisele because precious metals are available in too great quantities to find a profitably use merely for adornment and for technical purposes. The completion of the process conceived by the theory concerning the value of money as a metal would result in such a multitude of objects made of precious metal that their value would be reduced to a minimum. The valuation of money because of the possibility of converting it into other objects is possible only to the extent that this does happen or happens only on a very small scale. Even though at the beginning of the development, i.e. when there is a limited supply of precious metals, the value of money may have been determined by its alternative use for adornment, this condition disappears as production is increased. This argument is further supported by the fact that, although primitive people regard a particular style of self-adornment as a vital necessity, the subsequent elaboration of scales of value actually places this interest in the category of the 'dispensable' or 'superfluous'. In modern culture, adornment does not at all play the social role that we discover with amazement in ethnological and even in medieval accounts. This fact must also contribute to reducing the significance of money based upon the substance of which it is made. It may be said that the value of money moves increasingly from its *terminus a quo* to its *terminus ad quem*, and that metal money stands on an equal basis with paper money as a result of the growing psychological indifference to its value as metal. It would be wrong to consider the valuelessness of paper money as irrelevant on the grounds that it is simply a draft upon metal. This is refuted by the fact that unsecured paper money is still valued as money. Even if one points to the political force which alone imposes the current rate of exchange of paper money, this means precisely that other reasons besides direct material use can give, and actually do give, money value to a particular substance. The increasing replacement of metal money by paper money and the various forms of credit unavoidably react upon the character of money – in roughly the same way as in personal relations when somebody allows himself always to be represented by others, so that finally he receives no greater esteem than is accorded to his representatives. The functional value of money exceeds its value as a substance the more extensive and diversified are the services it performs and the more rapidly it circulates. Modern commerce tends more and more to eliminate money as a substantial embodiment of value, and this trend is unavoidable because, even if the production of precious metals were increased to the utmost extent, it would still be inadequate to allow all transactions to be conducted in cash. Clearing house business on the one hand and international bills of exchange on the other are only the outstanding examples of this general tendency, the earlier features of which will be discussed in the final section of this chapter.

Generally speaking, the less developed the economic concepts, the more strongly does measurement involve a direct physical relation between the values compared. The interpretation outlined earlier, according to which the equality of value between a commodity and a sum of money consists of an equality between two fractions – in which the individual commodity and sum of money are the numerators and the total quantities of all commodities and all money are the denominators – clearly holds universally, because only this interpretation transforms a particular kind of object into money. However, since money evolves only slowly, this mode will also emerge from the more primitive mode of direct comparison of the objects in exchange. The lowest stage is perhaps illustrated by a case reported from the island of New Britain. The natives there use cowry shells strung together, which they call *dewarra*, as money. This money is used for purchases according to a linear measure (e.g. an arm-length, etc.); fish are usually paid for by *dewarra* equal to their own length. It is also reported from the cowry money region that a type of purchase prevails in which equal measures of two commodities are considered to be of equal value; thus, a measure of grain is worth an equal measure of cowry shells. The direct equivalence of commodity and price has here attained its most complete and simple expression. The comparison of values between which there is no quantitative congruence represents a more highly developed mental process. There are rudiments of such a naive equation of values by equal quantities in the phenomenon that Mungo Park reports of some West African tribes in the eighteenth century. Iron bars circulated there as money and served to designate the quantities of other commodities; thus a certain measure of tobacco or rum used to be called a 'bar of tobacco' or a 'bar of rum'. In this case, the disposition to regard value equality as equality of quantities, which was obviously a powerful element – resulting from sense impressions – in the primitive construction of values has been transposed into a linguistic expression. Several other phenomena, very diversified in appearance, can be attributed to the same general attitude. Old coins of bronze from the city of Olbia on the Dnieper, a colony of Miletus, have been preserved which have the shape of a fish, with inscriptions which probably mean tuna fish and fish basket. It is assumed that this fishing tribe originally used tuna fish as a standard of exchange, and that it was considered necessary when coins were introduced – perhaps because of exchange with less developed neighbouring tribes – to represent the value of one tuna fish on each coin, thus symbolizing, by using the same form, that it had the same value and exchangeability. In other areas, the same visible association was made less emphatically by impressing a picture of the object (a bull, fish or axe), which was the basic unit of exchange in the period of barter and whose value the coin represented, upon the coin. The same basic sentiment prevails in the Zend-Avesta, when it is prescribed that a physician should ask as his fee for healing a house-owner the value of an inferior ox, for healing a village magistrate an ox of average quality, for curing a town official the value of a high-quality ox, for the governor of a province the value of a carriage-and-four. On the other hand, the physician would be entitled to a female donkey for curing the wife of a village magistrate, a mare for the wife of a patrician, a female camel for the wife of a governor. The identity between the sex of the patient and the sex of the value-equivalent demonstrates the inclination to base the equivalence of values upon a direct external equality. It is just the same with the fact that money originally consisted of large and heavy objects – hides, cattle, copper, bronze – or of large quantities, as in the case of cowry shell money. The first bank note of which we have knowledge, preserved from China at the end of the fourteenth century, is eighteen inches long and nine inches wide. The peasant saying, 'Much gets more', is still influential, reflecting a natural sentiment which is proven wrong only by a more refined and reflective empiricism. The largest coins even of precious metals are found almost exclusively among less developed peoples where barter still prevails. The largest gold coins are the *lool* of the Annamese, worth 880 marks, the Japanese *obang* (220 marks), and the *benta* of the Ashanti; Annam also has a silver coin worth 60 marks. The same sentiment about the importance of quantity reserved the privilege of minting the largest coins to the highest authorities, while the smaller coins, though of the same metal, were coined by lower authorities. The Persian Emperor coined the large coins, the satraps the small gold coins of less than a quarter the value. This feature of considerable quantity is characteristic not only of the early forms of metal money, but in some cases also of the preceding kinds of money. The Slavs who inhabited the area between Saale and Elbe during the first century AD, and who were a very barbarous primitive race, used linen cloth as money; the exchange value of one cloth was 100 chickens or grain sufficient for ten men for one month. Even in more elaborate money systems it is noteworthy how the concept of money becomes less and less determined by metal values. The medieval guilder was a gold coin worth a ducat, while today it equals only 100 copper farthings; the original *groschen* was a thick (*grossus*) silver coin; the original mark amounted to a pound of silver, the pound sterling equalled seventy marks. Under primitive barter conditions, money transactions took place not for the small needs of everyday life, but only for the acquisition of larger and more valuable objects. The desire for symmetry which characterizes those cultures that are not yet fully developed also regulated money exchange, and a large token of value was demanded for large objects. Only at higher stages of cultural development is it realized that a considerable quantitative inequality still permits equality of power, of significance and of value. Where practical life is based upon the equating of objects, a direct equality is demanded at first as the size of primitive money in relation to the objects for which it is exchanged illustrates. In the same direction, the abstraction which later recognizes a small piece of metal as the equivalent of an object of any size approaches the goal that one side of the equation no longer functions as a value in itself but is only the abstract expression of the value of the other side. The measuring function of money, which is loosely connected with its material content, has therefore varied least through all the changes of the modern economy.

The development of the purely symbolic character of money

One of the greatest advances made by mankind – the discovery of a new world out of the material of the old – is to establish a proportion between two quantities, not by direct comparison, but in terms of the fact that each of them relates to a third quantity and that these two relations are either equal or unequal. Two performances of entirely different quality are given; they become comparable if they display the same strength of will and self-sacrifice in relation to the required effort. Two destinies reveal very different degrees of happiness; yet they acquire a measurable relation if each is interpreted according to the extent to which its bearer deserved his fate. Two movements with quite different velocities can be related and equated if we observe that the acceleration from the initial stage is identical in each case. A kind of homogeneity emerges – and not only for our feelings – between two elements which, differing in their substance, have an equal relation to a third or fourth element. The one thereby becomes a factor for the calculability of the other. Furthermore, no matter how incomparable two people may be in their ostensible qualities, the relation of each to another person establishes an equality between them; as soon as one of them shows the same degree of love or hatred, domination or subjection, towards a third person as the other does towards a fourth person, these relations have established the separateness of personal identity. As a final example: the perfection of works of art of different kinds could not be compared and their values could not be arranged on a scale, unless each of them first had a definite relation to the particular ideal of its own kind. From the problem, the material and the style of each work of art, there evolves a norm which the actual work approaches more or less closely; and it is this relation that makes it possible to compare even the most diverse works of art. The possible conformity of such relations to a norm produces an aesthetic cosmos, a precise order, an ideal homogeneity in relation to value, from the individual works which are initially quite heterogeneous. This is not only true for the world of art. Out of the material of our isolated valuations there develops a pattern of graded significance. Disharmony is experienced only as a result of the desire for a consistent order and an inner relation of values. We owe this essential feature of our world view to our ability to balance against each other not only two things, but also the relations of these two to two others, and so unite them by judging them equal or similar. Money, as a product of this fundamental power or form of our mind, is not only its most extreme example, but is, as it were, its pure embodiment. For money can express the value relation between things realized in exchange only by equating the relation between a specific sum and some general denominator, with the relation between a corresponding commodity and the totality of commodities available for exchange. Money is not, by its nature, a valuable object whose parts happen to have the same proportion to each other or to the whole that other values have to each other. The significance of money is only to express the value relations between other objects. It succeeds in this with the aid of man's developed intelligence, which is able to equate the relations between things even though the things themselves are not identical or similar. This ability only gradually evolves from the more primitive capacity to judge and express the identity or similarity of two objects directly, which is the source of the phenomena mentioned earlier that reflect the attempt to establish a direct relationship between money and its exchange values.

In modern economies this transition began with the mercantilist system. The efforts of governments to get as much coin as possible into the country were also guided, of course, by the principle 'much gets more', but the final purpose that these measures were intended to promote was the stimulation of industry and the market. The next stage beyond this was the discovery that the values that sustained this purpose did not result from money as a substance, but from the direct product of labour. It was much the same with the aims of state policy in earlier times, to acquire as much land as possible and to 'populate' it with as many people as possible. Until the eighteenth century it did not occur to any statesman that real national greatness could be promoted in any other way than by the acquisition of new territory. The justification of such aims under particular historical conditions, however, has not prevented the discovery that this kind of abundance is important only as a basis for dynamic development, which needs in fact only limited gains of such objects (land or money). It has become evident that the physical availability of a money equivalent becomes less and less essential for the increase of production and wealth, even though large amounts of money are sought not so much for themselves as for definite functional purposes. These purposes can be realized by free-floating processes not involving money in a substantial form, as the international exchange of goods illustrates. The significance of money as expressing the relative value of commodities is, according to our earlier discussion, quite independent of any intrinsic value. Just as it is irrelevant whether a scale to measure space consists of iron, wood or glass, since only the relation of its parts to each other or to another measure concerns us, so the scale that money provides for the determination of values has nothing to do with the nature of its substance. This ideal significance of money as a standard and an expression of the value of goods has remained completely unchanged, whereas its character as an intermediary, as a means to store and to transport values, has changed in some degree and is still in the process of changing. Money passes from the form of directness and substantiality in which it first carried out these functions to the ideal form; that is, it exercises its effects merely as an idea which is embodied in a representative symbol.

The development of money seems to be an element in a profound cultural trend. The different levels of culture may be distinguished by the extent to which, and at what points, they have a direct relationship with the objects that concern them, and on the other hand by the extent to which they use symbols. The way of life is radically different according to whether religious needs are satisfied by symbolic services and formulas, or by a direct approach of the individual to God; whether the respect of people for each other is manifested through established rules that indicate relative positions by specific ceremonies, or through informal courtesy, attachment and respect; whether purchases, agreements and contracts are made by simply making their content known, or are legalized and made binding by an external symbol of solemn undertaking; whether theoretical knowledge deals directly with sense reality or with its representation through general concepts and metaphysical or mythological symbols. But of course, these differences are not rigid. Rather, the history of mankind shows a continuous fluctuation between them. On the one hand, the symbolic representation of reality increases, but at the same time, as a counter-movement, symbols are constantly analysed and reduced to their original foundation. I will mention a singular example of this. Sexual objects have long been concealed through propriety and shame, while the words referring to them were used without hesitation. Only in recent centuries have the words themselves come under the same interdict. The symbol was thus brought into agreement with the emotional attitude to reality. But in very recent times this connection has begun to be dissolved again. Naturalism in art has drawn our attention to the lack of differentiation and freedom in perception if the same sensations are attached to the word, which is a mere symbol used for artistic purposes, as to the object itself. The representation of indecency is not at all the same thing as an indecent exhibition; and the perception of reality must be distinguished from the symbolical world in which art, including naturalism, exists. Perhaps in these circumstances there emerges a greater freedom among educated people in talking about delicate subjects. So long as an objective and chaste attitude can be presupposed, what was formerly forbidden is now allowed; the sense of shame is restricted more to the matter itself and does not affect the word as a mere symbol. Thus the relation between reality and symbol fluctuates in narrower as well as in more general areas. One is almost inclined to think – though such generalities cannot be demonstrated – that either every stage of culture (and finally every nation, every group and every individual) displays a specific proportion between the symbolic and the directly realistic treatment of its interests, or else that this proportion is generally stable and only the objects that are affected by it are subject to change. But perhaps it may be stated more specifically that a conspicuous prevalence of symbolism is as much part of primitive and naive as of very highly developed and complicated stages of cultural development. It may be that the progressive development frees us from symbols in the realm of cognition, but makes us more dependent on them in practical matters. By contrast with the nebulous symbolism of mythological world views, modern philosophy shows an incomparable directness in its interpretation of objects. On the other hand, the extensive and intensive multiplication of life-experiences has the result that we have to subsume, condense and represent them by symbolic forms to a greater extent than was necessary under simpler and more restricted conditions. Symbolism, which at lower cultural stages often means detours and waste of energy, is expedient and saves energy at the higher stages. One may think here of diplomatic techniques in the international as well as the party political sphere. Certainly, it is the relation between actual degrees of power that determines the outcome of the struggle between interests. But these are no longer measured against each other directly in a physical fight; they are represented conceptually. Behind the representative of each collective power stands in condensed potential form the real power of his party, and it is just in proportion to the latter that his voice is effective and his interest able to prevail. He himself is the symbol of this power. The intellectual exchange between the representatives of different power groups symbolizes the course that a real battle would have taken, in such fashion that the vanquished accepts the result as though he had really been defeated. I call to mind, for instance, the negotiations between employees and employers to avoid an impending strike. Each party yields just at the point which, according to its estimate of the respective strength of the parties, would be enforced by an actual strike. The *ultima rationis* is avoided by anticipating its results through imaginative devices. If such a representation and measurement of real strength could always be made accurately by the imagination, then every battle could be avoided. The utopian suggestion to decide the outcome of future wars by a game of chess between the generals is absurd, because the result of a game of chess does not give any indication of what would have been the outcome of a struggle between the armies, and so cannot symbolize and represent it in a valid way. However, a war game in which the whole armed forces, all fortuitous occurrences, all the intelligence of the leaders, found an appropriate symbolical expression, might possibly eliminate the physical struggle if such a game could be conceived.

The multitude of factors – of powers, substances and events – that operate in modern life demand a concentration in comprehensive symbols which can be manipulated with the assurance that they will lead to the same result as if all the details had been taken into account, so that the result will be applicable and valid for all particulars. This should be possible to the extent that the quantitative relations between things become, so to speak, independent. The growing differentiation of our representations has the result that the problem of 'how much' is, to a certain extent, psychologically separated from the question of 'what' – no matter how strange this may sound from the logical point of view. It occurred first and most successully in the construction of numbers, by extracting the 'so and so much' out of 'so many things' and making it into independent concepts. The more stable the concepts become with reference to their qualitative content, the more attention becomes focused upon their quantitative relations. Finally, the ideal of knowledge is seen as the dissolution of all the qualitative categories of reality into purely quantitative ones. This specification and emphasis of quantity facilitates the symbolic treatment of things. Since those that differ in content may coincide with respect to quantity, the relations, characteristics and movements of one of them may provide a valid representation of those of another. The simplest examples are the tokens that represent the numerical value of any object, or the thermometer that shows the temperature in degrees. It may appear self-evident today that symbols should be created by segregating the quantitative aspects of things; but this is in fact an achievement of the human mind which has remarkable consequences. The institution of money depends upon it inasmuch as money represents pure quantity in a numerical form, regardless of all the specific qualities of a valued object. An account from ancient Russia illustrates a very characteristic transition from the qualitative to the quantitative symbolic representation. Originally, marten furs served as a means of exchange. As trade developed, the size and quality of individual pelts lost all significance for their exchange value; each pelt simply equalled any other, and only the number of pelts mattered. Eventually only the tips of the pelts were used as money, and finally pieces of leather, probably stamped by the government, circulated as a means of exchange. This clearly illustrates how the reduction to a quantitative viewpoint supports the symbolization of values, which is the basis for the genuine realization of money.

However, it appears that at first ideal money does not meet the higher economic needs, although it is particularly suited for general acceptance, since it has no relation to particular values, but an equal relation to all of them. The extraordinary spread of cowry-money – which was used for a thousand years in a large part of Africa, at an earlier time in the region of the Indian Ocean, and in prehistoric times in Europe – would not have been possible if it had not been so genuinely ideal. At the lower economic stages, extreme contrasts of money values exist side by side; on the one hand, there is money which is entirely concrete in value, such as cattle or cotton cloth, which circulates when large amounts of money are involved, and on the other, there is completely ideal money such as crowy shells, the bark of the mulberry tree which Marco Polo discovered in China, or the pieces of porcelain with Chinese characters, which circulated in Siam. A certain functional development beyond the types of money with concrete value begins where natural products which are at the same time export articles become means of exchange: tobacco in Virginia, rice in Carolina, cod in Newfoundland, tea in China and furs in Massachusetts. In the case of export articles, value becomes psychologically separated from the immediacy which prevails in the domestic use of money. However, the most useful compromise between abstract kinds of money, such as those just mentioned, and money which has intrinsic value, is still jewelry money, that is, gold and silver; this is neither so whimsical and senseless as the former, nor so crude and singular as the latter. Gold and silver are obviously the forms through which money can most easily and certainly become a symbol. Money has to pass through this incarnation in order to achieve its greatest effects, and it seems unlikely that it will escape from it in the foreseeable future.

As secondary symbols – as they may be called by contrast with the naive symbolism of naive states of mind – increasingly replace the direct substance of things and values in practical life, the importance of intellect in the conduct of life is extraordinarily enhanced. As soon as life no longer moves between particular sense impressions but is determined by abstractions, averages and synoptic views, then, particularly in the sphere of human relations, a more rapid and exact process of abstraction will produce an advantage. If public order today can be secured by the mere appearance of an official, whereas in former times it required physical force; if a mere signature binds us unconditionally, both externally and internally; if a mere hint, or a facial expression, suffices among civilized people to indicate a lasting relationship which, under less developed conditions can be shown only by lengthy explanations or long-term behaviour; if sacrifices can be imposed upon us by written accounts which could be wrested from more ignorant peoples only by the real working of the factors conceived – then this significance of symbolic things and acts is obviously possible only as a result of greatly enhanced intellectuality, and of the existence of such independent mental power that the particular details of phenomena no longer require attention.

I have made these observations in order to clarify the role of money too in this trend of cultural development. The increasingly influential principle of economizing strength and materials leads to more and more extensive experiments with representatives and symbols that have virtually no relation to what they represent. The same course is followed when operations with values are carried out by a symbol that loses more and more any material relation to the specific phenomena of its area and becomes merely a symbol. This form of life not only presupposes a remarkable expansion of mental processes (consider, for instance, the complicated psychological pre-conditions required to cover bank notes by cash reserves) but also their intensification, a fundamental re-orientation of culture towards intellectuality. The idea that life is essentially based on intellect, and that intellect is accepted in practical life as the most valuable of our mental energies, goes hand in hand with the growth of a money economy, as our further discussion will show plainly. Intellect is also undoubtedly sovereign in the field of commerce, and especially in financial transactions. The growth of intellectual abilities and of abstract thought characterizes the age in which money becomes more and more a mere symbol, neutral as regards its intrinsic value.

II

Renunciation of the non-monetary uses of monetary material

It must be kept in mind that thus far we have only established a trend of development which began when the intrinsic value of money was co-ordinated with all other values. Thus, some other conceptions have to be disproved which apparently coincide with our theory that money has no intrinsic value, in so far as they emphasize the distinction between money and all other values and thus seek to prove that money cannot possibly be a value of the same kind. As is so often the case, this establishes in a rigid form and by anticipation what can be established only by endless approximation. In arguing against the dogma of the intrinsic value of money, we should not become victims of the dogma that money is valueless – an error into which the following notions might lead us. It appears that even the most useful object must renounce its usefulness in order to function as money. If, for example, in Abyssinia specifically cut pieces of rock salt circulate as coins, they are money precisely because they are not used as salt. On the coast of Somaliland pieces of blue cotton cloth, each two ells long, used to circulate as money. This was a considerable progress over the use of cloth money that was cut and composed arbitrarily, but nevertheless it indicates a tendency to abandon the use of cloth as cloth. The possible use of gold and silver for technical and aesthetic purposes cannot be realized as long as they circulate as money, and the same is true of all other kinds of money. The various uses that the material of money has for our purposes must all be renounced if it is to be used as money. As soon as such materials reveal their practical, aesthetic or other value they are withdrawn from circulation and are no longer money. All other values may be compared with each other and exchanged according to the measure of their utility in order to acquire a specific value, but money is kept completely apart from this series. For as soon as it is used in the same manner as the value that it buys, it ceases to be money. It may be part of the unique suitability of precious metals as money material that they can easily be restored from some other form to the form of money. Neverthe-less, at any given moment they have the choice of being either money or jewelry, that is of functioning either as money or as use value. It may appear that money is then assimilated again to the other categories of value. For if I buy a yard of wood for fuel I value its substance only for the heat that it produces and not for any other possible use. In reality, however, the situation is quite different. If it is claimed that the value of money consists in the value of its material, this means that its value is embodied in the qualities or powers of the substance which are not those of money. The apparent paradox indicates that money does not necessarily have to be based upon substances that are intrinsically valuable, i.e. valuable in some other respect. It is sufficient if the ability to function as money is transferred to any substance, the other qualities of which are quite irrelevant. It remains to be seen whether the abandonment of all those value functions that support the theory that money must possess intrinsic value, justifies the conclusion that money can be only money and nothing but money.

The point in question is the very important phenomenon of an object that has several functions of which only one, to the exclusion of all others, can be realized; and whether this realized function is modified in its significance and its value by the retreat of the others. In order to understand the co-existence of different possibilities, it may be permissible to point out first how the succession of diverse functions affects the one that finally survives. If the repentant sinner is given a higher value in the moral order of the world than the righteous man who has never erred, then this valuation of the moral superiority of the sinner is not derived from the presently existing situation – for the ethical content of this situation is, according to our assumptions, exactly the same as that of the righteous man – but from the preceding situation, in which the moral behaviour was different and from the fact that this situation no longer exists. Again, if freedom and self-determination is restored after there has been obstruction of our activity and external enforcement of its direction, our actions then acquire a particular feeling of well-being and value, which arises not from their content or success, but exclusively from the fact that the form of dependency has been eliminated. The same activity, following an uninterrupted series of independent actions, would lack the attraction that springs simply from the passing of a preceding form of life. This influence of not-being on being appears – some-what modified and more obvious in spite of the differences of content – in the significance that immediate emotional life has for lyrical or musical art. For even though the lyric and music are based upon the strength of inner emotions, their character as art requires that the immediacy of these emotions should be overcome. Although the raw material of emotion, with its impulsiveness, its personal limitations, its unbalanced fortuitousness, is the prerequisite of a work of art, the purity of art requires a distance, a release from the emotion. This is the essential meaning of art, for the artist as well as for those who enjoy it, namely, that it raises us above the immediacy of its relation to ourselves and to the world. The value of art depends upon our overcoming this immediacy, which then operates as if it no longer existed. And if it is asserted that the attraction of the work of art depends, after all, upon the resonance of that autochthonous emotion, that original agitation of the soul, it will nevertheless be admitted that the specific element of art lies not in what is common to the immediate and aesthetic form of emotion, but in the new colouring which the aesthetic form receives to the extent that the immediate form has faded away.

Finally, let us consider the most decisive and most general instance, which is considered only rarely because it is deeply embedded in our fundamental valuations. It seems to me that a vast number of life experiences that we enjoy derive their intensity from the fact that, for their sake, we leave unexplored innumerable opportunities for other enjoyments and for other ways of proving ourselves. A regal extravagance, a careless grandeur of existence, is revealed by the way that people ignore each other or pass on after a brief encounter, by our total indifference towards many to whom we could give much and who could give much to us. But there also emanates from this unique value of non-enjoyment a new, enhanced and more concentrated charm in what we do actually possess. The fact that this one among innumerable possibilities has become reality gives it a triumphant tone; the shades of the untried, neglected richness of life provide its victor's retinue. Moreover, what is given to other people often derives its value from what is retained, or indeed resolutely withheld. A cordial expansiveness, especially towards those of lower status, loses its value if it goes too far, if one shows too little reserve. It is all the more important to the recipient that one even offers a part of oneself, when he feels that one has still kept back something of oneself. In the last resort, it is the same with the significance of our own actions and undertakings. Sudden and compelling demands often make evident to us that we have abilities and powers for tasks that have hitherto seemed remote; that we have energies that would have remained latent if by chance an emergency had not elicited them from us. This shows that, besides the energies that are actually used, there are indeterminate potentialities which lie dormant in everyone, so that each person could have become something different from what he actually became. Life allows only a very limited number among these many possibilities to be realized; consequently, these appear more significant and precious the more we understand that they are a selection from many, that many forms of activity remain undeveloped and have to be sacrificed in order to develop others. Since so many possible achievements have to be sacrificed for the sake of one particular accomplishment, the latter represents, as it were, the quintessence of a much wider range of life-energies. By denying growth to these other energies it acquires significance and sharpness, a tone of distinction and accumulated force, which makes it the focus and representative of our total personality, transcending the area with which it is directly concerned.

Money may be subsumed under this general type of value formation. It is certainly correct that the other values of money's substance have to be discarded for the substance to become money; but the value that money has, and that allows it to perform its function, may be determined by those other possible uses which have to be foregone. As in the cases that we have just discussed, the perceived value of the developed function is constituted by its positive content and also by the exclusion of all other functions. What is effective here is not the operation of other functions but the fact that they do not operate. If the value of any object is determined by the fact that something else is sacrificed for it, then the value of the money material is determined by giving up all its other uses so that it can become money. This kind of valuation is, of course, reciprocal; i.e. the value of the money material for other uses will also increase if its use as money is abandoned. The wampum of the North American Indians consisted of mussel shells, which served as money but could also be worn as a decorative belt. These functions are obviously correlated; the role of the shells as jewelry has acquired an air of distinction by virtue of the fact that it requires abstention from using them directly as money. This whole type of value may be regarded as an instance of scarcity value. This usually implies that an object is demanded by more individuals or in greater quantity than the supply is adequate to meet. If different needs that can be satisfied by the same object compete for it – whether these needs occur in a single individual or among several individuals – the situation is naturally affected by the restriction of the supply, which makes impossible the satisfaction of all the needs. Just as the exchange value of grain can be traced to the fact that there is not enough of it to satisfy all those who are hungry, so the exchange value of the money material is the result of the fact that there is not enough to satisfy all those needs for it additional to the need for money. So far from the renunciation of other uses reducing the value of the metal that is used for money to that of quite worthless materials, these unrealized uses of the material instead contribute largely to the value of money.

The first argument against money as merely a symbol

There is another argument which seeks to convince us more directly than the one we have just refuted that money cannot be a value. Let us imagine an all-powerful individual with despotic authority within a given group over everything that he desires; one, for example, such as those chiefs in Oceania of whom it is said that they 'cannot steal' because everything already belongs to them. Such an individual would have no occasion to seize the money of the group, since he can in any case take possession of everything that money can buy. If money were itself a value in addition to other available values, then he would desire it as much as those other values. If it is clear that this does not happen in the fictitious case that I have described, then it seems to follow that money is really only a representative of real values, and is unnecessary once the real values are attainable without money. But this simple idea presupposes what it wishes to prove, namely that the substance of money has no value of its own aside from its functioning as money. For if it had such value it would be desired by the wielder of power not so much as money but for its other value as a substance. If such a value does not exist, its absence does not need to be demonstrated again. Leaving aside its logical deficiency, however, this case illustrates what specific kind of value money has. Money has acquired the value it possesses as a means of exchange; if there is nothing to exchange, money has no value. For obviously, its significance as a means of storing and transporting values is not of the same importance, but is a derivative of the function of money as means of exchange; without the latter, the other functions could not be exercised, whereas its function as means of exchange is independent of them. Money has no value either for a person to whom the goods that it can buy are valueless, or for a person who does not need money to acquire them. In short, money is the expression and the agent of the relationship that makes the satisfaction of one person always mutually dependent upon another person. Money has no place where there is no mutual relationship, either because one does not want anything from other people, or because one lives on a different plane – without any relation to them as it were – and is able to satisfy any need without any service in return. Looked at in this way, the world of money is related to the world of concrete values as thought is related to extension in Spinoza's system: it is impossible that either one should interfere with the other, because each of them expresses the whole world by itself and in its language. Thus, the total amount of value does not consist of the sum total of the value of things plus the total value of money; there is a certain quantity of value that may be realized in either form, as things or as money.

If money were reduced entirely to this value and had divested itself of all co-ordination with valuable things, it would realize, in the field of economics, the extraordinary conception that is the basis of Plato's theory of ideas. Plato was led, by a profound dissatisfaction with the world of experience to which we are confined, to conceive a metaphysical realm of ideas outside space and time, in which the real, harmonious, absolute essence of things existed. Earthly reality, therefore, became void of all real being and significance; but on the other hand, something was reflected back upon it from the realm of ideas; it had at least some part in the glowing realm of the absolute, as its faint shadow, and so it acquired a significance which was at first denied to it. This relationship is repeated and confirmed in the realm of values. The reality of things that confronts the perceiving mind is devoid of values, as we asserted at the beginning of this investigation; it develops in a form indifferent to values, often destroying what is most noble and preserving what is most base, because it does not proceed in terms of a hierarchy of worth, interests or values. We then subordinate this natural objective existence to a hierarchy of values, constructed in terms of good and bad, noble and mediocre, precious and valueless. This construction does not in any way affect being in its tangible reality, but it is the source of all meaning that reality may have for us; and we experience it – in spite of our awareness of its human origin – as being quite the opposite of mere fancy and subjectivity. The value of things – ethical as well as eudaemonistic, religious as well as aesthetic – hovers, like the Platonic ideas, above the world; a realm that is governed by its own alien and intangible inner norms, but that lends relief and colour to reality. Economic value originates by derivation from these primary, directly experienced values, by weighing the objects in which values are incorporated against each other, so far as they are exchangeable. Within this area, however, economic value, no matter how it has constituted itself, has the same peculiar relation to the individual objects as has value in general. It is a world apart, in which the objects are classified and arranged according to particular norms which are not inherent in the objects. Objects that are ordered and related by their economic value form a cosmos that is entirely different from that formed by their natural and immediate reality. If money were really nothing but the expression of the values of things external to money, it would be related to things just as the idea, which Plato conceived also as a substantial, metaphysical entity, is related to empirical reality. The movements of money – balancing, accumulation, outflow – would directly represent the value relationship between things. The world of values, which hovers above the real world apparently unconnected yet without question governing it, would be represented in its 'pure form' by money. And just as Plato interprets the real world, from the observation and sublimation of which the ideas have arisen, as a mere reflection of these ideas, so then do the economic relations, stages and fluctuations of concrete things appear as derivatives from their own derivative, namely as representatives and shadows of the significance that their money equivalent possesses. No other species of values is more favourably situated in this respect than are economic values. Religious values are embodied in priests and churches, ethical–social values in administrators and the visible institutions of state-power, the values of knowledge in the norms of logic; but none of these is more detached than are economic values from concrete valuable objects or processes; none is more completely the mere abstract bearer of value; in none of them is the whole world of relevant values so faithfully reflected.

The development of money is a striving towards the ideal of a pure symbol of economic value which is never attained. At first, as we must clearly remember, money belongs to the same series as all other objects of value, and its concrete material value is balanced against these. With the growing need for means of exchange and standards of value it changes more and more from a connecting link between value equations to a symbol of these equations and thus becomes more independent of the value of its material. Yet money cannot cast off a residue of material value, not exactly for inherent reasons, but on account of certain shortcomings of economic technique. One of these has to do with money as a means of exchange. The substitution of symbolic meaning for the intrinsic value of money is made possible only by a number of factors which we noted earlier. These are that the proportion between the single commodity and the economically effective total quantity of commodities is, with certain qualifications, equal to the proportion between a certain amount of money and the economically effective total quantity of money; that the denominators of these fractions are practically but not consciously effective, since only the changing numerators are of real interest in determining the transactions; and that in this transaction a direct equation between the commodity and the sum of money appears to take place, although of course it is quite a different basis from that of the original equation between the object and the material value of money. Even if this development is accepted, it remains true that the factors arising from the respective total sums of value are situated within fluctuating limits, and the instinctively formed estimation of their size will always be rather inexact. Perhaps that is why it is impossible to do without a direct value equation between commodities and money. The portion of intrinsic material value contained in money provides the support and complementation that we need because our knowledge of the exact proportion is insufficient; otherwise an identity between the measured value and the standard, that is an intrinsic value of money, would not be required. So long as experience and economic practice show that the proposition is imprecise, the measuring process will require a certain qualitative unity of the standard and the values themselves. It may be of interest to point out a corresponding instance in the aesthetic use of precious metals. An expert reported from the London Exhibition of 1851 on the differences between English and Indian gold and silverware. The English craftsman seems to have striven to incorporate the largest possible amount of metal in the smallest possible form; the Indian craftsman however, 'used enamelling, damascene and filigree work, etc., in such a way as to incorporate the greatest possible amount of highly skilled work in the smallest possible quantity of metal'. Yet even in the latter case it is certainly not irrelevant for the aesthetic significance of the jewelry that the small amount of metal employed is precious metal. Even if this practice is carried to a point where the amount of metal has only a minimal value, this minimum still has to be of precious material for the purpose of decoration and aesthetic pleasure. The intrinsic value of the material is not important, only the fact that the sole adequate bearer of a perfect formal relationship between the parts is a very precious material.

It is, by the way, quite obvious that this attribution of the material value of money to a complementing and supporting principle with reference to the uncertain relations is only an interpretation of processes that occur in the sub-conscious of the economic subjects themselves. Economic interactions take place with such admirable expediency, by subtly organized dovetailing of innumer-able details, that it would be necessary to assume that they were integrated by a superior mind, operating with superhuman wisdom, if one did not fall back upon the unconscious power of adaptation of the human species. The conscious intentions and foresight of individuals would not suffice to maintain the harmony that economic activity displays alongside its fearful discords and inadequacies. We have to assume that there are unconscious experiences and calculations which accumulate during the historical development of the economy and which regulate its course. It should be remembered, however, that unconscious con-ceptions do not provide a satisfactory explanation, but are only aids to under-standing that are actually based upon a fallacy. We arrive at determinate thoughts and actions from particular conceptions, chains of reasoning, etc. But if these consequences emerge without the antecedents, we conclude that the latter nevertheless existed without our being conscious of them. From a logical point of view, this is clearly unwarranted. Surreptitiously, we turn the merely negative fact that we are ignorant of the causative conceptions into a positive assertion that unconscious representations exist. Actually we know nothing of the pro-cesses that produce a psychic effect without conscious antecedents, and the notion of unconscious representations, experiences and inferences only expresses the fact that the effects occur as if they were the result of conscious motivations and ideas. The urge to explain has to rest content with investigating these processes and treating them as (unconsciously) effective causes, although they merely symbolize the real course of events. In our present state of knowledge it is unavoidable, and thus legitimate, to interpret the formation of values – their consolidation and fluctuation – as unconscious processes which follow the norms and forms of conscious reasoning.

The second argument against money as merely a symbol

The second reason for not regarding money as being only a symbol is con-nected with its significance as an element in exchange. Although, in principle, the exchange function of money could be accomplished by mere token money, no human power could provide a sufficient guarantee against possible misuse. The functions of exchange and reckoning obviously depend upon a limitation of the quantity of money, upon its 'scarcity', as the expression goes. If the pro-portion between the single amount and the total sum of commodities and of money is accepted as valid, then the proportion appears to be unchanged by an arbitrary increase in the amount of money and is able to retain its significance for the establishment of prices. The money fraction would show a proportionate increase of both the numerator and the denominator, without changing the value of the fraction. In reality, however, these changes do not occur in the same proportions if the amount of money is considerably increased. The denominator of the money fraction is in fact increased, but the numerator is unchanged until all exchange transactions have been adjusted to the new basis. The price, which equals the absolute size of the numerator, is therefore unchanged for the time being, whereas, as a fraction of the total sum of money, it has become much smaller. Consequently, the owner of new quantities of money, and in the first place the government, occupies a highly privileged position in relation to all sellers of commodities. The most serious repercussions upon exchange transactions will follow from this situation, particularly at the moment when the government's own revenues are paid in devalued money. The numerator of the money fraction – the price of commodities – rises proportionately to the increased supply of money only after the large quantities of new money have already been spent by the government, which then finds itself confronted again with a reduced supply of money. The temptation then to make a new issue of money is generally irresistible, and the process begins all over again. I mention this only as an example of the numerous and frequently discussed failures of arbitrary issues of paper money, which present themselves as a temptation whenever money is not closely linked with a substance of a limited supply. This is shown most clearly by an apparently contradictory example. In the sixteenth century, a French statesman suggested that silver should no longer be used for money, and that coins should be made from iron, because the bulk import of silver from America was depriving this metal of its scarcity. The use of a metal that becomes valuable only by official coinage would provide a better guarantee for the required limitations of the quantity of money, since the supply of money would become unlimited if every owner of silver was thereby automatically an owner of money. This peculiar suggestion shows a very distinct understanding of the fact that a precious metal is not as such the proper material for money, but only in so far as it sets a necessary limit to the supply of money. If a metal fails to do this, then it has to be replaced by another substance, the supply of which can be more effectively controlled. The preference for metal as a means of exchange is the consequence of certain functional qualities; if for any reason these are lacking it is replaced by another currency better qualified in this respect. Owing to the poor condition and incalculable variety of coins coming into Genoa in 1673, transactions were based on bills of exchange. Today we know that only precious metals, and indeed only gold, guarantee the requisite qualities, and in particular the limitation of quantity; and that paper money can escape the dangers of misuse by arbitrary inflation only if it is tied to a metal value established by law or by the economy. The following instance illustrates how effective such a restriction is, even in controlling individual speculation. During the American Civil War the circulation of Confederate paper money – 'greenbacks' – was prohibited in the western states, and although they were legal tender, nobody dared to repay in paper money a loan received in gold, by which means he could have made a profit of 150 per cent. In the eighteenth century the situation was similar in respect of the treasury bonds that the French government had issued to meet its pressing need for revenue. It was decreed that only 25 per cent of any payment could be made in these bonds, but nevertheless the value of the bonds soon declined to a very small proportion of their nominal worth. Such cases show the extent to which the significance of specie is sustained by the laws of exchange themselves. This does not happen only in the type of case that I have quoted so far. When the Bank of England ceased to redeem its notes between 1796 and 1819 the fall in the value of gold was only 3–5 per cent, but commodities prices rose 20–50 per cent as a result! Whenever a compulsory rate of exchange leaves only paper money and small coins in circulation, serious harm can be avoided only if the exchange rates show only minimal fluctuation over long periods, and to ensure this the issue of paper money must be strictly limited. This indispensable regulating function of gold, and formerly of silver, is due not to the correspondence between its value and that of the objects for which it is exchanged, but to the relative scarcity of the metal, which prevents the flooding of the market with money and the consequent undermining of the proportion upon which the equivalence of a commodity with a certain amount of money is based. The disruption of this proportion may be brought about from both sides. The excessive increase in money creates pessimism and mistrust among the people, so that they attempt to dispense with money and to fall back upon barter and promissory notes. This reduction of the demand for money leads to a further decline in the value of the money in circulation. The authority responsible for issuing money attempts to counteract the decline in value by further increasing the supply of money; thus supply and demand drift further apart, and the reciprocal effects that we have noted produce a cumulative decline in the value of money. This distrust of the value of money produced by government coinage – in contrast to the confidence in the value of specie – may assume a form in which, as in the later Roman Republic, coin circulates only in the retail trade, whereas large-scale transactions are carried on with money which is reckoned by weight. Only in this fashion, it was believed, could trade be protected against political crises, party interests and government interference.

The supply of money

It may appear from the foregoing that the inconveniences of an unlimited increase in the volume of money are attributable not so much to the increase itself, but rather to the way in which it is distributed. Shocks, hypertrophy and stagnation occur only because the newly created money is initially in one hand and spreads from there in an uneven and inappropriate manner. This might be avoidable if a way could be found of distributing the money equally or according to some principle of equity. Thus, it has been said that if every Englishman were suddenly to find that he had twice as much money in his pocket, all prices would increase correspondingly but no one would gain any advantage; the only difference would be that the pounds, shillings and pence would have to be calculated in larger amounts. This would not only dispose of the objection to token money but would also illustrate the advantages of an increase in the volume of money, arising from the empirical fact that more money means more transactions, greater well-being, power and culture.

There is little to be gained from a discussion of such hypotheses, based upon quite unrealizable presuppositions, yet they lead to a better understanding of the real conditions which render a gradual elimination of the intrinsic value of money impossible. Let us assume an ideal condition in which an increase in the volume of money has brought about an equal increase in what every individual owns: then one conclusion – that nothing has changed because all prices rise equally – contradicts the other – that the increase in the volume of money brings about a stimulation and expansion of trade. It is tempting to assume that the relations between individuals, that is the relative social position of superiors and inferiors, would in this case remain unchanged, while the total sum of objective cultural goods would be increased; that the content and enjoyment of life in an absolute sense would have risen both generally and for each individual, without changing anything in the relationship between wealth and poverty, which mutually determine each other. It might be pointed out that the modern commercial culture has already made available to the poor a number of goods – public amenities, educational opportunities, means of subsistence, etc. – which even well-to-do people did not enjoy formerly, without changing the relative position of rich and poor. The possibility that an increase in the volume of money, distributed proportionately, extends objective culture and also the cultural content of the individual life in absolute terms, while the relations among individuals remain the same, deserves examination. On closer scrutiny, however, it appears that real success can be achieved only by an unequal distribution of the increased supply of money, at least in the first instance. Money, which is entirely a social institution and quite meaningless if restricted to one individual, can bring about a change in general conditions only by changing the relations between individuals. The increased liveliness and intensity of commerce that ensues from a plethora of money can be traced to the fact that the desire for money increases at the same time. The wish to acquire as much money as possible from other people, though always present, evidently becomes sufficiently urgent to lead to extraordinary exertion and diligence only when the individual becomes acutely aware of having less than others; this is the sense of the remark, '*Les affaires – c'est l'argent des autres.*' If what the above theory presupposes were true – namely, that an increase in the volume of money would leave the relations of people to each other and the relative prices of commodities completely unchanged – there would be no such stimulation of work energies. Moreover, the magical doubling of the volume of money will also affect the relations between individuals because the financial situation of the individuals is different to begin with. The doubling of three different incomes of 1,000, 10,000 and 100,000 marks, for instance, changes the relation between the recipients because the objects bought for the second 1,000, 10,000 marks, etc., are not simply duplicates of what was bought for the first 1,000 marks, and so on. In the first case there would be, perhaps, an improvement in nutrition, in the second a refinement of artistic culture, and in the third a greater involvement in financial speculation. If we assume a preceding absolute equality among individuals then no changes would be produced either in the subjective or in the objective aspects of their lives, because if the latter changed then it would be in an unpredictable way; they would show an upswing of activity only if the differences in individual incomes became, or were felt to be, more important than previously.

Even more relevant to our purposes are considerations about the factual implications of this theory; namely, that the doubling of all money incomes would leave everything unchanged, because all commodity prices would be simultaneously doubled. This reasoning is false, because it overlooks a peculiar and decisive characteristic of money, which might be termed its relative inelasticity. This consists in the fact that the distribution of an additional quantity of money in a given economic region does not raise all prices proportionately, but creates new price relationships which do not necessarily result from the power of individual interests. Inelasticity is a consequence of the fact that the money price of a commodity, despite its relativity and the absence of an inherent connection with the commodity, nevertheless acquires a certain stability and appears to be the objectively adequate equivalent. If the price of an object has remained stable within definite limits, then it does not usually change without resistance simply because the value of money has changed. The association – of concepts as well as of interests – between the object and its price has become psychologically so firmly fixed that the seller will not readily admit a decline or the buyer an increase, as would be a matter of course if the balancing of money value and commodity value were accomplished by the same unrestricted mechanism through which the thermometer rises or falls according to the temperature without any disturbance of the exact relation between cause and effect resulting from change in the degree of resistance to the movement. If one suddenly has twice as much money in one's pocket as a short time before, one is not inclined immediately to pay twice the amount for each commodity. Or it may be that with the bravado of the newly rich, reckoning the new wealth by the previous standards, one will not trouble about price at all. However, both the willingness to pay more and the disinclination to pay as much as the new appropriate price show that a proportional regulation of prices is out of the question during the initial period of abundant money, and that the established association between a commodity and a traditional range of prices has a continuously disturbing influence. Furthermore, the demand for commodities will change considerably following an increase or decrease in the quantity of money even if this affects everybody equally. If there is a decrease, for instance, objects that have a sufficiently steady sale may still be sold at half the price up to that amount or even in greater abundance, but beyond a certain limit they may not find any buyers at all. In the case of a general increase in the supply of money, on the other hand, a lively demand will develop for those goods that were desired by the mass of the people, i.e. for goods that are just above their present standard of living. The demand would not increase very greatly for those goods that satisfy basic needs, which can be met by a limited supply, or for those that satisfy the most refined and cultivated needs, which are significant only for a limited, scarcely expanding, circle. Price increases would affect mainly the goods between these extremes where prices would remain relatively stable. There would be no question of the increased supply of money affecting all prices equally. In general terms, the theory that the relativity of prices renders the absolute quantity of money a matter of indifference is incorrect, because this relativity is in practice continuously disrupted by a psychological process which makes the prices of certain commodities rigid and absolute.

It might be argued that these doubts about the harmlessness of an unrestricted increase in the supply of money are valid only for the transitional periods of adjustment between two different price levels. They presuppose that the whole process evolves from a proportional relationship between the quantities of goods and money. It must be possible to establish this relationship at a different level, and future fluctuations could be eliminated just as well as the preceding ones. The doubts can refer only to the period of change, not to the accomplished changes, which cannot be held responsible for the maladjustments, dislocations and difficulties of the transition period. It is impossible to conceive of any means of exchange that would not eventually enforce an adjustment, so that the money price of a commodity expressed the proportion between its value and the value of the total quantity of commodities; and therefore an arbitrary increase in money is unable to disrupt this proportion permanently. This reasoning is quite correct, but it does not prove that the removal of all limitations upon the increase in the supply of money is possible, taking into account the inadequacy of human circumstances. For the transitional period, the instability and difficulties of which are admitted, would then become a permanent condition, and the state of adjustment that is attainable in principle for any quantity of money would never be reached.

Reality and pure concepts

This argument may be summarized as follows. Money performs its services best when it is not simply money, that is when it does not merely represent the value of things in pure abstraction. Precious metals are also valuable as jewelry or for technical purposes, but this has to be conceptually distinguished as a primary fact from the secondary fact that they are valuable on account of it; whereas it is the first and only quality of money to be valuable. It is not technically feasible to accomplish what is conceptually correct, namely to transform the money function into a pure token money, and to detach it completely from every substantial value that limits the quantity of money, even though the actual development of money suggests that this will be the final outcome. This is not a contradiction. A great number of processes occur in the same manner; they closely approach a definite goal by which their course is unambiguously determined, yet they would lose precisely those qualities that led them towards the goal if they were actually to reach it. One phenomenon that is eminently characteristic of the money economy may illustrate this point and provide, at the same time, an analogy for the consequences of unlimited money supply with reference to individual circumstances. The striving of the individual to earn more and more money is of the greatest socioeconomic significance. By seeking the greatest possible gain, the stockbroker brings about liveliness of transactions, the adjustment of supply and demand, the introduction of otherwise sterile values into economic circulation. However, very high profits on the stock exchange can usually be realized only when there is excessive fluctuation of the rates of exchange and a preponderance of purely speculative elements. In such conditions, the production and consumption of goods, which is the ultimate interest of society, is excessively stimulated in one area and neglected in another, and in any case is diverted from the course of development which corresponds with its specific inner conditions and with real needs. Here the specific quality of money becomes a basis for the divergence between the individual and the social interest, which has previously coincided up to a point. Only through the fact that the value of things has become detached from the objects and has acquired an independent existence in a specific substance is it possible for money to develop interests, movements and norms that, on occasion, act contrary to those of the symbolized objects. The activities of private enterprise, which are connected with money, promote the social interest of the production and consumption of goods so long as they remain merely endeavours, whereas the final attainment of their ends might undermine the aims of society. This type of situation is most frequently and decisively produced in those cases where emotional impulses strive for a final objective without being aware that all the hoped-for satisfaction is the consequence of relative advances, and may perhaps turn into its opposite when the goal is reached. I would call your attention to love, which receives its content and colouring from the desire for the closest and most permanent union, and frequently loses both when its object is attained; or to political ideals, which provide the strength and spiritual fervour in the life of whole generations but which, once they are realized, do not bring about an ideal condition, but practical materialism, torpidity and philistinism; or to the longing for a peaceful and undisturbed way of life, which is the goal of all effort and labour, yet which once accomplished often ends in idleness and inner dissatisfaction. It has indeed become a platitude to say that even happiness, though it is the object of all our endeavours, would be mere boredom if it were ever achieved as an eternal state. Although our will drives us in this direction, the attainment of such a condition would contradict its striving, and only the admixture of the suffering that we want to avoid can give any sense to the pursuit of happiness. This kind of process may be summed up by saying that the effectiveness of some or perhaps all elements of life depends upon the concurrence of opposing elements. The proportion in which an element and its opposite are combined and co-operate are naturally variable, sometimes in the sense that one element steadily increases while the other declines, so that the trend of the development appears to be one in which one element will finally supplant the other. But as soon as this happened and every trace of the second element disappeared, the sense and effectiveness of the first element would also be paralysed. This happens, for instance, with the opposition between individualism and socialism. There are periods in which the latter determines historical development, not only in reality, but also as an inference from ideal convictions and an expression of a developing conception of society which strives toward perfection. But if, in the party politics of such an age, it is then concluded that, since all progress depends upon the growth of the socialist elements, their triumph will produce the most advanced and ideal state of things, this overlooks the fact that the whole success of socialist measures depends upon the circumstance under which they are introduced into an individualistic economic system. The progress resulting from the relative increase of socialist measures does not justify the conclusion that their complete implementation would represent further progress. It is the same with periods of increasing individualism. The significance of individualistic measures depends upon the fact that centralized socialist institutions continue to exist; these can be progressively reduced, but their complete disappearance would lead to unanticipated results differing widely from those that individualism had previously brought about. In the field of art, the contrary tendencies towards naturalism and towards mannerism show a similar pattern. At each particular moment in the development of art there is a mixture of simple reflection of reality and subjective transformation. From the standpoint of realism, art becomes more perfect through the growth of the objective element. But at the very moment when this became the sole content of a work of art the growing interest would suddenly turn to indifference, because the work of art would no longer be distinct from reality, would lose its significance as a separate entity. On the other hand, although enhancement of the generalizing and idealizing element may refine art for a time, it must reach a point where the relation to reality, which the idealistic movement was supposed to represent in a purer and more perfect form, is completely lost as a result of the elimination of all individualistic contingency. In short, a number of most important processes follow this pattern the growing importance of one element leads to greater success, but the complete hegemony of this element, and the total elimination of the contrasting element, would not result in total success; on the contrary, it would deprive the original element of its specific character. The relationship between the intrinsic value of money and its purely functional and symbolic nature may develop in analogous fashion; the latter increasingly replaces the former, but a certain measure of the former has to be retained because the functional and symbolic character of money would lose its basis and significance if this trend were brought to its final conclusion.

It is not only a formal analogy that is in question here, but the unity of the deeper meaning of life, which is expressed in this external similarity. In practice, we can only cope with the variety of elements and tendencies that make up life by allowing our behaviour, in every context and at every period of time, to be governed by a uniform and one-sided principle. But in this way the diversity of reality catches up with us again and again, and weaves our subjective striving, along with all those factors that oppose it, into an empirical existence which allows the ideal to enter reality. This does not imply a denial of the ideal; life is adapted to such absolute strivings as its elements, in the same way as the physical world is adapted to motions that, if left unimpeded, would have inconceivable consequences, but that, as a result of their meeting with counterforces, produce the orderly world of natural events. If the practical world is formed in such a way that our will is focused upon eternity and only attains the world of reality by being deflected and rebuffed, then here too the structure of practical life has predetermined the theoretical structure. On innumerable occasions, our concepts of things are made so unalloyed and absolute that they do not reflect experience, and only their qualification and modification by opposing concepts can give them an empirical form. However, these concepts are not for that reason thoroughly bad; it is precisely through this unique procedure of exaggeration followed by retraction in the formation of concepts and maxims, that a view of the world which is in conformity with our understanding emerges. The formula through which our mind establishes a relation with the oneness of things, which is not directly accessible, by supplementing and reproducing it, is in practice as well as in theory a primary too-much, too-high, too-pure. It gains the consistency and scope of reality and truth only by means of restraining contrasts. Thus, the pure concept of money as the mere expression of the reciprocally measured value of things, which has no intrinsic value of its own, remains completely justified, although in historical reality this concept is consistently disparaged and limited by the contrary concept of money as possessing intrinsic value. Our intellect can grasp reality only as a modification of pure concepts, which, no matter how much they diverge from reality, are legitimized by the service they render in the interpretation of reality.

III

The historical development of money from substance to function

We have now to consider the historical manifestations of our theoretical constructions. The broad cultural ramifications of the nature and significance of money are to be seen in the movements that lead money towards its pure concept and away from its attachment to particular substances – even though it never attains the goal that determines its course of development. Thus, money is involved in the general development which in every domain of life and in every sense strives to dissolve substance into free-floating processes. On the one hand, money forms part of this comprehensive development; on the other, it has a special relationship with concrete values, as that which symbolizes them. Furthermore, money is influenced by the broad cultural trends, and it is at the same time an independent cause of these trends. We are interested in this interrelation here in so far as the form of money is determined by the conditions and needs of human society. With the reservation that this process never reaches the goal, I shall now examine the growing importance of money as a function or symbol, which comes to overshadow its significance as a substance.

On a more profound examination, the dissolution of the concept of money as a substance is much less radical than appears at first sight; for, strictly speaking, the substance value of money is also a functional value. No matter how much precious metals are appreciated simply as substances, they are in fact appreciated only because they adorn, distinguish, are technically useful, give aesthetic pleasure, etc., that is to say, because they perform functions. Their value does not consist in their autonomous being, but always in their performance. Their substance as such, apart from their performance, like the substance of all practical objects, is totally irrelevant to us. It may be said of the majority of objects that they are not valuable, but become valuable; and in order to do so they must continually emerge out of themselves and interact with other objects. Our sense of value is bound up with the effects that objects produce. Even if a particular aesthetic mood were to attribute objective value to the precious metals on the ground that their mere existence, quite apart from all recognition and enjoyment, enriches the world, they would never enter the economic system through this kind of value. In the economy all value is connected with performance, and it is an arbitrary way of speaking, which conceals the actual condition, to say that precious metals have a substantial value which is distinct from their performance as money. Every value possessed by precious metals as substances is also a functional value, with the exception of their function as money. All the values of the precious metals form a series that is simply a series of functions. This is naturally less easily comprehended, the less lively these functions are in reality. All the misgivings of the Middle Ages about the taking of interest arise from the fact that money then appeared to be, and actually was, much more solid and substantial, more starkly contrasted with other things, than in modern times when it appears and operates in a much more dynamic, variable and pliable way. The adoption of the Aristotelian doctrine that it is unnatural for money to engender money; the condemnation of interest as theft, because the capital repaid equals the borrowed capital; the argument in favour of this interpretation by Alexander of Hales, that money did not wear out by use and that it was not profitable, as were the objects of a lease, to the creditor; the doctrine of Aquinas that in the case of money, whose sole end is to be spent, use and spending were identical, and that therefore the use of money, unlike the use of a house, could not be sold separately – all these doctrines illustrate how inflexible and dissociated from the fluctuations of life money appeared, how little it was regarded as a productive power. The actual insignificance of money's effects concealed its functional character. This is the same basic sentiment concerning money as that which regards it as a metallic substance. This view, like that of the Middle Ages, opposes money as an entity *per se* to the circulation of economic objects, instead of bringing money into this circulation and recognizing that money, whatever represents it, does not *have* a function, but *is* a function.

At the opposite pole from the mentality of the Middle Ages is the credit economy, in which the bill of exchange serves as money. The dominant idea in the Middle Ages was the substance of money, rather than its effects, which were in fact reduced to a minimum, though they could not really be eliminated altogether. In the modern conception of money based upon metal, the vital point is the working of the substance; and finally, in a credit economy there is a tendency to eliminate substance entirely, and to regard the effects as the only important matter.

This superficial view owes something to an earlier scheme of thought which distinguished in all phenomena between substance and accident. Certainly this was historically of tremendous importance: the analysis of every phenomenon into a substantial core and relative, changeable appearances and qualities was a first orientation, a first guiding thread through the mysterious formlessness of things, giving them a structure and subjecting them to a general category that was consonant with our intellect. The mere sense differences that appear at first thus become organized and determined in their mutual relations. But it is the nature of such forms, as of social organizations, to appear and to claim to be eternal. Just as the destruction of one social order in favour of another gives the impression that all order and regularity is being abandoned, so does reconstruction in the intellectual realm. The objective stability as well as the subjective understanding of the world seems to be destroyed when a category that formed the backbone of a world view is abrogated. But money value will be just as little able to resist its reduction to functional value as light, heat and life can retain their particular substantial quality or resist their dissolution into forms of motion.

Social interactions and their crystallization into separate structures

I shall now examine certain structural relationships of the economy. The extent to which it depends upon these relationships and not upon the substance of money, where money really functions as money, may be shown by a negative example based upon a general observation. We notice that, in a relationship between two people, the external form is rarely an adequate expression of its inner intensity. This inadequacy results from the fact that the inner relations develop continuously, while the external relations develop in a spasmodic fashion. Even if the two correspond at any given time, the latter persist in their traditional form whereas the former grow. At a certain point, there is a sudden development of the external relationship, and characteristically this does not usually stop at the point corresponding to the inner relationship but anticipates a more advanced intimacy. The use of the intimate form of address – 'du' – with friends as the final expression of an affection that has existed for a long time is often felt at first to be exaggerated, and it produces suddenly an external closeness which is usually followed only slowly by a corresponding inner intimacy. Sometimes it does not follow at all. Some relationships break down because the form, although to a certain extent justified, overtakes the inner relation. A corresponding phenomenon can be found in the impersonal realm. Social forces which seek expression in certain constellations of law, modes of exchange and conditions of government, often fail because the traditional forms in these areas easily become rigid. If the desired external change nevertheless takes place, then it often goes beyond the state of readiness of the inner forces, and their subsequent legitimation does not always succeed. In some instances, the money economy has been introduced in this way. When the general economic conditions have been tending towards it for a long time, it takes shape as such a powerful phenomenon that the general conditions can no longer accommodate it, and if the growth of the inner economic forces does not catch up rapidly enough with the anticipated forms the new institutions may come to a tragic end. Such was the situation when the Fuggers, and indeed all the great bankers of southern Germany, came to grief. Their financial operations, comparable with those of modern world bankers, took place in an age that had outgrown the barter economy of the Middle Ages but did not yet dispose of the communications, guarantees, or commercial practices that are an indispensable correlate of such transactions. The general conditions were not such that debts could be collected in Spain or from ruling princes without further ado. The new forms of the money economy misled Anton Fugger into extending them far beyond what was justified by the actual conditions in Europe. For the same reasons, the debtors of these financial magnates were no better off. The financial crisis in Spain in the sixteenth century resulted from the fact that, although money was usually available in Spain, it was not available in the Netherlands where it was most needed. Consequently, difficulties, delays and expenses arose which contributed to the ruin of Spanish finances. In other local conditions money functioned in quite a different fashion. The Netherlands had the tremendous advantage in their war with Spain in that their money could be used just where it was available. In the hands of the Dutch it was really 'money', because it could function unhampered, even though the Dutch actually owned much less money in a material form than did Spain, since their economic life was based upon credit. The function of money can be exercised with less money material, the more favourable are the local conditions; and one might say paradoxically that, the more it is really money in its essential significance, the less need there is for it to be money in a material sense.

Alongside the influence of local conditions, it is the stability and reliability of social interaction or, as it were, the consistency of the economic domain that prepares the dissolution of money as a substance. This is illustrated by the fact that money brings about a continually increasing number of effects while it remains itself immobile. The notion that the economic significance of money results simply from its value and the frequency of its circulation at any given time overlooks the powerful effects that money produces through the hope and fear, the desire and anxiety that are associated with it. It radiates these economically important sentiments, as heaven and hell also radiate them, but as pure ideas. The idea of the availability or shortage of money at a given time produces effort or paralysis; and the gold reserves that lie in the bank vaults as cover for their notes demonstrate clearly that the merely psychological representation of money is fully effective. In this instance, money can truly be described as the 'unmoved mover'. It is obvious that the effect of this merely potential money depends upon the refinement and stability of the economic organization. Wherever social relations are loose, sporadic and sluggish, sales will be made only for cash, and the immobile money will not make use of the many psychological channels through which it can operate. The dual role of money that is lent should also be considered here, first in the ideal but very significant form of active debts, and second as a reality in the hands of the debtor. As a claim it counts among the assets of the creditor, and although it is not immediately available it is still very effective; on the other hand, although it does not form part of the debtor's property he can still achieve the same economic effects as if it did. The lending of money divides its activity into two parts and increases enormously the product of its economic energy. But the intellectual abstraction on which this process rests can attain its results only in a firmly established and civilized social order, in which it is possible to lend money with relative security and to base economic activity on this partial function of money. A certain comprehensiveness and intensity of social relations is required for money to become effective – otherwise it does not differ at all from other goods that are exchanged – and a further intensification of social relations is needed in order to intellectualize its effects. These conspicuous phenomena illustrate clearly that the inner nature of money is only loosely tied to its material basis; since money is entirely a sociological phenomenon, a form of human interaction, its character stands out all the more clearly the more concentrated, dependable and agreeable social relations are. Indeed, the general stability and reliability of cultural inter-action influences all the external aspects of money. Only in a stable and closely organized society that assures mutual protection and provides safeguards against a variety of elemental dangers, both external and psychological, is it possible for such a delicate and easily destroyed material as paper to become the repre-sentative of the highest money value. In the Middle Ages, characteristically, leather money was very often used. If paper money signifies the progressive dissolution of money value into purely functional value, then leather money may be regarded as symbolizing the first step towards it. Leather money pre-serves, out of all the qualities that characterize money as a substance, the quality of relative indestructibility; this quality can be surrendered only when the structure of individual and social relations has reached an advanced stage.

Monetary policy

The theory and practice of monetary policy confirm the course of development from the substantial to the functional significance of money, as well as the dependence of the latter upon sociological conditions. The fiscalism of the Middle Ages, and mercantilism, may be regarded as materialistic monetary policies. Just as materialism incorporates the phenomena and values of spirit into matter, so fiscalism and mercantilism considered the nature and energy of socio-political life tied to the material of money. The same difference exists between them, however, as between the crude and the sophisticated form of materialism. The former claims that perception itself is a material process, that the brain produces thoughts just as the liver secretes bile; the latter asserts that

perception itself is not material, but is a form of movement of the material, that
thoughts consist of a special kind of oscillation of material elements, as do light,
heat or electricity. In accordance with this difference of intellectual outlook,
fiscalism discerns the interest of government as being to acquire as much ready
money as possible for direct use by the princes for government purposes, while
mercantilism, on the other hand, lays the greatest stress not upon the accumulation of money but upon the stimulation of economic activity. These materialistic
trends of monetary policy are still closely associated with the idea that the
money material represents value as such, but the change from a crudely objective to a functional significance of this material is already discernible. The
political constitutions of these periods correspond with this situation. Where the
medieval fiscal constitution prevails, the prince has only an external, not an
organic, relationship to his country, which is established by marriage or conquest and is well indicated by the tendency to extract as much money as
possible from the country. The frequent sale of whole territories for money was
a logical conclusion of this tendency. The purely monetary connection between
ruler and subject demonstrated the absence of any other relationship. The
continuous depreciation of the currency by medieval rulers was an appropriate
technique within such a sociological relationship; for these methods, which give
all the benefits to one side and the entire loss to the other, are possible only
when an organic relationship is lacking. The love of ready money, which seems
to be an innate characteristic of oriental peoples, has been traced to the fiscal
policy of their rulers, who use the royal prerogative of coinage as a means of
taxation without concern for the consequences of devaluation. The necessary
counterpart of this policy is the passion of their subjects for accumulating ready
money in the form of gold and silver. The emergence of the centralized despotic
state involved a much closer and more vital relationship among the various
political elements; and the idea of an organic whole provides a common basis
for the princely ideal, from '*l'état c'est moi*' to the notion of the king as the first
servant of his people. Although the interest of the government is still in this
case directed towards the import of ample quantities of money material (i.e.
bullion), the livelier interaction between the head and the members of the state
and the greater animation of political life are reflected in the fact that the
ultimate end of acquisition is no longer mere ownership but the nurture and
growth of industry by money. When these liberal tendencies had produced a
freer flow of political life, an unhampered flexibility and a less stable equilibrium
of elements, the material basis was prepared for Adam Smith's theory that gold
and silver are merely tools, no different from kitchen utensils, and that their
import increases the wealth of a country just as little as the multiplication of
kitchen utensils provides more food. When the traditional regulation of money
material has been abolished, in order to make way for more anarchistic ideas,
this new tendency of monetary theory, as might be expected, leads to another

extreme. Proudhon, who wants to abolish all established forms of the state and to recognize only the free and direct interaction of individuals as the proper form of social life, attacks the use of money in general, seeing it as exactly analogous to those forms of authority that absorb the living interaction of individuals and crystallize it within themselves. The exchangeability of values should be organized without money as an intermediary, just as the administration of society should be accomplished by all citizens without the intervention of the king. In the same way as every citizen has voting rights, so every commodity should represent value without the mediation of money. The trend towards this theory of money, which may be characterized as transcendental by contrast with the materialistic theory, began with the views of Adam Smith. While materialism asserts that mind is matter, the transcendental philosophy teaches that matter itself is mind. This does not refer to mind in the spiritualist sense, as a substance, an autonomous being (although of an immaterial kind), but to the knowledge that any object, whether physical or mental, exists for us only in so far as it is conceived by the active process of the mind, or more precisely, in so far as it is a function of the mind. If the materialistic interpretation of money now appears to be an error, historical analysis shows that this error was not accidental but was the appropriate theoretical expression of an actual sociological condition, which had first to be overcome by the real forces before its theoretical counterpart could be overcome in theory.

Social interaction and exchange relations: money's functions

There is a further context in which the sociological character of money appears. The interaction between individuals is the starting point of all social formations. The real historical origins of social life are still obscure, but whatever they were, a systematic genetic analysis must begin from this most simple and immediate relationship, which even today is the source of innumerable new social formations. Further development replaces the immediacy of interacting forces with the creation of higher supra-individual formations, which appear as independent representatives of these forces and absorb and mediate the relations between individuals. These formations exist in great variety; as tangible realities and as mere ideas and products of the imagination; as complex organizations and as individual existences. In this way, the objective laws of custom, law and morality developed from the necessities and practices, which originate incidentally in the relations between group members and which eventually become fixed. They are ideal products of human conceptions and valuation, which in our mind now stand beyond the will and action of the individual as 'pure forms'. Thus, in the continuation of this process, the law of the state is embodied in the judges and the whole administrative hierarchy; the cohesive power of a political party lies in its executive committee and its parliamentary representatives; the unity of a regiment is incarnated in its flag, and that of a mystical union rests in its Holy Grail, etc. The interactions between the primary elements that produce the social unit are replaced by the fact that each of these elements establishes an independent relation to a higher or intermediate organ. Money belongs to this category of reified social functions. The function of exchange, as a direct interaction between individuals, becomes crystallized in the form of money as an independent structure. The exchange of the products of labour, or of any other possessions, is obviously one of the purest and most primitive forms of human socialization; not in the sense that 'society' already existed and then brought about acts of exchange but, on the contrary, that exchange is one of the functions that creates an inner bond between men – a society, in place of a mere collection of individuals. Society is not an absolute entity which must first exist so that all the individual relations of its members – super- and subordination, cohesion, imitation, division of labour, exchange, common attack and defence, religious community, party formations and many others – can develop within its framework or be represented by it: it is only the synthesis or the general term for the totality of these specific interactions. Any one of the interactions may, of course, be eliminated and 'society' still exist, but only if a sufficiently large number of others remain intact. If all interaction ceases there is no longer any society. In the same way, a living organism can continue to exist if one or the other of its functions – which is an interaction between parts – ceases, but it cannot live if all functions cease, because 'life' is nothing but the sum of interacting forces among the atoms of the organism. It is, therefore, almost a tautology to say that exchange brings about socialization: for exchange is a form of socialization. It is one of those relations through which a number of individuals become a social group, and 'society' is identical with the sum total of these relations.

The frequently emphasized inconveniences and deficiencies of barter are comparable with those that appear in other social interactions when they are still in the stage of immediacy. If all governmental measures have to be discussed and approved by the whole body of citizens; if the defence of the group against external enemies is still assured by military service for all its members; if collective effort and organization depends entirely upon personal authority and force; if the administration of justice requires the verdict of the whole community – if all these things are necessary then the growing size and complexity of the group will produce all those inadequacies, hindrances and breakdowns that eventually suggest, on one hand, the transfer of these functions to specific organs and, on the other hand, the creation of representative and integrating ideals and symbols. The function of exchange leads in fact to both kinds of structure: to a class of merchants and to money. The merchant is the differentiated representative of the exchange functions, which otherwise are carried out directly by the producers; instead of the simple interaction between producers, a new relationship of each of them to the merchant is established, just as the direct cohesion and control of the group members is replaced by their common relation to the organs of government. Anticipating a more exact knowledge, one may say that money stands between the objects of exchange as the merchant stands between the exchanging subjects. The equivalence between objects of exchange is no longer effected directly, and its fluctuations are no longer concealed; instead, each object acquires a relationship of equivalence and exchange with money. The merchant is the personified function of exchange, and money is the reified function of being exchanged. Money is, as I noted earlier, the reification of the pure relationship between things as expressed in their economic motion. Money stands beyond the individual objects that are related to it, in a realm organized according to its own norms which is the objectification of the movements of balancing and exchange originally accomplished by the objects themselves. However, this is only a preliminary view. For, in the last analysis, it is not the objects but the people who carry on these processes, and the relations between the objects are really relations between people. The activity of exchange among individuals is represented by money in a concrete, independent, and, as it were, congealed form, in the same sense as government represents the reciprocal self-regulation of the members of a community, as the palladium or the ark of the covenant represents the cohesion of the group, or the military order represents its self-defence. All these are instances of a general type, in which a specific feature becomes detached from the primary phenomena, substances or events to which it was bound in the same way that a quality is bound to its substance or action to its subject. This feature then assumes a structure of its own and the process of abstraction is brought to a conclusion when it crystallizes in a concrete formation. Outside exchange, money has as little meaning as have regiments and flags outside the needs of communal attack and defence, or as have priests and temples independently of communal religiosity. The dual nature of money, as a concrete and valued substance and, at the same time, as something that owes its significance to the complete dissolution of substance into motion and function, derives from the fact that money is the reification of exchange among people, the embodiment of a pure function.

The developments in the material of money express its sociological character more and more clearly. The use of simple means of exchange such as salt, cattle, tobacco and grain is determined by a pure individual interest, in a solipsistic fashion; that is to say, they are eventually consumed by a single person since no one else has any interest in them at that particular time. The use of precious metals for jewelry, on the other hand, indicates a relation between individuals: people adorn themselves for others. Adornment is a social need, and precious metals are particularly apt for attracting the attention of others by their glitter. In consequence, certain kinds of ornament are reserved for particular social positions: in medieval France gold was not permitted below a certain rank. Since the whole significance of adornment lies in the psychological process that is incited in other people by the wearer, the precious metals differ fundamentally from the primitive, as it were, centripetal, means of exchange. Exchange, as the purest sociological occurrence, the most complete form of interaction, finds its appropriate representation in the material of jewelry, the significance of which for its owner is only indirect, namely as relation to other people.

If the embodiment of the action of exchange in a particular form is accomplished technically in such a way that each object is first exchanged for this form rather than directly for another object, the question arises: upon closer examination, what is the corresponding behaviour of the people behind the objects? Their general behaviour in relation to merchants, however much it is a cause and effect of monetary transactions, provides only an analogy. It seems clear to me that the basis and the sociological representative of the relation between objects and money is the relationship between economically active individuals and the central power which issues and guarantees the currency. Money serves as an absolute intermediary between all commodities only if coinage has raised it above its character as a mere quantity of metal – to say nothing of simpler kinds of money. The abstraction of the process of exchange from specific real exchanges, and its embodiment in a distinctive form, can happen only if exchange has become something other than a private process between two individuals which is confined to individual actions. This new and broader character of exchange is established when the value of exchange given by one party has no direct value for the other party, but is merely a claim upon other definite values; a claim whose realization depends upon the economic community as a whole or upon the government as its representative. When barter is replaced by money transactions a third factor is introduced between the two parties: the community as a whole, which provides a real value corresponding to money. The pivotal point in the interaction of the two parties recedes from the direct line of contact between them, and moves to the relationship which each of them, through his interest in money, has with the economic community that accepts the money, and demonstrates this fact by having money minted by its highest representative. This is the core of truth in the theory that money is only a claim upon society. Money appears, so to speak, as a bill of exchange from which the name of the drawee is lacking, or alternatively, which is guaranteed rather than accepted. It has been argued against this theory that metallic money involves credit, that credit creates a liability, whereas metallic money payment liquidates any liability; but this argument overlooks the fact that the liquidation of the individual's liability may still involve an obligation for the community. The liquidation of every private obligation by money means that the community now assumes this obligation towards the creditor. The obligation that arises from a service in kind can be removed in only two ways: either by providing an equivalent service, or by creating a claim for an equivalent service. The owner of money possesses such a claim and, by transferring it to whoever performed the service, he directs him to an anonymous producer who, on the basis of his membership of the community, offers the required service in exchange for the money. The distinction that has been made between paper money which is backed in some way (e.g. by gold) and that which is unbacked, with reference to the credit character of money, is quite irrelevant here. It has been assumed that only unredeemable paper money is really money, while redeemable paper money is only a claim for payment; but on the other hand, it has also been urged that this difference is meaningless for the transactions between buyer and seller, because even the guaranteed paper money does not function as a promise to pay but as final payment, in contrast to the cheque, which is only a promise between buyer and seller. This way of posing the question does not penetrate to the sociological background. Viewed from the sociological perspective, there is no doubt that metallic money is also a promise and that it differs from the cheque only with respect to the size of the group which vouches for its being accepted. The common relationship that the owner of money and the seller have to a social group – the claim of the former to a service and the trust of the latter that this claim will be honoured – provides the sociological constellation in which money transactions, as distinct from barter, are accomplished.

Metallic money, which is usually regarded as the absolute opposite of credit money, contains in fact two presuppositions of credit which are peculiarly intertwined. First, an examination of the metallic substance of the coin is not feasible in everyday transactions. Cash transactions cannot develop without public confidence in the issuing government, or perhaps in those persons who are able to determine the real value of the coin in relation to its nominal value. The inscription on the coins of Malta – *non aes sed fides* – indicates very appropriately the element of trust without which even a coin of full value cannot perform its function in most cases. The variety of reasons, often contradictory, for accepting a coin indicates that it is not some objective proof that is essential. In some parts of Africa the Maria-Theresa thaler has to be white and clean, in other parts it has to be greasy and dirty, in order to be accepted as genuine.

Secondly, there has to be confidence that the money that is accepted can be spent again at the same value. What is indispensable and conclusive is *non aes sed fides* – the confidence in the ability of an economic community to ensure that the value given in exchange for an interim value, a coin, will be replaced without loss. No one can make use of a coin without giving credit in these two respects. Only this twofold trust confers upon a dirty and perhaps unrecognizable coin a definite amount of value. Without the general trust that people have in each other, society itself would disintegrate, for very few relationships are based entirely upon what is known with certainty about another person, and very few relationships would endure if trust were not as strong as, or stronger than, rational proof or personal observation. In the same way, money transactions would collapse without trust. There are nuances of this trust. The assertion that money is always credit because its value rests upon the recipient's confidence that he will be able to acquire a certain quantity of goods in exchange for it is not entirely adequate. For it is not only a money economy, but any economy, that depends upon such trust. If the farmer did not have confidence that his field would bear grain this year as in former years, he would not sow; if the trader did not believe that the public would desire his goods, he would not provide them, etc. This kind of trust is only a weak form of inductive knowledge. But in the case of credit, of trust in someone, there is an additional element which is hard to describe: it is most clearly embodied in religious faith. When someone says that he believes in God, this does not merely express an imperfect stage of knowledge about God, but a state of mind which has nothing to do with knowledge, which is both less and more than knowledge. To 'believe in someone', without adding or even conceiving what it is that one believes about him, is to employ a very subtle and profound idiom. It expresses the feeling that there exists between our idea of a being and the being itself a definite connection and unity, a certain consistency in our conception of it, an assurance and lack of resistance in the surrender of the Ego to this conception, which may rest upon particular reasons, but is not explained by them. Economic credit does contain an element of this supratheoretical belief, and so does the confidence that the community will assure the validity of the tokens for which we have exchanged the products of our labour in an exchange against material goods. This is largely, as I have said, a simple induction, but it contains a further element of social–psychological quasi-religious faith. The feeling of personal security that the possession of money gives is perhaps the most concentrated and pointed form and manifestation of confidence in the socio-political organization and order. The subjectivity of this process is, so to speak, a higher power of the subjectivity that creates the value of precious metals in the first place. The latter is presupposed, but now it has a practical outcome in money transactions through that two-sided faith. This also illustrates that the development from material money to credit money is less radical than appears at first, because credit money has to be interpreted as the evolution, growing independence and isolation of those elements of credit which already exist in fact in material money.

The nature of the economic circle and its significance for money

The guarantee for the continuous usefulness of money, which is the essence of the relation of the contracting parties to the whole social group, has, however, a peculiar form. From an abstract point of view, this guarantee does not exist because the owner of money cannot force anybody to give him something for money, even for money that is indisputably good; this becomes evident in cases of boycott. Only where obligations already exist can the creditor be forced to accept money in settlement of the obligation, and even that is not the case in all legal systems. The possibility that the claim that money represents will not be satisfied confirms the character of money as mere credit; for it is the essence of credit that the probability of realizing it is never one hundred per cent, no matter how closely it may approach it. The individual is free, in fact, to transfer his product or other possessions to the owner of money or to retain them, whereas the community is duty-bound to him. This distribution of freedom and bondage, although paradoxical, frequently serves as a category of knowledge. Thus, the advocates of 'statistical laws' have asserted that society, in given conditions, must produce a definite number of murders, thefts and illegitimate births, but that the individual is not thereby constrained to such behaviour and remains free to act morally or immorally. The statistical law does not determine that a particular individual must commit such acts, but only that the social whole to which he belongs must produce a determinate number. Or we may be told that society or the species as a whole have a determinate role in the divine scheme of the universe, in the evolution of being towards its final transcendental purposes; but that the individual representatives of these purposes are irrelevant, are free to distribute the execution among themselves, and that any particular individual may opt out without impairing the total performance. Finally, it has been asserted that the actions of a group are always strictly determined in the manner of a natural law by the direction of their interests, as material masses are determined by gravitation; but that the individual may be misled by theories and conflicts, that he confronts numerous alternatives among which he may choose rightly or wrongly – in contrast with the actions of the collective entity which have no freedom because they are guided by deviating instincts and purposes. We do not have to investigate here whether these ideas are true or false. I want only to indicate that the model of a relationship between the collective entity and the individual is accepted in many different contexts; the former is conceived as being ruled by necessity, the latter as free; the restraint of the former is moderated by the freedom of the latter, and this freedom itself is limited by the collective restraint and adapted to the necessity of the total result. The guarantee of the general usefulness of money, which the ruler or other representative of the community undertakes by the coinage of metal or the printing of paper, is an acceptance of the overwhelming probability that every individual, in spite of his liberty to refuse the money, will accept it.

These circumstances lead to the conclusion that the currency must be of a higher value the larger the group for which it is supposed to be valid. Within a small local group money of inferior value may circulate. This happens in the most primitive culture: in Darfur, local means of exchange – hoes, tobacco, balls of cotton, etc. – circulated within each district; the better currency – cloth, cows, slaves – was valid for all of them. It may even happen that the paper money issued by a state is restricted to a single province; Turkey issued notes in 1853 that were supposed to be valid only in Constantinople. Very small and closely allied associations occasionally come to an agreement to accept any symbol, even a counter, as money. The spread of trade relations, however, requires a valuable currency, if only because the transportation of money over long distances makes it desirable that the value should be concentrated in a small volume. Thus, the historical empires and the trading states with extensive markets were always driven towards money with a high material value. Some contrary trends prove the same rule. The essential advantage of medieval rights of coinage consisted in the fact that the sovereign was allowed to coin new pennies in his domain at any time and to enforce the exchange of all old coins, or foreign coins, that entered the area as a result of trade, against the new ones; with each debasement of his coins he profited by the difference between the new and the exchanged coin. But this advantage depended upon a large domain, for in small areas the privilege of coinage did not pay because the market for the coins was too small. If the profit from debasement of the coinage had not been contingent upon the size of the area, the chaos of coins in Germany would have been much worse, because of the terrible frivolity with which the privilege of coinage was granted to every monastery and every small town. Just because the socioeconomic structure of a domain required stable money, the profit to be had from an enforced inferior money was considerable. This is illustrated further by the fact that the growth of European trade in the fourteenth century led to the acceptance of the *gulden* as the general unit of coinage, and the replacement of the silver standard by the gold standard. Shillings and pennies, that is the small coins minted by every small state or town for internal transactions, could be as base as desired. The privilege of coinage in the Middle Ages was at first restricted to silver coins; the privilege of minting gold coins needed special permission, which was granted only to the governments of larger territories. It is very characteristic of this relation that the last remnant of the Roman dominion which the Byzantine Court retained until the sixth century, was the exclusive right to mint gold coins. Finally, this relation is confirmed by the following instance. Among the cases of restriction of the circulation of paper money to a particular region within the state that issued it, there is that of France, where at one time paper money was legal tender throughout the country except at the seaports, that is at the points where there was extensive trade. When the scope of trading expands, the currency also has to be made acceptable and tempting to foreigners and to trading partners. The extension of the economic area leads, *ceteris paribus*, to a reduction of direct contact; the reciprocal knowledge of conditions becomes less complete, confidence is more limited, and the possibility of getting claims satisfied is less certain. Under such conditions, no one will supply commodities if the money given in exchange can be used only in the territory of the buyer and is of doubtful value elsewhere. The seller will demand money that is valuable in itself, that is to say accepted everywhere. The increase in the material value of money signifies the extension of the circle of subjects in which it is generally accepted, while in a smaller circle its negotiability may be secured by social, legal and personal guarantees and relationships. If we suppose that the usefulness of money is the reason for its acceptance, its material value may be regarded as a pledge for that usefulness; it may have a zero value if negotiability is assured by other means, and it will be high when the risk is great. However, expanding economic relations eventually produce in the enlarged, and finally international, circle the same features that originally characterized only closed groups; economic and legal conditions overcome the spatial separation more and more, and they come to operate just as reliably, precisely and predictably over a great distance as they did previously in local communities. To the extent that this happens, the pledge, that is the intrinsic value of the money, can be reduced. The view of the advocates of bimetallism, that it would be possibly only on an international scale, conforms with this consideration. Even though we are still far from having a close and reliable interrelationship within or between nations, the trend is undoubtedly in that direction. The association and unification of constantly expanding social groups, supported by laws, customs and interests, is the basis for the diminishing intrinsic value of money and its replacement by functional value.

It is significant that the expansion of trade relations, which originally increased the intrinsic value of the means of exchange, leads, in modern civilization, to its complete elimination by the inter-local and international balancing of accounts through banking operations and bills of exchange. The same development occurs in particular sectors of the use of money. Taxes today are levied principally on income, not on property. A wealthy banker who has incurred losses over the past few years pays no tax in Prussia, except for the small property tax recently introduced. It is not the ownership of money, but the profit from its use, the money yielded by money, that determines tax obligations and, in so far as voting rights depend upon tax liability, also determines rights in the community. A glance at the role of money capital in ancient Rome will reveal the general direction of development. Just as money was acquired by unproductive methods, through war, tribute and money-changing, so also it was lent for consumption, not for production. Thus, interest obviously could not be interpreted as a natural product of capital; and the vague, inorganic relationship between capital and interest that emerged from this situation is reflected in the difficulty of coming to grips with the problem of interest, which persisted far into the Christian era. Only the concept and fact of productive capital eventually provided a practical solution. The earlier situation forms a striking contrast with that of the present time, in which the significance of capital depends not on what it is, but on what it performs. It has changed from a rigid element, estranged from production, to a living function within production.

The guarantee, which is the vital nerve of money, naturally loses some of its force when the objective institution representing the community in fact represents only limited segments of the community and its interests. The private bank, for instance, is a relatively objective supra-personal entity interposed in the exchanges between individual interests. This sociological character enables it to issue money, but if its note issue is not soon transferred to a central institution under state supervision, the limitations of the area that it represents will become apparent in the imperfect 'money' character of its notes. The defects of the North American paper money economy result in part from the view that, while coinage is a state matter, the provision of paper money is a responsibility of the private banks with which the state should not interfere. This view overlooks the fact that the difference between metallic and paper money is only relative; that, as money, each consists merely in the substantiation of the exchange function through a common relation of the interested parties to an objective institution, and that money can perform its function only to the extent that the issuing institution represents and expresses the interests of the whole area. Consequently, local rulers sometimes attempt to give their coins at least the appearance of issuing from a more comprehensive institution. Even centuries after the deaths of Philip and Alexander, coins with their names and seals were minted at a number of places, giving the appearance of being royal coins although they were in fact the coins of particular cities. Progressive development strives in reality for the expansion, and consequently the centralization, of the institutions and powers that guarantee money values. It is a significant feature of this development that the treasury bonds that governments issued before the eighteenth century were the first to create a claim upon state revenues as a whole. In this case, the certainty of payment did not depend upon particular circumstances that had to be investigated, but upon a general confidence in the state's capacity to pay. This illustrates the great centralizing tendency of modern times, which does not at all contradict the trend towards individualization. They form parts of a single process of clearer differentiation and new concentration of the two parts of the personality, one of which is turned towards society and the other towards the self. This development eliminates all individualistic and isolating elements from the nature of money, and makes the centralizing forces of the most inclusive social circle the representatives of money. Personal credit as well as state credit profits by this development in the abstract form of money property. Individual princes had little personal credit in the fifteenth and early sixteenth centuries; it was not their own solvency that was considered, but the value of the guarantees and pledges that they gave. Personal credit is based upon the assumption that the total value of a debtor's property is adequate to cover his debt regardless of the changing composition of his property; only when the total value of an individual's property has been appraised in terms of money will he have permanent credit. Otherwise credit depends on the changing character of his property. Even in the eighteenth century, most debts were expressed as specific quantities of specific coins, and this seems to be a stage of transition to the present time. The concept of abstract value detached from any specific form – value that is no longer guaranteed by an objective quality but only by the state or the individual person – was not yet wholly effective.

The transition to money's general functional character

The main point, however, is that the significance of metal in monetary affairs recedes more and more into the background, as compared with safeguarding the functional value of money through community institutions. For metal is originally always private property, and public interests and public forces can never gain absolute control over it. One might say that money becomes increasingly a public institution in the strict sense of the word; it consists more and more of what public authorities, public institutions and the various forms of intercourse and guarantees of the general public make of money, and the extent to which they legitimize it. It is significant, therefore, that in earlier periods money could not yet be based only on its abstract function: money transactions were tied either to specific enterprises, to the technical production of coins, or to the trade in precious metals. At the beginning of the thirteenth century, the regular business of exchange was carried out in Vienna by the cloth-dyer, in England, and to some extent also in Germany, by the goldsmith. The exchange of coins, which was the core of money transactions in the Middle Ages (because payments everywhere had to be made in local coins), was originally the privilege of the mint itself, of the *Münzer Hausgenossen*. Only later, when the towns acquired the right of coinage, did the business of exchange and the trade in precious metals become separated from the mint. The function of a coin is originally bound to its material in what is almost a personal union; but when a public authority guarantees its value it acquires independence and exchange, and trade in the material from which it is made becomes open to everybody, precisely to the extent that its function as money is assured by the collectivity. The growing depersonalization of money and its closer relationship to a centralized and more extensive community are directly and effectively connected with the accentuation of those functions that are independent of the metallic value. The value of money is based on a guarantee represented by the central political power, which eventually replaces the significance of the metal. There is here an analogy with a neglected aspect of valuation. When the value of an object is due to the fact that it makes possible the acquisition of another object, its value is then determined by two factors: the intrinsic value of the object to be acquired, and the degree of certainty that it can acquire that object. A diminution in one of these factors may leave the total value unaffected, within certain limits, if it is accompanied by an augmentation of the other factor. Thus, for example, the significance of one of our perceptions depends both upon its reliability and upon the importance of what is perceived. In the natural sciences, the factor of reliability tends to be more important, in the social sciences the significance of the object perceived; and thus there may be equality in the value of perceptions in these two fields. Only if we follow Aristotle in not doubting the certainty of knowledge can the value of perception be regarded as depending solely upon the value of the object. The value of a lottery ticket is a product of the probability that it will be drawn and of the size of the possible prize; the value of an action is a product of the probability that its purpose will be accomplished and of the importance of this purpose; the value of a bond is composed of the security of the capital and the rate of interest. Money does not function in exactly the same way, for its growing reliability is not associated with a declining value of the object that it can acquire. But the analogy is still valid in so far as the growing certainty that coin will be accepted at its face value makes possible a diminution in the intrinsic value of the metal content without altering the total value. On the other hand, the causes as well as the effects of the sociological position of money bring about a situation in which the relations between the central power of the group and its individual elements become stronger and closer because the relations among these elements themselves are now channelled through the central power. The Carolingian rulers plainly attempted to replace barter and the exchange of cattle by a money economy. They frequently decreed that coins were not to be rejected and they punished rejection severely. Coinage was exclusively a royal privilege, and the enforcement of money transactions meant an extension of the royal power into areas in which private and personal modes of exchange had previously existed. In the same way, the Roman gold and silver coins after the time of Augustus were minted exclusively in the name and at the command of the emperor, while the right to issue small coins was assigned to the Senate and to local authorities. It is only a generalization of the same trend that great princes often created powerful coinage systems, as did Darius I, Alexander the Great, Augustus, Diocletian and others down to Napoleon I. The whole technique which supports a great social power in a barter economy encourages self-sufficiency and the creation of a state within the state, as happened with the large territorial domains from the time of the Merovingians, whereas the equivalent power institutions in a monetary economy have developed and persisted in alliance with the state organization. The modern centralized state, therefore, came into being partly as a result of the prodigious growth of the money economy which followed the opening up of the gold and silver resources of America. The self-sufficiency of feudalism was destroyed by the fact that every transaction depended upon the use of coins, involving a central power and extending the relationships of the contracting parties beyond the coinage itself, with the result that the power of money to bind the individual more closely to the crown came to be regarded as the deeper meaning of the mercantilist system. The fact that the territorial rulers wrested this means of centralization from the German emperors is considered one of the essential reasons for the breakdown of the German empire; the French and English kings of the thirteenth and fourteenth centuries, on the other hand, established the unity of their states with the aid of this trend towards money transactions. After the Russian empire was already unified, Ivan III gave sovereignty over parts of the country to his younger sons, but he retained for the central power the rights of coinage and the administration of justice. The area of loose trade relations outside political boundaries grows remarkably in extent and consistency once the stability of the official money makes it generally acceptable and thus enables it to draw all parts of the trading area into a closer relationship with the country in which it originates. The rate of exchange of the English sovereign gave considerable prestige to English trade in Portugal and Brazil and made the trade relations with these countries very close. In Germany soon after the Carolingian period the king granted the right of coinage to various individuals and religious establishments, but retained control over the alloy, quality and form of the coins. Before the twelfth century, however, those who had such rights of coinage were allowed to determine for themselves the standard and form of coinage, and were thus able to make as much profit as they wished. The separation of coinage from the central power goes hand in hand with debasement of the currency; the essential function of money declines the less strongly it is guaranteed by the largest sociological group or its central organ. The reverse process illustrates the same point: the debasement of the currency brought about the dissolution and collapse of the largest group, on the unity of which it depended. A purely formal and symbolic relationship may also have contributed to these phenomena. It is one of the essential characteristics of gold and silver that they are relatively indestructible, and since the amount added by mining is insignificant their total quantity remains almost stable over long periods of time. Whereas most other objects are used up, disappear and are replaced in an unending process, money with its almost unlimited durability remains unaffected by this change of individual objects. As a result, it is raised above these objects, just as the objective unity of a social group is raised above the variation of its individual members. It is precisely the characteristic form of life of these reified abstractions of group functions, that they exist outside their embodiment in real individuals, as stable formations amid the transitory individual manifestations, which are, so to speak, integrated into them, formed by them and then released again. Such, for example, is the immortality of a king, which is independent of the accidents of his personality, his particular acts, or the changing fortunes of his society; the well-nigh indestructible coin with his portrait upon it is a symbol and a demonstration of this fact. The business of finance on a large scale began only in the sixteenth century with the business transactions of princes; the intercourse with princes that followed raised the financiers to a position of royal dignity, while trade in commodities came to appear plebeian. The hatred that the socialists have for finance, therefore, may not only be directed against the power of the capitalist over the worker in private enterprise; it may also arise from anti-monarchical instincts, for even though the reification of the social whole, which is a prerequisite of money, need not necessarily take a monarchical form, it is in fact monarchy that has most strongly favoured the intervention of a central power in the economic functioning of the group. Moreover, the fixed residences of princes, which require centralization, are possible only with the emergence of money taxes, for taxes paid in kind cannot be transported and they are appropriate only to a wandering court which consumes them as it goes. It is in the same spirit that modern tax policy tends to leave taxes on real property to local authorities, and to reserve income tax for the state. By focusing the tax demands of the central power upon the money income of the individual, it grasps precisely the kind of property with which it has the closest relation. The development of officialdom, with its close relation to finance, is thus only a symptom of the trend towards centralization. Feudal administration was decentralized, and the interest of the vassal with his distant landed property separated him from the central power, whereas regular money payments draw the officials toward the central power, and continually reaffirm his dependence. At the beginning of the nineteenth century the *Sublime Porte*, as a result of the continuous debasement of the currency, was obliged to mint coins of double weight for the officials and officers, because it was precisely in its relations with state officials that money of full value was needed. The tremendous growth and differentiation of the civil service became possible only through a money economy; it is, however, only one symptom of the relation that exists between money and the objectification of group cohesion in a special central instituion. In Greek culture this relation was represented not by political, but by religious, unity. All Greek money was once sacred; it emanated from the priesthood, as did other generally valid concepts of measure referring to weight, size and time. This priesthood represented at the same time the unity of the various regions. The earliest associations developed on a religious basis, and in some cases they covered relatively large areas. The shrines had a non-particularistic centralizing significance, and money expressed this by bearing the symbol of the common God. The religious social unity, crystallized in the temple, became active again through the money that was put into circulation, and money acquired a basis and a function far beyond the significance of the metal content of the individual coin. Supported by, and supporting, these sociological constellations, the function of money grew in significance at the expense of its substance. A few examples and reflections will make this process clear. Among the many services of money, I will mention here only the facilitation of trade, the stability of the standard of value, the mobilization of values and the acceleration of circulation, and the distillation of values in a concentrated form.

I would like to emphasize, by way of introduction, that the debasement of the coinage by the sovereign (which I discussed earlier) reveals most clearly, through its defrauding of the masses, the significance of the functional value of money in contrast with its value as metal. What motivated the subjects to accept base coin and to give substantially better coin in exchange was the fact that the former fulfilled the exchange purpose of money. The lords of the mint extorted a disproportionately high recompense for the functional value of money; for the sake of which their subjects had to agree to the exchange of coins, that is to sacrifice the value of the metal. But this only exemplifies the very general phenomenon that money, which by its form serves trade better than anything else, is not superior only by virtue of its material, since it can also transcend the significance of its own material, as in the following case. In 1621, when the value of the *reichsthaler* rose from 48 to 54 shillings as a result of the debasement of the currency in Lower Germany, the authorities of Holstein, Pomerania, Lübeck, Hamburg and other areas issued a decree according to which the *reichsthaler* should, from a certain date, be worth only 40 shillings. Although this was generally regarded and accepted as being fair and sensible, the *reichsthaler* continued to be worth 48 shillings because this was more convenient for division and reckoning. At a more advanced and complicated stage, the same thing may happen when bonds are issued in large and small denominations; the stock exchange quotes the latter at a higher price because they are more in demand and serve transactions in small amounts better, although the value pro rata is exactly the same. Indeed, a committee on the currency in the American colonies stated in 1749 that in countries with an undeveloped economy which consume more than they produce, money should always be of lesser value than that of their wealthier neighbours, since otherwise it would inevitably flow out to these countries. This case illustrates in an accentuated way the fact, mentioned previously, that the suitability of a particular form of money for calculation and settling accounts creates a value for this form that is deliberately raised above the actually valid price. The functional value of money has here outgrown its material value to the point of reversing their significance. We may take as examples of the increase in the functional value as compared with the material value those cases in which inferior coins maintain a scarcely credible price in relation to precious metals. This happens for instance in gold mining districts, where the wealth acquired stimulates vigorous trading, but cash is lacking for everyday transactions. Among the gold miners in Brazil a need for small cash developed at the end of the seventeenth century which the King of Portugal exploited by supplying silver money in exchange for tremendous sums in gold. Subsequently, in California and Australia, it also happened that gold miners had to pay between twice and sixteen times the real value in gold in order to acquire small change. The worst phenomena of this kind are shown by the currency conditions that prevailed until recently in Turkey, but that are now being changed. No nickel or copper money existed; all small change consisted of a wretched silver alloy – *altiliks, beschliks* and *metalliques* – the supply of which was totally inadequate. In consequence, the value of these coins, which the government nominally reduced in 1880 by about 50 per cent, has remained unchanged, and the coins are exchanged at parity with gold; the *metalliques*, indeed, which are regarded as one of the worst money tokens in the whole world, sometimes rise above parity with gold. This is extremely characteristic; the smallest coin is the most important for exchange and is valued accordingly, so that these small coins are always the first to be debased. The price of *metalliques* illustrates the paradox that a coin may be more valuable the less valuable it is, because the lack of material value makes it suitable for certain functional purposes by which its value may be increased almost indefinitely.

The objections to a silver standard are based upon the increasing recognition, and the growing role, of the functional significance of money; namely, that convenience in handling is the primary requirement of money. A foodstuff may be retained even though its use is inconvenient, so long as it is nutritious and enjoyable, and an uncomfortable dress may be kept because it is beautiful or warm; but inconvenient money is like unpalatable food or an unbecoming dress, since its main purpose is to provide a convenient means for the exchange of goods. Its difference from other goods arises from the fact that it has, and should have, fewer secondary qualities aside from its principal quality. Because money is an absolute abstraction above all concrete goods, it is encumbered and distorted by every quality outside its original character.

The value of money may be increased or decreased independently of its material value by an expansion or contraction of the function of money, even in the case of its value stability, which is closely connected with its material value. The Roman emperors had the exclusive right to mint gold and silver coins, while copper coins, which were used in everyday transactions, were minted by the Senate or, in the eastern provinces, by the towns. This provided some kind of guarantee that the emperor would not inundate the country with small coins of no substantial value. The final outcome was that the emperors continued their debasement of the silver coinage which led, in due course, to the total collapse of the Roman coinage. This produced a strange reversal of value relationships: as a result of debasement, silver coins became the means for everyday transactions, while copper coins, which had not changed in value, became increasingly the standard of value. The original role of the metals as representatives of money value was reversed by a change in the relative stability of their value. It has been emphasized recently, with reference to the greater importance of stability value as against material value, that a transition from paper currency to the gold standard does not necessarily involve a resumption of gold payments. In a country such as Austria, where the currency notes are at parity with silver, a changeover to the gold standard would bring about the decisive advantage of a stabilization of money value, and would accomplish the vital function of gold without using the material itself. In recent times, the interest in the stability of money value has even led to proposals for abolishing the metal reserve against which notes are issued. So long as such a reserve exists, the various countries belong to a common system which submits domestic transactions in each country to all the fluctuations of political and economic events in all the other countries. Unguaranteed paper money, since it could not be exported, would have the advantage of being available for all kinds of enterprises within the country, and above all of having complete value stability. However much this theory may be open to criticism, the mere suggestion illustrates how the concept of money has been psychologically separated from the concept of a money material and how it is gradually being perfected through the notion of functional services. All these functions of money are obviously subject to the conditions that apply to the general dissolution of money into functions; at any given time they are only partially valid, and the concepts indicate a line of development the goal of which is never reached. The fact that the values that money is supposed to measure, and the mutual relations that it is supposed to express, are purely psychological makes such stability of measurement as exists in the case of space or weight impossible.

The declining significance of money as substance

In practice, the stability of value is accepted as a fact when any question arises concerning the repayment of a money loan after the value of money has changed. If the value of money has declined generally so that the same sum is of lesser value when it is repaid, then the law disregards this fact; the identical sum of money is taken to be of identical value. If the coinage has been debased by alloying or by changing the standard, then the law may decide that the debt shall be repaid according to the new standard, or according to the metal content of the new standard, or simply at its nominal value. Generally speaking, the view prevails that money retains its value unchanged. Such stability is, of course, also a fiction where other objects are concerned and no one doubts that, for example, fifty pounds of potatoes lent in the spring may be worth either more or less when they are later returned in kind. In such a case, however, reference can be made to the direct significance of the object; while the exchange value of potatoes may fluctuate, their value in providing satisfaction and nourishment remains unchanged. Money, however, has no value of this kind, but only exchange value, and the assumption of its value stability is thus all the more striking. Reasons of expediency will tend to ensure that this essential fiction becomes true. I have already indicated that in the case of money which is made from precious metals the connection with jewelry helps to maintain stability of value; as the demand for jewelry is highly elastic, it absorbs a larger quantity of the growing supply of precious metals and thus prevents too great a pressure upon their value, and on the other hand a growing need for money can be satisfied by drawing upon the stock of jewelry, from which the required quantity can be taken and a rise in the price of precious metals avoided. The continuation of this trend seems to imply as its goal the complete elimination of the material basis of money. For even a material as suitable as a precious metal cannot altogether avoid fluctuations that result from particular conditions of demand, production and processing, which have little to do with the fact that the metal also serves as a medium of exchange and as an expression of the relative value of goods. Perfect stability of the value of money could be attained only if it were nothing in itself, but only the pure expression of the value relationship between concrete goods. Money would then reach a neutral position which would be as little affected by the fluctuations in commodities as is the yardstick by the different lengths that it measures. The value of money established by the performance of this service would then also reach its maximum stability, because the relationship of supply and demand could be regulated more easily than when it depends upon a substance the quantity of which we can never fully control. This is not to deny that, under particular historical and psychological conditions, the value of money may be more stable if it is tied to a metal than if it is detached from it – as I observed earlier.

Thus, to return to the analogies used previously, while the deepest and most sublime love may be that between two souls, which excludes all carnal desire, so long as such love is unattainable, the sentiment of love will develop most fully where a spiritual relation is complemented and mediated by a close sensual bond. Paradise may fulfil the promise of eternal bliss under conditions in which the consciousness of bliss no longer requires the contrast of opposite emotions, but, as long as we remain human, positive happiness depends upon the contrast with our other experiences of pain, indifference and depression. Thus, although money with no intrinsic value would be the best means of exchange in an ideal social order, until that point is reached the most satisfactory form of money may be that which is bound to a material substance. This condition does not imply a deviation from the persistent trend towards the transformation of money into a purely symbolic representative of its essential function.

A particular stage in the process of differentiation between the functional and the material value of money is indicated by those cases in which a certain kind of money is used as a standard of value but not for actual payments. Money cannot exercise the function of exchange without, at the same time, measuring values; but the latter function is in certain respects independent of the former. In ancient Egypt prices were determined by the *uten*, a piece of coiled copper wire, but payments were made in all kinds of goods. In the Middle Ages price was often determined in money terms, but the buyer was free to pay in whatever manner was convenient. In many places in Africa at the present day the exchange of goods is carried out according to a monetary standard which is sometimes quite complicated, while money itself for the most part does not even exist. The business of the very important Genoese exchange market in the sixteenth century was based upon the standard of the *scudo de' marchi*. This standard was almost entirely imaginary and did not exist in any actual coinage: 100 of these *scudi* were worth up to 99 of the best gold *scudi*. All obligations were expressed in *scudi de' marchi* and, as a result of its ideal character, this standard of value was absolutely stable, unaffected by the fluctuations and inconsistencies of actual currencies. The East India Company, in order to counteract the debasement, depreciation and counterfeiting of Indian coins, introduced the *rupee current*, a coin that was not minted at all but corresponded to a definite amount of silver, and simply provided a standard by which to measure the value of the actual debased currency. Through the existence of such a stable ideal standard the actual coins also attained a stable relative value. In this way, a state of affairs was very nearly established which a theorist of the early nineteenth century conceived. He regarded all money, whether coined or in other forms, as a claim upon exchangeable goods, and finally arrived at the negation of the reality of money. Money in the strict sense is contrasted with the currency, which is simply the 'claim' expressed in money terms, while money itself is only the ideal standard by which all property values are measured. Here, the principle of the *scudo de' marchi* has become a general theory; money has been idealized to a pure form and a concept of relation, so that it is no longer identical with a tangible reality but relates to the latter as does an abstract law to an empirical case. In the cases cited above, the function of measuring value has been separated from its material representative; the coin used for calculation is deliberately set in opposition to the metal coin, in order to establish its position beyond the sphere of the latter. In this relationship the ideal money fulfils the same purposes as 'good money', which is 'good' only because it is a reliable measure of values.

This leads us to the subject of the representation of money values by equivalents, in so far as this illustrates that one of the essential services performed by money is to make values more mobile. The more the significance of money as a means of exchange, a standard of value and a method of storing value increases in relation to its material value, the more easily it can circulate in the world in a form other than metal. The same development that leads from the rigidity and the substantial determinateness of money to the representation of money occurs also in these representations themselves; for example, in the evolution of the bill payable to the bearer from the promissory note given by one individual to another. The various stages of this development have still to be traced. The stipulation, in the acknowledgment of a debt, that the bearer as well as the original creditor is entitled to collect the money, is found already in the Middle Ages; but its object was to facilitate collection of the debt by a representative of the creditor, not to allow the transfer of the value. This purely formal mobility of paper values was given a more real content in the French *billet en blanc* which was current on the stock exchange in Lyons. It was still worded to refer to an individual creditor, but without specifying his name; only after a name had been inserted in the vacant space was the individual creditor determined. The trade in bills of exchange was first properly established in Antwerp in the sixteenth century. Initially they were often rejected at the due date if they were not accompanied by a note of transfer, and an imperial order had to be issued asserting their general validity. Here we have a very clear succession of stages. The value in question is, at it were, confined between the creditor and the debtor by the individually designated promissory note. It acquires mobility first of all by becoming payable at least to another person, although still on the account of the original creditor, and this process is then extended by postponing but not yet eliminating the designation of an individual creditor, until finally the value becomes completely mobile with the bearer bill, which can change hands like a coin. This appears as the reverse, or the subjective, aspect of the development that we observed in respect of state treasury bonds. Inasmuch as these bonds were ultimately redeemable from general state revenues rather than specific revenues of the crown, they lost their rigidity from the point of view of the debtor; they emerged from their confined sphere into the general movement of the economy and became much more mobile representatives of value because a test of their particular worth was no longer needed.

The general acceleration in the circulation of values also determines the relationship between the material and the function of money. In opposition to a one-sided interpretation of the relation between money and money substitutes it has been asserted that the latter – cheques, bills of exchange, warrants and transfers – do not replace money but only give rise to a more rapid circulation. This function of money representatives is well illustrated by the fact that bank notes change consistently from large and slowly circulating values to smaller values. The Bank of England did not issue notes under £20 before 1759, while the Bank of France issued only 500-franc notes up to 1848. The money substitutes make it possible for the individual to dispense with a large reserve of cash, but the main advantage is that the available money can now be used in other ways, for example by the banks. What is economized is not money itself but its use as a passive reserve of cash. It may be noted more generally that credit and cash do not simply replace each other, but that each produces a more lively activity of the other. At times when there is most cash on the market, credit activities also often expand exuberantly, even to a pathological degree, as in the sixteenth century when large imports of precious metals were associated with a vast and insecure expansion of credit and feverish activity in company-promoting in Germany. The fact that the extent of money and credit increase together shows that they render the same services, and when the functions of one of them are enhanced the other is also provoked into more lively activity. This does not contradict the other relation between money and credit, in which credit makes cash superfluous; we are told, for instance, that there was less cash available in England in 1838 than fifty years earlier in spite of the tremendously increased production, and in France there was less than before the Revolution. This dual relationship between two phenomena, which arise from the same motive, on one side to stimulate each other and on the other side to limit or supplant each other, is easily conceivable and not at all rare. I would remind you that the fundamental emotion of love can manifest itself sensually and spiritually in such a way that these two forms strengthen each other, but also in such a way that the one seeks to eliminate the other; and that very often an interplay between the two possibilities expresses the basic emotion most fully and vividly.

I would remind you also that the diverse activities of the quest for knowledge, whether they incite each other or supplant each other, reveal the same unity in the fundamental interest; and finally, that the political energies of a group become concentrated in divergent parties, according to the nature and the milieu of individuals, yet these parties display their strength not only in the passionate struggle against each other but also in their occasional association for common action in the interest of the group as a whole. The significance of credit, both as inciting a greater circulation of cash and as taking the place of this cash circulation, indicates the unity of the service which these two means of exchange render.

The growth of trade leads to a more rapid circulation of money rather than an increase in the money material. I mentioned earlier that in 1890 the Bank of France put into circulation on current account 135 times as much as the amount deposited with it, while the German Reichsbank circulated 190 times as much as its deposits. It is rarely appreciated how incredibly small is the quantity of material with which money renders its services. The striking phenomenon that money disappears without trace on the outbreak of war or other catastrophes only means that there has been an interruption of its circulation, caused or intensified by the reluctance of individuals to part with their money even momentarily. In normal times the money stock seems to be larger than it actually is, because of the velocity of circulation – just as a glowing spark, rotated quickly in the dark, appears as a glowing circle, but dwindles again to a minute speck of material as soon as the movement ceases. This happens most violently in the case of debased money. For money belongs to that category of phenomena in which normal activity has determinate limits and extent, while any deviation or malfunctioning causes vast and almost inconceivable damage. Typical examples are the powers of fire and water. Good money does not have so many side-effects as does base money, and since its use need not be so strictly regulated or supervised, it can circulate more easily and more smoothly than can bad money. The more precise the form in which money renders its services, the smaller is the quantity of money required and the more easily can its place be taken by a more rapid circulation. The increase in transactions can also be accomplished by diminishing the value of coins instead of augmenting the quantity of tangible money in circulation. The trend of coinage is generally from larger to smaller coins. One characteristic example is the English farthing (equal to 0.12 grammes of silver), which was for a long time the smallest coin; only from 1843 were half-farthings minted. Until that time all values below a farthing were excluded from money transactions, and any exchanges that involved values lying between two whole farthings were rendered difficult. A traveller from Abyssinia reported (1882) that trade was considerably hampered because only one coin, the Maria Theresa Taler of 1780, was accepted, and small coins were practically non-existent. If somebody wanted to buy barley worth half a *taler*, he was obliged to take other goods for the balance of his coin. On the other hand, trade was reported to be particularly easy in Borneo in the 1860s since the value of the *taler* corresponded with approximately 4,000 cowry shells and thus poor people had money for even the smallest quantities of goods. It is true that, as a result of the divisibility of the coin, free assistance was no longer given; the loans and mutual help that are the rule in primitive conditions disappear as soon as a money equivalent is available, and consequently demanded, for even the smallest service. But mutual aid, which is at first a social necessity and later a moral obligation or simple kindness, does not yet signify the possibility of a proper economy, any more than does its opposite, robbery. The offering of gifts develops into an economic system only when trade and its objects become reified. This subjective procedure – the exchange of gifts – is certainly of great value, even economic value, but it sets very narrow limits to the economy, and these can be removed only by measures that destroy the values; one such measure is the introduction of small coins. The dissolution of the substance of money into atoms, so to speak, considerably increases the volume of transactions; and by accelerating the circulation of money it increases, in effect, the quantity of money. In other words, the manner in which money functions can be a substitute for an increase in the quantity of money material.

Finally, some of the effects of money have a sense that is incongruous with the nature of the money material itself. It is one of the functions of money to concentrate, as well as to represent, the economic significance of objects in its own idiom. The unity of the sum of money that is paid for an object incorporates the values of all the elements of its uses, extending perhaps over a long period of time, as well as the particular values of its spatially separate parts and the values of all the powers and substances that prepared, and finally ended in, money. A money price, no matter how many coins it includes, is still a unity. The complete interchangeability of its parts confines the meaning of money exclusively to its quantitative sum, and the parts form a total unity which scarcely exists elsewhere in practical life. If one says of an extremely valuable and complex object, for example a country estate, that it is worth half a million marks, then this sum, however many specific presuppositions and considerations it is based upon, concentrates the value of the property into a unitary concept, in just the same way as when a simple, unitary object is valued in terms of a unitary coin concept, for example that one hour of work is worth one mark. This can only be compared with the unity of a concept that brings together the essential characteristics from a number of individual instances. When I use the general term 'tree', for example, the characteristics that I abstract from very different manifestations in individual trees are not merely assembled side by side but are integrated in a unitary existence. It is the deeper significance of a concept that it is not simply an aggregate of characteristics but an ideal unity in which these characteristics encounter each other and are fused together in spite of their differences; and it is in this fashion that the money price brings together in a concentrated unity the numerous and wide-ranging economic meanings of objects. It may appear that the purely quantitative character of money would make this impossible; that one mark could never form a unity with a second mark, in the way that elements of an organic body or of a social group do, because any mutual relationship would be lacking and would remain always in mere juxtaposition. But this is not so in those cases where the sum of money expresses the value of an object. Half a million marks are, in themselves, only an aggregate of independent units, but as the value of a country estate they are a unitary symbol, the expression or equivalent of its value. They are not a mere aggregate of mark-units any more than a temperature of $20°$ is an aggregate of twenty particular degrees rather than a unitary state of heat. This corresponds with the above-mentioned ability of money to concentrate values. Money is thus one of the great cultural elements whose function it is to assemble great forces at a single point and so to overcome the passive and active opposition to our purposes by this concentration of energies. We should think of the machine in this context, not only for the obvious reason that machinery directs the forces towards our desired ends, but also because every improvement and speeding up of machinery imposes a greater intensity of work upon the worker. This is precisely the reason why progress in technology and the shortening of working time can and must go hand in hand, because the powers of nature and of man serve our purposes in a more concentrated form through improved machinery. We can observe the same cultural tendency at work in the growing pre-eminence of laws of nature in shaping our world view; compared with the preoccupation with individual phenomena, or the fortuitousness and narrowness of crude empiricism, a law of nature represents a tremendous concentration of knowledge, summarizing in a brief formula the characteristics and movements of innumerable instances. Through laws of nature the mind compresses the vast array of spatial and temporal events into an intelligible system which contains, so to speak, the whole world.

In a quite different sphere, the replacement of hand weapons by firearms shows the same form of development; gunpowder provides an enormous concentration of power, which unleashes with a minimum of muscular effort an effect otherwise unattainable. It may also be that the significance and the differentiation of the individual personality in the historical development that takes place through the organizations of the clan, the family and the association are subject to the same principle. The active forces radiate more and more from individualized, externally limited representatives; they appear to be more concentrated than before, and the elements that decide the destiny of a group, that are distributed over the group as long as the individual is closely connected with it, are now concentrated in the individual himself. The right of self-determination of modern man could not have emerged if an increased quantity of means of activity had not been brought together in the narrow form of personal existence. There is no contradiction in asserting that, at the same time, the functions of those earlier close communities have been transferred, for the most part, to a much more extensive association, the State. From the point of view of its actual achievements, the life of the modern state, with its bureaucracy, its powers and its centralization, is much more intensive than that of small primitive communities. The modern state is based upon an extraordinary collectivization, integration and unification of all political forces; compared with the waste of energy in a nation that is subdivided into small-scale autonomous communities, the free and differentiated personality on the one hand and the modern state on the other represent an unrivalled concentration of forces. In this way the energy of society acquires a form that allows a minimum effort to achieve the maximum effect in face of each particular need. It is interesting to note that money not only conforms with this historical trend towards the concentration of forces by expressing the value of things in the most concise and condensed way; but in addition, it confirms this trend by a direct relationship with many of the instances that belong to quite different spheres. For example, in the early stages of firearms money provided the sinews of war (*pecunia nervus belli*); it wrested weapons from the knights and citizens and handed them over to the mercenary, making the possession and use of weapons a privilege of the owner of wealth. It is hardly necessary to demonstrate how closely the origins and progress of machine technology are connected with the monetary system. But I shall show later that the formation of primary groups which liberated the individual and, concurrently, the development of the State, were very closely related to the

The Value of Money as a Substance

emergence of the monetary economy. We can see that the cultural trend towards a concentration of forces has many direct and indirect connections with the money form of values. All the implications of money for other parts of the cultural process result from its essential function of providing the most concise possible expression and the most intense representation of the economic value of things. The conservation and transfer of values have traditionally been regarded as the principal functions of money, but these are only the crude, secondary manifestations of its basic function. This function obviously has no inner relation to the material value of money, and indeed it becomes evident, through this function, that what is essential in money are the ideas incorporated in it, which point far beyond the significance of its material representatives. The greater the role of money becomes in concentrating values – and this occurs not simply through the increase in its quantity, but through an extension of its function to more and more objects and the consolidation of even more diverse values in this form – the less it will need to be tied to a material substance; for the mechanical sameness and rigidity of a substance will become increasingly inadequate compared with the abundance, mutability and variety of values which are projected upon and consolidated in, the concept of money.

This process might be called the growing spiritualization of money, since it is the essence of mental activity to bring unity out of diversity. In the sensible world, things exist side by side; only in the sphere of the mind are they integrated. The elements of a concept form a unity, as do subject and predicate in a proposition; there is no equivalent in the world of directly perceived phenomena. The organism, as the bridge between matter and mind, is the first step towards such an equivalent; interaction merges its elements and it strives constantly for an unattainable perfect unity. Only in the mind, however, does interaction become real integration. The interaction of exchange brings about a mental unity of values. The spatially extended substance is only a symbol of money, because the disconnectedness of what exists as substance contradicts the nature of money as an abstract representation of interaction. Only to the extent that the material element recedes does money become real money, that is a real integration and a point of unification of interacting elements of value, which only the mind can accomplish.

The increasing significance of money as value

If the functions of money can be exercised in part side by side with its material, and in part independently of the quantity of this material, and if therefore the value of money declines, then this does not mean that there is a general decline in the value of money, but only in determinate quantities of it. The two things do not coincide, and it might almost be said that the less valuable any given quantity of money becomes, the more valuable is money generally. For only when money is cheap and any given amount of it less valuable can it have the wide diffusion, rapid circulation and general utility that assure its present role. The same relationship between a particular quantity of money and money in general prevails in the individual mind. It is just the spend-thrifts, who part most easily with money for specific purchases, who are at the same time most dependent on money in general. This is one of the meanings of the saying that one can despise money only if one possesses it in abundance. In peaceful times and places, where the tempo of economical life is slow and money circulates sluggishly, a given quantity of money is valued more highly than it is in the economic jungle of modern urban life. The rapid circulation of money induces habits of spending and acquisition; it makes a specific quantity of money psychologically less significant and valuable, while money in general becomes increasingly important because money matters now affect the individual more vitally than they do in a less agitated style of life. We are confronted here with a very common phenomenon; namely, that the total value of something increases to the same extent as the value of its individual parts declines. For example, the size and significance of a social group often becomes greater the less highly the lives and interests of its individual members are valued; the objective culture, the diversity and liveliness of its content attain their highest point through a division of labour that often condemns the individual representative and participant in this culture to a monotonous specialization, narrowness and stunted growth. The whole becomes more perfect and harmonious, the less the individual is a harmonious being. The same phenomenon appears in impersonal things. The charm and perfection of certain poems consists in the fact that the individual words have no independent meaning; they serve the dominant emotion or the artistic purpose of the whole, and all the varied associations that make up the full meaning of the word are excluded, except for those that bear upon the central theme of the poem. The whole poem is artistically more perfect to the extent that its individual elements lose their meaning. Finally, a more trivial example: the costs of production and the aesthetic value of a mosaic are higher the smaller are the single pieces; the colours of the whole are most striking and most subtle when the single piece occupies a small area and is in itself insignificant.

In the sphere of valuation it is not at all unusual for the values of the whole and the parts to develop in inverse ratio. This is not fortuitous, but expresses a causal connection. The fact that a given quantity of money is less valuable today than it was centuries ago is a direct pre-condition for the enormously increased significance of money in general. This condition itself in turn depends upon the increase in the functional as against the material value of money. It is apparent not only in the case of money in general, but also in various derivative phenomena. For example, the rate of interest was extremely high so long as there were few interest-bearing loans, as a result of the Church's doctrine of usury and the general conditions of a barter economy. The rate of interest declined steadily with the growing importance of interest in economic life.

From a theoretical standpoint it would be a profound mistake to regard the change from substance to function as a process in which money becomes 'value-less', as though it were similar to depriving a man of his soul. This view misses the main point, namely that the functions into which money is dissolved are valuable in themselves, and that the value that money acquires is a supplementary value in the case of metallic money but the sole value in the case of token money. It is unquestionably a real value, like that of the locomotive whose value in providing transportation exceeds the value of the material from which it is constructed. It is true that money is able to function initially because it has intrinsic value, but subsequently it becomes valuable because it exercises these functions. To equate the value of money with the value of its material is like equating the value of a locomotive with the weight of iron that it contains plus the value of the labour employed in its construction. It may appear that this comparison does in fact disprove the assumption that there is a specific value originating from the function. The price of a locomotive (in this context we need not differentiate between value and price) in fact consists of the value of the material plus the value of the labour invested in it. The fact that a locomotive, like money, brings about the exchange of objects is only a reason for it to be valued at all; its actual value does not depend upon this fact. Similarly, the utility of countless other objects is responsible for their having a market price, but the actual level of market prices is determined by many other factors. Utility establishes, at most, a limit beyond which the price cannot rise, but it has no influence upon the actual price level. If this comparison is valid, then the value of money seems to be removed once again from its functions to its material. But the comparison is not valid in one decisive respect. The fact that a locomotive is priced according to the cost of materials and labour results entirely from the fact that anyone may build locomotives, and that consequently the concept itself, without which material and labour would never produce a locomotive, has no influence upon the formation of price. If there were a patent for the construction of locomotives, then its value, in addition to the value of materials and labour, would be reflected in a higher price. As soon as a concept becomes common property, its realizations in practice are no longer 'scarce', and only scarcity can give functional significance a special effect upon price. In the case of money there is something that corresponds with a patent, namely the governmental right of coinage, which forbids the realization of the concept of money by unauthorized persons. The 'scarcity' of money is based upon this governmental monopoly, to a limited extent when it consists of precious metals and totally when it is paper money or coinage. The monopoly of the government is formulated with characteristic rigour in a Chinese law which punishes the counterfeiter who uses genuine precious metals more severely than one who uses inferior materials; the former enters into a more improper competition with the government and infringes its prerogative more profoundly. If everyone were allowed to mint coins their value would indeed decline to the value of the material plus labour, and the advantages of monopoly would be eliminated. Thus, ethnologists have observed that the power position of wealthy men and chiefs is easily undermined when everyone can produce money, as in the case of shell money. Conversely, anyone who possesses money shares to that extent in the privilege of the State to coin money, just as the buyer of a patented object shares in the patent of the inventor. The privilege of the central power to coin money, which guarantees the functioning of money as money, ensures that these functions contribute an additional value to the value of the material and labour embodied in money, or, where the latter values are lacking altogether, endow money with its value. One of the decrees of Roman law is very characteristic in this respect. From the time that minted coins replaced weighed quantities of copper as money, the Roman law insisted that these coins be accepted at their face value, regardless of their material value. This independence from the metal content required a further provision, namely that only these coins should be accepted as money, while all other coins should be treated as mere commodities. Only as a claim for this particular coin can an action for debt be pursued in monetary terms; and all other actions for debts have to be formulated, like commodity debts, in terms of real value, independently of their nominal value as money (*quanti ea res est*). This means that the value of other coins was not monetary but material, because the function of money was reserved for the legal coin. Thus, the legal coin acquired a value which other coins could acquire only through the material of which they were made, and this justified its independence from any intrinsic value. Just as a quart measure has economic value, not because it is the product of material and labour – for if it were not useful for some purpose outside itself no one would want it – but because it is used for measuring, so too money has value because it serves as a means of measurement and in other ways. The fact that this value can itself be expressed only in money makes it less easy to recognize than the value of a quart measure, which can be expressed in terms other than itself. The services of money determine its 'use value', which must find expression in its 'exchange value'; money is one of these objects whose 'utility value', which depends upon the government monopoly of coinage, includes its 'scarcity value' which this monopoly establishes. The theory of money as having a material value is opposed to the general trend of knowledge in which the meaning of things is transposed from their *terminus a quo* to their *terminus ad quem*. Money has value not on account of what it is, but on account of the ends that it serves; and although an original intrinsic value of money made possible its later functions, it acquires its value subsequently from these functions, and gains at a higher level what it had given up at an earlier stage.

In the development that I have outlined, money tends towards a point at which, as a pure symbol, it is completely absorbed by its exchange and measuring functions. There are many parallels in the history of thought. Our original, untutored interest in phenomena usually comprehends them as undifferentiated wholes. They confront us as a unity of form and content, and our valuations are bound to the form because it is the form of this specific content, to the content because it is the content of this specific form. In higher stages of development these elements are separated and the function as pure form is appreciated in specific ways. The diverse contents of these forms are often treated as irrelevant. Thus, for instance, we appreciate the religious mood while being indifferent to the dogmatic content. We consider it valuable that this elevation, striving and appeasement of the soul, which is the universal element in the many different historical creeds, should exist. Similarly, an exhibition of strength often elicits a respect which is denied to its consequences. Thus, a more refined aesthetic interest turns increasingly towards what is pure art in a work of art, to the form of art in the broadest sense, and is increasingly indifferent towards the material of art; that is, towards its theme and towards the feeling that originally inspired it. The sublimation and objectification of such feelings is the aesthetic function in both the production and the consumption of art. In the same way, we value cognition as a formal function of the mind which reflects the external world, regardless of whether the objects and results of cognition are gratifying or distasteful, useful or merely ideal. This differentiation of value feelings has yet another important aspect. The evolution of the modern naturalistic spirit tends to dethrone universal concepts, and to emphasize singular instances as the only legitimate content of conceptions. In theory and in practice, the universal is treated as something purely abstract which acquires meaning only in its material embodiment, that is in tangible instances. In rising above these concrete instances one seems to enter a void. Yet the sense of the significance of universals, which reached its climax with Plato, has not altogether disappeared; and we should attain completely satisfying relation to the world only if every aspect of our world view reconciled the material reality of singular instances with the depth and scope of a formal universality. Historicism and a sociological world view are attempts to confirm universality and yet to deny its abstractness, to transcend the singular instance, to derive the singular from the general without sacrificing its material reality; for society is universal but not abstract. The valuation of functions as distinct from content has its place here. Function is universal in relation to the purpose that it serves. Religious sentiment is a universal by contrast with the content of a particular creed; cognition is universal as against any one of its particular objects; power is universal by contrast with the specific and varied problems to which it is always applied in the same way. All of these are forms and frameworks which comprehend a great variety of material. Money seems to participate in this trend when valuation becomes independent of the material of money and is transferred to its function, which is universal and yet not abstract. The valuation, which at first concerned a particular functioning substance, becomes differentiated, and while the precious metal continues to be valued, its function, which goes beyond the particular substance with which it is associated, attains a specific value of its own. The form in which money exists for us is that of mediating exchanges and measuring values. A metal becomes money by assuming this form, just as ideas about the supernatural become religion when they are incorporated into the function of religious sentiment, and as the block of marble becomes a work of art when artistic creativity endows it with a form that is simply the expression in space of the artistic function. The refinement of the sense of the original dissolves the interfusion of function and allows each to develop as an independent value. It is true that the functional value of money still needs to be represented. The decisive point, however, is that its value no longer arises from what represents it; on the contrary, the latter is quite secondary, and its nature has no importance except on technical grounds which have nothing to do with the sense of value.

CHAPTER 3

Money in the Sequence of Purposes

I

Action towards an end as the conscious interaction between subject and object

The great antinomy in the history of thought – whether the contents of reality are to be conceived and interpreted in terms of their causes or their consequences (i.e. the opposition between a causal and a teleological approach) – finds its original expression in a distinction within our practical motivations. The feeling that we call 'instinct' appears to be tied to a physiological process in which stored up energies strive for release. The instinctual drive terminates when these energies find expression in action. If it is simply an instinct then it is 'satisfied' as soon as it has dissolved into action. In contrast with this direct causal process, which is reflected in consciousness as a primitive instinctual feeling, are those actions that arise, so far as our consciousness is concerned, from a representation of the ends that they will achieve. In this case we experience ourselves as being drawn rather than driven. The feeling of satisfaction, therefore, does not arise from the action alone, but from the consequences that the action produces. If, for instance, an aimless inner unrest drives us to furious activity, then this belongs to the category of instinctual behaviour; if we undertake the same activity in order to attain some precise kind of well-being, then it belongs to the category of purposive behaviour. Eating exclusively to satisfy hunger falls within the first category; eating to enjoy the flavour of the dishes falls within the second. Sexual intercourse as an animal instinct belongs to the first category, but as an activity directed to the attainment of a particular kind of pleasure it belongs to the second. This distinction seems to me vital in two respects. To the extent that our actions are purely instinctual, that is causally determined in the strict sense, there is a fundamental incongruity between the psychological state, which is the cause of action, and the ensuing consequences. The state that moves us to action has no more significant qualitative relation to the action and its result than has the wind to the falling of the fruit that it blows from the trees. On the other hand, when the conception of an end is experienced as a motive, cause and effect are congruous in their conceptual and perceptible content. Nevertheless, in this case too, the cause of action is (even though this cannot be defined in a strictly scientific way) the real force of the conception or of its physical correlate, and this force or energy must be rigorously distinguished from the intellectual content of the conception. The content itself, as an ideal representation of action and events, has absolutely no force; it possesses only conceptual validity and can become real only to the extent that it is endowed with real energy, in the same way as justice and morality, as ideas, have no historical influence until they are adopted as determinants of action by real powers. The controversy over the relevance of causality or teleology to human action may thus be decided in the following way. Since the consequences of action exist in a psychologically effective form before they acquire an objective existence, a strict causal relation can be upheld. Only those intellectual conceptions that have become psychological forces need be taken into account, and thus cause and effect are entirely distinct, whereas the identity between the intellectual content of motive and consequences has absolutely nothing to do with the actual production of events.

Another difference between instinctual drives and purposive striving is still more significant for the present problem. To the extent that our action is simply causally determined (in the strict sense), the whole process comes to an end when the turbulent forces are discharged in activity, and the feelings of tension and constraint disappear as soon as the instinct culminates in action. The instinct consumes itself by its natural continuation in action and the whole process remains confined within the individual. The process that is guided by a conscious purpose is entirely different. It is directed to a definite objective result of action, and it attains its final end through the reaction of this result upon the subject or of the subject upon the result. The fundamental significance of purposive action is the interaction between subject and object. Our mere existence involves us in this interaction, and purposive action is therefore rooted in the nature of the mind. Our relationship to the world may be represented as an arc that passes from the subject to the object, incorporates the object and returns to the subject. It is true that every fortuitous and mechanical contact with things displays the same external character, but as purposive action it is suffused and held together by the unity of our consciousness. As natural beings we are in constant interaction with the world of nature, and co-ordinated with it. It is only in purposive action that the self as personality differentiates itself from the natural elements within and outside itself. Or regarded from another aspect, it is only when a purposive agent is distinguished from the purely causal system of nature that the unity of the two can be re-established at a higher level. This theoretical relationship is to be found, with some modifications, in the difference that is supposed to exist between the labour of civilized and primitive peoples. The former is said to be regular and methodical, the latter irregular and spasmodic; in other words, the former involves deliberate over-coming of our resistance to work, while the latter is only a release of nervous energy.

This does not meant that the real purpose of all purposive action is located in the acting subject, that the reason for attaining an objective always lies in the feelings that are retroactively aroused by the object. This may be the case in egoistic actions proper, but there are innumerable other actions in which the identity of motive and result is concerned only with the result in the sense of attaining the object, with the non-subjective happening. The inner energy which determines our action frequently takes into account consciously only the objec-tive result, and excludes from the teleological process any further retroactive effects upon ourselves. Yet unless the result of our activities ultimately produced an emotion in us, the conception of it would not generate any motive force to bring it into existence. This final link in the chain of action is not, however, its final purpose; our teleologically determined volition ends very often with the objective result and does not consciously inquire beyond this point. Purposive action in contrast to causal–instinctive action (it remains to be seen whether this distinction is, so to speak, only one of approach or method) may be formulated thus: purposive action involves the conscious interweaving of our subjective energies and the objective world, and a double impact of reality upon the subject; first, in an anticipation of the content of reality in terms of subjective intention, and second, in a retroactive effect of the realization of the object in terms of a subjective emotion. The role of purpose in life evolves from these conditions.

It follows from this that so-called unmediated purposes contradict the very concept of purpose. If purpose means a modification within objective being, this modification can be achieved only by an action that transmits the inner accept-ance of the purpose to the realization of the modification. Our actions are the bridge that makes it possible for the content of the purpose to pass from its psychological form to a real form. Purpose is necessarily bound up with its means. It differs in this respect from a mere mechanism and its psychological correlate, instinct – in which the energies of each moment dissolve in the immediate result without pointing to a further stage; the next stage arises only from the immediately preceding one. Purpose has three elements whereas mechanism has only two. On the other hand, purpose also differs, by virtue of its dependence upon means, from what one might call 'divine action'. In the case of a god, it is impossible that there should exist a temporal or material interval between the will and the deed. Human action that is interposed between these two elements is only the vanquishing of obstacles that cannot exist for a god; unless we think of him in terms of terrestrial imperfection, his will must be already the reality of whatever he wills. One may speak of God's final purpose for the world only in a very qualified sense, namely as the ultimate temporal condition that concludes its destiny. If this divine decree were related to the preceding stages as a human purpose is related to its means – namely as the only thing that is valuable and desired – then it would be incomprehensible why God did not bring it about directly, without those useless and retarding intermediate stages; for He does not need the technical means that we, confronted with an autonomous world and possessing only limited strength which must accept compromises, delay and laborious achievement, require. In other words, God can have no purpose because He employs no means.

The varying length of teleological series

This contrast makes clear the specific significance of what was emphasized above, that purposive action is an interaction between the committed self and external nature. The mechanism that exists between the will and its satisfaction constitutes, on the one hand, a bond and, on the other, a separation between them. This mechanism signifies the impossibility for the will to gain satisfaction by itself; it represents the obstacle that the will has to overcome. Purposefulness is essentially a relational concept since it always presupposes something alien to the purpose that has to be transformed. If such a transformation were not necessary, if the will contained its realization within itself, there would be no formation of purposes. Our own action in pursuit of our purposes is the first case in which we become aware of the dual character of the means; in such action we experience both the resistance of external reality and the directing energy which overcomes it, and the two experiences enter into consciousness, each developing its particular character. If our action is unable to produce the object of our purpose immediately, but must first bring about another external event which eventually produces the desired result, then the intermediate happenings have the same quality as our own action; both are mechanisms, but both are also mechanisms that connect mind with mind; both have a continuity in producing the arc of events which begins and ends in the mind. The average number of links in this arc within a given form of life indicates the degree of knowledge and control of nature, as well as the breadth and refinement of the way of life. It is here that social complexities begin which culminate in the creation of money.

The following interconnections are evident: if a purpose D is to be attained and a chain of mechanical processes A, B, C has to be produced so that B is caused by A, C by B and D only by C, then this series, the content and direction of which is determined by D, depends upon the knowledge of the causal relationship between the members. If I did not know that C can produce D, B can produce C and so on, I should be helpless in my desire for D. A teleological chain can never occur unless the causal connections between its elements are known. The purpose repays this service by providing the psychological impulse to seek out causal relations. Thus, the factual and logical possibility of the teleological chain depends upon the causal relation, but the interest of this causal chain, its psychological possibility, arises from the pursuit of an end. This interaction, which expresses in a general sense the relation between theory and practice, results in the fact that the more profound awareness of causality goes hand in hand with a more profound awareness of teleology. The length of the series of purposes depends on the length of the causal series; and on the other hand, the possession of suitable means produces very often not only the realization but also the very idea of a purpose.

In order to understand the significance of this interweaving of natural and mental life, one must bear in mind the apparently obvious fact that we can attain more, and more essential, ends with a long series of means containing numerous elements than with a short series. Primitive man, who has only a limited knowledge of natural causes, is consequently restricted in his purposive action. For him, the arc of purposive action will contain as intermediate links little more than his own physical action and the direct effect that he can have upon a single object. If the expected effect does not follow from this action, then the appeal to a magical authority, who is expected somehow to produce the desired result, will appear less as a prolongation of the teleological series than as a proof that the end is unattainable. Whenever this short series proves inadequate, therefore, the purpose will be abandoned or, more likely, will not be formed at all. The prolongation of the series means that the subject, to an increasing extent, makes the force of the objects themselves work for him. As the most basic needs are satisfied, the more links are needed in the teleological series, and only a very sophisticated knowledge of causation can then succeed in reducing the number of links by discovering more direct connections and shorter paths within the natural order of things. This may lead to a reversal of the natural relationship: in relatively primitive periods, the simple necessities of life are procured by simple series of purposes, while the satisfaction of higher and more differentiated needs require more roundabout methods; but the progress of technology usually provides relatively simple and direct means of production for the latter needs while the provision for the fundamental needs of life encounters growing difficulties which have to be overcome by more complicated means. In short, cultural development tends to prolong the teleological series for what is close to us and to shorten the series for what is remote.

The tool as intensified means

Here, the very important concept of the tool must enter into our consideration of purposive action. The primary form of the teleological sequence is that in which our action produces reactions in an external object, and these reactions, following a course determined by their own nature, culminate in the desired effects. The use of tools involves interposing another factor between the subject and this object, a factor that occupies an intermediate position not only in terms of space and time but also in terms of its content. For on the one hand a tool is a mere object which is mechanically effective, but on the other hand it is also an object that we not merely operate *upon*, but operate *with*, as with our own hands. The tool is an intensified instrument, for its form and existence are predetermined by the end, whereas in the primary teleological process natural objects are only later made to serve our purposes. The person who plants a seed in order to enjoy the fruit of the plant at a later date, instead of being satisfied with wild fruits, acts teleologically, but the purposive action is limited to his hand. If, however, he uses a spade and hoe he removes himself further from the point at which natural processes operate by themselves, and he enhances the subjective factor in relation to the objective factor. By using tools we deliberately add a new link to the chain of purposive action, thus showing that the straight road is not always the shortest. The tool is typical of what we might call our creations in the external world; on the one hand it is formed exclusively by our own powers, and on the other it is devoted entirely to our own purposes. Because the tool is not itself an end it lacks the relative independence that the end implies, either as an absolute value or as something that will produce an effect upon us: it is an absolute means. The principle of the tool is not only effective in the physical world. Where self-interest is not focused directly upon material production, but mental conditions or non-material events are involved, the tool attains a still more refined form, inasmuch as it is now really the creation of our will and does not have to compromise with the attributes of a material substance that is fundamentally alien to purpose. The most typical instances of this kind of tool are perhaps social institutions, by means of which the individual can attain ends for which his personal abilities would never suffice. Membership of a state provides the protection that is a prerequisite for most individual purposive action; but leaving aside this most general aspect, the particular institutions of civil law make possible for the individual achievements that would otherwise be denied to him. In the roundabout legal forms of contract, testament, adoption, etc., the individual possesses a collectively established tool that multiplies his own powers, extends their effectiveness and secures their ends. Fortuitous elements are eliminated and the homogeneity of interests makes possible an increase in the services rendered; from the interaction of individuals there develop objective institutions which become the junction of countless individual teleological sequences and provide an efficient tool for otherwise unattainable purposes. It is the same with religious rites, which are tools of the Church, serving to objectify the typical emotions of the religious community. They are, no doubt, a digression from the ultimate end of religious sentiment, but a digression by means of a tool which, in contrast to all material tools, serves exclusively those ends that the individual is otherwise unable to attain.

Money as the purest example of the tool

Here, finally, we reach the point at which money finds its place in the inter-weaving of purposes. I will begin with some generally accepted facts. All economic transactions rest upon the fact that I want something that someone else owns, and that he will transfer it to me if I give him something I own that he wants. It is obvious that the final link in this two-sided process will not always be present when the first link appears; on many occasions I want the object A which A possesses, but the object or service B which I am willing to give in return does not interest A; or else the goods offered are acceptable to both parties but no agreement can be reached about the respective quantities. Thus, it is of great value in the attainment of our purposes that an intermediate link should be introduced into the chain of purposes; something into which I can change B at any time and which can itself be changed into A – in much the same way as any form of power, from water, wind, etc., can be transformed into another form of power by means of a dynamo. Just as my thoughts must take the form of a universally understood language so that I can attain my practical ends in this roundabout way, so must my activities and possessions take the form of money value in order to serve my more remote purposes. Money is the purest form of the tool, in the category mentioned above; it is an institution through which the individual concentrates his activity and possessions in order to attain goals that he could not attain directly. The fact that everyone works with it makes its character as a tool more evident than was the case in the examples given earlier. The nature and effectiveness of money is not to be found simply in the coin that I hold in my hand; its qualities are invested in the social organizations and the supra-subjective norms that make this coin a tool of endlessly diverse and extensive uses despite its material limitations, its insignificance and rigidity. It is characteristic of the State and of religious rites that, since they are constituted entirely by mental powers and do not have to compromise with any independent material objects, they can express their purpose fully in themselves. Yet they are so close to their specific purposes, indeed almost identical with them, that we often hesitate to recognize that they are tools (which would make them instruments without value in themselves, brought to life only by the will behind them) and regard them as ultimate moral values. In the case of money, its character as an instrument is very rarely obscured. By contrast with the other institutions mentioned earlier, money has no inherent relation to the specific purpose the attainment of which it aids. Money is totally indifferent to the objects because it is separated from them by the fact of exchange. What money mediates is not the possession of an object but the exchange of objects. Money in its perfected forms is an absolute means because, on the one hand, it is completely teleologically determined and is not influenced by any determination from a different series, while on the other hand it is restricted to being a pure means and tool in relation to a given end, has no purpose of its own and functions impartially as an intermediary in the series of purposes. Money is perhaps the clearest expression and demonstration of the fact that man is a 'tool-making' animal, which, however, is itself connected with the fact that man is a 'purposive' animal. The concept of means characterizes the position of man in the world; he is not dependent as is an animal upon the mechanism of instinctual life and immediate volition and enjoyment, nor does he have unmediated power, such as we attribute to a god, such that his will is identical with its realization. He stands between the two in so far as he can extend his will far beyond the present moment, but can realize it only in a roundabout way through a teleological series which has several links. Love, which according to Plato is an intermediate stage between possessing and not-possessing, is in the inner subjective life what means are in the objective external world. For man, who is always striving, never satisfied, always becoming, love is the true human condition. Means, on the other hand, and their enhanced form, the tool, symbolize the human genus. The tool illustrates or incorporates the grandeur of the human will, and at the same time its limitations. The practical necessity to introduce a series of intermediate steps between ourselves and our ends has perhaps given rise to the concept of the past, and so has endowed man with his specific sense of life, of its extent and its limits, as a watershed between past and future. Money is the purest reification of means, a concrete instrument which is absolutely identical with its abstract concept; it is a pure instrument. The tremendous importance of money for understanding the basic motives of life lies in the fact that money embodies and sublimates the practical relation of man to the objects of his will, his power and his impotence; one might say, paradoxically, that man is an indirect being. I am here concerned with the relation of money to the totality of human life only in so far as it illuminates our immediate problem, which is to comprehend the nature of money through the internal and external relationships that find their expression, their means or their effects in money. I shall add here to the functions previously discussed one that shows with particular clarity how the abstract character of money is transposed into practical reality.

Money in the Sequence of Purposes

The unlimited possibilities for the utilization of money

I noted earlier that the representation and provision of means does not always depend upon an already formed purpose; the availability of materials and forces often provokes us to form certain purposes which these means will enable us to attain. Once a purpose has engendered the idea of means, the means may produce the conception of a purpose. This relationship, frequently modified but enduring, may be seen in the case of tools, which I characterized as the purest kind of means. While ordinary, simple means are entirely used up in achieving the purpose, a tool continues to exist apart from its particular application and is capable of a variety of other uses that cannot be foreseen. This is true not only for thousands of cases in daily life that need not be exemplified, but also in much more complicated situations. How often are military organizations, which were intended for external deployment, used by a dynasty for internal political ends? How often does a relationship among individuals which was originally established for a particular purpose grow beyond this and become the bearer of altogether different contents, with the result that one may say of all enduring human associations – familial, economic, religious, political or social – that they have a tendency to acquire purposes for which they were not originally conceived? It is obvious that a tool will be more significant and valuable – *ceteris paribus* – if it has various and extensive uses. At the same time, it must then become more neutral and colourless, more objective in relation to particular interests and more remote from any specific purpose. Money as the means *par excellence* fulfils this condition perfectly; from this point of view its importance is enhanced. The matter can be put as follows. The value of a given quantity of money exceeds the value of the particular object for which it is exchanged, because it makes possible the choice of any other object in an unlimited area. Of course, the money can be used ultimately only for one of the objects, but the choice that it offers is a bonus which increases its value. Since money is not related at all to a specific purpose, it acquires a relation to the totality of purposes. Money is the tool that has the greatest possible number of unpredictable uses and so possesses the maximum value attainable in this respect. The mere possibility of unlimited uses that money has, or represents, on account of its lack of any content of its own, is manifested in a positive way by the restlessness of money, by its urge to be used, so to speak. As in the case of languages such as French, which have a limited vocabulary, the need to employ the same expression for different things makes possible a wealth of allusions, references and psychological overtones, and one might almost say that their wealth results from their poverty; so the absence of any inner significance of money engenders the abundance of its practical uses, and indeed provides the impulse to fill its infinite conceptual categories with new formations, to give new content to its form, because it is never a conclusion but only a transitional point for each content. In the last analysis, the whole vast range of commodities can only be exchanged for one value, namely money; but money can be exchanged for any one of the range of commodities. By contrast with labour, which can rarely change its application, and the less easily the more specialized it is, capital in the form of money can almost always be transferred from one use to another, at worst with a loss, but often with a gain. The worker can hardly ever extricate his art and skill from his trade and invest it somewhere else. By comparison with the owner of money he is at a disadvantage so far as free choice is concerned, just as the merchant is. Thus, the value of a given amount of money is equal to the value of any object for which it might be exchanged plus the value of free choice between innumerable other objects, and this is an asset that has no analogy in the area of commodities or labour.

This surplus value of money appears all the more important if one considers the nature of the decision to which this power of choice leads in reality. It has been asserted that a commodity that is limited in quantity and has alternative uses will be valued by its owners with respect to its most important use; all other uses will appear uneconomic and unreasonable. On the other hand, a supply of goods that is sufficient or more than sufficient for all possible uses, so that the goods compete to be used, will be valued according to its least important use. The most important use becomes the measure of the object if there are competing uses. This is most fully and effectively demonstrated by money. Since money can be used for any economic purpose, a given amount of it can be used to satisfy the most important subjective need for the moment. The choice is not limited, as is the case with all other commodities, and, because human desires know no limit, a great variety of possible uses is always competing for any given quantity of money. Since the decision will always be in favour of the good that is desired most intensely, money must be valued at any moment as equivalent to the most important interest experienced at that moment. A supply of wood or a building plot that is adequate only for one of several desired uses, and which is therefore valued according to the most valuable of those uses, cannot have a significance beyond the region of things of its own kind. Money, however, has no such limitation, and so its value corresponds with the most important universal interest of the individual that can be satisfied with the available supply.

The opportunity of choice which money as an abstract instrument provides applies not only to the goods offered at any one time, but also to the date when it can be used. The value of a commodity is not determined simply by its practical significance at the moment of its use. The relative freedom of choice in timing the use is a factor that can increase or diminish considerably the value placed upon the commodity. The first of these possibilities of choice results from the coexistence of different uses, the second from the existence of alternative uses over time. Other things being equal, that commodity is more valuable which I *can* but do not *have to* use immediately. The range of commodities falls into a graduated series of values between two extremes: at one end is the commodity that can be enjoyed later but not now. If, for example, fish caught during the summer is exchanged for furs that are going to be worn in the winter, then the value of the fish is increased by the fact that I can consume it immediately, whereas the value of the furs is affected by the fact that the delay in using them involves the risk of damage, loss or devaluation. On the other hand, the value of the fish is diminished because it will no longer be fresh tomorrow, and the value of the furs is increased because they will still be serviceable at a later date. An object used as a means of exchange is most suitable for money, if it possesses both of these value-enhancing qualities. Money as a pure instrument represents their highest possible synthesis because it has no specific quality for a specific use, but is only a tool for acquiring concrete values, and because the opportunities for using it are just as great at any point of time and for any object.

The superiority of the owner of money over the owner of commodities results from this unique quality of money as being unrelated to all particular characteristics of things or moments of time, dissociated from any purpose, and a purely abstract means. There are some exceptions to this, such as the refusal to sell on ideological grounds, boycotts and cartels, but these arise only when the objects of exchange in that particular situation cannot be replaced by other objects. The freedom of choice and also the particular advantage that money confers upon its owner are then eliminated precisely because there is a single object of desire instead of a choice. In general, the owner of money enjoys this twofold liberty and he will demand a recompense if he relinquishes it in favour of the owner of goods. This is shown, for example, by the economically and psychologically interesting principle of the 'supplement'. When goods that can be measured or weighed are purchased the merchant is expected to 'measure liberally', that is to add at least one additional unit, and he usually does so. It must be taken into account that a mistake is more likely in measuring goods than in counting money, but the important feature is that the buyer has the power to enforce an interpretation of this possibility in his own favour even though the chances of advantage or disadvantage are equal for both parties. It is significant that the advantage is given to the buyer even when the other party is also dealing in money. The customer expects the banker, the insured expects the insurance company in case of a claim, to deal 'fairly', that is to give a little more, even if only in a formal way, than what is enforceable by law. The bank and the insurance company also trade only in money, but the customer for his part does not think of being 'fair' or 'liberal'; he only offers what has been agreed upon beforehand. The sums of money offered on each side have in fact quite a different significance. For the banker and the insurance company the money with which they operate is simply a commodity that they can use only in this particular way; for the customer it is 'money' in the sense with which we are here concerned, namely a value that he can, but need not necessarily, use for stock exchange business or insurance. The freedom to use the money for diverse purposes gives the customer an advantage which is compensated by the 'fairness' of the other party. Where a supplement is given by the owner of money, as in tipping waiters and taxi-drivers, this merely expresses the social superiority of the giver, which is the presupposition of tipping. Like all other monetary phenomena these are not occurrences isolated from the rest of human life; they display in a particularly clear and obvious manner a fundamental characteristic of life, namely that in every relationship the individual who has less interest in the substance of the relationship is at an advantage. This may appear paradoxical, since the more intense the desire to possess something or to establish a relationship, the more intense and passionate is the enjoyment of it. It is indeed the anticipated enjoyment that determines the strength of our desire. Yet it is just this situation that gives an advantage to the less interested party, for it is in the nature of things that the one who benefits less should be compensated by some concessions from the other party. This is apparent even in the most refined and intimate relations. In every love relationship, the one who is less involved has an advantage, because the other renounces from the very beginning any exploitation of the relationship, is more ready to make sacrifices, and offers a greater measure of devotion in exchange for the greater satisfaction that he derives. Equity is thus established: since the degree of desire corresponds with the degree of enjoyment it is right that the relationship should provide the individual who is less involved with a special gain, which he is able to exact because he is more hesitant, more reserved and more ready to make conditions. Thus the profit of the one who gives money is not altogether unfair; since he is usually less interested in the commodity – money transaction, an agreement between the two parties is brought about by the one who is more interested in the transaction giving to the other a gain over and above the objective equivalence of the exchange values. It should also be borne in mind that the owner of money has this advantage not because he possesses money, but because he is prepared to part with it.

The profit that accrues to money because it is detached from any particular content or process of the economy is also shown in other ways, and particularly in the fact that owners of money usually profit from violent and ruinous economic upheavals, often to an extraordinary extent. However many bankruptcies and business failures result from price slumps or from commodity market booms, experience has shown that the big bankers usually make a steady profit out of these dangers that confront sellers and buyers, creditors and debtors. The services of money, as the neutral tool of economic processes, have to be paid for regardless of the direction or pace of these processes. Of course, money has to pay something for this freedom; the uncommitted nature of money means that contradictory demands are made upon the dispenser of money from different sides, and that he excites the suspicion of betrayal more easily than does the individual who deals in specific commodities. In early modern times, when the great financial powers – the Fuggers, the Welsers, the Florentine and Genoan bankers – entered the political arena, particularly during the great struggle between the Habsburgs and the French monarchy for European hegemony, they were regarded with permanent mistrust by all parties, including those to whom they had lent vast sums of money. One never could be sure of the financiers, whose money transactions did not commit them beyond the present moment; and even the enemy against whom they had lent their financial support did not regard this as an obstacle to approaching them himself with requests and propositions. Money has the very positive quality that is designated by the negative concept of lack of character. The individual whom we regard as a weak character is not directed by the inner worth of persons, things or thoughts, but by the external pressure that is brought to bear upon him. The fact that money is detached from all specific contents and exists only as a quantity earns for money and for those people who are only interested in money the quality of characterlessness. This is the almost logically necessary reverse side of the advantages of finance and of the over-valuation of money in relation to qualitative values. The superiority of money is expressed first in the fact that the seller is more interested and eager than the buyer. A very significant feature of our whole attitude towards objects is involved here; namely, when two opposing classes of values are considered as a whole, the first class may be distinctly superior to the second, while the individual objects or representatives of the second group may be superior to those of the first. Faced with a choice between the totality of material goods and the totality of ideal goods, we should probably be obliged to choose the first, because to renounce it would be to negate life, including all its ideal contents; but on the other hand, we might not hesitate to give up any single material good in exchange for an ideal good. In our relations with other people we do not question that one relationship is much more valuable and indispensable than another, when viewed as a whole; but on particular occasions and in particular aspects the less valuable relationship may be more enjoyable and attractive. This is how matters stand in the relation between money and concrete objects of value; a choice between the objects as a whole and money as a whole would immediately reveal the intrinsic valuelessness of the latter, which provides us only with means, not with an end. Yet when a given sum of money is set against a given quantity of commodities, the exchange of the latter for the former is usually demanded much more strongly than vice-versa. This relationship exists not only between commodities and money in general, but also between money and particular categories of commodities. A single pin is almost worthless, but pins in general are almost indispensable and 'worth their weight in gold'. The case is similar with many kinds of commodities; the ease with which a single specimen can be supplied in return for money devalues it in relation to money, which now appears as a ruling power disposing over the object. But the significance of the class of object as a whole seems incommensurable with money; it has a value independent of money which is often concealed from our notice by the fact that the single specimen can so easily be replaced. However, since our practical economic interests are almost exclusively concerned with single units or with a limited number of units, our sense of the value of objects generally employs the measuring rod of money. This is evidently connected with the overriding interest in possessing money rather than commodities.

The unearned increment of wealth

This leads to a more general phenomenon, which might be termed the surplus value of wealth and which resembles the unearned rent of land. The wealthy man enjoys advantages beyond the enjoyment of what he can buy with his money. The merchant supplies him more reliably and more cheaply than he does poorer people; everyone he meets, whether likely to profit from his wealth or not, is more deferential; he moves in an ideal atmosphere of unquestioned privilege. One can observe everywhere all manner of small privileges being granted to the purchaser of expensive goods and to the first-class traveller; privileges that have as little connection with the objective value as has the friendly smile of the merchant with the more expensive goods that he is selling. These privileges are a gratuitous supplement, and their most painful feature is perhaps that the consumer of cheaper goods, who is denied them, cannot complain that he is being cheated. This can be best illustrated by a very minor instance. The streetcars in some cities have two separate classes which differ in price, although the more expensive class offers no material advantage in the way of greater comfort. What the traveller buys with his first-class ticket is the right to join the exclusive company of those who pay such a higher price in order to be separated from the second-class passengers. Thus the well-to-do individual can acquire an advantage simply by spending more money, without necessarily receiving a material equivalent for his expenditure.

Viewed from the outside, it may seem that this is the opposite of an unearned increment, because the well-to-do individual receives relatively less, not relatively more, for his money. But the unearned increment of wealth appears here in a negative, but pure, form; the rich man gains an advantage without recourse to an object and exclusively by virtue of the fact that other people cannot spend as much money as he can. Wealth, indeed, is often regarded as a kind of moral merit, as is indicated by the term 'respectability' and by popular references to the well-to-do as 'upright citizens' or 'the better-class public'. The same phenomenon is shown from the other side by the fact that the poor are treated as if they were guilty, that beggars are angrily driven away, and that even good-natured people consider themselves naturally superior to the poor. When it was decreed in 1536 that the journeyman locksmiths in Strasbourg who earned more than eight *kreuzer* should have a holiday on Monday afternoons, a bonus was given to those who were better off, when moral logic suggests that it should have been given to the needy. It is not uncommon for the unearned increment of wealth to attain such a degree of perversity: practical idealism, when it is manifested in the unpaid scientific work of a wealthy man, is generally more highly esteemed than is the work of a poor schoolteacher. This usurious interest upon wealth, these advantages that its possessor gains without being obliged to give anything in return, are bound up with the money form of value. For those phenomena obviously express or reflect that unlimited freedom of use which distinguishes money from all other values. This it is that creates the state of affairs in which a rich man has an influence not only by what he does but also by what he could do; a great fortune is encircled by innumerable possibilities of use, as though by an astral body, which extend far beyond the employment of the income from it on the benefits which the income brings to other people. The German language indicates this by the use of the word *Vermögen*, which means 'to be able to do something', for a great fortune. These possibilities, only a small number of which can be realized, are nevertheless put to account psychologically. They convey the impression of an indeterminate power which is not confined to the achievement of a particular result, and this impression is all the stronger the more mobile and more easily available for any purpose the possessions are; that is to say, the more the fortune consists of money or is convertible to money, and the more distinctly money itself has become a tool and a point of transition without any purpose of its own. The pure potentiality of money as a means is distilled in a general conception of power and significance which becomes effective as real power and significance for the owner of money. It is like the attraction of a work of art, which is produced not only by its content and the associated psychological reactions, but by all the accidental, individual and indirect complexes of feeling that it makes possible. Only the indeterminate sum of these feelings circumscribes the whole value and significance of a work of art.

The difference between the same amount of money as part of a large and of a small fortune

If this interpretation of the unearned increment of wealth is correct, then the increment will be greater when the circumstances of the owner provide better opportunities and more freedom to use it. A poor man has the fewest opportunities, because his money income is adequate only for the basic needs of life and allows almost no latitude in the choice of uses. This latitude increases with increasing income, and each unit of the growing income becomes more valuable to the extent that it differs from those units that are necessary for the satisfaction of basic and predetermined needs; that is, each additional unit of income includes a larger proportion of unearned increment, though of course this is only the case up to a relatively high level of income, beyond which each unit of income is equal in this respect. Here the phenomenon we are considering can be seen in a particular context, and in a way that seems to me especially fruitful. Many commodities are available in such abundance that they cannot all be consumed by the well-to-do members of society and they have to be offered to the poorer strata of society if they are to be sold at all. The prices of such goods cannot be higher than these strata are able to afford. One might refer to this as 'the law of consumer's price limitation', according to which the price of a commodity can never exceed the amount that the social strata to whom the available supply must be offered is able to pay. This may be interpreted as an application of marginal utility theory to the social scene; instead of the least urgent need that can still be satisfied by a commodity, it is the need of those with the least ability to pay that becomes decisive for price formation. This phenomenon involves a tremendous advantage for the well-to-do, since the indispensable goods are now available to him at a much lower price than he would be willing to pay if necessary. Because the poor man has to buy the simple necessities of life he makes them cheap for the wealthy man. Even if the latter had to spend the same proportion of his income as the poor man for his basic needs (food, shelter and clothing), he would still have more money left for luxuries. Instead, he has the additional advantage that he can satisfy his basic needs with a relatively smaller part of his income, and with the remaining part he has freedom of choice in the use of his money, which makes him an object of respect and deference beyond his actual economic income. The pecuniary resources of the poor are not surrounded by this sphere of unlimited possibilities, because they immediately and undoubtedly terminate in very definite purposes. For the poor, these resources are not simply 'means' at their disposal in the same pure and abstract sense as they are for the rich, because the purpose is already embedded in them and colours and directs them. The German language very subtly terms those who own a considerable amount of money *bemittelt*, that is, equipped with means. The freedom associated with such resources leads to yet another unearned increment. Wherever public functionaries are unpaid, it is only well-to-do people who are able to hold the leading positions. The general of the Achaean League, just as much as the English member of Parliament – at least until recently – had to be well off. For this reason, in countries that paid their officials very little, a complete plutocracy, a form of hereditary concentration of high officials in a few families, often developed. Whereas it seems that unsalaried positions separate money interests from the interest in service, the positions of officials, with all the honour, power and opportunities associated with them, become an annex of wealth. It is obvious that this situation is best served by the money form of wealth because its teleological indifference allows the personage completely free disposal of his time, his place of residence and the direction of his activities. The honours acquired by wealth and the moral esteem that it enjoys is condensed, through the unsalaried official functions, to a centre of power in leading offices that is unattainable to the poor. This is, in turn, related to a further unearned increment, associated with the fame of service to one's country, which, though often quite deserved, is granted on other than ethical grounds, namely on the purely technical grounds of mere money ownership. We observe the same situation at a higher level, when, at the end of the Middle Ages in Lübeck, wealthy people liked to join several fraternities to make their salvation more secure. The technical means for the attainment of religious blessing in the medieval Church were often such that only the wealthy could use them. Aside from their transcendental purpose, and as an unearned discount, they brought with them a certain amount of worldly prestige and advantage such as the membership in several fraternities. At the psychological level, the overstepping of the property boundary outlined above produces the following unearned increment: the question of how much a desired object costs in many cases plays no role at all for those who are extremely wealthy. This means much more than is usually associated with this everyday expression. As long as the income is tied to definite purposes, every expenditure is unavoidably burdened with the thought of the required costs; for the majority of people the question of 'How much?' stands between a desire and its satisfaction. It implies a certain materialization of things that does not exist for the real financial aristocrat. Whoever owns money beyond a certain level thereby gains the additional advantage of being allowed to be contemptuous of it. The way of life that does not have to consider the money value of things has an extraordinary aesthetic charm. The acquisition of things can be determined exclusively by objective points of view, dependent only on the content and the significance of the objects. Although the domination of money may depreciate the specific qualities of things and the awareness of them in so many respects, there are undeniably other phenomena that money enhances. The qualities of objects have at least the psychological chance, even though rarely realized, to be more in evidence, if what they have in common – economic value – is projected on to and localized in another form which lies outside them. Every way of life that does not have to take money into account avoids the distractions and shadows that arise for the purely objective quality and valuation of things through which these internally completely alien relations arrive at their money price. Wherever the less well-to-do person is able to purchase the same object as the very rich person, the latter enjoys the psychological unearned increment of ease and directness. Unlike the less prosperous person, the very rich person is not distracted in his acquisition and enjoyment by the problem of sacrificing money. In a contrary manner, we shall see later that the blasé attitude deadens the particularity and specific charms of things and reduces them to shadows of monetary wealth. Yet far from disproving the other relation, it merely illustrates the essential qualities of money: through its distancing from every specific determination, money is able to take up the threads of internal and external life that run in completely opposite directions and to act as a tool of decisive cultural and representational importance for any one of them. This is the incomparable significance of money for the evolutionary process of the practical mind; it achieves the utmost reduction of the specific qualities and the one-sided character of all empirical forms. What one might term the tragedy of human concept formation lies in the fact that the higher concept, which through its breadth embraces a growing number of details, must count upon increasing loss of content. Money is the perfect practical counterpart of such a higher category, namely a form of being whose qualities are generality and lack of content; a form of being that endows these qualities with real power and whose relation to all the contrary qualities of the objects transacted and to their psychological constellations can be equally interpreted as service and as domination.

The unearned increment of the ownership of money is nothing but a single instance of what one might call the metaphysical quality of money; namely, to extend beyond every particular use and, since it is the ultimate means, to realize the possibility of all values as the value of all possibilities.

Money's congruence with those who are marginal

I wish to extract from the sphere of activity of these relations a second series of relations. The importance of money as a means, independent of all specific ends, results in the fact that money becomes the centre of interest and the proper domain of individuals and classes who, because of their social position, are excluded from many kinds of personal and specific goals. The emancipated Roman slaves were predisposed towards monetary transactions because they lacked any chance of achieving complete citizen status. Already in Athens, at the very inception of pure monetary transactions in the fourth century, the wealthiest banker, Pasion, had started his career as a slave. In Turkey the Armenians, a despised and often persecuted people, are frequently merchants and money-lenders, as, under similar circumstances, were the Moors in Spain. In India these circumstances are a frequent occurrence. On the one hand, the socially oppressed and yet cautiously advancing Parsee are mostly money-changers or bankers, while on the other hand in some parts of southern India, money business and wealth are in the hands of the Chetty, a mixed caste, who, because of imperfect caste purity, have very little prestige. Similarly, the Huguenots in

France, like the Quakers in England, applied themselves with the greatest intensity to money acquisition because of their exposed and restricted position. To exclude someone in principle from the acquisition of money is almost impossible because all possible paths constantly lead to it. Money transactions require less technical training than any other trade and therefore more easily evade control and interference; in addition, people who require money are usually in desperate need and are willing both to contact people who would normally be despised and to go to normally shunned hiding places. Because the outlawed cannot be kept away from the sphere of pure money interests, there develops an association between these two factors operating in different directions: on the one hand, the person dealing merely with money is threatened with becoming socially *déclassé*, which usually he can escape only through his power and indispensability, and on the other hand the vagabonds of the Middle Ages, who were in other respects legally discriminated against, were treated impartially before the law in money matters. The same result will occur if the exclusion of social groups from the full rights and benefits of citizenship is enforced not through legal or otherwise imposed regulations, but through voluntary renunciation itself. After the Quakers had already attained full political equality, they themselves rejected the interests of others: they did not take an oath and therefore could not accept a public office; they refused everything that was associated with the adornment of life, even sport; they even had to give up farming because they did not want to pay tithe. Thus, in order to retain an external life interest, they were directed towards money as the sole interest in life to which they had access. In the same way, it has been pointed out that in the Herrenhuter community its members lack all interest in the sciences, the arts and cheerful sociability and that, aside from religious interest, only naked acquisitiveness as a practical impulse remains. The industry and greed of many Herrenhuter and pietists was not, therefore, a symptom of hypocrisy but of a degenerate christendom, decaying cultural interests and of a piety that does not tolerate the superior values of this world, but only those associated with the baseness of the world. Indeed, even at the opposite levels of the social scale, it is ominous that the interest in money remains the last, the most dogged and persistent interest after all others are gone. The French aristocracy of the *ancien régime* withdrew from its social obligations because of the growing centralization of the State which had taken over the administration of the rural areas. Since the State had taken away all tangible and valuable functions of domination from the aristocracy, land ownership lost all significance save as a basis for making money. This was the last remaining point of interest, and everything that formerly had been a living bond between aristocrat and peasant was now reduced to money interests. Whereas money transaction becomes the *ultima ratio* of the socially disadvantaged and suppressed elements, the power of money contributes positively to the attainment of positions, influence and enjoyments wherever people are excluded from achieving, by certain direct means, social rank and fulfilment as officials or in professions from which they are barred. Because money is indeed a mere means, though on an absolute scale, and since money lacks all particularity derived from whatever actual determinations, it is the unconditional *terminus a quo* to everything, as well as the unconditional *terminus ad quem* from everywhere. Therefore, equivalent circumstances emerge where sections of groups are not excluded from the sequence of purposes, and the identical teleological formation is valid for the whole group. The Spartans, to whom the pursuit of any economic interest was strictly forbidden, are reported to have been very greedy. It seems that the passion for possessions, whose distribution had been impractically systematized by the Lycian constitution, burst out precisely where ownership possessed the least specific character and where restrictions were least able to be imposed. It has also been mentioned that over a long period in Sparta there was no difference between the poor and the wealthy with regard to the practical enjoyment of possessions, and that the wealthy did not live any better than did the poor. Thus, acquisitiveness had to focus all the more on the possession of money. The same state of affairs came about when, as one of the Ephoros – the Spartan magistrates – reports, Aegina became a similar major trading place because the poor quality of the soil suggested trade to the inhabitants – and Aegina was the first place in Greece proper where coins were minted! Because money is the common point of intersection of the sequence of purposes that stretches from every point of the economic world to every other, it is accepted by everyone from everyone. At the time when the curse of 'dishonesty' weighed most heavily on certain occupations, people still accepted money from the hangman even though they were looking for an honest person to handle it first. Aware of this overriding power of money, Macaulay defended the emancipation of the Jews on the grounds that it would be nonsense to withhold political rights from them, because money already gave them the substance of power. They could buy voters or control kings; as creditors they could dominate their debtors, so that political rights would be nothing but the formal acknowledgment of what they already possessed. In order to really deprive them of their political rights one would have to kill them and rob them; if they kept their money – 'so we may take away the shadow, but we must leave them the substance', a very characteristic expression for the teleological inversion of the concept of money – then, in purely factual terms, one would certainly be inclined to characterize social, political and personal positions as possessing a real and substantial value while money – in itself the empty symbolization of other values – would be seen as a mere shadow!

There is no need to emphasize that the Jews are the best example of the correlation between the central role of money interests and social deprivation. I only want to mention two viewpoints as particularly important for the basic significance of money. Because the wealth of the Jews consisted of money, they became a particularly sought-after and profitable object of exploitation, for no other possessions can be expropriated as easily, simply and without loss. Just as one can rank economic goods in the light of their acquisition through labour on a scale of greater or less utility, so one can do the same for their acquisition by robbery. If one deprives somebody of his land, it is impossible – except by turning it into cash – to realize the benefit right away, since time, effort and expenses are required. Personal effects are naturally more practical to cope with, although here too differences exist: in medieval England, for instance, wool was most useful in this respect, since it was a sort of circulating medium used by Parliament to grant taxes to the king and used by the king to squeeze money from the merchants. Money is the extreme point of this scale. The same specific character of money as lacking in any specific determinacy which made it the most suitable and the least refusable source of income for the Jews in their position as pariahs, also made it the most convenient and direct incentive for exploiting them. If, with regard to the medieval pogroms, we are informed that in some cities the persecution was directed against the wealthy while in others against the poor Jews, then this is surely no counter-evidence, but is rather the other side to the growing power of money.

The relationship of Jews to money in general is more evident in a sociological constellation that gives expression to that character of money. The role that the stranger plays within a social group directs him, from the outset, towards relations with the group that are mediated by money, above all because of the transportability and the extensive usefulness of money outside the boundaries of the group. The relation between the nature of money and the stranger is already noticeable among some primitive people. Money consists there of tokens that are imported; for instance, in the Solomon Islands and among the Ibo on the Niger a kind of industry exists that manufactures tokens out of shells or other monetary symbols. These tokens circulate as money not in the place of production but in the neighbouring areas to which they are exported. This calls to mind fashion, which is so often particularly valued and powerful if it is imported. Money and fashion are forms of social interaction and it seems that social elements, just like the focusing of our eyes, sometimes converge best on a point that is not too close. The stranger as a person is predominantly interested in money for the same reason that makes money so valuable to the socially deprived: namely, because it provides chances for him that are open to fully entitled persons or to the indigenous people by specific concrete channels and by personal relationships. It has also been emphasized that it was strangers who, in front of the Babylonian Temple, threw money to the native girls who then prostituted themselves for it. There is another connection between the sociological importance of the stranger and of money. The pure monetary transaction is obviously something secondary; the basic interest in money expresses itself first and foremost in trade. For good reason, the trader is usually a stranger at the beginning of economic development. As long as the economic spheres are small and do not yet possess a highly developed division of labour, direct exchange or purchase suffices for necessary distribution; the trader is required only for the provision of goods produced in far-away areas. The decisiveness of this relationship is demonstrated by its reversibility: not only is the trader a stranger, but the stranger is also disposed to become a trader. This becomes evident as soon as the stranger is not only temporarily present in the society but settles and looks for permanent support within the group. Thus, the citizens in Plato's *Laws* are prohibited from owning gold and silver, and all trade and manufacturing is specifically reserved for strangers. The fact that the Jews became a trading people is due not only to their suppression but also to their dispersal throughout all countries. The Jews became familiar with money business only during the last Babylonian exile, prior to which time it was unknown to them. This is emphasized by the fact that it was particularly the Jews of the Diaspora who followed this profession in large numbers. Dispersed peoples, crowded into more or less closed cultural circles, can hardly put down roots or find a free position in production. They are therefore dependent on intermediate trade which is much more elastic than primary production, since the sphere of trade can be expanded almost limitlessly by merely formal combinations and can absorb people from outside whose roots do not lie in the group.

The basic trait of Jewish mentality to be much more interested in logical–formal combinations than in substantive creative production must be understood in the light of their economic condition. The fact that the Jew was a stranger who was not organically connected with his economic group directed him to trade and its sublimation in pure monetary transactions. With a most remarkable insight into the Jewish situation, a statute of Osnabrück at the turn of the thirteenth century permitted the Jews to take 1 per cent interest per week and thus $36\frac{1}{9}$ per cent yearly, whereas the usual rate was 10 per cent per year at the most. It was of particular importance that the Jew was a stranger not only with regard to the local people, but also with regard to religion. Since the medieval ban on taking interest was therefore not valid for him, he became the recognized person for money lending. The high interest rate charged by Jews was the result of their being excluded from land ownership: mortgages on landed property were never safe for them, and so they always feared that a higher authority would declare their claims null and void (as did King Wenzel for Franken in 1390, Charles IV in 1347 for the burgrave of Nuremberg, and Duke Henry of Bavaria in 1338 for the citizens of Straubing).

The stranger needs a higher risk premium for his enterprises and loans. This connection is not only valid for the Jews, but is deeply rooted in the essence of trade and of money and is just as important for a series of other phenomena. I will refer here only to those in modern times. The world stock exchanges of the sixteenth century, Lyons and Antwerp, gained their distinctive character through strangers on the basis of almost unlimited freedom of trade which the alien merchant enjoyed here. This again is bound up with the money transactions characteristic of these places: a money economy and free trade possess a deep inner relationship, no matter how often it may be obscured by historical accidents and mistaken principles of governments. The role of the stranger in financial transactions illustrates their inter-relationship clearly. The financial importance of some Florentine families during the Medici period was based on the fact that they were banished by the Medici or deprived of their political power. In order to regain strength and importance, they were dependent on financial transactions, since they could not pursue any other business away from home. It is worth observing how, on closer scrutiny, other concurrent but apparently contradictory events reveal the same relationship. When Antwerp in the sixteenth century was the undisputed centre of world trade, its importance rested upon the strangers, the Italians, Spaniards, Portuguese, British and Germans, who settled there and sold their merchandise. The native people of Antwerp played a very restricted role in trading and were employed mainly as commission agents and as bankers in financial business. In this international society unified by the interests of world trade, the native people played the role that is otherwise often played by the stranger. What is decisive here is the sociological relationship between a large group and some estranged individuals. The latter, because they do not have any direct relationship with more concrete interests, turn towards financial transactions. In most cases such a relation develops between the native people and strangers; when the Anglo-Saxons had absorbed the British population whom they had not expelled they called them 'the strangers'; wherever, as in Antwerp, strangers represent a large cohesive group and where it is the native people who are the dispersed minority, then the result shows that the same sociological cause has the same effect, whereas the question as to which of the elements is locally born and which is foreign is of no importance. Regardless of the private motives of the individual stranger within a group for choosing trade and particularly financial transactions, the first major transactions of modern bankers during the sixteenth century take place abroad. Money is emancipated from the local restrictedness of most teleological sequences, because it is the intermediate link from any given starting point to any given final point. And if, as one might put it, every element of historical existence searches for the form of activity in which it can express its specific quality and its genuine strength in its purest form, then the earliest modern substantial capital, like the expanding urge of youthful spirits, presses for investments which most strongly reveal its all-embracing power, its all-embracing usefulness and its impartiality. The hatred of the people for the major financial houses rested primarily on the fact that the owners and also their agents were usually strangers: it was the hatred of national sentiment against internationalism, the opposition of one-sidedness which, being aware of its specific value, feels overpowered by an indifferent, characterless force whose essence seems to be personified by strangers. This fully corresponds to the aversion of the conservative Athenian masses for the intellectualism of the Sophists and of Socrates, for this new uncanny power of the mind, which, neutral and heartless like money, often showed its strength first of all in the demolition of the surviving pockets of ridiculed power. Moreover, as if objectifying this tendency of money, the enormous expansion of financial transactions originated in endless wars, between the German Kaiser and the French King, the religious wars in the Low Countries, Germany and France, etc. War, which by itself is only pure unproductive movement, gained complete control of money funds, and the solid trade in goods – which is largely locally confined – became overgrown by financial trade. Indeed, in this way the transfer of financial capital into foreign countries actually became subversive. French kings have engaged in wars with Italy with the support of Florentine bankers: they have taken away Lorraine, and later Alsace, from the German Empire with the assistance of German money; the Spaniards have been able to use Italian financial power to dominate Italy. Only during the seventeenth century did France, England and Spain attempt to set an end to this fluttering to and fro of finance capital, which thereby disclosed its character as a pure means, and to satisfy the capital needs of governments within their own country. If finance in the most recent period has again become international in many respects, then it certainly has a completely different significance: 'strangers' in the original sense no longer exist today; trade relations, the customs and laws of even very remote countries, have come to form a more and more uniform organism. Money has not lost the character that originally made it a domain of the stranger, but has intensified it more and more into abstraction and colourlessness through the multiplication and variation of the intersecting teleological purposes that exist in it. The contrast that existed between the native and the stranger has been eliminated, because the money form of transactions has now been taken up by the whole economic community. The significance of the stranger for the nature of money seems to me to be epitomized in miniature by the advice I once overheard: never have any financial dealings with two kinds of people – friends and enemies. In the first case, the indifferent objectivity of money transactions is in insurmountable conflict with the personal character of the relationship; in the other, the same condition provides a wide scope for hostile intentions which corresponds to the fact that our forms of law in a money economy are never precise enough to rule out wilful malice with certainty. The desirable party for financial transactions – in which, as it has been said quite correctly, business is business – is the person completely indifferent to us, engaged neither for us nor against us.

II

The psychological growth of means into ends

In the preceding analysis we have presupposed one aspect of the sense of value whose self-evidence can easily obscure its significance for us. Money is valuable to us because it is the means for the acquisition of values: but one could just as well say that it is only the means. For it does not appear to be logically necessary that the emphasis of value that rests on the ultimate ends of our action is transferable to the means, which, in themselves and without reference to the teleological sequence, would be completely estranged from value. This value transference on the basis of purely external connections arranges itself in a very general form of our mental processes which one might call the psychological expansion of qualities. If an actual sequence of objects, forces or events contains a link that brings about certain subjective reactions in us, e.g. pleasure and displeasure, love or hate, positive or negative value sentiments, then not only do these values seem attached to their immediate representatives, but we also allow the other unspecified mental links of the series to participate in them. This is true not only for teleological sequences whose ultimate link reflects its significance on all the causes of its realization, but also for other regular linkages of the elements: all members of a family participate in the honour or degradation of one of its members; the insignificant works of a great poet enjoy an undeserved appreciation because his other works are important; preference and rejection of the individual in party politics extends to those points of the party programme that may otherwise be met with opposite feelings or with indifference; love for a human being originating from sympathy with one of his qualities finally encompasses his total personality, and therewith all kinds of qualities and utterances, with the same passion that would be unjustified without such a connection. In brief, wherever a number of people and objects exist as a unit through whatever connection, the sense of value derived from a single element is also transmitted by the common root of the system to the others, which by themselves do not provoke such feelings. Precisely because the sense of value has nothing to do with the structure of things but possesses its impassable realm beyond them, valuation does not strictly adhere to its logical boundaries but evolves liberally beyond the objectively justified relations to things. There is something irrational in the fact that the relatively high points of our mental life tinge the contiguous moments that do not have those qualities, but this reveals the whole happy wealth of the soul which wants to live out its interest in the once-sensitive significant elements and values, even according to the full measure of its inner resonance to things, without anxiously asking for the legitimate reason for their sharing this value.

The most rational and most plausible of all the forms of such expansion of qualities is certainly that of the sequence of ends. Yet this too does not seem to be absolutely necessary. The significance that the indifferent means acquires by realizing a valuable end does not have to consist of a transferred value. Rather, it could be a specific category grown out of the extraordinary frequency and importance of this configuration. However, the psychological expansion is in fact based on the value quality, the only difference being that the value of the end may be called absolute and the value of the means relative. The value of things is absolute – here in the questionable practical sense – where a process of the will definitely stops. This stopping naturally does not need to be an extensive pause in time, but only the end of a series of innervations so that the continued life of the will manifests itself in new innervations after the sense of satisfaction has been exhausted. On the other hand, an object is relatively valuable if the sense of its value is thereby conditioned by the realization of an absolute value; the relativity of its value is demonstrated by the fact that the value is lost at the moment when another means for the same end is discovered which is superior and more easily attainable. This contrast between absolute and relative value does not coincide with the contrast between objective and subjective value, since the former may evolve in both of these forms of value. I have used the concepts of value and purpose here as largely identical; in this context, they are in fact only different aspects of one and the same phenomenon: the actual conception which, according to its theoretical–emotive meaning, is a value is a purpose from a practical–volitional point of view.

The psychic energies that posit one or the other kind of values and purposes are of a very different nature. The creation of a final purpose is, under all circumstances, possible only by a spontaneous act of the will, whereas the relative value of a means can only be adjudged by way of theoretical knowledge. The setting of the goal arises from the character, from the mood and from the interest, but the road is determined by the nature of things. The notion that we are free with regard to the first step but slaves with regard to the second is nowhere more applicable than in the teleological sphere. However, this opposition, which discloses the great variety of relations between our inner forces and objective being, in no way hinders one and the same content from shifting from one category to the other. It is precisely the spontaneity in setting the final purpose, together with the fact that the means psychologically participate in the value of their goal, that enables the means to acquire the quality of a definite autonomous value for itself in our consciousness. This is possible only because the final authority of our will is independent of all rational logical foundation, yet the fact itself serves the expediency of the end even though it appears to run counter to it. It is in no way certain, but rather can only be valid at a cursory glance, that we attain our purposes best if we conceive them clearly. The concept of 'unconscious purpose' may seem difficult and imperfect, yet the fact that, on the one hand, our actions in their most precise adaptation are focused on certain final objectives and are incomprehensible without any effectiveness, whereas on the other hand our consciousness is unaware of it, repeats itself so often and is so crucial for our whole mode of existence that we cannot do without a specific term for it. The expression 'unconscious purpose' is intended not to explain this phenomenon, but merely to designate it. The problem becomes clearer if we constantly keep in mind the fact that our actions are never caused by a purpose – by something that will happen – but always only through it as a physio-psychic energy which exists prior to action. Consequently, we may assume the following state of affairs. On the one hand, all our activities are directed by the central forces of our innermost self; on the other they are directed by the coincidence of sense impressions, moods, external stimuli and determinations. Both sets of factors occur in very varied combinations. Our actions are more appropriate to the extent that the first factor prevails, by turning all the various given elements in the direction of the energies which emerge from the mental self in its restricted sense. If we have accumulated a considerable quantity of suspended energy to such an extent that its discharge persistently follows in the predominant direction – a constellation which, in its form, is realized identically in secondary and objectionable interests – then this real physio-psychic power, if it is mirrored in our conceptual consciousness is called purpose. The awareness of the purpose, as the mental reflection of this suspended energy, can disappear during the actual process of the further development of the purpose, because its real foundation is conceived as dissolving; by being slowly transposed into action it continues to exist only in its effects. Even though it is true that, according to the structure of our memory, the original notion of purpose may survive any real foundation and continue to exist in our consciousness, this is not necessary for the actions that seem to be permeated and guided by this foundation. Further, if this construction is correct, then it follows that, to deal with teleological sequences, only the presence of the original unit of energy, that is the original existence of purpose as such, is required. The substantial force of energy survives in the succeeding action, which remains guided from the outset by the purpose, regardless of whether or not the awareness of purpose accompanies the practical sequence any longer.

If the consciousness of purpose remains alive then it is not only something purely ideal, but also a process that consumes the organic strength and intensity of consciousness. The general practicality of life will therefore tend to eliminate it, since – apart from any complications and diversions – it is basically no longer necessary for the teleological guidance of our actions. This seems to make clear the phenomenon found in our experience, namely that the ultimate link of our practical sequences, which can be realized only through the means, will be all the better realized the more our strength is focused and concentrated on producing these means. The real practical question is then the production of means. The more it is completely solved, then the easier it is for the final purpose to dispense with the effort of the will, and this can be accomplished as the mechanical result of the means. If we are constantly conscious of the final purpose, then a certain amount of strength is withdrawn from the labour by the means. The most expedient attitude is that of the complete concentration of one's energies on that stage of the sequence of purposes that should be realized next; in other words, one cannot promote the final purpose any better than to treat the means as if it were the end itself. The distribution of psychological stress that is required when the available forces are limited does not coincide with the logical organization; whereas for the latter the means is completely indifferent and the whole emphasis is on the end, practical expediency requires the direct psychological reverse of this relationship. This apparently irrational fact is of immeasurable value to mankind. In all probability, we would never have advanced beyond the setting of the most primitive tasks if our consciousness had been preoccupied with them, and we would never have been free to develop a greater variety of means; or we would have experienced an unbearable and crippling fragmentation if we had had to be constantly aware of the whole sequence of means for the ultimate purpose while working on each subordinate means. Finally, we would have had neither the strength nor the interest for the immediate task, if we had realized the logical insignificance of the means in relation to the ultimate ends and if we had not focused the whole collective strength of our consciousness on what is necessary at any one time. It is obvious that this metempsychosis of the final end occurs more frequently and thoroughly, the more complicated are the technics of life. With increasing competition and increasing division of labour, the purposes of life become harder to attain; that is, they require an ever-increasing infrastructure of means. A larger proportion of civilized man remains forever enslaved, in every sense of the word, in the interest in technics. The conditions on which the realization of the ultimate object depends claim their attention, and they concentrate their strength on them, so that every real purpose completely disappears from consciousness. Indeed, they are often denied. This is encouraged by the fact that in culturally developed relations the individual is born into a teleological system composed of many links (for example, with reference to customs that are taken as categorical imperatives, whose origin as a pre-condition for social purposes no one questions any more); the individual accepts collaboration for long-established purposes, while even his individual goals are frequently seen as self-evidently given by the surrounding atmosphere and gain their validity more in his actual existence and self-development rather than through a clear consciousness. All these circumstances contribute to the fact that not only the final goals of life as such but also those within life are allowed to rise only imperfectly into the stream of consciousness and to concentrate and direct consciousness towards the practical task of the realization of means.

Money in the Sequence of Purposes

Money as the most extreme example of a means becoming an end

It is surely obvious that this antedating of the final purpose in its most comprehensive and radical form takes place not in the intermediate instances of life but rather in money. Never has an object that owes its value exclusively to its quality as a means, to its convertibility into more definite values, so thoroughly and unreservedly developed into a psychological value absolute, into a completely engrossing final purpose governing our practical consciousness. This ultimate craving for money must increase to the extent that money takes on the quality of a pure means. For this implies that the range of objects made available to money grows continuously, that things submit more and more defencelessly to the power of money, that money itself becomes more and more lacking in quality yet thereby at the same time becomes powerful in relation to the quality of things. Its growing importance depends on its being cleansed of everything that is not merely a means, because its clash with the specific characteristics of objects is thereby eliminated. Money's value as a *means* increases with its *value* as a means right up to the point at which it is valid as an absolute value and the consciousness of purpose in it comes to an end. The inner polarity of the essence of money lies in its being the absolute means and thereby becoming psychologically the absolute purpose for most people, which makes it, in a strange way, a symbol in which the major regulators of practical life are frozen. We are supposed to treat life as if each of its moments were a final purpose; every moment is supposed to be taken to be so important as if life existed for its sake. At the same time, we are supposed to live as if none of its moments were final, as if our sense of value did not stop with any moment and each should be a transitional point and a means to higher and higher stages. This apparently contradictory double demand upon every moment of life, to be at the same time both final and yet not final, evolves from our innermost being in which the soul determines our relation to life – and finds, oddly enough, an almost ironical fulfilment in money, the entity most external to it, since it stands above all qualities and intensities of existing forms of the mind.

Money as an end depends upon the cultural tendencies of an epoch

The extent to which money becomes absolute for the consciousness of value depends on the major transformation of economic interest from primitive production to industrial enterprise. Modern man and the ancient Greek have such different attitudes toward money largely because formerly it served only consumption whereas now it essentially serves production. This difference is of extreme importance for the teleological role of money which is the true index of the economy as a whole. Formerly, general economic interest was directed much more towards consumption than to production; agricultural production predominated and its simple and traditional stationary technology did not require as much expenditure of economic consciousness as did constantly changing industry. This consciousness was therefore predominantly focused on the other side of the economy, namely consumption. The development of labour as a whole reflects the same pattern. Native peoples work almost exclusively for immediate consumption and not for possessions, which would be the next stage further towards acquisition. Thus it is that the so-called socialist tendencies and the ideals of antiquity centre around an organization of consumption but not of productive labour: Plato's ideal state in this respect resembles the Athenian democracy which he sought to attack. One of Aristotle's arguments illustrates this particularly clearly. If political functions were to receive payment, then this would result in predominance of the poor over the wealthy in a democracy, because the poor would be less occupied by private business and have more time to exercise their public rights, which they would do if they received payment for it. Here it is taken for granted that the poor are less busy. If this situation, in contrast to later centuries, is not a matter of chance but rather is based in principle on the form that the economy takes, then it follows that the interest of the masses was simply in having enough to survive on. A social structure that presupposes the unemployment of the poor must basically possess an interest in consumption rather than production. The moral rules of the Greeks concerning the economic realm almost never refer to acquisition, perhaps if only because the numerically predominant primary producers, the slaves, were not the object of social or moral interest. It was Aristotle's opinion that only expenditure and not production provided the opportunity to develop a positive morality. This coincides with both Aristotle's and Plato's opinions on money, which was considered by both to be only a necessary evil. Money reveals its indifferent and empty character particularly clearly where the value emphasis is exclusively upon consumption because here it is immediately confronted with the final purpose of the economy, whereas, as a means of production, it is both more removed from the final goal and surrounded by other means in comparison with which it possesses a totally different relative significance. This distinction in the meaning of money can be traced back to the ultimate decisions in the spirit of each epoch. The conscious over-estimation of the interest in consumption over that in production has its origin in the predominance of agrarian production. Landed property, the relatively safe possession protected by law, was the only possession that could guarantee for the Greeks the continuity and unity of their awareness for life. In this respect, the Greeks were still Orientals, in that they conceived the continuity of life only if the fleetingness of time was supplemented by a solid and constant content. It is thus the adherence to the concept of substance that characterizes the whole of Greek philosophy. This does not at all characterize the reality of Greek life, but rather its failures, its longing and its salvation. It reflects the tremendous scope of the Greek mind in that it not only sought its ideals in the extension and completion of the given, as happened with lesser-spirited people, but further reflected this scope in their attempt to complete their passionately endangered reality – always disrupted by party strife – in another realm, in the secure bounds and quiet forms of their thoughts and creations. The modern view, in total contrast, views the unity and coherence of life in the interplay of forces and the law-like sequence of moments that vary their content to the utmost. The whole diversity and motion of our life does not dispose of the feeling of unity – at least not usually, and then only in cases where we ourselves perceive deviations or deficiencies; on the contrary, life is sustained by it and brought to fullest consciousness by it. This dynamic unity was foreign to the Greeks. The same basic trait that allowed their aesthetic ideals to culminate in their forms of architecture and plastic arts and that led their view of life to be one of a limited and finite cosmos and the rejection of infinity – this trait allowed them to recognize the continuity of existence only as something substantial, as resting upon, and realized in, landed property, whereas the modern view of life rests upon money whose nature is fluctuating and which presents the identity of essence in the greatest and most changing variety of equivalents. Moreover, commercial transactions based on money were further discredited in the eyes of the Greeks by the fact that such transactions are always somewhat long-sighted and operate on the calculability of the future. Yet to the Greeks the future was, in principle, something unpredictable; hope for the future was extremely delusive, even presumptuous, and such insight might provoke the wrath of the gods.

All these internal and external moments of life formation interact in such a way that one cannot designate any one of them as the unconditional fundamental one. The character of an agrarian economy is determined, on the one hand, by its reliability, by a small and less variable number of intermediate links, by the emphasis on consumption rather than production, and on the other by an attitude focused on the substance of things, and by an aversion to the unpredictable, the unstable and the dynamic. On the one hand, all these qualities are various broken rays of a unified historical basic formation refracted by the medium of differentiated interests. We cannot directly grasp or name these rays with the dissecting mind; perhaps they belong to those formations to which the question of priority is not applicable, because their essence basically rests upon the interaction of mutual dependence in an infinite process and in a circle that is defective as to the knowledge of the details but essential and unavoidable in its basic motives. No matter how we interpret it, the fact remains that, for the Greeks, the ends and means of the economy had not drifted so far apart as they did later; further, that the means had not the same psychological independent existence and that money had not developed so obviously and without inner resistance into an independent value.

Psychological consequences of money's teleological position

The importance of money as the outstanding and most perfect example of the psychological raising of means to ends becomes most apparent when the relationship between means and ends is inspected more closely. I have already mentioned a number of occasions in which we hide the real goals of our actions from ourselves, so that our will is in reality focused on goals other than we ourselves assume. Thus, it seems legitimate to search further for purposes beyond those reflected by our consciousness; but where does the limit to our search lie? If the teleological sequence does not terminate in the last consciously conceived link, then does that not open up the way to its continuation to the infinite? Is it not then necessary to be dissatisfied with any given purpose on which our action rests, and to search for a further reason for it in a purpose beyond the acknowledged one? In addition, no gain or condition attained grants us the final satisfaction which is logically bound up with the concept of an ultimate purpose. Rather, every point arrived at is actually experienced as only a transitional stage to a definitive one – both in the realm of the senses, because it is in constant flux and every enjoyment is followed by a new need; and in the realm of the ideal, because the demands are never fully met by empirical reality. To summarize, it appears as if what we call the ultimate purpose is floating above the teleological sequence, yet stands in the same relation to the horizon as the earthly paths that always lead towards it, yet which, after the longest wanderings, never seem to be any closer than at the outset. The question is not whether the ultimate purpose can be attained, but whether its form of presentation may be given any content. The teleological sequences, to the extent that they are directed towards what can be realized in this world, come to a standstill not with their realization but rather in accordance with their inner structure. Instead of the fixed point that each of them seems to have in its ultimate purpose, only the following heuristic regulative principle is offered: namely, that one should not consider any individually willed goal as the final one, but that one should leave the possibility open for a step to a higher purpose. In other words, the ultimate purpose is only a function or a request. Viewed as a concept, it is nothing other than the condensation of the fact that at first it seemed to nullify: that the path of human endeavour and valuation leads to infinity and that no points reached on that path can, in retrospect, escape being considered as a mere means, no matter how much it appeared to be definite before it was reached. The elevation of the means to the dignity of an ultimate purpose thereby becomes a much less irrational category. Certainly in the individual case, irrationality cannot be eliminated, but the nature of the totality of teleological sequences differs from that of the limited phases. That the means become ends is justified by the fact that, in the last analysis, ends are only means. Out of the endless series of possible volitions, self-developing actions and satisfactions, we almost arbitrarily designate one moment as the ultimate end, for which everything preceding it is only a means; whereas an objective observer or later even we ourselves have to posit for the future the genuinely effective and valid purposes without their being secured against a similar fate. At this point of extreme tension between the relativity of our endeavours and the absoluteness of the idea of a final purpose, money again becomes significant and a previous suggestion is developed further. As the expression and equivalent of the value of things, and at the same time as a pure means and an indifferent transitional stage, money symbolizes the established fact that the values for which we strive and which we experience are ultimately revealed to be means and temporary entities. In so far as the most sublimated means of life become the most sublimated purposes of life for most people, it forms the most unambiguous evidence that whether a teleological moment will be interpreted as a means or as an end depends only on one's standpoint – a proof whose extreme decisiveness corresponds to the completeness of a test case.

There is no period of time in which individuals have not been greedy for money, yet one can certainly say that the greatest intensity and expansion of this desire occurred in those times in which the modest satisfaction of individual life-interests, such as the elevation of the religious absolute as the ultimate purpose of existence, had lost its power. At present – as in the period of decline in Greece and Rome – and far beyond the inner state of the individual, the whole aspect of life, the relationships of human beings with one another and with objective culture are coloured by monetary interests. It may appear as an irony of history that, as the moment when the satisfying and ultimate purposes of life become atrophied, precisely that value that is exclusively a means and nothing else takes the place of such purposes and clothes itself in their form. In reality, money in its psychological form, as the absolute means and thus as the unifying point of innumerable sequences of purposes, possesses a significant relationship to the notion of God – a relationship that only psychology, which has the privilege of being unable to commit blasphemy, may disclose. The essence of the notion of God is that all diversities and contradictions in the world achieve a unity in him, that he is – according to a beautiful formulation of Nicolas de Cusa – the *coincidentia oppositorum*. Out of this idea, that in him all estrangements and all irreconcilables of existence find their unity and equalization, there arises the peace, the security, the all-embracing wealth of feeling that reverberate with the notion of God which we hold.

There is no doubt that, in their realm, the feelings that money excite possess a psychological similarity with this. In so far as money becomes the absolutely commensurate expression and equivalent of all values, it rises to abstract heights way above the whole broad diversity of objects; it becomes the centre in which the most opposed, the most estranged and the most distant things find their common denominator and come into contact with one another. Thus, money actually provides an elevated position above the particular and a confidence in its omnipotence, just as we have confidence in the omnipotence of a highest principle to grant us the particular and the baser at any moment and to be able to transform itself into them. The specific ability and the interest of the Jews in the nature of money has certainly been related to their 'monotheistic schooling'. The temper of a people who for thousands of years became used to lifting their eyes up to a single supreme being, to finding in him – especially as he possessed only a very relative transcendence – the goal and intersection of all particular interests, would be suited to devoting itself to the economic sphere and especially to that value which presents itself as the encompassing unity and the common focal point of all sequences of purposes. Nor does the wild scramble for money, the impulsiveness that money – in contrast with other central values, for example landed property – spreads over the economy and indeed over life in general at all contradict the final pacification in which the effect of money approaches that of a religious mood. Not only is the whole excitement and tension in the struggle for money the pre-condition for the blissful peace after the conquest, but that calmness of the soul that religion provides, that feeling of standing at the focal point of existence, attains its highest value for consciousness only at the price of having searched and struggled for God. Augustine's comment on the business man, *Merito dictum negotium, quia negat otium, quod malum est neque quaerit veram quietem quae est Deus*, is quite valid for the industriousness which, constantly compiling means of acquisition, strives for the final goal of financial gain, which is no longer *negotium* but is its outlet. The frequent animosity of the religious and clerical mentality towards money matters may perhaps be traced to its instinct for the similarity in psychological form between the highest economic and the highest cosmic unity and to its awareness of the danger of competition between monetary and religious interest – a danger that has been shown to exist not only where the substance of life is economic but also where it is religious. The rejection of the rate of interest in Canon Law reflects the general rejection of money as a whole, since the interest rate represents monetary transactions in their abstract purity. The principle of interest rates as such did not yet in itself reflect the full measure of sinfulness – it was frequently believed in the Middle Ages that this was avoided by paying interest in the form of commodities rather than money – but rather it reflected the fact that interest rates were the interest on money paid in money, which implied that the abolition of interest would hit the essence of money at its root. Money all too often easily gives the impression of being the final purpose; for too many people money signifies the end of the teleological sequences, and lends to them such a measure of unified combination of interests, of abstract heights, of sovereignty over the details of life, that it reduces the need to search for such satisfactions in religion. All these connections show that something more than the familiar points of comparison exist. Thus Hans Sachs, already a representative of popular opinion, concluded that 'Money is the secular God of the World'. This refers back to the basic reason for the position of money, which is that it is the absolute means which is elevated to the psychological significance of an absolute purpose. It has been stated – in a not altogether consistent manner – that the relativity of things is the only absolute, and in this respect money is indeed the strongest and most immediate symbol. For money is the embodiment of the relativity of economic values. It embodies the significance of each particular value as a means for the acquisition of another value – but really this mere significance as a means is detached from its particular concrete representative. Despite this, money can become, psychologically, an absolute value, because it does not have to fear being dissolved into something relative, a prospect that makes it impossible for many substantial values to maintain the claim to be absolute. To the extent that the absolute of our existence (I am not speaking here of the ideal meaning of things) dissolves into motion, relation and development, the latter replace the former with regard to our need for values. The economic sphere has exemplified this historical type perfectly in the psychologically absolute value character of money. To avoid popular misunderstanding on this point it must be noted that the formal uniformity of this development in all spheres does not imply the claim that it is uniformly welcome.

Greed and avarice

If the character of money as an ultimate purpose oversteps that intensity for an individual in which it is the appropriate expression of the economic culture of his circle, then greed and avarice emerge. I specifically wish to emphasize the dependence of these concepts on the current specific economic conditions, because the same degree of passion in acquiring and holding on to money may be quite normal for the particular importance of money in one context but may belong to the hypertrophied categories in another. Generally speaking, the threshold for the beginning of a real greed for money will be relatively high in a developed and lively money economy, but relatively low at primitive economic levels, whereas the reverse is true for avarice. Whoever is considered thrifty and reasonable in spending money under restricted circumstances little affected by the money economy will appear to be avaricious under conditions of a quick turnover and easy money. This already illustrates what will be made more evident later, namely that greed and avarice are not identical phenomena although they have a common basis in the evaluation of money as an absolute purpose. Like all phenomena that have their origin in money, both represent specific stages in the development of tendencies whose lower or higher levels also become visible with reference to other contents. Both manifest themselves, with reference to concrete objects and regardless of their monetary value, in some people's most remarkable psychological mania for accumulation, a trait that often leads people to compare them to hamsters: such people pile up precious collections of any kind without getting any satisfaction from the objects themselves, frequently without even caring about them. In such cases, value is located not in the subjective reflex of ownership that is normally the reason for acquisition and possession, but in the simple objective fact, unaccompanied by any personal consequences, that merely having these things in their possession is valuable for such people. This phenomenon, which is quite common in a limited and less extreme form, is usually interpreted as egoism since it shares with it the negative side of the common form of egoism – the exclusion of all others from ownership. However, it does differ from it in one respect which is explored in the following digression.

It must always be emphasized that the contrast between egoism and altruism in no way fully embraces the motivations for our actions. In fact we have an objective interest in whether certain events or things are realized or not, and this is so regardless of the consequences for the human subject. It is important to us that a harmony, an order based on ideas, and a significance – which does not have to fit the usual schemes of ethics or aesthetics – prevail in the world. We feel ourselves obliged to co-operate in this without always asking whether it gives pleasure or will be of advantage to any person, that is, whether it is of interest to oneself or to another. The three motivations come together to some extent in the religious sphere where the position of objective motivation is made quite clear. Compliance with religious commandments can occur out of purely egoistical reasons, either in a crude manner, out of fear or hope, or in a somewhat refined manner, for the sake of a good conscience or the feeling of inner satisfaction. Furthermore, it can be of an altruistic nature: the love of God, the surrender of our heart, may make us obey His commandments, just as we fulfil the wishes of a person we love because their joy and satisfaction is our greatest concern. Finally, we can be motivated by a feeling for the objective value of a world order in which the will of the highest principle continues uninterrupted in the will of all individual elements; the objective relation between God and ourselves can demand of us this obedience as its adequate expression or its inner necessary consequence, without any consequences for ourselves and without the joy and contentment of God entering this motivation. In many cases, then, the consciousness of purpose stops short of objective reality, and does not borrow its value primarily from its subjective reflexes. I will leave every psychological and epistemological interpretation of this impersonal motivation undecided here. It is, in any case, a psychological fact which only enters into a variety of combinations with the sequence of purposes of a personal nature. The collector who shuts away his valuables from everyone else and who does not even enjoy them himself, yet watches most jealously over them, colours his egoism with an admixture of supra-subjective valuation. Generally speaking, it is the function of possessions to be enjoyed and we may contrast this not only with those objects that one enjoys without wanting to own them, like the stars, but also those whose value is independent of all subjective enjoyment like the beauty, order and significance of the universe, whose value persists independent of human response. In the case of such possessive people, there exists an intermediate or mixed phenomenon: possession is certainly necessary, yet it does not extend to its regular subjective consequences but is experienced as a worthwhile and valuable goal without them. Here it is not the quality of the object that is the genuine bearer of value; rather, however much quality is indispensable and determines the measure of the value, the true motivation is the fact of its being possessed, the form of the relationship in which the subject stands to the object. The real value, at which the teleological sequence comes to an end, lies in this form – which is realizable only in a specific content: it lies in this ownership by the subject which exists as an objective fact.

The process of becoming an absolute economic value, the disruption of the teleological sequence before returning to the subject, is in a peculiar way illustrated by a certain significance of landed property which blends with its real economic significance in various ways – though often only as an overtone. Landed property would not have acquired a value except for the fact that it brought in a subjective gain in utility for the owner. Thus, its value is not completely created by such accountable value factors as its yield, the greater security of immobile possessions, the social power connected with it, etc. Over and above all these factors, though bound up with them, there often exists a certain ideal value, and the feeling that it is valuable in itself, that man has a relation of sovereign power over the soil, that he possesses such a close personal relationship to the basis of human existence. Landed property thus possesses and grants a certain dignity which distinguishes it from all other types of possession, even if their resultant utility is equal or greater for the owner. This accounts for the fact that it has often been preserved by sacrifices that are only made in a similar way for an objective ideal. An element of absolute value is therefore hidden in the significance of landed property; it is, or at least it was, connected with the idea that it is valuable to be a landowner even if this value is not expressed in terms of utility. The commitment to landed property may thus possess religious overtones as, for example, at the high point of Greek civilization. At that time, to sell landed property was an offence not only against the children, but also against the ancestors, because it disrupted the continuity of the family. The fact that the supply of land could not easily be increased favoured its function as the symbol of family unity which transcended individuals and was sacrosanct. Particularly in the Middle Ages, landed property was ranked as an absolute value to a far greater extent than today. Even though it was sought after, in the first place, because of its yield and the enjoyment of this yield, and thus represented a relative value, it had – over and above its role in the money economy – a specific importance both in and for itself since it was not constantly being turned into money and taxed according to monetary value. One might say that landed property had no equivalent; the sequence of values in which it stood terminated with landed property. Whereas movable objects might be exchanged against one another, immobile property was – *cum grano salis* – something incomparable: it was value as such, the immovable ground above and beyond which real economic activity was carried on. It was probably not only the economic–relativistic interest that motivated the Church to appropriate it: at the beginning of the fourteenth century, almost half of English soil, and at the time of Philip II more than half of the Spanish soil, is supposed to have been owned by the clergy, and even today two-thirds of all productive landed estates in the religious state of Tibet belong to the clergy. Just as the Church provided the stable, apparently externally grounded norms of life in the Middle Ages, so it seemed appropriate, in the real as well as the symbolic sense, that it encompassed in its hands that value which was the foundation for all other values. The inalienability of the Church's landed property was only the conscious and legal manifestation of this inner character. It demonstrated that the movement of values terminated here and that the ultimate limit and finality of the economic sphere had been attained. If one can compare the *mort main* with the lion's den, to which all footsteps lead but from which none emerge, then this is also a symbol of the all-embracing absolute and the timelessness of the principle on which the Church is founded.

This development of goods into a final purpose whose absolute value extends beyond that of the mere enjoyment of their benefits is found represented most clearly and decisively in avarice and greed, those pathological deformations of the interest in money which increasingly tend to draw in the other cases of the same type. Money that has become an ultimate purpose does not tolerate the co-ordinated definite values even of those goods that are of a non-economic nature. Money is not content with being just another final purpose of life alongside wisdom and art, personal significance and strength, beauty and love; but in so far as money does adopt this position it gains the power to reduce the other purposes to the level of means. This reorganization is all the more valid for actual economic goods. To insist on keeping them as if they were incomparable values must appear stupid as long as one can get them back for money at any time, and above all as long as the precise expressibility of their monetary value has robbed them of their existing individual significance and their significance outside the purely indifferent economy. The abstract character of money, its remoteness from any specific enjoyment in and for itself, supports an objective delight in money, in the awareness of a value that extends far beyond all individual and personal enjoyment of its benefits. If money is no longer a purpose, in the sense in which any other tool has a purpose in terms of its useful application, but is rather a final purpose to those greedy for money, then it is furthermore not even a final purpose in the sense of an enjoyment. Instead, for the miser, money is kept outside of this personal sphere which is taboo to him. To him, money is an object of timid respect. The miser loves money as one loves a highly admired person who makes us happy simply by his existence and by our knowing him and being with him, without our relation to him as an individual taking the form of concrete enjoyment. In so far as, from the outset, the miser consciously forgoes the use of money as a means towards any specific enjoyment, he places money at an unbridgeable distance from his subjectivity, a distance that he nevertheless constantly attempts to overcome through the awareness of his ownership.

Where the character of money as a means makes its appearance as the abstract form of enjoyment which, none the less, is not enjoyed, the individual's appreciation of ownership – to the extent that it is preserved intact – has a touch of objectivity about it. It couches itself in the subtle fascination of resignation which attends all objective final purposes and which unites the positive and negative aspects of enjoyment in a unique and inexpressibly unified fashion. In avarice both moments achieve their most extreme opposition to one another because money, as the *absolute* means, provides unlimited possibilities for enjoyment, while at the same time, as the absolute *means*, it leaves enjoyment as yet completely untouched during the stage of its unused ownership. In this respect the significance of money coincides with that of power; money, like power, is a mere potentiality which stores up a merely subjectively anticipatable future in the form of an objectively existing present. The notion of 'possibility' actually contains two aspects which are usually not sufficiently distinguished from one another. If one asserts that one 'can' do something, then this means not only the mental anticipation of a future event, but an already existent state of energy, physical and psychic co-ordinations, definite locations of existing elements; whoever 'can' play the piano, even if he does not do so, is different from someone who is unable to do so, not only in a future moment, but even at the present moment on account of the specific present state of his nerves and muscles. Secondly, this state of ability, which in itself contains nothing of the future, leads to the realization of what can be done only by meeting with further conditions whose occurrence we are unable to predict. This moment of uncertainty and that sense or knowledge of a certain strength or state make up the elements of what can be done, in a mixture of very diverse quantities. It commences, for example, with: 'I can play the piano' – where the moment of reality is paramount and the uncertainty of the other required conditions is at a minimum; it extends to: 'the next throw can be all the nines' – where the given and known conditions are, at the moment, in a minority in relation to the completely uncertain factors required for any success. Money represents, in a unique combination, the crystallization and embodiment of these two elements of capability. What one really possesses of this capability at the precise moment of possession is nothing. The decisive factor that ensures valuable results is completely extraneous to money. Yet the degree of certainty that it will materialize at the right moment is extremely high. Whereas, as a rule, the measure of reliability and unambiguousness contained in capabilities is determined by what actually exists at the present time, what will happen in the future is uncertain. With regard to money, however, this latter uncertainty has completely disappeared, whereas the actual possession in the present is, as such, of no account. The specific sense of capability is thereby sharply intensified: it is really nothing but capability, in the sense of chances for the future, which gives significance to what we presently own; but it is real capability in the sense of absolute certainty about the realization of such a future.

The certainty of satisfaction is further enhanced by the particular relationship between wish and fulfilment which money assumes in contrast to other objects of our interest. The subjective consequences of a fulfilled wish are not always the exact complement of the state of deprivation that originally brought about the wish. The desire for an object is not like a hole that is filled by the possession so that everything remains as it was before the wish. This is the way Schopenhauer presents it, since to him every satisfaction is only something negative, the elimination of a painful condition of deprivation. But if one accepts that satisfaction is something positive, then our wish fulfilment is not only the elimination of a negative state by a corresponding positive one, enhanced by a feeling of happiness; rather, the relation of the wish to its fulfilment is an infinitely diverse one, because the wish almost never allows for all aspects of the object and its effect upon us. Reality almost never corresponds to the wish as a category of possibility of wanting to possess. The trivial wisdom that the possession of something we wanted usually disappoints us is, for better or worse, correct and we become conscious of this otherness in possession only as a fact unaccompanied by any feelings. However, money takes on an exceptional position in this respect. On the one hand, it pushes to its limit any incommensurability between the wish and its object. Any endeavour that has been focused on money only finds in it something completely indeterminate, something that cannot satisfy a reasonable demand and to which we have no specific relation because it has no substance. If our wish does not extend beyond money towards a concrete goal, then a deadly disappointment must follow. Such a disappointment will always be experienced where monetary wealth, which has been passionately desired and considered an unquestionable happiness, reveals what it really is after it has been acquired: money is merely a means, whose elevation to an ultimate purpose cannot survive after it has been acquired. Whereas here the greatest discrepancy between wish and fulfilment exists, the exact reverse takes place if the psychological character of money as a final purpose has become permanently solidified and greed, too, has become a chronic condition. In this case, where the desired object is supposed to grant nothing but its possession, and where this limitation of desire is not only a passing self-deception, every disappointment is dropped. All objects that we want to possess are expected to achieve something for us once we own them. The often tragic, often humorous incommensurability between wish and fulfilment is due to the inadequate anticipation of this achievement of which I have just spoken. But money is not expected to achieve anything for the greedy person over and above its mere ownership. We know more about money than about any other object because there is nothing to be known about money and so it cannot hide anything from us. It is a thing absolutely lacking in qualities and therefore cannot, as can even the most pitiful object, conceal within itself any surprises or disappointments. Whoever really and definitely only wants money is absolutely safe from such experiences. The general human weakness to rate what is longed for differently compared with what is attained reaches its apogee in greed for money because such greed only fulfils consciousness of purpose in an illusory and untenable fashion; on the other hand, this weakness is completely removed as soon as the will is really completely satisfied by the ownership of money. If we desire to arrange human destiny according to the scheme of relationship between the wish and its object, then we must concede that, in terms of the final point in the sequence of purposes, money is the most inadequate but also the most adequate object of our endeavours.

The powerful character of money, to which I again return, appears at its most noticeable, at the least at its most uncanny, wherever the money economy is not yet completely established and accepted, and where money displays its compelling power in relations that are structurally antagonistic. The reason why money seems to have reached the pinnacle of its power at the highest stage of culture is due to the fact that innumerable, formerly unknown objects are now at its disposal; but from the very outset they are concerned with being obedient to money. There is nothing of that friction that the whole type and mode of evaluation of more natural conditions opposes to the alien nature of money and whose elimination the consciousness of power must particularly be concerned with. Since money is the value of values, an expert of Indian life terms the Indian village banker, the money-lender, 'the man of all men in the village' – his Indian name means 'the great man'. It has been emphasized that, when larger amounts of capital were first amassed during the thirteenth century, capital became a means of power which was as yet unknown to the mass of the people. Thus, to this effect was added the psychological compensation of the unprecedented and the supra-empirical. Quite apart from the fact that the Church and the people considered money transactions completely objectionable – even a patrician from Cologne in the thirteenth century confessed to support the clerical principle, *mercator sine peccamine vix esse potest* – the utilization of such a mysterious and dangerous power as capital necessarily appeared as immoral, as criminal misuse. Just as so often the mistaken prejudices promote their justification, so the descendants of the trading aristocracy of that period indulged in a ruthless misuse of their power, whose form and extent was possible only because of the novelty of monetary capital and the freshness of its impact on relationships that were differently organized. Thus it was that the masses – from the Middle Ages right up to the nineteenth century – thought that there was something wrong with the origin of great fortunes and that their owners were rather sinister personalities. Tales of horror spread about the origin of the Grinaldi, the Medici and the Rothschild fortunes, not only in the sense of moral duplicity but in a superstitious way as if a demonic spirit was at work.

In so far as the contradictory types of capacities embodied in money lend it a sublimated sense of power before it is spent – the 'fruitful moment' has, as it were, come to a halt – avarice is one form of the will to power that is not transformed in its exercise and its enjoyment, thereby illuminating the character of money as an absolute means. This is an important factor in explaining the avarice of old age. Such a tendency certainly may be expedient as provision for the next generation – although this motive is usually not in the mind of the miser, since the older he gets the less he is willing to part with his treasures. Subjectively, what is basic in old age is that, on the one hand, the sensual enjoyment of life has lost its charm, and on the other the ideals lose their agitating power through disenchantment and lack of nerve; thus there remains, as the last goal of the will and of life, only the power that manifests itself partly in the inclination of old people to tyrannize and in a mania for 'influence' on the part of elderly people in high positions. In part, however, this results in avarice because the same abstract 'power' seems to be embodied in the possession of money. I consider it a mistake to envisage every miser as being busy with the anticipation of all available enjoyments, all the attractive possible uses of money. Rather, the purest form of avarice is that in which the will does not really go beyond money; nor is money treated as a means for something else, not even in the imagination. On the contrary, the power that money-stored-up represents is experienced as the final and absolutely satisfying value. For the miser, all other goods lie at the periphery of existence and from each of them a straight road leads to the centre, to money. The whole specific sense of enjoyment and power would be misinterpreted if one were to reverse this direction and wished to lead it back again from the terminal point to the periphery. For the power of the centre would be lost as power if it were to be transposed into the enjoyment of specific things. Our essential nature is based on the duality of dominating and serving, and we develop relations and forms that do justice to both these complementary drives in a variety of combinations. In contrast to the power that money confers, the lack of dignity in avarice is well expressed by a poet of the fifteenth century who stated that whoever serves money is 'his slave's slave'.

Actually avarice is the most sublimated, one could almost say caricatured, form of inner subjugated existence in that it makes us a servant of an indifferent means as if it were the highest purpose. Yet on the other hand, avarice is supported by the most sublimated feeling of power. Here too, money displays its fundamental nature, namely, to permit an equable decisiveness and purest presentation of our antagonistic endeavours. In money, the mind has created a form of the greatest scope which, operating as pure energy, increasingly separates the poles of the mind, the more unified it represents itself – that is, as mere money, which rejects every specific determinateness.

It is very characteristic of the mastery that money attained over the general way of thinking that we are accustomed to designating a series of phenomena as avarice – in the sense of greed for money – which in reality are its exact opposite. Such phenomena are manifested in people who use a burned-out match again, who carefully tear off empty letter pages, who don't throw away a piece of string and who spend a lot of time in searching for every lost pin. We call these people 'avaricious' because we have grown accustomed to considering the money price of things quite naturally as their value. Actually, however, they do not think of the money value of these objects; rather, the strength of their feeling is applied to the practical value of things, which is not at all proportionately reflected in their money value. In many cases, it is not the fraction of a penny that the thrifty person is concerned to save; often they have no consideration for the money by which the object itself could be easily replaced, but instead merely value the object itself. In this category belong peculiar, but not altogether rare, people who give away a hundred marks without hesitation, but give away a sheet of paper from their writing desk, or something similar, only with true self-conquest. We encounter here the exact opposite of avarice: to the avaricious person the objects are of no concern – except to the extent that they represent money value – because money has robbed them of their character as ultimate purposes, whereas the behaviour of these other people would be totally senseless if it were determined by the money value of things. Yet it can also become unreasonable again by leaving money value completely out of account. Because of the purpose, these people forget the means that would make the purpose attainable, whereas the means make the avaricious person forget the purpose that alone gives significance to the means. Furthermore, there are those phenomena that – although they coincide in their outer form with practical thriftiness – help to clarify further the teleological character of money by the inner divergence from thriftiness. Many 'thrifty' people think it proper that everything that is paid for is also consumed, and even then not only if another necessary expenditure were to be saved, but also in relation to luxury goods which, in the meantime, have proved to be unenjoyable. The purpose has once more not been attained, but in order to make up for the failure another sacrifice is made. This kind of behaviour is illustrated by the German proverb, '*Lieber den Magen verrenkt als dem Wirt einen Kreuzer geschenkt'* ('Better to strain your stomach than tip the host'). Such behaviour, which is taken seriously by many people, is caricatured in the thrifty mother who was teased by her children that she would take the remains of unused medicine after illness in the family because she did not wish to waste it. In this case, consumption of the object is indifferent or worse than indifferent; the motive for such action cannot be not letting the object be wasted, for it has gone to waste since the need for it, and therefore its significance for the subject, has passed. Actually the object consumed is not the same as the intended object, but another which lacks the quality of motivation. The only possible motive for consuming it is at least to find an equivalent for the expenditure. Money has thus arrived at its next purpose; and with it a feeling of satisfaction and a peak in the teleological sequence is reached, aside from the failure of its subjective final purpose as a thing for itself which does not diminish that satisfaction. This trivial and basically uninteresting phenomenon reveals a very peculiar teleological constellation of money value. Although it is usually not in evidence in valuable objects and therefore appears to be bourgeois and insignificant, it is perhaps the most extreme expression of the role of money as an intermediary overgrowing the real final purpose. Not only is the genuine sense of economizing eliminated here as it is in avarice, but also the attraction of power and of the possibilities that enrich the idle possession of money are eliminated. The object, which has lost whatever might have been the meaning and purpose of its consumption, is consumed under conditions of discomfort and harmfulness merely because the money spent has bestowed an absolute value upon it. Not only is the purposive process arrested here by money but, in addition, it becomes retrogressive and perverse in so far as the valuation, which is purposive in itself, is realized by a procedure directly lacking in purpose.

Extravagance

By means of two negative instances, I now want to explore the extent to which money takes on the character of an independent interest beyond its role as a mere intermediary. Extravagance is more closely related to avarice than the opposition of these two phenomena would seem to indicate. It must be noted here that where the primitive economy exists the thrifty conservation of values is incompatible with their nature, with the very limited transferability of agricultural products. One rarely finds a genuine avaricious hoarding of products if they cannot easily or self-evidently be turned into unlimitedly transferable money; wherever agricultural products are immediately produced and consumed, a certain generosity often prevails, particularly in relation to guests or to the needy – a generosity that is probably less marked in a money economy since money can be more easily stored up. Peter the Martyr thus praised the sacks of cocoa that served as money to the ancient Mexicans, because they could not be secretly preserved and hoarded for long periods and therefore prohibited an avaricious attitude. Similarly, natural conditions limit the possibility and the attractiveness of extravagance. Aside from senseless destruction, the limit to lavish consumption and frivolous waste in a group lies in the capacity of its members and strangers for consumption. But the main point is that monetary extravagance possesses an altogether different meaning and a completely new aura when compared with extravagance with regard to concrete objects: the latter implies that its value for the rational sequence of purposes of the individual is simply destroyed, whereas the former implies that value is, in an inexpedient way, transposed into other values. The only type of squanderer in the money economy who is significant for the philosophy of money is not a person who senselessly gives away money *in natura*, but rather one who uses it for nonsensical purchases that are unsuited to his circumstances. The pleasure associated with squandering is attached to the moment of spending money upon any object whatsoever, and has to be distinguished from the pleasure provided by the fleeting enjoyment of objects, from the snobbery to which it is related, from the stimulating change between acquisition and use of objects; rather it relates to the pure function of squandering without regard for its substantial content and attendant circumstances. For the spendthrift, the attraction of the moment of squandering surpasses both the proper appreciation of money as well as of the objects. This specifically highlights the position of the spendthrift in relation to the sequence of purposes. If the final point of the sequence is enjoyment through the ownership of the object, then the first basic intermediate stage is the possession of money, the second is the expenditure of money upon the object. For the miser, the first stage becomes an enjoyable end in itself, for the spendthrift the second stage is the enjoyable one. To the spendthrift money is as important as it is to the miser, though not in the form of owning it but in squandering it. The spendthrift's sense of value depends on the moment of transposition of money into other forms of value, to such an extent that he is willing to pay for the enjoyment of this moment at the price of squandering all more concrete values.

It is therefore very noticeable that the indifference towards money value, which constitutes the essence and attraction of extravagance, presupposes this value as something experienced and appreciated. For, obviously, throwing away what is indifferent would itself be completely indifferent. The following case is typical of the wild extravagances of the *ancien régime*. When Prince Conti sent a diamond valued at 4,000–5,000 francs to a lady and it was returned to him, he ordered it to be crushed so that he might use it as writing sand for the letter he wrote to her in reply. Taine adds to this story the following remark about the conventions of that period: '*On est d'autant plus un homme du monde que l'on est moins un homme d'argent'* ('The less one cares about money, the more a man of the world one is'). However, this implied a degree of self-deception, for the conscious and emphatic negative attitude towards money is based – as in a dialectical process – on its opposite, which alone can give it significance and attraction. The same is true of certain shops in big cities which, in contrast to those that attract customers by cheap prices, stress with ostentatious self-indulgence that they have the highest prices. They thereby appeal to the finest circles of society who do not ask about prices. What is remarkable about this is that they do not emphasize the main point – the object itself – but rather its negative correlate, that the price is not important; and thereby they unconsciously place money in the foreground of interest again, even though in a negative manner. Because of its close relationship to money, extravagance very easily gains an immense increase in momentum and robs those who are subject to it of all reasonable standards, since the regulation that is given through the measure of receptivity of concrete objects is lacking.

Precisely the same extravagance characterizes the avaricious greed for money: instead of seeking out the enjoyment of real entities, it searches for the intangible, which extends to the infinite and has no external or internal reasons for its restriction. Wherever external positive fixations and barriers are absent, greediness discharges itself quite formlessly and with a growing intensity. This is the reason for the particular relentlessness and embitteredness of inheritance disputes. Because the individual's claim is not determined by work or by a concretely grounded measure, neither party is inclined *a priori* to acknowledge the claim of the other. There are thus no inhibitions to restrain the claim and any interference with it is felt to be a completely groundless injustice. The lack of inner relationship between the wish and any measure of its object, which in this case derives from the personal structure of inheritance relations, derives, as far as greed is concerned, from the structure of the object.

A revolt against new coinage in Brunswick in 1499 highlights the lack of principles that increases with greed and prevents the reduction of the claims. The authorities thought that, in the future, base money should be replaced by good coinage. And yet the same people who wanted good coinage for their products and as their wages revolted because others refused to accept their payments in base coinage! The frequent coexistence of good and base coinage provides the greatest possibilities for the inner excess of money mania – compared with which, other intense passions always seem to be psychologically based. We know that even in China revolutions occurred because the government paid in base coinage but requested taxes to be paid in good coinage. I assume, purely hypothetically, that this lack of moderation that is part of mere money interest itself is also the hidden root of a peculiar phenomenon found at the stock exchange, namely that the small grain speculators, the outsiders, almost without exception speculate for a rise in market prices. It seems to me that the logically correct but, in practice, irrelevant fact that gains in bear operations are limited, whereas in bull operations they are not, is the psychological motivation for such behaviour. Whereas the major grain speculators who actually have to deliver the object calculate the chances of both sides of the market, mere money speculation as is found in speculation in futures is interested in speculating in the one direction, which is potentially infinite. This tendency, which constitutes the internal form of the movement of financial interest, is even better represented by the following. In the period 1830–80, German agriculture produced steadily increasing annual returns, which gave rise to the idea that this was an infinite process; therefore, estates were not bought for a price that corresponded to their current value, but to the expected future profit – this is the reason for the present distressed condition of agriculture. It is the money form of profit which distorts the notion of value. Wherever profit appears only in terms of 'use-value' and where only its immediate concrete quantity is taken into account, then the idea of its growth is confined to sober limits, whereas the possibility and anticipation of money value grows infinitely. This is the basis for the essence of greed and squandering, since they both reject in principle the measurement of value that alone can secure a limit and a boundary to the sequence of purposes, namely by the final enjoyment of objects. The genuine spendthrift should not be mistaken for an Epicurean or somebody who is merely frivolous, although all these elements are mixed up in the individual representative. The spendthrift is indifferent towards the object once he possesses it; his enjoyment is doomed never to find repose and permanency; the moment of his possession of an object coincides with the negation of its enjoyment. In this respect, life has the same demonic form as for the avaricious: every goal attained arouses a thirst for more which can never be satisfied, for this whole tendency searches for satisfaction, as it flows out of an ultimate purpose, within a category that denies any purpose from the outset and limits itself to the means and to the penultimate moment. The miserly person is the more abstract of the two. His consciousness of purpose halts at an even greater distance from the final purpose, whereas the spendthrift comes closer to the objects since his movement towards a rational goal stops at a later stage in order to annex it, as if it were the final goal itself. On the one hand, this formal identity of the complete opposition of visible results, and, on the other the lack of a regulating concrete purpose which, with reference to the equal senselessness of both tendencies, suggests an uncertain interplay between them, explains the fact that avarice and extravagance are therefore often to be found in the same person, be it in their distribution over different spheres of interests or in connection with changing moods. Contraction and expansion of these moods is expressed in avarice and squandering as if, each time, the impulse were the same and merely its valency differed.

The dual significance of money for our will is the result of the synthesis of two tasks performed by money. The more pressing and general the need for food and clothing, the more is the desire for them limited by nature; there may be sufficient quantities, particularly of what are necessities, which originally therefore are the most intensely desired. In contrast with our natural needs, the demand for luxury goods is unlimited. The supply of luxuries will never exceed the demand for them. For example, precious metals, in so far as they are the materials for jewelry, have an unlimited number of uses. This is the result of their basic superfluousness. The closer values stand to our basic life and the more they are conditions of bare survival the stronger, but also the more limited as to quantity, is the direct demand and the more likely it is that the point of satiety is reached at an earlier stage. On the other hand, the more removed values are from primary needs, the less is their demand measured in terms of a natural need and the more they continue to exist relatively unchanged with regard to their available quantity. The scale of our needs moves between these two poles: either it is one of immediate intensity but then certainly limited by nature, or else it is the need for luxuries, in which case the lack of necessity is replaced by unlimited possibilities for their expansion. Whereas most cultural goods exhibit a certain mixture of these extremes, such that the approximation to the one corresponds to a growing distance from the other, money combines the maximum of both. Because it serves to satisfy the most indispensable as well as most dispensable needs of life, it associates the intense urgency or desire with its extensive unlimitedness. Money carries within itself the structure of the need for luxuries, in that it rejects any limitation upon desire for it – which would be possible only through the relation of definite quantities to our capacity to consume. Yet money, unlike a precious metal used for jewelry, does not need to balance the unlimited desire for it by a growing distance from direct needs, because it has become the correlate of the most basic needs of life as well. This remarkable dual character of money with reference to desire for it is presented in a detached form by avarice and extravagance, since in both instances money has dissolved into pure desire for it. Both exhibit the negative side of what we have also observed as a positive side to money, namely that money enlarges the diameter of the circle in which our antagonistic psychic drives flourish. What avarice exhibits, as it were, in material paralysis, extravagance reveals in the form of fluidity and expansion.

Ascetic poverty

On another level than extravagance and in contrast to greed and avarice, there exists a second negative phenomenon – poverty as a positive value, poverty in itself as a satisfying purpose of life. The growth of one link of the sequence of purposes to absolute importance has been transplanted in a direction completely different to avarice and greed. Whereas they come to a halt with the conversion of means to final ends, poverty persists regardless of the absence of means or moves into the section that lies behind the final purpose inasmuch as it is the result of the terminated sequence of purposes. Poverty, like avarice and greed, appears in its purest and specific form only at a certain stage of the money economy. In natural conditions which are not yet regulated by a money economy, and as long as agricultural products do not circulate merely as commodities, that is as money values, the total destitution of an individual is less common. Even in recent times, Russia prided herself on there being no personal poverty in those areas less affected by a money economy. As a general phenomenon, this may be attributed not only to the easier availability of what is absolutely necessary without having to depend upon money, but also to the fact that humane and sympathetic feelings towards poverty are more easily aroused in these circumstances than where what the poor lack and what one can help them with is not what is most immediately necessary to them. In purely monetary relationships, sympathetic feelings have to make a detour before they reach the point of their genuine interest. They often flag during this detour. For this reason, practically helpful and charitable people prefer to come to the aid of the poor with food and clothing rather than with money. If poverty emerges as a moral ideal, then correspondingly the possession of money is detested as the most dangerous temptation, as the primary evil.

Whenever the salvation of the soul is conceived as the final purpose, poverty is at the same time interpreted in many doctrines as a positive and indispensable means which rises above this position to the dignity of a value that is important and valid in itself. This may happen at different stages in the sequence of purposes and for different reasons. In the first place, the mere indifference towards all worldly enjoyments and interests may lead to it. This burden is removed from the aspiring soul as from itself without requiring a will which is specifically directed towards it. The first Christians may frequently have behaved in this way, that is, not directly antagonistic and aggressive towards tangible goods, but simply lacking any relation to them, just as to things that we cannot perceive because we lack the necessary organ. Therefore, the sporadic communism of early Christianity is fundamentally opposed to the attempts at modern communism since the former originates from indifference towards worldly goods, the latter from the greatest evaluation of them. A mixture of both occurred in the intervening period: the socialist–revolutionary movements at the end of the Middle Ages certainly struggled against poverty, but they were in part supported by ascetic movements with their ideal of complete frugality. However, at least with regard to money, asceticism has to abandon its mere dismissal of material interest and to acquire more positive and resolute forms, since one continually confronts it on the road to the most indispensable and since its acquisition requires more attentiveness and activity of the will than the resultant concern with subsistence. Whoever wished to be so indifferent to this interest that, like the Father of the Church who ate axle grease for butter without noticing it, can none the less, if he wants to exist at all in a period of money transactions, not permit the smallest amount of his consciousness to be distracted in this manner for its acquisition. Therefore, where in principle only indifference to everything external predominates, this, in contrast with money, will easily transform itself into real hatred. Second, the tempting character of money has an even more distinctive effect upon it. Because it is ready to be used at any moment, it is the worst snare of a moment of weakness, and since it serves all activities, it offers the soul its most tempting aspect at that time. All this is of even greater danger since money, as long as it really exists merely as money in our hands, is the most indifferent and innocent thing in the world. But for ascetic modes of sensibility it becomes the real symbol of the devil who seduces us under the mask of innocence and simplicity, so that the only safeguard against both the devil and money is to keep them at a distance and reject any relation to them, no matter how innocent it may appear to be.

This attitude found its general expression in the earliest Buddhist communities. The monk who joins the community surrenders his possessions as well as his family relations and his wife and he is not allowed – with occasional exceptions – to own anything but the little things of daily use, and even these only if they accrue to him as alms. The fundamental importance of this regulation is indicated by the name the monks chose to call themselves: the community of beggars. In as far as they begged for what they needed daily – though not even by asking for alms but by quietly expecting them none the less – attachment to any property was completely impossible. Just as certain Arab nomadic tribes were prohibited by law from sowing grain, from building a house, or similar things in order to avoid disloyalty to the tribal tradition by becoming settled, so the Buddhist monks accepted the same rules by a change of spirit. The monks, who liken themselves to the birds who do not carry anything with them but their wings wherever they fly, are not allowed to accept arable land, cattle or slaves as a present. But this prohibition is most severe with regard to gold and silver. The benefactor who has intended to give money to the monks cannot do so and has to give it to an artisan or trader instead, who thereupon hands over to the monks the value of the money in kind. If a monk does accept gold or silver he has to do penance before the community and the money is given to a friendly layman to purchase basic necessities since the monk himself is not allowed to provide them. If no layman is in the neighbourhood, then the money is given to the monk to be thrown away, and even then only to a monk who is 'free of desire, free of hatred and free of delusion' and who can be relied upon to throw it away. Here, money has become an object of fear and horror – although with the peculiar anaemic faintness of these benumbed souls – and poverty has become a jealously guarded possession, a precious part of the inventory of value in an existence estranged from the diversity and the interests of the world. Money represented the unified value, the rejection of which meant the rejection of the diversity of the world.

The inner formation that culminated in the elevation of poverty to an absolute value is represented most distinctly, and with unique passion, by the early Franciscan friars. Their order is not only a reaction against the intolerable secularization of the Italian Church in the twelfth and thirteenth centuries, which found its most articulate expression in simony – everything was attuned to money and available for money, from the election of the pope to the appointment of the most wretched country parson, from the spectacular establishment of a monastery to the enunciation of the formula by which the Florentine priests expiated and restored the wine in which mice had been drowned. The reform movement, which had never completely disappeared since the fifth century, had already proclaimed poverty as the ideal demand for the clergy because it would cut off both the root and the crown of the secularization of the Church. But it was the Franciscans who first made poverty an autonomous value and a correlate of the deepest innermost needs. An expert on the earliest period of the order states: 'The *gente poverella* found security, love, and freedom in poverty. It is no wonder then that all the thoughts and endeavours of the new apostles focused solely on the preservation of this precious treasure. Their glorification of poverty was boundless; every day they wooed anew their beloved with the full fervour of nuptual passion.' Poverty thus became a positive possession, which on the one hand mediated the acquisition of the supreme goods while on the other performed the same service as money does for worldly and contemptible goods. Like money, poverty was the reservoir which the practical series of values led to and from which they were nourished again. On the other hand, poverty was already quite clearly one side or expression of the fact that, in a higher and supreme sense, the world belongs to he who renounces, even though he does not really renounce; rather, in poverty he possesses the purest and finest extract of things, just as money possesses the same for the avaricious. Just as the Buddhist monks said, 'We who do not own anything live in an ecstasy of happiness; joyfulness is our nourishment as it is for the celestial Gods', so the Franciscans were characterized as *nihil habentes, omnia possidentes*. Poverty has here lost its ascetic essence. The values of the soul, for which poverty is the negative condition, have come directly to them; the renunciation of the means, which is usually the full representative of their final purposes, of the world, is similarly elevated to a final value. The tremendous and wide-reaching power of the process by which money is elevated from its intermediary position to absolute importance is best illuminated by the fact that the negation of its meaning is elevated to the identical form.

Cynicism

I want to close the circle of phenomena that illustrate and clarify the nature of money by two processes that are almost endemic to the heights of a money culture – cynicism and a blasé attitude – both of which are the results of the reduction of the concrete values of life to the mediating value of money. They are, so to speak, the reverse of avarice and greed in that, whereas this reduction manifests itself in them in the growth of a new ultimate value, in the case of cynicism and the blasé attitude it is manifested in the disparagement of all old values. The negativity of the teleological sequence, which money had already brought about in extravagance and the desire for poverty, is now completed by seizing upon not only the particularity of values, which are merely crystallized in money, but upon the existence of values as such. Although the attitude that we today term cynicism has nothing to do with the Greek philosophy from which the term originates, there exists none the less, one might say, a perverse relationship between the two. The cynicism of antiquity had a very definite ideal in life, namely positive strength of mind and moral freedom of the indivi-dual. This was such an absolute value for cynicism that all the differences between otherwise accepted values paled into insignificance. Whether a person is a master or slave, whether he satisfies his needs in an aesthetic or unaesthetic manner, whether he has a native country or not, whether he fulfils his family obligations or not – all this is completely irrelevant for the wise person, not only in comparison with any absolute value, but also in that this indifference is revealed in their existence. In the attitude which we nowadays characterize as cynical, it seems to me decisive that here too no higher differences in values exist and that, in general, the only significance of what is highly valued consists in its being degraded to the lowest level, but that the positive and ideal moral purpose of this levelling has disappeared. What was a means, or a secondary result, for those paradoxical adherents to Socratic wisdom is not central and in the process has completely altered its meaning. The nature of the cynic – in the contemporary sense – is most clearly demonstrated in contrast with that of the sanguine enthusiast. Whereas the curve of evaluation of the enthusiast moves upwards and lower values strive to be raised to the importance of higher values, the evaluation curve of the cynic moves in the opposite direction. His awareness of life is adequately expressed only when he has theoretically and practically exemplified the baseness of the highest values and the illusion of any differences in values. This mood can be most effectively supported by money's capacity to reduce the highest as well as the lowest values equally to one value form and thereby to place them on the same level, regardless of their diverse kinds and amounts. Nowhere else does the cynic find so triumphant a justification as here, where the finest, most ideal and most personal goods are available not only for anyone who has the necessary money, but even, more significantly, where these goods are denied to the most worthy if he lacks the necessary means, and where the movements of money bring about the most absurd combinations of personal and objective values. The nurseries of cynicism are therefore those places with huge turnovers, exemplified in stock exchange dealings, where money is available in huge quantities and changes owners easily. The more money becomes the sole centre of interest, the more one discovers that honour and conviction, talent and virtue, beauty and salvation of the soul, are exchanged against money and so the more a mocking and frivolous attitude will develop in relation to these higher values that are for sale for the same kind of value as groceries, and that also command a 'market price'. The concept of a market price for values which, according to their nature, reject any evaluation except in terms of their own categories and ideals is the perfect objectification of what cynicism presents in the form of a subjective reflex.

The blasé attitude

The other meaning of levelling, which refers to the differences in the nature of things rather than to their different evaluation – inasmuch as the central position of money focuses interest on what things have in common rather than on their particular level of development – finds its personal expression in the blasé attitude. Whereas the cynic is still moved to a reaction by the sphere of value, even if in the perverse sense that he considers the downward movement of values part of the attraction of life, the blasé person – although the concept of such a person is rarely fully realized – has completely lost the feeling for value differences. He experiences all things as being of an equally dull and grey hue, as not worth getting excited about, particularly where the will is concerned. The decisive moment here – and one that is denied to the blasé – is not the devaluation of things as such, but indifference to their specific qualities from which the whole liveliness of feeling and volition originates. Whoever has become possessed by the fact that the same amount of money can procure all the possibilities that life has to offer must also become blasé. As a rule, the blasé attitude is rightly attributed to satiated enjoyment because too strong a stimulus destroys the nervous ability to respond to it. Yet this does not yet close the circle of phenomena associated with the blasé attitude. The attraction of things is not the only cause of practical activity intent on gaining them; on the contrary, the kind and amount of practically necessary endeavours to acquire them often determines the depth and liveliness of their attraction for us. All individual particular strivings, all the tortuous turns on the way and all specific demands that the acquisition of the object imposes upon us – all are transferred to the object itself as particular qualities of its nature and its relation to us, and all are invested in the object as its fascination. In the opposite instance, the more the acquisition is carried out in a mechanical and indifferent way, the more the object appears to be colourless and without interest, just as everywhere it is the case that not only does the goal determine the way, but also the way determines the goal. Therefore their acquisition by money, which equalizes procurement and does not reserve specific methods for any object, makes the objects necessarily more indifferent. This is all the more the case where more and more objects are encompassed by wealth and their value differences are actually reduced. As long as we are not yet in a position to buy things, they affect us with their particular distinctive charms. Yet as soon as we easily acquire them with our money, those charms fade away, not only because we now own and enjoy them, but also because we acquired them by an indifferent method which effaces their specific value. This influence is, of course, almost unnoticeable in individual cases. But in the relationship of the wealthy person to the objects acquired by money, indeed, even in the total colouring which the public mind now attributes to these objects, this influence has grown considerably. Thus, cynicism and the blasé attitude are the answers to two different, sometimes to some extent mixed, natural dispositions to the same state of affairs. For the cynical disposition, the experience of how much can be obtained for money and the inductive conclusion that finally everything and everybody is purchasable excites a definite pleasurable sensation, whereas the same picture of reality viewed from a blasé attitude destroys all possibilities of being attractive. While, as a rule, the cynic does not wish to change his inner condition, the reverse is often the case for the blasé person: his membership of the human species demands the attractions of life that his individual condition makes intangible for him. Out of this there emerges the craving today for excitement, for extreme impressions, for the greatest speed in its change – it is one of the typical attempts to meet the dangers or sufferings in a situation by the quantitative exaggeration of its content. The satisfaction of such cravings may bring about a temporary relief, but soon the former condition will be re-established, though now made worse by the increased quantity of its elements. What is more important is that the modern preference for 'stimulation' as such in impressions, relations and information – without thinking it important for us to find out why these stimulate us – also reveals the characteristic entanglement with means: one is satisfied with this preliminary stage of the genuine production values. The search for mere stimuli in themselves is the consequence of the increasing blasé attitude through which natural excitement increasingly disappears. This search for stimuli originates in the money economy with the fading of all specific values into a mere mediating value. We have here one of those interesting cases in which the disease determines its own form of the cure. A money culture signifies such an enslavement of life in its means, that release from its weariness is also evidently sought in a mere means which conceals its final significance – in the fact of 'stimulation' as such.

III

I have mentioned before that greed and avarice, although they appear in most cases in unison, must none the less be precisely distinguished both conceptually as well as psychologically. There are, in fact, phenomena that illustrate them separately. The speed on the route towards money is often completely independent of the speed on the route away from money, not only with reference to greed and avarice in the narrow sense, but already on those levels on which the inner movements have not yet overstepped the boundary of the normal. This is largely brought about by that illegitimate elevation of money in the series of ends which, because it contains no objective standards, often changes the significance of the series, so that money, as long as it can still be gained, arouses different value sentiments than when it is considered for the purpose of spending upon further objects. The discrepancy between value sentiment and money on the path towards money declines once it has been obtained. This discrepancy is also expressed by the observation that, as consumers, most people do not economize as carefully as they do in business. Perhaps a regulation in ancient Jewish law has its origin in this experience that we are more strict, more exact and less careless in acquiring than in spending money. According to this law, the oath always had to be taken by the defendant in cases of disputes concerning money. Only the grocer was occasionally allowed, according to one passage of the Talmud, to swear on the entry in his account book. Under certain circumstances, the change in contraction and remission of the valuation of money emerges from the attitude of princes who, like Louis XI and many others, were very severe in collecting their revenues but very liberal in spending them. However, generally speaking, one cannot deny a proportionate relationship between the speed of acquisition and the speed of expenditure. Nobody spends money more light-heartedly and frivolously than the gambler, the gold-digger and the *demi-monde*. Spain's ruinous fiscal policy since Charles V has been attributed to the relative ease with which precious metals of America fell to the Spaniards. The saying, 'Easy come, easy go', refers not only to the objective structure of the economy where the security of what has been acquired is usually only the reward of a certain solidity in the process of acquisition. The objective circumstances in those professions in which particularly easy and quick profits can be made also provide channels that favour the natural tendency and chance for spending them. But a more effective argument for the proverb lies in the following psychological state: the faster the teleological series terminates at the point of monetary gain, the less the sentiments of energy and importance are concentrated in this point. Thus, the more superficially and therefore more easily separably monetary gain clings to the centre of value, the more we are willing to let it go. Even though the upward and downward leading sections of the series have a common characteristic of greater or lesser tension, there remains a difference between them, namely that money, before it has been acquired, has the value of a final purpose, which it loses as soon as it is gained and experienced in its role as a mere means – unless avarice prohibits this process.

The quantity of money as its quality

I have emphasized this turning point between the two sections of the teleological series because it reveals a most essential quality of money. As long as money serves in our consciousness as the only and closest goal of our endeavours it still possesses a quality. We would be hard pressed to formulate what kind of quality it is, but the interestedness of the will, the concentration of thoughts on it, the liveliness of the attached hopes and emotions shine on it with a warmth that lends it a colourful glow and renders the concept of money significant regardless of its amount. All our practical wishes develop in this way. As long as they stand before us unachieved, the whole genera attracts us, so that we often labour under the illusion that the smallest amount of it, inasmuch as it represents only this object and this concept, would satisfy us permanently. Our desire is concentrated on the qualitative character of the object and the interest in quantity usually asserts itself only after the quality has been realized and experienced to a certain extent. This typical evolution of our interests takes possession of money in a specifically modified form. Since money is nothing but the indifferent means for concrete and infinitely varied purposes, its quantity is its only important determination as far as we are concerned. With reference to money, we do not ask what and how, but how much. This quality or lack of quality of money first emerges in all its psychological purity, however, only after it has been acquired. Only when money is transformed into positive values does it become evident that the quantity exclusively determines the importance of money, namely its power as a means. Until the teleological series reaches this point, and as long as money is a mere object of desire, its purely quantitative character recedes from its general and, to a certain extent, qualitatively experienced nature on account of the emotional overtones attached to money as a general concept. This relationship is chronic for avarice, because avarice does not permit the teleological series to go beyond this critical point, with the result that the avaricious person constantly attaches sentiments to money as if it were a substance of qualitative and specific attraction. The limitation of the interest in money to the question 'How much' – in other words, the fact that *its quality consists exclusively in its quantity* – has many important consequences for our analysis.

In the first place, the quantitative differences of money ownership imply the most considerable qualitative differences for the owner. This is such a trivial fact of experience that to emphasize it would seem meaningless, were it not for the constant temptation to reverse the interpretation of the purely quantitative character of money and to conceive its importance and its effectiveness mechanically, that is to conceive of the more important as the multiplication of the less important. I wish first to mention a quite superficial case as proof of how drastically quantitative differences in the concentrations of money intervene in its qualitative consequences. The issue of small-denomination bank notes has a character totally different from the issue of large ones. People with a small income, who are usually the owners of small notes, cannot as easily present them for redemption as the owners of large notes can. On the other hand, if a panic breaks out, the former press for redemption more violently and thoughtlessly or give the notes away at any price. The following more general considerations support my basic argument.

Subjective differences in amounts of risk

All money outlays for the purposes of acquisition fall into two categories – with risk and without risk. Viewed abstractly, both forms exist in every single outlay if one excludes gambling. Even the wildest speculation must reckon with a very considerable loss of value, though it need not fear a nullification of the object of speculation, whereas on the other hand even the safest act of acquisition always contains an element of risk. In many cases the latter risk can be practically disregarded as an infinitely small factor, so that one can say of every transaction either that there is no risk at all or that a definite portion of the invested capital – in other words the assets of the subject – is at stake. It seems reasonable to determine the size of this possible risk by two objective factors: the probability fraction of the loss and the size of the possible profit. It is obviously unreasonable to invest 100 marks in a business where the chances of loss are 50 per cent and the highest possible gain is 25 marks. Under any circumstances it would appear rational to wager 20 marks on the same terms. But this objective calculation is not sufficient for calculating the reasonableness or unreasonableness of risking a definite amount. A personal factor must also be considered. In every economic situation, a certain fraction of one's possessions should not be risked at all, regardless of how large and how probable the chances of profit might be. The desperate risk of the final gamble, which is usually justified by the statement that one 'has nothing more to lose', indicates by this very argument that any vestige of rationality has been deliberately abandoned here. If, however, one presupposes rationality, then the question of the objective probability of the success of a speculation should be raised only for that part of the assets that lies above a certain fraction. The amount below this limit should, rationally, not be risked, even where a large sum might be gained with a very low probability of loss. The objective factors which otherwise determine the reasonableness of risk are totally irrelevant here. The money form of values easily tempts one to misjudge this economic dictate because it subdivides values into very small portions and so tempts the person with slender means to take a risk that, in principle, he ought to avoid. This has been typified, for example, in the gold shares to the value of one pound, which were issued by mining companies in the Transvaal and western Australia. In view of their relatively low value and the very high chance of gain, this share has been bought by people who normally have nothing to do with stock exchange speculations. A similar state of affairs is created in the Italian lottery. However, in many countries, modern legislation relating to shares attempts to counteract this danger to the welfare of the people by establishing a fairly high minimum for the nominal value of any share offered. If a speculative value – of an enterprise or a loan – is offered in very small shares, its objective insignificance in relation to the total amount easily deceives the buyer that its subjective value – that is, in relation to the buyer's assets – is considerable. And the further fact that it is possible to make a speculative profit with such a small sum makes people forget that their circumstances do not permit them to risk this sum. The tragedy in all this is that people whose income provides only the minimum level of existence, and who therefore should not risk anything at all, are most strongly subjected to such temptations. Not only is the profit that is based on probability denied to those whose situation places them in most need of it and who are prevented from obtaining it by the logic of their situation, but their security against losses based on probability is also denied them – and it is precisely these people who can least bear such losses. Often, many less well off families do not make use of the insurance which, for a relatively small premium, provides care for the servants in case of sickness. To take care of sick servants may be difficult but they would rather run that risk, because at a very low income even low fixed costs seem less tolerable than the mere chance of much higher costs – no matter how irrational such calculations may be. Clearly, within an income or fortune the limits beyond which the risk is economically justified are all the lower – that is, a larger part is free for speculative purposes – the better the person is situated, not only in terms of an absolutely larger amount – which is obvious – but also in terms of a relatively larger amount in proportion to the total income. Not only does such a difference exist between very high and very low financial circumstances, but also more minor differences may already indicate the justification of different amounts of risk. This is a further contribution to the unearned increment of wealth which was discussed earlier, since obviously a fortune has a greater chance of increasing, the larger the portion of it that may be invested in speculation without endangering the economic existence of its owner. This situation also illustrates how money takes on a completely different qualitative character through mere differences in quantity and how it subjects monetary matters to qualitatively different forms.

The completely external and, indeed, even the inner importance of a sum of money is different, depending on whether it lies below or above any dividing line. Whether it does lie above or below this line depends solely upon the total assets of the owner. Changes in the quantity of money produce totally new qualities.

The qualitatively different consequences of quantitatively altered causes

Finally, all this fits into a very general form of the behaviour of things, the most striking instance of which can be found in the sphere of psychology. A quantitative increase in phenomena that are operating as causes does not always call forth a proportionate increase in their consequences. Rather, the augmentation of a cause that resulted in a definite augmentation of the consequence cannot be sufficient for the same purpose on a higher stage of the scale; a much greater influence will be required in order to attain even the same effect. I remind you of the frequent phenomenon whereby the working capital that produces a definite return in a newly developed area of acquisition has later to be expanded considerably in order to continue to yield the same return. We might also point to the effect of medication which, in the beginning, can be increased by a small increment of the doses, whereas later exactly the same additional applications produce much reduced effects; or we may point to the joy brought about under strained financial circumstances by a profit which, however, will no longer produce a joyous reaction if it is continuously repeated. The most common example refers to the so-called threshold of consciousness: external stimuli that affect our nerves are unnoticeable below a certain strength; but when this threshold is reached the stimuli suddenly evoke sensations, and the stimuli's merely quantitative increase brings about an effect of qualitative determinateness. In some cases, however, the increase has an upper limit with regard to this effect, so that the simple continuation of an increase in the stimulus beyond this threshold results in the disappearance of the sensation. This points to the most extreme form of discrepancy between cause and effect which is brought about by the mere quantitative increase of the cause, namely, the direct transformation of the effect into its opposite. With reference to the example of medication, it should be specifically mentioned that homeopathic experiments have demonstrated a direct contrast in the effects that a purely quantitative change in the doses can bring about in one and the same patient. With reference to electric shock treatment, it has been observed that frequent repetition may turn the result into its opposite and again into the opposite of the opposite. It is an everyday experience of major and typical importance that almost all pleasure-affording stimuli can, after an original increase in pleasurable sensation, lead to its arrest and even to positive pain. Finally, the incommensurability of objective causal stimuli and the subjective sensation evoked is also illustrated in the following way. Very low economic values, which are values none the less, often do not incite us to behaviour that would otherwise correspond to economic values as such. There are objects of money value, such as stamps, whose money value is not at all taken into account and does not operate as a factor in dealing with these objects. We expect replies to inquiries from far-off people of whom we would or could not demand a penny, and who themselves have no interest in the issue. If the recipient of the letter is of equal social status, we would not dare to enclose a stamp for the reply. Someone who is thrifty with pennies in other matters is usually less concerned about thriftiness with regard to stamps or bus fares. It would appear that a threshold of economic awareness exists that varies according to the wealth and temperament of the subject, so that economic appeals below that level are not experienced as economic ones. This is probably a phenomenon common to all higher spheres. For such spheres emerge when already existing and perceptible elements converge towards a new form and are thereby elevated to a new and, as yet, unknown importance. In this way, things become objects of law, of aesthetic enjoyment and of philosophical interest – things whose well-known content attains a new aspect. In order that this may occur, a definite quantity of such elements is also presupposed in many cases, and if they remain below this quantity, then they do not enter that higher, more difficult to excite, stratum of consciousness in which these categories live. For instance, certain colours or combinations of colours may be visible in all their clarity, and yet they do not incite an aesthetic pleasure if the space which they cover does not have considerable dimensions; prior to that, they are simple entities which certainly overstep the threshold of sensory awareness but not that of aesthetic awareness. There is also a threshold of historical awareness which creates the remarkable disproportion between personal energies and their historical consequences. There have been many Indian ascetics who taught a similar doctrine to Gotama, but only he became Buddha; there were certainly many Jewish teachers whose sermons did not differ much from those of Jesus, but only he has influenced world history. This phenomenon can be seen everywhere. The importance of personalities forms a continuous scale, but there is a point above which the historical significance of a personality commences, whereas those who remain below this threshold of significance have not merely a lesser effect but none at all and they sink into oblivion. At a higher level, perhaps, lies the threshold of philosophical consciousness. The same phenomena that in minute quantity belong to the transitory irrelevancies of everyday life, and which, perhaps in somewhat greater quantity, provoke aesthetic interest, can become subjects of philosophical and religious reflection if they emerge in powerful and exciting dimensions. In a similar way, there exists a quantitative threshold regarding the sentiments of tragedy. All kinds of contradictions, futilities and disappointments that are negligible as single events of daily life, or that even have a humorous trait, take on a tragic and deeply disquieting quality when we become aware of their tremendous diffusion, the unavoidability of their repetition and their colouring not only of a single day but of life in general. In the legal sphere, the threshold is marked by the principle: *minima non curat praetor*. The theft of a pin is quantitatively too insignificant – even though qualitatively and logically it constitutes a theft – to set the complicated psychological mechanism of legal consciousness into motion. This too has a threshold, and stimuli that remain below this threshold, although they may stimulate other areas of consciousness, cannot arouse a psychic-legal reaction – let alone a reaction by the State.

The threshold of economic awareness

The fact that economic awareness is also equipped with a specific threshold explains the general inclination to prefer a continuous series of small expenses that each pass 'unnoticed' to a single, once-and-for-all larger one. When Pufendorf suggested to the prince that it would be preferable to impose a modest tax on many objects rather than a high tax on a single object, on the grounds that people do not like to part with money (*fort dur à la desserre*), he did not mention the crucial point of this argument. Even though the people have to hand over their money in one form or the other, only in one form does handing over the money remain below the threshold of economic consciousness and the single sum of money that is handed over is not elevated into the category of economie calculation, sensation and reaction – just as two weights, each of them below the threshold of awareness of pressure, do not produce any sensation when placed on the hand one after the other, but do produce one if placed on the hand at the same time.

This may be interpreted as a passive resistance on the part of our simple or complicated sensations, which first has to be overcome in order to transfer the influence to our consciousness. This resistance can, however, be an active one. One can imagine that our receptive physical–psychic organs are, at any moment, in a state of agitation so that the effect of a new stimulus depends on the relation between the direction and strength of the new and the preceding inner movement. The effect can be in the same direction, spreading without restraint, or it can be in the opposite direction, becoming totally or partly counterbalanced so that the receptive organ can move in the proper direction only after overcoming a definite resistance. This kind of conduct also encounters what we term differential sensitivity. Our sensitivity measures not absolute, but only relative amounts; that is, we can determine the amount only by the difference of one sensation from another. This experience – whose modification can here be disregarded, since it is valid for us only in so far as its critics are willing to admit its validity – is obviously the foundation of the series of phenomena discussed above. This experience may be illustrated by a very simple example. If a motion in the tactile nerves of the strength of one has increased by one-third, then this is the same as if the motion of the strength of two had increased by two-thirds. The fact that we attach the same reaction to the relatively equal difference in the scale of sensations results in the fact that objectively equal stimuli have very different subjective consequences. The farther the sensation of a new stimulus deviates from the original state of that sensation, the stronger and the more obviously will we become conscious of it. As we might expect, this clashes with the fact that often the stimulus must first overcome an opposing disposition of our physical–psychic organs before it can affect our consciousness. For whereas the stimulus is – according to differential sensitivity – all the more noticeable the further it deviates from the preceding condition, it is – according to the other principle – less noticeable, up to a certain point, the more the direction differs from the inner motion in operation. This is associated with the observation that, if the stimulus is stable, sensations require a certain time, however short, before they reach their peak. Whereas the first sequence of phenomena can be traced to fatigue – the nerve no longer reacts to the second stimulus with the same energy because it is fatigued by the first stimulus – the latter sequence shows that fatigue does not immediately follow the reaction to the stimulus, but that this reaction accumulates almost autonomously if the stimulus reaches an adequate level, from which, however, it declines again through subsequent fatigue. This dualism of effects is also very much in evidence in complicated phenomena. An occasion for joy, for instance, will be experienced by a generally unhappy individual with a passionate reaction and the release of unused eudaemonistic energies, and this occasion will stand out boldly from the dark background of his previous existence. On the other hand, we also notice that a certain stimulus to happiness may not be fully responded to if the mind is already adjusted to continuously contrasting experiences. The especially delicate charms of life at first recoil without effect from a rhythm of life that is determined by misery and sorrow, and the strength of the experience that, by contrast, was supposed to be strong comes about only after the extended influence of the eudaemonistic moments. If they do persist and the overall state of the mind is eventually transposed in a corresponding rhythm or structure, then the amount of the stimuli – which could not be completely perceived before – will now also go unnoticed because of the opposite constellation since the mind has now become accustomed to eudaemonistic conditions and the necessary difference goes unnoticed.

Differential sensitivity towards economic stimuli

The major teleological significance of this antinomy is also manifested in economic life. The differential sensitivity drives us from every given state of affairs to the acquisition of new goods, to the production of new objects of enjoyment. The limit to this differential – through the passive or active resistance of the existing organic constitution – forces us to pursue this new direction with persistent energy and to continue to acquire more and more goods. However, the differential sensitivity sets an upper limit to this increase, because it weakens the inurement to a certain stimulus and finally becomes so indifferent to any increment that it moves on to qualitatively new stimuli. Just as the regular quantitative increase of objects here brings about an alternation of internal consequences, so the simple increase in the money value of objects may lead to a reversal in the demand for them. In the beginning, an object that does not cost anything or is available at a minimum price is often not valued and not in demand at all. As soon as its price rises, however, its desirability increases; its desirability, in turn, increases parallel to the price for a while up to its ultimate point of attraction. If the price continues to increase so that acquisition is no longer possible, then the first stage of this abandonment will perhaps exhibit the greatest desire. Subsequently, however, an adjustment will be made and the useless longing will be overcome, indeed even a direct aversion to the unattainable – a 'sour grapes' attitude – may develop. In many spheres such a change of positive and negative behaviour is the result of the quantitative change of economic demands. The pressure of taxation on the Russian peasant is offered as an explanation for his poor, primitive and less intensive agriculture, since it would not pay him to be industrious because he does not retain anything save his bare livelihood. Obviously somewhat less pressure, which would make industrious work profitable, would motivate him to intensify cultivation; but if taxation were reduced considerably he might return to his former indolence if the return were sufficient to satisfy all the needs of his cultural level. To take a further example: if a social class or an individual is condemned to a low standard of living and therefore knows only crude and ordinary entertainments and forms of relaxation, then a somewhat higher income will only have the effect of extending these enjoyments still further. Yet if income rises dramatically, the demands for entertainment will move into a completely different sphere. If, for example, a bottle of gin is the main pleasure, then higher wages will lead to an increased consumption of gin; but if wages are raised still further and more considerably, then the desire for very different categories of enjoyments will follow. The fact that the threshold of awareness for different pleasure and pain sensations have totally different levels here leads to complications that defy any analysis. Recent research in physiology has demonstrated the enormous difference in sensitivity to pain between the nerves of various parts of the body; for some, the threshold is six hundred times higher than for others, and it is characteristic that even the threshold value of sensitivity to pressure on the same place possesses no constant relation to them. A comparison of the threshold value for different higher and non-sensory feelings is very dubious because the factors that give rise to them are completely heterogeneous and cannot be quantitatively compared in the same manner as mechanical or electric stimuli of sensory nerves. But in spite of the fact that measurement seems impossible at this level, one must concede the different sensitivity of the realm of higher sentiments and also – since the life situations under discussion always refer to a plurality of areas – the enormous theoretically incomprehensible variety of relations between external conditions and the internal sequence of feelings.

The fate of sentiments determined by money ownership permit an approximate insight into these threshold values and proportions. Money operates as a stimulus to all kinds of possible sentiments because its unspecific character, devoid of all qualities, places it at such a great distance from any sentiment that its relations with all of them are fairly equal. This relation is only rarely a direct one since it requires intermediate objects that are partly – in so far as they can be purchased for money – unspecific, but which, viewed from the other side, are also specific because they evoke certain sentiments. Inasmuch as money makes us anticipate the enjoyment value of particular objects obtainable by money, the attraction of these objects is transferred to money and represented by money. Thus, money is the only object in relation to which the threshold values of various sensitivities to enjoyment are in any way comparable. The reason why measurement none the less seems impossible is obvious: it is the extraordinary diversity in the money value of those things that, in different spheres, produce seemingly equal amounts of satisfaction. If the threshold of enjoyment on the monetary scale lies at totally different levels for a gourmet, a book collector or a sportsman, then this is not due to any difference in sensitivity to enjoyment, but to the fact that the various objects of attraction have very different prices. Yet it is conceivable that the fortuitousness of the threshold values tends towards a balance between amounts of money and eudaemonistic effects, at least in the sense that it becomes obvious to individuals, or even to types, what money value those purchasable objects or impressions possess that overstep the threshold of enjoyment. This development is brought about by the fact that our intuitive appraisal of the fairness or unfairness of the price of an object is a consequence not only of the price demanded for the object elsewhere, but also of the completely different absolute prices of qualitatively very different types of goods. The balancing of these factors signifies the evolution of a general standard of money prices which is certainly the final result of many subjective and fortuitous deviations. From what we know, for instance, of the economic circumstances of the Palestinian Jews in an earlier period, it seems that they were struck by the extraordinary cheapness of certain articles and enormous prices of others. Since the relationship to present prices is so varied that it defies rational analysis, one cannot say – and this is perhaps true of any period of antiquity – that the general money value at that time differs by such and such an amount from the present. Actually, a general money value did not formerly exist at all. This phenomenon has been tentatively explained by the economic gulf between rich and poor which was not reduced by any ambitions on the part of the poor with regard to their standard of living. This was due to the lower strata's great and stable contentedness, with the result that they generally did not have any desire for certain goods. Therefore, two totally different standards of money prices evolved: one for what the poor were able to pay and one for the domain of the rich to whom money did not matter. This might have been the case among all ancient peoples. In this connection, it must be emphasized that, according to recent social views, the middle classes wish to be equal to the upper classes, and the lower classes to be equal to the middle classes with regard to clothing, food, comfort and entertainment. For the first time, this has opened up the possibility of a uniform and general money value. General economic culture, in view of this development, may be said to tend towards making what were originally cheap objects more expensive and vice-versa. This levelling process is first displayed in an objective manner, and finds its truly astounding manifestation in the 'average rate of profit'. Through an almost unbelievable and unconscious process of mutual adjustment of all the economic factors concerned, industrial enterprises which in a developed economy are independent of each other and quite different as to materials, labour conditions and rates of return, neverthe- less yield, *ceteris paribus*, the same rate of interest in relation to the capital invested in them. Any similar adjustment of the subjective eudaemonistic results of money values is obviously out of the question in view of the individual differentiation of human beings. However, a somewhat similar adjustment might be reached in the cultural process because all objects will gradually become expressible in money terms, and a general standard of money prices, that is the uniform importance of money for all commodities, will gradually be established. On the scale of the quantity of money, certain points might possibly emerge as the equivalents of those objects that mark the economic, enjoyment or blasé threshold for a specific individual or type. In the sphere of threshold pheno- mena – a sphere that is the most difficult to examine in view of its complications and individualizations – money remains the only object which, through its purely quantitative character and its uniform response to all differences between things, provides the possibility of arranging the manifold sensitivities in one uniform series. In addition, however, certain occurrences indicate the very direct importance that money has for the threshold of economic awareness, in the sense that our consciousness responds as specific economic awareness only to a pecuniary stimulus. Bourgeois narrow-mindedness often refuses to give an object away for altruistic reasons on the grounds that it has cost money – and this is perceived as the justification for proceeding according to the rigid ego- istical principle of sheer economy! In the same way, foolish parents attempt to hold their children back from wilful destruction by asserting that the things they wish to destroy cost money! Instead of explaining to their children the value of the object itself, they immediately react economically only to the idea of money spent. Two totally different phenomena illustrate this in a very characteristic way. Presents are often valued only if the giver has spent money on them; to make a present out of one's own possessions seems to be shabby, illegitimate and inadequate. Only very refined and superior people will appreciate a present most if the giver has owned it. In the former case, the awareness of a sacrifice on the part of the giver develops in the receiver only if the sacrifice is made in terms of money. On the other hand, a money present seems to be incompatible with the standards of the upper circles of society, and even servants, coachmen or messengers often appreciate a cigar more than a tip of perhaps three times its value. The decisive fact here is that the gift should not appear as economically significant or at least that, allowing its economic nature to recede into the background, it should bring about considerable cordiality. In all these cases, only the money form of value stimulates economic awareness, and the same procedure will be desired or rejected depending on the sentiments evoked. Even though the fully developed money economy arranges economic objects in a continuous series, there remains such a general difference between these objects and money – a fact that is less true for barter economies – that the emergence of a threshold of awareness that reacts only to the money value becomes quite understandable.

Relations between external stimuli and emotional responses in the field of money

There is another reason that specifically relates the phenomena of the threshold of awareness to money. The existence and accumulation of causes whose real proportional effect is excluded are more likely to prevail above a certain limit, and, to push the limits of these effects still higher, the more stable and motionless is the whole system that surrounds the occurrence. As is well known, water can be cooled considerably below zero point without freezing it if it is protected from any motion, whereas the slightest vibration immediately causes it to ice up. Similarly it is possible to keep one's hand in gradually heated water much longer than it would otherwise be bearable if one avoids any motion. Thus, in higher and more complicated areas, numerous influences and circumstances evoke corresponding sensory reactions only when our whole being is aroused, perhaps from a totally different angle. In the same way, the possession of values as well as the privation of values or the unworthiness of certain situations can exist for a long time and even gradually grow before we become aware of their importance. There must first be an impulse that causes the internal elements to dash into one another in order for us to become aware of their real strength through their newly discovered relations or through the difference of relations to all other elements. Indeed, emotions like love and hate may live inside us for a long time, and accumulate below the surface, exercising certain disguised effects, until some occurrence – most often the interruption of the formal regularity of a relationship–causes the emotions to explode into our consciousness and thus first provides the unfolding and the profusion of their consequences. Social developments take a similar course. Senselessness and abuses not only creep into once consolidated states of affairs but also accumulate and increase below the threshold of social awareness, often to the extent that their endurance is no longer conceivable from that moment when the general process of putting things in order – which often has its origins in totally different impulses – brings about an awareness of these disturbances. As is well known, the convulsions of a country experiencing a foreign war first openly reveal the contradictions and the total defects of a state. This explains, for instance, our earlier observation that very crass social differences and the insurmountable distance between classes usually go hand in hand with social harmony. The call for egalitarian reforms or for revolutions is usually raised only after the rigidity of class barriers has been alleviated and a livelier movement within society has brought about certain intermediate transitional phenomena and a degree of contact between the social orders which allows mutual comparison. As soon as this happens, however, the lower classes become aware of their subjugation and the upper classes of their moral responsibility as well as their interest in defending their position, and social harmony is disrupted. Within the money economy, that turbulence in the system of life that incites the awareness of differences and thresholds is particularly widespread and lively. The consolidation of relationships that prevents the consequences of this growing inducement from taking effect in the reactions of consciousness is constantly interrupted by being based upon money. This is because all such relationships are somewhat unstable and resistant to stabilization, particularly since money has no objective relation to personalities and does not – as does a status or lack of it, an occupation or a moral value, an emotional relation or an activity – become a part of personality. All relations based on these other life-contents have some sort of stability because of the relative constancy with which they belong to the person. They resist the influence of elements of change which can take effect only after considerable growth. Money, however, lacking any quality and lacking any relation to a qualitatively determined personality as such, moves from one personality to the other without any internal resistance, so that the relations and situations that pertain to it can easily and adequately adjust to any change. Or, to formulate the problem in terms of our present interest, the fact that money can be accumulated, which reflects the mere quantitative character most clearly, means that it will most frequently and distinctly make itself felt on the determinate content of life. The threshold phenomena, so frequently associated with money, explain its basic character, part of which is also the unearned increment. Indeed, this is only one of the phenomena characterized in this way. For it testifies not only that the importance of more money lies in a proportional multiple of the importance of less money, but that this differential importance represents an abrupt change – despite the purely quantitative change in its basis – in qualitatively new, indeed opposite, results.

Significance of the personal unity of the owner

This fact is based on an obvious presupposition which nevertheless requires further explanation. It can be expressed in the following way. Every sum of money has a different qualitative significance if it belongs to a number of people rather than to one person. The unit of the personality is thus the correlate or the pre-condition for all qualitative differences of possessions and their importance; here the assets of legal persons are, in terms of their function, on the same level because of the uniformity of their administration. Similarly, we may speak of a nation's wealth only if we conceive of the nation as a unified possessing subject. That is to say, we have to conceive the assets owned by the individual citizens as being unified by their interaction within the national economy, in the same way as the fortune of one individual comes together as a practical unity through such interactions – for example distribution, the relation of individual expenditures to the total, balance between income and expenditure, etc. Money, whose importance as a value rests on its quantity, appears as many single quantities standing side by side, so that every sum, in order to operate as a unity, requires an extraneous principle which forces the partial quantities into a relationship and interaction, that is, into a unity. Just as the image of one world emerges from the separate contents of perception which are integrated into a personal unity of consciousness, and just as the sum of the elements of the world becomes more than a mere sum, and the whole attains a new significance beyond its separate parts, so, in the same manner, the personal unity of the owner affects money and confers upon its total quantity the possibility of realizing more or less of it in its qualitative importance. The contribution of this fact to our knowledge can perhaps be made clearer if we refer to a proposition in marginal utility theory. Every unit of quantity of a supply of goods has the value of that unit which is valued least, that is, which is used for the most inessential purpose. For if any unit were lost, the remainder would naturally be used for all more important needs and only the least important would remain unsatisfied. Thus, whichever unit would have to be foregone would be the least important. The value of a supply of goods is therefore determined not by the uses to which the goods might be put, that is not by the sum of the very diverse uses of individual units, but by the use of the least useful unit, multiplied by the number of units of the same size. One exception to this theory is generally admitted, and that is in the case where a sum of goods forms a unity and as such provides a certain utility effect which is not the same as the sum of uses of its individual parts.

For instance, the existence of a forest, so we are given to believe, has an influence on the climate and weather, and therewith also on soil fertility, the health of the population and the stability of part of the national wealth, etc. In short, the forest as a whole has a value which would remain totally outside our calculations if we were to estimate the utility of individual trees. Similarly, the value of an army cannot be judged according to the marginal utility of the individual soldier, nor can the value of a river be judged according to the marginal utility of a single drop of water. This distinction is also valid for the assets owned by an individual. Not only does one million marks in the possession of a single individual accord him a status and a social qualification that is totally different from the thousandfold multiple of its corresponding significance to the owner of one thousand marks. Rather, at the basis of this subjective consequence, it is also true that the objective economic value of one million marks cannot be calculated in terms of the marginal utility of its thousand parts at a thousand marks each. On the contrary, it forms a comprehensive unit in the same way as the value of a living creature, acting as a unit, differs from the sum total of its individual organs. In the previous chapter I argued that the money price of an object, no matter how many coins it consists of, is none the less a unit. I stated there that one million marks are, as such, a mere aggregate composed of unconnected units. Yet as the value of a landed estate they are the unified symbol, expression or equivalent of the amount of its value and not at all a mere agglomeration of single-value units. This practical determination has its personal correlate. The quantity of money is realized in relation to the unity of a person as a quality and its extensiveness is realized as intensity – a process that could not be achieved by the mere summation of its constituent parts.

The material and cultural relation of form and amount

Perhaps we can also express this in the following way. As a purely arithmetical addition of value units, money can be characterized as absolutely formless. Formlessness and a purely quantitative character are one and the same. To the extent that things are considered only in terms of their quantity, their form is disregarded. This is most evident if they are weighed. Therefore, money as such is the most terrible destroyer of form. No matter what the reason is that the forms of things a, b and c cost the same price of m, their differentiation – the specific form of each of them – does not affect their fixed value at all but is submerged in the m which equally represents a, b and c. Form is not a determining factor within economic valuation. As soon as our interest is reduced to the money value of objects, their form – even though it may have brought about their value – becomes irrelevant just as it is irrelevant to their weight. This may also explain the materialism of modern times which, in its theoretical significance, necessarily has a common root in the money economy. Matter as such is simply formless, the counterpart of all form, and if it is accepted as the only principle of reality, reality is submitted to broadly the same process that the reduction to money value exercises on the objects of our practical interest. I shall come back to the problem of how money in extraordinarily great quantities – and fundamentally in connection with the threshold importance of money quantities – attains a particular and, at the same time, more individual form, thereby removing it from its empty quantitative nature. The formlessness of money declines relatively and even outwardly the more its quantity increases: the small coins of the earliest Italian copper currency remained shapeless or had only a crude round or cubical form; the biggest pieces, however, were usually cast in a four-sided ingot form and provided with a mark on both sides. But the universal formlessness of money as money is certainly the root of the antagonism between an aesthetic tendency and money interests. Aesthetic interests are so much focused on pure form that, for instance, design was considered to be the primary aesthetic value of all fine arts, because as pure form it can be realized unchanged in any amount of material. This is now known to be an error; indeed, we must go further and admit that the absolute size of a form of art considerably influences its aesthetic significance, and that this significance is readily modified by the very smallest change of dimensions even if the form remains the same. Nevertheless, the aesthetic value of things remains attached to their form, for example to the relation between its elements, although we now know that the character and the effect of this form is essentially co-determined by the amount of its realization. Perhaps it is no coincidence that a great many proverbs, but only a few of the innumerable folk songs, appear to deal with money despite its predominant importance. Thus, when a rebellion broke out owing to a change in coinage, the folk songs generated by the people on this occasion by and large disregarded the coinage problem. The irreconcilable and, for all aesthetic interests, decisive antagonism always remains in the emphasis placed on whether we value things according to their form or ask for the amount of their value. This value is a merely quantitative one which replaces all quality by a mere sum of equal units.

One can even say that the more the value of an object rests on its form, the more irrelevant is its monetary value. If the greatest works of art that we possess – for example, the Delphic charioteer and Praxiteles' 'Hermes', Botticelli's 'Spring', the Mona Lisa, the Medici tombs and Rembrandt's self-portrait – existed in a thousand identical copies, then it would make a big difference to the happiness of mankind, but their ideal, objectively aesthetic value or their value in the history of art would in no way be enhanced above the point that a single, already existing copy represents. It is certainly different in the case of handicraft works where the aesthetic form and the practical purpose are completely unified, so that often the most perfect realization of this practical purpose is its real aesthetic attraction. Here it is essential, for the whole value created in this way, that the object is also used and therefore its ideal importance grows with its popularity. If the object makes room for value elements other than form, then the number of times the object is created becomes important. This is also the basis of the deepest connection between Nietzsche's ethical value theory and his aesthetic frame of mind. According to Nietzsche, the quality of a society is determined by the height of the values achieved in it no matter how isolated they may be; the quality of a society does not depend on the extent to which laudable qualities have spread. In the same way, the quality of an artistic period is not the result of the height and quantity of good average achievements but only of the height of the very best achievement. Thus the utilitarian, who is interested solely in the tangible results of action, is inclined towards socialism with its emphasis on the masses and on spreading desirable living conditions, whereas the idealistic moralist, to whom the more or less aesthetically expressible form of action is crucial, is usually an individualist, or at least, like Kant, someone who emphasizes the autonomy of the individual above all else. The same is true in the realm of subjective happiness. We often feel that the highest culmination of *joie de vivre*, which signifies for the individual his perfect self-realization in the material of existence, need not be repeated. To have experienced this once gives a value to life that would not, as a rule, be enhanced by its repetition. Such moments in which life has been brought to a point of unique self-fulfilment, and has completely subjected the resistance of matter – in the broadest sense – to our feelings and our will, spread an atmosphere that one might call a counterpart to timelessness, to *species aeternitatis* – a transcendence of number and of time. Just as a law of nature does not derive its significance for the state and coherence of the world from the number of its instances but from the fact that it exists and is valid, so the moments of the highest transcendence of the self have meaning for our life because they once occurred. No repetition that did not add anything to their content could enlarge this meaning. In brief, the concentration of our evaluations on form brings about an indifference towards its quantitative moments, whereas it is precisely its formlessness that points towards its decisiveness for value.

As long as an innumerable sequence of purposes does not yet intersect in money as at the height of a culture based on a money economy, and as long as the specific structure of a culture is not yet atomized and converted to absolute flexibility, we encounter phenomena in which money still displays specific forms. This is the case if greater sums cannot be replaced by the addition of smaller ones. Traces of this phenomenon are exhibited in barter transactions. Among some peoples, cattle can be exchanged only against iron or cloth, but not against tobacco despite its easy exchangeability. Elsewhere, on the Island of Yap for example, the extraordinary variety of types of money (bones, mother of pearl shells, stones, pieces of glass, etc.) are graded. Despite the fact that the relationship between lower and higher kinds of money is well established, certain valuable objects such as boats or houses cannot be paid for with an equivalent amount of many pieces of money with a low denomination, but have to be paid for by a specific kind of money which stands high in rank order of types of money. This same restriction to money of a specific quality is also to be found in the purchase of women and cannot be replaced by a larger quantity of other kinds of money. The reverse is also true: in some places gold is never used to pay for large quantities of goods of small value, but is used exclusively to buy particularly expensive things. This group of phenomena does not correspond to the regulation of our gold standard in which payments above a certain level can be asked for in gold whereas other metals have to be accepted for smaller amounts. Such a fundamental and technical distinction between money as a standard and token money does not seem to exist for every usage. Rather, different kinds of money appear to form a unified series in which only the upper units link their quantitative content to a particular form of value that cannot be expressed quantitatively. This is an excellent means of preventing the trivialization of the function of money which is the necessary consequence of its purely quantitative character, and of preserving the sacred character that money originally so often conveys. It is also an indication that the importance of such forms or qualities of money belongs to a primitive epoch in which money is not only money but, in additon, is something else. This nuance, in a much weaker form and dying away, is still present in a very few phenomena at the highest stages of development. The following habit probably goes back to the significance of money as a form. The French prefer to speak of 20 sous instead of 1 franc, or *pièce de cent* sous instead of a 5 franc piece, etc.; also one can not very easily speak of half a franc, so this sum is expressed in sous and centimes. The same sum, represented in this form rather than in any other, seems to provoke other reactions of sentiment to some extent. When ordinary people prefer to use the name of a coin, a specific form of money – instead of the abstract word 'money' – even if they refer exclusively to money as a quantity – it still has the same meaning: for example, 'No *Schweizer* without a *Kreuzer*'; 'Whoever knocks with the *taler* has all doors opened for him.' It is also apparent that when ordinary people are calculating low values they prefer to denote certain amounts of money by adding small sums rather than dividing large ones. Not only does the sum derived from the multiplication of a familiar unit seem to provide a more wide-ranging and distinctive expression of its significance, but also this subjective moment is objectified in a feeling as if the sum thus expressed has more weight than if it presents itself in other factors. Differences of this kind could be observed in northern Germany when the *taler* was replaced by the mark. During the transitional period '300 marks' was frequently accompanied by totally different psychic overtones than '100 *taler*'; the new form in which the identical content was expressed appeared more comprehensive and plentiful than the other, which on the other hand seemed to be more concise and specific. Such are the phenomena in which form, which is so essential for all other objects, is at least limited in relation to money; and the otherwise unconditional identity of money with the sum, regardless of the form in which it is borrowed, is here, to some extent, interrupted.

What else in money might be generally characterized as form comes out of the unity of the personality which transforms discretely separated parts of a fortune into a unity. Hence, a fortune, particularly a large one, does not possess the aesthetic awkwardness of money. This is due not only to the aesthetic possibilities that wealth provides. Rather – partly in addition to these possibilities and partly by giving them a basis – the image of a fortune lies in the form that money attains through its relationship to a personal centre, which differs completely from the abstract notion of money. This form clearly indicates its character as form by the difference between such a unified fortune and the same amount of money distributed among many people. The extent to which personal ownership determines and emphasizes its form is illustrated not only by money. The hide of land held by the old Germanic freeman was indivisible because it was identical with membership of the mark community. The ownership of this land flowed from the person and thus possessed the same qualities of unity and indivisibility as he did. If we consider English landed property in the Middle Ages, and the fact that the complete equality of lots always indicated bonded possession – a rational distribution of land by a lord to the small farmer – even here it was the unified personality, though unindividual and unfree, that imparted the distinctiveness and form to the possession. The reification of possessions, their detachment from the person, meant at the same time the possibility, on the one hand, of uniting the portions of land of many people in the hands of a single owner and, on the other, of breaking up single pieces of land at will. The stability as well as the importance of the form of land ownership was lost with the disruption of the personal relations; the form of land ownership fluctuated, it was continuously dissolved and reshaped through practical circumstances (which naturally also imply personal circumstances), whereas the identity of the possession with the person had been penetrated by the internally constituted form and unity of the individual self. Life in earlier times seems much more closely tied to established unities, which means nothing less than that it was controlled by a rhythm which in modern times is dissolved into an arbitrarily divisible continuum. The contents of life – as they become more and more expressible in money which is absolutely continuous, rhythmical and indifferent to any distinctive form – are, at it were, split up into so many small parts; their rounded totalities are so shattered that any arbitrary synthesis and formation of them is possible. It is this process that provides the material for modern individualism and the abundance of its products. The personality clearly creates new unities of life with this basically unformed material and obviously operates with greater independence and variability compared with what was formerly done in close solidarity with material unities.

The relation between quantity and quality

Within the historical–psychological sphere, money by its very nature becomes the most perfect representative of a cognitive tendency in modern science as a whole: the reduction of qualitative determinations to quantitative ones. This reminds us of the oscillations of indifferent media which are the objective cause of our senses of colour and sound. Purely quantitative differences in oscillations determine whether we perceive such qualitative differences as green or violet, or hear the contra A or the high C. Within the objective reality that affects our consciousness casually and incoherently only by fragments, everything is arranged by amount and number, and the qualitative differences in our subjective reactions correspond quantitatively to their actual counterparts. Perhaps all the infinite diversity of substances, which becomes evident in their chemical relations, are only different oscillations of one and the same basic material. Wherever mathematical science penetrates certain given materials, constellations and causes of motion, it tends to express structures and developments by purely quantitative formula. The same basic tendency is apparent in another form and area of application, namely in all those cases where the earlier assumptions of original forces and formations is now replaced by the theory of the mass effect of otherwise known but unspecified elements. Thus, for example, the formation of the earth's surface is now explained not as the result of sudden and unique catastrophes, but in terms of the slow accretia and infinitesimal consequences of an immense variety of effects which the continuously observable forces of water, air, plants, and changes in temperature exert. The same viewpoint can be observed in the historical sciences: language, the arts, institutions and cultural products of any kind are interpreted as the result of innumerable minimal contributions; the miracle of their origin is traced not to the quality of heroic individual personalities but to the quantity of the converging and condensed activities of a whole historical group. The small daily events of the intellectual, cultural and political life, whose sum total determines the overall picture of the historical scene, rather than the specific individual acts of the leaders, have now become the object of historical research. Where any prominence and qualitative incomparability of an individual still prevails, this is interpreted as an unusually lucky inheritance, that is as an event that includes and expresses a large quantity of accumulated energies and achievements of the human species. Indeed, even within a wholly individualistic ethic this

277

democratic tendency is powerful and is elevated to a world view, while at the same time the inner nature of the soul is deprecated. This corresponds to the belief that the highest values are embedded in everyday existence and in each of its moments, but not in a heroic attitude or in catastrophes or outstanding deeds and experiences, which always have something arbitrary and superficial about them. We may all experience great passions and unheard-of flights of fancy, yet their final value depends on what they mean for those quiet, nameless and equable hours when alone the real and total self lives. Finally, despite all appearances to the contrary and all justified criticism, modern times as a whole are characterized throughout by a trend towards empiricism and hence display their innermost relationship to modern democracy in terms of form and sentiment. Empiricism replaces the single visionary or rational idea with the highest possible number of observations; it substitutes their qualitative character by the quantity of assembled individual cases. Psychological sensualism, which considers the most sublime and abstract forms and faculties of our reasons to be the mere accumulation and intensification of the most ordinary sensual elements, corresponds to this methodological intention. It would be easy to multiply the examples that illustrate the growing preponderance of the category of quantity over that of quality, or more precisely the tendency to dissolve quality into quantity, to remove the elements more and more from quality, to grant them only specific forms of motion and to interpret everything that is specifically, individually and qualitatively determined as the more or less, the bigger or smaller, the wider or narrower, the more or less frequent of those colourless elements and awarenesses that are only accessible to numerical determination – even though this tendency may never absolutely attain its goal by mortal means. The interest in how much, although it has a given real meaning only in connection with what and how and by itself is only an abstraction, belongs to the basis of our intellectual makeup, and is the envelope that contains the note on our interest in qualities. Although only both types of interests together provide a texture, the exclusive emphasis upon one of them, even though it cannot logically be justified, is certainly psychologically one of the major factors of differentiation between periods, individuals and mental provinces. What separates Nietzsche from all socialist evaluations is most distinctly characterized by the fact that, for him, only the quality of mankind has any significance, so that a single highest example determines the value of an era, whereas for socialism only the degree of diffusion of desirable conditions and values is relevant.

The examples mentioned above of the modern quantitative tendency clearly indicate two different types. Firstly, the objective substances and events, which are the basis for the qualitatively different subjective conceptions, are, for their part, only quantitatively different. Secondly, the mere accumulation of elements and forces produces subjective phenomena whose character differs both specifically and according to value standpoints from those that are quantitatively conditioned. In both directions, money is the example, expression or symbol of the modern emphasis on the quantitative moment. The fact that more and more things are available for money and, bound up with this, the fact that money becomes the central and absolute value, results in objects being valued only to the extent to which they cost money and the quality of value with which we perceive them appearing only as a function of their money price. Their high or low money price has two consequences. Firstly, money arouses contradictory emotions in the human subject, the deepest sorrow and the highest bliss as well as all intermediate stages between these poles, just as it is arranged by others into the equally diversified scale between contemptuous indifference and subservient devotion. In another dimension, money radiates equal value significance in both directions of plenty and of scarcity: the typical modern man appreciates things because they cost very much and also because they cost very little. That the significance of money is substituted for the significance of things cannot be more radically expressed than by the effect – in the same direction although not in the same direction in every particular case – of much and of little money. The more centrally a thought or a value controls its sphere, the more will its positive as well as its negative character have an equal force. On the other hand, objectively, the increase in the quantity of money and its accumulation in individual hands brings about an improvement in practical culture, the production of goods, enjoyments, and forms of life, the qualities of which cannot be attained through less or differently distributed quantities of money. Indeed, one is tempted to consider the quantitative tendency to be more radically realized in money than in any other empirical area. For whenever we retrace qualitative actualities back to quantitative relations, the elements – of a physical, personal, psychic kind – whose quantity more or less determines the specific result remain in some measure qualitative ones. It is possible to push this determination further and further back, so that what yesterday appeared to be an insoluble quality of the element today becomes a modification that is recognizable by amount and number. But this process can go on infinitely, and at any moment leaves a qualitative determination of the elements intact and the question of quantity unanswered. Only metaphysics can construct entities completely lacking in quality, which perform the play of the world according to purely arithmetical relations. In the empirical world, however, only money is free from any quality and exclusively determined by quantity. Since we are unable to grasp pure being as pure energy in order to trace the particularity of the phenomena from the quantitative modifications of being or energy, and since we always have some kind of relationship – even though not always exactly the same one – with all specific things, their elements and origins, money is completely cut off from the corresponding relationships that concern it. Pure economic value has been embodied in a substance whose quantitative conditions bring about all kinds of peculiar formations without being able to bring into being anything other than its quantity. Thus, one of the major tendencies of life – the reduction of quality to quantity – achieves its highest and uniquely perfect representation in money. Here too, money is the pinnacle of a cultural historical series of developments which unambiguously determines its direction.

Synthetic Part

CHAPTER 4

Individual Freedom

I

Freedom exists in conjunction with duties

The development of each human fate can be represented as an uninterrupted alternation between bondage and release, obligation and freedom. This initial appraisal, however, presents us with a distinction whose abruptness is tempered by closer investigation. For what we regard as freedom is often in fact only a change of obligations; as a new obligation replaces one that we have borne hitherto, we sense above all that the old burden has been removed. Because we are free from it, we seem at first to be completely free – until the new duty, which initially we bear, as it were, with hitherto untaxed and therefore particularly strong sets of muscles, makes its weight felt as these muscles, too, gradually tire. The process of liberation now starts again with this new duty, just as it had ended at this very point. This pattern is not repeated in a quantitatively uniform manner in all forms of bondage. Rather, there are some with which the note of freedom is associated longer, more intensively and more consciously than with others. Some accomplishments that are no less rigidly required of some than of others and that are generally no less demanding on the powers of the personality none the less seem to allow the personality a particularly large amount of freedom. The difference in obligations which leads to this difference in the freedom compatible with obligations is of the following type. Each obligation that does not exist with regard to a mere idea corresponds to the right of someone else to make demands. For this reason, moral philosophy always identifies ethical freedom with those *obligations* imposed by an ideal or social imperative or by one's own ego. The other person's demands can consist of the personal actions and deeds of the person under obligation. Or they can be realized at least in the immediate outcome of personal labour. Or, finally, it need only be a certain object, the use of which someone can rightly lay claim to, although he has no influence whatsoever concerning the manner in which the person under obligation procures this object for him. This scale is also that of the degrees of freedom that exist with the performance of a duty.

The graduations of this freedom depend on whether the duties are directly personal or apply only to the products of labour

Naturally, every obligation is generally resolved through the personal actions of the human subject, but it makes a great deal of difference as to whether the rights of the person entitled to some service extend directly to the person under obligation himself or simply to the product of the latter's labour or, finally, to the product in itself – regardless of whether the person under obligation acquired the product through his own labour or not. Even if the advantages of the entitled person remained objectively the same, the first of these forms of obligation would completely bind the obligated person, the second would permit him a little more latitude and the third considerable latitude. The most extreme example of the first type is slavery; in this case, the obligation does not involve a service that is in some way objectively defined, but instead refers to the person himself who performs the service. It includes the employment of all the available energy of the human subject. If, under modern conditions, duties that involve the whole capacity to work as such but not the objectively defined result of this capacity – as with certain categories of workers, civil servants and domestic servants – do not offend against freedom in too crass a manner, then this is a result either of the temporal restriction in the periods of service or of the possibility of selecting the people whom one wishes to be obligated to, or a result of the magnitude of what is offered in return, which makes the obligated person feel, at the same time, that he too has rights. The bondsmen are about at this level, as long as they belong completely, and with their entire working capacity, to their lord's domain, or rather, as long as their services are 'unmeasured'. The transition to the second level occurs when the services are temporally limited (but this does not imply that this level was always later historically; on the contrary, the deterioration in peasants' freedom very often leads from the second to the first level of obligation). This second level is definitely reached when, instead of a fixed amount of labour time and energy, a specific product of labour is required. At this level, one can observe a certain gradation, namely, that the manorial serf had to hand over either an aliquot part of the yield from the soil – for example, every tenth sheaf of corn – or a permanently fixed amount of corn, cattle, honey, etc. Although the latter arrangement might possibly be the more severe and more difficult, it none the less creates great individual freedom for the obligated person, for it makes the lord of the manor more indifferent towards the peasant's type of husbandry. If the serf only produces what is sufficient for his payment to the lord of the manor, then the latter has no interest in the total yield. But this is most important in the case of the aliquot payment, where supervision, coercive measures and oppression are the consequences. The fixing of payments with regard to an absolute rather than to a relative quantity is in itself a transitional phenomenon which suggests that it will be replaced by money. In principle, at this level as a whole, the complete freedom and release of the personality as such from the relationship of obligation could, in fact, be realized, for the person entitled to some service is concerned only with receiving a given objective payment, regardless of where the obligated person procures it. But in view of the economic organization it can actually only be procured by the latter through his own labour, and it is upon this basis that the relationship is constructed. The employment of the person was clearly determined by a person's obligations. This is typically the case wherever in a barter economy the performance of a service commits someone to perform one in return. Service and personality, however, soon diverge to such an extent that the person under obligation would, in principle, be entitled to withdraw his personality completely from the service and perform it in a purely objective manner by producing it, for instance, through the labour of another person. But in reality this is virtually ruled out by the economic system and by means of the product which must be given in payment. In this product the human subject himself remains under obligation and his personal energy is still confined in a certain direction. To what extent the principle of objectivity none the less represents a development towards freedom when compared with the principle of personality is shown, for example, by the greatly increased capacity of estate officials to hold a fief during the thirteenth century. For, as a result, their previous personal dependency was transformed into a merely objectified [*dingliche*] one and thereby placed under common law; that is, they were given freedom in all matters except those connected with feudal service. One finds a similar phenomenon today when talented people, who are forced to work for a wage, prefer to work for a company with its strictly objective organization rather than for an individual employer; or when a shortage of domestic servants occurs because girls prefer factory work to service with people of authority, where they are certainly in a better position materially but feel themselves less free in their subordination to individual personalities.

Money payment as the form most congruent with personal freedom

The third level, where the person is actually excluded from the product and the demands no longer extend to him, is reached with the replacement of payment in kind by money payment. For this reason, it has been regarded, to some extent, as a *magna charta* of personal freedom in the domain of civil law. Classical Roman law declared that, if a payment in kind were refused, then any demand for payment could be met with money. This is, therefore, the right to buy oneself out of a personal obligation by means of money. The lord of the manor who can demand a quantity of beer or poultry or honey from a serf thereby determines the activity of the latter in a certain direction. But the moment he imposes merely a money levy the peasant is free, in so far as he can decide whether to keep bees or cattle or anything else. Formally, in the sphere of personal labour services, the same process takes place with the right of appointing another person as a substitute, and the other party has to accept the latter unless his competence is in doubt. This right, which sets the whole conception of the relationship on a new basis, must often be fought for since it is felt that, like the right to make payment in money, it is a step on the way towards a dissolution of the entire obligation. The authors of the *Domesday Survey* characteristically selected terms for the peasants who replaced their socages by regular money payments which were intended to show that they were neither totally free nor totally subordinate. For a long time, however, the names of the money levies continued to reveal their origin in payments in kind: kitchen tax, barrel money, lodging money (instead of the provision of accommodation for the lords of the manor and their officials as they travelled around), honey tax, etc., were all levied. It is often the case, in a transitional phase, that the original payment in kind was estimated in money and that this sum was demanded as a substitute. This transitional phenomenon also occurs in relationships that are far removed from the example dealt with here. In 1877 in Japan all levies and taxes were still either paid in rice *or calculated in rice and paid in money*. Similarly, under Elizabeth I, the rent for certain estates belonging to the universities was fixed in terms of corn although payment was apparently made in silver. At least the identity of the value of the obligation is still emphasized in this manner, but any personal bondage resulting from rigidly fixed contents has already been thrown off. If the *ius primae noctis* had really existed anywhere, then its development would have followed analogous steps; every one of the feudal lord's rights extended to the whole of the obligated person who had to forfeit his most fundamental possessions or rather his being. This would have been the price at which the lord would have granted his female subjects the right to marry. The next stage is that he grants this right – which he can deny at any time – in exchange for a sum of money; the third stage is that the lord's veto as such is abolished and the subject is now free to marry if he or she pays the lord of the manor a fixed sum: bride-wealth, marriage money, bridal money, etc. Personal liberation is certainly linked with money, though not exclusively at the second stage, since the approval of the lord of the manor still had to be won and could not be attained by force. The relationship is completely depersonalized only when no factors other than money payment are involved in the decision. Before the abolition of every right of this nature that the lord of the manor possesses, personal freedom cannot rise any higher than when the obligation of the subject is transformed into a money payment which the lord of the manor has to accept. Consequently, the reduction and eventually the complete replacement of peasants' services and payments frequently took place through their transformation into sums of money. This connection between a payment of money and liberation can perhaps be regarded by the person entitled to some service as being so effective that he himself suppresses the liveliest interest in cash payments. The transformation of peasant socages and payments in kind into money levies took place in Germany from the twelfth century onwards and the process was interrupted simply because in the fourteenth and fifteenth centuries the feudal lords also fell prey to capitalism. For they realized that payments in kind were far more elastic and susceptible to arbitrary extension than were money payments, which – once they had been quantitatively and numerically fixed – could not be altered. This advantage of payments in kind seemed, in their eyes, great enough to make them seize it in their greed at the moment when otherwise money interests were predominant. It is precisely for this reason that people were completely unwilling to allow the peasant to become rich. The English copy-holder was not generally allowed to sell any cattle without the special permission of his lord. For by selling cattle he obtained money with which he could acquire land elsewhere and extricate himself from his obligations to his previous lord. The greatest step forward in the process of liberation is achieved through a development within money payment itself when a single capital payment replaces the periodical levy. Even if the objective value is identical in both forms of payment, the effect upon the human subject is quite different. As we have pointed out, the various payments levied certainly give the obligated person complete freedom in terms of his actions, provided that he obtains the money required. But the regularity of the payments forces such action into a fixed scheme, imposed by an alien power, and so it is only with the capitalization of the payments that the form of all kinds of obligations is attained which corresponds to the greatest personal freedom.

Thus, it is only with the capital payment that the obligation is entirely converted into a money payment, whereas the money levy with its regular recurrence still preserves at least a formal element of bondage over and above the value required in payments. This distinction is manifested in the following manner. In the thirteenth century and later the English Parliament often decided that the counties had to provide a certain number of soldiers or workers for the king. The representatives of the counties, however, regularly replaced the provision of men with a money payment. But no matter how much personal freedom was saved in this manner, there is a fundamental distinction between this and the rights and freedoms that the English people purchased from their monarchs through single votes on money. If the person receiving the capital is then freed from all the insecurities to which he is subjected in the case of individual levies, then the corresponding equivalent on the side of the obligated person is that his freedom is converted from the unstable form that it possesses when recurrent payments have to be made into a stable form. The freedom of the English people with regard to their monarchs depends partially upon the fact that, by means of capital payments, the people had settled matters with their king once and for all with respect to certain rights: a document from Henry III states, for example, '*pro hac concessione dederunt nobis quintam decimam partem omnium movilium suorum*'. It is not in spite of but precisely because of the fact that such an agreement concerning the freedoms of the people reveals a somewhat brutal, external and mechanical character that it implies the most complete antagonism contrary to the feelings of the king that 'no piece of paper should come between him and his people'. Yet precisely for this reason it also constitutes a radical abolition of all the imponderables of more emotional relations which, when freedoms are attained in a form less tied to money transactions, often provide the means for revoking them or making them illusory. A good example of the gradual development in which the substitution of money payment for payment in kind secures the liberation of the individual is revealed in the obligation upon subjects, citizens and copy-holders to accommodate and feed their monarchs, civil servants, patrons and manorial lords in the course of their travels. This burden stemmed from the old service to the monarch and achieved great significance in the Middle Ages. The first step towards an objectification and depersonalization of this obligation occurs when it is strictly defined. Consequently, we can find, even at an early date, an exact specification of how many knights and servants have to be accommodated, how many horses and dogs can accompany them and how much bread, wine, fish, dishes, tablecloths, etc., must be provided. Nevertheless, the moment that accommodation and feeding were actually required, on the one hand the limits to the services provided must easily have become vague and, on the other, such services definitely reflected the character of a personal relationship. In contrast, we are dealing with a more developed stage when we find that mere deliveries of payments in kind took place without any accommodation. In such cases, the measurement of the quantity could be much more precise than if people had to be accommodated and their appetites satisfied. We learn, for instance, that Count von Rieseck was to receive a certain payment of corn: 'From this corn bread must be baked for his retinue when he is in the village of Krotzenburg so that he will not molest or harm the poor people in the village any further.' Another consequence of this development is that fixed money payments are stipulated for the occasions when people of high rank appear on their travels or at court sessions. Eventually even the variable and personal element that is still present here is removed when these services are commuted into *permanent levies* which are imposed in the form of subsistence money, masters' daily allowance, mercenary money, even when the former official journeys of the judges, etc., were replaced by completely different organizations. It was in this way that services of this kind were ultimately completely abolished and were absorbed into the general tax contribution of the lower orders. This development was, as it were, one that lacked any specific form and is, therefore, the correlate of personal freedom of modern times.

In such cases of the replacement of natural services by money payments the advantage is usually mutual. This is a most remarkable fact which calls for an analysis within a wider context. If one starts out from the assumption that the quantity of goods available for consumption is limited; that this quantity does not satisfy the given demands; that, finally, 'the world has been given away', that is, that in general every good has its owner, then it follows that whatever is given to one person must be taken away from another. Even if one disregards all cases where this obviously does not hold, there still remain countless others where the satisfaction of one person's needs is at the expense of that of another. If one were to consider this as the, or as one, characteristic or basis of our economic life, then it would accord with all those world views that hold as immutable the total amount of values given to mankind – such as ethics, happiness, knowledge – so that only the forms and agents of these values can change. Schopenhauer is inclined to assume that the amount of suffering and joy that each individual experiences is predetermined by his essential nature, that this amount can neither be exceeded nor remain void, and that all extraneous circumstances to which we are accustomed to ascribe our situation only represent a difference in the form in which we experience that unchangeable amount of happiness and sorrow. If one extends this individualistic conception to mankind as a whole, then it appears as if all our striving for happiness, all evolution of material conditions, all the struggle for possessions and being is a mere shifting back and forth of values whose total amount cannot be changed in this way. As a result, all changes in distribution merely reflect the basic phenomenon that one person now owns what the other, voluntarily or not, has given away. This conservation of values obviously corresponds to a pessimistic–quietistic view of life; for the less we consider ourselves able to produce really new values, the more important it is that none are really lost. The widespread notion in India that, if a holy ascetic yields to temptation his merits are transferred to the tempter, teaches this with paradoxical consistency.

But exactly opposite phenomena must also be considered. In all those emotional relationships where happiness lies not only in what one receives but just as much in what one gives, where each is mutually and equally enriched by the others, there develops a value the enjoyment of which is not bought by any deprivation on the part of an opposite party. Similarly, the communication of intellectual matters does not mean that something has to be taken from one person so that another can enjoy it. At least, only an almost pathological sensibility can bring about a feeling of deprivation if an objective intellectual idea is no longer an exclusive personal property but is also shared by others. Generally speaking, one may assert that intellectual property – at least to the extent that it does not extend into economic property – is not gained at the expense of others, since it is not taken from a limited supply but, even though its content is given, ultimately has to be produced by the thought process of whoever acquires it. This harmonization of interests, which emanates from the nature of the object, should obviously also be provided in those economic spheres where competition for the satisfaction of individual needs is gained only at the expense of someone else. There are two types of means for transferring this situation into a more perfect one. The nearest at hand is the diversion of the struggle against fellow men towards the struggle against nature. To the extent to which further substances and forces are incorporated into human uses from the available supply of nature, competition for those that are already obtained will be reduced. The thesis of the preservation of material and energy is, luckily, valid only for the absolute total of nature, but not for that section of it which human purposive action designates. This relative total can, indeed, be multiplied indefinitely by bringing more material and forces into a form that accords with our purposes, that is by annexing them. A progressive technology teaches us to gain even more uses for things, even from what is already completely occupied. The transition from an extensive to an intensive economy is applicable not only to the cultivation of the land, but to any substance that can be subdivided into smaller and smaller parts for more and more specific usages or to the substance's latent forces that are to be released to an even greater extent. The extension of human spheres of power in a variety of dimensions, which belies both the statement that the world is given away free and that the satisfaction of needs is tied to theft of whatever sort, could be termed the substantive progress of culture. Alongside this, there is what might be termed functional progress. The concern here is with finding the appropriate forms that make it advantageous for both parties to exchange ownership of specific objects. Such a form can originally have been attained only if the first owner had the physical power to keep the object wanted by others until he was offered a corresponding advantage, because otherwise the object would simply have been taken away from him. Robbery, and perhaps the gift, appear to be the most primitive stages of change in ownership, the advantage lying completely on one side and the burden falling completely on the other. When the stage of exchange appears as the form of change in ownership, or as stated earlier as a mere consequence of the equal power of both parties, then this would be evidence of the greatest progress that mankind could have made. In view of the mere differences of degree that exist in so many respects between man and the lower animals, many have often attempted to establish the specific difference that separates mankind unmistakably and unequivocally from other animals. Thus, man has been defined as the political animal, the tool-creating animal, the purposeful animal, the hierarchical animal – indeed, by a serious philosopher, as the megalomaniac animal. Perhaps we might add to this series that man is the exchanging animal, and this is in fact only one side or form of the whole general feature which seems to reflect the specific qualities of man – man is the *objective* animal. Nowhere in the animal world do we find indications of what we term objectivity, of views and treatment of things that lie beyond subjective feeling and volition.

I have already indicated how this reduces the human tragedy of competition. Such is the civilizing influence of culture that more and more contents of life become objectified in supra-individual forms: books, art, ideal concepts such as fatherland, general culture, the manifestation of life in conceptual and aesthetic images, the knowledge of a thousand interesting and significant things – all this may be enjoyed without any one depriving any other. The more values are transposed into such objective forms, the more room there is in them, as in the house of God, for every soul. Perhaps the wildness and embitterment of modern competition would be completely unbearable were it not accompanied by this growing objectivation of the contents of existence which remain untouched by all *ôte-toi que je m'y mette*. It is surely of deep significance that whatever separates man on the purely factual and psychological level from lower animal species, namely the capacity for objective contemplation, the disregard of the ego with its impulses and conditions in favour of pure objectivity, contributes to the noblest and most ennobling result in the historical process: to build a world that may be acquired without conflict and mutual repression, to possess values whose acquisition and enjoyment by one person does not exclude that of another, but opens the door a thousand times for him to acquire such values as well. This problem, which is successfully solved in the world of objectivity in a substantial form, comes close to a solution in a functional form.

In contrast to the simple taking-away or gift, in which the purely subjective impulse is enjoyed, exchange presupposes, as we saw earlier, an objective appraisal, consideration, mutual acknowledgment, a restraint of direct subjective desire. It does not matter that originally this may not be voluntary but enforced by the equal power of the other party; rather, the decisive, specifically common factor is that this equivalence of power does not lead to mutual theft and struggle but to a balanced exchange in which the one-sided and personal possession or desire for possession enters into an objective concerted action arising out of and beyond the interaction of the subjects. Exchange – which to us appears to be something entirely self-evident – is the first, and in its simplicity really wonderful, means for combining justice with changes in ownership. In so far as the receiver is, at the same time, the giver, the mere one-sidedness of advantage that characterizes changes of ownership dominated by a purely impulsive egotism or altruism disappears – though this does not imply that the latter relationship is always the first stage of development.

The maximization of value through changes in ownership

But the mere justice that is implied in exchange is certainly only formal and relative: any one person should have neither more nor less than any other. Over and above that, exchange brings about an increase in the absolute number of values experienced. Since everybody offers for exchange only what is relatively useless to him, and accepts in exchange what is relatively necessary, exchange effects a continuously growing utilization of the values wre :.ed from nature at any given time. If the world were really 'given away' and a' activity consisted only in the mere moving back and forth of an objectively una:terable quantity of values, then exchange would nevertheless produce, as it were, an intercellular growth of values. The objectively stable sum of values changes through a more useful distribution, effected by exchange, into a subjectively larger amount and higher measure of uses experienced. This is the great cultural task of every new distribution of rights and duties, which always implies an exchange. Even in the case of an apparently quite one-sided transfer of advantages, a truly social procedure will not disregard them. Thus, for example, it was essential during the liberation of peasants in the eighteenth and nineteenth centuries not only to ensure that the landowners forfeited what the peasants were supposed to gain, but also to find a mode of distributing property and rights which enlarged the total amount of utilities.

There are two qualities of money that, in this respect, suggest that the exchange of goods or services is best served by money: its divisibility and its unlimited convertibility. The former ensures that an objective equivalence between service and its return can take place. Natural objects can seldom be so determined and scaled in value that their exchange has to be accepted as completely just by both parties. Only money – because it is nothing but the representation of the value of *other* objects, and because there is almost no limit to its divisibility and accretion – provides the technical possibility for the exact equivalence of exchange values. However, this represents only the first stage in the progressive development away from the one-sidedness of exchange of ownership. The second quality of money derives from the fact that exchange in kind seldom gives both parties the desired object to an equal extent or is able to release them from equally superfluous ones. As a rule, the more lively desire will be on the side of one party to the transaction while the other party will enter into the exchange only by being forced to do so or where they receive a disproportionately high compensation for doing so. In the case of the exchange of services or benefits against money, however, one party receives the object that they especially need while the other receives something that anyone in general desires. Because of its boundless usefulness and therefore its permanent desirability, every exchange becomes, at least in principle, equally advantageous to both parties. The one who takes the object will certainly do so only if he needs it at this point in time; the person who takes money will accept it because he can use it at any time. The exchange against money makes possible an increase in satisfaction for both parties, whereas with exchange in kind it is frequently the case that only one party will have a specific interest in the acquisition or disposal of the object. Thus exchange against money is so far the most perfect form of solution of the great cultural problem that evolves from the one-sided advantage of exchange of possessions, namely, to raise the objectively given amount of value to a greater amount of subjectively experienced values merely through the change in its owners. This, alongside the original creation of values, is clearly the task of social expediency as part of the general human task: to set free a maximum of the latent value that lies in the form that we give to the contents of life. Wherever we see money serving this purpose, the technical role of money also reveals that exchange is the essential social mode of solving this problem and that exchange itself is embodied in money.

The increase in the amount of satisfaction that in principle is always made possible through the commodity–money exchange process – and despite its eudaemonistic devaluation by virtue of other consequences – does not rest solely on the subjective state of one or the other parties involved in the exchange. Obviously the objective, economic fruitfulness and the intensive and extensive growth in the amount of goods in the future depends upon the manner in which any given quantity of goods is distributed at the present time. The economic consequences will be completely different depending upon who disposes of the various quantities. The mere transfer of goods from one hand to the other can subsequently considerably modify the quantity of goods in an upward or downward direction. We can even say that the same quantity of goods in different hands means a different quantity, just as the same seed in different soils produces different results. This result of the variation in distribution is most marked with regard to money. However changeable the economic importance of a landed estate or a factory may be for different owners, these variations in returns, over and above quite insignificant amounts, bear the mark of chance and abnormality. Yet the fact that the same amount of money in the hands of a stock exchange speculator or a rentier, or the State or the large industrialist produces extraordinarily different returns is a normal phenomenon that corresponds to the incomparable scope which the ownership of money provides to objective and subjective, to good and bad factors for its realization. One can at least say, with regard to the sum total of money owned by a group, that the inequality and change in its distribution is only a change in form that leaves its significance for the whole unchanged. This very change in form produces in this material the most fundamentally diverse results for the economy and for wealth as totalities. It is, furthermore, not merely a question of quantitative differences but rather of differences in quality that on the one hand are absolutely basic to our problem at hand, and on the other also lead back to the question of quantity.

In general, the same commodity in different hands implies, economically, only a quantitative difference in the money return, whereas the same amount of money in different hands signifies a qualitative difference in its objective effects. The social expediency that is undoubtedly at work here explains why modern wealth tends to remain for much shorter periods of time in any one family than was formerly the case in non-money economies. Money, so to speak, seeks out the more profitable hand, and this is all the more conspicuous and must result from all the more compelling reasons because the ownership of money may be enjoyed more tranquilly, safely and passively than any other form of property. Since money, by virtue of its mere distribution at a given moment, displays a minimum as well as a maximum of economic profitability, and, further, since change in the ownership of money does not bring about as much loss through clashes and loss of time as do other objects, economic usefulness here possesses a particularly wide scope for its task of attaining a maximum of its total importance by means of the type of distribution of ownership.

We are here especially concerned to resume our interrupted investigation of how far the money economy is able to increase individual liberty to its fullest extent, that is to release it from that primary form of social values in which one person has to be deprived of what the other receives. In the first place, the purely surface phenomenon of the money economy indicates this bilateral advantage. The everyday exchange of commodities in which the commodity is directly inspected and handed over obliges the buyer to undertake in his interest a careful and expert examination of the commodity because the seller – after having offered this opportunity – may reject any later complaint. When trade has developed to the extent that purchases are made on the basis of samples, responsibility is transferred to the seller not only for the exact concurrence of the sample with the delivery, but also for any error, since the buyer will naturally profit ruthlessly by any error that he may find in the quality of the sample. Transactions carried out at our modern commodity exchanges have taken on a form that relieves both parties of these responsibilities by being carried out not according to samples but by generally accepted standards that are set once and for all. In this case, the buyer no longer has to rely upon a preliminary testing of the whole or upon the sample with all its chances of error; the seller too is no longer required to supply, according to the individual, the relatively arbitrary sample which entails all kinds of risks. Rather, both now know exactly, when they agree to a contract for a certain standardized quality of wheat or petrol, that they are obliged to deliver an objectively fixed standard of the commodity – a standard that has no regard for personal uncertainties and deficiencies. There has thus been established a mode of bargaining at the peak of the money economy which lightens the burden of responsibility for both parties but transposes the subjective basis of the transaction into an objective one and alleviates the disadvantage of one party at the expense of the other. Credit transactions exhibit an exact parallel to this. In the Middle Ages it was very difficult to ascertain the credit-worthiness of an individual businessman, a difficulty that impaired and hampered both his actions and those of the creditors. Only at the stock exchanges of the sixteenth century, particularly at Lyons and Antwerp, were the bills of exchange of certain trading houses considered safe from the very outset. At these exchanges the concept of absolute credit-worthiness emerged, which gave an objective interchangeable value to obligations that were independent of personal considerations of credit-worthiness. None the less, trading houses might still vary in their qualifications, but they were reliable as far as their money obligations were concerned, and such obligations – adequate for this objective purpose – were thereby severed from any other individual characteristics. Just as the stock exchange raises the essence of money to its purest form, so it has, through the creation of the general and objective concept of being 'credit-worthy', typically developed a relief for one side that is not outweighed by a burden for the other but which, on the contrary, provides the same facilities to the creditors as to the debtors by transforming uncertain individual assessments into an objectively valid quality.

Cultural development increases the number of persons on whom one is dependent

The importance of the money economy for individual liberty is enhanced if we explore the form that the persistent relations of dependence actually possess. As already indicated, the money economy makes possible not only a solution but a specific kind of mutual dependence which, at the same time, affords room for a maximum of liberty. Firstly, on the face of it, it creates a series of previously unknown obligations. Dependency upon third persons has spread into completely new areas ever since a considerable amount of working capital, mostly in terms of mortgages, had to be sunk into the soil in order to wrest from it the required yield. Such dependency upon third parties also spreads once tools that were directly produced with raw materials are produced indirectly by certain amounts of prefabricated components and once the labourer uses means of production which he does not own. The more the activity and life of people becomes dependent upon objective conditions by virtue of a complicated technology, the greater necessarily is the dependence upon more and more people. However, these people gain their significance for the individual concerned solely as representatives of those functions, such as owners of capital and suppliers of working materials. What kind of people they are in other respects plays no role here.

This general fact, the significance of which we shall examine later, presupposes the process by which a person acquires a definite personality in the first place. It is obviously a result of the fact that a majority of qualities, characteristic traits and forces coalesce in a single person. Even though this person is, relatively speaking, a unity, this unity can become real and effective only by unifying a variety of determinants. Just as the essence of the physical organism lies in the fact that it creates the unity of the life-process out of the multitude of material parts, so a man's inner personal unity is based upon the interaction and connection of many elements and determinants. Each individual trait, viewed in isolation, bears an objective character; that is, it is, in and for itself, still not something personal. Neither beauty nor ugliness, neither the physical nor the intellectual centres of power, neither occupations nor intentions, nor indeed all the other innumerable human traits, unambiguously determine a personality as such. For each of them may be combined with any other quality, even with mutually incompatible elements, and may still be found in the make-up of an unlimited variety of personalities. Only the combination and fusion of several traits in one focal point forms a personality which then in its turn imparts to each individual trait a personal–subjective quality. It is not that it is this *or* that trait that makes a unique personality of man, but that he is this *and* that trait. The enigmatic unity of the soul cannot be grasped by the cognitive process directly, but only when it is broken down into a multitude of strands, the re-synthesis of which signifies the unique personality.

Such a personality is almost completely destroyed under the conditions of a money economy. The delivery man, the money-lender, the worker, upon whom we are dependent, do not operate as personalities because they enter into a relationship only by virtue of a single activity such as the delivery of goods, the lending of money, and because their other qualities, which alone' would give them a personality, are missing. This, of course, only signifies the ultimate stage of an on-going development which, in many ways, is not yet completed – for the dependency of human beings upon each other has not yet become wholly objec-tified, and personal elements have not yet been completely excluded. The general tendency, however, undoubtedly moves in the direction of making the individual more and more dependent upon the achievements of people, but less and less dependent upon the personalities that lie behind them. Both pheno-mena have the same root and form the opposing sides of one and the same process: the modern division of labour permits the number of dependencies to increase just as it causes personalities to disappear behind their functions, because only one side of them operates, at the expense of all those others whose composition would make up a personality. The form of social life that would evolve were this tendency to be completely realized would exhibit a profound affinity to socialism, at least to an extreme state socialism. For socialism is con-cerned primarily with transforming to an extreme degree every action of social importance into an objective function. Just as today the official takes up a 'position' that is objectively pre-formed and that only absorbs quite specific individual aspects or energies of his personality, so a fully fledged state socialism would erect, above the world of personalities, a world of objective forms of

social action which would restrict and limit the impulses of individual personalities to very precisely and objectively determined expressions. The relationship of this world to the former is similar to that of the relationship of geometric
figures to empirical bodies. The subjective tendencies and the whole of the
personality could then turn into activity by restricting themselves to one-sided
functional modes into which the necessary societal action is subdivided, fixed
and objectivated. The qualification of acts of the personality would thereby be
completely transferred from the personality, as the *terminus a quo*, to objective
expediency, the *terminus ad quem*. Thus, the forms of human activity would
stand far above the full psychological reality of man, like the realm of Platonic
ideas above the real world. Traces of such formations do frequently exist: often
a function in the division of labour confronts its holders as an independent
imaginary formation so that they, no longer individually differentiated, simply
pass through this function without being able or allowed to put their whole
personality into these rigidly circumscribed individual demands. The personality
as a mere holder of a function or position is just as irrelevant as that of a guest in
a hotel room. In such a social formation, taken to its logical conclusion, the
individual would be infinitely dependent; the one-sided determination of his
performance would make him dependent upon supplementation by the action of
all others and the satisfaction of needs would result not so much from the
specific abilities of the individual but rather from an organization of work which
confronted him externally and which was conceived in accordance with a completely objective standpoint. If state socialism were ever to develop to its fullest
extent then it would pave the way for this differentiation of life-forms.

Money is responsible for impersonal relations between people

The money economy, however, exhibits such differentiation in the sphere of
private interests. On the one hand, money makes possible the plurality of
economic dependencies through its infinite flexibility and divisibility, while on
the other it is conducive to the removal of the personal element from human
relationships through its indifferent and objective nature. Compared with
modern man, the member of a traditional or primitive economy is dependent
only upon a minimum of other persons. Not only is the extent of our needs
considerably wider, but even the elementary necessities that we have in common
with all other human beings (food, clothing and shelter) can be satisfied only
with the help of a much more complex organization and many more hands. Not
only does specialization of our activities itself require an infinitely extended
range of other producers with whom we exchange products, but direct action
itself is dependent upon a growing amount of preparatory work, additional help
and semi-finished products. However, the relatively narrow circle of people

upon whom man was dependent in an undeveloped or under-developed money economy was established much more on a personal basis. It was these specific, familiar, and at the same time irreplaceable people with whom the ancient German peasant or the Indian tribesman, the member of a Slav or Indian caste, and even medieval man frequently stood in economic relations of dependency. The fewer the number of interdependent functions, the more permanent and significant were their representatives. In contrast, consider how many 'delivery men' alone we are dependent upon in a money economy! But they are incomparably less dependent upon the specific individual and can change him easily and frequently at any time. We have only to compare living conditions in a small town with those in a city to obtain an unmistakable though small-scale illustration of this development. While at an earlier stage man paid for the smaller number of his dependencies with the narrowness of personal relations, often with their personal irreplaceability, we are compensated for the great quantity of our dependencies by the indifference towards the respective persons and by our liberty to change them at will. And even though we are much more dependent on the whole of society through the complexity of our needs on the one hand, and the specialization of our abilities on the other, than are primitive people who could make their way through life with their very narrow isolated group, we are remarkably independent of every *specific* member of this society, because his significance for us has been transferred to the one-sided objectivity of his contribution, which can be just as easily produced by any number of other people with different personalities with whom we are connected only by an interest that can be completely expressed in money terms.

This is the most favourable situation for bringing about inner independence, the feeling of individual self-sufficiency. The mere isolation from others does not yet imply such a positive attitude. Stated in purely logical terms, independence is something other than mere non-dependence just as, say, immortality is something other than non-mortality; stone and metal are not mortal but it would not be proper to call them immortal. Even the other meaning of isolation – loneliness – reflects the erroneous impression of pure negativity. If loneliness has a psychological reality and significance then it in no way refers merely to the absence of society but rather to its ideal and then its subsequently negated existence. Loneliness is a distant effect of society, the positive determination of the individual through negative socialization. If mere isolation does not produce a longing for others or satisfaction at being remote from others – in brief, a dependency of feeling – then man is placed completely beyond the question of dependency or freedom and actual freedom takes on no conscious value because it lacks its opposite – friction, temptation, proximity to differences. If freedom means the development of individuality, the conviction to unfold the core of our being with all its individual desires and feelings, then this category implies not a mere absence of relationships but rather a very specific relation to others. These others have to be there and to be experienced as there in order to become irrelevant. Individual freedom is not a pure inner condition of an isolated subject, but rather a phenomenon of correlation which loses its meaning when its opposite is absent. If every human relationship consists of elements of closeness and distance, then independence signifies that distance has reached a maximum, but the elements of attraction can just as little disappear altogether as can the concept of 'left' exist without that of 'right'. The only question is then one of what is the most favourable concrete formation of both elements for promoting independence, both as an objective fact and as a subjective awareness. Such a situation seems to exist when, although extensive relations to other people exist, all genuinely individual elements have been removed from them; as in the case of mutual influences which are, however, exerted anonymously or regulations established without regard for those to whom they apply. The cause as well as the effect of such objective dependencies, where the subject as such remains free, rests upon the interchangeability of persons: the change of human subjects – voluntarily or effected by the structure of the relationship – discloses that indifference to subjective elements of dependence that characterizes the experience of freedom. I recall the experience referred to at the beginning of this chapter, namely that a change in obligations is often experienced as freedom; it is the same form of relationship between obligations and freedom that continues here only in the individual obligation. A simple example is the characteristic difference between a medieval vassal and a serf: the vassal could change his master whereas the serf was unalterably tied to the same one. This reflects an incomparably higher measure of independence for the vassal compared with the serf, even though their obligations, considered by themselves, would have been the same. It is not the bond as such, but being bound to a particular individual master that represents the real antipode of freedom. Even the modern status of domestic servants is characterized by the fact that employers can choose by references and personal recommendations, whereas the servant has neither the chance nor the criteria for making similar choices. Only in most recent times has the scarcity of domestic servants in large cities occasionally provided the possibility of turning down a position for imponderable reasons. Both sides consider this a major step towards the independence of servants, even though the actual demands of the job are no less heavy than they previously were. If we consider the same form of relationship in an altogether different area, we can say that if an anabaptist sect justifies polygamy and the frequent change of wives on the grounds that this destroys the inner dependency or the female role then this is merely the caricature of a basically sound observation. Our overall condition is at any moment composed of both a measure of obligation and a measure of freedom, such that, within a specific sphere of life, the one is to a greater extent realized in its content, the other in its form. The restraints imposed upon us by a specific interest are felt to be less oppressive if we can

299

choose for ourselves the objective, ideal or personal authorities to whom we are obliged without reducing the degree of dependence. A formally similar development emerges for wage labourers in a money economy. In view of the harshness and coerced nature of labour, it seems as if the wage labourer is nothing but a disguised slave. We shall see later how the fact that they are slaves of the objective process of production may be interpreted as a transitional stage towards their emancipation. From the subjective aspect, however, the relationship to the individual employer has become much more loose compared with earlier forms of labour. Certainly the worker is tied to his job almost as the peasant to his lot, but the frequency with which employers change in a money economy and the frequent possibility of choosing and changing them that is made possible by the form of money wages provide an altogether new freedom within the framework of his dependency. The slave could not change his master even if he had been willing to risk much worse living conditions, whereas the industrial worker can do that at any time. By thus eliminating the pressure of irrevocable dependency upon a particular individual master, the worker is already on the way to personal freedom despite his objective bondage. That this emergent freedom has little continuous influence upon the material situation of the worker should not prevent us from appreciating it. For here, as in other spheres, there is no necessary connection between liberty and increased well-being which is usually automatically presupposed by wishes, theories and agitations. The absence of such a connection is largely the result of the fact that the freedom of the worker is matched by the freedom of the employer which did not exist in a society of bonded labour. The slave-owner as well as the lord of the manor had a personal interest in keeping his slaves and his serfs in a good and efficient condition; his authority over them entailed his obligation to them in his own interest. Either this is not the case for the capitalist in relation to the wage labourer or, wherever it may be so, it is usually not realized. The emancipation of the labourer has to be paid for, as it were, by the emancipation of the employer, that is, by the loss of welfare that the bonded labourer enjoyed. The harshness or insecurity of his present condition is very much an indication of the process of emancipation which begins with the elimination of individually determined dependence. Freedom in a social sense, like lack of freedom, is a relationship between human beings. Its growth implies that the relationship changes from one of stability and invariability to one of liability and interchangeability of persons. Since freedom means independence from the will of others, it commences with independence from the will of specific individuals. The lonely settler in the German or American forests is non-dependent; the inhabitants of a modern metropolis are independent in the positive sense of the word, and even though they require innumerable suppliers, workers and co-operators and would be lost without them, their relationship to them is completely objective and is only embodied in money. Thus the city dweller is not dependent upon any of them as particular individuals but only upon their objective services which have a money value and may therefore be carried out by any interchangeable person. In that the purely money relationship ties the individual very closely to the group as an abstract whole and in that this is because money, in the light of our earlier deliberations, is the representative of abstract group forces, the relationship of individual persons to others simply duplicates the relationship that they have to objects as a result of money. By means of the rapid increase in the supply of commodities, on the one hand, and through the peculiar devaluation and loss of quality that objects undergo in a money economy on the other, the individual object becomes irrelevant, often almost worthless. In contrast, not only does the whole class of these objects retain its significance, but as that culture develops our dependency on these and a steadily increasing number of objects grows; one particular pin is just as good or as worthless as any other but the modern civilized individual could not manage without pins. Finally, the significance of money develops according to this very same tendency. The enormous cheapening of money makes specific amounts of money increasingly less valuable and important, while the role of money as a whole becomes more and more powerful and comprehensive. Within the money economy, as these phenomena illustrate, the specificity and indivi-duality of objects becomes more and more indifferent, insubstantial and inter-changeable to us, while the actual function of the whole class of objects becomes more important and makes us increasingly dependent upon it.

This development is part of a much more general pattern which is valid for an extraordinary number of aspects and relationships of human life. These usually have their origin in an integral unity of the material and the personal. This does not mean – as it appears to us today – that the contents of life such as property and work, duty and knowledge, social position and religion possessed some kind of independent existence, a real or conceptual independence, and that they entered any close and solidaristic union only after they had been taken up by the personality. Rather, the primary state is a complete unity, an unbroken indiffer-ence which is completely removed from the opposition of the personal and objective sides of life. At lower levels of human development, for example, imagination is as yet unable to distinguish between objective, logical truth and subjective, psychological formations. Both the child and primitive man im-mediately conceive of the psychological forms of the transitory moment, the fantasy, and the subjective impression as reality. The word and the object, the symbol and what it represents, the name and the person are identical, as has been shown by innumerable ethnological findings and by child psychology. This process does not derive from the fact that two separate series mistakenly con-verge and become confused. Rather, a duality does not yet exist at all, either abstractly or in any concrete manifestation. The notional contents appear from the outset as a completely undivided whole whose unity does not lie in the dissolution of opposites but in their being passed over in silence. Thus, the contents of life – as mentioned above – develop immediately in a personal form. The emphasis on the Ego on the one hand, and the object on the other, evolves from the originally naive unified form as the result of a long, never-ending process of differentiation. The way in which the personality grows out of the state of indifference to the contents of life, the way in which, from the other side, the objectivity of things evolves, is at the same time the process of the emergence of freedom. What we term 'freedom' has such a close relationship to the principle of personality that moral philosophy frequently proclaims both terms to be identical. That unity of psychic elements, their tendency to convergence in one centre, that fixed distinctness and uniqueness of the entity that we term 'personality' actually means independence from and exclusion of all extraneous factors, and development exclusively according to the laws of one's own being which we call freedom. Both concepts of freedom and personality contain, in an equal measure, emphasis upon an ultimate and fundamental point in our being which stands opposed to all that is tangible, external and sensual, both within and outside our own nature. Both are but two expressions of the single fact that a counterpart to the natural, continuous and objectively determined existence has emerged that indicates its distinctiveness not only in the claim to an exceptional position *vis-à-vis* that existence but equally by striving for reconciliation with that existence. If the notion of the personality as counterpart and correlate must grow in equal measure to that of objectivity, then it becomes clear from this connection that a stricter evolution of concepts of objectivity and of individual freedom go hand in hand. Thus we can observe the distinctive parallel movement during the last three hundred years, namely that on the one hand the laws of nature, the material order of things, the objective necessity of events emerge more clearly and distinctly, while on the other we see the emphasis upon the independent individuality, upon personal freedom, upon independence (*Fürsichsein*) in relation to all external and natural forces becoming more and more acute and increasingly stronger. Even the development of art in recent times exhibits the same dual character. The naturalism of Van Eyck and Quattrocento is, as it were, an elaboration of what is most individual in phenomena. The simultaneous appearance of satire, biography and drama in their first forms exhibit a naturalistic style that centres upon the individual as such. This occurred, by the way, at a time when the money economy began perceptibly to display its social implications. Even at the high point of Greek culture we find a quite objective view of the world that is close to the laws of nature as one side of their view of life, the other side of which embraced the complete inner freedom and self-directedness of the personality. To the extent that the Greeks lagged behind in the theoretical formulation of the concept of freedom and the self, a corresponding shortcoming prevailed in the rigorousness of their theories of nature. Whatever difficulties metaphysics may find in the relationship between the objective determination of things and the subjective freedom of the individual, as aspects of culture their development runs parallel and the accentuation of the one seems to require the accentuation of the other in order to preserve the equipoise of inner life.

And here these general reflections touch upon the specific problems with which we are concerned. In the economy, too, the personal and objective sides of work are originally not yet separated. At first, the indifference slowly splits into opposites and the personal element increasingly recedes from production, product and exchange. This process, however, releases individual freedom. As we have just seen, individual freedom grows to the extent that nature becomes more objective and more real for us and displays the peculiarities of its own order so that this freedom increases with the objectivation and depersonalization of the economic universe. Just as the positive sense of individual independence is not awakened in the economic isolation of an unsocial existence, then neither is it awakened in a world view which is as yet unfamiliar with the law-like regularity and strict objectivity of nature. The sense of a distinctive force and of a distinctive value of being independent is a concomitant of this opposition. Indeed, even with regard to our relationship to nature, it appears as if, in the isolation of a primitive economy – in other words, in the period of ignorance of the laws of nature in the modern sense – a much stronger bondage was reinforced by the superstitious interpretation of natural processes. Only through the growth of the economy to its full capacity, complexity and internal interaction does the mutual dependence of people emerge. The elimination of the personal element directs the individual towards his own resources and makes him more positively aware of his liberty than would be possible with the total lack of relationships. Money is the ideal representative of such a condition since it makes possible relationships between people but leaves them personally undisturbed; it is the exact measure of material achievements, but is very inadequate for the particular and the personal. To the discriminating consciousness, the restrictedness of objective dependencies that money provides is but the background that first throws the resulting differentiated personality and its freedom into full relief.

II

Possession as activity

One is accustomed to understanding the dynamics of life, especially where they relate to external objects, as either acquisition – within which, in its broader sense, we also include labour – or as the enjoyment of things. The possession of things, however, does not appear as movement but as a stationary and, as it were, substantial condition that relates to those other dynamics just as being relates to becoming. In contrast with such a notion, I believe that one must also characterize possession as an action if one wishes to grasp the whole depth and breadth of its meaning. The habit of considering possession as something passively accepted, as the unconditionally complying object which, to the extent that it is really possession, does not require any activity on our part, is false. This fact, misjudged in the realm of being, has taken refuge in the ethical realm, as is the case for instance of pious wishes, whenever we hear it as an *exhortation* that we should acquire what we want to own, that every possession entails at the same time an obligation, that one should make the most of one's opportunities, etc. At most, it will be conceded that one has to do something further with one's property. On its own, however, it is supposed to be something static, a terminal point, perhaps a point of departure for action but not action itself. If one looks more closely, this passive concept of property proves to be a fiction, a fiction that is particularly well illustrated in certain primitive circumstances. In ancient northern Peru and ancient Mexico too, the tilling of the fields – redistributed every year – was a common task, but the yield was privately owned. Not only was no one allowed to sell or give away his share, but he also completely lost his share if he voluntarily travelled to other parts and did not return in time for the cultivation of his tract of land. In the same way, the possession of a tract of land in the ancient German marches did not yet signify that one was a real member of the march; in order to be a full member one also had to till the soil oneself and, as was stated in early judicial sentences, make use of water and grazing facilities and have one's own hearth. Ownership that is not to some extent activity is a mere abstraction. Ownership as the point of indifference between the movement that leads towards it and the movement that leads beyond it shrinks to zero. The static concept of property is nothing but the active enjoyment or treatment of the object transposed into a latent condition, and the guarantee for the fact that one can at any time enjoy it or act upon it. The child wants to 'have' every object that interests him; one should 'give' it to him. This only means that the child wants to do something with the object, frequently only to look at it and touch it. The concept of property among primitive peoples is not at all characterized by the permanence or the fundamental timelessness of our concept of it. Rather, it encompasses only a momentary relationship of enjoyment and action with the object which is often, in the next instant, given away or lost with complete indifference. Thus, ownership in its original form is much more unstable than stable. Every higher form of ownership develops as a gradual increase in durability, security and permanency of the relation to the object. Mere momentariness of the object transforms itself into a permanent possibility of falling back upon it without the content or the realization of the object meaning anything other or more than a series of individual undertakings or fructifications. The notion that ownership means something qualitatively new and substantial in contrast to individual acts of disposing with things belongs to the class of typical errors which, for instance, has become so important in the history of the concept of causality. After Hume had called attention to the fact that any factually necessary connection that we term cause and effect could never be established, that the empirically real is only the temporal succession of two events, Kant seems to preserve the security of our image of the world by the proof that the mere sense perception of a temporal sequence is not yet experience as such; rather this experience, even in the empiricist's sense, presupposes a real objectivity and necessity of causal sequences. In other words, whereas in the first case perception was to be confined merely to subjective and individual impressions, Kant pointed to the objective validity of our knowledge independent of the individual case and the individual perceiving subject – just as property exists over and above its individual usage. What is at issue here is an application of the very same category by which we sought to establish the essence of objective value in the first chapter. Beyond the specific contents of our consciousness – perceptions, impulses and emotions – lies a realm of objects, in the awareness of which there hovers the thought that they have a lasting objective validity, independent of their singularity and chance of being perceived. The enduring substance of things, the regular order of their fate, the steadfast character of men and the norms of morality, the demands of the law and the religious meaning of the whole universe – all this has, as it were, an ideal existence and validity which can only be expressed in terms of the independence of the individual facts in which that substance and lawfulness presents itself or in which those demands and norms are or are not satisfied. Just as we distinguish the permanent character of a person from the individual acts by which he expresses himself or which may even contradict him, so the moral imperative exists in unbroken dignity regardless of whether or not it is obeyed in practice. Just as a geometrical proposition is valid independently of the individual figures that represent it more or less exactly, so the substance and powers of the world as a whole exist regardless of which parts of it are alternately conceived by human perception.

Of course, epistemology must distinguish the eternal law of nature from the temporal sum of its realizations. But I do not see what it is supposed to achieve *within the activity of cognition* except the determination of every single possible realization. The objective entity certainly has to be distinguished from the subjective perceptions in which it is reflected. Yet its importance lies only in the fact that it unambiguously determines every possible perception of the object. It is true that the ethical norm lies beyond those individual actions to which it may be positively or negatively applied, but its sole meaning is to determine the value of any such action, and if there were to exist or could exist no individual actions at all to which it referred, then its actual significance would be zero. Briefly, the category of these substances and values is generally different from each individual case and from the relative sum of these cases, no matter how large it may be. Its *absolute* sum total, however, is its exact equivalent. Apart from their metaphysical meaning, they are nothing but the abbreviated expression for the totality of individual events, perceptions and actions. One should not be misled by the fact that certainly no empirical series of particulars – which is always incomplete and relative – covers or exhausts the contents of these categories.

This is the form in which the concept of property is employed. Both conceptually and legally property must clearly be distinguished from individual rights and from the enjoyment of the object's benefits. What anybody will do with their property can never be so determined beforehand that one could say that this sum of actions and enjoyments coincides with his property rights. But the totality of possible and actual uses is nevertheless equal to it. No matter how much the *jura in re aliena* may differ from property rights, there is only a difference of degree between them in terms of their content: property is nothing but a sum total of rights over the object. Even such an apparently unified and circumscribed possession as the Roman principate consisted – in terms of the history of law – of access to a series of offices acquired in different ways, just as the lord of the manor owned the serf as 'property' only in the sense that the lord exerted a sum total of individual, slowly expanding rights over him. Yet property expresses and guarantees not a relative sum but, in principle, the absolute sum total of rights over an object. It is precisely for this reason that property as a reality – even though not as a conceptual abstraction – presupposes, as a necessary corollary, action on the part of the proprietor. Static possession exists only in the imaginary aftermath of the processes that precede it, and in the imaginary anticipation of future enjoyment or use. If one disregards these processes which one falsely considers to be only secondary, then nothing remains of the concept of property.

The mutual dependence of having and being

The various kinds of this subjective movement that is termed ownership are, to some degree, dependent upon the quality of the object concerned. Money, however, is the object of possession that suffers least from this dependency. Acquisition and use of objects other than money depends upon particular forces, specific qualities and endeavours. It follows directly from this that the specific possession, in turn, exercises an influence upon the quality and activity of the owner. Whoever owns an estate or a factory, in so far as he leaves the management to somebody else and becomes a rentier and invests his money in a picture gallery or training stables, no longer has a completely free existence. This means not only that his time is governed in a particular way and form: above all it means that a specific capacity is presupposed as well. Specific material possession entails, at the same time, a retrospective predestination. The possession of different objects is a different type of ownership as soon as it is a question of more than the juridical meaning of property. The ownership of a distinctive object which seeks to be more than the abstract concept of property is nothing that cannot be immediately attached, as if from outside, to every personality. Rather, it exists through an interaction between the forces or qualities of the subject and those of the object and this interaction can only emerge out of a certain relationship of both, that is out of a definite capacity of the subject as well. This is only the reverse of the notion that the owner is determined by the effect of the possession upon him. Just as the possession of specific objects is all the more genuine and active the better and more certainly the human subject is suited for it, so the reverse is just as true: the more fundamentally and intensively the possession is really owned, that is is made useful and enjoyed, then the more distinct and determining will be the effects upon the internal and external nature of the subjects. Thus there is a chain from being to having and from having back to being. Marx's question of whether the consciousness of men determines their being or their being determines their consciousness is here answered in one sphere of existence since men's being in Marx's sense includes having. This peculiar connection, by means of which a person, through a specific investment, is directed towards a particular possession which, on the other hand, determines his being, is tighter or looser depending upon the object that forms its pivot. In the case of objects of a purely aesthetic importance, economic values that are determined by an advanced division of labour and objects that are hard to acquire and utilize, the connection will be very strict, and it will be more and more relaxed along the scales of increasingly indeterminate objects, until it finally seems to disintegrate altogether in relation to money.

The dissolving of this dependency by the possession of money

The independence of being from possessing and of possessing from being that is accomplished by money is first illustrated in its acquisition. Because of the abstract nature of money, it is the end of all possible investments and activities. Just as all roads lead to Rome – Rome being conceived as lying beyond every local interest and as standing in the background of every individual action – so all economic roads lead to money. Just as Irenaeus called Rome the compendium of the world, Spinoza called money the *omnium rerum compendium*. It is at least the constant by-product of all different kinds of production. The peculiarity of money lies in its being acquired by dealing successfully with other objects. The able farmer will produce many fruits of the earth, the diligent shoe-maker lots of shoes; but lots of money is gained by efficiency in any specific trade. To earn money, therefore, does not require those specific qualities by which the acquisition of other objects is tied to the subject's being. There are, it is true, personalities that exhibit a specific ability for dealing with the money side of all transactions. However, since economic transactions are generally expressed in money, the persistent general commercial ability presents itself as a talent for making money. On the other hand, our interpretation is strengthened precisely by the fact that some people are conspicuous for their lack of understanding of all money matters. That such persons are so much in evidence – more than those who, for example, have no talent for agriculture or for literary or technical tasks – itself illustrates that making money refers to a wider circle of qualities than the production of any other value. The fact that money completely divests itself of its origins – that is, the specific activity by which it is deserved, both in the economic as well as the moral sense of 'deserve' – explains why the enjoyment of a well-deserved fortune easily appears to be snobbish and produces a feeling of hatred in the proletarian that does not arise out of other prerogatives, such as birth, office, superiority, unless more embittering and aggravating factors are added to them.

On the other hand, an analogous exception may be observed at the very peak of the money economy. The expert may perhaps recognize the 'hand' of a certain personality at work in the transactions of the great financier or speculator, a specific style and rhythm that characteristically distinguishes the actions of the one from those of another. However, we must first of all take into account what has yet to be demonstrated in the case of other phenomena, namely that in the case of extraordinarily large sums of money the purely quantitative character of money actually provides a place for a nuance of qualitative distinctiveness. The indifference, the refinement and banality that are peculiar to money that is constantly circulating do not affect, to the same extent, these rare and spectacular concentrations of immense fortunes in a single hand. It is also essential to point out here that money as a whole takes on a very distinctive character in specific monetary transactions; that is, when it does not function as a medium of exchange to other objects, but as the central content, as the object of a transaction sufficient to itself. Money is an end in itself in the purely bilateral financial operation not only in the sense that it has suspended its qualities as a means, but also in the sense that it is, from the outset, the self-sufficient centre of interest, which also develops its own distinctive norms and, at the same time, completely autonomous qualities and a corresponding technique. Under these circumstances in which money possesses its own colouring and specific qualifications, a personality may be expressed more readily in the management of this money than when it is the colourless means to altogether different ends. Most important of all in such a case is the fact that money requires a quite specific and actually highly developed technique and only such a technique enables the personality to develop its own individual style. Only when the phenomena of a specific category emerges in such abundance and internal isolation that a special technique evolves to master them, only then does the material become so malleable and pliable that the individual is able to express his own style when handling it.

The particular conditions of these cases in which a specific relationship between money and personality springs up, should not be interpreted as contradicting money's alleged function, namely the separation of having and being. This function presents itself from the point of view of utilization in the following way. As we have seen, what distinguishes property from instantaneous enjoyment is the guarantee that use in any direction and at any time can result from property. The fact of ownership of an object is equal to the sum total of all its uses and enjoyments. The form in which this fact appears at any particular moment is the guarantee for all future enjoyments, the certainty that no one else may use and enjoy this object without the consent of its owner. Under pre-legal conditions – and also, naturally, in those areas within our civilization that lie outside any direct legal control – such a guarantee is secured only through the strength of the owner to protect his property. As soon as this strength diminishes, the owner can no longer exclude others from the enjoyment of what was hitherto his property, and it will be transferred without further ado to another person to whom it will belong, as long as his strength in turn serves to guarantee the exclusive use of the object. There is no need for such personal strength where laws do exist inasmuch as the totality of owners guarantee to the owner permanent ownership and the exclusion of all others from such ownership. In this case we can say that property is the socially guaranteed potentiality for the exclusive enjoyment of an object. This concept of property is enhanced, as it were, if it is realized in terms of money. For if somebody owns money he is assured by the constitution of the community not only of the possession of the money, but thereby of the possession of many other things as well. If the ownership of an object means only the possibility of some specific use of that object that the nature of this object permits, then the possession of money implies the possibility of the enjoyment of an indefinite number of objects. With regard to all other possessions, public order can only guarantee what the particular type of object is endowed with. The public order can guarantee to the landowner that nobody else is allowed to reap the fruits of his land, that he alone may till the soil or let it lie fallow; to the owner of the forest that he may cut timber and hunt game, etc. By minting money, however, the community guarantees to the owner of money that he can acquire grain, wood, game, etc., with his money. Money thus produces a higher potential of the general concept of property, a potential for which the specific character of any other type of property is already dissolved by law and the money-owning individual is confronted with an infinite number of objects the enjoyment of which is equally guaranteed by public order. This means that money alone, unlike one-sidedly determined objects, does not determine its further use and fructi-fication. What applies to states, namely that they are preserved only by the same methods on which they were founded, in no way applies to money – even though it is valid for many other possessions, particularly intellectual ones, and also for various possessions acquired by money, which can be preserved only by the very same interest that led to their acquisition in the first place. The com-plete independence of money from its origins and its eminently ahistorical character is projected in the complete indeterminacy of its use. Hence it seems to us completely unfounded and eccentric to imbue money with personal significance such as resulted from the church's prohibition of interest. Even in the sixteenth century a merchant considered it a sin to practise usury with his own money though not with other people's money which he had borrowed. This distinction appears to be possible only if there exists an inner ethical relation-ship between money and personality as such. Yet the impossibility of under-standing this distinction demonstrates the absence of such a relationship. Wherever such a relationship occurs none the less, it exists not in relation to money as a whole but only with reference to differences in its quantity. It is true that the effect of other kinds of property on the owner and his effect on them is different depending upon their respective amounts; for example, in the case of land the difference between a small farm and a large estate. Yet even here a certain equality of interests and necessary talents exists through which the quality of what is possessed becomes the bond between the owner's possession and his existence. But wherever a definite connection exists between the person and the ownership of money, it is the sheer *quantity* of money itself that operates as the characteristic cause or effect, whereas in the case of other possessions mere quality is incidental to specific personal causes and effects. Only the possession of an enormous amount of money gives a decisive direction to the life of its owner which the wealthy person can hardly escape from. Otherwise, there are only very rare and awkward phenomena that illustrate the personality's direct relationship to money. It has been stated, for instance, that a miser as well as a spendthrift lies hidden in every human being. This means that every individual deviates from the purely average spending pattern of his cultural sphere both downwards as well as upwards. It is almost unavoidable that it appears to the individual, from his subjective sense of values, as if others spend too much or too little on certain items. The reason for this is obvious. The difference in the valuation of specific objects bought with money is, however, not the sole reason; in addition, the person's individual attitude towards money as such has to be considered. This comprises whether someone is inclined to spend a large amount of money at once or prefers a number of smaller expendi-tures; whether the gain of a large sum induces him to wastefulness or to greater economy; whether he is apt to go off the deep end in spending such that every expenditure psychologically facilitates the next one, or whether every purchase leaves behind it an inner obstruction so that a justified purchase is made only reluctantly. All these are individual differences rooted in the depths of the personality that become most apparent or appear at all only in a money economy. But here, too, the source of this expression lies in mere quantity. All these differences in behaviour with regard to money only reflect a matter of degree, in complete contrast to the differences between personalities which we find in their various relationships to things and people. In general it remains true that any possession other than money places more definite demands upon the individual and exerts more definite effects upon him in such a way that it appears to the individual as a determination of or shackle upon his life. Only the possession of money provides complete freedom in both directions, at least up to a very remote and rarely attained point.

For this reason, those professional classes whose productivity lies outside the economy proper have emerged only in the money economy – those concerned with specific intellectual activity such as teachers and literary people, artists and physicians, scholars and state officials. As long as a barter economy prevails there are only very few of them and then mostly on the basis of substantial land ownership. This is the reason why, during the Middle Ages, the Church, and to some extent the nobility, were the supporters of intellectual life. The rank of this category of professional people depends upon the uncompromising question that determines the whole value of their personalities, namely whether they strive for their own betterment or for the realization of an objective goal. Wherever acquisitive activity basically has no other motive than acquisition itself, such a criterion does not exist and may be replaced only through the alternative of ruthless egotism and a reasonable fair-mindedness – though here it would have a basically prohibitive effect. Curiously enough, money, although or rather because it is the most sublimated economic value, may release us from economic bondage – though only, it is true, at the price of confronting us with that relentless question of those activities whose meaning does not lie in economic success. Just as the differentiation of life at a higher stage of development produces new units that form new syntheses, so we already see here that the monetary alienation of possession and the core of the personality provide a new significance for each other.

For the practical content of the activity of the artist, the official, the preacher, the teacher and the scholar is measured against an objective ideal and gives subjective satisfaction to the performer according to these standards. But then there is also the economic success of these activities, which as we know is not always a constant function of their objective and ideal success. Not only can the economic success of these activities be pushed by the lowest dispositions so much into the foreground that it relegates the objective ideals merely to a means; but also, for more sensitive and idealistic people, the material success of the performance may be a consolation, a substitute, a salvation for the insufficiency that is felt with regard to the primary goal. At the very least, it will be something like a respite and a momentary shift of interest which will finally channel new strength into the main objective. Much more difficult and dangerous is the lot of those who do not make any money with their activities, but can only evaluate them objectively and in accordance with their inner demands. They lack the beneficial diversion and consolation of the thought that they have, at least in the economic sense, held their own and have received acknowledgment for it. They feel themselves confronted with an 'all or nothing' ideal and have to adjust to a law that recognizes no extenuating circumstances. Such is the compensation for the advantage of those who are envied because money is of no concern to them and who can devote themselves to a cause. They have to pay for this advantage by the fact that the value of their action is determined by only one type of success. If their action fails they do not have the comfort, however small, that they at least accomplished a tangible secondary success. Since this success is embodied in the form of *money* earned, it thereby greatly facilitates the gaining of such importance. First, it demonstrates in the unambiguous manner the fact that the achievement, in spite of falling short of its own or the objective final value, must still be of value to other people. Furthermore, the structure of money is particularly well suited to operating as a relatively satisfactory substitute for an absent ideal major success because, by virtue of its tangibility and its quantitative determination, it provides a certain support and psychological release from the oscillations and fluctuations of qualitative life-values, particularly where these are still in a state of being conquered. Finally, the complete inner estrangement of money from ideal values prevents an entanglement of the sense of values which would be extremely disquieting to sensitive people. Both consequences remain completely separate, the one may sometimes gain a certain inner importance when the other fails, but they do not mix with one another. Money thus succeeds – after having made the purely intellectual professions possible through the separation of having and being – in supporting, through a new synthesis of what is differentiated, the production of purely intellectual values, not only, as it were, on an absolute, but also on a relative level – precisely where one is not yet accustomed to the indeterminacy of that decision.

Lack of freedom as the interweaving of the mental series

It is precisely through this fundamental separation that the money economy contributes towards the realization of a concept of freedom that is worthy of consideration. Man's lack of freedom is characterized only superficially by the fact that he is dependent upon external powers. This external dependency has its counterpart in those internal relations that intertwine our interests and our actions so closely with other people's that their independent movement and development is hindered. The external lack of freedom often extends to the inner personality. It gives to one psychic realm or energy an unwarranted emphasis such that it interferes with the development of other abilities and cripples their own autonomy. Of course, this constellation may have other causes than that of external dependence. If moral philosophy seeks to define moral freedom as the independence of reason from sensual–egotistic impulses, then this is just a one-sided instance of the whole general ideal of freedom that exists in the specific evolution, the independent living to the full, of a single energy of the soul in relation to all others. Sensuality, too, is 'free' if it is no longer bound up in the norms of reason, that is, no longer restrained by them. Thought is free when it only follows its own inner motives and has detached itself from its involvement with emotions and volitions that influence it in a direction that is alien to it. Thus, one may define freedom as an internal division of labour, as a mutual detachment and differentiation of impulses, interests and capacities. That man is a free person whose various individual energies develop and are alive exclusively for their own purposes and norms. This includes freedom in the ordinary sense of independence from external forces. When closely analysed, the lack of freedom that we endure means nothing other than that the inner strength to combat it, the realm of the soul committed to an imposed purpose, involves other energies and interests which would otherwise not be taken up. We would not view work imposed upon us as lack of freedom unless it hindered us in other activities or enjoyments; we would never view an imposed privation as lack of freedom unless it distorted or suppressed other normal or desired sensual energies. The old saying that freedom means living according to one's own nature is nothing but the concise and abstract expression for what is meant here in a specific concrete sense. Since man consists of a variety of qualities, strengths and impulses, so freedom signifies the independence and evolution of each one of them according to their own laws of life.

The avoidance of the mutual influence of the individual psychic sequences can never be complete; its limit lies in the actual and indispensable psychic connections by which man, with all the diversity of his being and action, ultimately appears as a relative unity. The complete differentiation or freedom of an inner series is an inconceivable concept. The form that may be attained in this respect is that the entanglements and bonds affect increasingly fewer individual points of the series. Wherever one series is unavoidably connected with another psychic sphere, it will achieve its most independent formation if it is bound up with this sphere only generally, but not specifically with each of its elements. Whereas, for example, intelligence is closely connected with the will in such a way that its greatest depths and achievements depend upon the energetic vitality of the latter, thinking will deviate from its own norms and from the independence of its inner consistency as soon as the will that drives it possesses a specific colouring, a special content. Intelligence definitely requires fusing with general life-energy. However, the more it coalesces with specific forms of that energy, for example, religious, political, sensual, etc., the more it is in danger of being unable to develop its own independent direction. Thus, artistic production at the levels of particular refinement and spirituality depends on a higher degree of intellectual training; but it will be able to profit by that development, or even to bear it, only if the training is not too specialized but rather unfolds its range and its depth only in more general fields of knowledge. Otherwise, the independence and purely artistic motivation of production experiences distortions and constraints. For instance, the feeling of love may have the most intimate knowledge of the beloved person as a cause or as an effect or simply as an accompanying phenomenon. Yet the enhancement of the emotions to their limits and their capacity to remain there will easily be handicapped if consciousness is focused one-sidedly on some particular quality of the other person. Rather, only if the overall picture of the beloved determines the consciousness of them, and thereby offsets every specific and one-sided quality they possess, does it become a basis on which the feeling of love can unfold its strength and sincerity undisturbed, and can follow its own impulse. The unavoidable coalescence of psychic energies impedes the free development of the particular energies if they are connected not with a specialized side or stage of development of the other, but rather with its general character. Only in this fashion can the distance be established that enables each of them to develop on their own.

Its application to limitations deriving from economic interests

The case that interests us here is of the same type. The purely intellectual sequences of the psychic process cannot be completely separated from those that carry economic interests whose basic character prevents such a separation, not so much in individual or exceptional cases but in the general context of individual and social life. If this restricts the absolute independence and freedom of purely intellectual labour, then it will be more unlikely to do so, the less the bond concerns a specific economic object. If it is possible, in this context, to base the sequence of economic interests solely upon their most general interest, then the intellectual sequence will gain a distance from it which could not be maintained if the sequence of economic interests were to centre around a specific object requiring specific attention. In this respect, the most suitable kind of property was, for a long time, the ownership of land. Its kind of management, the immediate utility of its products and their regular marketability all permit a relative differentiation and uninterruptedness of intellectual energies. Yet only the money economy heightened this quality to such an extent that someone could be an intellectual worker and nothing else. Money is so much an exclusively economic value and is so far removed from any economic specificity that, within psychological contexts, it grants the greatest amount of freedom to purely intellectual activity. The latter's diversion is minimized; differentiation of the inner series, which here too may be termed 'being and having', is maximized. Thus, a complete concentration of consciousness upon non-material interests makes possible the independence of intellectuality within the division of labour, which in turn results in the evolution of the above-mentioned classes of purely intellectual production. The intellectual flowering of Florence in comparison with Genoa and Venice, which were equally wealthy and endowed with talents, has been attributed partly to the fact that these two had become rich during the Middle Ages largely through commerce, whereas the Florentines, ever since the thirteenth century, had become rich mainly as bankers. The nature of banking required less specific work and left them more freedom for the development of higher interests!

One phenomenon that at first glance seems to contradict money's emancipatory effects is the development of direct taxation. It seems to contradict them because it intensifies the relationship of the person to money while nevertheless eventually having the same importance. During the early decades of the nineteenth century, direct taxes were all tied to the object: land, buildings, enterprises, possessions of all kinds bore the tax regardless of the personal circumstances of the owner or manufacturer, regardless of whether he was in debt or really managed to secure a normal profit. This type of tax is no more commensurate with the individual than is the poll tax which is the most impersonal of all known forms of taxation. The bearer of the tax on real estate and trading capital is the owner of the object who is somehow determined individually by this ownership and differs from others who do not own exactly the same object. Even in the Middle Ages in Germany there was a distinction between the dependent and the more privileged tenant farmer; the former paid a *per capita* rent, every member of the court or the district the same, while in the case of the latter individually arranged rents were raised and were differentiated according to the objective situation. The tax on objects, which forms systematically, though not historically, the second stage that moves toward personalism, is followed historically by taxes on social classes. Their basis was not yet the real individual income of the citizen, but rather was formed according to the main social and economic differences between the major classes within whose wider limits the individual was placed according to his overall social and economic circumstances. Only the present state tax seizes upon the exact personal income, so that all that is individually specific is reduced to mere elements which are not decisive at all. Viewed more closely, this increasingly precise adjustment of tax to one's personal situation in a growing money economy implies increased personal freedom. For this process belongs to the trend towards that differentiation of life processes by which each single one remains strictly within its own area and leaves every other as far as possible unaffected. The most objective principle, the poll tax, most thoughtlessly ignores personal differences in circumstances. Every other tax that is not an exact function of individual income but has to be paid out of this income also transgresses its proper sphere and enters into others where it does not at all belong. As is so often the case, the same process that we observed between the economic and other spheres of life repeats itself among the various elements of the economy. Such a relationship was already present when it was demanded, at the first dawning of liberal ideas in the eighteenth century, that the individual's minimum level of subsistence be free of taxation and that the minimum level of existence of the different estates be set accordingly. Here too we find the tendency for taxes to be adjusted – at first negatively by what they exempted – to particular circumstances while leaving purely personal existence completely untouched. And if recently property taxes have reversed this trend to some extent by being imposed on money and physical assets regardless of the income they produce, then this has its origin in the social standpoints that are quite alien to the interest in individual liberty. Both positive and negative instances illustrate the fact that, with the growing importance of money, taxes – as the shadow of property – are located in an increasingly differentiated manner in their appropriate series and, through pliant flexibility, leave as much liberty as possible to the totality of economic life and to life in general.

The fact that the relationship of the State to its citizens is determined basic-ally by a monetary relationship has its origin primarily in taxation. This refers to a correlation which is important in the present context and may be presented in the following manner. If social strata are primarily differentiated by their money income, then a policy based on the various strata is very restricted because the most divergent objective interests are bound up with the same money income, and therefore any measure taken in the interests of one stratum unavoidably harms many interests within that particular stratum. It is, for instance, impossible to have a uniform middle-class policy if one understands by middle-class levels of income those between 1200 and 3000 marks. For those who are included in this group – businessmen, manual workers, peasants, artisans, white-collar workers, people of independent means and civil servants – have almost no parallel interests in other points of legislation. The problems of tariff policy, of the protection of labour, of rights of association, the furthering of wholesale or retail trade, of trade regulations including those of residence requirements and of sabbath observance will be answered in the most contra-dictory manner within this complex. The same is true for big business and large landed estates which, in terms of their income, belong to the same stratum but, in terms of political interests, belong to completely different camps. The fusion of any one class on the basis of the formal criterion of money income thus loses practical, political significance altogether. The State thereby becomes more dependent upon measures that fit the totality and diversity of interests. This development may be diverted or covered over by countless countervailing forces. However, in principle, one consequence of the replacement of groupings in terms of vocation and birth by groupings in terms of income is that the qualitative interests that are inexpressible in quantitative terms destroy the external significance of status complexes and thereby direct public policy towards an objective level that exists above any kind of classification. This is part of a very typical correlation between the most perfect objectivity and the most perfect consideration of the subjective which has been revealed by the development of taxation.

Furthermore, I wish to show that money provides the technical possibility for the creation of this correlation in basic social relationships as well. I have emphasized several times the medieval theory which gave to every commodity a just price, that is an objectively fair price, an arithmetical equilibrium between money and real value, and which sought to regulate legally against its upward or downward movement. The result had to be subjective in the worst sense of the word – an arbitrary, inadequate valuation that made a momentary constellation into a fetter for future developments. A just and appropriate price could not be brought about through a process of direct levelling but rather by taking account of the overall state of the economy, the many-sided forces of supply and demand, the fluctuating productivity of people and objects as price-determining factors. Although this excluded the individually binding fixing of prices, and had to abandon to the individual the estimation of a continually changing situation, prices were now determined by much more real factors and were, as a result, objectively more commensurable and just. This development could be improved upon still further. A thoroughgoing ideal of fairness would shape prices, not only by co-determining the complications and changes of supra-individual moments but also the extent of the state of the personal assets of the consumers. Individuals' circumstances, too, are objective facts that are very important for the carrying out of individual purchases. However, in principle they do not find any expression at all in price formation. None the less, the fact that one can readily observe this gives this notion its basic paradoxicality. This paradoxicality confronts us in a very obvious manner within the phenomena that I earlier termed the superadditum of wealth: the poor paid more for the same commodity than the rich. On many occasions, however, the contrary is also the case: the poor person often understands his needs to be cheaper and no more difficult to satisfy than the rich person. In a certain sense, the regulation of the price of a doctor's fee appears to be determined according to the circumstances of the consumer. Within certain limits, it is legitimate for the patient to pay the doctor 'according to his circumstances'. Of course, this is particularly justified by the fact that the sick person finds himself in a situation of constraint; he must have a doctor and this must therefore be organized from the outset on the basis of unequal payment for the same services. The citizen too finds himself in a similar situation of constraint in relation to the State whose services he cannot dispense with or even, if he wished, refuse. Therefore it is not surprising that the State takes from the poor a lower compensation for its services and less in taxes, and this not only because it offers greater benefits to the more wealthy. This external objectivity in adjusting reciprocal services has long been recognized as inappropriate and has been replaced by the principle of financial circumstances. The new equation is no less objective than the old one; it is only that it also incorporates personal circumstances among its elements. The new equation has a more appropriate objectivity because the elimination of the general economic circumstances of the individual from price formation – particularly where indispensable items are concerned – seems rather arbitrary and disregards the state of things. The variation in the fee for lawyers according to the value of what is contested points in the same direction. Whoever engages in a lawsuit over 20 marks may ask from the lawyer the same effort as a person in a position to contest a case concerning many thousands. In this way, the lawyer is also paid 'according to circumstances' even though they appear in a more objective form than in relation to the doctor. This principle is the basis for further suggestions which will be dealt with in detail later: for example, that the law fixes fines not on a general level but according to level of income, or that the value of the object of litigation which is set as a limit for appeal to the highest court is no longer, as it was previously, an absolute amount but rather a percentage of the yearly income of the plaintiff. Indeed, the system of unequal prices corresponding to the means of the consumer has recently been declared a general remedy in social policy which would possess the advantages of socialism without its shortcomings. We are interested here not in the correctness but only in the existence of this proposal, which signifies in a peculiar way the completion of the economic development of trade. We saw its beginnings in the purely subjective–personal change of possession – through gifts and theft. By placing objects rather than people in relation with one another, exchange achieves a level of objectivity. At first it is rigidly formal and realized by fixed naturalistic quantities of exchange or by publicly imposed prices which, despite their objective form, remain completely subjective and arbitrary in their content. The more liberal trade of modern times enlarged this objectivity by incorporating all variable elements resulting from accidental circumstances into price formation. The objectivity of trade became more elastic and thus more comprehensive. The above suggestion finally attempts to objectify the most individual factors, such that the economic circumstances of the individual buyer are supposed to modify the price of those objects that he needs. This would be a counterpart or at least an extension of cost theory which claims that prices depend on the conditions of production. Now it would become dependent on the conditions of consumption, or at least vary according to them. If the latter conditions were to hold then the interests of the producers would be secured – which, though utopian, is still logically possible – and prices then would adequately express at every sale all the individual circumstances on which they were based. Everything subjective would have become an objective–legal element of price formation. Such a development would correspond to a philosophical view of the world which sees all original objective data as subjective formations. But through this absolute retracing to the Ego, it would gain the unity, cohesion and palpability that give meaning and value to what we call objectivity. Just as in this case the subject would transcend its antithesis to the object which it has completely absorbed and transcended, so, in the other case, the antithesis is overcome by the fact that the objective behaviour has swallowed up all subjectivity without leaving a residue upon which the antithesis could survive.

What is important in this context is that this ideal formation and the fragmentary approximations to reality are made possible by the concept of money. The sum total of economic situational elements can be fully used for price determination only if there is a uniform equivalent expression of value. Only the reduction to a common denominator provides that uniformity among all elements of an individual situation, which would allow their concurrence for the determination of prices according to just standards. Money's remarkable achievement is to make possible the most adequate realization and effectiveness of every individual complication through the equalization of the greatest diversity – as if all specific forms must first be returned to the common primary element in order to secure complete freedom for individual reorganization. This achievement is the pre-condition for a line of development that will eliminate from the prices of things everything rigid that might distort the individual situation and which is expressed with a certain vehemence in the social principle of unequal prices. These prices, however, possess a relative equality in relation to consumer's circumstances and thereby form the subjective pre-conditions – through their total inclusion – according to a principle of complete objectivity. We first become conscious of objectivity through its absolute contrast with the subject. The distinction can in no way be sharp enough to release the object from its naive or confused identity with the subject. Only the higher level of intellectual development encompasses once more the comprehensive concept of objectivity which includes the subject within it. It no longer requires the immediacy of the contrast to be fixed and clear, but rather it raises the subject to a component part of an objective view of the world or to one of its aspects.

In the earlier formulation – which also includes this development – of the situation in which money favours the separation of owning and being, money clearly expresses and correspondingly concludes a process that had already developed on other levels of historical life. As long as the social order was based on the clan, a stable connection between the individual and the soil prevailed. For the clan was the overall owner of the soil, and its interests were identical with those of the individual. The clan formed the tie that connected being and owning before owning became individualistic. The subsequent transformation of the soil into private property – although it appeared to connect the person with his possession – nevertheless loosened any fundamental connection between them in so far as any arbitrary action with regard to the possession was now possible. The emergent money economy, first of all in the medieval cities, brought about a situation in which land could be mortgaged and rents received from it without affecting the owner personally or reducing his social position. The money economy separated the soil and its owner as a person to such an extent that a limitation upon the full property ownership – as indicated by the mortgage – would no longer be interpreted as the degradation of the owner. Mortgaging and selling appear only as the most extreme consequences of that separation between the person and the soil that is first made possible by money. However, this process had already *commenced* before money existed and at the moment when the institution of the clan dissolved. There is a similar process in the later development which transformed the patriarchal order into the constitutional state with equal rights before the law for all citizens. It also means the detachment of being from owning and of owning from being. Social position is no longer determined by landed property, and property, for its part, is no longer determined by membership of the nobility. This is the result of a whole variety of social movements such as the weakening of the nobility by the numerical increase in the lower strata; the division of labour among the lower strata which on the one hand creates a kind of aristocracy and on the other makes them indispensable to the landed aristocracy; the greater freedom of movement of those strata not tied to the land, etc. All these forces were in operation, for example, at the end of the 'Greek Middle Ages', when maritime trade and colonialism developed and Athens gained the upper hand economically from the seventh century onwards. When the money economy develops it only completes this process. The landowner too now needs money to keep up with the wealthy upstart. Money as a mortgage, as the proceeds from produce or even from land itself moves between the landowner and his property and, by making him more independent of the specific quality of his property and by depriving it of its individual flavour, brings about a growing equality between nobility and other strata. The principle of equal rights for all which finally predominated in the Greek democracies dissolves the mutual dependence of owning and being. But here, too, the money economy only presents itself as the most powerful, and at the same time as the most obvious, factor and expression of a much more broadly based movement. In Germany in the earliest times we see that landed property was not an independent object but the result of the personal membership of the individual to his local community. Land in itself was not the kind of qualified object whose ownership would have given the individual his significance and his following. Rather, because the person possessed this specific importance he was endowed with a specific piece of landed property. This personal tie had already disappeared in the tenth century and had been replaced by an independence of land and soil that might almost be termed a personification of it. This led to the tendency to split up the land and to draw it into the restlessness of economic life. When this tendency was finally checked by the stability inherent in the soil, it was replaced by money, by the most personally estranged economic object. Yet money was the most suitable substance for the clear expression of that separation of being and owning that had already started to affect the conditions of land ownership. Finally, the same phenomenon was displayed from its other side and from the other end of the social ladder in the thirteenth century. In this period, the peasantry had gained a very high level of freedom, particularly in the eastern German provinces, which had been colonized by free peasants in close connection with the then relatively highly developed money economy. However, after a short period of time a sudden reversal occurred: the manorial system was extended, particularly east of the Elbe, and successfully endeavoured to bind the peasant to the soil. At the same time, however, monetary exchange was once more replaced by barter. The binding of the peasants to their economic position, the binding of their existence to their possessions, runs parallel to the decline of the money economy. And even though the money economy has been interpreted as the cause of manorial estates, it is certainly only the most striking of a whole complex of causes which led to the formation of manorial estates at that time. If money as such is considered as an object of property, separated and isolated to some extent from the owner's existence, then, in the historical relations between owning and being, money represents the most definite and decisive and, I would say, the most symptomatic among the factors that bring about the world-historical changes in the contraction and the loosening of that relationship.

Freedom as the articulation of the self in the medium of things

If freedom indeed means the ability to bring about the independence of being from owning, and if money ownership most decisively loosens and breaks the dependence of the one upon the other, then there exists another contrasting and more positive concept of freedom which ties being and owning together again on a higher plane, and yet still finds its strongest realization in money. I refer to the earlier assertion that ownership is not, as it superficially appears to be, a passive acceptance of objects but an acting with and upon them. Ownership, however comprehensive and unlimited, can do with things nothing other than provide an opportunity for the will of the Ego to find its expression in them. For to own something actually means that the object does not resist my intentions, that they can prevail over it. If I state that a person 'belongs' to me, it means that he yields to my wishes, that by natural harmony or suggestive compulsion my being and willing continue to be effective in him. Just as my body is mine and 'mine' to a higher degree than any other object because it obeys my psychic impulses more directly and completely than any other object and because these impulses are almost completely expressed in it, so, to the same extent, every object for which this is valid is mine. The fact that one can 'do what one wishes' with an object is not only a consequence of ownership but actually means that one owns it. Thus, the Ego is surrounded by all its possessions as by a sphere in which its tendencies and character traits gain visible reality. Possessions form an extension of the Ego which is only the centre from which impulses extend into things. The objects are mine if they yield to the right and the strength of my Ego to shape them according to my will. This close relationship to the Ego – as if ownership were, at the same time, its sphere and its expression – is not only embodied in ownership as long as it is retained and persists; rather, it is compatible with our conception of ownership as a sum of activities that the *giving away of values*, whether it is in exchange or as a gift, may heighten the feeling of personal relation to the possession – the attraction that is bound up with self-deprivation and self-sacrifice and which, in a roundabout way, in a reduction in the Ego implies a strengthening of the Ego. Possessive ties are often realized only when the property is given away, just as one experiences a part of one's body most strongly at the moment of extirpation. The fascination of owning is so intensified at the moment of giving property away – painfully or joyfully – that it is not possible to do so without paying this price. This instant – just like the moment of making a profit – is an eminently 'fruitful moment'. The ability of the personality that ownership represents appears visibly intensified by disposing of what is owned, just as, with some modification, also occurs in the urge to destroy. It is said that among the bedouin Arabs begging, giving presents and plundering are interchangeable concepts and necessarily interrelated actions. This shows, particularly in the light of the individualistic character of these tribes, how all these diverse actions with regard to ownership express – with different premises and in different directions – one and the same importance and value of all objects of possession, namely that the personality expresses, reveals and expands itself in possession. To understand the concept of property it is decisive to recognize that the rigid demarcation between it and the self, between internal and external life, is quite superficial and that it should be made more fluid for the purpose of a deeper interpretation. On the one hand, the whole significance of property lies in the fact that it releases certain emotions and impulses of the soul, while on the other hand the sphere of the Ego extends both over and into these 'external' objects just as the process in the mind of the violinist or the painter is continually transferred to the movement of the violin's bow or the brush. Just as the possession of any external object would be meaningless if it did not have a psychic value, so, at the same time, the Ego would collapse and lose its dimensions if it were not surrounded by external objects which become the expression of its tendencies, its strength and its individual manner because they obey or, in other words, belong to it. It seems probable to me that the development of private property originally and most intensively did not take up the *products* of labour as such but the *tools* of labour, including weapons. For tools function most directly as extensions of the limbs, and the resistance of the objects against our impulses is usually experienced only at their end-point. The activity factor present in owning tools is greater than for other possessions and therefore, next to the body, they are the possession that is most completely incorporated into the Ego. Such an interpretation of property indicates the way in which the world views of idealism and freedom are complemented by their counterparts: objects must enter into the Ego, just as the Ego enters into objects.

One might say that the acquisition of property also reflects a growth of the personality beyond the individual – just as procreation has been characterized as such a growth. In both cases, the sphere of the individual extends beyond its original limits, and extends into another self which, however, in a wider sense, is still 'his'. In some Malayan tribes, the father owns only those children who are born after bride wealth has been paid, while those born earlier – though undoubtedly to the same parents – belong to the mother's family. The reason for this rule is naturally a purely practical one, namely, that the children represent objects of value which are given away to the husband by the daughter's marriage but which are retained until the price of the mother has been paid. And yet this custom reveals the deep relationship between possessions and their proliferation. The husband has, as it were, a choice as to whether he wishes to widen his sphere of power by owning his children or retain the values due to his wife's parents. With reference to the earliest Brahmin monks, the Veda states: 'They leave off their activities to strive for sons and to strive for property. For the striving for sons is also the striving for possessions. Both are equally aspirations.' In itself this statement does not yet express the identical content of both endeavours. But it is certainly significant that both examples are chosen to illustrate the identity of all endeavours. In the creation of equals the Ego translates its original limitations on to itself, just as when the Ego is in control of property it enforces the form of its will upon that property. This concept of property as a mere enlargement of the personality is not refuted but rather is strongly confirmed by cases in which the self-awareness of the personality has been transposed from the core of the Ego to its surrounding layers, to property. In the same way, the interpretation of proliferation and of family formation as an expansion of the Ego is not affected by the fact that direct self-interests can recede behind the children's interests. In medieval England it was a mark of bondage if one was not allowed to give away one's daughter or sell an ox without the lord's permission. In fact, whoever was entitled to do so was considered to be free, even if he had to render personal services. That self-awareness has transcended its immediate boundaries, and has become rooted in objects that only indirectly concern it, really proves to what extent property as such means nothing other than the extension of the personality into the objects and, through its domination of them, the gaining of its sphere of influence. This explains the strange phenomenon that sometimes the *sum total* of possessions appears to be identical with the *totality* of the personality. There was a certain class of serfs in medieval France whose legal right it was to enter the state of freedom if they gave over all their property to the lord.

Such an interpretation has a number of consequences for the understanding of different types of property. If freedom means that the will may be realized unhampered, then we seem to be freer the more we own, since we have accepted as the meaning of property that we 'can do whatever we want' with its content. We do not have 'freedom' to do so with other people's property or with objects which cannot be possessed at all. Therefore the Latin, and for a long time also the German, language associated the meaning of the word 'freedom' with that of privilege, or of a special favour – precisely in the sense of our interpretation of freedom. Only the nature of the object owned limits this freedom itself. This is already manifest in relation to our body which we consider our own totally unrestricted property. The body obeys psychic impulses only within the laws of its own constitution and certain movements and performances cannot be requested by our will with any success at all. Such is the case with all other objects. The freedom of my will in relation to a piece of wood that I own extends as far as my being able to carve all kinds of tools out of it, but as soon as I want to make a tool that requires the elasticity of rubber or the hardness of stone my freedom diminishes. What our will is able to do with things is comparable with what an artist can elicit from his instrument. No matter how deeply his emotions and artistry may penetrate his instrument, no matter whether the limits of his powers are predetermined, somewhere such limits do exist. Beyond a certain point, the structure of the instrument does not permit any further yielding to the power of the soul. That is the point at which things no longer 'belong' to us. At the present time, we easily overlook the fundamental limits of ownership when our disrupted adaptations and unbridled strivings after freedom and possessions cause us to demand of objects innumerable things which they cannot possibly provide by virtue of their own and our nature. I recall here the lack of understanding – which has only very recently been corrected – of the substance of art, and the fact that we increasingly tend to expect happiness and peace of mind predominantly from external conditions of life, true culture from technological progress, and contentment and perfection of the individual from the objective structure of society.

By and large, the will is so adjusted to our conditions of life that it does not expect from objects what they cannot perform, and the limitation of our freedom by the inherent laws of possession does not result in positive experiences. Despite this, it would be possible to construct a scale of objects based on the extent to which the will can take command of them and the point on this scale at which they become impenetrable, or the extent to which they can really be 'possessed'. Money would be located at the extreme end of such a scale. That unattainable entity that other objects, as it were, reserve for themselves and which is denied to even unlimited ownership, has completely disappeared in the case of money. Money lacks that structure by which other specific objects, even if we legally own them, refuse to yield to our will. It adjusts with equal ease to every form and every purpose that the will wishes to imprint it with. Obstacles may spring only from the objects that lie behind it. Money itself complies equally with every directive with regard to the object, the extent of expenditure, the speed of spending or retaining. In this manner, money grants to the self the most complete freedom to express itself in an object, although only within the limits set by its own lack of specific qualities. Such limits, however, are merely negative and not a result of money's own positive nature, as is the case with all other objects. All that money is and has to offer is given without reservation to the human will and is completely absorbed by the will. When money can no longer achieve this, then this is due to the fact that nothing remains of money beyond that limit which, for all other objects, represents a reserved and un-yielding part of their existence.

Formally, money is both the most responsive and, because of its complete emptiness, the most irresponsive object. Since the money we own belongs to us absolutely and without reservation, we are unable, in other words, to extract anything more from it. In general it is true to say that an object can mean something to us only by being substantially something in itself; only then, to the extent that the object sets limits to our freedom, does it give way to our freedom. This logical antithesis, in whose tension the unity of our behaviour towards objects is realized, reaches its maximum in money. Money means more to us than any other object of possession because it obeys us without reservation – and it means less to us because it lacks any content that might be appropriated beyond the mere form of possession. We possess it more than anything else but we have less of it than all other objects.

The flexibility of money, as with so many of its qualities, is most clearly and emphatically expressed in the stock exchange, in which the money economy is crystallized as an independent structure just as political organization is crystal-lized in the state. The fluctuations in exchange prices frequently indicate subjec-tive–psychological motivations, which, in their crudeness and independent movements, are totally out of proportion in relation to objective factors. It would certainly be superficial, however, to explain this by pointing out that price fluctuations correspond only rarely to real changes in the quality that the stock represents. For the significance of this quality for the market lies not only in the inner qualities of the State or the brewery, the mine or the bank, but in the relationship of these to all other stocks on the market and their conditions. Therefore, it does not affect their actual basis if, for instance, large insolvencies in Argentina depress the price of Chinese bonds, although the security of such bonds is no more affected by that event than by something that happens on the moon. For the value of these stocks, for all their external stability, none the less depends on the overall situation of the market, the fluctuations of which, at any one point, may for example make the further utilization of those returns less profitable. Over and above these stock market fluctuations, which even though they presuppose the synthesis of the single object with others are still objectively produced, there exists one factor that originates in speculation itself. These wagers on the future quoted price of one stock *themselves have the most considerable influence on such a price.* For instance, as soon as a powerful financial group, for reasons that have nothing to do with the quality of the stock, becomes interested in it, its quoted price will increase; conversely, a bearish group is able to bring about a fall in the quoted price by mere manipulation. Here the real value of the object appears to be the irrelevant substratum above which the movement of market values rises only because it has to be attached to some substance, or rather to some name. The relation between the real and final value of the object and its representation by a bond has lost all stability. This clearly shows the absolute flexibility of this form of value, a form that the objects have gained through money and which has completely detached them from their real basis. Now value follows, almost without resistance, the psychological impulses of the temper, of greed, of unfounded opinion, and it does this in such a striking manner since objective circumstances exist that could provide exact standards of valuation. But value in terms of the money form has made itself independent of its own roots and foundation in order to surrender itself completely to subjective energies. Here, where speculation itself may determine the fate of the object of speculation, the permeability and flexibility of the money form of values has found its most triumphant expression through subjectivity in its strictest sense.

The possession of money and the self

In the light of this, the extension of the self that the possession of money signifies is a very distinctive one. In one sense it is the most complete extension that can be derived from an object; in another sense it is a very limited one because money's flexibility is only that of an extremely liquid body which takes on any form, and does not shape itself but receives any form it may possess only from the surrounding body. This constellation explains psychological facts of the following type. Somebody told me that he felt the urge to buy everything that he liked very much, but not for himself or in order to possess it; his only concern was to give an active expression to his liking of the things, to let them pass through his hands and, in so doing, to set the stamp of his personality upon them. Money thus provides a unique extension of the personality which does not seek to adorn itself with the possession of goods. Such a personality is indifferent to control over objects; it is satisfied with that momentary power over them, and while it appears as if this avoidance of any qualitative relationship to objects would not offer any extension and satisfaction to the person, the very act of buying is experienced as such a satisfaction, because the objects are absolutely obedient to money. Because of the completeness with which money and objects as money-values follow the impulses of the person, he is satisfied by a symbol of his domination over them which is otherwise obtained only through actual ownership. The enjoyment of this mere symbol of enjoyment may come close to the pathological, as in the following case related by a French novelist. An Englishman was a member of a bohemian group whose enjoyment in life consisted of his sponsorship of the wildest orgies, though he himself never joined in but always only paid for everybody – he appeared, said nothing, did nothing, paid for everything and disappeared. The one side of these dubious events – paying for them – must, in this man's experience, have stood for everything. One may readily assume that here is a case of one of those perverse satisfactions that has recently become the subject of sexual pathology. In comparison with ordinary extravagance, which stops at the first stage of possession and enjoyment and the mere squandering of money, the behaviour of this man is particularly eccentric because the enjoyments, represented here by their money equivalent, are so close and directly tempting to him. The absence of a positive owning and using of things on the one hand, and the fact on the other that the mere act of buying is experienced as a relationship between the person and the objects and as a personal satisfaction, can be explained by the expansion that the mere act of spending money affords to the person. Money builds a bridge between such people and objects. In crossing this bridge, the mind experiences the attraction of their possession even if it does in fact not attain it.

This relationship also forms one side of the very complex and important phenomenon of avarice. To the miser who finds his happiness in owning money without ever getting round to the acquisition and enjoyment of particular objects, his sense of power must be more profound and more valuable than any control over specific things could ever be. For every possession – as we saw earlier – has its own limitations. The greedy soul who seeks complete satisfaction and wants to penetrate the ultimate, innermost and absolute nature of things, is painfully rejected by them. Objects are, and remain, something for themselves which resists their complete integration into the sphere of the self and allows the most passionate ownership to end in dissatisfaction. The possession of money is free of this hidden contradiction that exists in all other kinds of possession. At the price of not attaining the objects at all and of removing all specific enjoyments that are dependent upon specific things, money can provide a sense of power that is far enough removed from specific empirical objects that it does not come up against the limitations of ownership. It is only money that we own completely and without reservations; it is only money that merges completely into the function we assign to it. The miser's pleasures must be aesthetically similar to this. For such pleasures lie beyond the impenetrable reality of the world and cling to its light and glimmer which are fully accessible to the mind and can fuse completely with it. However, the phenomena associated with money are but the purest and most transparent parts of a series that also realizes the same principle in other forms. I once met a man who, though no longer young and a well-to-do family man, spent his whole time in learning all kinds of things such as languages without ever using them – dancing without doing it, and skills of all sorts without making use of them or even intending to do so. This is precisely the miserly type – gaining satisfaction from having fully acquired potentialities without ever conceiving of their actualization. Here, too, the attraction must be associated with aesthetic attractions: the control over the pure form and ideal of things or of action in the light of which any progress towards their realization has to be viewed as a decline through unavoidable obstacles, reverses and insufficiencies which must reduce the enjoyment of perfect control over things. Aesthetic contemplation – which as a mere function is possible with regard to any object though is particularly easy with respect to the 'beautiful' – most thoroughly removes the barrier between the self and the objects. To aesthetic contemplation, the notion of the objects unfolds so easily, effortlessly and harmoniously as if they were solely determined by the basic laws of the self. Hence the feeling of liberation which is part of the aesthetic mood, the release from the dull pressure of things, the expansion of the joyful and free self into things, the reality of which usually oppresses it. Such must be the psychological flavour of the enjoyment of merely owning money. It means a peculiar coalescence, abstraction and anticipation of actual ownership and gives to consciousness that free scope, that ominous self-extension through an un-resistant medium, that self-absorption of all possibilities without doing violence or denying reality, all of which are part of any aesthetic enjoyment. The defini-tion of beauty as *une promesse de bonheur* also points to the similarity between the psychological form of aesthetic attraction and the attraction of money; for where else can the latter lie if not in the promise of pleasures that money may provide?

There are, incidentally, attempts to combine the attraction of a still unformed value with that of a formed value. This is one of the ways in which jewelry and precious stones are important. The owner appears as a representative and master of potentially very valuable assets, which on the one hand represent a concen-trated power at his disposal and on the other reveal that the absolute liquidity and mere potentiality that this significance otherwise entails is already congealed into a certain determinate form and specific quality. A particularly striking example of the attempt to combine these two functions is found in India where it has long been customary to save money in the form of jewelry; that is, the rupees were melted down and manufactured into jewelry (this involved only a small loss in value) and then stored in order to spend again as silver in an emergency. Such value obviously has a more concentrated effect and is richer in quality. By giving value a specific quality and eliminating its atomistic structure, it appears to belong more closely to the individual. This is very clearly illustrated by the fact that, since Solomon's day, the royal hoarding of precious metals in the form of utensils has been based on the belief that the treasure was thereby most closely tied to the family, and safe from the enemy's grasp. The direct use of coins as jewelry frequently means that one wishes to have one's assets immediately by one's person and under control. Jewelry exists as an irradiation of the personality and it is therefore essential that it is something valuable when it radiates the personality. Its ideal as well as its practical importance rests upon its close relationship to the self. It has been pointed out that, in the Orient, all wealth is conditional upon the fact that the owner is able to flee with it, to make it, as it were, absolutely dependent upon what may happen to him. On the other hand, the enjoyment of money ownership undoubtedly contains an idealistic element. To stress this element appears to be paradoxical only because, on the one hand, the means of making money usually lacks this element, and on the other, the person who utters the joy usually does so in a form altogether different from the idealistic one. This should not disguise the fact that the pleasure of money ownership as such is one of the most abstract enjoyments and is most remote from sensual immediacy since it is exclusively experienced through a process of thought and fantasy. It resembles the joy of victory which is so strong in some people that they do not even ask what they gain by such a victory.

The peculiar way in which money ownership represents the extension of the personality and which is inherent in any possession, is supported and complemented by the following observation. Every sphere of objects that I imbue with my will is limited by laws inherent to the objects, by laws that my will is unable to break. Such a limit is set not only by the passive resistance of the object but also, from the other side, by the limitations on the capacity of the subject to expand. The range of objects that obey the will may be so large that the self is no more able to fulfil its task. If we say that possession equals freedom; if my freedom – that is, the predominance of my will – increases with the quantity of my possessions, then this is really possible only up to a certain point, beyond which the self is unable to exert and enjoy its potential control over objects. Of course, greed may pass beyond this point, but it reveals its absurdity both in the lack of satisfaction that is part of its own fulfilment, and in the occasional constraint and restriction with which an excess of possessions turns into the opposite of their original character and goal. This leads to such phenomena as that of unprofitable property because the activity of the owner is insufficient to realize a return on it; the despot who becomes tired of ruling his slaves, because his will to power ceases at the unconditional surrender and the lack of resistance which would make him aware of himself; the property-owner who has neither the time nor the strength for the enjoyment of his property because both are completely spent in the administration and nurture of that property. The objects differ only as to the question of what amount of the personality they can absorb at the same time, that is at what point possession becomes meaningless, because the self is able to control it only up to this point. Here, too, money occupies a special position. One might say that the administration, control and enjoyment of money requires less of the person than do other possessions, and that therefore the size of the possessions he may control and build up to an economic sphere of his personality is larger than it is for other forms of property.

Apart from real enjoyment, the appetite for all other things is also, as a rule, limited by the receptivity of the subject, regardless of whether the limitations of both coincide and regardless of how far the distance between them may be. It is only money – as we stated in another context – that does not remain within the bounds that assert themselves as the limitations of the appetite for the object. Naturally, this is all the more the case, the more money is really nothing but 'money', that is a pure medium of exchange without any directly enjoyable value of its own. As long as cattle, food, slaves, etc. – that is, consumer goods – function as money, its ownership means lavish consumption rather than an expanding purchasing power. In other words, here are two different formulae for the extension of the personality alongside one another. In the case of primitive barter, it consists of the acquisition of objects by immediate consumption. One might say that the self extends continuously from the centre, whereas in the case of abstract metal money, to say nothing of credit, these direct stages are of no consequence and are omitted. In contrast with the 'wealthy' man in the barter economy, a rich person in modern society may lead the most modest and restricted life without any gratification in the direct sense. One can, for example, in the culinary sphere discover two tendencies that are a consequence of a developed money economy; namely that, apart from festivities, rich people tend to eat more simply, and that the middle class at least in the cities eats much better. Through the distant effects of money, the self may enjoy his power, his satisfaction and his will in relation to the remotest objects in as far as he neglects and passes over the more direct strata which wealth, in a less developed society, puts at his sole disposal. The ability of the individual to expand, which is limited by his own nature, exhibits a greater elasticity and freedom in relation to money than to any other possession. The difference between this and our earlier considerations is this: earlier it was the specific character of objects that broke down the expansion of the self, whereas here it is the limitations in personal power that must diminish after a certain quantity of possessions has been reached, even with the complete elasticity of the objects. This is a phenomenon that is postponed if the possessions take the form not of specific objects but of money.

III

Differentiation of person and possession

In the history of ideas we are confronted with a development which, despite its simple outline, belongs to the most significant forms of intellectual life by virtue of its comprehensive and penetrating realization. Certain areas are originally completely dominated by one characteristic trait. In the course of time, the unity is split into more and more sub-sections, one of which represents the character of the whole in a limited sense and contrasts with the other parts. Formulated differently, despite any relative contrast between two elements of a whole, both may none the less exhibit the character of one of them, though in an absolute form. For instance, the moral–philosophical justification of egoism may be correct in claiming that we cannot possibly act other than in our personal interest and for personal satisfaction. But then one would have to differentiate between egoism in the narrower and in the broader sense. Whoever satisfies his egoism in the well-being of others, possibly by sacrificing his own life, we must undoubtedly continue to call an altruist and to distinguish from a person whose actions are detrimental and repressive towards others. Such a person would simply be an egotist, even though egoism in its absolute and broadest sense as reflected in any action may also be included in the former. Furthermore, the epistemological assertion that all cognition is a purely subjective process that is exclusively experienced and determined by the Ego may be correct. None the less, we distinguish such conceptions that are objectively true from those that are only subjectively true and are the result of fantasy, arbitrariness and deception of the senses, even though, taken absolutely, this more objective knowledge may also be of merely subjective origin. The trend is towards an increasingly basic and more conscious separation between objective and subjective conceptions which originally moved in a vague psychological state of indifference. This kind of progress seems to repeat itself in the relationship of man to his possessions. Generally speaking, every possession is an extension of the self, a phenomenon within subjective life, and its whole meaning lies in the conscious and emotional reflexes that are the mind's response to the self's relations to objects. In the same sense, everything that happens to possessions is a function of the subject who imposes his will, his emotions, his way of thinking upon them and finds his expression in them. However, historically, this absolute importance of practical as well as intellectual possessions is first embedded in a state of indifference which, located beyond the opposition of the self and the objects, unites them both. The ancient Germanic constitution which tied property directly to the person; the later feudalism which, conversely, tied the person to the property; the close connection with the group as a whole which allows its members *a priori* to grow into their economic positions; the hereditary character of occupations by means of which activity and position on the one hand, and the familial person on the other, became interchangeable terms; every organization of society based on estates and guilds that is conditioned by an organic interplay of the person with his economic position – all these are instances of the lack of differentiation between property and person. Their economic contents or functions and those that represent the self in a more limited sense are very closely and mutually dependent. Such a relationship is observable in the ancient custom of allowing the personal belongings to go with the dead into their grave. It was present too, while this custom existed, when the Anglo-Saxon king had a claim to his vassal's armour when he died, since it was due to the king as a vestige and substitute for the person bound to him. Generally speaking, just as the thought of primitive peoples has no separate categories for distinguishing merely subjective imaginings and the objectively true conception, so it is unable to distinguish clearly in practice between the particular lawfulness of things (wherever this is recognized it readily appears as the personified form of a divine principle) and the self-centred personality that is independent of external factors. The development beyond this stage lies in the separation of these elements. All more advanced economic technology rests upon an increasing independence of economic processes. These processes become detached from the immediacy of personal interests; they function as if they were ends in themselves; their mechanical process becomes less and less disturbed by the irregularities and unpredictability of the personal element. On the other hand, the personal element becomes more and more independent, the individual becomes capable of developing more independently, not of his economic situation as a whole but of the *a priori* factors that determine it. In the course of this distinctive development that separates the objective and subjective elements of practical life, the fact that, in the last analysis, the totality of this practice is based on human subjectivity naturally remains hidden. The organization of mechanical equipment or a factory, even though it accords with objective laws, is, after all, enclosed in personal purposes by the subjective intelligence of man. But this general and positive character is, in a relative sense, focused on one of the elements in which the whole of the area has become fragmented.

Spatial separation and technical objectification through money

If we investigate the role of money in this process of differentiation, it first of all becomes apparent that the role of money is associated with the spatial distance between the individual and his possession. The owner of shares who has absolutely nothing to do with the management of the company; the creditor of a state who never visits the indebted country; the owner of a large landed estate who has leased his lands – they all leave their property to purely technical management, with which they have nothing to do, even though they reap the rewards from their property. And this is possible only by means of money. Only if the profit of an enterprise takes a form that can be easily transferred to any other place does it guarantee to property and the owner, through their spatial separation, a high degreee of independence or, in other words, self-mobility.It enables the property to be managed exclusively according to objective demands while it gives its owner a chance of leading his life independently of the specific demands of his possessions. The power of money to bridge distances enables the owner and his possessions to exist so far apart that each of them may follow their own precepts to a greater extent than in the period when the owner and his possessions still stood in a direct mutual relationship, when every economic engagement was also a personal one, and when every change in personal direction or position meant, at the same time, a corresponding change in economic interests. For primitive peoples in all parts of the world, the solidarity between the person and his possession is expressed in the custom that the possession, to the extent that it is personal, conquered or acquired by work, goes into the grave with the owner. It is obvious from such customs how much objective cultural development, whose progress depends upon the continuous accumulation of inherited goods, became retarded. It is only through inheritance that possessions reach beyond the boundary of the individual and begin to lead an objective and independent existence. The personal type of property, firmly united with the owner, is exemplified in early German law, which stated that every gift could be revoked in cases of ingratitude on the part of the recipient, and in some other cases too. The completely personal character of early forms of ownership is rarely illustrated so acutely: a purely individual–ethical relationship between giver and receiver has a direct legal–economic consequence. The money economy resists such a mode of interpretation even in its external form. The natural gift can be returned in kind whereas the money gift very rapidly becomes not 'the same', but only equal in value. Thus the emotional relationship that might have continued between the natural gift and the giver, and that might have been the basis for the counter-demand, is weakened or negated. A gift in the form of money distances and estranges the gift from the giver much more definitely. Because of this separation of object and person, the ages of highly developed and independent technology are also the epochs of the most individualistic and subjective personalities. The beginning of the Roman Empire and the last 100–150 years are both periods of a highly developed money economy. The technically refined character of legal concepts is also a corollary of that abstract individualism that goes hand-in-hand with the money economy.

Individual Freedom

Prior to the time when Roman law was adopted in Germany – at the same time as the money economy was also adopted – German law had the concept neither of representation in legal affairs, nor of the institution of the juristic person, nor of property as an object of free individual will, but only as a representative of rights and obligations. A legal system that operates with such concepts is no longer possible once the individual has been separated from his fusion with the particular conditions of possession, of social position and of the material contents of existence and has become completely free and self-reliant, and yet has become conceptually divorced from all specific existential tendencies that belong solely to a money economy. Thus, those life interests that have become purely objective may be abandoned legal techniques of Roman law. The relationship between land and its owner in Germany has gone through several stages. First, landed property was the result of personal position in the community, and then, conversely, the person was determined by his property, until finally the independence of landed property took on a totally different meaning, one in which, at the opposite extreme, the personality was allowed to emerge as completely independent of it. In primeval times the personality covered and absorbed the objective relations, while during the patrimonial period the reverse was the case. The money economy differentiates them both, and possession and personality become independent opposites. The culmination that this formal process experiences in money itself is most clearly illustrated by the expression that appears in the most fully developed money economy, namely that money 'works', that is, that it exercises its functions according to forces and norms that are in no way identical with those of its owner but are relatively independent of them. If freedom means only obeying one's own laws, then the distance between property and its owner that is made possible by the money form of returns provides a hitherto unheard-of freedom. The division of labour between subjectivity and the norms of the object is now complete; each has to solve its tasks as they are given by its very nature and this is done free from determination by internally alien elements.

The separation of the total personality from individual work activities

This differentiation by means of money and this individual freedom brought about by differentiation affects not only the rentier. The labour relationship too develops similar features although they are more difficult to recognize. Earlier economic organizations and their present remaining forms in crafts and the retail trade rest upon relationships of personal subordination of the apprentice to the master, the employee to the store-owner, etc. At such levels economic activity is carried out through the interaction of factors that are entirely of a direct personal nature. In each case, this activity is carried out in the spirit of

334

the leading personality and with the subordination of all others to his subjectivity. Through the growing superiority of technical and objective elements over personal ones this relationship takes on a different character. The production manager and the labourer, the director and the salesman in the large department store are now equally subordinated to an objective purpose, and only within this common relationship does subordination continue as a technical necessity in which the requirements of production as an objective process are expressed. Even though this relationship may be harder on the worker in some essential personal respects, it none the less contains an element of freedom in that his subordination is no longer of a subjective–personal nature but is now a technical one. It is now clear that any basic liberation that lies in the transition of subordination into an objective form is very closely related to the complete effectiveness of the money principle. As long as the wage labour relationship is interpreted as a contractual one it certainly contains an element of subordination of the labourer to the employer, because the *working person* is hired – as is still most drastically the case with our domestic servants. In reality, the person as a total, unlimited complex of labour power is hired and thus enters the relationship of dependence and subordination to another person as a complete person. However, as soon as the labour contract emerges as the purchase of labour as a commodity – and this is the final result of the money economy – we are dealing with the offer of a completely objective work activity which, as has been stated, is introduced as a factor in the process of co-operation and is thus combined and co-ordinated with the work of the employer. The growing self-confidence of the modern worker is the result of the fact that he no longer feels subordinate as a person, but rather contributes only an exactly prescribed amount of work – prescribed on the basis of its monetary equivalent – which leaves the person as such all the more free, the more objective, impersonal and technical work and its regulation become. The established money economy has similar consequences for the manager inasmuch as he now produces *for the market*, that is for totally unknown and indifferent consumers who deal with him only through the medium of money. His work is thus objectified in a way that is less concerned with and less dependent upon the individual person than was the case when local and personal considerations for particular buyers – especially where natural exchange relationships still prevailed – affected it. The development of personal freedom for domestic servants too is just as much the result of the increased importance of money. The personal bond that is reflected in domestic servants' 'unmeasured' services is basically connected with their being members of the household. It seems unavoidable that, if the servant lives under the same roof with his master, is fed and sometimes clothed by him, his services will be quantitatively undetermined and dependent only upon the changing needs of the domestic situation, and that he has also to conform to the general rules of the household. Increasingly the tendency seems to be towards transferring different services to people outside the household who have only to contribute quite specific services and who are paid solely in cash. The dissolution of the natural economic household community would therefore lead, on the one hand, to an objective fixing of service and to the more technical nature of services, and, as a direct consequence of this development, to the total independence and self-reliance of servants.

If the development of working conditions continues to proceed in this direction – one made possible by money – then the elimination of certain abuses may perhaps be achieved, abuses for which the modern money economy has largely been blamed. The hostile rejection of relations of superordination and subordination is the motive for anarchism, and although socialism replaces this formal motive by a more material one it is nevertheless one of socialism's basic tenets to remove the differences in human conditions that entitle one person to command and force the other to obey. To a mode of thought that takes the degree of freedom to be the measure of everything socially necessary, the abolition of superordination and subordination is a self-evident demand; but a social order based on superordination and subordination would in itself be no worse than one based on a constitution of complete equality if sentiments of oppression, suffering and degradation were not connected with the former. If socialist theories possessed more psychological clarity with regard to themselves, then they would reflect an awareness of the fact that the equality of individuals is not at all the absolute ideal or the categorical imperative, but only the means for removing certain feelings of affliction for promoting certain feelings of well-being. The only exceptions are those abstract idealists to whom equality is a formal, absolute value demanded at the price of all kinds of possibly practical disadvantages, even at the price of *pereat mundus*. Wherever the significance of a demand does not lie in the demand itself but in its consequences it is *in principle* always possible to replace it, since the same consequences may be attained by very different causes. Such a possibility is very important in this context since all experience has so far shown that superordination and subordination are quite indispensable means of organization and their disappearance would destroy one of the most fruitful forms of social production. It is thus our task to preserve superordination and subordination as long as they have these positive consequences, while at the same time eliminating those psychological consequences that make such relationships abhorrent. This goal is clearly approached to the extent to which all superordination and subordination become merely technical forms of organization, the purely objective character of which no longer evokes any subjective reactions. The point is to separate the organization and the person in such a way that the objective requirements of the organization leave the individuality, freedom and essential life-experience of the person completely undisturbed, no matter what his position in the processes of production and circulation may be. One aspect of such a condition is already realized within a status order – that of the officer corps. Blind subordination to one's superiors is not experienced as degrading since it is nothing but a technically indispensable requirement for military purposes to which every superior is also subjected in the same strict and objective manner. Personal honour and dignity are completely separate from this super- and subordination, which is only attached to the uniform and is merely an objective condition that has no reflection upon the person. Such differentiation also appears, in a different form, in connection with purely intellectual activities. There have always been persons who, despite the total subordination and dependence of their external positions in life, have preserved complete intellectual freedom and individual productivity, particularly in those periods when well established social orders were traversed by the influx of new cultural interests. The old orders continued to exist while the new interests created altogether new internal hierarchies and categories – as in the age of humanism and in the last stages of the *ancien régime*. It is possible to conceive of a situation in which these casually evolving and one-sided conditions become the form of social organization as a whole. Super- and subordination in all its possible forms is now the technical pre-condition for society accomplishing its goals. Yet it also reflects upon the intrinsic significance of the person, upon his freedom to develop, upon his personal relationship with other individuals. By dissolving this amalgamation, all upper and lower positions, all commanding and obeying would become a purely external technique of the social order, which could throw neither light nor shade upon an individual's position and development. Furthermore, all the resentment that is due to the too-close association of the formalities and mere expediency of the social hierarchy with the personal–subjective qualities of the individual, and which calls for an abolition of that hierarchy, would disappear. Through this objectification of performances and its organizational pre-conditions one could preserve all the technical advantages of the latter and avoid the disadvantages for subjectivity and freedom which today are the source of anarchism and, to some extent, of socialism. This is the direction of culture for which, as we have seen, the money economy paved the way. The separation of the worker from his means of production, the ownership of which is considered the focal point of social misery, would in a completely different sense appear as a salvation. This would be true if such a separation were to mean the personal differentiation of the worker as a person from the purely objective conditions in which the techniques of production placed him. Thus, money would bring about one of those frequent developments in which the importance of one factor turns into its opposite as soon as it has unfolded a basic, consistent and all-pervasive effectiveness out of its original limited efficiency. Money, by driving a wedge between the person and the object, not only goes on to destroy the beneficial and supporting connections, but also paves the way for the independence of both from each other so that each of them may find its full satisfactory development undisturbed by the other.

Wherever the organization of labour, or rather social relationships in general, change from the personal to the objective form – and, parallel with this, from a barter to a money economy – we find first of all, at least partially, a deterioration in the position of the subordinate. Payment in kind, in spite of its dangers, undoubtedly possesses certain advantages for the worker compared with money wages. For the greater external exactitude of money wages – in other words, their logical precision – is outweighed by the greater uncertainty of their final value. Bread and shelter possess an absolute value for the worker which, as such, remains the same at all times. The fluctuations in value, which is a general inescapable phenomenon, are at the employer's expense and thus relieve the worker from this risk. The identical money wage, however, may mean something altogether different today than it did a year ago – the chances of fluctuation are shared by the payer and the receiver. This uncertainty and irregularity, which often enough may be quite tangible, is the unavoidable corollary of freedom. The manner in which freedom presents itself is as irregularity, unpredictability and asymmetry. This is why liberal political constitutions like the British are characterized by internal anomalies, lack of organization and systematic structure, whereas despotic compulsion culminates in symmetric structures, uniformity of elements and avoidance of anything that is improvised. Price fluctuations, from which the worker receiving money wages suffers more than if he is paid in kind, have a profound connection with the life-form of freedom whose corollary is the money wage, just as payment in kind reflects a life-form of bondage. According to the maxim, 'where there is a freedom there is also a tax', whose relevance extends far beyond politics, the worker pays the tax, in the form of the instability of money wages, for the freedom made possible by the introduction of money wages. We may observe a corresponding case where, conversely, the contributions of the socially subordinate pass from contributions in kind to money payments. Payment in kind provides a more informal relationship between the beneficiary and the indebted. The serf's labour power is directly embodied in the grain, the fowl and the wine that he delivers to the manor house. They are parts of himself, not yet fully separated from his past and his interests. Correspondingly, they are directly enjoyed by the receiver, who has an interest in their quality and who receives them as personal contributions just as they are given as such. There is, therefore, a much closer relationship here between the obligated and the entitled person than is the case in monetary contributions where the personal element disappears on both sides. Thus we find that during the early Middle Ages in Germany, the custom of alleviating the contributions of the serfs by little favours prevailed. Upon delivering their dues they would receive a small gift in return, at least food and drink. Such a benevolent and, one might even say, gracious treatment of the bondsman has largely disappeared to the extent that money payments increasingly replaced contributions in kind and more severe officials replaced the lord of the manor who lived close to the serfs. The appointment of officials indicated the objectification of management. The official managed according to impersonal technical requirements which were supposed to produce maximum objective results possible; he stood between the serf and the lord with the same depersonalizing effect as money moves between the service of one and the enjoyment of the other. This separate independence of the mediator is also illustrated by the fact that the change from services in kind to money payment provided the bailiff with new opportunities for dishonesty in relation to the absent lord of the manor. However much the peasant profited from the personal character of the relationship, and in this respect suffered from its objectification and transformation into a money relationship, it still remained the indispensable road to the abolition of serfdom as a whole.

Alongside this series of phenomena that tend toward this final goal, there stands another series which, at first glance, has quite opposite consequences. It appears, for example, as if piece wages rather than hourly wages would more readily correspond to the development of a society based on money relationships. Hourly wages stand much closer to the bondage of the whole person with his total but not clearly determinable powers than do piece wages by which the individual, precisely determined and completely objectified service is paid for. Yet at present the worker is, in general, better off with hourly wages – except, for example, where technical advances such as machinery with greatly increased productivity is introduced and piece rates are paid – precisely because payment is not tied to the performance with the same rigidity as are piece rates. Hourly wages remain the same even if stoppages, slow-downs, or mistakes alter the output. Thus, the hourly wage seems more worthy of human beings because it presupposes a greater trust and also grants somewhat more actual freedom within the work situation than do piece wages, in spite of (or rather because of) the fact that the whole person becomes part of the labour process and thus the relentlessness of the purely objective standard is mitigated. The enhancement of this relationship is to be seen in the 'appointment', in which individual performance hardly provides the direct standard of payment; rather, the sum total of performances, including the chance of any interference owing to human deficiencies, is paid for. This is best illustrated by the position of the higher civil servant whose salary no longer has any quantitative relationship to his various achievements, but is supposed to grant him an appropriate standard of living. A recent court decision cancelled part of the salary of a Prussian civil servant who, through his own responsibility, has been unable to function for some time; the Supreme Court rescinded the verdict on the grounds that the salary of an official is not a *pro rata* compensation for his services but an 'annuity' assigned to secure for him a standard of living that corresponds to his social position. Payment is here focused on the personal element and excludes an exact objective equivalent. It is true that these salaries are always fixed for longer periods; so that if the value of money fluctuates, then the stability of living is threatened by the stability of the income, whereas payment on the basis of individual achievement may be more easily adjusted to changes in money value. But this hardly refutes my interpretation, which emphasizes the decisive independence of the personal from the economic element. That the salary is generally fixed and not adjusted to individual fluctuations in economic development certainly signifies the detachment of the person as an independent unit from the particularity of economically assessable work activities. The stable salary relates to the changing level of its particular uses just as the whole personality relates to the necessarily changing quality of its individual performances. The most extreme stage of this series of phenomena – though not always recognizable as such – is remuneration for those ideal functions whose incommensurability with any amount of money renders the notion of 'appropriate' fees illusory. The importance of such payments can only be to contribute so much as is necessary to provide a proper standard of living to the performer, but not to provide an objective equivalent between payment and performance. Therefore, an honorarium is paid to the artist whether or not the portrait turns out well; an admission fee is paid to the musician even if he plays badly; a fee is paid to the physician whether the patient gets well or dies. In contrast, at lower levels, payment is more directly and precisely related to the quality of the work performed. The extent to which the objective relation of the performance and its equivalent is here discarded is illustrated, at first glance, by the disproportion in the various amounts of money paid. If someone pays twice the amount for one portrait, theatre ticket or lecture, as for another and assumes he has paid the appropriate amount in either case, then he certainly cannot say that this picture is exactly twice as beautiful as the other, or that this lecture is twice as true as the other. Even if one wished to relate the payment – independently of objective measurements – to the different quantities of subjective enjoyment, one could not logically claim an exact relationship as indicated by money equivalents, and the higher one moved up the scale of achievements the less satisfactory would be the assessment. Finally, the complete irrelevance of remuneration to performance is vividly illustrated when one pays a few marks for the performance of a music virtuoso which lifted us to the highest levels of our senses. The only meaning we can give to such an equivalent lies not in our supposing it to be equal to the value of the performance, but in its contributing to the artist's support as a proper basis for his performance. For the highest productions the general trend seems to be reversed. The money equivalent is no longer related to individual performance without reference to the person standing behind that performance but is now related directly to this person as a whole regardless of his individual performance.

On closer scrutiny, however, this series of phenomena tends towards the same point as the other series which found its ideal in the pure objectivity of the economic position. Both of them equally culminate in a complete, mutual, independence of economic achievement and personality. For this is surely the meaning of the fact that an official or an artist is not remunerated for his specific activity but is given an honorarium to allow him a certain personal standard of living. In any case, and in contrast to the former series, the personal element is here connected with the economic, but in such a manner that the achievements for which – in the last analysis – the equivalent is given are very sharply contrasted with the total person as the basis of the achievement. The liberation of the personality that is secured by its differentiation from the objective achievement is carried out in the same manner. This liberation commences either from the growing objectivation of the achievement, which finally enters into economic circulation on its own account and leaves the person outside it, or from the honorarium or support of the person as a whole, from which the individual achievement emerges without a direct and individual economic equivalent. In both cases the person is liberated from the constraints that would be imposed on him by a direct economic linkage with the particular objective achievement.

The second series certainly seems to be less conditioned by the money economy than the first. If the mutual independence between person and achievement is the result of emphasis upon the latter, then money has to play a greater role than if the person is, so to speak, the active element in the process of separation. For money, because of its impersonal character and its unconditioned flexibility, has a strong affinity with the individual achievement as such and has a specific power to accentuate it. In contrast, the level and security of the standard of living, which is equivalent to the success of the person as a whole, could just as well be secured in more primitive economic forms by granting to the person a piece of land or some kind of regalia. The specific importance of money within this series arises not out of the part played by the receiver, but that played by the giver. For money enables us to compare the total equivalent for the life-work of a single worker *with the contributions of many people*, whether these contributions are the entrance fees of concert-goers or the expenditures of book-buyers or the taxes of citizens from which the civil servants are paid. This is particularly evident in the connection which the money economy evidently has with the emergence of mechanical reproductions. After the invention of book printing, the same price per sheet of paper is paid for the most miserable trash as for the most sublime poem; after photography had been invented, a copy of the Bella di Tiziano is no more expensive than that of a cabaret singer; after the mechanical production of utensils was developed, utensils in excellent taste are no more expensive than those in poor taste. If the creator of one kind makes more money than the other, then this is only the result of *the larger number of buyers* who all pay the same price regardless of quality. Herein lies the democratic character of money when compared with giving gifts to honoured persons as in forms of feudalism or patronage. In contrast, the anonymity of the person who gives money certainly supports the subjective independence and free growth of the person who offers the goods. The rapid growth of mechanical modes of reproduction in particular, and consequently the tendency of money prices to become independent of the quality of the product, breaks the bond that a specific payment for a specific achievement had created between buyer and producer. In the process of differentiation between the person and his achievement, money supports the independence of the person regardless of whether the separation of the originally intertwined elements has its origins in the growing independence of the person or of the achievement.

The development of the individual's independence from the group

If we look back to the beginning of our analysis, then the whole process of separation between person and object appears predominantly as a differentiation of the person. His different interests and spheres of activity gain relative independence through the money economy. When I stated that money separates economic achievement from the total personality and that, taken absolutely, the achievements always remain a part of the personality, then, on the other hand, this no longer means his total entity, but rather only those psychic contents and energies that remain after the economic ones have been excluded. Thus, one may characterize the effect of money as an atomization of the individual person, as an individualization that occurs within the person. This is, however, a general tendency of the whole society that extends inside the individual. Just as money affects the elements of the individual, so it also acts primarily upon the elements of society, that is upon individuals. This latter consequence of the money economy is often emphasized and is associated with the fact that money is a transfer to the achievements of others. Whereas in the period prior to the emergence of a money economy, the individual was directly dependent upon his group and the exchange of services united everyone closely with the whole of society, today everyone carries around with him, in a condensed latent form, his claim to the achievements of others. Everyone has the choice of deciding when and where he wants to assert this claim, and therefore loosen the direct relations of the earlier form of exchange. The extremely significant power of money to lend to the individual a new independence from group interests is manifested not only in the basic differences between a barter and a money economy but also within the money economy itself. Towards the end of the sixteenth century the Italian writer Botero wrote, 'We have two flourishing Republics in Italy, Venice and Genoa. The Venetians who deal with trade in goods are only fairly wealthy as private citizens, but they have developed an extremely great and wealthy state. The Genoans, on the other hand, are totally devoted to monetary transactions, and in so doing have increased their private fortunes whilst impoverishing their state.' Inasmuch as interests are focused on money and to the extent that possessions consist of money, the individual will develop the tendency and feeling of independent importance in relation to the social whole. He will relate to the social whole as one power confronting another, since he is free to take up business relations and co-operation wherever he likes. Those who trade in general merchandise, however, even if geographically extended as far as that of the Venetians, have to look much more for co-operation and employees within adjacent groups since its complicated and substantive techniques impose local bonds from which money transactions are free. This difference is even more decisive in the relationship between landed property and money. It is a tribute to the depth of this sociological connection that, a hundred years after Botero's statement, men were led to observe that the State would be greatly endangered if the possessions of the ruling class consisted largely of movable personal property which could be removed in times of public emergency, whereas the landowner's interests were inextricably bound up with their native state. The increasing share of industrial wealth as against landed property in England has been held responsible for the decline in ruling class communal social interests. The original self-government was based on personal participation of this class which has now given way increasingly to organs of the State. Mere money taxes, to which we are now reconciled, illustrate the connection between the growing pecuniary character of all relationships and the decline of the old social obligations.

New forms of association brought about by money

Money not only renders the relations of individuals to the group as a whole more independent, but also makes the content of that particular association and the relationship of its members to it undergo a completely new process of differentiation. The medieval corporation embraced the whole individual: a guild of cloth-makers was not an association of people who merely represented the interests of cloth-making, but a living community in technical, social, religious, political and many other respects. Even though such an association was centred around objective interests, it rested directly on its members and they were absorbed in it. In contrast to this unified form, the money economy has made possible innumerable associations that either only take money contributions from their members or tend to pursue merely monetary interests. This is particularly true of the joint stock company whose shareholders are united solely in their interest in the dividends, to such an extent that they do not even care what the company produces. The objective lack of connections between the subject and the object in which the individual has a merely monetary interest is reflected in his personal lack of connection with other human subjects with whom he shares only money interests. Here we have one of the most effective cultural formations, namely the possibility of the individual participating in associations, the objective purpose of which he wants to promote and enjoy, without that connection implying any commitment on his part. Money has made it possible for people to join a group without having to give up any personal freedom and reserve. This is the fundamental, extremely important divergence from the medieval form of unification which did not distinguish between man as such and man as a member of an association. It enclosed within its sphere the general economic, religious, political and familial interests alike. The permanent association at that early stage did not yet know the form of a mere 'contribution', least of all the provision of its main funds from them and from 'limited liabilities'. By and large, and with the reservations necessary for such a general assertion, one might say that the relationships between people were formerly more close, less modified by mediations, mixtures and reserve, and that there were less problematical and noncommittal relationships. The relationship of the individual to the association stood under the banner of 'all or nothing'; it did not tolerate a divisibility by which only a small particle of the otherwise independent personality might enter into it; and it did not find its ideal in giving and receiving money as the sole bond of association. This is valid not only for the individual but also for collective individuals. The money form of common interests also ensures that associations have the possibility of joining a higher unit without its members having to forgo their independence and distinctiveness. After 1848 in France, syndicates of workers' associations of the same trade grew up, each of them delivering its indivisible fund to this syndicate and thereby providing an indivisible common fund whose main purpose was wholesale purchasing and offering of loans, etc. It was never the purpose of the syndicates, however, to unite the participating associations in a single unit; rather, each of them was supposed to preserve its particular organization. This case is particularly instructive since, at that time, workers had a genuine obsession for forming associations. If they expressly rejected this amalgamation, then there must have been particularly strong reasons for mutual reserve; and yet they found a way of realizing the existing unity of their interest in that communality through the mere possession of money. Certain associations were made possible only on the basis of this completely subjective freedom which is guaranteed to the members of an association by their money contributions. The Gustav-Adolf Association, the large community for the support of needy evangelical congregations, could never have come into existence and into operation unless the character (or rather lack of character) of money contributions had blurred the contributors' doctrinal differences. Lutheran, Reformed and United congregations would have been unwilling to take part in any other form of amalgamation. The same is true when the common monetary interest becomes, as it were, a passive one. Until well into the Middle Ages, the English clergy did not form a unified group. In particular, the bishops as feudal lords belonged to the lords and were socially and politically distinct from the lower clergy. This was true as long as taxes were imposed only on landed property, of which the lower clergy had no part. As soon as the special taxation of all clerical income was introduced, a common interest for the whole stratum was created, either in terms of their opposition to it or acceptance of it. An expert on that period considers this event to be one of the most important bonds that first made the clergy a unified estate. With the beginning of a money economy, economic associations developed out of the same basic motive. The increase in capital and its growing importance from the fourteenth century onwards made it necessary to keep it undivided within the family. By keeping the shares of all the heirs together the shares became much more profitable to each heir than they would have been had they been apportioned. In Germany, the participation of all heirs in the undivided legacy began to take place, as well as the continued existence of the old enterprise under joint ownership. This had two consequences. The separation of the household economy from the enterprise evolved within the family so that members of the family in which the domestic economy and other capital were separated could remain partners in an undivided 'firm'. While the importance of money capital had dissolved the traditional family economy, it now created a new unification of these separate elements, in which pure objectivity – released from specific private interests – entered into the interests of capital. Secondly, this communal mode of interests was also taken over by others who did not even have family relations. After the 'business' had been severed from the household economy, the unifying form of working capital was also chosen by people unrelated to each other, so that by the beginning of the fifteenth century the general partnership was already in use. Only after the money economy became prevalent did purely corporate property develop in which the commonly owned capital was objectified in an independent unit and legal entity over and above the various partners, who participated in it with only a limited part of their assets and not as individual persons. Only money could bring about such associations which in no way prejudiced the individual member; only money could create, in its pure form, the association for particular purposes – a type of organization that united individuals' non-personal elements in a project. Money has provided us with the sole possibility for uniting people while excluding everything personal and specific.

The disintegrating and isolating effect of money is not only the general precondition and corollary of this conciliatory and unifying quality; under specific historic conditions, money simultaneously exerts both a disintegrating and a unifying effect. For instance, the organic unity and narrowness of family life has on the one hand been destroyed as a consequence of the money economy, while, acknowledging this as a fact, it has been emphasized that the family has become almost nothing more than an organization for inheritance. If, among several interests that determine the cohesion of the group, one of them has a destructive effect upon all the others, then this interest will survive the others and become the only bond between the different elements whose other relationships it has destroyed. It is not only because of its immanent character, but precisely because it destroys so many other kinds of relationships between people, that money establishes relationships between elements that otherwise would have no connection whatsoever. Today there probably exists no association between people that does not include some monetary interest, even if it is only the rent for a hall for a religious association.

The more the unifying bond of social life takes on the character of an association for specific purposes, the more soulless it becomes. The complete heartlessness of money is reflected in our social culture, which is itself determined by money. Perhaps the power of the socialist ideal is partly a reaction to this. For by declaring war upon this monetary system, socialism seeks to abolish the individual's isolation in relation to the group as embodied in the form of the purposive association, and at the same time it appeals to all the innermost and enthusiastic sympathies for the group that may lie dormant in the individual. Undoubtedly, socialism is directed towards a rationalization of life, towards control of life's chance and unique elements by the law-like regularities and calculations of reason. At the same time, socialism has affinities with the hollow communistic instincts that, as the residue of times long since past, still lie in the remote corners of the soul. Socialism's dual motivations have diametrically opposed psychic roots. On the one hand, socialism is the final developmental product of the rationalistic money economy, and on the other it is the embodiment of the most basic instincts and emotions. The distinguishing feature of its power of attraction lies in rationalism as well as a reaction to rationalism. Socialism has found its inspiring ideal in the ancient clanhood with its communistic equality, while the monetary system leads the individual retrospectively to concentrate upon himself and to leave as objects of personal and emotional devotion on the one hand only the closest individual relations, such as family and friends, and on the other the most remote spheres such as the mother country or mankind. Both social formations are completely estranged – even though for different reasons – from the objective association for specific purposes. One of the most comprehensive and fundamental sociological norms is in operation here. One of the few rules that may be established with some degree of generality concerning the form of social development is this: that the enlargement of the group goes hand in hand with the individualization and independence of its individual members. The evolution of societies usually commences from relatively small groups which hold their elements in strict and equal bonds and then proceeds to a relative larger group which affords freedom, independence and mutual differentiation. The history of family formations such as that of religious communities, the development of economic co-operatives and political parties all illustrate this type. The importance of money for the development of individuality is thus very closely related to the importance that it possesses for the enlargement of social groups. This latter role requires no further elaboration here. I have previously analysed the interaction between the money economy and the size of the economic unit. The more people develop relationships with one another, the more abstract and generally acceptable must be their medium of exchange; conversely, if such a medium exists, then it permits agreements over otherwise inaccessible distances, an inclusion of the most diverse persons in the same project, an interaction and thereby a unification of people who, because of their spatial, social, personal and other discrepancies in interests, could not possibly be integrated into any other group formation.

General relations between a money economy and the principle of individualism

How close the relationship is between the money economy, individualization and enlargement of the circle of social relationships is exemplified by the character of commercial trade, which stands in an obvious relationship on the one hand to the advancing money economy and on the other to the enlargement of relationships that extend beyond the close, self-sufficient group of primitive times. Therefore, trade has a distinctive character because – except at its highest levels – it possesses no techniques that are as complicated as the crafts or as traditionally established as agriculture. The merchant is, to a lesser extent than other economic pursuits, dependent upon training – which always involves a closer and closer relationship with the direct environment – or upon personal and objective tradition – which levels individual specialities – or upon inheritance – upon which the crafts were originally dependent and upon which land ownership still is dependent. It is reported from India that the hereditary nature of occupations is less decisive in commercial trade than it is in manufacturing. It is the techniques of trade that enable the travelling merchant – the pioneer of the money economy who breaks the boundaries of the group – to resist the equalization and amalgamations of other vocations and to insist on his individual ability and risk-taking. I can demonstrate the same correlation in a somewhat far-fetched case. It makes a great deal of difference whether the winner of a competition is awarded an honorary or a money prize. The money prize pays him off; he receives what he deserves. The honorary prize has further consequences; it gives distinction to the whole person (which, under specific circumstances, a money prize may also do, although it is not part of its nature). The money prize refers to the performance, the honorary prize to the performer. But in this latter sense, a tribute to a person is often possible only within a relatively small circle. Such honour, which implies no distinction for the individual, originates only within a small group that keeps itself closed, powerful and unassailable by means of the distinctly defined integrity of its members – as, for instance, the officer's honour, the merchant's honour, the honour of the family, even the often-cited rogue's honour. Every kind of honour is originally the honour of an estate or class, and the honour of man in general or of the single individual only places such demands upon the person as are agreed upon by all the smaller groups within the larger. The honour that does not subordinate its representative to others but brings him into prominence also requires a certain narrowness and solidarity of the group; the name of the victor at the Olympics resounded through the whole of that part of Greece that was closely knit together by this interest. The money prize has an egotistic quality which suggests itself to members of a large group. The unegotistic character which corresponds to the solidarity of the small group is most beautifully symbolized by the custom that the golden wreath presented by the Athenian Council of the Five Hundred for good administration was set aside in the temple. Within smaller and closed interest groups, as for instance for sport affairs or for industrial experts, the honorary prize is fully justified even today. But in so far as the restriction and homogeneity of the group is replaced by openness and heterogeneity, the honorary prize, which reflects the co-operation of the whole group, has to be replaced by the money prize, which reflects the ultimate recognition of the performance. The enlargement of the social group requires the transition to expressing merit in money terms because it means the inescapable atomization of such a group. Since it is impossible to provoke the same sentiment in the same manner in a large group as in a small one, distinction within a large group requires a means by which the recipient is no longer dependent upon the agreement and co-operation of the whole group.

It may be emphasized in this context that money has just as close a relationship to the widening of the social group as to the objectification of the contents of life. This parallel is no mere coincidence. What we term the objective significance of things is, *in practice*, their validity for a larger circle of subjects. In that they outgrow their first connection with the individual person or a small group, and the fortuitousness of subjective interpretation, their perception or formation becomes valid and significant for an increasingly large circle (even if in reality the obstacles in the situation make their general acceptance impossible). In the course of this development, they gain what we call their objective reality or their objectively adequate form – even though the actuality of the ideal validity that is indicated by these concepts rejects all relations with becoming or not becoming recognized. In both respects, the importance of money confirms the closeness of this correlation, which asserts itself in many specific areas. Commercial law in the Middle Ages in Germany was originally only the co-operative law of the individual merchant groups. It developed into a common law on the basis of the universalistic notion that the whole merchant class of the German empire, or even of the world, in fact formed a huge guild. Thus, the common law of the merchant class developed into a common law of commercial transactions. This development clearly shows how the law, in its extension from a narrow to a much wider group, detaches itself from a relationship to mere persons and becomes a law of objective transactions. It was this development that was favoured by and that also favoured an increasing extension of money transactions.

Whereas the technical difficulty of transporting the values of a barter economy over long distances already restricts it to a relatively small number of individual economic spheres, money, by virtue of its perfect mobility, forms the bond that combines the largest extension of the economic sphere with the growing independence of persons. The concept that mediates this correlation between money on the one hand and the extension of the group as well as the differentiation of individuals on the other is often private property as a whole. The small group with a barter economy tends towards common property. Every enlargement of such a group forces it towards the allocation of portions of property. With the very considerable growth in the number of participants, the administration of common property becomes so complicated and conflict-laden, the probability of quarrelsome individuals pressing for escape from communistic restrictions grows to such an extent, the division of labour that conflicts with communal property and a higher degree of efficiency become such a necessity, that one is justified in interpreting private property as a direct consequence of the quantitative increase in the group. A twelfth-century Irish manuscript states that the distribution of land was carried out because the number of families had grown too large, while in Russia, where we still have occasion to observe the transition from communal to private property, it is quite clear that the mere increase in population favours and accelerates this process. However, money is clearly the best-suited foundation for the private and personal form of property. The distribution in separate parts, the fixing of property rights, the realization of individual claims has been made possible only by money. Exchange as such is the primary and purest scheme for the quantitative enlargement of the economic spheres of life. Through exchange, the individual fundamentally extends himself beyond his solipsistic circle – much more so than by robbing or giving presents. Exchange in its basic features is possible, however, only with private property. All collective property tends towards *mortmain*, whereas the specific wishes of the individual and his need of supplementation make exchange necessary for him. Possessions must first be concentrated in the individual for them to spread out from there through the process of exchange. Money as the absolute representative and embodiment of exchange becomes – by means of private property, with its dependence upon exchange – the vehicle for the expansion of the economy, for the inclusion of innumerable contracting parties through the give-and-take of the exchange process. In so doing, however, money resists – and this is the reverse side of the same fact – certain collectivist arrangements that are quite natural in a barter economy. During the Middle Ages the theory prevailed that money payment could be demanded only from those who had personally promised it; therefore the members of the estates that had not been present in the voting assembly often refused to pay. In early thirteenth-century England, it was not yet officially decreed that the decision of the Supreme Council of estates should be binding with respect to taxation for all subjects and against the will of individuals. When, towards the end of the Middle Ages, the provincial estates in Germany formed a corporation that acted as a single unit – often in opposition to the feudal lord – and when its decisions were not the sum total of individual decisions but a decision of all the estates, the former interpretation remained valid for a long time with regard to the granting of taxes. The totality of estates was for a long time considered to be only the sum total of individuals, so that any individual could withdraw himself from the common decision. The same motive becomes effective under very changed circumstances where, with the growing centralization of state administration, local associations none the less remain relatively free concerning their financial policy. German legislation in recent decades, for example, has tended to restrict the social, political and moral obligations of local communities and to reduce them to local organs of the government, while, in contrast, the communities have been given considerable autonomy regarding financial administration. Similar considerations prevail if one emphasizes as the main disadvantage of money fines that money is economically less useful in the hands of the State than in those of the individual. Therefore it is more expedient to grant a certain degree of freedom with reference to the handling of money to whomever is limited in all other respects – a somewhat disguised practical consequence and form of the difficulties with which collectivistic disposal of money has to cope.

Such a difficulty exists despite money's suitability for representing the common interest for the unification of otherwise incompatible individuals. Both aspects may ultimately be traced back to one and the same effect of money, namely to grant separation and mutual independence to those elements that originally existed as a living unity. On the one hand, this disintegration concerns individual personalities and thereby makes possible the convergence of similar interests – however divergent and irreconcilable – in a collective form. On the other hand, this disintegration also affects the communities and makes internal and external communalization difficult for the now sharply differentiated individuals. The form that this contradiction takes permeates the whole of social life far beyond this particular case. It has its origin in the fact that the individual is only one element and member of the social unity, while at the same time being himself a whole entity, whose elements form a relatively closed unity. The role of the individual as a mere organ will frequently clash with the role that he can or wants to play as a separate organism. The same influence that affects both the social entity composed of individuals and the individual as a whole entity, produces the same formal effects in both cases. This often results in actual opposition, since the individual represents these two completely heterogeneous consequences. Therefore it may be a practical though not insoluble logical contradiction that money brings about the differentiation of elements in society just as much as in the individual. In society's case, money impedes; in the individual's case it facilitates the same phenomenon. The impediment of the collectivistic disposal of money is, in general, connected with this. All other possessions refer to a certain type of usage by virtue of their technical condition; the freedom of disposition over them therefore has an objective limit. Money's usage completely lacks such a limitation and its common arrangement by many people therefore provides the broadest scope for opposing tendencies. Thus, the money economy stands in decisive contrast to the living conditions of small economic groups who are frequently dependent upon common orders and uniform regulations. One might say – though greatly simplifying the case – that the small group supports itself through individualization and the division of labour. Money as an abstract form evolves out of the economic interactions within a relatively large circle and at the same time, through its merely quantitative character, permits the most exact mechanical expression of every specific demand, of the value of every individual work activity, of every personal tendency. In so doing, money first completes in the economic sphere the general sociological correlation between the expansion of the group and the development of individuality.

The relationship of money to private property and thereby to the free development of the personality is largely conditioned by its movability, and this becomes particularly obvious in its opposite, the ownership of land. Landed property extends beyond the connection with the individual in two directions: breadthwise because, more than anything else, it is suited to the collective property of a group, and depthwise because it is the best object for inheritance. If the whole property of a primitive group consisted of landed property, then development would take place in two main directions. First, by producing food from property it gains a more mobile character; as soon as this happens, private property emerges. As a rule, nomadic peoples hold land as common property of the tribe and assign it only for the use of individual families; but livestock is always the private property of these families. As far as we know, the nomadic tribe has never been communistic with regard to cattle as property. In many other societies too movables were already private property while land remained common property for a long period thereafter. On the other hand, the origin of private property is connected with those activities that are independent of land as a factor of production. In the law of the Indian extended family, the notion developed that whatever had been acquired independently of the family fortune – which consisted predominantly of land – did not have to be incorporated into it. The acquisition of an individual skill – for example learning a craft – is mentioned as the main method for acquiring property and personal independence. The craftsman who carries his skill with him has thereby acquired a mobile commodity which – just like the ownership of cattle, though in a different fashion – severs the individual from landed property and from its collectivistic character. Finally, the transition from a communal to an individual form of life is a useful means for preserving the co-operation that resulted from it after the barter economy dissolved. Until the thirteenth century, the assets of the religious communities consisted largely of landed property and their management was based on the principle of the social economy. The decline in farming profits led to a serious economic crisis, but the emergent money economy that had brought about this crisis also provided a remedy. The revenues of the benefactors and even of the monasteries were more or less extensively split up into salaries and benefactions; and now more of them, from various distant areas, could be given to a single person because the revenue was calculated in money terms. In this way it was still possible – with sinking total revenues – to maintain the income of at least the leading and representative persons of the communities at the same level, although this occurred at the expense of the lower clergy who now had to serve the community as hirelings. This chain of events clearly shows how the declining importance of land pushes even those groups – such as the Church – that are specifically intended for co-operation and unity from collectivistic to individualistic forms of life and how the intruding money economy forms the cause just as much as the means for this process – by the subdivision and mobilization of land. The reason why the peasant today is the most unyielding adversary of socialistic tendencies lies firstly in the fact that, in practical contrast with the techniques of his trade, he is extremely conservative. Since private property now exists he clings to it, just as he did centuries ago to the German mark community and much later still to mixed crop farming. Modern socialism has one main feature which is totally antipathetic to the earlier collectivism of landed property and quite alien to the farmer's impulses in life, namely the complete control of production by reason, the will and the organizing calculations of man. The organization of the factory and the construction of machinery demonstrates daily to the industrial worker that efficient movements and effects can be accomplished with absolute accuracy and that personal and other internal disturbances must be avoided at all costs. This attainment of ends by a transparent and controllable mechanism paves the way for a social ideal that seeks to organize the social totality with the supreme rationalism of the machine and the exclusion of all private impulses. In contrast, the peasant's work and its success is dependent upon independent and unpredictable powers, and his thoughts are concerned with a favour that is not subject to reason and with the respective utilization of irregular conditions. Thus his ideals are opposed to those of socialism which aims not at favours but at the elimination of all that is fortuitous and at an organization – impossible in agricultural pursuits – that makes all elements of life calculable. The complete control of total production by reason and willpower is technically possible only with total centralization of the means of production in the hands of 'society' – but it is obvious how different the ancient collectivity of a primitive economy is in its core and in its meaning from socialism, whose ideal grew out of the most mobilized property conditions determined by the money economy. This is true in spite of the fact that primitive collectivism as an instinct and as a nebulous ideal may have contributed to the driving forces of socialism.

Historically at any rate, the correlation between the primitive economy and collectivism and, on the other hand, the mobilization of possessions and their individualization does exist. Closely associated with its character as a collective good, land also possesses a distinctive character as inherited property. If we analyse the economic content of family organizations we often discover that the difference between inherited property and self-acquired property coincides with the difference between immovable and movable assets. In the north-western districts of India, the same word (*jalm*) covers the right of both primogeniture and landed property in the narrower sense. In the contrary case, the connection between movable property and the individual may be so close that among primitive and often very poor tribes the transference of property by inheritance is not carried out at all. Rather, as is reported from many parts of the world, the belongings of the deceased are destroyed. Mystical ideas undoubtedly play a role here: as if the spirit of the dead might be tempted by these things and might return to do damage! However, this merely testifies to the close relationship that exists between the individual and his possessions such that superstitions dwell upon it. It is reported that in the Nicobar Islands it is considered wrong to inherit from kinsfolk and therefore, except for trees and dwellings, assets are destroyed. Trees and dwellings have the character of immovable property, so their connection with the individual is a loose one and they are thus suitable for being transferred to others. We have a dual relationship to things: man persists and things change, and things remain and men change. Where the former predominates, as in movable property, the accentuation is on man, and one is inclined to emphasize the individual as the essential element. Where, in contrast, the objects persist and survive in relation to man, the individual recedes in importance. Land appears as the rock upon which individual life, like the wave, rises and runs off. Therefore immovable property is disposed towards allowing the individual to move into the background, his relationship to the collectivity here being analogous to his relationship to objects. This also accounts for the close relationship of landed property and aristocracy based on the principle of inheritability. I again recall how much, in ancient Greece, the aristocratic principle of *family continuity*, supported by religion, interacted with the central position of landed property. To sell landed property was a violation of duty not only towards one's children, but to a higher degree towards one's ancestors!

It has also been pointed out that royal fiefage was merely in kind, as in early medieval Germany – whereas in countries somewhat closer to a money economy, vassalages could be based also on other benefices – and favoured an aristocratic character of the whole institution. The principle of inheritance is, by and large, opposed to the principle of individuality. It ties the individual person to the sequence of generations, just as collectivism ties him to his contemporaries. In biology inheritance similarly guarantees equality to the generations. The principle of inheritance acts as a barrier to economic individualization. During the thirteenth and fourteenth centuries the individual German family was economically emancipated from 'ancestry' and acted as an independent subject with regard to property. But that was also the end of its differentiation. Neither the father, nor the wife, nor the children had clearly defined individual property rights; the assets remained common property to that particular generation of the family. The various members of the family were not yet individualized in this respect. The emergence of economic individuality begins at the point where inheritance ends. It commences with the individual family and it ceases where inheritance still prevails – *within* the individual family. Only in modern times, where property consists mostly of movables, does this aspect of inheritance with its individualistic consequences predominate over its anti-individualistic nature. Even practical exigencies are powerless against the latter if the property consists of land. Some drawbacks of the peasant's inheritance rights could be remedied in specific cases if the peasants disposed of their property by means of a will. But they do not do this very often. The will is too individualistic when compared with intestate inheritance. To dispose of his property according to personal wishes that differed from tradition and general customs would subject the peasant to too great a strain. Everywhere the immovability of property – whether connected with the collectivity or with inheritance – testifies to the obstacle whose removal would permit a corresponding progress in differentiation and personal freedom. Money, as the most mobile of all goods, represents the pinnacle of this tendency. Money is really that form of property that most effectively liberates the individual from the unifying bonds that extend from other objects of possession.

CHAPTER 5

The Money Equivalent of Personal Values

I

Wergild

The importance of money within the system of appreciation is measurable by the development of the money fine. We first encounter in this area, as its most peculiar manifestation, the atonement of murder by payment of money – an occurrence so frequent in primitive cultures that it makes specific examples unnecessary, at least for its simplest and most direct form. Less appreciated, however, is not so much the frequency as the *intensity* with which the relationship between human value and money value dominates legal conceptions. In early Anglo-Saxon England a *wergild* – the atonement of murder by money payment, a manbote – was even attached to killing the king; a law set it at 2,700 shillings. Such a sum was, for that period, totally imaginary and impossible to obtain. Its real meaning was that, in order to compensate for the deed, the murderer and his whole family had to be sold into slavery, though even then, as one interpreter of the law suggests, the difference remained so large that – as a mere money debt! – it could be cleared only by death. Only by resorting to the money fine was it possible to fix upon the person the magnitude of the crime. Thus within the same culture, at the time of the Seven Kingdoms, the typical *wergild* for an ordinary free man was 200 shillings and that of members of other estates was calculated *according to this norm either in fractions or multiples*. This indicates, in a different manner, the way in which money provided a quantitative concept of the value of human beings. Thus one finds, even at the time of the Magna Carta, the statement that the knight, baron and earl relate to each other as shilling, mark and pound, since these are the proportions of their escheat – a conception that is as typical as its basis is inaccurate. For it illustrates that the tendency to reduce the value of man to a monetary expression is so powerful that it is realized even at the expense of objective accuracy. This tendency not only makes money the measure of man, but it also makes man the measure of the value of money. From time to time, we come across a monetary unit as the sum to be paid for homicide. According to Grimm, the 'perfect skillan' means: I have killed or wounded, therefore I have become penitent. The *solidus* was the basic fine according to which payments were calculated in common law. On the basis of the meaning of 'skillan' we can assume that the word 'shilling' means a simple fine. The value of the human being is considered here to be the principle of classification for the monetary system and as the determinate basis for the value of money. This is similar to the situation where the standard rate of *wergild* among the bedouin – whom Mohammed incorporated into Islam – is one hundred camels, and this rate is at the same time used as the typical ransom money for prisoners and also as dowry money. The same role of money is in evidence where fines are imposed not only for murder but for any offence. In the Merovingian period the *solidus* was no longer 40 but was only 12 *denari*. One may speculate that the reason for this change was that the fine at that time imposed according to *solidi* should be reduced and it was decreed that whenever a *solidus* was required the fine should be no longer 40 but 12 *denari*. From this there evolved the *solidus* fine of 12 *denari* which finally became the generally accepted one. And it is reported that in the Palau Islands any kind of payment is simply called a fine. Here it is not the different coins that determine the scale against which the relative seriousness of the offence is measured, but rather the contrary, that the valuation of the offence creates a measure for establishing money values.

This way of looking at things – in so far as it relates to atonement for murder – is based on a sentiment of general importance. Since the very essence of money rests upon quantity, since money in itself without the determining factor of 'how much' is a completely empty concept, it is of the utmost importance and quite essential that each monetary system possesses a unit, the multiple or part of which represents each specific money value. This original determination without which no monetary system is possible, and which becomes technically refined as a 'standard of coinage', is, as it were, the absolute foundation for the quantitative relations in which money transactions operate. Conceptually speaking, of course, the size of this unit is quite irrelevant, for whatever it may be the necessary amount may be obtained by division or multiplication. Especially in later centuries, the fixing of this unit is actually only partly determined by historical-political or by technical reasons with regard to the coinage. And yet, that amount of money that stands as the measure of all others whenever money is mentioned, and which is, as it were, the representative of money as a whole must have some relationship to man's central sense of value in order to be used as the equivalent for an object or performance that stands uppermost in his mind. This may also explain the often mentioned fact that in countries with a high monetary unit the cost of living is higher than in countries with a lower unit – thus, *ceteris paribus*, dearer in dollar countries than in mark countries, dearer in mark countries than in franc countries. The value of many necessities of life is expressed in these units or some multiple of them, regardless of their absolute size. Yet, both as a cause and a consequence, the monetary unit within a social circle none the less has profound relations with the economically explicable type of life values – no matter how irrelevant this unit seems to be because it can be divided and multiplied at will. It was as a consequence of this connection that the first French Constitution of 1791 adopted the daily wage as the standard of value. Every fully qualified citizen had to pay a direct tax of at least three days' work, and, in order to vote, required an income of 150–200 labour days. Thus, there emerged the notion in value theory that the absolute standard of value was equal to the daily necessities – that is, that which had the most basic value for men – in relation to which precious metals and all money as commodities rose or fell in value. The suggestion of 'labour money' as the basic unit that ought to be equal to the labour value of one hour or one day points in the same direction, namely of using a central limited object determined by an essential human interest as the unit of value. There is only a quantitative difference between this approach and using the equivalent of the human being, the *wergild*, as the basic money unit.

The transition from the utilitarian to the objective and absolute valuation of the human being

The origin of *wergild* is obviously purely utilitarian, and even though it does not altogether pertain to civil law it none the less belongs to that state of indifference with regard to private and public law with which social development begins. The tribe, the clan and the family demanded a substitute for the economic loss which the death of one of its members implied and was willing to accept it instead of an impulsive vendetta. This transformation finally occurs in cases where the vendetta, which was supposed to be superseded, would itself be impossible. Among the Goajiro Indians, someone who accidentally hurt himself had to compensate his own family because he shed the blood of the family. Among some Malayan peoples it is common for the word for 'blood money' to also mean: to get up, to stand up. It reflects the idea that by imposing blood money the slain person is resurrected for his people, that the void created by his death is filled again. In addition to the payment to relatives, a special payment for disturbing the peace of the community was imposed very early on, at least among the Germans. In the same vein, in some Anglo-Saxon kingdoms *wergild* for the family of the king was demanded a second time from the people

357

for the life of their king. Similarly, *wergild* in India was transferred from the royal family to the Brahmins. In the light of such further developments of *wergild*, severed from its private economic origins, it contained from the very beginning an objective supra-individual element since the amount was determined by custom and law, even though it differed according to social status. Thus the value of each person was fixed from birth onwards, quite regardless of his real value to his relatives. Not only was the person thereby valued as substance in contrast to the sum of his concrete achievements, but also the notion was introduced that he, by himself and not only for others, was worth such and such an amount. A characteristic transitional phenomenon from a subjective–economic to an objective evaluation is illustrated in the following instance. In the Hebrew state of around the third century, the regular price for a male slave was 50 *schekel*, for a female slave 30 *schekel*. But as atonement for the killing of a slave one had to pay 30 *sela* (almost twice the amount) since the Pentateuch maintained that the amount was 30 *schekel* and this was mistakenly considered to be 30 *sela*. They clung not to the calculable economic value of the damage done, but rather to a regulation that stemmed from non-economic sources which contrasted considerably – in size as well as lack of differentiation – with the former. The notion that the slave had a definite value, regardless of his utility to his owner, was not yet firmly established. Only the difference between the slave's price which expressed this utility and the atonement payment for killing him – even though brought about by a theological misinterpretation – suggested, none the less, that a specific economic value of a person might be derived from an objective order which revealed his valuation out of the merely private utility for those entitled to it. This transition is facilitated to the extent to which *wergild* becomes purely an institution of the State. In many cases the value of the legal oath was estimated to be proportional to the amount of the *wergild*. And it is significant that sometimes only the freeman has *wergild*, but not the serf. In the Middle Ages in the area around Florence we find many gradations of serfs as *coloni, sedentes, quilini, inquilini, adscripticii, censiti*, etc., whose bondage was probably in reverse relation to their *wergild* so that there was no *wergild* at all for the totally dependent. Even as late as the thirteenth century such a long outdated and merely formal criterion was put forward before the courts in order to grade testimonies accordingly. From the standpoint of individualistic utility, *wergild* should have been maintained all the more strongly, the more someone was the property of a third person. The fact that it happened differently, and that the rank order functioned as a symbol for the weight to be attached to personal testimony, serves to underline the point at which *wergild* became an expression of the objective value of the person.

This development, which elevated the valuation of man from a merely utilitarian to an objective price valuation, reflects a very common mode of thinking. If all human subjects receive one and the same impression of an object, then it seems to be explained only by the fact that the subject in itself possesses this specific quality that is the content of the impression. Very different impressions may, in their differentiation, originate in the subjects who absorb them, but the identity of impressions – if we exclude the most improbable chances – can spring only from the fact that the object of these qualities is reflected in our minds, while admitting of course that this is only a symbolic expression that requires further supplementation. Within the sphere of valuation, this process repeats itself. If the same object is valued differently in different cases and by different persons, then the whole valuation appears as a subjective process which consequently produces different results according to personal circumstances and dispositions. If, however, the object is valued equally by different persons, the conclusion seems unavoidable that the object is worth that much. If, therefore, the relatives of a murdered person demanded different amounts of *wergild*, then it was clear that they wanted to replace their personal loss. As soon, however, as the amount of *wergild* for one particular estate is fixed once and for all, and the same payment is made even for widely different persons and cases, the notion was formed that the man in himself was worth such and such an amount. This indifference to personal differences no longer allows a person's value as a whole to consist of what other individuals enjoy and lose by them; their value is, as it were, embodied in themselves as an objective quality expressible in money. The fixing of *wergild* carried out in the interests of social peace and in order to avoid endless feuds therefore seems to be the psychological origin of the transformation of the originally subjective utilitarian valuation of human life into the objective notion that man has this specific value.

The idea, which is so very important in cultural history, that man as such can be compensated for by money is actually realized in only two or three phenomena: certainly in blood money and in slavery, and perhaps also in bridal purchase, which we shall consider later. The tremendous difference in views that make slavery and blood money quite alien to our thought today might, none the less, from the standpoint of purely economic concepts, be considered to be only a gradual and quantitative difference. For in purchasing slaves, the sum total of their labour services is paid for by money and yet we also pay for various units of those services today by money. The equivalent for the money expended nowadays is, as it was formerly, the labour of man, the difference being that formerly it was acquired as a whole, and now it is acquired from case to case; and formerly the price was paid not to the worker but to another person – apart from cases of one's voluntarily selling oneself into slavery. With regard to blood money too, there is nowadays no contradiction between such payments and our feelings that money compensation be fixed for minor injuries, be they of a physical or mental nature such as slander or breach of promise. Even today, a whole range of less serious crimes are expiated by money according to some penal codes as, for instance, is the case in the state of New York, in the Netherlands and in modern

Japan. From the purely economic standpoint, the killing of a person may be considered to be a merely gradual extension of such partial paralyses and reductions of energies and trials in the same way as death has been seen physiologically as an intensification and spreading of processes that are also to be found to a certain extent, or limited to specific areas of the body, in the 'living' organism.

However, this economic perspective is not the common one. Actually the whole development of the value of life out of predominantly Christian doctrine is based on the idea that man has an *absolute* value. Over and above all the details, relativities, particular forces and expressions of his empirical being stands 'man', as something unified and indivisible whose value cannot possibly be measured by any quantitative standard and cannot be compensated for merely by more or less of another value. This is the basic notion that negates the ideal basis of blood money and slavery, because they place the whole and absolute man in an equation with money, with a relative and merely quantitatively determinable value. That such heightening of the value of human beings occurred is, so to speak, to the credit of Christianity, whose views were anticipated in many other appraisals while at the same time the historical development of its consequences was postponed for a long time; for the Church did not fight against slavery as energetically as it was really obliged to do and it actually supported the atonement for homicide by *wergild*, if only for public peace and in order to avoid bloodshed. Yet despite this removal of human value from any relativity, from any merely quantitatively determined sequence, it corresponds to the mentality of Christianity. What distinguishes a higher culture from a lower one is the multiplicity as well as the length of teleological series. The needs of primitive man are limited in number, and if they are satisfied at all then this is accomplished by a relatively short chain of means. A developing culture not only increases the demands and tasks of men, but also leads the construction of means for each of these individual ends even higher, and already often demands merely for the means a manifold mechanism of interlocking preconditions. Because of this relationship, the abstract notion of ends and means develops only at a higher cultural level. Only at that level, and because of the numerous purposive sequences striving for some kind of unification, because of the continuous removal of the specific purpose by a larger and larger chain of means – only then does the question of the ultimate purpose, that lends reason and dignity to the whole effort, and the question of why emerge. In addition, the life and actions of civilized man pass through an infinite number of purposive systems of which he can control, or even conceive, only a very small part, so that, compared with the simplicity of primitive existence, a frightening differentiation of the elements of life emerges. The idea of an ultimate purpose in which everything is again reconciled, but which is dispensable to undifferentiated conditions and men, stands as peace and salvation in the disunited and fragmentary character of our culture. The further the elements of existence are set apart by qualitative differentiation, the more removed on an abstract plane must that final purpose be which enables us to experience life as a unity. Such longings need not be articulated in a conscious formulation but may exist, no less strongly, as a faint desire, longing or dissatisfaction on the part of the masses. At the beginning of our era, Greco-Roman culture had obviously arrived at this point. Life had become such a finely woven tissue of purposes that, as its result and *focus imaginarius*, a feeling arose with tremendous power: what is the *ultimate* purpose of this whole, the final end of which does not – as does everything else we strive for – reveal itself as a mere means? On the one hand, the resigned or resentful pessimism of that period, its senseless indulgence – which in its momentary existence certainly did not look for a transcending purpose – and on the other the mystical ascetic tendencies are all the expression of the unconscious search for an ultimate purpose of life, and of an anxiety as to the ultimate purpose of the whole diversity and hardship of its apparatus of means. To this end, however, Christianity brought a glorious fulfilment. For the first time in Western history, a real ultimate purpose for life was offered to the masses, an absolute value of existence, quite independent of all the details, fragments and contradictions of the empirical world: salvation of the soul and the kingdom of God. Now there was room in God's house for every soul, and every single one, the meanest and the lowest as well as the soul of the hero and the sage, because each was infinitely valuable by being the representative of its eternal salvation. Through their relationship to the one God, all significance, absoluteness and transcendency was reflected back upon them. The tremendous authoritative dictum that preached an eternal destiny and infinite significance of the soul suspended with one stroke all that was merely relative, all merely quantitative differences in worthiness. The idea of an ultimate purpose which Christianity tied to the absolute value of the soul has clearly undergone a peculiar transformation. Just as every need becomes more permanent the more it is satisfied, so Christianity has ingrained to a large extent the need for an ultimate purpose by its continuous consciousness of it over a long period, so that those who now reject the doctrine shall leave behind them the heritage of an empty longing for a definite purpose of their whole existence: the need has outlived its fulfilment. In so far as Schopenhauer's metaphysics proclaimed the will to be the substance of existence – a will that must necessarily remain unfulfilled because, as the absolute, there is nothing apart from itself that might satisfy it and so can only continue to grasp itself – this metaphysics is the perfect expression of this cultural situation which has retained the vehement need for an absolute final purpose but has lost its compelling content. The weakening of religious sentiments and, at the same time, the vital reawakening need for such sentiments are both a consequence of the fact that modern man is deprived of an ultimate purpose. But what this notion has achieved for the evaluation of the human soul has not been lost but may be counted to the credit of its inheritance. In that Christianity proclaimed the human soul to be the vehicle of God's grace, it became incommensurable with all wordly measures and has remained so. No matter how remote and alien this interpretation really is for actual human beings, its repercussions cannot be avoided where the whole person is at stake. His individual fate may be of no concern, but the absolute sum total cannot remain so. Actually, Hebrew law had already directly proclaimed the religious value of man to be irreconcilable with slavery. If destitution compels an Israelite to sell himself as slave to a clansman, then he shall treat him – as Jahveh commands – as a wage labourer and not as a slave 'for those are *my* servants whom I have led out of Egypt, they should not be sold as one sells slaves'.

But the value of the person, which makes him incommensurable with the purely quantitative scale of money, may have two very different meanings. It may refer to man as man in general or to man as this particular individual. If one states, for instance, that the human personality possesses the highest scarcity value, because it is not interchangeable but is absolutely irreplaceable, then the question remains as to which other values it is isolated from in this way. If the specific qualities of a person – which are different from those of any other person – determine his value, then this scarcity refers to the individual person in relation to all the others. This interpretation, which in part is common to antiquity and modern individualism, leads inescapably to a grading of humanity, and only to the extent that the representatives of the lowest values come into contact with the representatives of the highest values do they participate in the absoluteness of these values. This is the reason why the classical view that slavery is justified is taken over by some modern individualists. The viewpoint of Christianity, the Enlightenment of the eighteenth century (including Rousseau and Kant) and ethical socialism is totally different. From these standpoints, value lies in human beings merely because they are human beings; the scarcity value refers to the human soul as such in contrast to everything else. What is decisive here is that the absolute value of all men is the same. This view is thus that of abstract individualism – 'abstract' because it attaches the whole value, the whole absolute importance to the general concept of man and only transfers it from there to the individual members of the species. In contrast, the nineteenth century since the Romantics has given a totally different content to the concept of individualism. Whereas the contrast from which the individual as such gained his specific significance during the eighteenth century was that of the individual and the collectivity and bonds of the State, Church, society and guild, so that the ideal was the free independence of the individual, the meaning attached to the subsequent individualism lies in the differences between individuals and their qualitative peculiarities. It is the former mode of interpretation, upon whose basis 'human dignity' and 'human rights' have developed, that marks most decisively the development that made every sale of human beings for money, and atonement for their death by money impossible. This is a development whose origins must lie in the situation in which the collectivistic bonds of the earliest social forms wear thin, where the individual raises himself out of the merging of interests with his group companions and insists upon his independence.

Punishment by fine and the stages of culture

I have traced the development of expiation of murder up to the point at which, out of the restitution of actual damage to the survivors calculated according to their status, the notion evolved that the value of man, as a member of a particular estate, was equal to a specific *wergild*. Out of this a further development commences whose result is that the expiatory sacrifice of the criminal is interpreted not as compensation for the destroyed value, but as punishment – and this is true not only for murder but also for other serious offences. Every punishment, as a pain imposed by the idea of expediency, can, as far as I can see, possess only two starting points: the protection of society and the obligation to indemnify for the damage done to society or the victim – no matter how far their subsequent idealistic meanings are removed from these original ones. For if one traces punishment back to vengeance, then it seems to me that vengeance itself requires further explanation. This can be found only in the need for protection which forces man to get the criminal out of the way, a process that can often occur only through the imposition of pain or death. This kind of utility and necessity has developed into an independent impulse such that the damage to those who have done damage, originally merely a means of ensuring against further damage, has become satisfactory in itself, and has given rise to an impulse that is independent of its utilitarian roots. Finally, the origin of punishment as revenge can be traced back to the need for protection. It is this need that makes intelligible the fact that highly civilized ages request the the criminal should be rendered harmless, whereas less civilized ages are satisfied with a milder compensation. For nowadays murder is usually committed only by completely corrupt and morally deprived persons, whereas in rougher or more heroic ages it was also committed by people with quite different qualities, whose superiority and energy in conserving society was in everyone's interest. Thus, it is the difference in the basic traits of the murderer at various stages of historical development that, for reasons of social self-preservation, requires sometimes the destruction and at other times an expiation of the culprit's life. Here we are interested mainly in the other origin of punishment–compensation for damages. As long as or in so far as the consequences of an act of damage for the perpetrator are carried out by the victim himself, it will – apart from impulses of vengeance – be restricted to compensation of the victim. The victim is not interested in the personal situation of the criminal; his action is determined by utility and not by consideration for the person. This situation changes as soon as an objective power, such as the State or the Church, takes over the responsibility for the expiation of the crime. Because the damage to the victim is now no longer a personal event but rather a disturbance of public order or a violation of an ethical–religious law, the condition of the criminal becomes the final purpose of the action taken, whereas formerly his situation was only an indifferent accident for the person who sought compensation. Only here can we talk about *punishment* in the full sense of the word.

The purpose is now to affect the subject himself, and any penalty as practical action is merely a means towards this end. Money fines thus take on a totally different meaning from the former monetary compensation for wounding and killing. They are not supposed to compensate for the damage done, but to inflict pain upon the culprit. Hence modern law, in cases of insolvency, replaces it with imprisonment which not only brings in no money to the State but also requires considerable expense by the State. In so far as fines are imposed because of the subjective reflexes with which the criminal experiences them, fines can, in fact, produce an individual trait that is alien to money as such. This trait is documented by some qualities that make fines superior to other kinds of punishment: it can be well graded, it can be completely cancelled; and it does not, as did imprisonment or even mutilation in former times, paralyse or reduce the labour power of the delinquent, but rather encourages the delinquent to make up for the loss. This personal element that accrues to money fines, however, does not have very far-reaching effects, if they are intended to cause pain and be more than just a substitute for it. This is illustrated, for example, by the fact that nowadays being sentenced to pay the highest possible fine does not endanger the social position of the person it is inflicted upon as much as does even the shortest imprisonment. Only where self-respect is not yet highly developed, as for instance, among the Russian peasantry, is corporal punishment preferred over the fine by the criminal himself. The weakness of the personal element in money fines is further displayed in the fact that – at least as it has been dealt with so far – its basic gradation is not at all adjusted to actual individual circumstances. The law generally sets lower and upper limits to fines, but there is no doubt that the minimum is a much harsher punishment for the very poor than is the maximum for the very rich. Whereas, because of a fine of one mark, the very poor person perhaps has to go hungry for one day, a fine of several thousand marks to which the very rich person may be sentenced does not impose the slightest deprivation upon him. In the one case, the subjective purpose of the punishment is exaggerated and in the other it is not accomplished at all. In order to attain a more effective individualization of fines, it has therefore been suggested that the law should not set definite limits to money fines at all, but rather percentage amounts of the guilty person's income. However, it has rightly been objected that the punishment of a minor violation of the law would be several thousands for a multi-millionaire, which would undoubtedly be considered to be objectively disproportionate to the offence. This internal contradiction in the attempt to achieve a genuine individualization of fines, which seems desirable in the light of major differences in standards of living, illustrates how much lower its subjective suitability is for a highly developed economic culture with pronounced differences of wealth than for more primitive and equitable conditions. Finally, it must be emphasized that fines are completely inadequate where only man's innermost relationships are concerned – from the seventh century onwards penance could be absolved in money. The Church had taken over a large part of the administration of criminal law which was really the State's domain, and the travelling bishop as a judge punished the sinner from the viewpoint of the violated *divine* order. Therefore, the moral improvement of the *soul*, the turning away from sinful pursuits, was the real intention of the punishment and was based on a deep-seated and effective tendency in religious morality. This resulted in the paradox that the positive moral obligation of man lay in gaining his own salvation, whereas secular morality transposes its final goal out of the self and on to the other person and his condition. As a result of this tendency to internalize and individualize punishment, even crimes such as murder and perjury were punished by penance through fasting. But, as noted above, these religious punishments could very soon be absolved by the payment of money. That such payment was later considered to be totally insufficient and inappropriate penance testifies not against but in favour of the growing importance of money. It is precisely because money represents the value of incommensurable things and has become more colourless and indifferent that it cannot be used as an equivalent in very special and uncommon conditions where the innermost and most basic aspects of the person are concerned. This is not in spite of the fact that one can obtain almost anything for money, rather, it is precisely for this reason that money was no longer used to settle the moral–religious demands upon which religious penance rested. The increasing valuation of the human soul with its uniqueness and individuality meets with the opposite trend in the development of money and in so doing accelerates and secures the abolition of penance as a fine. Money first attains the quality of cool indifference and complete abstractness in relation to all specific values to the extent that it becomes the equivalent of increasingly diverse objects. As long as the objects that may be acquired by money are limited in number, and as long as an essential part of economic values is excluded from being purchasable (as was the case, for example, with landed property over very long periods), money itself retains a more specific character and is not yet indifferent to either side. Under primitive circumstances, money may even possess the exact opposite quality of its real nature, namely sacred dignity, the quality of an exceptional value. I refer to the strict norms mentioned earlier which reserved certain kinds of money exclusively for important or ceremonial transactions, and specifically to evidence from the Caroline Islands. The islanders, it appears, do not need any money to support themselves because they all are self-sufficient. And yet money plays a significant role, because the acquisition of a wife, membership of the local state and the political significance of the community are all dependent upon the ownership of money. From such circumstances we can understand why money is not as common there as in our society in which it satisfies the lower needs rather than the higher ones. Certainly, the merely quantitative fact that there is not yet enough money to slip continuously through one's fingers delays – during periods of production for one's own requirements – the emergence of its prevalence and its precision. Therefore, it seems more apt to serve as a satisfactory equivalent for extraordinary objects such as human life. The progressive differentiation of people and the equally progressive indifference of money combine to make expiation for murder and other serious crimes by money completely impossible.

The increasing inadequacy of money

It is interesting to note that awareness of this intrinsic inadequacy of money is aroused at a very early stage. In the earliest periods of Jewish history, when money was already used in exchange for women and for atonement, contributions to the temple always had to be delivered in kind. Whoever, because of his remoteness from the shrine, brought his tithe in money had to exchange it again into commodities at the appropriate place. Similarly, in Delos, the ancient sacred shrine, the ox remained for a long time the standard unit of monetary value. Among the medieval journeymen's associations, the older, church-related brotherhoods imposed punishments for specific offences in terms of wax (for holy candles); the secular associations, on the other hand, imposed punishments mostly in money. In the same vein is the ancient Hebrew regulation that stolen domestic animals have to be replaced in duplicate, but if they are no longer available they have to be paid for in money four or five times their value. Only a disproportionately inflated fine could substitute for the replacement of the original goods. Long after cattle money in Italy had been replaced by metal coinage, fines were still calculated, at least formally, in terms of cattle. Among the Czechs, where cattle had originally been the medium of exchange, they continued to serve for a long time later as the standard for penance for murder. The same kind of phenomenon was found among the Californian Indians, where, even after shell money had been taken out of circulation, it remained the gift to the dead for the Happy Hunting Grounds. The religious flavour of atonement or payment as a whole in its archaic form already at this stage of development takes current money to be inadequate for the sacredness of the events. It leads to the same debasement of money as the contrary movement mentioned earlier, and at a later stage it further severs the value of man from the value of money, thereby producing one of the most important factors in the development of the importance of money. I want to mention here just one more manifestation of this trend. The medieval prohibitions upon taking interest rest on the assumption that money is not a commodity. On the contrary, money was considered to be inflexible or unproductive and therefore it was deemed a sin to demand a price for its use as one would for the use of a commodity. During the very same period, however, it was considered not in the least sinful to treat a person as a commodity. If one compares this standpoint with the practical and theoretical notions of modern times, then it becomes clear how the concepts of money and of man move continuously in exactly opposite directions; the oppositeness of the directions remains the same, however, whether the concepts, with reference to a specific problem, develop towards or away from each other.

The dissociation of the value of the person from the value of money which is expressed in the down-grading of fines to the most minor offences is itself counteracted by another tendency. The legal retribution for injustice and injury that one person inflicts upon another becomes more and more restricted to cases in which the interest of the victim is expressible in money terms. If we survey the sequences in the stages of culture, then it will be seen to be less frequent at a lower level than at a higher one, and here again less than at the next higher one. This is especially noticeable in urban life, where circumstances ascribe considerably greater importance to money than do rural circumstances in those instances in which the general level of both remains relatively low. In modern Arabia, for instance, the vendetta prevails amongst desert-dwellers, whereas *wergild* is paid in the cities. In urban areas dominated by economic interests, the value of a human being is more likely to be interpreted in terms of a sum of money. This culminates in a situation in which damage measured in money terms is granted a specific claim to expiation by criminal law. The concept of fraud which could be clearly defined only in a social order based on money, illustrates this point very clearly. German criminal law recognizes an act to be criminal fraud only if somebody misrepresents the facts 'with the intention of procuring an illegal advantage for himself or somebody else'. There are only two or, at most, three other cases in which German law punishes the misrepresentation of facts and in which individual damage inflicted upon a person is the grounds for punishment – the seduction of a girl by the promise of marriage, marriage with fraudulent concealment of impediment to marriage, and the intentionally false denunciation. In all other instances where fraudulent cases are threatened with punishment, the damage is done not to the individual but to the interests of the State – perjury, falsification of elections, false excuses by witnesses and jurors, giving wrong names and titles to proper officials, etc. Even in these instances involving the interests of the State, the punishment in general, or its amount, is often dependent upon the fact that the culprit was motivated by an economic interest. Thus, the falsification of passports, work rosters, etc., are subject to punishment where they are falsified for reasons of 'improving one's position'. Typical in this respect is the fact that the falsification of personal status (substitution of a child, etc.) is punished by a prison sentence of up to three years, but 'if the action was done for reasons of economic profit', with imprisonment of up to ten years. Even though the substitution of a child may undoubtedly occur for more immoral and criminal reasons than economic profit, so that the worst criminal receives less punishment because he has no money interest, it none the less generally remains true that numerous fraudulent misrepresentations may destroy people's happiness, honour and belongings without ever being punished unless the swindler attempts to gain a 'pecuniary advantage'. In that financial interests are involved from the outset in the concept of fraud, this gives to penal practice the simplicity and clarity that is inherent in the reduction to money, but at the price of leaving the sense of justice very much unsatisfied. Out of the whole group of damages that may be inflicted by fraud, only that which can be expressed in money is subject to criminal prosecution and is thus specified as the one that requires expiation from the standpoint of the social order. Since it must be the intention of the law to punish every fraudulent destruction of personal values, this can be based only on the assumption that all such destructible values possess a money equivalent. The concept of *wergild* is again relevant here, though in a rudimentary form. If a negation of a personal value can be compensated for by giving money to the injured party, then it must be presupposed that this value can be reduced to money. None the less, modern criminal law rejects the conclusion that fraudulent damage is sufficiently expiated by the exchange of money; yet with reference to the object of the act, the notion prevails that any fraudulently acquired value may be represented by a sum of money.

Just as the need for greater explicitness in legal norms has led to the enormous restriction of personal values that can be protected against fraud to those expressible in money terms while the other values are reduced to negligible quantities, so the same need leads to corresponding regulations in civil law. Breach of promise and chicanery which may involve someone in considerable inconvenience and losses are, according to German law, no basis for a claim by the injured party unless the money value of the damage can be proven. I need mention here only some cases pointed out by lawyers themselves: the landlord who does not permit the tenant to use the garden despite his contractual right to do so, the traveller to whom the hotel owner refuses lodging despite written assent, the school principal with whom the teacher breaks his contract without being able to secure a substitute. All these people, although their claim to compensation is as clear as daylight, cannot raise this claim because the damage cannot be equated with a specific amount of money. Who could demonstrate the precise money equivalent of these subjective and objective inconveniences and impairments? If such a proof is not given, then the damages in question are only negligible quantities to the judge; they do not exist as far as he is concerned. In a tremendous number of instances in life the injured party has no rights at all; he has neither the moral satisfaction of seeing the person responsible for the damage prosecuted by the law nor the economic satisfaction of being compensated for his losses and his troubles. It must be emphasized once more that the presumption of the law is to secure all individuals' possessions against illegal damage, but this assurance does not include a whole series of goods whose value cannot be realized in money terms. It follows that the whole of this legal interpretation is based on the assumption that all personal goods do possess a money equivalent, with the obvious exception of the inviolability of the body and, in some respects, of matrimony which are also guaranteed by law. The extraordinary simplification and uniformity of the legal system which this reduction to money interests implies has, in association with its actual domination, led to the fiction of the autocratic rule of money – a fiction that also corresponds to the peculiar practical indifference towards those values that cannot be expressed in money terms, even though they are theoretically recognized to be the highest values.

It is interesting to observe how Roman law, in its middle period, took the opposite view in this respect. Monetary conviction, the same as was established in civil suits, was a penalty that went beyond the value of the object and was awarded to the injured party in order to compensate him for the particular insidiousness or malice from which he had to suffer by the defendant. The deposit that had been malevolently denied, the money held in trust for a ward by the guardian and similar obligations, were not simply refunded; in addition the judge, and under certain circumstances the plaintiff, was entitled to determine compensation not only for the objective damage directly equivalent to a certain amount of money, but for malevolent violation of the personal legal sphere as a whole. Such regulations reflect the feeling that the personal values that the law is supposed to guarantee are not confined to the money value of the object. Rather, their violation requires a penalty over and above that. At the same time, however, this expiation is achieved by offering a certain amount of money, so that the damage that extends beyond the objective money interest is made good by money. In the one instance, money here plays a lesser role, but in the other a more important one, than is the case today. For that very reason, the present situation displays a combination of both of those typical tendencies that modern culture imposes upon the function of money. On the one hand, it gives money an importance that, as it were, makes it the world soul of the universe of practical interests and which, in continuing its motion beyond its proper limits, stifles personal values as well. On the other hand, however, modern culture distances money from these personal values, makes its significance less and less compatible with all that is really personal, and suppresses the assertion of personal values rather than accept such an inadequate equivalent. Our sense of justice is less satisfied by the momentary effect of the concurrence of these two tendencies than it was in the Roman period, but this should not prevent us from being aware that we are concerned here with the combination of much more advanced cultural tendencies that reflect the antagonism and the irreconcilability of their directions in the insufficiency and low standards of some phenomena in which they are both simultaneously effective.

Marriage by purchase

There are some analogies to the earlier state of affairs in which the whole person was compensated for by money in the particular development connected with the monetary purchase of women. Marriage by purchase, its extraordinary frequency in the history of civilized nations and today in less civilized countries, the extent of its variations and forms are all well known. We are interested here only in the conclusions that can be drawn from the facts as to the nature of values that are purchased. The feeling of degradation that modern man possesses concerning the purchase of a person for money or money equivalents is not always justified with reference to earlier historical circumstances. We have seen that, as long as the person has elevated himself above his species kind, and as long as money value has not yet been generalized into a completely colourless entity, both, as it were, stand in close proximity to one another; and the personal dignity of the early Germans certainly did not suffer from the fact that they permitted its value to be expressed in *wergild*. Marriage by purchase is a similar case. Ethnological data show that marriage by purchase is neither solely nor chiefly to be found only at the lowest stages of cultural development. One of the best experts in this area states that the uncivilized peoples who are unfamiliar with marriage by purchase are usually extraordinarily barbarous races. No matter how degrading the purchase of women may appear to be in higher cultures, it may enhance women's status under primitive conditions for two reasons. In the first place, marriage by purchase never occurs – as far as we know – in any kind of individualistic economy. Even at the very lowest level of culture, marriage by purchase is tied to rigid forms and formulas, consideration of family interests, exact conventions about the kind and amount of payment. The whole way in which it is carried out has a definite social character. This is evident from the fact that the groom is often entitled to demand a contribution to the price of the bride from each clansman and that this is often distributed among the bride's relatives – just as among the Arabs, for example, the expiation money for a murder was collected from the whole tribe, from the clanship of the murderer.

Among one Indian tribe, the suitor who has only half the necessary price for the bride is entitled to a 'partial marriage'; that is, instead of taking the woman as slave in his own house he must live in her house until he has paid in full. In many instances in which patriarchal and matriarchal conditions coexist the patriarchal form is valid only after payment of the price for the bride, while the poor man has to accept the matriarchal form. There is no doubt that this businesslike attitude completely suppresses the individuality of the persons and their relationships. And yet the organization of marriage affairs as found in marriage by purchase signifies considerable progress when compared with the more brutal conditions of marriage by robbery or of completely primitive sexual relationships which, although not completely promiscuous, were none the less probably carried out without that stabilizing norm that was supplied in the socially regulated purchase of a wife. Time and time again, the development of mankind reaches stages at which the suppression of individuality is the unavoidable transitional point for its subsequent free development, at which the mere externality of the determinations of life favours spiritual growth, at which oppressive formation results in a reservoir of forces that later emerge as personal quality. Viewed from the ideal of fully developed individuality, such periods certainly appear to be brutal and undignified. However, they not only plant the positive germs of later higher development, but are in themselves manifestations of the spirit in its organizing control of the material of fluctuating impulses, activities of specifically human expediency that creates for itself, no matter how brutal, extraneous, or even stupid, the norms of life instead of merely receiving them from natural forces. Nowadays there are extreme individualists who are none the less in practice adherents of socialism because they consider socialism to be the indispensable preparation and even the severe training for a purified and just individualism. Thus the relatively stable order and external standardization of marriage by purchase was a first, very violent and eminently non-individual, attempt to give a certain mould to the marriage relationship which was just as appropriate for primitive stages as the more individualistic marital form is for more highly developed stages. The importance of marriage for social cohesion is already indicated by the exchange of women, which, as a barter-agreement, might be considered a preparatory stage to the purchase of women. Among the Australian Narinyeri, marriage is conducted by the exchange of the sisters of two men. If, instead of this arrangement, one of the girls elopes with a lover, then not only is she considered to be socially inferior, but she also loses the claim for protection which the clan into which she was born otherwise owes her. This clearly illustrates the social significance of this non-individual type of marriage. The clan no longer protects the girl; it severs its relationship with her because it has not received an equivalent for her.

Marriage by purchase and the value of women

The transition to the second culturally advanced motive for marriage by purchase commences here. The fact that women are useful objects of possession, that their acquisition requires sacrifices, ultimately makes them appear to be valuable. It has been stated that possession universally engenders love of possessing. One not only makes sacrifices for what one loves, but also one loves that for which one has made sacrifices. If motherly love is the source of innumerable sacrifices for the children, then so too the trouble and worries that the mother endures for the child form an ever closer bond with the child. This explains why sick or handicapped children, who require the greatest devotion on the part of the mother, are often the most beloved ones. The Church has never hesitated to demand the greatest sacrifices for the love of God, since it was well aware that we become all the more closely tied to a principle the more sacrifices we have made, the more capital – so to speak – we have invested in it. However much the purchase of women directly expressed their suppression, exploitation and valuation solely as an object, the woman nevertheless gained value both for the parents, who received the purchase price, as well as for the husband, to whom she represented a relatively high sacrifice and who therefore had to treat her considerately in his own interest. Compared with modern standards, her treatment was still miserable enough, and certainly the better aspects of the purchase of women could become so paralysed by the humiliating aspects that women found themselves in the most wretched and slave-like position. But it remains equally true that the purchase of women has given meaningful and eloquent expression to the fact that women are valuable – and, in the psychological context, not only to the fact that they are purchased because they are valuable, but that they are valuable because one has to pay for them. Therefore it is understandable that among certain American tribes the giving away of a girl without payment is considered a great deprecation of the girl and her whole family, so much so that their children would be considered to be nothing better than bastards.

Although the purchase of women always implies a tendency towards polygamy and thereby the degradation of women, the necessity of spending money, on the other hand, sets a limit to such trends. The pagan Danish kind Frotho is reported to have legally prohibited the vanquished Ruthenians from contracting any marriages except by the purchase of women. His intention was to suppress lax morals since he saw the purchase of women as a guarantee of stability. Indirectly, by necessarily restricting the polygamous instincts with which it has affinities, the purchase of women must lead to a higher appreciation of the woman owned. Not only is the stability a consequence of appreciation of the wife; but conversely, her valuation is a consequence of the established stability, just as it is the consequence of direct expenses. It is of the utmost importance that the differences in prices – in the socially controlled as well as the free market prices – reflects the difference in value of the women. It is said that the Kaffir women do not consider being sold to be in the least way humiliating. On the contrary, the girl is proud of it, and the more bulls and cows are paid for her the more valuable she considers herself to be. One may frequently notice that a certain category of objects acquires a stronger awareness of value if each single one has to be appraised individually and if considerable differences in prices develop an increasing sense of value. At other levels of evaluation however – as in the case of *wergild* – the identical nature of the compensation favours the objective significance of the equivalent value. The purchase of women is one of the first, though very crude, methods of emphasizing the individual value of a particular woman and also – according to the psychological rule of valuation – the value of women in general. Even when the woman is sold as a slave, the variation in prices is probably much greater than it is for male slaves. The male slave, as a mere working animal, has at the same age about the same conventional price (in ancient Greece and in Ireland equal to three cows), whereas the female slave, who serves purposes other than work, changes in value according to her personal attractiveness – although the impact of this aesthetic factor is not very great among primitive people. In any case, at the lowest stage of development the price is usually fixed by custom, as in the purchase of women among several African tribes.

All these instances strongly underline the fact that a woman is treated as a mere genus, an impersonal object. This is itself, bearing in mind all the qualifications mentioned earlier, the distinguishing feature of marriage by purchase. Therefore among some people, particularly in India, the purchase of women is considered dishonourable, while in other areas it may take place, but the term is avoided and the price paid to the parents is interpreted as a voluntary present. The difference between money proper and other contributions is relevant here. The Laplanders are said to give their daughters away in return for presents, but they consider it improper to take money for them. If one takes account of the other very complicated conditions that determine the position of women, it seems as if purchase for money degrades them more than being given away in return for presents or in return for personal services to their parents on the part of the suitors. The gift contains something more personal – because of the indeterminateness of the gift's value and the individual freedom of choosing, even if governed by conventions – than a definite sum of money with its uncompromising objectivity. In addition, the gift builds the bridge to that later form which is the transition to the dowry, where the gifts of the suitor are matched by the gifts of the bride's parents. The unconditional disposal of the woman is thereby broken, because the value that the man has accepted implies a certain obligation and he is now no longer merely the creditor since the other side also has a claim. It has also been asserted that the acquisition of women by labour tasks instead of by direct purchase represents a higher marital form. Nevertheless, it seems that this is the older and uncivilized form which does not rule out the possibility that it is associated with better treatment of women. For the emergent money economy has often worsened the condition of women, just as it has worsened the situation of weaker groups as a whole. Among present-day primitive peoples we sometimes find both forms existing side by side. This proves that there is no essential difference in the treatment of women here although, by and large, the sacrifice of such a personal value as service elevates the acquisition of a woman over that of a slave in a very different manner than purchasing her for money or substantial money value. It must be emphasized here that what is generally true is that the degradation and humiliation of human value decreases if the purchase prices are very high. For money value in very great sums contains an element of rarity which makes it more individual and less interchangeable and thus more appropriate as an equivalent of personal values. Among the Greeks in the heroic period, a bridegroom's gifts to the bride's father – which do not appear to suggest direct purchasing – were quite common, while the position of women was particularly favourable. But it must be emphasized that these gifts were quite considerable. Although it appears degrading if the essence or the whole of a person is made equivalent to a sum of money, an unusually large sum offered may, as later examples clearly demonstrate, somehow counterbalance this, particularly in view of the social position of the person concerned. We know that Edward II and Edward III gave their friends away as hostages for the repayment of their debts and in 1340 it was planned to send the Archbishop of Canterbury to Brabant – not as a guarantor, but as a pawn for the debts of the King. The size of the respective sums averted the disparagement that would have affected these persons if only a negligible amount of money had been at stake.

Division of labour among the sexes, and the dowry

The transition from the principle of marriage by purchase, which was probably prevalent among most peoples at some time, to its opposite, the principle of the dowry, probably evolved when the bridegroom's gifts to the parents were passed on to the bride as a means of providing a certain amount of economic independence. The provision of the woman's dowry by her parents continued to exist and to develop further even after its original basis – the purchase money paid by the suitor – had disappeared. It is not worth while tracing this evolution here, about which we know very little. But it is safe to assume that the general custom of the dowry commences with the emergent money economy. The connections between the two may be as follows. Under primitive conditions, where the purchase of women prevails, the wife is not only a glutton for work – that is also true later on – but also her work is not yet specifically 'domestic', as is that of the woman in the money economy who has to organize the household consumption of whatever the husband has acquired. The division of labour is not yet sufficiently advanced in such periods. The wife still participates more directly in production and therefore represents a more tangible economic value to her possessor than she does subsequently. This connection has occasionally been confirmed in much more recent times. Whereas Macaulay regarded the performance of agricultural work by women in Scotland as a symptom of the barbaric low position of the female sex, an expert emphasized, in contrast, that it gave them a certain degree of independence and prestige among men. In addition, under primitive circumstances, children possess an immediate economic value for the father, whereas in a more advanced culture they are often an economic burden. The original owner, the father of the clan, has no reason to abandon this value to others without compensation. At this level, not only do women provide their own subsistence, but also the husband may extract her purchase price directly from her work. This situation changes when the economy is no longer based on the family household and consumption is no longer restricted to home production. In this new situation, the household's interests split off in a centrifugal and a centripetal direction. Money makes possible separate production for the market and for the household economy and this separation initiates a more rigorous division of labour between the sexes. For very obvious reasons, the wife takes over the domestic activities and the husband the activities outside the home, the domestic activities becoming more and more an administration and application of the proceeds from the latter. In so doing, the wife's economic value loses, as it were, its substance and its obviousness since she now appears to be supported by the work of her husband. Not only do the grounds for asking and obtaining a price for her disappear, but she becomes – at least from a superficial standpoint – a liability which the husband takes over and has to cope with. Thus the basis is laid for the dowry which will accordingly become more extensive the more the spheres of activity of husband and wife are separated in this way. Among peoples like the Jews, whose men – because of a restless temperament and other reasons – are very mobile and whose women, as a necessary corollary, are more strictly confined to the home, the dowry as a legal requirement was to be found even before the money economy became fully developed, and before it had time to produce the same result. Only the money economy brings together in the sphere of production the objective technology, the spread and wealth of relationships and at the same time the one-sidedness of the division of labour, through which the earlier state of indifference between home interests and interests in acquisition becomes split and a specific representative becomes necessary for each of them. Under these circumstances, there can be no doubt about the roles of husband and wife. Similarly, the price for the bride by which the man purchases the productive capacity of the woman is replaced by the dowry, which compensates for his having to support the wife or which is supposed to give her an independence and security side by side with her productive husband.

The typical relation between money and prostitution

This close connection between the dowry in the money economy and the whole constitution of married life – be it to secure the husband's or the wife's position – serves to explain the fact that in Greece as well as in Rome the dowry became the distinguishing attribute of the legitimate wife in contrast to the concubine, who had no further claim on the husband so that both compensation for her as well as security measures for her would be out of place. This leads on to the problem of prostitution, which places the significance of money in the relationship between the sexes in yet another light. Whereas all the gifts of the man for or to the wife – including the dowry and the *pretium virginitatis* – may take the form of a gift in kind or in money, the price paid for sexual relations outside marriage usually takes the form of money. Only a monetary transaction corresponds to the character of a completely fleeting inconsequential relationship as is the case with prostitution. The relationship is more completely dissolved and more radically terminated by payment of money than by the gift of a specific object, which always, through its content, its choice and its use, retains an element of the person who has given it. Only money, which does not imply any commitment, and which in principle is always at hand and welcomed, is the appropriate equivalent to the fleetingly intensified and just as fleetingly extinguished sexual appetite that is served by prostitution. Money is never an adequate mediator of personal relationships – such as the genuine love relationship, however abruptly it may be broken off – that are intended to be permanent and based on the sincerity of the binding forces. Money best serves, both objectively and symbolically, that purchasable satisfaction which rejects any relationship that continues beyond the momentary sexual impulse, because it is absolutely detached from the person and completely cuts off from the outset any further consequences. In as far as one pays with money, one is completely finished with any object just as fundamentally as when one has paid for satisfaction from a prostitute. Since in prostitution the relationship between the sexes is quite specifically confined to the sexual act, it is reduced to its purely generic content. It consists of what any member of the species can perform and experience. It is a relationship in which the most contrasting personalities are equal and individual differences are eliminated. Thus, the economic counterpart of this kind of relationship is money, which also, transcending all individual distinctions, stands for the species-type of economic values, the representation of which is common to all individual values. Conversely, we experience in the nature of money itself something of the essence of prostitution. The indifference as to its use, the lack of attachment to any individual because it is unrelated to any of them, the objectivity inherent in money as a mere m eans which excludes any emotional relationship – all this produces an ominous analogy between money and prostitution. Kant's moral imperative never to use human beings as a mere means but to accept and treat them always, at the same time, as ends in themselves is blatantly disregarded *by both parties* in the case of prostitution. Of all human relationships, prostitution is perhaps the most striking instance of mutual degradation to a mere means, and this may be the strongest and most fundamental factor that places prostitution in such a close historical relationship to the money economy, the economy of 'means' in the strictest sense.

This is the basis for the fact that the terrible degradation that is inherent in prostitution is most clearly expressed by its money equivalent. It certainly signifies the nadir of human dignity if a woman surrenders her most intimate and most personal quality, which should be offered only on the basis of a genuine personal impulse and also only with equal personal devotion on the part of the male – in so far as this might have a different importance for the man compared with the woman – for a totally impersonal, purely extraneous and objective compensation. We experience here the fullest and most distressing incongruity between giving and taking. More accurately, we can say that the degradation of prostitution lies in the fact that it so degrades a woman's most personal possession, one that is dependent upon the greatest reserve, that the most neutral value devoid of all personal qualities is considered to be an appropriate equivalent. The foregoing characterization of prostitution in terms of money payment leads, however, to certain contradictory considerations which have to be explored in order to place the significance of money into full relief.

There seems to be an inconsistency in emphasizing, on the one hand, the personal, intimately individual nature of the sexual surrender of a woman and on the other the fact that the merely sensual relationship between the sexes is of a generic character and that it is something we have in common with the animal kingdom in which the personality and individual inner feelings are extinguished. If men are so inclined to speak of women 'in the plural', to judge them by lumping them all together in the same pot, then one of the reasons is certainly that the men of crude sensuality are interested in a quality of women that is identical for the seamstress and the princess. Thus, it seems out of the question to find a specifically personal value in this function. All the other functions of a similar level of generality, such as eating, drinking, the regular physiological and even psychological reactions, the instinct of self-preservation and the typical logical functions, are never strongly entwined with the personality as such. One is never inclined to imagine that the practice or presentation of what is indistinguishably common to all men would express or exhaust his innermost, essential and comprehensive nature. Yet such an anomaly does exist with regard to the sexual surrender of women. This completely general act that is identical for people of all strata is experienced, at the same time – at least for the woman – as an extremely personal and intimate one. This anomaly may be understood on the basis of the opinion that women as a whole are more deeply rooted in the species type than are men, who are more greatly differentiated and more specifically individualized. It would follow from this view that the species and the personal elements coincide more readily in women. If, in fact, women are more closely and more deeply rooted in the dark primitive forces of nature than are men, then their most essential and personal qualities must also be rooted in those natural, universal functions that guarantee the uniformity of the genus. Furthermore, it follows that the uniformity of the female sex, in whom the general qualities are less clearly distinguished from individual traits, is also reflected in a greater uniformity in the nature of each individual woman. Experience seems to confirm that the various forces, qualities and impulses of the woman are more directly and closely connected with each other than are those of men, whose qualities are more independent, so that the development and fate of each are relatively independent. Women, however – at least according to general opinion – live under the sign of all or nothing; their inclinations and actions are more closely associated and it is easier, commencing from a single point, to arouse the whole of their being, with all its emotions, volitions and thoughts. If this is indeed the case, then there is a certain justification in the supposition that a woman gives herself up more completely and unreservedly by surrendering this one part of her self than does the more differentiated man under the same circumstances. The significance of this difference for both is already evident at a more harmless stage of the relationship between man and woman. Even primitive peoples request a different payment for the bridegroom and the bride respectively for dissolving an engagement. Among the Bakaks, for example, she has to pay 5 and he 10 guilders, while among the inhabitants of Bengkula the disloyal bridegroom pays 40, the bride only 10 guilders. The significance and the consequences that society attaches to the sexual relations between man and woman are correspondingly based on the presupposition that the woman gives her total self, with all its worth, whereas the man gives only a part of his personality in the exchange. Society therefore denies to a girl who has once gone astray her whole 'reputation'; society condemns the adultery of the wife much more harshly than that of the husband, of whom it is supposed that an occasional sexual extravagancy is still reconcilable with loyalty to his wife in all its inner and essential elements; society irredeemably renders the prostitute *déclassé*, while the worst rake can, as it were, still save himself from the morass by other facets of his personality and can rise to any social position. The purely sexual act that is at issue in prostitution employs only a minimum of the man's ego but a maximum of the woman's – if not in every particular case, then certainly taking all cases together. This relationship explains the role of the pimp as well as the frequently reported cases of lesbianism among prostitutes. Because the prostitute has to endure a terrible void and lack of satisfaction in her relations with men, she searches for a substitute relationship in which at least some other qualities of the partner are involved. Neither the notion that the sexual act is something universal and impersonal, nor the fact that, on the face of it, men and women are equally involved in it changes this relationship in which the stake of the woman is infinitely more personal, more essential, encompassing more of her ego than that of the man and for which, therefore, a money equivalent is most unsuitable and inadequate, the giving and taking of which means the extreme abasement of the female personality. The degradation of the woman by prostitution is not in itself explained by its polyandric character, or by the fact that she has sexual relationships with many men. Genuine polyandry often gives a decisive superiority to the woman as, for instance, among the relatively high-caste Nayars in India. What is important here is not that prostitution means polyandry, but that it means polygamy, which degrades the personal value of women and causes the woman to lose her scarcity value. Viewed superficially, prostitution combines polyandric with polygamic features. But the advantage of the person who gives the money over the person who provides the commodity grants a tremendous superiority to the male and determines the character of prostitution as polygamous. Women consider it embarrassing and degrading to take money from their lover under circumstances that have nothing to do with prostitution, whereas this feeling often does not extend to non-monetary presents. On the contrary, women find pleasure and satisfaction in giving money to their lovers. It has been said that the reason for Marlborough's success with women was that he accepted money from them. The superiority of whoever gives over whoever takes money, which in the case of prostitution has brought about the most terrible social distance, gives to the woman in these contrary instances the satisfaction of imposing dependency upon those whom she would otherwise consider her superiors.

But we are confronted with the remarkable fact that in many primitive cultures prostitution is not considered to be humiliating or socially degrading. For instance, it is reported that in ancient Asia the girls of all classes prostituted themselves in order to obtain a dowry or an offering for the temple, and we hear of the same custom being practised for reasons of marriage among certain African tribes. The girls, often including the prince's daughter, do not lose their reputation in the eyes of the public, nor is there subsequently any prejudice against them in their later married life. This profound difference from our own feelings indicates that the two factors – women's sexual honour and money – are basically related in a different way. Prostitution in our culture is characterized by an unbridgeable gulf, by the total incommensurability of these two values; but under circumstances that develop a different view of prostitution, they must be closer to each other. This is similar to the results of the development of *wergild*, the money atonement for homicide. The rising value of human life and the declining value of money conspired to render *wergild* impossible. The same cultural process of differentiation that gives to the individual a special significance which renders him relatively unique and irreplaceable makes money the standard and equivalent of such a divergent range of objects that the growing indifference and objectivity makes it increasingly less suitable as an equivalent of personal values. That disproportion between commodity and price that gives prostitution its character in our culture does not yet exist to the same extent in lower cultures. When travellers report that the women of many barbaric tribes display a striking physical and often mental similarity to men, then this is because they lack that differentiation which lends a value to the more highly civilized woman and to her sexual honour that cannot be compensated for in money terms, even though she may appear comparatively less differentiated and closer to the species type than a man of the same status. The attitude towards prostitution thus undergoes the same changes which may be observed in ecclesiastical penance and in blood money. In primitive epochs, man and his inner values do not yet bear the mark of individuality, whereas money, because of its scarcity and its limited use, possesses a relatively more unique value. In so far as cultural development rends both of these positions asunder, it thus renders the compensation of the one by the other impossible or – where that relationship persists, as in prostitution – it leads to a terrible degradation of personal value.

Marriage for money

Of the great variety of opinions concerning 'marriage for money', the following three are important with reference to the development of the importance of money. Marriages based exclusively upon economic motives have not only existed in all periods and at all stages of development, but are particularly common among primitive groups and conditions where they do not cause any offence at all. The disparagement of personal dignity that nowadays arises in every marriage that is not based on personal affection – so that a sense of decency requires the concealment of economic motives – does not exist in simpler cultures. The reason for this development is that increasing individualization makes it increasingly contradictory and discreditable to enter into purely individual relationships for other than purely individual reasons. For nowadays the choice of a partner in marriage is no longer determined by social motives (though regard for the offspring may be considered to be such a motive), but rather pertains to the personal and inner directed part of the relationship, in so far as society does not insist upon the couple's equal social status – a condition, however, that provides a great deal of latitude and only rarely leads to conflicts between individual and social interests. In a quite undifferentiated society it may be relatively irrelevant who marries whom, irrelevant not only for the mutual relationship of the couple but also for the offspring. This is because where the constitutions, state of health, temperament, internal and external forms of life and orientations are largely the same within the group, the chance that the children will turn out well depends less upon whether the parents agree and complement each other than it does in a highly differentiated society. It therefore seems quite natural and expedient that the choice of the partner should be determined by reasons other than purely individual affection. Yet personal attraction should be decisive in a highly individualized society where a harmonious relationship between two individuals becomes increasingly rare. The declining frequency of marriage which is to be found everywhere in highly civilized cultural circumstances is undoubtedly due, in part, to the fact that highly differentiated people in general have difficulty in finding a completely sympathetic complement to themselves. Yet we do not possess any other criterion and indication for the advisability of marriage except mutual instinctive attraction. But happiness is a purely personal matter, decided upon entirely by the couple themselves, and there would be no compelling reason for the official insistence on at least pretending love as the sole erotic motive for marriage if society did not have an interest in it regarding its advisability for the descendants. No matter how much love may be misleading – particularly in the higher strata, whose complicated circumstances often retard the growth of the purest instincts – and no matter how much other conditions may affect the final result, it remains true that, with reference to procreation, love is decidedly superior to money as a factor of selection. In fact, in this respect, it is the only right and proper thing. Marriage for money directly creates a situation of panmixia – the indiscriminate pairing regardless of individual qualities – a condition that biology has demonstrated to be the cause of the most direct and detrimental degeneration of the human species. In the case of marriage for money, the union of a couple is determined by a factor that has absolutely nothing to do with racial appropriateness – just as the regard for money often enough keeps apart a couple who really belong together – and it should be considered as a factor in degeneration to the same extent to which the undoubted differentiation of individuals makes selection by personal attraction more and more important. This case too illustrates once more that the increasing individualization within society renders money increasingly unsuitable as a mediator of purely individual relationships.

The second view of marriage for money is that it is a variation on prostitution, in a different form but subject to the same observations as on prostitution. This view holds that it is polyandric just as much as it is polygamic but because of the social superiority of the male only the consequences of the polygamous element, the degradation of the female, takes effect in marriage for money. Thus it seems as if marriage for money, as a means of permanently prostituting oneself, would degrade either partner that is motivated by money, regardless of whether they were male or female. However, this is usually not the case. The woman, by marrying, submits the whole of her interests and energies to this relationship most of the time and offers her personality, both the centre and the periphery, without reservation. In contrast, the married man is from the outset customarily granted much greater freedom of movement while in addition withholding the essential part of his personality that is taken up by his professional interests. In accordance with the relationship that exists between the sexes in our culture, the man who marries for money does not give away as much as the woman who marries for the same reasons. Since she belongs to her husband more than he belongs to her, it is more fatal for her to enter into a marriage relationship without love. I am inclined to believe – and empirical material must be replaced by psychological interpretation here – that marriage for money has more tragic consequences, particularly where sensitive natures are concerned, if it is the woman who is bought. Here, as in many other instances, the characteristic quality of money relations is displayed, namely that the potential superiority of one party leads to the radical exploitation and even aggravation of the other. Such, in fact, is the tendency in every relationship of this kind. The position of the *primus inter pares* very easily becomes that of a simple *primus*; the advantage once gained in any sphere forms the stage for a further advantage that heightens the contrast; again, a privileged position is often the easier achieved the higher the initial rank. In brief, positions of superiority usually develop in growing proportions, and the 'accumulation of capital' as an instrument of power is but a particular instance of a very general norm that is valid in many other non-economic spheres of power. There are, however, certain reservations and counterbalancing forces that set limits to the avalanche-like growth of superior power, such as, for example, tradition, reverence, law and the inherent limits to the expansion of power. But money, with its absolute flexibility and lack of quality, is least suited to put a stop to such a trend. Where a relationship based on money interests exists in which superiority and advantage rest from the outset on one side, these tendencies may grow further, more radically and more thoroughly in this direction, as if other motives of a more objective and objectifying nature are the basis for this relationship.

The third view of marriage for money is very clearly illustrated by that very peculiar phenomenon – the advertisement for a marriage partner. The fact that it plays a very small role that is limited to the middle classes might appear strange and regrettable. For despite the individualization of the modern personality which we mentioned earlier, and despite the resultant difficulties in choosing a partner, there is undoubtedly a partner of the opposite sex for everybody – no matter how unique – a partner who has complementary qualities and who would be the 'right' partner. The whole difficulty, however, lies in how the two people who are, so to speak, predestined for each other manage to find each other. The tragic absurdity of the human lot is nowhere better illustrated than by the remaining single or by the unhappy marriage of two estranged people, who cannot make one another happy because they did not learn to understand each other. There is little doubt that the proper use of marriage advertisements would rationalize these conditions based on chance. Advertising in general is one of the most powerful cultural factors because it provides the individual with an infinitely higher chance of achieving satisfaction than if he were to depend upon the chance of finding the object directly. It is the increasing degree of individualization of needs themselves that makes advertising necessary as a means of enlarging the range of offers. Yet, particularly in the stratum of more differentiated people, who, generally speaking, seem to be the most dependent on it, advertising for marriage is completely out of the question. There must be a positive reason for such a repudiation of this means of finding a partner. In analysing the published marriage advertisements one discovers that the financial status of both parties is the real, though sometimes disguised, centre of interest. This is quite logical. All other qualities of the person cannot be stated in an advertisement with any degree of accuracy. Neither the outward appearance nor the character, neither the degree of affability nor the intelligence can be described in such a way that a clear picture emerges which will incite a direct individual interest. The only factor that can be given with complete exactness in all cases is the financial situation of the persons concerned and it is a basic trait of the human imagination to consider that quality of an object among others to be the most decisive that can be stated and recognized with the greatest exactitude and precision. This peculiar, as it were, methodological merit of money ownership really renders the marriage advertisement impossible for precisely those social strata who would need it most, because it implies the admittance of mere money interests.

With regard to prostitution we find that, beyond a certain quantity, money loses its dignity and ability to be the equivalent of individual values. The abhorrence that modern 'good' society entertains towards the prostitute is more pronounced the more miserable and the poorer she is, and it declines with the increase in the price for her services, to the point at which even the actress whom everybody knows is kept by a millionaire is considered presentable in their salons, although she may be much more extortionate, fraudulent and depraved than many a streetwalker. This is also the result of the general attitude of allowing the really big thieves to go free and of hanging the small ones, and of the fact that the big success engenders a certain respect relatively independently of its sphere and content. Yet the basic and more fundamental reason is that the exorbitant price saves the object for sale from the degradation that would otherwise be part of the fact of being offered for sale. Zola, in one of his stories of the Second Empire, tells of the wife of a man in a high position who was generally known to be worth 100,000–200,000 francs. Zola narrates an incident, which must be based on historical fact, in which not only did this woman herself move in the highest social circles, but where to be known as her lover ensured a man an outstanding reputation within this society. The courtesan who sells herself for a very high price thereby acquires a 'scarcity value'. For not only do scarce objects have a high price, but so also do those whose value is determined by any other reason, even if it is only a fashionable whim. As with many other commodities, the favours of some courtesans are greatly appreciated and in great demand only because they have the courage to ask quite extraordinary prices. There must be a similar basis for English legal judgment when it grants money compensation to a husband whose wife has been seduced. There is nothing that more contradicts our feelings than this procedure which reduces the husband to being his wife's procurer. Yet these fines are extraordinarily high. I know of a case in which the wife had intercourse with several men and each of them was sentenced to pay compensation of 50,000 marks to the husband. It seems as if here too one tries to compensate through the size of the sum for the baseness of the principle of making amends for such values by money. It may also have been that, in a rather naive way, one wishes to express respect for the husband's social position by the size of the sum. Certainly, the author of the Junius letters reproaches a judge that, in a law suit concerning a prince and the wife of a lord, he had not taken the status of the offended husband into account when assessing the compensation.

Bribery

The significance of this viewpoint is shown most clearly in instances of the 'purchase' of a person in the commonly accepted sense of the word, namely in bribery. I wish to discuss this phenomenon in its specific monetary form. There is, in a certain sense, a justification for this if it concerns persons in relatively comfortable economic circumstances. Here one assumes that the mind that is unable to resist a small temptation must be particularly niggardly and weak, whereas to succumb to a large temptation may happen to a stronger mind as well! Similarly, bribery – that is the purchase of office or assurances – is judged to be so much more contemptible if it is carried out for small amounts. Thus, bribery is in fact interpreted as the purchase of a person according to whether he is 'unpurchaseable', expensive or cheap. The justice of the social evaluation seems to be guaranteed here, since it is only the reflection of the self-evaluation of the subjects concerned. The strange dignity that the person open to bribery uses to preserve or at least hide his position originates in bribery's relationship to the whole person. It is reflected either in his being inaccessible to smaller sums or (where even this does not exist) in a certain grandeur, a strictness and superiority of behaviour which seems to reduce the giver to the role of the receiver. Such external behaviour is supposed to present the person as someone who is unassailable and aware of his own value. Inasmuch as it is a charade – since the other party enters into compliance with it by tacit agreement – it provides a certain inner reflex and protects the bribable person against self-negation and self-devaluation which would result from his sacrificing his personality for a certain amount of money. Among the ancient Jews, and often in the Orient even today, such buying and selling is carried out by exchanging civilities as if the buyer were taking the object as a present. The peculiar dignity of the oriental would appear to favour hiding a genuine interest in money, even in the case of such legitimate transactions.

Such an attitude among bribable persons and in the whole phenomenon of bribery as such is most readily facilitated and encouraged to spread through the money form itself. Money, more than any other form of value, makes possible the secrecy, invisibility and silence of exchange. By compressing money into a piece of paper, by letting it glide into a person's hand, one can make him a wealthy person. Money's formlessness and abstractness makes it possible to invest it in the most varied and most remote values and thereby to remove it completely from the gaze of neighbours. Its anonymity and colourlessness does not reveal the source from which it came to the present owner: it does not have a certificate of origin in the way in which, more or less disguised, many concrete objects of possession do. Whereas for the owner himself the fact that values can be expressed in money provides a clear and unveiled insight into the state of his possessions, for other people it allows a concealment and disguise of possessions and transactions that would be impossible for other tangible forms of property. The concealability of money is the symptom, or the extreme form, of its relationship to private ownership. Compared with all other goods, money can be made invisible and non-existent to others and thus has affinities with intellectual possessions. Just as the private and, as it were, solipsistic character of mental possessions both begins and ends with keeping silent, so the private individualistic nature of money finds its complete expression in the possibility of keeping it secret. Herein undoubtedly lies a great danger for those who have claims and interests in the management of the economy without being able to control and influence it themselves. Modern law requires publicity for the financial policy of governments and corporations in order to try to avoid the dangers inherent in the money form of management with its ease of concealment, its misleading estimates and its illegitimate use. Such dangers are of concern to all outsiders with an interest in these affairs and can only be prevented to a certain extent by giving general publicity to such management. A general cultural trend towards differentiation is thus reflected both within and by means of money relationships – what is public becomes more public; what is private becomes more private. This differentiation was unknown to smaller groups in former times, in which the private circumstances of the individual could not be so well concealed, or so well protected against the interference of others as the modern way of life permits. On the other hand, the representatives of the public interest in those small circles disposed of more mystical authority and concealment than those of large groups in which the extension of their area of authority, the objectivity of their techniques and their distancing from the individual person allowed them to tolerate the public nature of the behaviour of the authorities. Thus politics, administration and the law lose their secrecy and inaccessibility to the same extent as the individual gains the possibility of even greater withdrawal and of exclusion of all outsiders from his private affairs. One need only compare English with German history or survey the cultural history of the last two centuries in order to recognize this correlation. Even in the religious sphere, this process of differentiation is distinguishable, especially during the Reformation. Whereas the Catholic Church wraps authority in a mystical form that reigns from above over the faithful and refuses any questions, any critique and any co-operation, it does not itself permit them undisturbed religious independence, but makes its followers into confidants and itself a constantly interfering authority on their religious circumstances. Conversely, the Reformation gave to church organization publicity, accessibility and control, and rejected in principle all concealment and entrenchment before the eyes of individual believers. They, for their part, also gained the undisturbed liberty of religious inner feelings; their relationship to God became a private one and they did not have to account for it to anyone.

We now return from the privacy and secrecy that, in accordance with the general cultural trends, become part of the economic conditions in the money economy back to the sale of people, to bribery, which reaches its highest form through the specific qualities of the money economy. Not only can a bribe in the form of a piece of land or a herd of cattle not be concealed from the eyes of the neighbours, but also the bribed person himself cannot behave as if nothing at all had happened by pretending ignorance in the manner in which – as characterized earlier – the representative dignity of bribery requires. With money, however, one can bribe a person, as it were, behind his own back; he can pretend – even to himself – not to know anything about it, since it is not specifically and personally connected with him. Secrecy, undisturbed representation, the continuation of all other relationships in life is more completely secured by bribery with money than even by bribery with a woman's favour. Even though the latter form is completely exhausted by the act, so that, viewed from the outside, less is attached to the person than is the case with a present of money, the inner consequences none the less leave a greater mark upon the person than is the case with bribery by money. In the case of money bribes, the giving and receiving of the money terminates any relationship between the people involved, whereas in the case of bribery by offering a woman's favours, aversion, remorse or hatred rather than indifference are more likely to ensue. This advantage of bribery by money is, however, usually counterbalanced by the drastic degradation of the people concerned if the case becomes known. There is a distinctive parallel here with theft. Servants steal money less frequently, that is only where they are extremely demoralized, than they do food or other trifles. Some such experiences indicate that they flinch from stealing amounts of money that are equal to a bottle of wine or a toilet article which they would appropriate without any scruples. Accordingly, from this standpoint, our penal code considers stealing a small amount of food and consumer goods for direct use to be only a slight violation of the law whereas the theft of an equivalent amount of money would be severely punished. It is obviously assumed that in the case of a momentary need the availability of the respective commodity is so tempting that to succumb is too human a frailty to be punished severely. The more the object is distanced from its immediate use and the longer the detour necessary to satisfy the need, the weaker is the attraction, and the greater is the degree of immorality involved in satisfying the impulse to steal it. Therefore, according to a decision of the highest court, heating material, for example, is not considered to be in the same category as food and is not subject to the same reduction of punishment. Undoubtedly, the need for heat may be just as urgent a need and just as necessary for survival as bread. But its use is certainly less direct than that of bread. There are more intermediate stages on the way to survival, and it is only fair to assume that the tempted person has more time for reflection than would otherwise be possible for more immediate needs. Money is the farthest removed from such direct enjoyments; the interest is always focused on what lies behind it, so that the temptation that, as it were, radiates from it is not a natural instinct and does not possess the force of such an instinct to act as an excuse for succumbing to it. Therefore, just as with the theft of money, so bribery by money appears – as opposed to an immediately enjoyable value – as the symptom of shrewder and more thoroughly corrupted moral standards, so that the secrecy that the nature of money makes possible acts as a kind of protection for the subject. Inasmuch as it represents a tribute to the sense of shame, it belongs to a familiar type: that immoral behaviour is combined with a set of moral factors, not in order to reduce the total amount of immorality, but rather to be able to realize it. Here too it is evident that money that exceeds a certain quantity changes its qualitative characteristics. There are gigantic briberies that expediently change that security device and dispense with secrecy, to the extent that it is technically impossible to uphold it, by giving them an official character. During the twenty years between the granting of legislative and administrative independence of Ireland and the union with England, the English ministers were confronted with the apparently insoluble problem of governing two different states with a uniform policy and of establishing harmony between two independent legislatures. They found a solution in permanent bribery. All the various trends in the Irish parliament were brought together into the desired unity simply by buying the votes. Thus one of the greatest admirers of Robert Walpole stated: 'He himself was absolutely incorruptible; but to attain his political ends, which were wise and just, he was willing to bribe the whole lower house, and he would not have recoiled from bribing a whole nation.' How the clearest conscience with regard to bribes, a conscience proud of its own moral standards, can coexist together with the passionate condemnation of bribery is indicated by the statement of a Florentine bishop at the height of the medieval struggle against simony – he wished to buy the papal chair, even at the price of a £1,000, only in order to drive out the cursed Simonists! And perhaps the most striking example of the fact that it is the tremendous measure of sums of money that removes the stigma of shamelessness and of secrecy from bribery – as it does from prostitution – is this: the biggest financial transaction of early modern times was the procurement of financial means that Charles V required in order to bribe the people for his election as emperor!

In addition, the extraordinary height of purchase prices for goods that should not be subject to such trade often provides a certain guarantee that the public interest does not suffer too much damage. The fact that English kings used to sell the important public offices at least had the effect that the buyer strove to behave well. It was stated that a man 'who had paid £10,000 for the seals was not likely to forfeit them for the sake of a petty malversation which many rivals would be ready to detect'. Just as I stated earlier that the secrecy of bribery is a safety device for the subject, so publicity is a corresponding safety device for public interests. This is the corrective through which these gigantic corruptions were legitimized to some extent – they were not allowed to be hidden and thus one could, as it were, come to terms with them. For this reason, bribes are easier to bear under simple circumstances. It has been emphasized as something unheard of that Aristides, despite his many discretionary powers, died a poor man. In the small ancient city-states, the dishonesty of a single person did not yet shake the foundations of the whole society, because only a very small part was based on a money economy and because relationships were transparent and uncomplicated and could easily be kept in balance. Therefore it has been rightly said that the fate of Athens was every day dependent upon the decisions on the Pnyx. Under the modern highly complex circumstances of public life with its innumerable subterranean forces of the money economy that extend in all directions, the bribery of officials has much more detrimental effects.

In all the cases mentioned so far, we have dealt with the sale of values of a personal but not subjective nature and, by safeguarding them, the person experiences an objective value in them – in contrast to the values of subjective enjoyment. That the complex of life-forces that are vested in marriage thereby coincide with the direction of our own instincts; that the woman surrenders only if the man responds with similar emotions; that words and deeds are the corresponding expression of convictions and obligations – all this signifies not so much a value that we have but a value that we are. By surrendering all this for money, one exchanges one's being against one's possessing. Certainly both concepts are interrelated; for all the contents of our existence present themselves to us as possession of that purely formal, insubstantial centre that we experience as our centrifugal Ego and as the owning subject, in contrast to the objects owned in terms of qualities, interests and emotions. On the other hand, possessions are, as we saw, an extension of our sphere of influence, a power of disposal over objects which thereby enters into the circle of our Ego. The Ego, our desires and feelings, continues to live in the objects we own. On the one hand, the innermost core of the Ego – inasmuch as it is a single definite capacity – is located outside the centre as an objective ownership belonging to its central point; on the other, even the most extraneous factors, if they are true possessions, rest within the Ego. In owning the objects, the Ego becomes competent to deal with them and without any one of them it would change into something else. Looked at logically and psychologically, it would therefore be arbitrary to draw a dividing line between being and owning. If we none the less consider it to be objectively justified, then this is because being and owning, in terms of the distinction between them, are not theoretical objective concepts, but value concepts. If we designate our being as being different from our owning, we attribute a certain kind of value and standard of value to our contents of life. If one interprets those that lie close to the enigmatic centre of the Ego as our being and the more remote ones as our owning, then their arrangement in this series – excluding, of course, any sharp demarcation – is only produced through the diversity of feelings of value that accompanies both of them. If in any transaction we allocate what we give away to our being and what we receive to our owning, then this is only an indirect expression of the fact that we have exchanged a more intensive, more durable sense of value which permeates the whole sphere of life for a more direct, urgent and momentary one.

Money and the ideal of distinction

If the sale of personal values implies a diminution of this specific being – in the sense used here – and the direct opposite of 'self-respect', then we may term a personal ideal which can serve as a decisive yardstick for those modes of behaviour one of distinction [*Vornehmheit*]. This value is decisive because it signifies the most radical criterion in money matters. Measured against it, prostitution, marriage for money and bribery are the extreme points of a series that commences with the most legitimate forms of money transactions. To explain this phenomenon we have first to define the concept of distinction itself.

The usual division of our objective norms of valuation into logical, ethical and aesthetic norms is quite incomplete when viewed in the light of our practical judgments. To take a very striking example, we value the distinct formation of individuality, the mere fact that a personality possesses a specific and concise form and power. We experience as valuable the incomparability and uniqueness with which a person represents, as it were, only his own idea as valuable to us, often indeed in contrast to the ethical and aesthetic inferiority of the content of such a phenomenon. We are interested not in the completion of that system of norms but rather in pointing out that the systematic approach as such is just as erroneous here as it is with regard to the five senses or the twelve Kantian categories of reason. The development of our species continuously creates new possibilities for responding to the world both sensually and intellectually and new categories for evaluating it. And just as we constantly form new and effective ideals, so our growing consciousness discloses ever new ones of which we were unconscious, even though they were already effective. I believe that among the senses of value with which we respond to phenomena there is one that we can characterize only as the evaluation of 'distinction'. The independence of this category is indicated in the fact that it emerges in connection with phenomena of a totally different kind and value: with ways of thinking as well as works of art, with lineal descent as well as literary style, with highly developed taste just as much as with the corresponding objects, with the manners of high society as well as an animal of noble stock – all these we may term 'distinguished'. Even though this value bears some relationship to those of morality and beauty, it remains essentially independent of them since it appears to the same degree in combination with very varied ethical and aesthetic levels. The social meaning of distinction such as an exceptional position set apart from a majority; the separation of the individual phenomenon within its autonomous area, which would be immediately destroyed by the intrusion of any heterogeneous element – all this obviously provides the model for all the concept's applications. The actual bearer of the value of distinction establishes a quite specific kind of distinction. On the one hand, the distinction accentuates the positive exclusion of being interchangeable, of the reduction to a common denominator and of 'common activity'; on the other, the distinction should not be so conspicuous as to entice what is distinguished away from its independence, its reserve and its inner self-containment and to transpose its essence into a relationship to others, be it only a relationship of difference. The distinguished person is the very person who completely reserves his personality. Distinction represents a quite unique combination of senses of differences that are based upon and yet reject any comparison at all. It seems to me that a conclusive example is that the House of Lords not only is recognized to be the sole judge of each of its members, but in 1330 it explicitly rejected the suggestion that it should sit in judgment on persons other than peers – so that even an authority relationship to persons other than of its own rank was interpreted as degradation! Yet the more money dominates interests and sets people and things into motion, the more objects are produced for the sake of money and are valued in terms of money, the less can the value of distinction be realized in men and in objects. Various historical phenomena point to this negative connection. The ancient aristocracies of Egypt and India detested maritime trade and considered it to be incompatible with the purity of the castes. Like money, the ocean is a mediator, it is the geographical version of the means of exchange. In itself it is completely characterless and therefore, just like money, it is utilizable for the interaction of the most diversified things. Ocean traffic and money transactions are historically very close and the reserve and rigid exclusiveness of the aristocracy has to fear a wearing away and levelling from both phenomena. Thus, at the heights of aristocratic rule, trade was forbidden to the Venetian aristocracy and only in 1784 did a law authorize noblemen to trade under their own name. Previously they could do so only as sleeping partners of the business of the *cittadini*, that is at a distance and under cover. In Thebes there once existed a law that only allowed those who had not participated in any market transactions for ten years to be eligible for state offices. Augustus prohibited the senators from participating in customs monopolies and in shipping trade. If Ranke characterizes the fourteenth and fifteenth centuries of German history as the 'plebean' age, then this refers to the emergent conditions of a money economy that are represented by the cities that were antagonistic to the traditional aristocracy. Already at the beginning of the early modern period in England, it was found that the differences in wealth prevailing in the city could never produce such a decisively closed aristocracy as did the barriers between the estates in the country. The poorest apprentice could hope for a prosperous future if this future lay only in money ownership, whereas a completely rigid line separated landed aristocracy from the yeomanry. The existence of the infinite, quantitative grading of money ownership permits the levels to merge into one another and removes the distinctive formations of aristocratic classes which cannot exist without secure boundaries.

As with the aesthetic ideal that I mentioned earlier, so the ideal of distinction is indifferent to quantitative evaluation. The question of quantity completely recedes when faced with the secluded detachment of the value that is conveyed in its participating essence. The purely qualitative significance of this ideal is relatively unaffected by whether more instances achieve this level or not. What is decisive is that life has succeeded in accomplishing distinction, and to be its single valid representative in itself gives the specific character to the distinguished being – whether human or subhuman. Yet at that moment at which things that are viewed according to their money value are so evaluated, they are removed from the realms of this category, their qualitative value is subordinated to their quantitative value and their total independence – the dual relationship to others and to itself – that we experience on a certain level as distinction has lost its basis. The essence of prostitution, which we recognized in money, is imparted to the objects that function exclusively as its equivalent, perhaps to a more noticeable degree because they have more to lose than money is able to. That extreme opposite of the category of distinction – doing things in common with others [*Sichgemein-machen*] – becomes the typical relationship of objects in a money economy because all things are connected by means of money as through a central station, all float with the same specific gravity in the constantly moving current of money, and all, since they are on the same level, are distinguished only by the size of the pieces that they cover.

The tragic consequence of any levelling process inescapably takes effect where the higher level is pulled down to a greater extent than the lower level can be raised. This is obvious in the relationship between people. Where an area of communication is formed – particularly of an intellectual kind – in which a majority of people find understanding and common ground, the standards must be considerably closer to the person of the lowest than of the highest level. For it is always easier for the latter to descend than it is for the former to ascend. The circle of thoughts, information, strength of will and shades of feelings of the less perfect person can be covered by that of the more perfect person but not vice-versa; the former circle is common to both, but the latter is not. Apart from certain exceptions, the base of common interests and actions among the higher and lower elements can be accomplished only if the higher elements are able to disclaim their individual superiority. The same result also follows from the fact that the level of common ground cannot be as high for equally outstanding personalities as for each of them existing independently. For it is precisely the highest attainments of different people that are usually differentiated according to very diverse aspects, and they meet only on a much lower general level, beyond which the individually significant potentialities often diverge to such an extent that any communication at all becomes impossible. What is common to people – in the biological aspect; the oldest and therefore the most secure inheritance – is, in general, the cruder, undifferentiated and unintellectual element of their nature.

In the typical relationship in which the contents of life must pay for their common elements, their service to understanding and conformity by their relatively low standards, in which the individual has to reduce himself to what is common to all and has to renounce his personal level, either because the other person has lower standards or because, although their standards are the same, they apply to another field – the form of this relationship is illustrated by objects no less than by persons. The only difference is that what in this case is a process in real entities in the other case happens not to the objects themselves but to the conceptions of their value. The fact that the most refined and unique object can be had for money just as much as the most trivial and crude one creates a relationship between them which is foreign to their quality, and occasionally it may result in a trivialization and a loss of the specific valuation of the unique object, whereas the trivial one has neither anything to lose nor to gain.

The fact that the one is expensive and the other cheap is not always a compensation, particularly for general valuations which do not lend themselves to individual comparisons. Nor can it be offset by the undeniable psychological occurrence that the common denominator of money itself sets individual differences between objects more sharply into relief. The levelling effect of the money equivalent becomes quite evident as soon as one compares a beautiful and original but purchasable object with another equally significant one which is not purchasable. We feel from the outset that this latter object possesses a reserve, an independence, a right to be exclusively evaluated according to the objective ideal – in short, it possesses a distinction that the other object cannot attain. Even for the best and most exquisite object, the characteristic of being available for money purchase is a *locus minoris resistentiae* that cannot resist the importunity of the inferior searching for contact with it. For in so far as money, because it is nothing by itself, gains greatly in value by this possibility, so, conversely, is the individual significance of different objects of equal value degraded through their exchangeability – however indirectly or imaginary this may be. After all, this is probably the underlying motive for the way in which we characterize certain things such as well-worn phrases, modes of behaviour, musical tunes, etc., somewhat contemptuously as 'negotiable currency'. It seems that coinage – the most negotiable object of all – calls not only for negotiability as the point of comparison and as its expression; sometimes, at least, the factor of exchange must be added. Everyone accepts them and everyone uses them again, without any specific interest in their content – just as is the case with money. Everyone has it in his pocket, in stock; it does not require any transformation to serve its purpose under any circumstances. Whether given or received, its relation to the individual does not obtain any individual colouring or specific qualities; it does not – as do other contents of speaking or acting – affect the style of the personality, but slips through it unaltered like money through a purse. Levelling is the cause as well as the effect of the exchangeability of objects, just as certain words may be exchanged without further ado because they are trivial and they become trivial because they are usually exchanged without further ado. The coldness and frivolity that so much distinguishes the present from earlier treatment of objects is certainly due, in part, to the mutual de-individualization and levelling brought about by the common levels of money value.

The exchangeability that is expressed in money must inevitably have repercussions upon the quality of commodities themselves, or must interact with it. The disparagement of the interest in the individuality of a commodity leads to a disparagement of individuality itself. If the two sides to a commodity are its quality and its price, then it seems logically impossible for the interest to be focused on only one of these sides: for cheapness is an empty word if it does not imply a low price for a relative good quality, and good quality is an economic attraction only for a correspondingly fair price. And yet this conceptual impossibility is psychologically real and effective. The interest in the one side can be so great that its logically necessary counterpart completely disappears. The typical instance of one of these cases is the 'fifty cents bazaar'. The principle of valuation in the modern money economy finds its clearest expression here. It is not the commodity that is the centre of interest here but the price – a principle that in former times not only would have appeared shameless but would have been absolutely impossible. It has been rightly pointed out that the medieval town, despite all the progress it embodied, still lacked the extensive capital economy, and that this was the reason for seeking the ideal of the economy not so much in the expansion (which is possibly only through cheapness) but rather in the quality of the goods offered; hence the great contributions of the applied arts, the rigorous control of production, the strict policing of basic necessities, etc. Such is one extreme pole of the series, whose other pole is characterized by the slogan, 'cheap and bad' – a synthesis that is possibly only if we are hypnotized by cheapness and are not aware of anything else. The levelling of objects to that of money reduces the subjective interest first in their specific qualities and then, as a further consequence, in the objects themselves. The production of cheap trash is, as it were, the vengeance of the objects for the fact that they have been ousted from the focal point of interest by a merely indifferent means.

All this has probably clearly illustrated what a radical contrast exists between a money economy and all its consequences and the values of distinction that have been sketched out earlier. Money thoroughly destroys that self-respect that characterizes the distinguished person and becomes embedded in certain objects and their appreciation; it forces an extraneous standard upon things, a standard that is quite alien to distinction. By arranging things in a series in which only quantitative differences are valid, it deprives them, on the one hand, of their difference and distance of one from another and on the other of the right to reject any relationship or any qualification by comparison with others – these are precisely the two factors whose combination determines the peculiar ideal of distinction. The enhancement of personal values that characterizes this ideal seems to be so transcended, even in its projection into objects, as far as the effectiveness of money is concerned, that the objects are made 'common' in every sense of the word and are thus completely opposed, even in terms of language, to distinction. In contrast with this concept of distinction, the effect of money becomes evident among the whole range of purchasable goods, an effect that prostitution, monetary marriage and bribery have illustrated in a personally accentuated form.

II

The transformation of specific rights into monetary claims

We have demonstrated in the chapter on individual freedom how much the transformation of obligations in kind into money payments are to the advantage of both parties, and to what extent particularly the dependent person gains liberty and dignity. Money's importance for personal values must now be extended by a line of development in the opposite direction.

The favourable result of that transformation was due to the fact that the obligated person had hitherto contributed a personal strength and individual determinateness to the relationship without receiving a proportional equivalent. What the other party offered him was of a purely impersonal nature. The rights that he received from the relationship were relatively impersonal; the obligations that he accepted were completely personal. In that these obligations became depersonalized by taking on the form of money payments, the disproportion between them was removed. However, the result will be completely different if the obligated person cannot simply be paid off with a concrete return, but if he has acquired a right, an influence, a personal importance through this relationship; and this is precisely because he contributes such a definite personal service to that relationship. Under such circumstances, the objectification of the relationship brought about by changing to the money form of payment will have unfavourable results just as in the first case the results were favourable. The subjugation of Athens' allies into a more or less direct position of dependency commenced with changing their tribute from ships and troops into mere money payments. This apparent liberation from their more personal obligations also included the renunciation of their own political activity, which by implication could be claimed for only on the basis of the sacrifice of a specific contribution, of the deployment of actual power. The original obligation still contained direct rights such as that the warpower delivered could not be used against their own interests as was possible with the money that they supplied. In Kantian terms, provision in kind consists of the obligations as its form and of the specific content and object as its substance. However, this substance may have certain side-effects. For example, as the statute labour of the peasant it may considerably restrict his freedom of person and movement but it may also, as the natural contribution to the military undertakings of a supreme power, enforce a certain regard for the contributors. Whereas the obligation itself is the same in both cases, the substance that determines its form will make things difficult for the obligated person in one case and relatively favourable in the other. However, if money payment replaces contributions in kind, then the substantive element is virtually eliminated; it loses every effective quality so that only the purely economic obligation, in its most abstract realization possible, remains. In the first case, this reduction in obligations will imply the elimination of a burden, in the second the elimination of a relief; and the obligated person will be as elevated in the one case as he will be subjugated in the other. Therefore we more frequently encounter the transformation of forced labour into money payment as a conscious political move by which the power position of the obligated person is supposed to be reduced as, for instance, when Henry II of England decided that the knights, instead of following him to the continental wars, could discharge their obligations by money payments. Many may have accepted the proposal because, at first sight, it appeared to be an alleviation and liberation of this obligation. In fact, however, it brought about a disarmament of the feudal faction which the King had reason to fear most, and this was precisely because of its belligerent qualities upon which he himself had hitherto been dependent. Since such an equivalent specific factor did not exist for the enrolment of men in the districts and towns, the result for them was quite the opposite – they gained liberty by discharging their obligations in money. What makes all these phenomena so important is the fact that one can derive from them the connection between very basic sentiments in life and completely extraneous facts. It is also essential to realize that the qualities by which money is able to mediate these connections are apparent in money in their purest and most precise form, even though not in money alone. The historical constellations that are intrinsically supported by this implication can be arranged in an ascending series in which each link, in accordance with the particular relations between the elements, provides room for their freedom as well as for their suppression. It is clear that the purely personal relationship may be represented just as much by the harshness of personal subjugation to a person as by the dignity of free association. Both elements change if the determining factor has an impersonal character, whether this impersonality is the material one of an external object or a majority of persons in which the subjectivity of the individual disappears. The previous chapter has shown how the transition operates in this case as liberation and how often people prefer subordination to an impersonal collectivity or a purely objective organization to subordination to a person. I only wish to mention here that slaves, as well as serfs, used to have a relatively easy time if they belonged to the State, that the employees in modern warehouses with impersonal management are usually better situated than in small business units where they are personally exploited by the owner. Conversely, where very personal values are engaged, the change to impersonal forms is experienced as loss of dignity and liberty. The aristocratic voluntary devotion, including extreme sacrifices, has often been replaced by a feeling of humiliation and degradation, where the sacrifices, even at a reduced level, were changed to objective legal obligations. Even during the sixteenth century, the princes of France, Germany, Scotland and the Netherlands met with considerable resistance when they ruled through trained substitutes or administrative bodies. Authority was experienced as something personal to which one was willing to comply solely for reasons of personal devotion, whereas, in relation to an impersonal body, there was only subjugation.

The last link of this series consists of relationships based on money, the most objective of all practical institutions. Depending upon their origin and content, money payments represent either complete liberty or total suppression. Therefore we find that they are also occasionally resolutely refused. When Peter IV of Arragon asked the Arragon estates for money credit, they replied that this was not customary and that though his Christian subjects would be willing to serve him personally, to offer money would be a matter for Jews and Moors. In Anglo-Saxon England, too, the king had no right to impose direct taxation; instead, the old Teutonic principle prevailed that the commonwealth was based on personal service in the army and the court. When the king raised Danegeld, ostensibly as a protective measure against new invasions, this signified the decay of the State. In so far as it is in their power, the people under obligation accept a change from personal service to money payments only if their traditional position does not imply participation in the sphere of power of the beneficiaries. Different sections of the same group often take a very different attitude according to this point of view. The territorial rulers in medieval Germany who were entitled to conscript freemen and serfs for purposes of war later frequently raised taxes instead. However, the lords of the manor remained free from this tax because they themselves performed cavalry service, that is, 'they served with their blood'. This is the origin of the old legal rule: 'The peasant earns his goods with the sack, the knight with the horse.' If the modern state has re-introduced military service for its subjects instead of raising taxes and hiring mercenaries, then such a substitution of money payments by direct service is an adequate expression of the growing political importance of the individual citizen. Thus, to state that universal suffrage is the corollary of compulsory military service is justified by the relationship of money payments to personal services.

The enforceability of demands

The fact that despotic tendencies strive to reduce all kinds of obligations to money payments can be deduced from very basic relationships. The concept of coercion is mostly used in an indistinct and loose fashion. One usually says that somebody has been 'coerced' if his action is motivated by the threat or fear of a very painful consequence – punishment or loss, etc. – should he not perform the act. In fact, in all such cases no real coercion exists. For if somebody is willing to take the consequences, he is completely free to abstain from the action that he is supposed to be coerced into performing. Real coercion is exclusively that which is immediately exercised by physical power or by hypnotic suggestion.

For instance, I can be forced to give my signature only if somebody stronger than me takes my hand and performs the writing with it, or if I do it by hypnotic suggestion. But no threat of death can compel me to do it. It is therefore inaccurate to say that the State enforces compliance with its laws. The State cannot actually compel anybody to serve his military service, or to respect the life and property of others, or to testify, as long as the person is ready to accept the punishment for breaking the law. What the State can do in such circumstances is only to ensure that the guilty person accepts the punishment. Only with respect to one single category of the law is the enforcement of positive compliance possible, namely liability to taxation. The discharge of this duty can be enforced in the strict sense of the term – as can monetary private legal obligations – by removing the appropriate value from the liable person by force. Certainly it is true that this compulsion refers only to money payments and not even to economic services of any other kind. If someone is obliged to give a definite contribution in kind, he can never really be coerced into delivering it if he does not wish, under any circumstances, to produce it. However, something else that he owns can be taken away from him and transferred into money. For any such object has a money value and can replace the other in this relationship, even though perhaps it can do so in no other. The despotic constitution that aims at the unconditional compulsion of subordinates should probably, for reasons of expediency, request only money payments from them right from the outset. In relation to the demand for money, there is nothing like the resistance that may develop on the occasion of a claim for other contributions that are impossible to enforce. It is therefore internally and externally useful to reduce claims that may meet any kind of resistance solely to money. Perhaps this is one of the more basic reasons why, in general, the despotic regime is often associated with the promotion of the money economy (the Italian despots, for example, usually tended to sell their domains), and why the mercantilist system, with its greatly increased evaluation of money, developed at the time of unlimited monarchical power. Of all demands, the demand for money is the demand whose fulfilment is the least dependent on the good will of the obligated person. In contrast, that freedom which exists with reference to all other demands and whose substantiation and confirmation depends only upon the willingness to resist declines. This in no way contradicts the fact strongly underlined earlier that the conversion of contributions in kind into money payments usually implies a liberation of the individual. For the shrewd despot will always choose a form for his demands that grants to his subjects the greatest possible freedom *in their purely individual relationships*. The terrible tyrannies of the Italian Renaissance are, at the same time, the ideal breeding ground for the most unrestricted growth of the individual with his ideal and private interests; and at all times – from the Roman Empire to Napoleon III – political despotism has been found to be accompanied by a licentious private libertinism. For its own benefit, despotism will restrict its demands to what is essential for it and will make its measure and kind endurable by granting the greatest possible freedom for everything else. The demand for money payments unites the two viewpoints in the most practical way possible. The freedom that is granted in purely private affairs in no way prohibits the disfranchisement in the political sphere which it has so often achieved.

The transformation of substantive values into money values

Alongside this type of instance in which the monetary discharge of obligations corresponds to a degradation of the obligated person, there stands a second supplementation of the results analysed in the last chapter. We have seen what progress it meant for the serf if he could discharge his obligations by money payments. The opposite result occurs for him when the change in his relationship to money is instigated by the other party, that is when the lord of the manor buys from him the piece of land which he hitherto possessed with more or less extended rights. The grounds for the prohibitions issued in the eighteenth century and far into the nineteenth in the area of the old German Empire against the buying out of the peasant are, it is true, basically associated with fiscal or very general agricultural policy. Yet occasionally the sentiment seems to have prevailed that it was unjust to the peasant if land was taken away from him even in exchange for a very fair monetary compensation. Certainly it is possible to experience the transformation of a tangible possession into money as liberation. With the aid of money, we can convert the value of the object that was hitherto fixed in one form into any other; with money in our pocket we are free, whereas previously the object made us dependent upon the conditions for its conservation and realization. In principle, obligation to an object seems to be no different from the obligations to a person, for the object determines our activities no less rigidly than does a person if we want to avoid the worst consequences. Only the reduction of the whole relationship to money – whether we receive it or give it away – releases us from the determination that comes to us from something outside ourselves. So it is true that the frequent conversion of obligations into money payments in the eighteenth century gave to the peasants a monetary freedom. Yet such conversions took away from him what cannot be bought by money and what primarily gives freedom its value – the trustworthy object of personal activity. To the peasant, the land meant something altogether different from a mere property value; for him it meant the possibility of useful activity, a centre of interest, a value that determined his life, which he lost as soon as he owned only the money value of his land instead of the land itself. The reduction of his landed property to its mere money value pushes him on the road to proletarianization. A different level of agricultural social relations exhibits the same form of development. On the farms in Oldenburg, for example, the hired labour relationship often prevails. The hired labourer is obliged to work a certain number of days per year for a lower wage than the day wage labourer; in exchange, he receives from the farmer his dwelling, use of land, transport, etc., for less than the going price. This is, at least in part, an exchange of values in kind. It has been pointed out that this relationship is characterized by social equality of the farmer and the hireling, who does not feel inferior by being forced to work for wages on account of less favourable property conditions. At the same time, however, it has been stated that the emerging money economy destroys this relationship, and that the transformation of the natural exchange of services into money payments degrades the hireling – even though he would, in this way, gain a certain freedom of action concerning his work contract, in contrast to being restricted to receiving a definite amount of goods. In the same area, the same development is evident in another respect. As long as the threshers on the farms were paid by a certain share of the threshing they had a lively personal interest in their master's successful management of the farm. The threshing machine displaced this type of payment, and the money wage that replaced it does not favour a personal relationship between master and labourer, who gained more self-respect and moral support from it than from a higher cash income.

The negative meaning of freedom and the extirpation of the personality

Money's importance in gaining individual freedom serves to illustrate a very far-reaching definition of the concept of freedom. At first glance, freedom seems to possess a merely negative character. It only has meaning in contrast to a form of bondage; it is always freedom from something and corresponds to the concept by expressing the absence of obstacles. However, the concept of freedom is not confined to this negative meaning. Freedom would be without meaning and value if the casting off of commitments were not, at the same time, supplemented by a gain in possessions or power: freedom from something implies, at the same time, freedom to do something. Phenomena in many varied spheres confirm this. In political life, wherever a party demands or attains freedom the issue is not at all one of freedom as such, but those positive gains, increases and spreading of power from which the party was previously excluded. The importance of the 'freedom' which the French Revolution gave to the Third Estate was that a Fourth Estate was in the making which could now be required to work 'freely' for that estate. The freedom of the Church means the direct extension of its sphere of influence, for example, that with reference to its 'freedom of instruction' the State permits its citizens to be exposed to and influenced by the Church's suggestions. The liberation of the peasant-serfs all over Europe was followed up by endeavours to make the peasant the owner of his plot of land – just like the ancient Jewish regulations, which requested that the indebted slave had to be liberated after a certain number of years, while adding that he should be handed over some property, preferably that which he formerly owned. Wherever the purely negative sense of freedom operates, freedom is considered to be incomplete and degrading. Giordano Bruno, in his enthusiasm for the unified regular life of the cosmos, considered free will to be a defect that characterized man in his imperfection since God alone was subject to necessity. After this very abstract example we can give a very concrete one. The land of the Prussian cottagers was located outside the community farmland where the various holdings lay in mixed strips. Since such strips could be cultivated only according to common rule, the cottager had much more individual freedom. Yet since he stood outside the community, he possessed not the positive freedom to participate in decisions concerning the fields, but only the negative freedom of not being bound by communal decisions. This is the reason why the cottager, even with considerable property, remains in a subjugated position with very little social prestige. In itself, freedom is an empty form which becomes effective, alive and valuable only in and through the development of other life-contents. If we analyse the events by which freedom is gained, we always notice, alongside the formal and pure concept of freedom, a substantively determined content which, however, by giving it a positive significance, also contains a certain limitation, a directive as to what has to be positively accomplished by this freedom. All the actions by which freedom is gained may be arranged on a scale on the basis of how much greater its material content and gain is in relation to its formal and negative moments of freedom from former bondage. For example, to the young man who, released from the pressures of school, enters the free life of a university student, the latter moment is the more acute. The new substance of life and aspirations that forms its positive side is at first very indefinite and ambiguous, so that the student, because mere freedom is something completely empty and unbearable, voluntarily accepts a constraint of the most rigid kind – the German student's code of behaviour. The situation for a businessman who is released from a troublesome commercial restriction is altogether different. Here, the new activity that makes that freedom valuable is definitely determined in content and orientation; he not merely accepts freedom but knows immediately how to make use of it. To the girl who leaves the confined order of her parents' home to make herself economically independent, freedom has a more positive meaning as to quantity as well as quality than if she gets married. In the latter case, the essence and purpose of the freedom leads to the management of her own household. In short, every act of liberation exhibits a specific proportion between the accentuation and extension of the situation that has been surmounted and the situation that is thereby acquired. If one were to construct such a series according to the slowly growing preponderance of the one moment over the other, then the freedom gained by exchanging an object against money would be placed at one extreme, at least if the object had hitherto determined the content of life. Whoever exchanges his landed estate for a house in the city is thereby freed from the troubles and anxieties of agricultural pursuits, but this freedom means that he now has to devote himself to the problems and chances that urban property ownership confers. However, if he sells his property for cash then he is really free; the negative factor of the liberation from former burdens predominates, and his newly created situation as a money-owner entails only a minimum of specific directives for the future. The positive factor in the liberation from the constraints of an object has been reduced to its marginal value. Money solves the task of realizing human freedom in a purely negative sense.

Thus the extreme danger for the peasant of being 'liberated' by cash payments is part of the general pattern of human freedom. It is true he gained freedom, but only freedom *from* something, not liberty *to do* something. Apparently, he gained freedom to do anything – because it was purely negative – but in fact he was without any directive, without any definite and determining content. Such freedom favours that emptiness and instability that allows one to give full rein to every accidental, whimsical and tempting impulse. Such freedom may be compared with the fate of the insecure person who has forsworn his Gods and whose newly acquired 'freedom' only provides the opportunity for making an idol out of any fleeting value. The tradesman who, burdened and worried by his business, urgently wants to sell it at any cost meets with the same fate. But when finally, cash in hand, he is really 'free', he often experiences that typical boredom, lack of purpose in life and inner restlessness of the rentier which drives him to the oddest and most contradictory attempts to keep busy in order to give a substantive content to his 'freedom'. A similar situation often confronts the official who wants, as quickly as possible, to attain a position whose pension will enable him to lead a 'free' life. Thus, amidst the torments and anxieties of the world, the state of repose often appears to us as the absolute ideal until we learn by experience that peace from specific things is valuable or even bearable only if it is, at the same time, peace to engage in specific things. Whereas the peasant who has been bought out, the merchant who has become a rentier or the pensioned civil servant seem to have freed their personalities from the constraints that are bound up with the specific conditions of their property or their position, in reality the opposite has occurred in the instances cited here. They have exchanged the positive contents of their self for money which does not offer any such contents. A French traveller relates a very characteristic story of Greek peasant women, who do embroidery and are very attached to their toilsome products: 'They give them away, they take them back, they look at the money, then at their job, then again at the money. The money finally is always the right thing and they are shattered to find themselves so rich.' Because the freedom that money offers is only a potential, formal and negative freedom, to receive money in exchange for the positive contents of life implies the selling of personal values – unless other values take their place immediately. For this reason, the Prussian distribution of communal land in the early nineteenth century greatly favoured the growth of a shiftless and rootless stratum of day wage labourers. The natural rights to the use of the woods and meadows were an aid to the standard of living of the poorer peasants for whom *in abstracto* there was no equivalent. If compensation for the removal of these rights were to be paid in money, then it would soon disappear; if it were to be paid in land, then it would be too small to yield results. Thus, such compensations for land were quickly changed to money and they increased rather than reduced the trend towards proletarianization and the loss of the substance of life. An exact parallel with the behaviour of the Greek peasant women is, as ethnologists report, the extreme difficulty in buying commodities from native people. This has been explained by the fact that each object has a decidedly individual stamp of originality with regard to its origin and use. The tremendous labour applied to producing and decorating it and its exclusive personal usage makes it part of the person himself. To part with it thus meets with the same resistance as parting with a limb of the body, so that instead of an expansion of the Ego – which the endless 'possibilities' of money ownership temptingly but vaguely suggest – a contraction takes place. Once we clearly recognize this it is not without significance for the understanding of our times. Ever since money has existed, everyone is by and large more inclined to sell than to buy. As the money economy expands, this inclination becomes stronger and increasingly affects those objects which are not meant to be sold but which have the character of permanent possessions and seem to be destined to be tied to the personality rather than to break loose from it in a rash exchange: businesses and factories, works of art and collections, landed property, rights and positions of all kinds. An extraordinary amount of freedom is realized by the fact that, where all this remains the property of one person for an increasingly shorter period, the person changes the specific conditions of such property more quickly and frequently. However, since money with its indeterminateness and its inner lack of direction is the other side of these processes of liberation, they often do not advance beyond this uprooting, and fail to sink new roots. In fact, since under very rapid money transactions possessions are no longer classified according to the category of a specific life-content, that inner bond, amalgamation and devotion in no way develops which, though it restricts the personality, none the less gives support and content to it. This explains why our age, which, on the whole, certainly possesses more freedom than any previous one, is unable to enjoy it properly. Money makes it possible for us to buy ourselves not only out of bonds with others but also out of those that stem from our own possessions. It frees us both when we give it away and when we take it. Thus the continuous processes of liberation occupy an extraordinarily broad section of modern life. At this point, too, the deeper connection of the money economy with the tendencies of liberation is revealed, exhibiting one of the reasons why the freedom of liberalism has brought about so much instability, disorder and dissatisfaction.

However, since so many objects continuously detached by money lose their direction-giving significance for us, there develops a practical reaction to the change in our relationship to them. If that insecurity and disloyalty in relation to specific possessions which is part of the money economy has to be paid for by the very modern feeling that the hoped for satisfaction that is connected with new acquisitions immediately grows beyond them, that the core and meaning of life always slips through one's hand, then this testifies to a deep yearning to give things a new importance, a deeper meaning, a value of their own. They have been worn away by the easy gain and loss of possessions, by the transitoriness of their existence, their enjoyability and their change. In short, the consequences and correlations of money have made them void and indifferent. Yet the lively motions in the arts, the search for new styles, for style as such, symbolism and even theosophy are all symptoms of the longing for a new and more perceptible significance of things – regardless of whether it is that each thing has its own more valuable and soulful emphasis, or gains such an emphasis through establishing a connection by release from its atomization. If modern man is free – free because he can sell everything, and free because he can buy everything – then he now seeks (often in problematical vacillations) in the objects themselves that vigour, stability and inner unity which he has lost because of the changed money-conditioned relationship that he has with them. Just as we saw earlier that, through money, man is no longer enslaved in things, so on the other hand is the content of his Ego, motivation and determination so much identical with concrete possessions that the constant selling and exchanging of them – even the mere fact that they are saleable – often means a selling and uprooting of personal values.

The difference in value between personal achievement and monetary equivalent

The money economy will increasingly gloss over the fact that the money value of things does not fully replace what we ourselves possess in them, that they have qualities that cannot be expressed in money. Wherever it is undeniable that the valuation and abandonment of the object for money cannot save it from the cheapening banality of daily transactions, we search, at least sometimes, for a form of money that is far removed from the everyday kind. The oldest Italian coin was a piece of copper without definite form which was therefore not counted but weighed. And until the period of the Roman Empire, by which time money matters had already reached a stage of refinement, this formless piece of copper was favoured for use in religious offerings and as a legal symbol.

It is quite evident that the value of things none the less exacts recognition over and above their money value if a personally performed task rather than a substance is sold, and if this task possesses an individual character not only in its external realization but also in its content. The following group of phenomena may make this clear. When money and performances are exchanged, the buyer claims only the specific object, the circumscribed performance. The actual performer, on the other hand, requests, or at leasts hopes in many cases, for more than just money. Whoever attends a concert is satisfied with their money outlay when they hear the expected programme with the expected perfection. The artist, however, is not satisfied with the money; he also expects applause. Whoever wants a portrait of himself is satisfied if he receives it, whereas the painter is not content if he gets the price agreed upon, but rather only if, in addition, he receives subjective recognition and supra-subjective fame. The minister asks not only for his salary, but also for the gratefulness of the ruler and the nation; the teacher and the priest demand not only their salary, but also reverence and loyalty; even the better class of businessman not only wants money for his wares, but also wants the buyer to be satisfied – and even then not only to ensure that the customer returns. In short, many performers of specific tasks – apart from money which they objectively recognize to be a sufficient equivalent for their achievement – also demand a personal acknowledgment, some kind of subjective token from the purchaser that exists quite apart from the agreed money payment and that will be a contributory complement to the full equivalent of his achievement. Here we have the exact opposite of the phenomenon that I described in the third chapter as the superadditum of money ownership. In that case, the buyer received something more than the exact equivalent of his expenditure because of money's capacity to extend beyond every particular object's value. But it is precisely the nature of money that, of all empirical things – to quote Jakob Böhme – it combines movement and countermovement, and expresses this adjustment. Personal performances demand something over and above their money equivalents. Just as on the part of money, so here too on the part of the achievement, the claim that exceeds direct exchange expresses itself in a sphere that surrounds the person as the geometric focus of his demands and exists independently of each individual demand. The balance in favour of the performer, which develops in this manner with the exchange of money and personal performance, may be considered to be so paramount that the acceptance of a money equivalent appears to disparage both the performance and the person. This is as if one were to accept in money terms what would be written off from that immaterial payment from which one allows no deductions. We know that Lord Byron accepted fees from publishers only with the greatest embarrassment. Wherever the activity of money-making itself already lacks prestige, as in classical Greece (because the social significance and productivity of money capital was not yet known, money was believed to serve only egotistical consumption), the degradation increases, particularly with reference to personal–intellectual achievements. Thus, to teach or to engage in intellectual work in general for money appeared to be a degradation of the person. As to all those activities that have their source in the core of the personality, it is superficial and unreal to assume that one could be paid for them in full. Is it at all possible completely to remunerate a person for the sacrifices of love by some other action, however equally valuable it may be and however much it may spring from equally strong emotions? A relationship of total personal obligation always remains, a relationship that perhaps is mutual but that none the less basically resists the balancing of accounts by that mutuality. In the same way, no subjective offence can be atoned for as if it had not happened, as is the case with external damages. If the guilty person feels he is completely rehabilitated after he has suffered the punishment, then this is the result not of the offence being equal to the punishment, but of an inner transformation which destroys the roots of the sin. That mere punishment alone is incapable of really wiping out the misdeed is indicated by the persistent distrust and degradation to which the sinner is exposed despite having undergone the punishment. I showed earlier that between qualitatively diverse elements there is no direct equivalence as there is between the debit and credit side of a balance sheet. This is most conclusively confirmed by the values that are embodied in the individual personality and it becomes invalid to the extent that these values lose their roots and take on an independent objective character. Such values unendingly draw towards money as the absolutely commensurable entity because it is absolutely objective in contrast to the absolutely incommensurable personality. On the other hand, there is something dreadful about realizing the profound mutual inadequateness of the things, achievements and psychic values which we constantly weigh against each other like real equivalents; on the other, it is preciesely this incommensurability of these elements of life that gives them the right not to be compared with any particular equivalent and that gives to life an irreplaceable charm and wealth. One of the reasons for the numerous injustices and tragic situations in life may be that personal values cannot be balanced by or equated with the money that is offered for them. Yet, on the other hand, the awareness of personal values, the pride in individual aspects of life arises precisely through the knowledge that they cannot be outweighed by any amount of merely quantitative values. As is so often recognized, this inadequacy is modified by very large sums as equivalents because they, for their part, are imbued with that 'super-additum', with fantastic possibilities that transcend the definiteness of numbers. They correspond to the personality incarnated in but yet transcending every individual achievement. The willingness to offer certain objects or performances for a very large amount of money seems justified; but if this cannot be obtained then one would rather make a present of them than take a small amount of money for them. Only the latter would be degrading, not the former. For this reason, among refined and sensitive people presents that are meant to pay tribute to a person must make the money value imperceptible. The *fleeting perishability* of flowers and candy that one may venture to give to a lady of distant acquaintance indicates the elimination of any substantial value.

The difference in value between a particular task and its money equivalent is neither always noticeable nor, even when that is true, always expressible, as in the earlier instances of the artist and the physician, the official and the scholar. If the activity is a very unindividual one and the performer an average person, as for example the unskilled worker, then the point of incommensurability is lacking, as is the process of expressing a unique personality recognizable by distinctive qualities in the work. On the other hand, whether the performer receives a compensation for the excess value rests, in principle, on whether his social position allows such ideal acknowledgments; wherever they are absent because of his general subordinate position he is all the more degraded the more personal is the value he is forced to offer for money and only for money. Thus, the reason why medieval minstrels were looked down upon was accounted for by the fact that they sang cheerful as well as sad songs upon request and thereby prostituted their personal emotions by taking money instead of honourable recognition. In order to exclude any ideal compensation, it was therefore quite consistent with this fact that they were treated very correctly at least with regard to their economic wage in order to exclude non-material compensations. Although the minstrels by and large fared badly, they were treated impartially, particularly with reference to what was due to them. Wherever genuine personal values have to be offered for money without any further non-material compensation, one finds that a loosening, almost a loss of substance in individual life, takes place. The feeling that personal values are exchanged in monetary transactions for an inadequate compensation is certainly one of the reasons why money transactions have so often been rejected with horror by proud and high-minded people and why agriculture, its opposite, has been praised as the only proper pursuit. For example, this was the case among the nobility in the Scottish Highlands who, until the eighteenth century, led an isolated and purely autochthonous life – one that was guided, however, by the ideal of greatest personal freedom. Yet however much money encourages such freedom, it cannot be denied that, from the standpoint of a free, independent and self-sufficient existence, the exchange of property and achievements for money depersonalizes life after a tight network of transactions originally enclosed and intertwined people. If the subjective and objective sides of life have been separated, then depersonalization, by increasingly concentrating on the objective side, might serve the pure elaboration of the subjective side. Conversely, in a more primitive and uniform existence, it must appear unreasonable and as a loss if property and achievement, hitherto only personally enjoyed and personally granted, are reduced to a mere element of monetary transactions and to an object of its objective laws. In the transition from the medieval manorial estate to modern farming we find that the concept of the knight's status is thereby enlarged. In addition to military activity, gainful activity is now considered permissible for him – yet this refers only to the management of his own estates, a type of acquisition whose peculiarity made him look down on the merchant and the tradesman even more than had been the case previously. Here, the specific impression that monetary transactions are undignified is brought clearly into relief since both economic forms are now pushed close to each other. One of the most general sociological phenomena is that the contrast between two elements appears most clearly if they have developed out of a common soil. Sects of the same religion hate each other more intensely than totally different religious communities; the antagonism between small neighbouring city-states was always more passionate than that between large countries with their spatially and objectively different spheres of interest; in fact, it has been claimed that the most fervent hatred that exists is that existing among blood relatives. This increase in antagonism out of a background of a community of interests in some cases seems to reach a peak when the common interest or similarity is in the process of increasing. Thus there is a danger that the difference and contrast, the preservation of which is in the interest of at least one of the parties, will become blurred. The more a lower and a higher element approach each other, the more vigorously will the latter emphasize the points of difference that still exist and the higher will it value them. Hence passionate and aggressive class hatred does not emerge where the classes are separated by an unbridgeable gulf, but rather at that moment at which the lower class has already begun to rise, and when the upper class has lost some of its prestige and the levelling of both classes can be discussed. The lord of the manor, during the process of becoming a managing estate farmer, therefore felt an increased need to distinguish himself from the money-minded merchant. He managed the estate but originally only for his own needs, and did not sell his produce for money. If he did do so then it was only his own product; he was not in the service of the money lender, as is the merchant with his direct personal skill. For a similar motive – although in co-operation with others – the Spartan citizen was allowed to own land, but not to farm it himself. It was very important for aristocratic interests to emphasize any difference with other sellers because money transactions have democratic levelling consequences, especially if the person in the higher social position takes the money, and the person in the lower position takes the product, since both parties are easily considered to be 'equal' to one another. Therefore the aristocrat considers money transactions degrading, whereas the peasant, if he pays the lord of the manor in money rather than in goods, thereby experiences an elevation of his position.

The sale of personal values for money also illustrates the unique quality of money which, with its own indecision and lack of content, cultivates all the opposites of historical–psychological possibilities and moulds them into definite entities. In such an increasingly practical world money, the embodiment of the relativity of things, appears, as it were, to be the absolute which embraces and upholds the oppositions of all that is relative.

III

'Labour money' and its rationale

The importance of the money equivalence of work has been referred to so often in these pages, both directly and indirectly, that here I only wish to examine one more question of principle that is relevant to it, namely, whether labour itself is indeed the value that actually forms *in concreto* the element of value in all economic items to the same extent that it is expressed *in abstracto* through money. The attempts to derive all economic values from a single source and to reduce them to a single expression – such as labour, costs, uses, etc. – would certainly not have arisen had not the convertibility of all these values into money, into a unit of their essence, suggested it and had it not served as a security for the recognizability of precisely this unit. The concept of 'labour money' that arises in socialist plans expresses this connection. Thus, work performed as the sole value-creating factor alone gives the right to claim the products of others' labour, and for this one knows of no other form for characterizing the symbol and recognition of a specific amount of labour than money. Therefore, money must itself be conserved here as a unified form of value whereas its momentary character will be rejected because its own existence prevents it from being the adequate expression of the fundamental power of value. If one permits nature as well as labour to be a creator of value, so that labour also possesses value out of the material extracted from nature and thus, as the saying goes, although work is the father of wealth, earth is the mother, then the socialist line of thought must none the less lead to labour money. For since the treasures of nature should no longer be private but common property, and *a priori* each should, in the same manner, be the accessible basis of economic life as such, then that which each person has to give in exchange is thus ultimately only his labour. Of course, if he has exchanged a valuable product of nature with the aid of his labour and exchanged it once more, an individual can take its material value into account. Yet the amount of its value is still only the same as the value of his labour for which he has acquired it and this thus forms the measure of its exchange value for the product of nature in question. If labour is thus the ultimate authority to which all the value determinations of the object must be referred, then it is inappropriate and a diversion to measure it in terms of an alien object such as money. Rather, one must certainly search for a possibility of expressing the pure and immediate unity of labour in a symbol that functions as a means of exchange and measurement, that functions as money.

/Without pronouncing on which of the proposed unifications of value is the sole legitimate one, I wish to assert that the labour theory of value is, at least philosophically, the most interesting theory. The material and intellectual aspects of human beings, their intellect and their will gain a unity in work that remains inaccessible to these potentialities so long as one views them, as it were, in peaceful co-existence. Work is the unified stream in which they mix like river sources, extinguishing the diversity of their nature in the similarity of the product. If work was really the sole agent of value, then the latter would thus be submerged in the specific point of unity of our practical nature, and this would have to choose the most adequate expression that it can find in external reality. It seems to me, in the light of this importance of work, that it is a secondary question as to whether or not one has to deny that, as a result, labour itself first *produces* values – just like the machine that works on a material that does not yet itself possess the form that it confers upon it. Certainly, if one only accords value to the products of human labour, then labour can not itself possess value – it is a physiological function – rather, only labour *power* possesses value. Clearly, this can be produced only by human beings, namely through the means of subsistence which in turn stem from human work. That it is then transposed into real work clearly does not require more work and thus itself implies no value; rather, this only adheres to the products of such labour. None the less, I take this to be a basically terminological issue. For since labour power is certainly not a value if it remains latent, and if it is not transposed into real work but rather only operates in this value-forming work, then one can employ labour for all purposes of calculation and expression. Furthermore, this situation is not changed by the consideration that the values consumed as subsistence are not produced by labour but by labour power and therefore only labour power as the bearer of these values can itself be a *value*. Therefore, the means of subsistence cannot be the sufficient cause of the value realized by human beings because this value exceeds that invested in the former since it can otherwise never supply an increase in value. The division between labour power and labour is important only for the purposes of socialism, because it illustrates the theory that the worker retains only a part of the value that he produces. His work produces more values than are invested in his labour power in the form of means of subsistence. In so far as the employer purchases the whole of the labour power for the value of the means of subsistence, he profits from the whole of the surplus by which the ultimate product of labour exceeds this value. But even viewed from this standpoint, it seems to me that one could, instead of labour power, characterize labour itself as value and separate out from one another the amounts whose values comprise, on the one hand, a wage to the worker and, on the other, the employer's profit. I wish not to go into this any further here but to investigate in what follows only the more immediate evaluation with which the labour theory of value confronts us so frequently. It searches for a concept of labour that is equally valid for manual and mental labour and, in so doing, actually appeals to manual labour as the primary value or value-producing entity that is valid as the measure of work as a whole. It would be erroneous to see in this merely proletarian spite and fundamental depreciation of intellectual achievements. On the contrary, deeper and more varied causes are at work here.

The unpaid contribution of mental effort

With regard to the share of the intellect in work, it is first of all asserted that it is not a 'cost', since it requires no compensation owing to depreciation and therefore does not raise the costs of the product. Thus, only manual labour is left as the foundation of exchange value. If, on the contrary, one emphasizes that mental energy is also creative and must be maintained and compensated for by nourishment to exactly the same degree as labour power, then the element of truth is overlooked that this theory may be the basis for this view, even if only as an instinctive feeling. The share of the intellect in a product of labour implies two aspects that must be sharply distinguished. If a joiner makes a chair according to a well tried model, then this is certainly not accomplished without a share of mental activity. The hand must be directed by the mind. Yet this is by no means all the mental activity that is invested in the chair. It could also not be produced without the mental activity of those who, perhaps generations ago, had invented such a design. The mental energy used here also forms a practical precondition for this chair. However, the content of this second mental process exists in a further form that no longer involves any mental expenditure of energy, namely as tradition, as objectivated thought which anyone can take up and reflect upon. In this form it affects the production process of the contemporary joiner and forms the content of the real mental function, which, of course, must be carried on and completed by its subjective power and by means of which it enters into the product as its form. The two mental activities of which I first spoke are quite certainly subordinated to the depreciation and the necessity of physiological compensation: both that of the joiner and that of the inventor of the chair. But the third mental factor that is certainly decisively important for the present production of the chair is indeed removed from potential consumption, and on the basis of the plan of this chair thousands of copies can be produced. The plan itself thereby suffers no depreciation, requires no restoration and certainly does not increase the cost of such chairs even though it constitutes the form-giving, material–intellectual content of each individual chair of this type. If one distinguishes with the necessary precision between the objective–mental content contained in a product and the subjective–mental function that produces the product according to the model of its content, then one can see the relative justification for the assertion that mental activity has no cost. One can, of course, also see the relative injustice of this assertion, since this uncompensatable and unusable notion of the object is itself realized not in products but only by means of an intellect which demands this idea of the appropriate functioning of organic energy and contributes to the cost value of the product on the same grounds as does manual labour – even though the mental expenditure that is associated with such a preformed content is much less than if it had, at the same time, originally produced this content. The difference between the two is the gratuitous achievement of the mind. And it is this ideal factor that so completely distinguishes mental from economic possession in two respects: on the one hand, it can be so much more basic; on the other, it can be so much less accepted than the latter. The thought that has been once expressed can no longer be captured again by any amount of power in the world; its content is irrevocably the public property of all who apply the mental energy necessary to recall it. By the same token, however, once it has appeared, it cannot be stolen again by any amount of power in the world. Once expressed, the thought remains indivisibly bound up with the personality as a constantly reproducible content in a manner that has no analogy in the economic sphere. In so far as, in terms of its content, the intellectual process possesses this supra-economic importance, and as such constitutes the psychological process, we are obviously concerned here only with the latter, with the question of the role that the mental expenditure of energy plays in the creation of value alongside manual labour.

The reduction of the importance of mental labour to that of physical labour is ultimately only one side of the whole general tendency to produce a unified concept of labour. What has to be discovered is the common factor in all the diverse types of labour – a much broader and more differentiated diversity than is expressed in the mere opposition of physical and mental labour. If this were achieved, then an extraordinarily large theoretical and practical gain would be made, as much in fact as the gain from the existence of money. One would then gain the general, qualitative unit on the basis of which all value relationships between the results of human activity could be expressed purely quantitatively through greater or smaller amounts. In all spheres this has implied the basic progress of knowledge, namely that the qualitative weighing of objects one with another, which always remains a relatively uncertain and inexact process, is transferred to a quite unambiguous quantitative process in which a universal internal unit is secured in the objects. This unit is universally the same and self-evident and no longer has to be considered in the calculation of the relative importance of individual elements. From the socialist standpoint, this is clearly a mere extension and consequence of the attempt to reduce all values as a whole to the economic sphere as their starting point and their substance. Such an attempt must necessarily follow from this standpoint if its levelling tendency is thought out to its conclusion. For in the economic sphere one can at least conceive of an equality of individuals as being possible; in all other spheres – the intellectual, emotional, character, aesthetic, ethical, etc. – the quality of the 'means of labour' is, from the very outset, hopeless. If, none the less, one wishes to undertake this task, then there is no other possibility than to somehow reduce these interests and qualities to that which alone permits an approximate uniformity of distribution. I am well aware that present-day scientific socialism rejects mechanical–communist egalitarianism and merely wishes to establish an equality of conditions of work out of which the diversity of talent, strength and effort would also lead to a diversity of position and satisfaction. Despite the present situation in which hereditary descent, class distinction, the accumulation of capital and all the possible chances of economic opportunities produce much greater corresponding distances than do individual differences in activities, this would, in fact, mean not only a basic equalization in *every* respect but also the equalization of the elements of ownership and satisfaction which seem to me today still to be the genuine effective means of agitation for the masses. If historical materialism is made the scientific demonstration of the socialist doctrine, then what is of concern here, as so often, is the systematic construction of the path that is the reverse of that of the creative movement of thought. Therefore socialist theory has not been logically derived from the independently established historical materialism; rather, the practically established socialistic–communistic tendency must furthermore first produce the only base that is possible for it: it must declare economic interests to be the source and common denominator of all others. Once this has taken place, however, the same tendency in the economic sphere must itself then be pursued, and the diversity of its contents reduced to a unity which, over and above all individual achievements, asserts the possibility of an equalization and an externally verifiable equitableness.

Differences in types of labour as quantitative differences

For the assertion that the value of all valuable objects rests upon their labour costs still does not suffice for this purpose. It would still be possible to unify the qualitative diversity of labour in such a manner that a smaller amount of higher labour formed a similar or higher value to a considerably larger amount of lower labour. In so doing, however, a completely different scale of value would be introduced than the one considered here. The decisive qualities of specialization, intellectuality and complexity would certainly still be produced both with and in labour, but would be realized as a mere attribute of that labour. Yet the *element of value* itself would rest no longer upon labour as labour but upon the order of qualities constructed according to a quite independent principle for which labour as such, which is the general element of all labour qualities, would still be only the irrelevant agent. In this way, the labour theory would be confronted with the same dilemma that underlies the doctrines of moral philosophy, namely that the production of happiness is the absolute ethical value. That is, if trade is really moral to the extent that it results in happiness, then this means a break-down of principle and the introduction of new specific elements of value if the purer, more intellectual, more exclusive happiness is priced as being the more valuable. For then one could conceive of the situation in which such happiness, though quantitative – i.e. considered as mere happiness – would be less than that of a lower, sensuous, selfish happiness, despite the fact that the former would be morally more worth striving for. The ethical theory of happiness is therefore consistent only when all the ethical distinctions between moral and intellectual, epicurean and ascetic, egotistic and altruistic happiness in the last instance – all accompanying and related phenomena – are taken into account as the mere quantitative distinctions of one and the same – qualitatively always the same – type of happiness. Equally, a consistent labour theory must be able to sustain the view that all the unambiguously experienced and indisputable value distinctions between two achievements that appear both as labour-extensive and -intensive only means, in the last instance, that more labour is concentrated in the one than in the other, that only a first and fleeting glance would take them to be the same amounts of labour, but that a deeper penetrating view actually reveals more or less labour as the basis of their greater or lesser value.

In fact, this interpretation is not as deficient as it at first sight appears to be. One need only interpret the concept of labour widely enough. Firstly, if one views labour solely with reference to its individual agents, then it is evident that in some 'higher' labour product it is in no way the case that only that amount of labour is invested in it that can be directly applied to this particular product. Rather, the whole prior efforts without which the present relatively easier pro-duction would be impossible must be included in the calculation on a *pro rata* basis as labour necessary for its production. Of course, the 'work' of a musical virtuoso at an orchestral concert is often less in relation to its economic and ideal assessment. However, the situation is completely different if one includes in the calculation the efforts and the extent of the preparation as the pre-condition for the immediate performance of this amount of labour. Thus, in countless other instances of *higher* labour, a form of *more* labour is implied. Yet this does not lie in the sensory perceptibility of momentary exertion but rather in the condensation and accumulation of previous achievements and the present performance of exertions so conditioned; in the playful ease with which the master solves his tasks an infinitely greater labour effort can be embodied than in the sweat that the bungler must shed in order to perform a much lower task. However, this interpretation of the qualitative distinctions of labour as quantitative ones can be extended to the merely personal pre-conditions. For certainly this interpretation is inadequate for reducing, in the specified manner, those qualities of labour that gain their high estimation through an inherited gift or through the good will of the objective pre-conditions that offer themselves. At this point, one must make use of a hereditary hypothesis which of course, here as elsewhere, where it specifically enters into inherited qualities, only offers a very general line of thought. If we were to accept the enlarged explanation of instinct, namely that it emerges out of the accumulated experiences of ancestors, that these have led to specific efficient co-ordinations of nerves and muscles and are inherited in this form by the offspring in such a manner that for them the efficient effect upon the necessary nervous stimulation results purely mechanically and without requiring their own experience and practice – if we were to accept this explanation, then one could view the particular inborn inheritance as an especially fortuitous instance of instinct. This example is one in which the accumulation of such physically assimilated experiences resolutely results in a specific direction and in such a stratification of the elements that the slightest disturbance calls forth a fruitful interaction of important and efficient functions. The fact that a genius needs to learn so much less than the average person for a similar achievement, that a genius knows things that they have not experienced – this wonder seems to indicate an exceptionally full and easy impressive co-ordination of inherited energies. If one traces this inheritance sequence far enough back and makes clear that all experiences and accomplishments within the same series can be gained and developed further only through real labours and through practising, then the individual distinctiveness of the genius's achievement also appears as the condensed result of the *work* of generations. The 'well-endowed' person would, consequently, be the one in whom a maximum of his predecessors' work is accumulated in a latent form that is designed for further accumulation. Thus, the higher value that the labour of such a person possesses because of its quality also rests, in the last instance, upon a quantitatively larger amount of labour that of course he personally does not have to perform but rather that the quality of its organization makes possible further results. If we presuppose the same actual labour effort on the part of the individual, then the achievement would be distinctively higher in so far as the structure of its psychic–physical system embodied with noticeably greater ease a distinctively greater sum of experiences and abilities gained by the ancestors. And if one were to express the amount of value of the achievements not through the amount of labour necessary but through the 'socially necessary labour time' for their production, then this too would not avoid the same interpretation: that the higher value of achievements containing special endowments means that society must always live through and function for a specific longer period before it can again produce a genius. It requires the longer period of time, which determines the value of the achievement, not, in this case, for its immediate production but for the production of – though appearing only in relatively longer intervals – the producers of such achievements.

The same reduction can also result in objective change. The higher valuation of the results of labour from the same subjective effort occurs not only as a result of personal talent; rather, there are specific categories of labour which, from the outset, represent a higher value than others, so that the individual achievement within one category requires neither more effort nor more talent than is contained within another in order, none the less, to acquire a higher status. We are well aware that countless work activities in the 'higher professions' in no way place higher claims upon the subject than they do upon 'lower' ones; that workers in coal mines and factories must often possess a circumspection, a capacity for resignation, a defiance of death which raises the subjective value of their achievement far above that of many bureaucratic occupations or those requiring education; that the achievement of an acrobat or a juggler requires exactly the same perseverance, proficiency and talent as that of some pianists who do not ennoble their manual dexterity with an admixture of spiritual depth. None the less, it appears to be the case not only that we reward the one category of labour much more highly in relation to the other, but also that in many cases a socially unprejudiced sense of value goes in the same direction. With full awareness of the same or higher subjective labour that a product requires, one will none the less award the other a higher status and value so that it at least appears as if other elements than the amount of labour determine its evaluation. This illusion is certainly not insuperable. One can, for instance, place the working capacities of higher cultures on a series of levels according to what amount of labour is already accumulated in the objective, technical pre-conditions on the basis of which individual work is at all possible. In order for there to be higher positions at all in a hierarchy of officials, an immense amount of work in administration and in general culture must, first of all, already have been achieved, a labour whose spirit and results increase the possibility of a necessity for such positions. Secondly, each individual activity on the part of higher functionaries presupposes the preparatory work of many subordinates that is concentrated in it. Thus, the quality of such work can emerge only through a very large amount of work that has already been carried out and which contributes to the higher form. Certainly, compared with 'unqualified' labour, all qualified labour as such in no way rests solely upon the higher education of the worker but rests equally upon the higher and more complicated structure of the objective conditions of work, of materials and the historical–technical organization. Similarly, however mediocre the pianist may be, he requires such an old and broad tradition, such an immense supra-individual supply of technical and artistic labour products, that of course these, in their collective ennoblement of his work, extend far beyond the possibly subjectively much more considerable talents of the tightrope walker or the conjurer. The same is true more generally. What we treasure as the higher achievements – viewed solely according to the category of the occupation and without personal elements affecting their level – are those achievements that, in the development of culture, have been relatively conclusively and almost completely prepared over a long period of time. Within such achievements is included a maximum amount of work on the part of predecessors and contemporaries rather than of their technical pre-conditions, however unjust it may be to award a particularly high payment or estimation for the fortuitous holder of such talents that are derived from this emergent value in view of the completely supra-personal origins of the objective performance. It is also quite evident that this measure is not closely adhered to. The valuation of performances and products based upon such talents are transferred to others unworthy of this title – whether because of external–formal similarity, because of historical association with them, or because the holders of the particular occupation use a social power that flows from other sources in order to increase its estimation. Without considering such coincidences that result from the complexities of historical life, it would be not at all possible to maintain a single basic connection in social matters. It seems to me that, by and large, one can maintain the view that the diverse valuation of qualities of performance embodying the same subjective labour effort none the less expresses the diversity of *amounts* of labour that are contained in the particular achievements in a mediated form. In this manner, the gain for the theoretical unification of economic values, from which the labour theory commences, is provisionally secured.

In this way, however, only the general concept of labour becomes relevant and the theory therefore rests upon a very artificial abstraction. One could counter it with the view that it rests upon the typical illusion that original labour and fundamental labour as such exist, and exist primarily, to a certain extent as second-order determinations, and its specific qualities enter into it in order to make them determine it; as if those qualities by means of which we characterize an action as labour as such did not, with their remaining determinations, form a complete unity, as if each distinction and rank order did not rest upon a completely arbitrarily drawn demarcation line! It is just as if man was straightaway man as such and then, in real distinction from this, was straightaway the determinate individual! Of course, this is a common error and has been made the basis of social theories. The concept of labour with which the whole previous argument is concerned is, in fact, only determined negatively as that which remains after one has removed everything from all types of labour that distinguishes them from each other. In fact, however, what remains left over in no way corresponds to the physical concept of energy – as a tempting analogy might suggest – which, in its quantitative invariateness, can sometimes appear as heat, as electricity, as mechanical motion. Indeed, a mathematical expression is possible here which represents the common element of all these specific phenomena and represents them as expressions of this one basic fact. In general, however, human labour permits no such abstract but none the less determinate formulation. The assertion that all labour is simply labour and nothing else means, as the basis for the equal valuation of such labour, something so inconceivable, so abstractly empty, as the theory that each person is merely a person and therefore all are of equal value and qualify for the same rights and obligations. Thus, if the concept of labour – which in its hitherto accepted generality has given a vague feeling rather than a definite content to its meaning – is to acquire such a definite meaning, then it requires that a greater precision be given to the real process which one understands as labour.

Manual labour as the unit of labour

I now wish to return to what has been asserted to be this ultimate concrete element of labour, namely manual labour. We investigated the accuracy of this assertion and limited its validity in the light of the evidence for the absence of a cost for mental labour. From the outset I admit that I do not simply rule out the possibility that in the future the mechanical equivalent as well as the psychic activity will be discovered. Of course, the importance of its content, its factually determined position in logical, ethical and aesthetic contexts is completely separate from all physical movements, roughly in the same manner as the meaning of a word is quite separate from its physiological–acoustic sound. Yet the energy that the organism must expend upon the thought of this content as a cerebral process is, in principle, just as calculable as that necessary for a muscular exertion. If this were to be achieved one day, then one could at least make the amount of energy necessary for a specific muscular exertion a unit of measurement on the basis of which the mental use of energy would be determined. Mental labour would then be dealt with on the same footing as manual labour, and its products would enter into a merely quantitative balancing of value with those of the latter. This, of course, is a scientific utopia which can only prove that the reduction of all scientifically calculable labour to manual labour does not itself need to contain, even for a by no means dogmatic–materialistic standpoint, the basic absurdity with which the dualism of intellectuality and corporality appears to strike this attempt.

In a somewhat more concrete manner, the following conception seems to approach the same goal. I start out from the fact that our means of subsistence is produced through physical labour. Yet no work is purely physical; all manual labour becomes a practical achievement only through an effective consciousness, so that the work that prepares the pre-conditions for higher mental labour itself already contains an admixture of an intellectual kind. However, this psychic achievement of the manual labourer is, for its part, made possible only through the means of subsistence. Specifically, the more mential the worker is, that is the more negligible the intellectual element of his work is in relation to manual activity, the more is his means of subsistence (in the broadest sense) produced by essentially physical labour – with one exception that pertains to the modern period and which is to be dealt with in the next chapter. Since this relationship is repeated only in these two categories of labour, this results in an infinite series out of which mental labour can certainly never vanish but in which it is pushed back further and further. Thus the means of subsistence of the highest categories of labour also rests upon a series of labour activities in which the mental admixture of each member is borne by a member of purely physical value, so that each, at the last stage, approaches the marginal value of zero. It may also be imagined that, in principle, all external pre-conditions for mental labour are expressible in quantities of manual labour. If the old theory of cost value were recognized as being valid, then the value of mental labour, in so far as it equals the costs of its production, would be the same value as certain manual activities. Perhaps this theory is tenable in a modified form. The value of a product is certainly not to be equated with its costs, although the values of two products could relate to one another as those of their conditions of emergence. A psyche, fed and stimulated by the means of subsistence, will yield products, the value of which may exceed that of their used up pre-conditions by many times. In this way, however, the value relationship of two complexes of pre-conditions could still be the same as that of two products – just as the values of two crop yields, of which each is a multiple of its seed, can so relate to one another like the values of the seeds; for the factor that increases value could be a constant for the average of persons. If all these presuppositions were true, then the reduction of mental to physical labour would be achieved in the sense that one could certainly express not the absolute but the relative value importance of that of the former through specific relations of the latter.

Yet the assumption that the level of value of mental activity should relate proportionally to the value of the means of subsistence appears to be completely paradoxical, even meaningless. None the less, it pays to seek out the point at which reality at least approximates to it because this reaches down into the internal and cultural relationships of intellectual values to their economic pre-conditions and equivalents. We must surely imagine that, as the focal point of organic development, a very large amount of energy lies stored up in the brain. The brain is certainly capable of giving out a large amount of energy which, among other things, explains the astonishing efficiency of weaker muscles which can be set in motion by mental impulses. The great exhaustion of the whole organism after intellectual labours or changes also indicates that mental activity, viewed from the standpoint of its physical correlate, consumes a very large amount of organic energy. The restoration of this energy is achieved not only through a mere increase in the level of the subsistence that the manual worker requires, since the capacity of the body is quite considerably restricted with regard to the amount of nourishment it can consume, and for predominantly mental labour this is reduced rather than increased. Therefore the restoration of energy, just like the necessary nervous stimulation of mental labour, can as a rule be achieved only through a concentration, refinement and individual adaptation of the means of life and the general conditions of life. Two culturally and historically significant elements are important here. Our daily means of existence were selected and developed in a period in which the common life conditions differed sharply from the present ones for intellectual strata in which manual labour and fresh air predominated over nervous tension and a sedentary mode of life. The countless direct and indirect digestive illnesses on the one hand, the hasty search for concentrated and easily assimilable foodstuffs on the other, indicate that the adaptation between our bodily constitution and our means of nourishment has broken down to a considerable extent. From this very general observation it is obvious how justified it is for people with very different occupations to require different nourishment and that it is not merely a matter of gastronomy but of the health of the people for the most highly developed worker to secure the means for an above-normal, specialized diet that is also determined by personal needs. More important, however, and at the same time more concealed, is the fact that mental labour extends much more into the whole of life and is surrounded by a much wider periphery of mediated relationships than is manual labour. The conversion of bodily energy into work can, as it were, occur immediately, whereas mental energies in general can achieve their complete task only if, quite apart from their immediate–real milieu, the whole complicated system of bodily–mental dispositions, impressions and impulses are contained in a specific organization, tone and proportion of rest and movement. Even to those who, in principle, wish to reduce mental and manual labour to the same level, it would appear trivial to say that the higher reward for the intellectual worker is justified by the physiological pre-conditions for his activity.

In this context, it is evident that the modern intellectual person seems to be so much more dependent upon his milieu than was the case previously, and this is true not only in the sense that, educationally, he is qualitatively more specialized but also in the sense that the development of his specific energies, his internal productivity, his personal quality is not possible without particularly favourable conditions of life that suit him as an individual. The unbelievably humble circumstances under which, in earlier times, a highly intellectual life often developed would be oppressive to the vast majority of present-day intellectual workers. They would not find in such circumstances the encouragements and stimulants that they need – sometimes each one different from the other – for their individual production. This is completely at odds with any epicureanism and perhaps arises – as the genuine pre-condition for achievement – on the one hand out of the enlarged sensitivity and weakness of the nervous system and on the other out of the accentuated individualization which cannot react upon that simple, that is, typical general life-stimulus, but rather emerges only out of specifically individualized stimuli. If the most recent times have implemented the historical milieu theory as the most decisive, then here too real circumstances, through their exaggeration of one element, may have opened up to us the view of its reality at the levels of its more limited development – in exactly the same way as the real increased importance of the masses in the nineteenth century first became the occasion for making us scientifically aware of their importance in all earlier epochs as well. In that these circumstances exist, there really is a certain proportion between the values that we consume and those that we produce; that is, the latter, as intellectual achievements, are functions of muscular inputs which are invested in the former.

The value of physical activity reducible to that of mental activity

However, this possible reduction of the values of mental labour to those of physical labour is very soon confronted with limitations from many sides. First of all, this proportion is certainly not reversible. Very considerable personal expenditures belong to specific achievements, but such expenditures for their part do not everywhere produce these achievements. The untalented person, transposed to equally favourable and refined living conditions, will none the less never achieve what the talented person can achieve under the same conditions. The series of products thus could be a constant function of the series of expenditures only if the latter resulted in the circumstance of natural personal talents. Yet if the impossible itself were to occur – namely that personal talents were permitted to be exactly produced and an ideal adaptation, measured exactly according to this establishment of the means of subsistence, were to be made the index of the extent of achievements – then this undertaking would always find its limits in the lack of equivalence in the conditions of existence which themselves exist between persons qualified for the same performances. Herein lies one of the major limitations upon social justice. Just as it is certain that, in general, the higher intellectual achievement also requires better living conditions, so human talents in the very claims that the development of their highest energies make are themselves extremely unequal. Of two natures that are capable of an objectively similar achievement, the one must necessarily, according to its level, have a completely different milieu, completely different material pre-conditions, completely different stimuli for the realization of this possibility compared with the other. This fact, which establishes an irreconcilable disharmony between the ideals of quality and justice and the maximization of tasks, is still by no means sufficiently taken into account. The diversity of our physical–mental structures, the relationships between efficient and restricting energies, the interaction between the intellect and the nature of the will results in the fact that the achievement, as a product of the personality and its living conditions, finds a highly inconsistent factor in the former, so that, in order to produce the same result, the other factor must also suffer particularly large variations. And it certainly seems as if these natural differences in relation to the conditions of realization of their inner possibilities are more considerable the higher, the more complex and the more intellectual is the sphere of achievement. The people who possess only muscle power for a specific work activity will require for its realization roughly the same nourishment and general standard of life. However, where leading, intellectual abstract activities are in question, the diversity between all those who ultimately could achieve the same comes to the fore as being important.

Personal talent is so variable that the same external circumstances act upon it, produce the most diverse end results and thereby make the comparison of one individual with another, of each value proportion between the material conditions of life and the mental achievements built upon them completely illusory. Only where major historical epochs or whole classes of people can be compared with one another as averages can the relative extent of physically creatable conditions exhibit the same relationship as that of mental achievements. Thus, for example, one can observe that, where very low prices for necessary foodstuffs prevail, the culture as a whole progresses only slowly and luxury articles, in which a considerable amount of mental labour is invested, are extremely dear. In contrast, increases in the price of basic foodstuffs usually go hand in hand with a reduction in the price and further increase in luxuries. It is characteristic of lower cultures that indispensable foodstuffs are very cheap whereas higher means of life are very expensive, as is still the case, for example, in Russia in comparison with central Europe. The cheapness of bread, meat and shelter, on the one hand, does not create the pressure that forces the worker to struggle for higher wages, whereas the expensiveness of luxury goods, on the other hand, pushes these goods completely out of his view and prevents their dissemination. It is primarily making dear what was originally cheap and making cheap what was originally dear – I have already shown the connection between the two – that implies and brings about an increase in intellectual activities. Beneath all the enormous incommensurability of individual elements, these proportions none the less reveal a general relationship – one that takes effect in these individual elements – between physical and mental labour that would certainly allow the amount of value of the latter to be expressed through the former if its effectiveness were not drowned out by the much stronger force of individual differences in talent.

Finally, there is a third standpoint from which the reduction of all labour value to the value of manual labour reveals its crude and plebeian character. If we look more closely upon what it is that really makes physical labour valid as value and expenditure, then it follows that this is certainly not a pure physical achievement of strength. By this I do not mean what has already been referred to, namely, that as such this would be quite useless for human purposes without a certain intellectual guidance. From this standpoint, however, the mental element remains a mere value admixture and the genuine value could still reside in the purely physical except that, in order to receive the necessary guidance, it would require this additional element. Rather, I mean that physical labour acquires its whole tone of value and valuableness only through the expenditure of mental energy embodied in it. If all work, viewed externally, implies the overcoming of obstacles, the formation of matter into a form that it did not originally possess but that it at first resisted, then the internal side of work exhibits the same form. Work is certainly effort, burden and difficulty. Therefore, where it is none of these things it is usual to assert that it is not really work at all. Viewed from the standpoint of its meaning for the emotions, work consists of the progressive overcoming of the impulse towards laziness, enjoyment and the relaxation of life. In this context it is irrelevant that this impulse, if one really continuously gave way to it, would similarly make life into a burden. For the burden of not working is experienced only in the rarest exceptional cases whereas the burden of working is almost always felt. Therefore no one is accustomed to taking on the pain and effort of work upon themselves without receiving something for it in exchange. What is actually rewarded for work, the legal title on the basis of which one demands a reward for it, is the *mental* expenditure of energy that is required in order to discipline oneself and overcome the internal feelings of constraint and aversion.

Language well illustrates this state of affairs in that it characterizes both the external economic and the internal moral results of our action as earnings. For in the latter sense too this certainly already enters into the situation if the moral impulse has overcome the restrictions of temptation, egoism and sensuousness but not if the moral action stems from a completely self-evident drive that, from the very outset, excludes the possibility of its opposite. Thus, in order for the moral ideals not to deny the moral earnings, the structure of myth among peoples everywhere allows their religious founder to conquer a 'temptation' and every Tertullian holds the glory of God to be greater *si laboravit*. Just as the real moral value connects with the restriction that is overcome in a contradictory impulse, so too does economic value connect in the same way. If man performed his work in the same way as the flower performs its flowering or the bird its singing, then no remunerative value would be attached to it. The reason for this lies not only in its external appearance, in the visible act and result, but also, in the case of physical labour, in the expenditure of will, in emotional reflexes – in short, in the conditions of the soul. Thus we gain the completion of the basic knowledge at the other end of the economic series, namely that all value and all the importance of objects and their possession lies in the feelings that they evoke; that their possession would be indifferent and meaningless as a mere external relationship if it did not include internal factors, emotions of desire, the elevation and expansion of the self. In this way the visibility of economic goods is limited from both sides – that of obtaining them and of enjoying them – by mental facts which alone ensure that an equivalent is demanded for the single achievement. However inessential and unconnected an object of possession that does not extend into a psychic emotion may be to us, it would be the suitable action for us if it did not arise out of an internally felt state of affairs whose aversion and sense of sacrifice alone bore within itself the demand for a remuneration and its measure. With reference to value, one can thus say that physical labour is mental labour. An exception to this could only be those forms of work that man accomplishes as a competitor to the machine or animals. For although these, like all others, conduct themselves in relation to internal exertion and the mental expenditure of energy, they none the less have no reason to improve in any way upon this internal achievement, since the only external effect that is important to them is also attainable through a purely physical potentiality, and cost-conscious production will never be rewarded so long as a cheaper one is possible. But at a slightly deeper level, perhaps this exception to the all-inclusiveness of the external may also be traced back through the soul. What is rewarded in the achievements of a machine or an animal is certainly the human achievement which is inserted into the invention, manufacture and control of the machine, and the rearing and training of the animal. Thus one can say that any human work is not rewarded in the same way as this physical sub-human work, but on the contrary the latter is, as it were, indirectly valued as mental–human work. This is only a practical extension of the theory that ultimately we also interpret the mechanism of inanimate nature according to the feelings of strength and exertion that guide *our* movements. If we insert our own essence into the general order of nature in order to understand it in its context, then this is possible only because we already place the forms, impulses and feelings of our intellectuality in nature in general and connect the 'underlay' and the 'cover' inevitably in a single act. When we extend this relationship to the world to our practical question of whether to compensate the performance of sub-human energies only through the counter-performance of human achievement, then the basic border-line becomes visible between that human work whose reward rests upon its mental element and that which, because of the similarity of its result with purely external–mechanical work, appears to reject this basis for its reward. One may therefore assert in very general terms that, from the standpoint of the value to be compensated, the distinction between mental and manual labour is not one between mental and material nature; that rather the reward is ultimately required in the latter case only for the internal aspect of work, for the aversion to exertion, for the conscription of will power. Of course, this intellectuality, which is, as it were, the thing-in-itself behind the appearance of work and which forms its interior value, is not really intellectual but resides in emotion and the will.

It follows from this that it is not co-ordinated with mental labour but rather is its basis. For at first the objective content of the intellectual process, the result separated off from the personality, the demand for reward is produced not in it but in the subjective function guided by the will that it embodies, the work effort, the expenditure of energy that it requires for the production of this intellectual content. In that an act of the *soul* is revealed to be the source of value not only from the standpoint of what is taken up but also of what is achieved, physical and 'mental' labour contain a common – one might say, morally – value grounding base through which the reduction of labour value as such to physical labour loses it philistine and brutal materialistic appearance. This is roughly the case with theoretical materialism which acquires a completely new and more seriously discussable basis if one emphasizes that matter itself is also a *conception*, not an essence which, outside us in the absolute sense, stands opposed to the soul but which in its cognizability is completely determined by the forms and presuppositions of our intellectual organization. From this standpoint, on the basis of which the basic distinction between material and mental phenomena becomes a relative instead of an absolute one, the claim to search for the explanation of mental phenomena in the restricted sense in their reduction to material phenomena is much less unacceptable. Here, as in the case of practical value, the external must only be freed from its rigidity, isolation and opposition to the internal in order for it to form the simplest expression and unit of measure for higher 'intellectual' things. This reduction may or may not be successful. Yet its assertion is at least compatible, in principle, with methodological demands and the fundamental composition of value.

Differences in the utility of labour as arguments against 'labour money'

These comments not only prove that the equivalent for work is exclusively related to the amount of muscular activity but also eliminate certain considerations that are commonly brought against this connection. None the less, a difficulty is encountered which seems to me to be insurmountable. This has its origin in the quite trivial objection that valueless, superfluous work also exists. For the refutation, according to which one naturally subsumes under labour as the fundamental value only efficient work justified through its result, contains an admission that is fatal for the whole theory. That is, if valuable and valueless labour exist, then undoubtedly intermediate stages, amounts of labour undertaken also exist which contain some but not distinct elements of purpose and value. Thus, the value of a product which, it is presupposed, is determined by the labour invested in it is greater or smaller according to the efficiency of this labour. This means, however, that the value of labour is measured not by its amount but by the utility of its result! And here the method sought to deal with the quality of labour is no longer helpful. The higher, more specialized, more intellectual labour indeed implies, compared with lower labour, *more* labour; it implies an accumulation and concentration of exactly the same general 'labour' of which crude and unqualified labour only represents, as it were, a larger dilution, a lower potentiality. For this distinction of types of labour was an internal one which allowed the question of utility to be left completely aside and one in which the utility of the labour in question was always presupposed to exist in it in increasingly similar amounts. From this perspective, the work of the street-sweeper is no less 'useful' than that of the violinist and its lower estimation arises out of its inner quality as mere labour, out of the lower condensation of labour energies in it. This shows, however, that this presupposition was too simple and that the diversity of external utility did not allow the distinctions in the evaluation of labour to be independent of their merely internal determinations. If one could create and produce from the world the useless labour, or more accurately the differences in the usefulness of labour, and show that labour is more or less useful to precisely the same extent to which it is more or less concentrated and uses energy, in a word is a greater or lesser amount of labour, then it would certainly be demonstrated that physical labour is still not the sole creator of value. However, labour as such could then exist as the standard of value of objects since its other element, that of utility, would always be the same and the value relations would no longer alter. Yet differences in utility do indeed exist, and it is a fallacy to reverse the postulate that is perhaps ethically groundable in the statement that 'all value is labour' into the one 'all labour is value', that is, of equal value.

This demonstrates the fundamental connection between the labour theory of value and socialism, for socialism in fact strives for a constitution of society in which *the utility value of objects, in relation to the labour time applied to them* forms *a constant*. In the third volume of *Capital*, Marx argues that the precondition of all value, of the labour theory too, is use value. Yet this means that so many parts of the total social labour time are used in each product as come in relation to its importance in use. It thus presupposes a qualitative unified total societal need – accordingly, to the motto of the labour theory, that labour is indeed labour and as such is of equal value, is here added the further motto, that need is indeed need and as such of equal value – and the equivalence of utility for all labour is reached only in so far as only that amount of labour is performed in each sphere of production that exactly covers the part of each need that is circumscribed by it. On the basis of this presupposition of course no labour would be less useful than any other. For if one holds, for example, that today piano playing is a less useful task than locomotive construction, then the reason for this lies merely in the fact that more time has been applied to it than the real need subsequently required. If it were limited to the measure outlined here, then it would be just as valuable as locomotive construction – just as the latter would also be useless if one applied more time to it, that is built more locomotives than are subsequently needed. In other words, there is, *in principle*, no distinction in use value at all. For if a product momentarily possesses less use value than another (that is if the labour applied to the former is less valuable than that applied to the latter), then one can simply continue to reduce labour to its category, that is the quantity of its production, until the need for it is just as great as that of the other object, that is until the 'industrial reserve army' is completely wiped out. Only under these conditions can labour truly express the amount of value of a product.

The essence of all *money*, however, is its unconditional interchangeability, the internal uniformity that makes each piece exchangeable for another, according to quantitative measures. For there to be labour money, labour must create this interchangeability, and this can occur only in the manner already described; that is, it creates exactly the same degree of utility and this, in turn, is attainable only by the reduction of labour for each production need to that amount by which the subsequent need is exactly as great as that of any other. Of course, in so doing the actual labour time could be valued still higher or lower. But now one would be certain that the higher value, derived from the greater utility of the product, indicated a proportionally more concentrated amount of labour per hour. Or conversely, it would be the case that as long as the hour partook of a higher value in the concentration of labour, it would also contain a higher amount of utility. However, this obviously presupposes a completely rationalized and providential economic order in which each labour activity regularly resulted from the absolute knowledge of needs and the labour requirements for each product – that is, an economic order such as socialism strives for. The approximation to this completely utopian state of affairs seems to be technically possible only if, as a whole, only the immediately essential, unquestionably basic life necessities are produced. For where this is exclusively the case, one work activity is of course precisely as necessary and as useful as the next. In contrast, however, as long as one moves into the higher spheres in which, on the one hand, need and estimation of utility are inevitably more individual and, on the other, the intensity of labour is more difficult to prove, no regulation of the amounts of production could bring about a situation in which the relationship between need and labour applied was everywhere the same. On these points, all the threads of the deliberations on socialism intertwine. At this point it is clear that the cultural danger with reference to labour money is in no way so *direct* as it is usually judged to be. Rather, it stems from technical difficulties in holding constant the utility of things, as its basis for evaluation in relation to labour and as its agent of value – a difficulty that increases in relation to the cultural level of the product and a difficulty whose avoidance, of course, must limit production to that of the most primitive, most essential and most average objects.

This result of labour money, however, throws light most clearly upon the nature of money as such. The importance of money lies in the fact that it is a unit of value that is clothed in the plurality of values. Otherwise, the quantitative differences in the unit of money would not be equivalently experienced as the qualitative differences of things. However, this often occurs in a quite unjust manner and personal values are specifically attired in a power that extinguishes their nature. Labour money strives to escape from this condition of money and wishes to undermine money with a concept that, though it is certainly even more abstract, is none the less closer to concrete existence. By means of labour money, an eminently personal, one could even say, *the* personal value would become the standard of value as such. And yet it is clear that labour money, because it should none the less possess the qualities of all money – unity, fungibility, universal validity – would be more threatening to the differentiation and personal creation of life's contents than money as it already exists! If it is the incomparable power of money not to oppose the exact opposite of a desired result, if we see it serve on the one hand the suppression and on the other the often much exaggerated accentuation of personal differentiation, then it denies the attempt to make it both more concrete and even more general; it denies the attempt to establish its position, as it were, above the parties and places it on the one side of the alternative to the exclusion of others. However much one must recognize the tendency for labour money to place money back into a closer relationship to personal values, each consequence none the less shows how closely the hostility to this is bound up with its essence.

CHAPTER 6

The Style of Life

ˋ

I

The preponderance of intellectual over emotional functions brought about by the money economy

We have frequently mentioned in these investigations that intellectual energy is the psychic energy which the specific phenomena of the money economy produces, in contrast to those energies generally denoted as emotions or sentiments which prevail in periods and spheres of interest not permeated by the money economy. Above all, this is the consequence of money's character as a means. All means as such imply that the conditions and concatenations of reality are incorporated in the process of our will. They are possible only because we possess an objective image of actual causal relationships, and certainly a mind that commands a perfect view of the total situation would also master the most appropriate means for every purpose and from every starting point. Yet this intellect that had a perfect knowledge of the appropriate means would not yet be able to transpose them into reality because their use is dependent on setting a *purpose*, only in relation to which those actual energies and connections acquire the status of *means*. For its part, a purpose can be created only by an act of will. Just as nothing is purposeful in the objective world unless there is a will, so too in the intellectual world, which is only a more or less perfect representation of the content of the world. It has been correctly stated, but mostly misunderstood, that the will is blind. The will is not blind in the same sense as Hödhr or the blinded cyclops who rush at a venture; the will does not produce anything irrational, in the sense of the value concept of reason. Rather, it is unable to effect anything at all unless it gains some kind of *content* that is completely external to it. For by itself, the will is nothing but one of the psychological forms (such as being, duty or hope, etc.) which make up the content of our life. It is one of those categories – probably realized psychologically by concomitant muscular or nervous reactions – by which we comprehend the ideal content of the world in order to give it a practical significance for us. Just as the will – the mere name of the form raised to a certain degree of independence – does not by itself choose any definite content whatsoever, so too the mere awareness of the word's content, that is from an intellectual standpoint, does not bring about any purposefulness. Rather, the contents of the world are completely neutral, but at one point or another they unpredictably become coloured by the will. Once this occurs, one finds that the will is transferred in a purely logical objective manner to other conceptions that are causally related to the earlier ones and that now possess the status of 'means' to that 'final purpose'. Wherever the intellect leads us, we are completely dependent, since it leads us solely through the actual connections between things. The intellect is the mediator through which volition adjusts itself to independent being. If we conceive of a rigid conception of the calculation of means and abide by it, then we are purely theoretical, absolutely non-practical beings when we act in this manner. Volition only accompanies the series of our considerations like an organ pedal note or like the general presupposition of a domain in whose peculiarities and conditions it does not interfere, yet which alone can give life and reality to it.

The number of means and the length of their series which form the content of our activity thus develop in proportion to intellectuality as the subjective representative of the objective world order. Since every means is, as such, completely indifferent, so all emotional values are in practice tied to the ends, to the critical point of action whose attainment radiates no longer upon our activity but only on the receptivity of our souls. The more such termini we have in our practical life, the stronger will be the emotional function in relation to the intellectual. The impulsiveness and emotional intensity so frequently reported among primitive peoples is probably connected with the shortness of their teleological series. Their life work does not possess that cohesion of elements which is prevalent in higher cultures, where an 'occupation' uniformly pervades life. Rather, their activity consists of a simple series of interests which, if they attain the end at all, do so with relatively few means. In this connection, the direct effort to obtain food is an important contributing factor which, in higher cultures, is replaced by an almost continuous multi-linked series of purposes. Under these circumstances, the conception and enjoyment of final goals is relatively frequent; the awareness of objective connections and of reality, that is intellectuality, operates less frequently than emotional connotations which characterize both the immediate conception as well as the real emergence of final purposes. Even during the Middle Ages there existed a larger number of specific points of satisfaction for purposive action than at present, and this was due to the prevailing production for one's own needs geared to the various kinds of craftsmen's establishments, to the variety and closeness of associations particularly through the Church. Today, when roundabout ways and preparations for such moments of satisfaction have become endless, the goal of the moment more usually lies beyond that moment, or even beyond the horizon of the individual. This extension of the series is brought about by money because money creates a common, central interest for otherwise unrelated series, thereby connecting the different series so that the one series can become the preparation for another which is objectively quite unrelated (for example, where the money returns of one series and therewith the whole series itself, serves as the basis for financing another series). However, the crux of the matter is the general fact, the emergence of which has been discussed earlier, that money is everywhere conceived as purpose, and countless things that are really ends in themselves are thereby degraded to mere means. But since money itself is an omnipresent means, the various elements of our existence are thus placed in an all-embracing teleological nexus in which no element is either the first or the last. Furthermore, since money measures all objects with merciless objectivity, and since its standard of value so measured determines their relationship, a web of objective and personal aspects of life emerges which is similar to the natural cosmos with its continuous cohesion and strict causality. This web is held together by the all-pervasive money value, just as nature is held together by the energy that gives life to everything. Like money, energy appears in innumerable forms, but the uniformity of its very nature and the possibility of transforming any specific form into any other results in a relationship between all of them and makes each of them a condition of any other. Just as every emotional accentuation has disappeared from the interpretation of natural processes and has been replaced by an objective intelligence, so the objects and relationships of our practical world, inasmuch as they form increasingly interconnected series, exclude the interference of emotions. They become merely objects of intelligence and appear only at the teleological terminal points. The growing transformation of all elements of life into means, the mutual connection of sequences that previously terminated in autonomous purposes with a complex of relative elements, is not only the practical counterpart of the growing causal knowledge of nature and the transformation of its absolutes into relativities. Rather, since the whole structure of means is one of a causal connection viewed from the front, the practical world too increasingly becomes a problem for the intelligence. To put it more precisely, the conceivable elements of action become objectively and subjectively calculable rational relationships and in so doing progressively eliminate the emotional reactions and decisions which only attach themselves to the turning points of life, to the final purposes.

Lack of character and objectivity of the style of life

This relationship between the significance in life of the intellect and money characterizes the epochs or spheres of interest where both predominate. It does this firstly in a negative way: by a certain lack of character. If character always means that persons or things are definitely committed to an individual mode of existence as distinct from and excluding any other, then the intellect is in no way affected by such factors. For the intellect is the indifferent mirror of reality in which all elements enjoy equal rights, because here their rights exist in nothing other than their mere existence. To be sure, people's intellects have different characteristics, but strictly speaking these are either only differences of degree – depth or superficiality, breadth or narrowness – or they are differences originating in the addition of other mental energies, of emotion or volition. The intellect, as a pure concept, is absolutely lacking in character, not in the sense of being deficient in some necessary quality, but because it exists completely apart from the selective one-sidedness that determines character. There is obviously a lack of character in money too. Just as money *per se* is the mechanical reflex of the relative value of things and is equally useful to everyone, so within money transactions all persons are of equal value, not because all but because none is valuable except money. However, the lack of character of both intellect and money transcends this purely negative meaning. We demand – perhaps not always rightly so – that all things have a definite character and we resent purely theoretical people who, because they understand everything, are inclined to condone everything: an objectivity that would certainly befit a god but never a man, since man places himself in obvious contradiction both with his nature and with his role in society. Thus we resent the money economy offering its central value as a fully compliant instrument for the meanest machinations. This is not compensated for by the fact that the high-minded enterprise gets the same credit as the meanest; rather, the completely fortuitous relationship between the series of monetary operations and the series of our higher value concepts, and the meaninglessness of the one measured in terms of the other, is most glaringly illustrated. The peculiar levelling of emotional life that is ascribed to contemporary times in contrast to the forthrightness and ruggedness of earlier epochs; the ease of intellectual understanding which exists even between people of the most divergent natures and positions (whereas even such an intellectually outstanding and theoretically committed person as Dante tells us that one should respond to certain theoretical opponents not with arguments but only with the knife); the trend towards conciliatoriness springing from indifference to the basic problems of our inner life, which one can characterize at its highest level as the salvation of the soul and as not being soluble by reason – right up to the idea of world peace, which is especially favoured in liberal circles, the historical representatives of intellectualism and of money transactions: all these are positive consequences of the negative trait of lack of character. This colourlessness becomes, as it were, the colour of work activity at the high points of money transactions. There are a large number of occupations in modern cities, such as certain categories of general and trading agents and all those indeterminate forms of livelihood in large cities, which do not have any objective form and decisiveness of activity. For such people, economic life, the web of their teleo-logical series, has no definite content for them except making money. Money, the absolutely entity, is for them the fixed point around which their activity circulates with unlimited scope. It is a peculiar kind of 'unskilled labour' com-pared with which what is usually characterized as unskilled is still highly quali-fied. The essence of this latter type of work consists in mere muscular work where the *amount* of energy employed completely outweighs the *form* of its expression. Yet this kind of work, even among the lowest labourers, retains a specific colouring without which the recent attempts in England to organize such labour into trades unions would not have been possible. Those people who pursue the most divergent opportunities to make money lack that predetermined distinctiveness in their lives to a much higher degree than the banker, for whom money is not only the final purpose but also the raw *material* of his activity, and as such can in time give rise to specific, prescribed directives, particular con-stellations of interests, and traits of a specific professional character. But in those problematical means of livelihood the routes to the ultimate goal of money have strayed from any actual unity or affinity. There is only a minimum of resistance to the levelling process which money as a goal exerts on various activities and interests. The determination and colouring that might affect the personality through his economic activity disappears. Obviously such a livelihood can be successful or even possible only with a superior intellectuality in a form that one terms 'shrewdness', which means severing prudence from any determination by objective or ideal norms and making it absolutely subservient to relevant personal interests. As might be expected, uprooted people in particular are dis-posed towards these 'occupations' – ones that lack the 'professional existence', that is the fixed ideal line between the person and his life – and equally they meet with the suspicion of being unreliable. Even in India the name of a com-missioner or agent has sometimes become the name for someone 'who lives by cheating his fellow-creatures'. Those products of an urban existence whose sole aim is to make money by any means possible therefore need the intellect as a general function all the more because specialized knowledge is out of the question for them. They form a major contingent of that type of insecure personality which can hardly be pinned down and 'placed' because their mobility and their versatility saves them from committing themselves, as it were, in any situation. These phenomena presuppose that money and intellect possess the common traits of neutrality and lack of character. They could develop only where these two factors coexist.

The dual roles of both intellect and money: with regard to content they are supra-personal

The intensity of modern economic conflicts in which no mercy is shown is only an apparent counter-instance of such features of the money economy since these conflicts are unleashed by direct interest in money itself. For it is not only that they take place in an objective sphere in which the importance of the person lies not only in his character but also in his embodiment of a particular objective economic potential, and where the deadly antagonistic competitor of today is the cartel ally of tomorrow. Rather, what is of primary importance is that the rules established within one sphere may be totally different from those considered valid outside that sphere but which are none the less influenced by them. A religion, for instance, can preach the gospel of peace to its members and still be very belligerent and cruel towards heretics and towards neighbouring spheres of life. Similarly, a person may provoke in another emotions and thoughts that are completely antithetical to his own philosophy so that he gives what he himself does not possess. A movement in art may be completely naturalistic according to its own precepts and artistic ideas, and have a direct relation to nature and aim at the mere reproduction of it, yet the fact that there is such a loyal devotion to the appearance of reality and an artistic endeavour to reflect it represents an absolutely ideal moment in the system of life that, compared with its other constituent element, far transcends any naturalistic reality. Just as the acrimony of theoretical–logical controversies does not affect the principle of conciliation inherent in intellectuality – for as soon as the dispute has shifted from the contrast of emotions or volitions, or the undemonstrable axioms based on sentiments, to theoretical discussion it can, in principle, be resolved – so equally the conflict of interests in the money economy does not affect the principle of neutrality that raises the controversy above personal involvement and that ultimately provides a basis for mutual understanding. Certainly there is something callous about the purely rationalistic treatment of people and things. Yet this is not a positive impulse but simply results from pure logic being unaffected by respect, kindness and delicacies of feeling. For this reason, the person who is interested solely in money is also unable to comprehend why he is reproached with callousness and brutality, since he is aware of the logical consistency and pure impartiality of his behaviour but not of any bad intentions. It must be borne in mind here that we are dealing only with money as the *form* of economic transactions which, on the basis of very different substantive motives, may acquire quite divergent features. The fact that life, regardless of all other consequences of intellectuality that sharpen conflicts and of the money economy that intensifies these conflicts, is thus no longer determined by the distinctness of character may be designated as the objectivity of the life-style. This is not a trait that is added to intelligence; rather it is the very essence of intelligence itself. It is the only way open to man of acquiring a relationship to things that is not determined by the arbitrariness of the subject. Even if we presuppose that the whole of objective reality is determined by the functions of our mind, we still identify as intelligence those functions of our mind through which reality appears to us as objective in the specific sense of the word, regardless of how much intelligence itself may also be enlivened and directed by other forces. The most brilliant example of this is Spinoza, in whose philosophy we see a most objective attitude towards the world; every single act of inwardness is required to be a harmonious continuation of the inevitability of existence; nowhere are the incalculabilities of individuality allowed to break through the logical–mathematical structure of the unity of the world. The function that this concept of the world and its norms serves is a purely intellectual one. This world view is itself subjectively built upon the mere understanding of things, and understanding suffices to fulfil its demands. This intellectuality itself is, however, based on a deep religious feeling, upon a completely supra-theoretical relationship to the foundation of things which, however, never intervenes in the autonomous intellectual process. Generally speaking, the Indian people display the same combination. It is said of the most remote as well as the most modern times that the peasant could till his land undisturbed by the fighting armies of Indian states or by a hostile party. For the peasant is the 'common benefactor of friend and foe'. Clearly this is an extreme instance of the objective treatment of practical affairs. What appear to be natural subjective impulses are completely eliminated in favour of a practice concerned only with the objective importance of the elements. The differentiation of behaviour is governed only by its objective expediency, not by personal passion. But this nation was also fully attuned to intellectuality. It was at all times superior to others in strict logic, in the meditative profundity of its interpretation of the world, even in the austere intellectuality of both its most gigantic fantasies and its highest ethical ideals; yet it was inferior to many in radiating warmth of sentiments and in will power. It became a mere spectator and a logical designer of the course of the world, but this rested ultimately upon emotional decisions, upon the immensity of suffering out of which grew a metaphysical–religious sense of its cosmic necessity, because the individual cannot cope with it, either in the emotional sphere or by diverting it into a vigorous life practice.

   This same objectivity of living conditions is itself also a result of their relationship to money. I have pointed out in an earlier context why trade represents such a considerable improvement over the originally undifferentiated subjectivity of man. There are still peoples today in Africa and Micronesia who know of no other change in ownership than in the form of theft and the gift. However, just as for more advanced peoples objective interests are joined by and transcend the subjectivistic impulses of egoism and altruism – alternatives in which ethics unfortunately still confines human motivations – and just as devotion and commitment to such interests has nothing to do with the relationships among human subjects, but deals with objective expediency and ideals, so exchange evolved a change of ownership according to criteria of objective correctness and fairness transcending the egoistical impulsiveness of theft and the no less altruistic impulsiveness of the gift. Money represents the moment of objectivity in exchange activities, as it were, in pure isolation and independent embodiment, since it is free of all the specific qualities of the individual things exchanged and thus *per se* has no biased relationship to any subjective economic element. Similarly, theoretical laws represent the independent objectivity of nature, in relation to which every individual case appears to be accidental – the counterpart to the subjectivity of man. The fact that, none the less, different people have very different relationships to money demonstrates money's complete independence from any subjective particularity. Money shares this quality with the other major historical forces which can be compared to large lakes from which one may draw from any side and draw all that the available receptacle allows according to its form and size. The objectivity of human interaction – which, however, is only a formation of material originally offered by subjective energies, but one that ultimately takes on its own independent existence and norms – finds its highest expression in purely monetary economic interests. Whatever is sold for money goes to the buyer who offers most for it, quite regardless of what or who he is. Where other equivalents play a role, where a possession is given away for reasons of honour, service or gratitude, then the character of the person who receives it is taken into consideration. Conversely, whenever I buy for money's sake it is irrelevant from whom I buy what I want as long as it is worth its price. But wherever one pays for something with a service or personal commitment of an internal or external kind, then one carefully checks the person one is dealing with because we do not wish to give away to anybody anything that belongs to us except money. The statement on bank notes to the effect that their value is paid to the bearer 'without proof of identity' typifies the absolute objectivity with which money transactions operate. Within this area, there is a counterpart to the Hindu peasant's exemption from acts of war even among a much more emotional people. Among some American Indian tribes the trader is permitted to move freely among tribes who are at war with his own! Money places the actions and relations of men quite outside of men as human subjects, just as intellectual life – in so far as it is purely intellectual – moves from personal subjectivity into the sphere of objectivity which it only reflects. This obviously implies a relationship of superiority. Just as he who has money is superior to he who has the commodity, so the intellectual person as such has a certain power over the more emotional, impulsive person. For however much the latter may be more valuable as a whole person, and however much his powers may ultimately surpass the other, he is more one-sided, more committed and prejudiced than the intellectual person; he does not have the superior view and the unlimited possibilities of the use of all practical means that the purely intellectual person has. It is this factor of superiority, common to both money and intellectuality by virtue of their objectivity towards any particular life contents, that prompted Comte to place bankers at the head of secular government in his utopian state, because bankers formed the class with the most general and abstract functions. This interrelationship is already discernible in the medieval journeymen's associations in which the treasurer was, at the same time, the head of the association.

The dual roles of intellect and money : with regard to function they are individualistic and egoistic

This explanation of the correlation between intellectuality and the money economy, based on the objectivity and indeterminacy of character that was common to both, may be seriously challenged with a powerful counter-argument. Alongside the impersonal objectivity inherent in the content of intelligence there exists an extremely close relationship between intelligence and individuality and the whole principle of individualism. Money, for its part, no matter how much it translates impulsive–subjective modes of behaviour into supra-personal and objective normative modes, is none the less the breeding ground for economic individualism and egoism. Here we obviously confront the ambiguities and complexities of concepts that must be clearly distinguished in order to understand the style of life that is designated by them. The dual role which both the intellect and money play becomes intelligible if one distinguishes their essentially objective content from their function or, in other words, from the uses to which they are put. In the first sense, the intellect possesses a levelling, one might almost say communistic, character; first, because the essence of its content is that intellect is universally communicable and that, if we presuppose its correctness, every sufficiently trained mind must be open to persuasion by it. There is absolutely no analogy to this in the realms of the will and the emotions. In the case of the intellect, every transference of the same inner constellation depends upon the individual's given frame of mind and any compulsion will be only conditionally submitted to. In the case of the will and the emotions, there are no *proofs* like those which, at least in principle, the intellect commands in order to spread the same conviction among the public at large. The ability to learn which belongs solely to the intellect implies that one is on the same level as anyone else. In addition, the contents of the intellect, leaving aside quite fortuitous complications, do not possess the jealous exclusiveness that is common in the practical contents of life. Certain emotions, for example involved in intimate personal relationships, would completely lose their significance and value if others were entitled to share them. It is also essential

437

for certain objectives of the will that other people are excluded from both pursuing them as well as gaining them. It has been rightly suggested that theoretical notions, on the other hand, are like a torch whose light does not become dimmer by igniting innumerable others from it. Inasmuch as their potential boundless dissemination has no influence whatsoever upon their importance, they elude private ownership more than any other contents of life. Finally, they present themselves in a way that, in principle, excludes all individual contingencies from the assimilation of their content. We have no possibility of formulating emotional changes and energies of the will in such a clear and unambiguous way that everyone can refer back to them at any time and use their objective structure to continually reproduce the same inner process. In contrast, only in intellectual matters do we possess an adequate means that is relatively independent of individual disposition, and this is found in language that proceeds through concepts and their logical interrelationship.

But the significance of the intellect develops in a totally different direction as soon as real historical forces begin to channel these abstract objectivities and possibilities. First of all, it is precisely the general validity of knowledge and its consequent forcefulness and irresistibility that makes intelligence such a powerful weapon for its outstanding representatives. One can offer resistance to a superior will if one does not possess a suggestible nature, but one can elude a superior logic only by a stubborn 'I don't want to', which implies a confession of inferiority. Furthermore, the daily struggle for existence and possessions is decided by a certain measure of intelligence, even though the great decisions among men originate from supra-intellectual energies. The power of superior intelligence rests upon the communistic character of its quality: because, in terms of its content, intelligence is universally valid and everywhere effective and recognized, the mere quantity of intellectual endowment of the individual confers a more unconditional advantage than can any more individual possession, which, because of its individuality, cannot be universally used or cannot find some domain for itself anywhere in the practical world. Here, as elsewhere, it is precisely the basis of equal rights for all that brings individual differences to their full development and utilization. It is because the mere intellectual conception and organization of human relations, which disregards the irrational emphases of volition and emotion, recognizes no *a priori* difference between individuals that it has just as little grounds for curtailing differences *a posteriori*. This might be attained subsequently as so often happens through a sense of social duty and the feeling of love and pity. This is why the rationalistic interpretation of the world – which, as impartial as money, has also come close to the socialist image of life – has become the advocate of modern egoism and the ruthless assertion of individuality. According to the usual and not exactly profound point of view, the Ego is, in practice no less than in theory, man's obvious basis and unfailing primary interest. Any selfless motives appear not to be natural and autochthonous but secondary and, as it were, artificially implanted. As a result, only self-interested action is considered to be genuinely and simply 'logical'. All devotion and self-sacrifice seems to flow from the irrational forces of feeling and volition, so that men of pure intellect treat them ironically as a proof of lack of intelligence or denounce them as the disguise of a hidden egoism. This is certainly mistaken since even the egoistic will is just as much a will as the altruistic will and can just as little be squeezed out of merely rationalistic thought. Rather, as we saw, rationality can only supply the means for either of them; it is totally indifferent to the practical purposes which either of them choose and realize. Yet this connection between pure intellectuality and practical egoism is none the less broadly accepted and it may have some basis in reality, if not in terms of the logical immediacy claimed for it then in some indirect psychological manner. Yet not only genuine ethical egoism but social individualism too appears as the intellect's necessary corollary. Any collectivism that establishes a new living unity transcending its individual constituents seems to the sober intellect to contain an element of impenetrable mysticism, in so far as it is not reducible to the mere sum of its individual members – just like the living unity of an organism, in that the intellect cannot understand the unity as a mechanism of the parts. Hence the rationalism of the eighteenth century, which culminated in revolution, is bound up with a strict individualism and only the opposition to rationalism from Herder to the Romantics has, in acknowledging the supra-individual emotional potential of life, thereby also recognized the supra-individual collectivities as unities and historical realities. The universality of intellectuality, in that it is valid for each individual intellect, brings about an atomization of society. By means of the intellect and viewed from its standpoint, everyone seems to be an enclosed self-sufficient element alongside every other, without this abstract universality somehow being resolved into the concrete universality in which the individual person only forms a unity in combination with others. Finally, the inner accessibility and reflectiveness of theoretical knowledge which cannot basically be withheld from anybody, as can certain emotions and volitions, has a consequence that directly offsets its practical results. In the first place, it is precisely because of their general accessibility that factors quite independent of personal capacities decide on the factual utilization of knowledge. This leads to the enormous preponderance of the most unintelligent 'educated' person over the cleverest proletarian. The apparent equality with which educational materials are available to everyone interested in them is, in reality, a sheer mockery. The same is true of the other freedoms accorded by liberal doctrines which, though they certainly do not hamper the individual from gaining goods of any kind, do however disregard the fact that only those already privileged in some way or another have the possibility of acquiring them. For just as the substance of education – in spite of, or because of its general availability – can ultimately be acquired only through individual activity, so it gives rise to the most intangible and thus the most unassailable aristocracy, to a distinction between high and low which can be abolished neither (as can socio-economic differences) by a decree or a revolution, nor by the good will of those concerned. Thus it was appropriate for Jesus to say to the rich youth: 'Give away your goods to the poor', but not for him to say 'Give your education to the underprivileged'. There is no advantage that appears to those in inferior positions to be so despised, and before which they feel so deprived and helpless, as the advantage of education. For this reason, attempts to achieve practical equality very often and in so many variations scorn intellectual education. This is true of Buddha, the Cynics, certain currents in Christianity, down to Robespierre's *'nous n'avons pas besoin de savants'*. In addition, there is the very important fact that the location of knowledge in speech and writing – which, viewed abstractly, are a manifestation of its communal nature – makes possible its accumulation and, especially, its concentration so that, in this respect, the gulf between high and low is persistently widened. The intellectually gifted or the materially independent person will have all the more chances for standing out from the masses the larger and more concentrated are the available educational materials. Just as the proletarian today has many comforts and cultural enjoyments that were formerly denied to him, while at the same time – particularly if we look back over several centuries and millennia – the gulf between his way of life and that of the higher strata has certainly become much deeper, so, similarly, the rise in the level of knowledge as a whole does not by any means bring about a general levelling, but rather its opposite.

I have analysed this phenomenon at length because the contrasts in meaning which the concept of intellectuality exhibits are completely analogous to those found in money. The understanding of the essence of money is not only facilitated by its interaction with intellectuality, which gives them a formal similarity, but perhaps also by an underlying common principle that is manifested in the similarity of their development – perhaps by reference to the fundamental condition or disposition of those historical elements which, by giving them form, constitute their style. We have pointed out in the preceding chapters how much money, on the basis of its general availability and objectivity, none the less facilitates the growth of individuality and subjectivity, how much its unchanging uniformity, its qualitatively communistic character, leads to each quantitative difference becoming a qualitative one. This extension of the power of money that is incomparable with that of any other cultural factor, and which gives equal rights to the most contradictory tendencies in life, is manifested here as the condensation of the purely formal cultural energy that can be applied to any content in order to strengthen it and to bring about its increasingly purer representation. I therefore propose to emphasize only some specific analogies with intellectuality in terms of its content, to the effect that the impersonality and universal validity of its abstract objective nature, at least with reference to its function and use, supports egoism and differentiation. The rational and logical character that is displayed by egoism also adheres to the full and ruthless exploitation of the possession of money. Earlier, we pointed to the distinctive feature of money compared with other forms of property, namely that it does not point to any specific use and therefore implies no inhibition as to its use. Money is completely adaptable to any use without any relationship of its quality to that of the real objects thereby bringing about any specific encouragement or obstruction. Money is therefore similar to the forms of logic which lend themselves equally to any particular content, regardless of that content's development or combination. It thus grants the same chances to representation and formal correctness to the objectively most nonsensical and detrimental contents as it does to the most valuable. Furthermore, money is also analogous to the schemes of law which often enough lack safety devices for preventing the most serious injustice from being endowed with an unimpeachable formal righteousness. This unrestricted possibility for fully exploiting the power of money appears not only as a justification but also, as it were, as a logical–conceptual necessity for doing so. Since money intrinsically contains neither directives nor obstacles, it follows the strongest subjective impulse that within all money matters appears to be the egoistic impulse. The inhibiting notion that certain amounts of money may be 'stained with blood' or be under a curse are sentimentalities that lose their significance completely with the growing indifference of money – that is, as money increasingly becomes nothing but mere money. Money's purely negative quality, that its use, unlike other forms of ownership, is in no way restricted by objective or ethical considerations, inevitably develops into inconsiderateness as a completely positive kind of attitude. Money's flexibility, which follows from its being detached from particular interests, origins and relations, entails as a necessary logical consequence the invitation to us not to restrain ourselves in those spheres of life in which money predominates. The absolute objectivity that results from the elimination of all one-sided objectivity makes a clean sweep in favour of egoism, as did pure intellectuality, for no other reason than because this guiding principle is logically the simplest, the closest at hand, so that the purely formal and indifferent forces of life attain in it their primary, as it were, natural, and congenial fulfilment.

Money's relationship to the rationalism of law and logic

It is not only, as I mentioned earlier, that the form of law in general, together with intellectuality and money transactions, disregards the objectively and morally most perverse contents, but rather it is that this discrepancy between form and real content culminates in the principle of *equality* before the law. All

441

three factors – the law, intellectuality and money – are characterized by their complete indifference to individual qualities; all three extract from the concrete totality of the streams of life one abstract, general factor which develops according to its own independent norms and which intervenes in the totality of existential interests and imposes itself upon them. In that all three of them have the power to lay down forms and directions for contents to which they are indifferent, they necessarily inject those contradictions into the totality of life which concern us here. Wherever equality impinges upon the formal foundations of human relationships, it serves to express individual inequalities most pointedly and far-reachingly. By observing the limits imposed by formal equality, egoism need no longer concern itself with internal and external barriers. It possesses, in the general validity of that equality, a weapon which, by serving anyone, may also be used against anyone. The forms of legal equality are the typical forms that intellectuality as well as money share: their general availability and validity; their potential communism which removes for everyone, those of higher, lower and equal position alike, certain barriers that resulted from the *a priori*, status-related demarcation of types of property. As long as landed property and the professions were in the hands of certain classes, they entailed certain obligations toward the lower orders, solidarity with others of the same class, and clear limits to the ambition of outsiders. Yet an 'enlightened' rationalism has no reason for retaining these any longer if every property can be transferred into a value, the unlimited acquisition of which is, in principle, denied to no one. This, of course, does not answer the question as to whether the *total* amount of egoism increases or decreases in the course of history.

Finally, I want to refer to the very characteristic fact that the accumulation of intellectual achievements, which gives a disproportionate and rapidly growing advantage to those who are favoured by it, also has its analogy in the accumulation of money capital. The structure of monetary relationships, the way in which money yields returns and profits, is such that, beyond a certain amount, money multiplies without a corresponding effort on the part of the owner. This corresponds to the structure of knowledge in the cultural world which requires, beyond a certain point, decreasing self-acquisition on the part of the individual, because the cognitive content is increasingly offered in a condensed and, beyond a certain level, concentrated form. The highest stages of education require less effort for every step further than the lower stages, and yet at the same time produce greater results. Just as the objectivity of money permits 'work' that is ultimately relatively independent of personal energies and the accumulating returns lead automatically to more accumulation in growing proportions, so the objectification of knowledge, the separation of the results of intelligence from its process, causes these results to accumulate in the form of concentrated abstractions, so that, if only one stands high enough, they may be picked like fruits that have ripened without any effort on our part.

As a result of all this, the tendencies in favour of general equality most decisively reject money, even though it is by nature a basically democratic levelling social form that excludes any specific individual relationships. Here we have the same result, for the same reason as we observed with regard to intellectuality. Universality in a logical–substantive sense and universality in a social–practical sense fall asunder in the two spheres. In other spheres they often enough do coincide. For instance, it has been stated – regardless of whether this is an exhaustive definition – that the essence of art is to represent in its content the typical general features of phenomena so as to appeal to the typical human emotions that reside in us, and that art's principal claim to subjective acceptance is based on the exclusion of all fortuitous and individual elements from its object. In the same manner, the forms of religion transcend all temporal particularity to the level of the absolute and universal and, in so doing, secure a relationship to what is most common to all individuals and to what unites them in the human world. By their all-embracing unity, the forms of religion release us from our merely individual attributes, by relating them back to the basic traits that are felt to be the common roots of everything human. The same is true of morality as conceived by Kant. The mode of action that may be logically generalized without contradicting itself should also be the moral law for everyone regardless of his identity. The criterion operating here is that one might conceive of the practical maxim as natural law, such that its conceptual, objective universality establishes the universality for all subjects, for whom it becomes a moral imperative. In contrast to these forms, modern life in other spheres seems rather to increase the tension between objective universality of content and universality of personal relationships. Certain elements gain an increasingly larger universality of content; they become more significant for an increasing number of details and relationships; their definition includes, directly or indirectly, an increasingly larger part of reality. This is true, for example, of law, the processes and results of intellectuality, and money. It is accompanied by their elevation to subjectively differentiated forms of life, by the utilization of their all-embracing importance for the practice of egoism, and by the full development of personal differences on the basis of this levelling material, since it is generally accessible and valid and therefore offers no resistance to any individual will. The confusion and the feeling of secret self-contradiction which in so many points characterizes the style of modern life is partly based on this imbalance and tension between the content and objective significance of these spheres and their personal use and development with regard to universality and equality.

The calculating character of modern times

I want to mention a final trait in the style of contemporary life whose rationalistic character clearly betrays the influence of money. By and large, one may characterize the intellectual functions that are used at present in coping with the world and in regulating both individual and social relations as *calculative* functions. Their cognitive ideal is to conceive of the world as a huge arithmetical problem, to conceive events and the qualitative distinction of things as a system of numbers. Kant believed that natural philosophy was scientific only to the extent that mathematics could be applied in it. Yet it is not only the physical world that has to be intellectually conquered by measuring and weighing; for pessimism as well as optimism wishes to establish the value of life by balancing pleasure and pain and its ideal is the quantitative calculation of both factors. The frequent determination of public life through majority votes is a manifestation of the same trend. To subject the individual to majority decision through the fact that others – not superior, but equal – hold a different opinion is not as natural as it may appear to us today. It is unknown in ancient German law, which states that whoever does not agree with the decision of the community is not bound by it; outvoting did not exist in the tribal council of the Iroquois, in the Cortes of Aragon up to the sixteenth century, or in the parliament of Poland and other communities; decisions that were not unanimous were not valid. The principle that the minority has to conform to the majority indicates that the absolute or qualitative value of the individual voice is reduced to an entity of purely quantitative significance. The corollary or the presupposition of this arithmetical procedure whereby the numerical majority or minority of unspecified units expresses and guides the inner reality of the group is the democratic levelling where everyone counts as one and no one counts for more than one. This measuring, weighing and calculating exactness of modern times is the purest reflection of its intellectualism which, however, on the basis of abstract equality, also favours the egoistical impulses of the elements. Language, with fine instinctive subtle insight, interprets a 'calculating' person simply as one who 'calculates' in an *egoistic* sense. Just as in the use of 'reasonable' or 'rational', so here too the apparently non-partisan formalism of the concept is basically a disposition to cover over a specific biased content.

This psychological feature of our times which stands in such a decisive contrast to the more impulsive, emotionally determined character of earlier epochs seems to me to stand in a close causal relationship to the money economy. The money economy enforces the necessity of continuous mathematical operations in our daily transactions. The lives of many people are absorbed by such evaluating, weighing, calculating and reducing of qualitative values to quantitative ones. Gauging values in terms of money has taught us to determine and specify values down to the last farthing and has thus enforced a much greater precision in the comparison of various contents of life. Where objects are conceived in their direct relationship to other objects, that is where they cannot be reduced to the common denominator of money, a much more spontaneous evaluation, a comparison of one unit against another, is to be found. Exactness, precision and

444

rigour in the economic relationships in life, which naturally affect other aspects of life as well, run parallel to the extension of monetary matters, though not exactly for the benefit of a superior style of living. The ideal of numerical calculability has been made possible in practical, and perhaps even in intellectual, life only through the money economy. Viewed from this standpoint, the institution of money appears as a mere intensification and sublimation of the economic sphere in general. With regard to commercial transactions between the English people and their kings, when, particularly in the thirteenth and fourteenth centuries, all kinds of rights and liberties were bought, a historian writes, 'This made possible a practical solution to difficult problems which seemed theoretically insoluble. The king has rights as the ruler of his people, the people have rights as free men and as estates of the realm that the king personifies. Though the determination of the rights of each of them is extremely difficult in principle, it became easy in practice as soon as it was reduced to a question of buying and selling.' This means that, as soon as a qualitative relationship of practical elements is represented by their significance as a part of business transactions, it gains an exactitude and possibility of precise determination that remains denied to the phenomenon as it stands, with all its qualitative differences. However, this process does not yet make money indispensable since such transactions are often carried out through payment in kind, for example in wool. Yet it is evident that money can accomplish in a much sharper and more exact manner what commercial transactions contributed to the accuracy of values and demands. In this respect, one could perhaps say that monetary transactions relate to commercial transactions as a whole as money relates to the exactness and relationship of objects before exchange existed. Money expresses, as it were, the purely commercial element in the commercial treatment of things, just as logic represents comprehensibility with reference to comprehensible objects. Since the abstract form that represents the immanent value of objects takes the form of arithmetical precision and thus of unequivocal rational accuracy, its characteristics must reflect upon the objects themselves. If it is true that the art of a period gradually determines the way we look at nature, and if the artist's spontaneous and subjective abstraction from reality forms the apparently immediate sensuous picture of nature in our consciousness, then so too will the superstructure of money relations erected above qualitative reality determine much more radically the inner image of reality according to its forms. The mathematical character of money imbues the relationship of the elements of life with a precision, a reliability in the determination of parity and disparity, an unambiguousness in agreements and arrangements in the same way as the general use of pocket watches has brought about a similar effect in daily life. Like the determination of abstract value by money, the determination of abstract time by clocks provides a system for the most detailed and definite arrangements and measurements that imparts an otherwise unattainable transparency and calculability to the contents of life, at least as regards their practical management. The calculating intellectuality embodied in these forms may in its turn derive from them some of the energy through which intellectuality controls modern life. All these relationships are brought into focus by the negative example of those types of thinkers who are most strongly and fiercely opposed to the economic interpretation of human affairs: Goethe, Carlyle and Nietzsche on the one hand are fundamentally anti-intellectual and on the other completely reject that mathematically exact interpretation of nature which we recognized as the theoretical counterpart to the institution of money.

II

The concept of culture

If we define culture as the refinement, as the intellectualized forms of life, the accomplishment of mental and practical labour, then we place these values in a context in which they do not automatically belong by virtue of their own objective significance. They become manifestations of culture to us inasmuch as we interpret them as intensified displays of natural vitality and potential, intensified beyond the level of development, fullness and differentiation that would be achieved by their mere nature. A natural energy or allusion, which is necessary only in order that it may be surpassed by actual development, forms the presupposition for the concept of culture. From the standpoint of culture, the values of life are civilized *nature*; they do not have here the isolated significance that is measured from above, as it were, by the ideals of happiness, intelligence and beauty. Rather, they appear as developments of a basis that we call nature and whose power and intellectual content they surpass in so far as they become culture. Therefore, if a cultivated garden fruit and a statue are both equally cultural products, then language indicates this relationship in a subtle manner by calling the fruit tree 'cultivated', whereas the bare marble block is not 'cultivated' to produce a statue. For in the first case one assumes a natural driving force and disposition of the tree to bear these fruits which, through intelligent influence, grow beyond their natural limits; whereas we do not presuppose a corresponding tendency as regards the statue. The culture embodied in the statue constitutes an enhancement and refinement of certain human energies whose original manifestations we term 'natural'.

At first glance, it seems reasonable to describe impersonal objects as cultured only as a figure of speech. For to develop through will and intelligence what is naturally given beyond the limits of its merely natural capacities is reserved for ourselves or such objects whose growth is connected with our impulses and, in their turn, stimulate our feelings. The material products of culture – furniture and cultivated plants, works of art and machinery, tools and books – in which natural material is developed into forms which could never have been realized by their own energies, are products of our own desires and emotions, the result of ideas that utilize the available possibilities of objects. It is exactly the same with regard to the culture that shapes people's relationships to one another and to themselves: language, morals, religion and law. To the extent that these values are interpreted as cultural, we distinguish them from such levels of growth of their innate energies that they may accomplish, as it were, by themselves, and that are only the raw material for the process of civilization, like wood and metal, plants and electricity. By cultivating objects, that is by increasing their value beyond the performance of their natural constitution, we cultivate ourselves: it is the same value-increasing process developing out of us and returning back to us that moves external nature or our own nature. The fine arts reflect this concept of culture most clearly because they display the greatest tension between these opposites. For the shaping of the object seems completely to escape being adapted to the process of our subjectivity. The work of art interprets the meaning of the phenomenon itself, whether it is embedded in the shaping of space or in the relations of colours or in the spirituality that exists, as it were, both in and beneath the visible. Yet everything depends on discovering the meaning and secret of things in order to represent them in a form that is purer and clearer than their natural development – not, however, in the sense of chemical or physical technology, which explores the law-like nature of objects in order to incorporate them into human purposes that are intrinsic to them. Rather, the artistic process is completed as soon as it has succeeded in presenting the object in its unique significance. This, in fact, also fulfils the purely artistic ideal, since the perfection of the work of art is an objective value in itself, completely independent of its success in our subjective experience. The slogan '*l'art pour l'art*' characterizes perfectly the self-sufficiency of the purely artistic tendency. But from the standpoint of a cultural ideal the situation is different. Here it is essential that the independent values of aesthetic, scientific, ethical, eudaemonistic and even religious achievements are transcended in order to integrate them all as elements in the development of human nature beyond its natural state. More accurately, they are the milestones which this development has to pass. At each moment cultural development is located somewhere along this road; it never can proceed purely formally and independently of some content even though it is not identical with this content. Cultural contents consist of those forms, each of which is subordinate to an autonomous ideal, though here they are viewed from the standpoint of the development of our energies or our being beyond the degree considered to be purely natural. In refining objects, man creates them in his own image. The cultural process, as the supra-natural growth of the energies of things, is the manifestation or embodiment of the identical growth of *our* energies. The borderline at which the development of specific life-content passes from its natural form into its cultural form is indistinct and is subject to controversy. But this is merely one of the most universal difficulties of thought. The categories under which specific phenomena are subsumed in order to incorporate them into knowledge, its norms and relationships, are marked off from each other and often gain their meaning only from this contrast. These concepts form sequences with discontinuous levels. Yet the particulars that are supposed to be covered by these concepts usually cannot be located with the same degree of certainty. Rather, their quantitative characteristics often determine whether they belong to the one or the other concept so that, because of the continuity of everything quantitative and the ever-possible *intermediate position* between two entities, each of which corresponds to a specific category, the specific phenomenon may well be placed sometimes with one, sometimes with the other. Thus there seems to be an indeterminacy between them, even a mixture of concepts which, according to their actual meaning, exclude one another. The fundamental certainty of the demarcation between nature and culture, that the one starts where the other leaves off, is just as little affected by the uncertainty as to where to locate individual phenomena as are the concepts of day and night which do not merge into one another because dawn and dusk may sometimes be attributed to the one, sometimes to the other.

The increase in material culture and the lag in individual culture

I will now contrast this discussion of the general concept of culture with a specific relationship within contemporary culture. If one compares our culture with that of a hundred years ago, then one may surely say – subject to many individual exceptions – that the things that determine and surround our lives, such as tools, means of transport, the products of science, technology and art, are extremely refined. Yet individual culture, at least in the higher strata, has not progressed at all to the same extent; indeed, it has even frequently declined. This does not need to be shown in detail. I only wish, therefore, to emphasize some aspects of it. Linguistic possibilities for expression, in German as well as in French, have become much more refined and subtle in the last hundred years. Not only do we now have Goethe's language, but in addition we have a large number of refinements, subtleties and individual modes of expression. Yet, if one looks at the speech and writing of individuals, they are on the whole increasingly less correct, less dignified and more trivial. In terms of content, the scope of objects of conversation has been widened during that time through advances in theory and practice, yet, none the less, it seems that conversation, both social as well as intimate and in the exchange of letters, is now more superficial, less interesting and less serious than at the end of the eighteenth century. The fact that machinery has become so much more sophisticated than the worker is part of this same process. How many workers are there today, even within large-scale industry, who are able to understand the machine with which they work, that is the mental effort invested in it? The same applies to military culture. The work of the individual soldier has essentially remained the same for a long time, and in some respects has even been reduced through modern methods of warfare. In contrast, not only the material instruments but, above all, the completely impersonal organization of the army have become extremely sophisticated and a real triumph of objective culture. In the purely intellectual sphere, even the best informed and most thoughtful persons work with a growing number of ideas, concepts and statements, the exact meaning and content of which they are not fully aware. The tremendous expansion of objective, available material of knowledge allows or even enforces the use of expressions that pass from hand to hand like sealed containers without the condensed content of thought actually enclosed within them being unfolded for the individual user. Just as our everyday life is surrounded more and more by objects of which we cannot conceive how much intellectual effort is expended in their production, so our mental and social communication is filled with symbolic terms, in which a comprehensive intellectuality is accumulated, but of which the individual mind need make only minimal use. The preponderance of objective over subjective culture that developed during the nineteenth century is reflected partly in the fact that the eighteenth century pedagogic ideal was focused upon the formation of man, that is upon a personal internal value, which was replaced during the nineteenth century, however, by the concept of 'education' in the sense of a body of objective knowledge and behavioural patterns. This discrepancy seems to widen steadily. Every day and from all sides, the wealth of objective culture increases, but the individual mind can enrich the forms and contents of its own development only by distancing itself still further from that culture and developing its own at a much slower pace.

How can we explain this phenomenon? If all the culture of things is, as we saw, nothing but a culture of people, so that we develop ourselves only by developing things, then what does that development, elaboration and intellectualization of objects mean, which seems to evolve out of these objects' own powers and norms without correspondingly developing the individual mind? This implies an accentuation of the enigmatic relationship which prevails between the social life and its products on the one hand and the fragmentary life-contents of individuals on the other. The labour of countless generations is embedded in language and custom, political constitutions and religious doctrines, literature and technology as objectified spirit from which everyone can take as much of it as they wish to or are able to, but no single individual is able to exhaust it all. Between the amount of this treasure and what is taken from it, there exists the most diverse and fortuitous relationships. The insignificance or irrationality of the individual's share leaves the substance and dignity of mankind's ownership unaffected, just as any physical entity is independent of its being individually perceived. Just as the content and significance of a book remains indifferent to a large or small, understanding or unresponsive, group of readers, so any cultural product confronts its cultural audience, ready to be absorbed by anyone but in fact taken up only sporadically. This concentrated mental labour of a cultural community is related to the degree to which it comes alive in individuals just as the abundance of possibilities is related to the limitations of reality. In order to understand the mode of existence of such objective intellectual manifestations, we have to place them within the specific framework of our categories for interpreting the world. The discrepant relationship between objective and subjective culture, which forms our specific problem, will then find its proper place within these categories.

The Platonic myth implied that the soul had seen the pure essence, the absolute significance, of worldly objects during its pre-existence, so that the subsequent knowledge of it is but a *remembrance* of this truth emerging through sensory stimuli. The prime motive underlying this myth is the perplexity as to the origins of our knowledge if one denies its origin, as Plato does, in experience. However, this metaphysical speculation – aside from the specific cause of its emergence – basically indicates an epistemological attitude of the mind. Whether we interpret our cognition as a direct result of external objects or as a purely internal process in which everything external is an immanent form or relationship of mental elements, we always conceive of our thought – to the extent that it is accepted as the truth – as the fulfilment of an objective demand, the reproduction of an imaginary model. Even if our cognition were an exact reflection of the objects as they are in themselves, the unity, correctness and completeness that knowledge approaches by mastering one thing after another would not derive from the objects themselves. Rather, our epistemological ideal would always be their content *in the form of ideas*, since even the most extreme realism wishes to gain not the objects themselves but rather knowledge of them. If we describe the sum total of fragments that make up our knowledge at any one moment in relation to the goal we want to attain and which determines the significance of each stage, then we can do so only by presupposing that which lies at the basis of the Platonic doctrine: that there is an ideal realm of theoretical values, of perfect intellectual meaning and coherence, that coincides neither with the objects – since these are only its objects – nor with the psychologically real knowledge that has been attained. On the contrary, this real knowledge only gradually and always imperfectly approximates to that realm which includes all possible truth. It is true-only in the sense that it is successful in doing this. Plato seems to have accepted this basic feeling that our knowledge at any moment is only a part of a complex of knowledge that exists only in an ideal form and invites and demands psychological realization on our part. Yet he expressed this as a decrease in real knowledge from the former grasp of this totality, as a 'no-longer', instead of our present-day interpretation of it as a 'not-yet'. But the relationship itself can obviously be experienced in both interpretations as basically the same – just as the identical number may be derived by subtractions from a higher number or by addition of lower numbers. The mode of existence peculiar to this cognitive ideal that confronts our real cognitions as a norm or as a totality is the same as the totality of moral values and prescriptions that confront the actual behaviour of individuals. Here, in the ethical realm, we are more aware of the fact that our behaviour corresponds well or badly to an intrinsically valid norm. This norm – which may differ in its content for different people and for different periods of their lives – is not to be found in time and space, nor does it coincide with moral awareness, which is instead conscious of being dependent upon that norm. Ultimately, the formula of our life as a whole, from the trivial practice of everyday to the highest peak of intellectuality, is this: in all that we do, we have a norm, a standard, an ideally preconceived totality before us, which we try to transpose into reality through our actions. This refers not to the simple generalization that our will is guided by some kind of ideal; rather, it refers to the specific, more or less distinct, quality of our actions, which can only be described in the following way: in our action, regardless of whether its value contradicts ideals, we follow some prefigured possibility and, as it were, carry out an ideal programme. Our practical existence, though inadequate and fragmentary, gains a certain significance and coherence, as it were, by partaking in the realization of a totality. Our actions, even our total being, beautiful or ugly, right or wrong, great or petty, seem to be drawn from a wealth of possibilities such that, at every moment, they relate to its ideally determined content just as the concrete object relates to the concept that expresses its immanent law and its logical essence without the significance of this content thereby being dependent upon whether, how and how often it is realized. We cannot conceive of cognition in any other way except as the realization in our consciousness of those conceptions which were, so to say, waiting to be conceived at that particular point in question. The fact that we term our knowledge necessary knowledge, that is that there is only *one* specific way in which its content can exist, is only a different expression of the conviction that we consider it to be the mental realization of the pre-established ideal content. This *one* specific way does not mean that there is only *one* truth for the great variety of minds. Rather, if on the one hand a definitely structured intellect and, on the other, a certain objective reality is given, the 'truth' for this mind is objectively pre-formed in the same way as is the answer to a calculation if its factors are given. With every change in the endowed mental structure, the content of this truth changes, without being any the less objective or more dependent upon the awareness of this mind. The unswerving conclusion that we derived from certain facts of knowledge, that other facts of knowledge also have to be assumed, is the accidental cause that illustrates the nature of our comprehension: every single piece of knowledge means becoming aware of something that is already valid and established within the objectively determined context of the contents of knowledge. Finally, from the psychological point of view, this is associated with the theory according to which everything held to be true is a certain *feeling* which accompanies a mental image; what we call proof is nothing other than the establishment of a psychological constellation which gives rise to such a feeling. No sense perception or logical derivations can directly assure us of a reality. Rather, they are only the conditions that evoke the supra-theoretical feeling of affirmation, of agreement or whatever one may call this rather indescribable sense of reality. It forms the psychological mediator between the two epistemological categories: between the valid purpose of things, brought forth by its inner coherence that assigns each element to its proper place, and our perception of things that signifies their reality for a human subject.

The objectification of the mind

This general and basic relationship is paralleled to a lesser extent in the relationship between the objectified mind and culture, and the individual. Just as, from an epistemological standpoint, we draw our life-contents from a realm of objectively valid entities, so, viewed historically, we draw the major part of them from the stock of accumulated mental labour of the species. Here too we find preformed contents that are ready to be realized by individual minds but yet preserve their determinateness which does not coincide with that of a material object. For even where the mind is tied to matter, as in tools, works of art and books, it is never identical with that part of them that is perceptible to our senses. The mind lives in them in a hardly definable potential form which the individual consciousness is able to actualize. Objective culture is the historical presentation or more or less perfect condensation of an objectively valid truth which is reproduced by our cognition. If we can say that the law of gravity was valid before Newton formulated it, then the law itself does not rest in the substance of matter. Instead, it only illustrates the manner in which the relations of matter present themselves to a specifically organized mind, and the validity of the law is independent of the fact that matter exists in reality. If this is the case then the law resides neither in objective things themselves nor in the subjective mind, but in that sphere of the objective spirit which, stage by stage, is condensed into reality by our sense of truth. Once this has been accomplished by Newton with respect to the law in question, that law has been incorporated into the objective historical mind, and its ideal significance within that mind is now, in its turn, basically independent of its reproduction by particular individuals.

By establishing this category of the objective mind as the historical manifestation of the valid intellectual content of things in general, it becomes clear how the cultural process that we recognize as a subjective development – the culture of things as a human culture – can be separated from its content. This content, by entering that category, acquires, as it were, another physical condition and thus provides the basis for the phenomenon of the separate development of objective and personal culture. The objectification of the mind provides the form that makes the conservation and accumulation of mental labour possible; it is the most significant and most far-reaching of the historical categories of mankind. For it transforms into a historical fact what is biologically so doubtful: hereditary transmission. If to be not only a descendant but also an heir denotes the superiority of man over animals, then the objectification of the mind in words and works, organizations and traditions is the basis for this distinction by which man takes possession of his world, or even of any world at all.

If this objective mind of historical society is its cultural content in the widest sense, then the practical cultural significance of its individual elements is measured by the extent to which they become factors in individual development. If we presuppose that Newton's discovery was only preserved in a book which no one knew, it would still be part of the objectified mind and a potential possession of society, but no longer a cultural value. Since this extreme case can occur on countless levels, it follows that in society at large only a certain proportion of objective cultural values become subjective values. If one looks at society as a whole, that is if one arranges the objectified intellectuality in a temporal–objective complex, then the whole cultural development, assuming it has a uniform representative, is richer in content than each of its elements. For the achievement of each element is incorporated in the total heritage, but this heritage does not permeate each element. The entire life-style of a community depends upon the relationship between the objectified culture and the culture of the subjects. I have already mentioned the significance of numerical factors. In the small community of a lower culture, this relationship will be almost one of perfect equality; the objective cultural possibilities will not extend much beyond the subjective cultural reality. An increase in the cultural level – particularly if it coincides with an enlargement of the group – will favour a discrepancy between both. The unique situation of the golden age of Athens was due to the fact that it was able to avoid this, except perhaps with reference to philosophy at its peak. Yet the size of the social circle does not yet in itself fully explain the divergence of the subjective and the objective factor. On the contrary, we must now search for the concrete, effective causes of this phenomenon.

The division of labour as the cause of the divergence of subjective and objective culture

If we wish to confine the cause and its present magnitude in a single concept, then it is that of the *division of labour*, in terms of its importance within production as well as consumption. With regard to production, it has been emphasized often enough that the product is completed at the expense of the development of the producer. The increase in psycho-physical energies and skills, which is the result of specialized activity, is of little value for the total personality, which often even becomes stunted because of the diversion of energies that are indispensable for the harmonious growth of the self. In other cases, it develops as if cut off from the core of the personality, as a province with unlimited autonomy whose fruits do not flow back to the centre. Experience seems to show that the inner wholeness of the self basically evolves out of interaction with the uniformity and the completion of our life task.

The unity of an object is realized for us only by projecting our self into the object in order to shape it according to our image, so that the diversity of determinations grows into the unity of the 'ego'. In the same manner, the unity or lack of unity of the object that we create affects, in a psychological–practical sense, the corresponding formation of our personality. Whenever our energies do not produce something whole as a reflection of the total personality, then the proper relationship between subject and object is missing. The internal nature of our achievement is bound up with parts of achievements accomplished by others which are a necessary part of the totality, but it does not refer back to the producer. As a result, the inadequacy that develops between the worker's existential form and that of his product because of greater specialization easily serves to completely divorce the product from the labourer. Its meaning is not derived from the mind of the producer but from its relationship with products of a different origin. Because of its fragmentary character, the product lacks the spiritual determinacy that can be easily perceived in a product of labour that is wholly the work of a *single* person. The significance of the product is thus to be sought neither in the reflection of a subjectivity nor in the reflex of a creative spirit, but is to be found only in the objective achievement that leads away from the subject.

This relationship is equally well illustrated by its extreme opposite, the work of art. The nature of the art work completely resists a subdivision of labour among a number of workers, none of whom on his own achieves a whole unity. The work of art, of all the works of man, is the most perfectly autonomous unity, a self-sufficient totality, even more so than the State. For the State, though it may be autonomous under specific circumstances, does not envelop all its elements so completely that each may not lead a separate life with its own interests: only one part of our personality is interwoven with the State, while the other parts may revolve around other centres. Art, however, does not grant significance to any of the elements within the context in which they are set; the individual work of art destroys the manifold meanings of words and of tones, of colours and of forms in order to preserve in our consciousness only such aspects as are relevant to the work. This autonomy of the work of art, however, signifies that it expresses a subjective spiritual unity. The work of art requires only one *single* person, but it requires him totally, right down to his innermost core. It rewards the person by its form becoming that person's purest reflection and expression. The complete rejection of the division of labour is both cause and symptom of the connection between the autonomous totality of the work and the unity of the spirit. Conversely, where the division of labour prevails, the achievement becomes incommensurable with the performer; the person can no longer find himself expressed in his work; its form becomes dissimilar to the subjective mind and appears only as a wholly specialized part of our being that is indifferent to the total unity of man. Where the work is based on a marked division of labour and achieved with an awareness of this division it thrusts itself inherently towards the category of objectivity. It becomes more and more plausible for the worker to consider his work and its effect as purely objective and anonymous, because it no longer touches the roots of his whole life-system.

The more completely an entity composed of subjective components absorbs the parts, and the more the character of each part serves only as a part of the whole, then the more objective is that whole and the more is its life independent of the subjects who produced it. Generally speaking, a broadening of consumption corresponds to the specialization of production. Even the most intellectually and occupationally specialized people today read the newspaper and thereby indulge in a more extensive mental consumption than was possible a hundred years ago, for even the most versatile and widely interested person. The broadening of consumption, however, is dependent upon the growth of *objective* culture, since the more objective and impersonal an object is the better it is suited to more people. Such consumable material, in order to be acceptable and enjoyable to a very large number of individuals, cannot be designed for subjective differentiation of taste, while on the other hand only the most extreme differentiation of production is able to produce the objects cheaply and abundantly enough in order to satisfy the demand for them. The pattern of consumption is thus a bridge between the objectivity of culture and the division of labour.

Finally, the process that is characterized as the separation of the worker from the means of production and which is itself also a kind of division of labour clearly operates in the same direction. In that it is the function of the capitalist to acquire, organize and allocate the means of production, these means acquire a very different objectivity for the worker than for those who work with their own material and their own tools. This capitalistic differentiation fundamentally separates the subjective and the objective conditions of work, a separation for which there was no psychological reason as long as both were united in the same hands. In so far as work itself and its direct object belongs to *different* persons, the objective character of these objects must loom extremely large in the worker's consciousness, all the more so as labour and its materials themselves form a unity and their usual proximity makes the present polarity all the more

455

noticeable. This process is continued and reflected in the fact that, in addition to the means of production, work itself is separated from the worker. This is the significance of the phenomenon indicated in the statement that labour power has become a commodity. Where the worker works with his own materials, his labour remains within the sphere of his own personality, and only by selling the finished products is it separated from him. Where there is no possibility for utilizing his labour in this way, the worker places his labour at the disposal of another person for a market price and thus separates himself from his labour from the moment it leaves its source. The fact that labour now shares the same character, mode of valuation and fate with all other commodities signifies that work has become something objectively separate from the worker, something that he not only no longer *is*, but also no longer *has*. For as soon as his potential labour power is transposed into actual work, only its money equivalent belongs to him whereas the work itself belongs to someone else or, more accurately, to an objective organization of labour. The process by which labour becomes a commodity is thus only one side of the far-reaching process of differentiation by which specific contents of the personality are detached in order for them to confront the personality as objects with an independent character and dynamics.

Finally, the result of this fate of the means of production and labour power is also exhibited in its product. The fact that the product of labour in the capitalist era is an object with a decidedly autonomous character, with its own laws of motion and a character alien to the producing subject, is most forcefully illustrated where the worker is compelled to *buy* his own product if he wishes to have it. This general pattern of development is valid far beyond the situation of the wage-labourer. The immense division of labour in science, for instance, results in a situation in which only very few scholars are able to procure for themselves the prerequisites for their work; innumerable facts and methods have simply to be accepted from outside as objective materials, as the intellectual property of others that is to be used for further research. I recall that in the sphere of technology even at the beginning of the nineteenth century, when the most spectacular inventions in textile and iron industries followed one upon the other, the inventors not only had to produce the new machines by their own hands and without the help of other machines, but most of the time they had to devise and produce the necessary tools for doing so. In a broader sense, and in any case in the sense implied here, the present situation in science can be designated as a separation of the worker from his means of production. For in the actual process of scientific investigation the objective material of the producer is certainly separated from the subjective process of his work. The less differentiated the scientific process was, the more the scholar had to work out the presuppositions and materials for his work himself and the less apparent was the contrast between his subjective achievement and a whole world of objectively given scientific facts. This contrast also extends to the product of his work: even the result itself, no matter how much it is the fruit of subjective effort, becomes elevated to the category of an objective fact independent of the producer, the more the work of others is already contained and combined in the final result. Therefore we can also observe that, in the disciplines with the most limited division of labour such as philosophy (and particularly metaphysics), on the one hand the objective material used plays only a secondary role, and on the other the product is the least detached from its subjective origin. Rather it appears entirely as the achievement of a single person.

The division of labour, understood in its widest sense to include the division of production, the differentiation of work processes and specialization, separates the working person from the work produced and endows the product with objective independence. Something similar happens in the relationship between production based on the division of labour and the consumer. The aim here is to derive the psychological consequences from well known concrete facts. Custom work, which predominated among medieval craftsmen and which rapidly declined only during the last century, gave the consumer a personal relationship to the commodity. Since it was produced specifically for him, and represented, as it were, a mutual relationship between him and the producer, it belonged, in a similar way as it belonged to the producer, also to him. Just as the radical opposition between subject and object has been reconciled in theory by making the object part of the subject's perception, so the same opposition between subject and object does not evolve in practice as long as the object is produced by a *single* person or for a *single* person. Since the division of labour destroys custom production – if only because the consumer can contact a producer but not a dozen different workers – the subjective aura of the product also disappears in relation to the consumer because the commodity is now produced independently of him. It becomes an objective given entity which the consumer approaches externally and whose specific existence and quality is autonomous of him. The difference, for instance, between a modern highly specialized dress store and the work of a tailor who worked at the customer's house sharply emphasizes the growing objectivity of the economic cosmos and its impersonal independence in relation to the individual consumer with whom it was originally closely identified. It has been emphasized that, with the splitting up of work into increasingly specialized partial operations, exchange relations become increasingly complicated and mediated with the result that the economy necessarily establishes more and more relationships and obligations *that are not directly reciprocal*. It is obvious how much this objectifies the whole character of transactions and how subjectivity is destroyed and transposed into cool reserve and anonymous objectivity once so many intermediate stages are introduced between the producer and the customer that they lose sight of each other.

This autonomy of production with reference to the consumer is connected

457

with another very common aspect of the division of labour, the significance of which is not yet appreciated. The simple notion generally prevails, derived from earlier forms of production, that the lower strata of society work for the upper strata; that the plants live from the soil, the animals from the plants and man from animals. It is assumed that this is repeated – with or without moral justification – in the structure of society. The more superior the position of individuals, both socially and intellectually, the more their existence is based on the work of those lower down the scale, in exchange not for their work but for money. This notion, however, is totally wrong nowadays since the needs of the subordinate masses are satisfied by large enterprises which have engaged countless scientific, technical and managerial energies of the upper strata in their service. The eminent chemist who reflects in his laboratory upon the description of dyed colours is working for the peasant woman who buys the most colourful scarf at the haberdasher; if the wholesale merchant, through global speculations, imports American grain to Germany, then he is the servant of the poorest proletarian; a cotton mill that employs people of the highest intelligence is dependent on customers in the lowest social strata. There are innumerable examples today of this feed-back of services, whereby the lower classes purchase the labour products of the higher classes; they affect our whole culture. This phenomenon is possible only through the objectification of production which has set it apart from the producing and the consuming individual and has thus placed production above social and other differences. This commissioning of the services of the highest cultural producers by the lowest consumers means that there is no relationship between them, but rather that an object has been thrust between them. On the one side of this object one group works on it while others on the other side consume it; the object separates them both and at the same time establishes a connection between them. The basic reason for this is obviously the division of labour: the techniques of production are so specialized that the handling of its different parts is transferred not only to more but also to increasingly more diverse people until the point is reached at which one part of the work on the humblest necessities is performed by individuals of the highest rank. Conversely, the subdivision of work by machine technology brings about a situation in which the roughest hands collaborate in the production of the most sophisticated products (one need mention here only the present printing press in contrast to the production of books before the invention of printing). This inversion of the typical relationship between the upper and lower strata of society indicates most clearly that the division of labour causes the upper strata to work for the lower strata. The only form, however, in which this may occur is through the complete objectification of the productive process itself in relation to both groups. This inversion is nothing other than a final consequence of the relationship that exists between the division of labour and objectification of culture.

So far the division of labour has been interpreted as a specialization of personal activities. Yet the specialization of objects themselves contributes no less to the process of their alienation from human subjects, which appears as an independence of the object, as the individual's inability to assimilate it and subject the object to his or her own rhythm. In the first place, this is true of the means of production. The more differentiated these means are, the more they are composed of a multitude of specialized parts, the less is the worker able to express his personality through them, and the less visible is his personal contribution to the product. The tools that the artist uses are relatively undifferentiated and thus afford the personality the widest scope for releasing all its capacities. They do not confront the artist as does the industrial machine, whose specialized complexity itself possesses a form of personal solidity and cohesiveness so that the worker is unable to imbue it with his personality as he can with other less elaborate tools. The tools of the sculptor have not changed for thousands of years in their total lack of specialization. Wherever the artistic tools have changed decisively, as with the piano, its character too has become quite objective. It has become much too autonomous and has set a more rigid limit to the expression of subjectivity than has, for instance, the violin, which is technically much less differentiated. The automatic character of modern machinery is the result of a highly advanced breakdown and specialization of materials and energies, akin to the character of a highly developed state administration which can evolve only on the basis of an elaborate division of labour among its functionaries. In that the machine becomes a totality and carries out a growing proportion of the work itself, it confronts the worker as an autonomous power, just as he too is no longer an individual personality but merely someone who carries out an objectively prescribed task. One has only to compare the worker in a shoe factory with the craft shoemaker in order to see to what extent the specialization of tools paralyses the effectiveness of personal qualities, whether superior or inferior, and allows both object and subject to develop as basically independent entities. Whereas the undifferentiated tool is merely a prolongation of the arm, the specialized tool is elevated to the pure category of an object. This process also operates in a very typical and obvious manner with reference to military equipment; its pinnacle is the most specialized and most perfect piece of machinery – the warship. With the warship, the process of objectification has advanced to such a degree that in a modern naval war almost the only decisive factor is the mere relative number of ships of equal quality!

The process of objectification of culture that, based on specialization, brings about a growing estrangement between the subject and its products ultimately invades even the more intimate aspects of our daily life. During the first decades of the nineteenth century, furniture and the objects that surrounded us for use and pleasure were of relative simplicity and durability and were in accord with the needs of the lower as well as of the upper strata. This resulted in people's attachment as they grew up to the objects of their surroundings, an attachment that already appears to the younger generation today as an eccentricity on the part of their grandparents. The differentiation of objects has broken down this situation in three different respects, with the same result in each case. First, the sheer quantity of very specifically formed objects makes a close and, as it were, personal relationship to each of them more difficult: a few and simple utensils are more easily assimilated by the individual, while an abundance of different kinds almost form an antagonistic object to the individual self. This is expressed both in the housewife's complaint that the care of the household becomes a ceremonial fetishism and in the occasional hatred on the part of persons of a more serious disposition of the innumerable articles with which we encumber our lives. The former case is very typical of our culture because the caring and sustaining activity of the housewife was formerly more extensive and strenuous than it is today. But a sense of dependence upon the objects never developed because the work was more closely united with the personality. A woman could express her individuality more easily with the few undifferentiated objects than she could when confronted with the independence of a host of specialized objects. We experience their independence as an antagonistic force only when we are at their service. Just as freedom is not something negative but rather is the positive extension of the self into the objects that yield to it, so, conversely, our freedom is crippled if we deal with objects that our ego cannot assimilate. The sense of being oppressed by the externalities of modern life is not only the consequence but also the cause of the fact that they confront us as autonomous objects. What is distressing is that we are basically indifferent to those numerous objects that swarm around us, and this is for reasons specific to a money economy: their impersonal origin and easy replaceability. The fact that large industrial concerns are the breeding ground for socialist ideas is due not only to the social conditions of their workers, but also to the objective quality of their products. Modern man is so surrounded by nothing but impersonal objects that he becomes more and more conditioned into accepting the idea of an anti-individualistic social order – though, of course, he may also oppose it. Cultural objects increasingly evolve into an interconnected enclosed world that has increasingly fewer points at which the subjective soul can interpose its will and feelings. And this trend is supported by a certain autonomous mobility on the part of the objects. It has been pointed out that the merchant, the craftsman and the scholar are today much less mobile than they were at the time of the Reformation. Both material and intellectual objects today move independently, without personal representatives or transport. Objects and people have become separated from one another. Thought, work effort and skill, through their growing embodiment in objective forms, books and commodities, are able to move independently; recent progress in the means of transportation is only the realization or expression of this. By their independent, impersonal mobility, objects complete the final stage of their separation from people. The slot machine is the ultimate example of the mechanical character of the modern economy, since by means of the vending machine the human relationship is completely eliminated even in the retail trade where, for so long, the exchange of commodities was carried out between one person and another. The money equivalent is now exchanged against the commodity by a mechanical device. At another level, the same principle is also at work in the five cents store and in similar stores where the psycho-economic process runs not from the commodity to the price, but from the price to the commodity. The *a priori* equivalence of prices for all commodities will eliminate the numerous deliberations and examinations of the buyer, the numerous efforts and elucidations of the seller, so that the economic transaction will very quickly and indifferently pass through its personal channels.

This concurrent differentiation has the same effect as consecutive differentiation. Changes in fashion disrupt that inner process of acquisition and assimilation between subject and object which usually does not tolerate a discrepancy between the two. Fashion is one of those social forms which combines, to a particular degree, the attraction of differentiation and change with that of similarity and conformity. Every fashion is essentially the fashion of a social class; that is, it always indicates a social stratum which uses similarity of appearance to assert both its own inner unity and its outward differentiation from other social strata. As soon as the lower strata attempt to imitate the upper strata and adopt their fashion, the latter create a new one. Wherever fashions have existed they have sought to express social differences. Yet the social changes of the last hundred years have accelerated the pace of changes in fashion, on the one hand through the weakening of class barriers and frequent upward social mobility of individuals and sometimes even of whole groups to a higher stratum, and on the other through the predominance of the third estate. The first factor makes very frequent changes of fashion necessary on the part of leading strata because imitation by the lower strata rapidly robs fashions of their meaning and attraction. The second factor comes into operation because the middle class and the urban population are, in contrast to the conservatism of the highest strata and the peasantry, the groups in which there is great variability. Insecure classes and individuals, pressing for change, find in fashion, in the changing and contrasting forms of life, a pace that mirrors their own psychological movements. If contemporary fashions are much less extravagant and expensive and of much shorter duration than those of earlier centuries, then this is due partly to the fact that it must be made much easier for the lower strata to emulate these fashions and partly because fashion now originates in the wealthy middle class. Consequently, the spreading of fashion, both in breadth as well as speed, appears to be an independent movement, an objective and autonomous force which follows its own course independently of the individual. As long as fashions, and we are talking here not only of dress fashions, lasted longer and held relatively restricted social circles together, it was possible for a personal relationship to exist, as it were, between the individual and the particular content of the fashion. But the speed of change, that is its consecutive differentiation, and the growing extension of fashion dissolve this connection. What has happened to some other social shibboleths in recent times has also happened to fashion: it becomes less dependent upon the individual and the individual becomes less dependent upon fashion. Both develop like separate evolutionary worlds.

The concurrent and consecutive differentiation of omnipresent aspects of culture helps to establish their independent objectivity. I wish now to elaborate on one of the factors that brings about this development. I refer to the multitude of styles that confronts us when we view the objects that surround us, from the construction of buildings to the format of books, from sculptures to gardens and furniture with their juxtaposition of Renaissance and Japanese styles, Baroque and Empire, the style of the Pre-Raphaelites and realistic functionalism. This is the result of the enlargement of our historical knowledge, which in turn is associated with modern man's penchant for change mentioned earlier. All historical understanding requires a flexibility of the mind, a capacity to empathize with and reconstruct casts of mind altogether different from one's own. For all history, however much it may deal with the visible, has meaning and becomes intelligible only as the history of the basic interests, emotions and strivings that lie at its roots. Even historical materialism is nothing but a psychological hypothesis. In order to grasp the content of history, a plasticity and pliability of the perceiving mind, a sublimated liking for change is necessary. The historicizing preference of our century, its unique ability to reproduce and bring back to life the most remote entities, both in time as well as in space, is only the internal aspect of the general development of its adaptability and its wide-ranging mobility. This is the root of the bewildering plurality of styles that are absorbed, presented and appreciated by our culture. If every style is like a language unto itself, with specific sounds, inflexions and syntax for expressing life, then as long as we know only a single style that forms our environment we are not aware of style as an autonomous factor with an independent life. No one speaking his mother tongue naively senses the objective law-like regularities that he has to consult, like something outside of his own subjectivity, in order to borrow from them resources for expressing his feelings – resources that obey independent norms. Rather, what one wants to express and what one expresses are, in this case, one and the same, and we experience not only our mother tongue but language as such as an independent entity only if we come to know foreign languages. In the same way, people who know only one uniform style which permeates their whole life will perceive this style as being identical with its *contents*. Since everything they create or contemplate is naturally expressed in this style, there are no psychological grounds for distinguishing it from the material of the formative and contemplative process or for contrasting the style as a form independent of the self. Only where a variety of given styles exists will one detach itself from its content so that its independence and specific significance gives us the freedom to choose between the one or the other. Through the differentiation of styles each individual style, and thus style in general, becomes something objective whose validity is independent of human subjects and their interests, activities, approval or disapproval. The fact that the entire visible environment of our cultural life has disintegrated into a plurality of styles dissolves that original relationship to style where subject and object are not yet separated. Instead, we are confronted with a world of expressive possibilities each developed according to their own norms, with a host of forms within which to express life as a whole. Thus these forms on the one side, and our subjectivity on the other, are like two parties between whom a purely fortuitous relationship of contacts, harmonies and disharmonies prevails.

Broadly speaking, this is the orbit in which the major process of objectification of modern culture is carried out through the division of labour and specialization in both its personal and objective sense. The total picture is composed of all these phenomena, in which the cultural content becomes an increasingly conscious *objective mind* in relation not only to recipients but also to producers. To the extent to which this objectification increases, the strange phenomenon from which we started our investigation becomes more comprehensible, namely that the cultural growth of the individual can lag considerably behind the cultural growth of tangible as well as functional and intellectual objects.

The occasional greater weight of subjective culture

The fact that the opposite occasionally occurs demonstrates that both forms of the mind have become mutually independent. The following phenomenon illustrates this in a somewhat disguised and modified manner. The peasant economy in north Germany seems to be able to survive only if one kind of hereditary succession to an undivided estate prevails, whereby one of the heirs succeeds to the estate and the other heirs are compensated by an amount that is smaller than the corresponding market value. If the property were to be appraised according to its market value – which is at present much higher than its value based on returns – then it would be burdened with mortgages to such an extent that only a much reduced and impoverished enterprise would be possible. Yet the modern individualistic sense of justice requires such a mechanical equality of rights in terms of money for all heirs and does not give to one single offspring any benefit even though this is the pre-condition for an objectively viable enterprise. This procedure has undoubtedly often improved the cultural standards of particular individuals at the price of leaving behind the objective culture. Such a discrepancy is distinctly discernible in actual social institutions whose evolution takes place at a more sluggish and conservative pace than does that of individuals. This is the case, for instance, where the relations of production, after having existed for a definite period, are outstripped by the forces of production which they themselves have developed, so that these forces are no longer permitted an adequate expression and utilization. These productive forces are to a large extent personal in nature: people's abilities and justified ambitions can no longer find a place in the objective forms of the enterprise. The necessary transformation occurs only when the pressing factors have become overwhelming. Up to that point, the objective organization of production lags behind the growth of individual economic energies. Many reasons for the women's movement may be explained by this process. The advances of modern industrial technology have transferred an extraordinarily large number of economic household activities previously incumbent upon women to outside the home, where they can be produced more cheaply and more expediently. Consequently, many middle-class women have thus lost the core of their activity without having it replaced by other activities and goals. The frequent 'dissatisfaction' of modern women, the waste of their energies, which may bring about all kinds of disturbances and destruction; their partly sound, partly abnormal search to prove their worth outside the home, is all the result of the fact that technology with its objectivity has progressed more independently and more quickly than have the possibilities for human development. The widespread unsatisfactory character of modern marriages may be traced back to similar circumstances. The fixed forms and habits of married life that are imposed upon individuals run counter to the personal development of the partners, particularly to that of the wife, who may have completely outgrown them. Individuals are now said to be inclined towards a freedom, a mutual understanding, an equality of rights and training, for which traditional married life does not provide any scope. One might say that the objective spirit of marriage lags behind its subjective spiritual development. The same is true of jurisprudence: developed logically on the basis of certain fundamental facts, laid down in a code of definite laws and represented by a particular stratum, it acquires a rigidity towards the changing conditions and needs of life which is passed on like an eternal illness, in which reason becomes nonsense and a blessing becomes a curse. As soon as the religious impulses have crystallized around a wealth of specific dogmas and these are represented, through the division of labour, by a corporate entity that is reserved for the faithful, religion meets the same fate. If one bears in mind this relatively independent life with which objective cultural forms, the result of elementary historical dynamics, confront human subjects, then the question of progress in history loses much of its perplexity. If every interpretation may be proved and disproved with equal plausibility, the fault may often lie with the fact that they do not centre around the same object. For instance, one may assert with equal justification the progress or the unchangeability of the moral order, depending upon whether one

464

focuses upon the stabilized principles, the organization and the imperatives that have been absorbed in the community's consciousness, or upon the relationship of the individual person to these objective ideals, to the adequacy or inadequacy of the moral behaviour of individuals. Progress and stagnation may exist side by side, not only in different spheres of historical life but in one and the same sphere, depending upon whether the evolution of individuals or institutions is focused upon; for the institutions, although they have grown out of contributions of individuals, have acquired an independent objective spiritual life of their own.

After establishing the possibility that the evolution of the objective mind may outpace the subjective mind but that the reverse of this may also occur, I wish to return now to the significance of the division of labour for the realization of the former case. Stated briefly, the twofold possibility arises in the following manner. The fact that the objectified mind, incorporated in all kinds of production, is superior to the single individual is due to the complexities of the mode of production which presupposes an extremely large number of historical and material factors, forerunners and collaborators. As a result, the product may contain energies, qualities and additional potentialities that lie quite outside the grasp of the individual producer. This is particularly common in specifically modern technology as a result of the division of labour. As long as the product was manufactured by a single producer or by a relatively unspecialized form of co-operation, the content of mind and power objectified in the product could not greatly exceed those of the individuals involved. Only a sophisticated division of labour imbues the individual product with energies derived from a very large number of individuals, so that the product, viewed as a unity and compared with single individuals, is bound to be superior in many different respects. This accumulation of quality and excellence in the object that forms their synthesis is unlimited, whereas the growth of individuals in any period of time and by their very nature has quite definite natural limits. Yet although the fact that the objective product absorbs many qualities of a number of persons and provides supreme possibilities for development, it none the less forfeits that perfection which can only be the result of the synthesis of energies of a *single* human subject. The State, especially the modern State, is the clearest illustration of this. When rationalism denounces as logically contradictory the situation in which the monarch, who is after all only a single individual, rules over an extremely large number of other people, this criticism overlooks the fact that the people, to the extent that they constitute this monarchic State, are not 'human beings' in the same sense as the monarch. They participate in the State only with a small fraction of their existence and their energies; the remainder extends to other groups and the whole of their personality is in no way incorporated in any one of them. But the monarch does identify himself with the State and engages himself in it more than any of his subjects. As long as the régime is an absolute one, in the sense that the ruler has unlimited power of disposal over his subjects, this discrepancy will exist. In contrast, the modern constitutional State delineates precisely the area in which people are committed to the State; the State differentiates people in order to constitute itself by certain selected elements. The greater this differentiation is, the more distinctly does the State as an objective institution – whose form contradicts personal individuality – differ from the individual. The State thus becomes a synthesis of the differentiated elements of its subjects, an entity that obviously stands both below and above the individual person. The same is true of all institutions of the objective mind that are based on the combination of differentiated individual efforts. For however much they may surpass the individual intellect in objective intellectual content and evolutionary potential, we none the less conceive of them in the same way as we do a mere inanimate and soulless mechanism to the extent that differentiation and the number of co-operating factors increase. The difference between mind and soul comes to the fore here. Mind is the objective content of what the soul becomes aware of as a living function. The soul is, as it were, the form that the mind, that is the logical–conceptual content of thought, assumes for our subjectivity, as our subjectivity. The mind in this sense, therefore, is not tied to the formation of a unity without which no soul exists. It is as if the mental contents are somehow dispersed in their existence and only the soul assembles them as a unity, almost as inorganic matter is incorporated into an organism and the unity of its life. Herein lies the greatness as well as the limitation of the soul in relation to the individual contents of consciousness when looked at in terms of their independent validity and objective significance. Plato depicted the realm of ideas in glowing perfection and complete self-contentedness. These ideas are nothing other than the objective contents of thought detached from all the arbitrariness of their actual representation, and so the soul of man with its pale, vague and chimerical reflection of things of true significance appeared to him imperfect, conditioned and obscure. Yet for us such graphic clarity and logical determination of form are not the only evaluative standards for ideals and realities. For us personal unity, towards which the consciousness of the objective intellectual meaning of things also leads, is of supreme value. Only here does that friction that is life and strength develop; only here do those mysterious strands of warmth of feeling develop that have no place and no sympathy in the clear perfection of purely objectively determined ideas. The same is true of the mind which, as the objectification of our intelligence, is juxtaposed to our soul as an object. Certainly, distance between both increases to the extent that the object is the result of the co-operative division of labour of a growing number of people; for it becomes increasingly impossible to incorporate the total personality, which is part of the value, the life-blood and the distinctiveness of the soul, into the product. Because of modern differentiation, and closely connected with this the mechanical nature of our cultural products, the objective mind lacks this spirituality. This may be the ultimate reason for the present-day animosity of highly individualistic and sensitive people to the 'progress of culture'. Certainly, the more objective culture, determined by the development of the division of labour, is a part or consequence of the general phenomenon, the more it is true that, in our present epoch, important things are carried out not by individuals but by the masses. The division of labour actually produces a situation in which even the individual object is a product of the mass. The breakdown of individuals into their particular energies which is determined by our organization of the labour process, and the re-integration of what has been differentiated into an objective cultural product, results in the object being deprived of a soul, the more people participate in its manufacture. The splendour and greatness of modern culture possesses some analogy with Plato's radiant realm of ideas in which the objective spirit of things exists in unblemished perfection, but yet lacks the values of the particular personality that cannot be dissolved into objectivities. This is a deficiency that persists despite any amount of awareness of the fragmentary, irrational and ephemeral character of these values. Indeed, personal spirituality possesses a value as mere form that asserts itself despite all the mediocrity and counter-idealism of its content. It retains its particular significance for our existence and, in contrast to all its objective aspects, even for those instances from which we commenced, where individual subjective culture declines while objective culture progresses.

The relationship between objectified mind and its evolution to the subjective mind is of extreme importance to every cultural community and especially with reference to its style of life. For if the importance of style lies in its ability to express any number and variety of contents in related forms, then the relationship between objective and subjective mind with reference to quantity, size and pace of development can be the same, even for quite different *contents* of the cultural mind. The general way of living, the framework that the social culture offers to individual impulses, is circumscribed by the following questions: is the inner life of the individual close to or estranged from the objective cultural evolution of his age? Does the individual experience this evolution, of which he has only a marginal comprehension, as superior, or does he consider his personal value to be higher than that of all reified mind? Are the objective, historically given elements an autonomous power within his own mental life, so that they and the specific core of his personality develop independently of each other? Is the soul, so to speak, master in its own house, or is there at least a harmony with regard to standards, meaning and rhythm established between its innermost life and what it has to absorb into that life as impersonal contents? These abstract formulations indicate the outline of innumerable concrete daily and life-long interests and moods, and in so doing also denote the extent to which the relationships between objective and subjective culture determine the style of life.

The relation of money to the agents of these opposing tendencies

If the present form of this relationship is sustained by the division of labour, then it is also an offshoot of the money economy; first, because the splitting up of the productive process into a large number of partial operations requires an organization that functions with absolute precision and reliability which, since the end of slave labour, has only been possible if workers are paid in money. Any other mediated relationship between employer and worker would entail incalculable elements, partly because payment in kind cannot be so easily provided and determined and partly because only the pure money relationship possesses the exclusively objective, automatic character that is the prerequisite for highly specialized and complex organizations; second, because the essential reason for the emergence of money becomes more and more pressing as production becomes more specialized. For it is the essence of economic transactions that one person gives up what another person desires, provided this other person acts in the same manner. The moral rule that one should do unto others as one would have done unto oneself finds the clearest example of its formal realization in the economy. If, for instance, a producer finds a purchaser for the object A which he wishes to exchange, then it is often the case that object B, which the purchaser wishes to offer in return, is not what the producer desires. That such a difference in the demand of two persons does not always coincide with the difference in the products they have to offer requires, as is well known, the intervention of a means of exchange. Thus, if the owners of A and B are unable to agree on a direct exchange, one can exchange A for money with which he can obtain the C that he desires, and the owner of B can procure the money to buy A by means of a similar transaction with a third party. Since money is required because of the *diversity* of products, or of demand for products, its role becomes obviously greater and more indispensable the greater the variety of objects that are included in the transaction. Or, conversely, a considerable specification of operations can evolve only if direct exchange is no longer necessary. The chance that the buyer of a product has to offer an object that is equally desired by the producer declines as the specialization of products and of human wants increases. So far there is nothing new about the way in which modern differentiation is connected with the predominance of money. Rather, the interrelationship between both cultural values is to be found at their very roots; and the fact that the interactions between the conditions of specialization and the money economy form a historical entity is only the gradual intensification of a synthesis that is inherent to both of them.

By means of this connection, the style of life too, in so far as it is dependent on the relationship between objective and subjective culture, is tied up with money transactions. The nature of this relationship is clearly revealed by the fact that money transactions represent the preponderance of objective over subjective mind, as well as the reverse, independent enhancement and autonomous development of the subjective mind. The superior power of the culture of objects over the culture of individuals is the result of the unity and autonomous self-sufficiency that the objective culture has accomplished in modern times. Production, with its technology and its achievements, seems to be a cosmos with definite and, as it were, logical determinations and developments which confront the individual in the same way as fate confronts the instability and irregularity of our will. This formal autonomy, this inner compulsion, which unifies cultural contents into a mirror-image of the natural context, can be realized only through money. On the one hand, money functions as the system of articulations in this organism, enabling its elements to be shifted, establishing a relationship of mutual dependence of the elements, and transmitting all impulses through the system. On the other hand, money can be compared to the bloodstream whose continuous circulation permeates all the intricacies of the body's organs and unifies their functions by feeding them all to an equal extent. Thus money, as an intermediate link between man and thing, enables man to have, as it were, an abstract existence, a freedom from direct concern with things and from a direct relationship to them, without which our inner nature would not have the same chances of development. If modern man can, under favourable circumstances, secure an island of subjectivity, a secret, closed-off sphere of privacy – not in the social but in a deeper metaphysical sense – for his most personal existence, which to some extent compensates for the religious style of life of former times, then this is due to the fact that money relieves us to an ever-increasing extent of direct contact with things, while at the same time making it infinitely easier for us to dominate them and select from them what we require.

These counter-tendencies, once started, may press forward to an ideal of completely pure separation in which all the material contents of life become increasingly objective and impersonal, so that the remainder that cannot be reified becomes all the more personal, all the more the indisputable property of the self. A typical individual instance of this trend is the typewriter. Writing, an external concrete activity but one that still has a typically individual form, can now abandon this form in favour of mechanical uniformity. On the other hand, this has a dual advantage: first, the written page now conveys only its pure content without any support or disturbance from its written form, and second, it avoids revealing the most personal element which is so often true of handwriting, in superficial and unimportant as well as in the most intimate communications. No matter how socialistic all such mechanical contrivances may be, the remaining private property of the intellectual self becomes all the more jealously guarded. Clearly the expulsion of subjective spirituality from everything external is as hostile to the aesthetic ideal of life as it may be favourable to pure introspectiveness. Such a combination may explain why it is that aesthetically minded people despair of the world today as well as why a slight tension develops in subterranean forms – quite unlike those in the age of Savonarola – between these people and those who are concerned only with inner salvation. In so far as money is the symbol as well as the cause of making every-thing indifferent and of the externalization of everything that lends itself to such a process, it also becomes the gatekeeper of the most intimate sphere, which can then develop within its own limits.

Whether this will lead to personal refinement, distinctiveness and intro-spection or whether, on the contrary, the subjugated objects, in view of the ease with which they may be acquired, will gain control over men, depends no longer upon money but upon man himself. Here again the money economy reveals its formal affinity to a socialist society. For what is expected of socialism – release from the individual struggle for survival, secure access to life's necessities and access to the higher economic values – would probably exercise the same differ-entiating effect, such that a certain sector of society might rise to unprecedented heights of spirituality far removed from earthly concerns, while another sector might plunge into a correspondingly unprecedented practical materialism.

Money, by and large, is most influential in those parts of our life whose style is determined by the preponderance of objective over subjective culture. That it may also support its converse places the nature and extent of its historical power in the clearest light. In some respects, money may be compared to language, which also lends itself to the most divergent directions of thought and feeling. Money belongs to those forces whose peculiarity lies in a lack of peculiarity, but which, none the less, may colour life very differently because their mere formal, functional and quantitative nature is confronted with qualita-tively determined contents and directions of life, and induces them to generate qualitatively new formations. The significance of money for the style of life is not negated but enhanced, not refuted but demonstrated by the fact that it favours *both* possible relations between the objective and the subjective mind.

III

Alterations in the distance between the self and objects as the manifestation of varying styles of life

We rarely realize to what extent our notions of spiritual processes possess a merely symbolic importance. The basic needs of life have forced us to consider the tangible external world as the first object of our attention. The concepts by which we conceive of an existence perceived outside the observer are therefore valid primarily for *its* contents and conditions; it is the class of objects in general, and every perception that is to become an object for us has to adjust to its forms. This demand refers to the mind itself which becomes the object of its own observation. First of all, however, the observation of the 'You' suggests itself as certainly being the most imperative prerequisite for communal life and individual self-assertion. But since we are never able to directly observe the other person's soul, and since all our perceptions are never anything more than our sense impressions, all psychological knowledge is nothing but an interpretation of the processes of consciousness that we perceive in our own mind. We transfer such an interpretation to the other person when confronted by physical impressions of them, even though this transference, focused as it is exclusively on its goal, is unaware of its point of origin. When the mind becomes an object of its own understanding, then this is possible only through images of spatial processes. When we speak of impressions and their relationships, of their elevation into consciousness and their sinking below the threshold of consciousness, of inner propensities and inhibitions, of mood with its elations and depressions, each of these expressions, and countless more, is clearly taken from observations of the external world. We may be quite sure that the laws that govern the life of our mind are of a totally different nature to those that govern an external mechanism, primarily because our mind lacks the clear circumscription and secure recognizability of its individual elements. Yet we unfailingly apprehend these 'conceptions' as a kind of essence that enters into the mechanical relationships of connecting and separating, or rising and falling. We are thus convinced, and experience confirms it, that this interpretation of the mind according to visible processes represents the inner reality of the mind, just as, for the astronomer, the movement of the stars is so successfully represented by his written computations that their outcome represents the picture that is verified by the outcome of the real forces.

This relationship is also valid in the opposite direction, namely in the interpretation of external events according to the contents of our inner life. I do not mean to say that the former is nothing but a world of notions, but that, once a relatively external phenomenon confronts a relatively internal one on some kind of epistemological basis, the specific internal phenomena serve to form the external phenomena into a comprehensible image. Thus it is that the object as a whole is realized by the sum of its qualities that it presents to us only by our lending it the unified form of our ego. In so doing, we basically experience how a wealth of determinations and fates may be attached to a fixed entity. The same may be true, as has often been suggested, of energy and the causality of external objects: we project the feelings of physio-psychic tension, impulses, wilful action, on to the objects, and if we place these interpretative categories behind their immediate perceptibility, then we orientate ourselves towards them according to the emotional experiences of our inner nature. Perhaps this is how one comes across the opposite interrelationship as soon as one hits the substantiality of a deeper stratum below that primary symbolization of the inner life. If we characterize a mental experience as an association of conceptions, then this knowledge is achieved according to spatial categories. Yet perhaps this category of association itself gains its meaning and significance in a merely internal and in no way visible process. What we characterize as association in the external world, that is as entities somehow unified and existing in each other, actually always remain adjacent to each other, and in referring to this association we *mean* something that we can project only from within ourselves into the object, something that is incomparable to everything external, namely the symbol for what we are unable to state and what cannot immediately be expressed. Thus there exists a relativism, an unending process between internal and external life: the one as the symbol of the other, making it conceivable and representable, being neither the first nor the second, but realizing the unity of their – that is, our – being by their mutual dependency.

The mental and physical aspects of existence are all the more open to this mutual symbolizing interpretation the simpler they are. In the simple processes of association, fusion and reproduction of notions we can adhere to the idea of a general lawfulness of form that calls for an analogous response from both the inner and the outer world and thus makes the one the suitable representative of the other. Characterization in terms of analogies of spatial vividness becomes more difficult for more complicated and distinctive mental forms. It becomes more dependent upon its applicability to a large number of instances, in order not to appear arbitrary and playful and in order to possess a secure, though only symbolic, relationship to psychological reality. Starting out from itself, this psychological reality will find the comprehension of things, the interpretation of their own meaning and significance, all the more difficult and uncertain the more specialized or complex are the processes on both sides. For the mysterious identity of form in internal and external phenomena, which provides a bridge from the one to the other, becomes less probable and more difficult to conceive. This is intended as an introduction to considerations that should encompass a series of various internal cultural phenomena and thereby make it clear that they all belong to one and the same style of life, because they all allow for an interpretation according to one and the same illustrative analogy.

One of the most frequent images that is used to illustrate the organization of life's elements is their arrangement in a circle with the individual at its centre. There is a type of relationship between this self and objects, people, ideas and interests that we can characterize only as *distance* between the two. Whatever our object may be, it can, with its content remaining unchanged, move closer to the centre or to the periphery of our sphere of interests and concerns. But this does not bring about a change in our inner relationship to this object; on the contrary, we can *characterize* certain relationships between the self and its contents only by the illustrative symbol of a definite or changing distance between the two. From the very outset, a symbolic expression for a verbally inexpressible state of affairs is created when we divide our inner existence into a central self and a surrounding array of contents. In view of the tremendous differences in sensory–external impressions of things according to their distance from our sensory organs – differences not only in distinctness, but also in the quality and whole character of the images received – an extension of this symbolization suggests itself whereby the diversity of the innermost relationship to objects is interpreted as a diversity in our distance from them.

From among the phenomena that, from this standpoint, form a unified series, I first wish to emphasize that of art. The inner significance of artistic styles can be interpreted as a result of the differences in distance that they produce between ourselves and objects. All art changes the field of vision in which we originally and naturally place ourselves in relation to reality. On the one hand, art brings us closer to reality; it places us in a more immediate relationship to its distinctive and innermost meaning; behind the cold strangeness of the external world it reveals to us the spirituality of existence through which it is related and made intelligible to us. In addition, however, all art brings about a distancing from the immediacy of things; it allows the concreteness of stimuli to recede and stretches a veil between us and them just like the fine bluish haze that envelops distant mountains. There are equally strong attractions on both sides of this duality of effects. The tension between them, their distribution over the wide variety of demands upon the work of art, gives a specific character to each artistic style. Indeed, the mere existence of style is in itself one of the most significant instances of distancing. Style, as the manifestation of our inner feelings, indicates that these feelings no longer immediately gush out but take on a disguise the moment they are revealed. Style, as the general form of the particular, is a veil that imposes a barrier and a distance in relation to the recipient of the expression of these feelings. Even naturalism which specifically aims at overcoming the distance between us and reality, conforms to this basic principle of all art: to bring us closer to things by placing them at a distance from us. For only by self-deception do we fail to recognize that naturalism is also a style, that is, that it too organizes and remodels the immediacy of impressions on the basis of quite definite presuppositions and demands. This is irrefutably demonstrated by the course of art history in which everything that one era considers to be a faithful and true picture of reality is recognized by a later period to be highly prejudiced and falsified, whereas this later period now claims to present things as they *really* are. Artistic realism makes the same mistake as scientific realism by assuming that it can dispense with an *a priori*, with a form that – springing from the inclinations and needs of our nature – provides a robe or a metamorphosis for the world of our senses. This transformation that reality suffers on its way to our consciousness is certainly a barrier between us and its immediate existence, but is at the same time the precondition for our perception and representation of it. Indeed, in a certain sense naturalism may bring about a quite distinctive distancing from things if we observe its preference for the objects of everyday life, for the trite and the banal. For since naturalism is undoubtedly a stylization too, this style is more appreciated by a refined artistic sense – which sees art as lying in the work of art and not, by whatever method it may be represented, in its object – if it is executed on some immediate, raw, earthly material.

Modern tendencies towards the increase and diminution of this distance

On the whole, the aesthetic interest of recent times has tended towards an increase in the distance produced by transposing objects into art. I have in mind the tremendous attraction that artistic styles far removed both in time and space have for the artistic sense of our time. Many lively, stimulating notions are aroused by what is far away and this satisfies our many-sided need for stimulation, although, because of the absence of any relationship to our most personal and direct interests, all these strange and distant notions have a faint ring about them and are therefore more than a comforting stimulation for weakened nerves. What we today call the 'historical spirit' perhaps not only is a favourable condition for this phenomenon, but also has the same origin. Through the wealth of inner relationships to spatially and temporally far removed interests, the historical spirit makes us more sensitive towards shocks and confusions that come to us from direct proximity and contact with people and things. The flight from the present is made easier, is less of a loss and is to some extent justified if it leads to the recognition and enjoyment of concrete realities, even though they are far away and can be experienced only very indirectly. Out of this process there springs the present vividly felt charm of the fragment, the mere allusion, the aphorism, the symbol, the undeveloped artistic style. All these forms, familiar to all the arts, place us at a distance from the substance of things; they speak to us 'as from afar'; reality is touched not with direct confidence but with fingertips that are immediately withdrawn. The most extreme refinement of our literary style avoids the direct characterization of objects; it only touches a remote corner of them with the word, and grasps not the things but only the veil that envelops them. This is most clearly demonstrated by the symbolistic tendencies in the fine arts and in literature. Here, the distance that art already places between ourselves and the objects is extended yet a stage further, in that the notions that form the content of the ultimately stimulating psychic experience no longer have a visible counterpart in the work of art itself, but are only provoked by perceptions of quite a different kind. In all this we discover an emotional trait whose pathological deformation is the so-called 'agoraphobia': the fear of coming into too close a contact with objects, a consequence of hyperaesthesia, for which every direct and energetic disturbance causes pain.

The delicacy, spirituality and differentiated sensitivity of so many modern people therefore finds expression in a negative taste; that is, they are easily offended by the unacceptable, they determinedly reject what they find unsympathetic, they often abhor much if not most of what is offered to them as attractions; whereas the positive taste, the energetic affirmation, the cheerful and unreserved acceptance of what they like – in short, the actively appropriating energies – are decidedly lacking.

Yet this inner tendency that the symbol of distance represents extends far beyond the aesthetic realm. Philosophical materialism, for instance, which believed that it could apprehend reality directly, today again gives way to subjectivist or neo-Kantian theories which allow objects to be reflected or distilled by the medium of the mind before they may become cognitions. The subjectivism of modern times has the same basic motive as art: to gain a more intimate and truer relationship to objects by dissociating ourselves from them and retreating into ourselves, or by consciously acknowledging the inevitable distance between ourselves and objects. When confronted with a stronger self-awareness, this subjectivism inevitably leads to an emphasis upon our inner nature, while on the other hand it is associated with a new, deeper and more conscious modesty, a delicate reticence towards expressing the ultimate, or towards giving a naturalistic form to a situation that would constantly reveal its innermost foundation. In other scientific areas, for instance, and with regard to ethical considerations, the trite utility as the evaluative standard of volition recedes still further. Here we can see that this characterization of action only refers to those relationships that are nearest at hand, and that therefore, in order to raise it beyond its mere technique as a means, it has to obtain its specific general instructions from higher and often religious principles that are unrelated to sensual immediacy. Finally, in the case of specialized detailed work, the call for integration and generalization arises from all sides; that is, a call for that distance which commands an overview of all concrete details, for a bird's-eye view in which all the restlessness of the present is transcended and where what was previously only tangible now also becomes intelligible.

Perhaps this tendency would not be so effective and noticeable were it not for the fact that it is accompanied by the opposite trend. One can interpret the intellectual relationship of modern science to the world in two different ways. It is true that the infinite distances between ourselves and objects have been overcome by the microscope and the telescope; but we were first conscious of these distances only at the very same moment in which they were overcome. If one adds to this the fact that every problem solved throws up more than one new one, and that coming closer to things often only shows us how far away they still are from us, then one has to admit that the period in which mythology predominated, in which there was a very general and superficial knowledge of an anthropomorphism of nature, made possible, from a *subjective* standpoint and with reference to sensations and beliefs (however mistaken), a shorter distance between men and objects than exists at present. All those ingenious methods by which we penetrate the internal aspects of nature can only very slowly and in a piecemeal manner replace that intimate familiar closeness that was secured for the mind by the Greek gods, by the interpretation of the world according to human impulses and emotions, by their being linked to a personally efficacious god with a teleological concern for the welfare of man. We could first of all characterize this difference by saying that, the more the distance in the external world is conquered, the more it increases the distance in the spiritual world. The justification for this symbolic expression can again be shown by applying it to a completely different sphere. Modern man's relationship to his environment usually develops in such a way that he becomes more removed from the groups closest to him in order to come closer to those more remote from him. The growing dissolution of family ties; the feeling of unbearable closeness when confined to the most intimate group, in which loyalty is often just as tragic as liberation; the increasing emphasis upon individuality which cuts itself off most sharply from the immediate environment – this whole process of distancing goes hand in hand with the formation of relationships with what is most remote, with being interested in what lies far away, with intellectual affinity with groups whose relationships replace all spatial proximity. The overall picture that this presents surely signifies a growing distance in genuine inner relationships and a declining distance in more external ones. Cultural development brings about the fact that previously unconscious and instinctive accomplishments later occur with clear accountability and fragmented consciousness. On the other hand, what originally required careful attention and conscious effort becomes mechanical routine and instinctive matter-of-factness. Thus, correspondingly, the most remote comes closer at the price of increasing the distance to what was originally nearer.

The part played by money in this dual process

The extent and intensity of the role that money plays in this dual process is first manifested as the *conquest* of distance. It is not necessary to elaborate upon the fact that only the translation of values into the money form makes possible those associations of interests in which the spatial distance of the interested parties is absolutely negligible. To give but one of hundreds of possible examples: only by means of money is it possible for a German capitalist and also a German worker to be actually involved in a ministerial change in Spain, in the profits of African gold mines, and in the outcome of a South American revolution. However, money as the agent of the opposite tendency seems to me to be of greater significance. The loosening of family ties has its origin in the special economic interests of its individual members, which is possible only in a money economy. Above all, it brings about a situation in which the means of livelihood can be based on completely individual talents. For only their equivalent money form makes possible the evaluation of very specialized tasks, and without their conversion into a general value they could hardly arrive at mutual exchange. The money form of equivalents makes individual relations with the outside world and entrance into unfamiliar groups that are interested only in the money value of tasks or the money contributions of their members more easy. The family, whose structure is based on collective ownership, particularly upon land ownership, is the exact opposite. Collective ownership resulted in a solidarity of interests which sociologically represented a continuity in the connections between family members; whereas the money economy makes possible, indeed even enforces, a mutual distancing. Certain other forms of modern existence, aside from those of family life, rest upon the distancing brought about by money transactions. Money transactions erect a barrier between persons, in that only one of the two parties to the transaction receives what he *actually* wants, what corresponds to his specific needs, whereas the other party to the transaction, who only receives money, has to search for a third party to satisfy his needs. The fact that both enter the transaction with a completely different *kind* of interest adds a new element of estrangement to the antagonism that is already brought about by opposing interests. In the same manner, it has already been suggested that money results in a universal objectification of transactions, in an elimination of all personal nuances and tendencies, and, further, that the number of relationships based on money is constantly increasing, that the significance of one person for another can increasingly be traced back, even though often in a concealed form, to monetary interests. In this way, an inner barrier develops between people, a barrier, however, that is indispensable for the modern form of life. For the jostling crowdedness and the motley disorder of metropolitan communication would simply be unbearable without such psychological distance. Since contemporary urban culture, with its commercial, professional and social intercourse, forces us to be physically close to an enormous number of people, sensitive and nervous modern people would sink completely into despair if the objectification of social relationships did not bring with it an inner boundary and reserve. The pecuniary character of relationships, either openly or concealed in a thousand forms, places an invisible functional distance between people that is an inner protection and neutralization against the overcrowded proximity and friction of our cultural life.

The same function that money has for the style of life also penetrates even more deeply into the individual human subject, not as the distancing from other persons but from the material objects of life. The mere fact that wealth today arises out of the means of production instead of out of the means of consumption as in primitive epochs indicates an enormous degree of distancing. Just as an increasing number of stages are introduced into the production of cultural objects themselves – in that the finished product becomes more and more removed from the raw material – so property ownership places the owner technically, and therefore also personally, at a much greater distance from the ultimate goal of all wealth than during the period when wealth merely meant an abundance of immediate possibilities for consumption. The division of labour, conditioned by its interaction with the monetary system, supports similar internal consequences in the sphere of production. The less each individual produces a complete final product, the more his activity appears to be merely a preliminary stage, and the more the source of his activity seems to be removed from the ultimate meaning and purpose of his work. Stated directly: just as money intervenes between person and person, so it intervenes between person and commodity. Since the emergence of a money economy we are no longer directly confronted with the objects of economic transactions. Our interest in them is disrupted through the medium of money, their own objective significance becomes dissociated from our consciousness because it is more or less excluded from its proper position in our constellation of interests by their money value. If we recall how often awareness of purpose is arrested at the level of money, then it becomes clear that money and the enlargement of its role places us at an increasingly greater mental distance from objects. This often occurs in such a way that we lose sight of their qualitative nature so that the inner contact with their whole distinctive existence is disrupted. This is true not only of cultural objects; our whole life also becomes affected by its remoteness from nature, a situation that is reinforced by the money economy and the urban life that is dependent upon it. To be sure, the distinctive aesthetic and romantic experience of nature is perhaps possible only through this process. Whoever lives in direct contact with nature and knows no other form of life may enjoy its charm subjectively, but he lacks that distance from nature that is the basis for aesthetic contemplation and the root of that quiet sorrow, that feeling of yearning estrangement and of a lost paradise that characterizes the romantic response to nature. If modern man finds his highest enjoyment of nature in the snow-bound regions of the Alps or on the shores of the North Sea, then this can hardly be explained solely in terms of the heightened need for excitement. It is also to be explained by the fact that this inaccessible world, which actually rejects us, represents the extreme enhancement and stylization of what nature as a whole still means to us: a spiritual distant image that confronts us even in moments of physical proximity as something internally unattainable, a promise that is never fully kept and an entity that responds to our most passionate devotion with a faint resistance and strangeness. Landscape painting, which as an art depends upon distance from the object and upon a break in our natural unity with it, has only developed in modern times as has the romantic sense of nature. They are the result of that increasing distancing from nature and that particularly abstract existence that urban life, based on the money economy, has forced upon us. This in no way contradicts the fact that it is precisely the possession of money that has allowed us to take flight into nature. For the very fact that nature can only be enjoyed by urban people under these conditions thrusts an entity between them and nature – no matter in how many transformations and mere after-effects – which forms a link between the two at the very same time that it separates them.

Credit

This significance of money is much more evident in its extended form as credit. Credit extends the series of conceptions still further and with a greater awareness of their unrestricted breadth than does the intermediate instance of cash. The pivot of the relationship between creditor and debtor lies, at it were, outside the straight line of contact between them and is set at a farther distance from them: the individual's activity and transactions thereby gain the qualities of far-sightedness and enhanced symbolism. In that the bill of exchange or the concept of money debt in general represents the values of distant objects, they are condensed, as it were, in the bill just as the view over a spatial distance condenses the contents of the view by a perspectival shortening. And just as money places a distance between ourselves and objects, and also brings them closer to us – thereby displaying its specific indifference in these contrasting effects – so too the instrument of credit has a dual relationship to our total assets. On the one hand, it has been pointed out that cheque transactions are a palliative against extravagance; some people are more easily inclined towards unnecessary spending when they have cash in hand than if the money is deposited with a third party and can be used only by drawing a cheque. On the other hand, it seems to me that the temptation to imprudence is particularly strong if one does not have all the disposable money before one's eyes but can dispose of it merely by the stroke of a pen. On the one hand, the form of cheque transactions, through the multiple mechanism that we have set in motion, dissociates us from money, while on the other it makes the transaction easier, not only because of the technical convenience but also psychologically, because money as cash gives us a visual impression of its value and makes it harder for us to part with it.

I wish to cite but one instance of the relevant features of credit transactions which, although not common, is none the less very apposite. A traveller relates that an English businessman once gave this definition: 'The common man is one who buys goods by cash payment; a gentleman is one to whom I give credit and who pays me every six months with a cheque.' It is primarily the basic attitude that is worthy of note here: namely that it is not necessary to be a gentleman in order to obtain credit, but rather that whoever demands credit is a gentleman. That credit transactions seem to reflect *greater distinction* may be traced back to two different sentiments. First, they demand trust. It is the essence of distinction not to demonstrate its views and their value but simply to presuppose adherence to them. Similarly, this is also the reason why the ostentatious display of wealth is a sign of lack of distinction. Certainly, any trust always implies a risk; persons of distinction demand that one takes this risk in doing business with them, the implication being that they do not recognize a risk and are unwilling to pay a premium for it because they consider themselves to be absolutely reliable. This attitude is reflected in Schiller's epigram, that noble characters pay only with what they are and not with what they do. It is understandable that mere payment in ready cash suggests something petty bourgeois to this businessman, since in this instance the stages of the economic series are anxiously compressed, whereas credit creates a distance between them that he controls on the basis of trust. It is a feature of higher stages of development everywhere that the original closeness and immediate unity of the elements is dissolved in order to unite them, as independent and distinct entities, in a new, more abstract and comprehensive synthesis. In credit transactions the immediacy of value exchange is replaced by a distance whose poles are held together by trust in the same way as religiosity is more intense the greater is the distance – in contrast to anthropomorphism and all sensual conceptions – between God and the individual soul in order to call forth the most considerable degree of *belief* so as to bridge the distance between them. The reason why the element of distinction in credit is no longer felt in larger transactions in the business community is because credit has become an impersonal organization and trust has lost its specific personal character – without which the category of distinction cannot be applied. First, credit has become a technical form of transaction either with or without very much reduced psychological overtones. Second, the accumulation of small debts up to the final payment by cheque brings about a certain reserve on the part of the buyer in relation to the trader. The continuous and direct interaction that is common to cash payments is eliminated. Viewed from the outside and, as it were, aesthetically, delivery by the businessman has acquired the form of a tribute, of an offering to the powerful that is accepted, at least in individual cases, without a corresponding return. Since payment at the end of the credit period is made not from person to person but by a cheque, by an order, as it were, to the objective account at the bank, this reserved behaviour persists on the part of the individual. Thus, from all sides the distance that is the basis of the concept of the 'gentleman' and the appropriate expression for this kind of transaction is accentuated between the 'gentleman' and the tradesman.

I will content myself with this singular example of credit's distancing effect on the style of life and only add one of its very general traits that refers back to the significance of money. Modern times, particularly the most recent, are permeated by a feeling of tension, expectation and unreleased intense desires – as if in anticipation of what is essential, of the definitive of the specific meaning and central point of life and things. This is obviously connected with the over-emphasis that the means often gain over the ends of life in mature cultures. Aside from money, militarism is perhaps the most striking example in this respect. The regular army is a mere preparation, a latent energy, a contingency, whose ultimate goal and purpose not only very rarely materializes but is also avoided at all costs. Indeed, the enormous buildup of military forces is praised as the only means of preventing their explosion. With this teleological web we have reached the very pinnacle of the contradiction that lies in the drowning out of the end by the means: the growing significance of the means goes hand in hand with a *corresponding* increase in the rejection and negation of the end. And this factor increasingly permeates the social life of the people; it directly inter-feres with personal, political and economic relationships on a large scale and indirectly gives certain age groups and social circles their distinctive character.

The pre-eminence of technology

The tendency towards making final ends illusory appears less crass, but more dangerous and insidious, in the advances and evaluation of technology. If the relationship of technological achievements to the meaning of life is, at best, that of a means or an instrument or very often no relationship at all, then, from among the many causes of the failure to recognize technology's role here, I only wish to mention the splendour that it has autonomously developed. It is one of the most common and almost unavoidable human traits to confuse the height, magnitude and perfection that has been achieved within the boundaries and internal presuppositions of a particular sphere with the significance of the sphere as a whole. The wealth and perfection of individual parts, the degree to which the sphere approximates to its own immanent ideals, is all too easily interpreted as a value and dignity in itself, and in its relationship to other elements of life. The realization that something might be outstanding within its genre and in relation to the demands of its type, while this genre and type is itself evaluated as something minimal and low – this realization presupposes, in each individual case, a very astute mode of thought and a differentiated sense of values. How often do we submit to the temptation to exaggerate the importance of our own achievements by ascribing an extravagant significance to the whole sphere to which they belong, by elevating their relative superiority to that of an absolute! How often does the possession of an exquisite detail of any kind of value – from the objects of the collector's mania to the specialized knowledge of a specific scientific discipline – deceive us into thinking that this particular kind of value is as valuable within the context of all values as the individual piece is in relation to its particular sphere! Basically, this derives from the same old metaphysical mistake: to transfer the attributes that the elements of a whole possess in relation to each other to the whole. It is this mistake through which, for example, the demand for a causal foundation valid for all *parts* of the world and their relationship to one another is also raised with reference to the whole world. It will probably appear most strange to the enthusiasts of modern technology that their attitude is based on the same formal mistake as that of the speculative metaphysician. And yet such is the case: the *relative* height that the technical progress of our time has attained in comparison with earlier circumstances and on the basis of the recognition of certain goals is extended by them to an *absolute* significance of these goals and this progress. It is true that we now have acetylene and electrical light instead of oil lamps; but the enthusiasm for the progress achieved in lighting makes us sometimes forget that the essential thing is not the lighting itself but what becomes more fully visible. People's ecstasy concerning the triumphs of the telegraph and telephone often makes them overlook the fact that what really matters is the value of what one has to say, and that, compared with this, the speed or slowness of the means of communication is often a concern that could attain its present status only by usurpation. The same is true in numerous other areas.

This preponderance of means over ends finds its apotheosis in the fact that the peripheral in life, the things that lie outside its basic essence, have become masters of its centre and even of ourselves. Although it is true to say that we control nature to the extent that we serve it, this is correct in the traditional sense only for the outer forms of life. If we consider the totality of life, then the control of nature by technology is possible only at the price of being enslaved in it and by dispensing with spirituality as the central point of life. The illusions in this sphere are reflected quite clearly in the terminology that is used in it and in which a mode of thinking, proud of its objectivity and freedom from myth, discloses the direct opposite of these features. To state that we conquer or control nature is a very childish formulation since it presupposes some kind of resistance, a teleological element in nature itself, an animosity towards us. Yet nature is merely indifferent and its subjugation does not affect its own regularities. In contrast, all notions of domination and obedience, conquest and subjugation have a proper meaning only if an opposing will has been broken. This is merely the counterpart to the expression that the effectiveness of natural laws exerts an inescapable coercion upon things. In the first place, however, natural laws do not *act* at all since they are only formulae for the activity of specific materials and energies. The naivety of this misunderstanding of natural scientific methods – the assumption that natural laws direct reality as real forces just as a sovereign controls his empire – is on the same level as believing in God's direct control over our earthly life. The alleged *coercion*, the necessity to which natural events are supposed to be subject, is no less misleading. But the human mind feels chained to laws under these categories only because stirrings that seek to lead us in another direction exist. Natural events as such are not subject to the alternatives of freedom and coercion, and the 'must' injects a dualism into the simple existence of things that only makes sense to the conscious mind. Although all this seems to be just a matter of terminology, it does lead astray those who think superficially in the direction of anthropomorphic misinterpretations and it does show that the mythological mode of thought is also at home within the natural scientific world view. This concept of human control over nature supports the self-flattering delusion of our relationship to nature which could be avoided, even on the basis of this comparison. Indeed, the objective picture certainly suggests a growing domination of nature by man; but this does not yet determine whether the subjective reflex, the psychic significance of this historical fact, cannot run in the opposite direction. One should not be misled by the tremendous amount of intelligence that created the theoretical foundations of modern technology and which, indeed, seems to put Plato's dream of making science reign supreme over life into practice. Yet the thread by which technology weaves the energies and materials of nature into our life are just as easily to be seen as fetters that tie us down and make many things indispensable which could and even ought to be dispensed with as far as the essence of life is concerned. It has been asserted with reference to the sphere of production that the machine, which was supposed to relieve man from his slave labour in relation to nature, has itself forced him to become a slave to it. This is even more true of the more sophisticated and comprehensive internal relationships: the statement that we control nature by serving it implies the shocking obverse meaning that we serve it in so far as we dominate it. It is quite erroneous to believe that the significance and intellectual potential of modern life has been transferred from the form of the individual to that of the masses. Rather, it has been transferred to the form of the objects: it lives in the immense abundance, the marvellous expediency and the complicated precision of machines, products and the supra-individual organizations of contemporary culture. Correspondingly, the 'revolt of the slaves' that threatens to dethrone the autocracy and the normative independence of strong individuals is not the revolt of the masses, but the revolt of objects. Just as, on the one hand, we have become slaves of the production process, so, on the other, we have become the slaves of the products. That is, what nature offers us by means of technology is now a mastery over the self-reliance and the spiritual centre of life through endless habits, endless distractions and endless superficial needs. Thus, the domination of the means has taken possession not only of specific ends but of the very centre of ends, of the point at which all purposes converge and from which they originate as final purposes. Man has thereby become estranged from himself; an insuperable barrier of media, technical inventions, abilities and enjoyments has been erected between him and his most distinctive and essential being.

There has never been an age in which such an emphasis on the intermediate aspects of life in contrast to its central and definite purposes was totally alien to that age. Rather, since man's mind is completely focused upon the categories of ends and means, it is his lasting fate to oscillate between the contradictory demands of means and ends. The means always implies the internal difficulty of using a force and awareness that are not really meant for it but for something else. However, the meaning of life does not really lie in realizing the permanent reconciliation of conditions for which it strives. In fact, the vitality of our inner life may indeed depend upon the continuation of that contradiction, and the styles of life probably differ fundamentally in terms of the intensity of this contradiction, the preponderance of the one or the other side and the psychological form of either one. In the case of the present age, in which the preponderance of technology obviously signifies a predominance of clear intelligent consciousness, as a cause as well as an effect, I have emphasized that spirituality and contemplation, stunned by the clamorous splendour of the scientific-technological age, have to suffer for it by a faint sense of tension and vague longing. They feel as if the whole meaning of our existence were so remote that we are unable to locate it and are constantly in danger of moving away from rather than closer to it. Furthermore, it is as if the meaning of life clearly confronted us, as if we would be able to grasp it were it not for the fact that we lack some modest amount of courage, strength and inner security. I believe that this secret restlessness, this helpless urgency that lies below the threshold of consciousness, that drives modern man from socialism to Nietzsche, from Böcklin to impressionism, from Hegel to Schopenhauer and back again, not only originates in the bustle and excitement of modern life, but that, conversely, this phenomenon is frequently the expression, symptom and eruption of this innermost condition. The lack of something definite at the centre of the soul impels us to search for momentary satisfaction in ever-new stimulations, sensations and external activities. Thus it is that we become entangled in the instability and helplessness that manifests itself as the tumult of the metropolis, as the mania for travelling, as the wild pursuit of competition and as the typically modern disloyalty with regard to taste, style, opinions and personal relationships. The significance of money for this kind of life follows quite logically from the premises that all the discussions in this book have identified. It is only necessary to mention here the dual role of money. Money stands in a series with all the means and tools of culture, which slide in front of the inner and final ends and ultimately cover them up and displace them. Money is most important in

illustrating the senselessness and the consequences of the teleological disloca-
tion, partly because of the passion with which it is craved for, and partly
because of its own emptiness and merely transitional character. However, in this
sense, money is only the highest point on the scale of all these phenomena. It
carries out the function of imposing a distance between ourselves and our
purposes in the same manner as other technical mediating elements, but does it
more purely and completely. Here, too, money shows itself to be not an isolated
instance but rather the most perfect expression of tendencies that are also
discernible in a series of lower phenomena. Yet in another respect, money
stands outside this whole series by frequently being the agent that brings about
the transformations in the sequence of purposes. Money interweaves this
sequence as the means of means, as the most general technique of practical life
without which the specific techniques of our culture could not have developed.
Indeed, even in this respect, money exhibits the duality of its functions through
whose unification it repeats the form of the greatest and the deepest potentialities
of life: on the one hand, it is an equal member or even a first among equals *in*
the series of human existence, and, on the other, it stands *above* them as an
integrating force that supports and permeates every single element. In the same
way, religion is a force in life, one interest among others and often opposed to
them. It is one of those factors that are the constituents of life and yet, on the
other hand, it expresses the unity and the basis of our whole existence – on the
one hand it is a link in life's organism, and on the other it stands opposed to that
organism by expressing life through the self-sufficiency of *its* summit and
inwardness.

The rhythm or symmetry of the contents of life

I now move on to a second determinant of the style of life that is characterized,
as is distancing, not by a spatial analogy but by a temporal one. Since time
encompasses internal just as much as external events, so reality is characterized
more directly and with less recourse to symbolism than in the former case. We
are concerned here with the *rhythm*, in which life's contents advance and recede,
with the question as to what extent different cultural epochs themselves favour
or destroy the rhythm of their course, and whether money takes part in this
process not only through its own movements but also through its influence on
the strengthening or weakening of the periodicity of life. All the sequences of
our life are regulated by upward and downward rhythm; the undulation that we
immediately recognize in nature and as the basic form of so many phenomena
also holds sway over the soul. The alternation of day and night which determines
our whole form of life indicates rhythm as a general scheme. We are unable to
pronounce two meaningfully co-ordinated terms without giving a greater
emphasis to the one than to the other: thus, for example, 'truth and poetry' is

something totally different from 'poetry and truth'. And if, out of three elements, the third is co-ordinated to the second, it cannot be completely realized psychologically; but rather the modulating form of the psychic tends to give an accent to the third that is similar to the first. Thus, the metre $-\smile\smile$ cannot be expressed absolutely correctly, but rather the third syllable is inevitably somewhat more accentuated than is the second. The proportioning of sequences of activity, both large and small, into rhythmically repeated periods serves to conserve energy. By means of the change within each period, the physically or psychologically active organs are alternately spared, while at the same time the regularity of the rotation favours an adjustment to the whole complex of movements, whose regularity makes each repetition easier. Rhythm satisfies the basic needs for both diversity and regularity, for change and stability. In that each period is composed of different elements, of elevation and decline, of a quantitative or qualitative variety, the regular repetition produces a reassurance, uniformity and unity in the character of the series. Simplicity or complication of rhythm, the length or brevity of its individual periods, its regularity and its interruptions provide, as it were, the abstract scheme for individual and social, objective and historical life-sequences. Within the cultural development under discussion here we first encounter a series of phenomena that takes a rhythmical course in its earlier stages but a continuous or irregular course in its later stages. Perhaps the most striking of these phenomena is that man, unlike most other animals, for whom periods of sexual excitement and indifference are distinctly separated, no longer has a definite mating period, though primitive peoples still exhibit aspects of this periodicity in their behaviour. The difference in the mating period of animals is basically determined by the fact that birth has to take place during seasons that are the most favourable with regard to feeding and climatic conditions for the raising of the young; indeed, some very primitive Australian aborigines, who possess no domestic animals and are therefore regularly faced with famines, have children only at a definite time of the year. Through his control over food and protection against the weather civilized man has become more independent, so that, with regard to mating, he can follow his individual rather than his general, necessarily rhythmically determined impulses. Hence the above-mentioned variations in sexuality have been transformed into a more or less fluctuating continuum. In any case, it has been established that the still observable periodicity in the maximal and minimal number of births is more marked in agricultural than in industrial areas, in the country than in cities. Furthermore, the child lives in an insurmountable rhythm of sleeping and waking, of activity and relaxation, and something similar may be observed in rural areas. Conversely, the regularity of these needs (and not only their satisfaction!) has long been disrupted for city-dwellers. And if it is true that women represent a less highly differentiated stage of human development and one that is still closer to nature, then the periodicity of their physiological life would serve to confirm this. As long as man is directly dependent upon the harvest or the fruits of hunting and also upon the arrival of the pedlars or periodic fairs, life in many respects has to move in a rhythm of expansion and contraction. For some nomadic tribes who are already more developed than the Australian aborigines – for instance some African peoples – the seasons in which no pasture land is available mean to them an annually recurring period of semi-famine. And even where no specific periodicity exists, the primitive subsistence economy exhibits its essential characteristic with regard to consumption as the direct change from one contrast to another, from want to surplus and from surplus to want. The levelling effect of culture is quite obvious here. It not only ensures that the necessities of life are available throughout the whole year in roughly equal quantity, but also reduces wasteful consumption by means of money. For now a temporary surplus can be transferred into money and its enjoyment can be evenly and continuously distributed over the whole year.

Finally, I wish to mention here – though only as a characteristic symbol of this development and quite independent of the economy – that in music too the rhythmic element is the first distinct and most accentuated element in its primitive stages. A missionary in Ashanti is impressed by the marvellous way in which the musicians keep time despite the chaotic disharmony of the music; Chinese theatre music in California – although an unmelodious noise that grates upon one's ears – is supposed to possess rigid rhythmic measures; a traveller says of the festivals of the Wintun Indians: 'Then come songs in which each Indian expresses his own emotions, and in which, strangely enough, they keep time perfectly.' If we move further down the scale of development we find that certain insects produce a sound that consists of one and the same sharp, rhythmically repeated note in order to enchant the female; in contrast, the more highly developed birds produce love songs whose rhythm is quite subservient to the melody. And at the highest levels of music one notices that the recent trend seems to be to move away completely from the rhythmical, not only in Wagner's music but also in that of certain of his opponents who choose texts that do not lend themselves to rhythm and put the Letter to the Corinthians and Solomon's sermons to music; the acute change from raising to lowering the tone gives way to more balanced or more irregular forms. If we apply this analogy to economic and general cultural life, then it becomes more easily comparable, since it is possible to buy anything at any time for money and so the emotions and stimulations of the individual need no longer to cling to a rhythm that would enforce a periodicity in order to satisfy them. When critics reproach the present economic order for its regular change between overproduction and crises, what they wish to indicate by this is that it is still imperfect and that a continuity of production and consumption ought to be established. At this point I would point to the extension of means of transport which have progressed from the infrequency of the mailcoach to the almost uninterrupted connections between the most important places and to the telegraph and telephone which makes communication possible at any time; the improvement of artificial lighting which increasingly eliminates the difference between day and night and, as a result, the natural rhythm of life; printed literature, which provides us, at any suitable moment and independent of the natural alternation in thought processes between exertion and rest, with thought and stimuli. In short, if culture, as one is accustomed to saying, overcomes not only space but also time, then this means that definite periods of time no longer determine the compelling framework for our activities and enjoyments, but rather they now depend only upon the relationship between the will and our ability and upon the purely objective conditions for carrying them out. Thus, the general conditions of life are freed from rhythm; they are more even and provide individual freedom and possible irregularity. The elements of regularity and diversity that are *united* in rhythm are now separated by means of this differentiation.

It would, however, be quite wrong to reduce the development of the style of life to the temptingly simple formula that it proceeds independently of any framework from the rhythm of its contents to a realization of its content. This is valid only for certain periods of development which require more profound and complex interpretations. Therefore, I first wish to investigate the psychological and historical significance of rhythmics while omitting its purely physiological conditioning which only repeats the fluctuations of external nature.

The sequence and simultaneity of rhythm and symmetry

Rhythm may be defined as symmetry in time, just as symmetry is rhythm in space. If one draws lines to represent rhythmical movement then they become symmetrical; conversely, the study of symmetry implies a rhythmic conception. Both are different forms of the same basic motif. Rhythm is for the ear what symmetry is for the eye at the start of all formations of raw material. In order to imbue things with an idea, a meaning and harmony, one has to form them symmetrically, organize the parts within the whole and order them evenly around a central point. Thus, the creative power of man when confronted with the arbitrariness and chaos of merely natural formations is illustrated in the quickest, most visible and direct manner. Symmetry is the first indication of the power of rationalism to relieve us of the meaninglessness of things and to accept them as they are. Therefore, the languages of primitive people are also often much more symmetrical than those of civilized people, and even the social structure exhibits – for instance, in the 'hundreds', which form the organizational principle of the most diverse primitive peoples – the symmetrical arrangement as a first attempt by the intellect to place the masses in a readily visible and controllable form. The symmetrical structure is completely rational in origin; it facilitates the control of the multitude from one vantage point.

Impulses are transmitted further with less resistance, and are more readily calculable through a symmetrically structured medium than where the inner structure and the boundary of the parts is irregular and fluctuating. If objects and men are brought under the yoke of the system – that is, if they are arranged symmetrically – then they can best be dealt with rationally. For this reason, both despotism and socialism possess particularly strong inclinations towards symmetrical constructions of society. This is true of both of them because they imply a strong centralization of society that requires the reduction of the individuality of its elements and of the irregularity of its forms and relationships to a symmetrical form. To give a practical manifestation of this: Louis XIV is supposed to have endangered his health by having doors and windows arranged symmetrically. Similarly, socialist utopias always construct the local units of their ideal cities or states according to the principle of symmetry: localities and buildings are arranged in the form of either circles or squares. In Campanella's Sun-state, the design of the capital is mathematically measured with compasses, as are the daily arrangements for the citizens and the gradation of their rights and obligations. Rabelais's order of Thelemites, in contrast with More's utopia, displays an absolute individualism – no clocks are allowed in this utopia but rather everything is supposed to happen according to need and occasion. Yet the style of unrestricted calculability and rationalization of life nevertheless tempts him to arrange the buildings of his ideal state in a distinctly symmetrical manner: a gigantic building in the shape of a sextangle, a tower at each corner, sixty steps in diameter. The stonemasons' lodge of the medieval association of builders with its strictly regulated, standardized mode of life and constitution was built in the form of a square. This general trait of socialist projects indicates in a crude form the deep attraction of a notion of the harmonic, stabilized organization of human activity that has overcome the resistance of irrational individuality. The symmetrical–rhythmic formation emerges as the first and simplest structure, through which, as it were, reason stylizes the material of life, and makes it controllable and assimilable. It is the first framework by means of which reason is able to penetrate things. But this also indicates the limits to the meaning and justification of this style of life. It is oppressive in two respects: first, in relation to the human subject whose impulses and needs always arise only in a happy, fortuitous harmony with a fixed scheme rather than in a pre-established harmony; and second, and no less significantly, in relation to external reality whose powers and relationships to us can only be forcibly integrated into such a simple framework. With due regard to the different areas of validity, one might formulate this in terms of an apparent paradox: nature is not as symmetric as the mind would like it to be and the mind is not as symmetric as nature would like it to be. All the acts of violence and inadequacies that a systematic method imposes upon reality are also due to the rhythm and symmetry in the formation of the contents of life. Just as the individual person's assimilation of people and objects by imposing upon them the form and law of his own being testifies to a considerable strength, and just as the more superior person, too, does justice to the uniqueness of objects and shows regard for them in the process of making them subservient to his ends and his power, so it is an eminently human quality to force the theoretical and practical world into a framework that is provided by us. But it is more noble to recognize the specific laws and requirements of things and to integrate them into our existence and activities by following them. For this not only demonstrates the much greater capacity for expansion and malleability of the latter, but it also can make much more creative use of the wealth and possibilities of objects. Thus it is that we observe in some spheres of life that rhythm as the rationalistic–systematic principle appears as the later stage of development, whereas in other spheres this stage is resolved according to circumstances, and the rigidity of the framework is adjusted to the changing requirements of the conditions themselves. For instance, we observe that only at a higher cultural level does the institution of regular meals divide the day rhythmically, whereas a number of regular daily meals is unknown among primitive peoples. On the contrary, we have already mentioned that they often have a regular cycle of periods of privation and times of frivolous jubilation that has been completely abolished by more advanced economic technology. However, this regularity of daily meals achieves its stability at very high levels of development but perhaps not at the highest levels of the social and intellectual scale. It is discontinued by the highest strata of society on account of their professional and social obligations, and complicated considerations of all kinds. The changing requirements of objective circumstances and the mood of the day may also cause the artist and the scholar to do the same. This already indicates how much the rhythm of meal times, and its opposite, corresponds to the rhythm of work. Here too different sequences exhibit quite different relationships. Primitive man works just as irregularly as he eats. Tremendous exertions of energy, brought about by need or whim, are followed by periods of complete laziness which alternate with the former quite fortuitously. It is probably correct to assume that, at least in northern countries, a fixed order of activities, a meaningful rhythm of exertion and relaxation of strength, first commences with ploughing in agriculture. This rhythm reaches its highest degree in more complex factory work and in office work of all kinds. At the peak of cultural activity – in scientific, political, artistic and commercial work – it tends to decrease considerably. For instance, if we learn that a certain writer picks up his pen and puts it down again at the very same minute every day, then we suspect that this stationary rhythm of production lacks inspiration and inner significance. But among wage-earners too this development leads at a later stage to irregularities and unpredictability even though for completely different reasons. With the advent of large-scale industry in Britain, the workers suffered greatly from the fact that any slump in sales disturbed a large enterprise to a far greater extent than it had disturbed the many smaller enterprises previously, because previously the guild would have distributed the losses. Formerly, the craftsman continued to work in bad times in order to accumulate a reserve, but now workers were simply discharged; formerly, the wages were fixed by the authorities, but now every decline in prices led to a reduction in wages. Under these circumstances it is reported that many workers preferred to continue to work under the old system, rather than to work for higher wages at the cost of the greater irregularity of work. Capitalism and the economic individualization that corresponds to it have, at least in part, made work as a whole – and therefore its content too! – much more insecure and have subordinated it to many more fortuitous constellations than existed at the time of the guilds when the greater stability of working conditions imparted a much stricter rhythm to other aspects of life during the day and the year. Recent investigations have shown that, whereas the arrangement of the content of work formerly had a predominantly rhythmic character, particularly in the case of primitive co-operative work, and was accompanied by songs, with the perfection of tools and the individualization of work this rhythmic character was subsequently lost. The modern factory, it is true, still possesses strong rhythmic elements, but, to the extent that they require regularly repeated motions, they possess an altogether different subjective significance than do the earlier work rhythms. Whereas this earlier rhythm corresponded to the inner demands of physiological–psychological energies, the present rhythm is related either directly to the indifferent objective movements of the machine or to the necessity for the individual worker who performs only a small part of the process to keep pace with the other members of the work-group. Perhaps this brings about a deadening of the sense of rhythm as such. The old guild associations struggled, just like modern trade unions, for a reduction in hours of work. But whereas the journeymen's associations accepted a working day from 5 or 6 am to 7 pm, that is for the whole day until bedtime, and as compensation pushed strenuously for one whole day off, trade unions today demand a shorter working day. The period of regular change between work and rest has become shorter for the modern worker. For the earlier workers, the sense of rhythm was enduring enough for them to be satisfied with a weekly period. Today, however, more frequent stimulation is needed – perhaps as a consequence or expression of declining nervous energy – and the alternation between work and rest has to become speeded up in order to produce the subjectively desired effect.

Analogous developments in money

The development of money as an institution follows the same pattern. It exhibits certain rhythmic phenomena as a kind of intermediate stage. From the chaotic fortuitousness that must have characterized its first appearance, money passed through a stage that at least reflects a principle and a meaningful form, until, at a still further stage, money gains a continuity in availability through which it is able to adjust itself to all objective and personal needs, free from the constraint of a rhythmic and, in a deeper sense, still fortuitous framework. For our purposes it is necessary here only to illustrate the transition from the second to the third stage with some examples. Even in the sixteenth century, in a city like Antwerp, in which a tremendous number of money transactions took place, it was almost impossible to get hold of a considerable amount of money outside the regular fairs where bills of exchange were bought and sold. The extension of this availability to any time when a person requires money indicates the transition to the establishment of a fully developed money economy. Yet it is typical of the fluctuation between rhythmical and non-rhythmical forms of money transactions and of people's awareness of them that the transactions at Antwerp were called 'the permanent fair' by those who were used to the difficulties and irrationality of money transactions in a medieval economy. Furthermore, as long as the businessman makes and receives all payments in cash, he must secure a considerable amount of cash whenever larger sums are due, and on the other hand he has to know how to invest such sums efficiently at times when his receipts arrive. The concentration of money transactions in large banks relieves him of the periodic necessity of accumulating and disposing of money. For since he and his business colleagues use the same clearing bank, assets and liabilities are now simply balanced by transferring the necessary amount from one account to another, so that the individual businessman needs only a relatively limited and stable amount of cash for daily expenses while the banks too need relatively less cash than the individual businessman did formerly because the credits and debits of different customers offset one another. Finally, I wish to give one more example. The more or less periodic fluctuations between scarcity and abundance in a period in which a money economy is not yet fully developed produces a corresponding periodic fluctuation in the interest rate from extreme cheapness to exorbitant expensiveness. The perfection of the money economy tends to eliminate these fluctuations, so that the rate of interest, in comparison with earlier periods, remains stable. Hence a change of 1 per cent in English discount rates becomes an event of major significance. In this way, the arrangements of the individual businessman become more easily adjustable and independent both of fluctuations that are beyond his control and of those fluctuations that often reluctantly forced him into bad forms of business practice.

The forms that rhythm or lack of rhythm bestow upon the contents of existence finally lost their form as alternating stages of development and present themselves simultaneously. The two principles of life that one can characterize with the symbols rhythmic–symmetrical and individualistic–spontaneous are two profoundly different trends whose opposition is not, as in previous examples, always reconcilable through integration in the course of development, but rather ultimately characterizes the permanent character of individuals and groups. Not only is the systematic form of life – as I emphasized above – the *technique* of centralizing tendencies, whether of a despotic or a socialistic kind, but also it gains an independent charm. The inner harmony and external conciseness, the harmony of the parts and the calculability of their fate, confer an attraction upon all symmetrical–systematic organizations, the effects of which exert a formative power that extends far beyond politics to countless public and private interests. Such organizations are supposed to give the individual contingencies of existence a unity and transparency that transposes them into a work of art. It is the same aesthetic attraction that is aroused by the machine. The absolute regularity and reliability of the movements, the complete removal of oppositions and frictions, the harmonious dovetailing of the smallest and largest parts, imparts to the machine, even at superficial glance, a distinctive beauty. It is this beauty that is repeated, to a greater extent, in the organization of the factory and which the socialist state is supposed to give the widest possible application. But this attraction, like all aesthetics, is based upon an ultimate direction and significance of life, upon an elemental quality of the soul. This aesthetic attraction or verification is manifested only in tangible material. We do not *possess* that elemental quality as we do its aesthetic, moral, social, intellectual, eudaemonistic manifestations in practical life, but rather we *are* that quality. These ultimate decisions of human nature cannot be put into words, but can only be sensed in those individual representations as their ultimate and guiding force. Therefore, it is impossible to argue about the relative attractions of opposing forms of life in the experience of which the aristocratic and individualistic tendencies – no matter which area of our interests is affected – confront one another. Historically, aristocracies prefer to steer clear of systematics, of the general form that places the individual in a structure that is external to him. Genuine aristocratic sentiment demands that every form of a political, social, objective or personal nature develops independently and thus proves its own value. The aristocratic liberalism of English life therefore finds the typical and, as it were, organic expression of its innermost motives in asymmetry, in freeing each individual case from the prejudices formed by similar cases. Macaulay, the enthusiastic liberal, specifically emphasizes this as the genuine strength of English constitutional life when he says: 'We do not think of symmetry, but rather of expediency; we never remove an anomaly merely because it is an anomaly; we do not set up other norms than those which are required by the specific case under consideration. These are the rules which have guided the considerations of our 250 Parliaments from King John to Queen Victoria.' The ideal of symmetry and logical roundness, which relates the meaning of every single event to a central point, is here rejected in favour of the ideal that permits every element to develop independently according to its own circumstances and allows the whole to appear as an irregular and unbalanced phenomenon. It is obvious that this contrast profoundly affects personal styles of life. On the one hand, there is the systematization of life, with its different provinces organized harmoniously around a central point, with all interests carefully graded and each content of these interests permitted only to the extent that the system makes allowance for. These comprise specific regularly alternating activities, a fixed alternation between activity and rest – in short, a rhythm in both co-ordination and sequence – that makes no allowance either for fluctuations in needs, energies and moods or for the chance of extraneous stimulations, situations and incidents. Instead, the form of existence that is established is completely secure because it excludes everything that does not accord with it or could not be successfully adjusted to its system. On the other hand, there is the formation of life from case to case, establishing the most favourable relationships between the inner demands of every moment and the corresponding exigencies of the external world, a continuous readiness for experiencing and acting combined with a constant respect for the autonomous life of things in order to do justice to their representations and requests as they arise. In this way, the calculability and secure equilibrium of life is indeed sacrificed and so is the style of life in the narrower sense. Life is not controlled by ideas whose application always leads to systematization and strict rhythms; rather, it is formed out of individual elements regardless of the symmetry of the whole, which is experienced only as a constraint rather than as an attraction. The essence of symmetry lies in the fact that every element of a whole derives its position, its justification and its significance only in relation to other elements and to a common centre. Conversely, if every element follows its own impulse and evolves autonomously and only for its own sake, the whole becomes necessarily asymmetrical and fortuitous. This conflict, in view of its aesthetic reflex, is the basic motif of all processes that are played out between a social whole – of a political, religious, familial, economic, social or any other kind – and its individual members. The individual strives to be an organic totality, a unity with its own centre from whence all the elements of his being and his action derive a coherent and consistent meaning. But if the supra-individual whole is supposed to be independently coherent and to realize its own objective notion of itself with self-sufficient significance, then it cannot possibly tolerate any independence on the part of its members. Hence it is impossible to expect a tree growing out of different trees, but only out of cells, or a painting out of other paintings, but only out of strokes of the brush not one of which on its own possesses any completeness, independent life or aesthetic significance. The totality of the whole – although it gains practical reality only in certain actions of the individual and perhaps even only within the individual – stands in eternal conflict with the totality of the individual. The aesthetic expression of this struggle is particularly impressive because the charm of beauty is always embedded in a whole, no matter whether it has immediate distinctiveness or a distinctiveness that is supplemented by fantasy as in the case of a fragment. The essential meaning of art lies in its being able to form an autonomous totality, a self-sufficient microcosm out of a fortuitous fragment of reality that is tied with a thousand threads to this reality. The typical conflict between the individual and supra-individual existence can be interpreted as the irreconcilable striving of both elements to attain an aesthetically satisfying expression.

Money, however, seems to serve the expression of only *one* of these two contrasting forms. For money itself is completely formless: it does not contain within itself the slightest suggestion of a regular rising and falling of the contents of life; it offers itself at every moment with the same freshness and efficiency; by its far-reaching effects and by reducing things to one and the same standard value, that is by levelling out countless fluctuations, mutual alternations of distance and proximity, of oscillation and equilibrium, it levels out what would otherwise impose far-reaching changes upon the possibilities for the individual's activities and experiences. It is significant that we term money in circulation 'liquid' money: like a liquid it lacks internal limits and accepts without resistance external limits that are offered by any solid surroundings. Thus, money is the most decisive and completely indifferent means for transposing the supra-individual rhythm in the conditions of life into the harmony and stability that allow a freer, more individual and more objective confirmation of our personal energies and interests. Yet it is precisely this insubstantial nature of money that enables it to support the systematization and tempo of life wherever the level of development or personal trends press for it. While we have observed that there is a close correlation between liberal constitutions and the money economy, it is just as worthy of note that money provides an extremely efficient technique for despotism, as a means for incorporating the most remote places into its rule which, in a barter economy, always tend to separate and become autonomous. And whereas the individualistic society of England has developed and become a major power through the growth of its financial system, money is also the precursor of socialistic forms of society not only through the dialectical process of turning liberalism into its negation, but also quite directly because, as we have seen, specific monetary conditions present the blueprint or type of social form that socialism strives to establish.

Money here becomes a category among the forces of life whose distinctive characteristic is that their essence and meaning is to rise above the antagonisms that exist within their respective sphere of interests and to be quite indifferent towards them while at the same time participating in these antagonisms by taking sides where once they had been unconcerned or judges. First, this is true of religion which man needs in order to reconcile the dichotomy between his wants and their satisfaction, between his moral demands and his practice, between his ideal notion of the world and reality. If such conciliation is accomplished, however, religion no longer remains upon the heights that its highest moments have achieved but steps down to the battle arena and identifies with one side of the dualism of existence which it had previously unified. On the one hand, religion confronts what we experience as our whole life as an equivalent power; it is a totality that exists above all the relativity of human nature. On the other hand, religion is part of life as one of its elements, and the whole of life depends on its interplay with all other elements. Thus, religion is both a whole organism and at the same time a single organ; it is a part of existence and at the same time existence itself on a higher internalized level. The same form is disclosed by the behaviour of the State. It is certainly in the nature of the State to stand above parties and their conflicting interests; the power of the State owes its unimpeachability and its position as the highest authority in society to this abstract level. Though the State is imbued with all these qualities, it none the less participates in the struggle of specific social forces, supports the party of one group against that of the other, which, in a narrower sense, confronts the State as another force, although in a wider sense it is a part of it. It is this dual position of the highest authorities that repeats itself in metaphysics wherever, for instance, the totality of existence is interpreted as a spiritual essence and the absolute – which creates and manifests itself in all phenomena – as a spiritual substance. Yet this absolute must, at the same time, be recognized as something relative. For in reality the spirit is confronted not only with a corporality, such that in this opposition it first realizes its own essence, but also with spiritual phenomena of an inferior kind such as wickedness, indolence and hostility. Such a metaphysics will not consider these qualities to be part of *the* spirit which is the absolute substance of being. Instead, the spirit is juxtaposed to all worldly and imperfect existence as a party, a balancing factor, a specific value, even though spirit as an absolute incorporates everything. This dual existence is most radically effective in the concept of the self. The self who conceives the world confronts all the specific contents of the world on an equally high level, independent of all qualities, differences and conflicts that exist *within* the individual, as it were, as his own private affair. But our actual sense of life does not permit the individual to remain at this high level, but identifies with certain contents more than with others – just as religion has God interfere at some points, whereas He should be equally effective at all other points. The self becomes identical with a particular content of itself, it differentiates itself, positively or negatively, aligns itself at a high or low level against the rest of the world and its distinctive features, whereas the meaning of the self had placed it above all these.

This then is the kind of form that money, in relation to its sphere of domination, shares with these other forces that are so different in terms of their content. The essence of money also lies in the abstract height to which it raises itself above all individual interests and styles of life; it gains its significance in and through the movements, conflicts and the balancing of all these, as an impartial entity which does not reveal the slightest clue for or against serving a particular interest. And then, supplied with all the unique qualities of being able to transcend distances, of concentrating power and of penetrating everywhere – qualities that are the result of its *distance* from all that is specific and one-sided – money enters the service of specific wants or forms of life. And here, despite all the general similarities that money as a form shares with religion, the State and metaphysical thought, a remarkable difference emerges. All these forces, where they identify themselves with particular interest and standpoints, become distinctly partisan with regard to one side of the conflict and opposed to the adversary; they align or identify themselves with *one* of the specific differences to which they were previously indifferent, and in so doing exclude the other differences. Money, however, offers its services equally to almost every purpose within its sphere of influence. It does not exist in an antagonistic relationship to other things as do the other forces as soon as they transform their general meaning into a particular one. Money actually preserves the comprehensive quality of its general meaning by the uniformity with which it serves protagonists when they use their general relation to money in order to work out their differences and to fight out their conflicts. In practice, the objectivity of money is not something that lies above oppositions so as to be subsequently used illegitimately by one side against the other, but is rather, from the very outset, of service to both sides of the conflict.

In so doing, however, money does not belong to the broad category that includes air, which is breathed equally by the most diverse living organism, or weapons, which are used equally by all parties to a conflict. Yet money is the most all-embracing instance of the fact that even the most radical differences and antagonisms in the human world always leave room for similarities and community of interests. But money is more than this. The other types of non-partisan entities simply remain aloof from the inner purposes that they serve. Money, however, no matter how alien it is as an abstract entity to all subjectivity and qualities, and as the economic abstract of the full extent of the universe of values, frequently displays the mysterious capacity for serving the *distinctive* essence and orientation of two antagonistic parties. The one extracts from the general reservoir of values that money represents those forces, means of expression, possibilities of communication or independence that are appropriate for its specific nature, while the opposite party receives monetary support that is no less flexible and pliable and no less helpful to *its* inner nature. The importance of money for the style of life lies in the fact that, precisely because of its complete detachment from all one-sided entities, it may be used by any one of them as its own instrument. Money is the symbol in the empirical world of the inconceivable unity of being, out of which the world, in all its breadth, diversity, energy and reality, flows. The indiscernible structure of things has to be subjectively interpreted by metaphysics in such a manner that the contents of the world form a merely spiritual context, that they exist in a mere ideality

497

and that only then – of course not in a temporal process – does existence emerge above them. It has been expressed in this manner: that the 'what' gains its 'thatness'. No one is able to say what this being actually is, which qualitatively determines the difference between the real object and the merely logically valid objective content. And this being, however empty and abstract its pure notion may be, appears as the warm stream of life, flowing into the schemata of concepts of things, allowing them to blossom and unfold their very essence, no matter how diverse or antagonistic their content and attitude may be. And yet this is nothing extraneous or strange to them, but rather it is their own essence which accepts being and develops it into an effective reality. Of all external practical things – for which any analogy to the absolute is only partially valid – money comes closest to this power of being. In its very essence it too is quite external to things and completely indifferent to their differences, so that each entity can fully absorb it and develop *its* specific nature to its fullest extent. I have particularly emphasized the significance of money for the development of the rhythmical and the specific–objective styles of life, because the incomparable depth of their opposition illustrates very clearly this kind of activity on the part of money.

The pace of life, its alterations and those of the money supply

Finally, there is a third influence by which money contributes to determining the form and order of the contents of life. It deals with the *pace* of their development, which is different for various historical epochs, for different areas of the world at any one time and for individuals of the same group. Our inner world extends, as it were, over two dimensions, the size of which determines the pace of life. The greater the differences between the contents of our imagination at any one time – even with an equal number of conceptions – the more intensive are the experiences of life, and the greater is the span of life through which we have passed. What we experience as the pace of life is the product of the sum total and the depth of its changes. The significance of money in determining the pace of life in a given period is first of all illustrated by the fact that a *change* in monetary circumstances brings about a *change* in the pace of life.

It has been asserted that an increase in the quantity of money – whether through the import of metals or the debasement of currency, through a positive balance of trade or through the issue of paper money – would leave the internal situation of a country completely unchanged. For aside from the few people whose income is fixed and not multipliable, every commodity or piece of work would increase in money value if the supply of money increased; but since everyone is a producer as well as a consumer, then the individual would earn only that much more as he had to spend, and the situation would remain unchanged. Even if such a proportionate increase in prices were the objective effect of an increase in money supply, quite basic psychological changes would occur. No one readily decides to pay a higher price for a commodity than he did hitherto even if his income has increased in the meantime; on the other hand, everyone is easily tempted by an increased income to spend more, without considering that the increased income is balanced by price increases in daily needs. The mere increase in the supply of money that one has in one's hand intensifies – quite regardless of any awareness of its mere relativity – the temptation to spend money, and in so doing promotes a greater turnover in commodities, an increase, acceleration and multiplication in economic conceptions. The basic human trait of interpreting what is relative as an absolute conceals the transitory character of the relationship between an object and a specific amount of money and makes it appear as an objective and permanent relationship. This brings about disturbance and disorientation as soon as one link of the relationship changes. The alteration in what is active and passive is in no way immediately balanced by its psychological effects. When such changes occur the awareness of the economic processes in their previous stability is interrupted from every side and the difference between present and previous circumstances makes itself felt on every side. As long as the new adjustment does not occur, the increase in the quantity of money will cause a constant sense of disorder and psychic shocks, and will thus deepen the differences and the comparative disparity between current conceptions and thereby accelerate the pace of life. It would therefore be to invite misinterpretation were one to infer a 'consolidation of society' from the continuous increase in income. It is precisely because of the increase in money income that the lower strata become agitated, a condition that – depending upon one's political viewpoint – is interpreted either as rapacity and mania for innovation, or as healthy development and energy, but which in any case is avoided where a greater stability of income and prices exists. The latter implies at the same time the stability of social distances.

The accelerating effects of an increase in the supply of money on the development of the economic–psychic process are most conspicuously displayed by the after-effects of debased paper money, in the same way as some aspects of normal physiology are most clearly illustrated by pathological and abnormal cases. The unnatural and unfounded influx of money brings about, first of all, a shaky and illogical increase in all prices. The first plethora of money only suffices to satisfy the demand for certain categories of goods. Therefore one issue of unreliable paper money is followed by another, and the second issue by yet another. 'Any pretext' – it was stated of Rhode Island at the beginning of the eighteenth century – 'served for the additional multiplication of notes. And if paper money had driven all coins out of the country, *the scarcity of silver* would have been an additional reason for further paper money issues.' The tragic consequence of such operations is that a second paper money issue is unavoidable in order to satisfy the demands that are the result of the first issue. This will make itself felt all the more where money itself is the immediate centre of the movements: price revolutions that are the result of the inundation of paper money lead to speculation, which in turn requires constantly growing supplies of money. One might say that the acceleration in the pace of social life that is brought about through an increase in the supply of money is most clearly discernible when the purely functional importance of money, without reference to its substantial value, is in question. The acceleration in the whole economic tempo is here raised to a still higher pitch, because, as it were, its origin is purely immanent; that is, it first manifests itself in the acceleration in the printing of money. This interrelationship is demonstrated by the fact that, in countries with a rapid pace of economic development, paper money is particularly apt to increase in quantity. A monetary expert states with reference to North America: 'One cannot expect people who are so impatient with small gains, so convinced that wealth can be produced out of nothing or at least out of very little, to be willing to impose upon themselves the self-restrictions which in England or Germany reduce the dangers of paper money issues to a minimum.' In particular, however, the acceleration in the pace of life that is brought about through an increase in the supply of paper money results from the upheaval in ownership. This is clearly discernible in the North American paper money economy prior to the War of Independence. The abundantly printed money which had originally circulated at a high value suffered tremendous losses in value. Whoever was wealthy yesterday could be poor today; and conversely, whoever had secured fixed values for borrowed money paid his debts back in devalued money and thus became rich. Not only did it become everyone's urgent interest to transact his economic operations as quickly as possible, to avoid long-term transactions and to learn to take up opportunities immediately; but also, these fluctuations in ownership brought about a sense of continuous change, sudden rifts and convulsions within the economic scene that spread to many other areas of life and were thus experienced as the growing intensity in the trend of economic life or as a quickening of its pace. Compared with stable money, debased money has even been considered to be of specific utility: it has been claimed that it is desirable to have debts repaid in debased money, because debtors are generally active economic producers, whereas creditors are mostly passive consumers who contribute much less positively to economic transactions. The fiduciary note-issue was not yet legal currency at the beginning of the eighteenth century in Connecticut and at the begnning of the nineteenth century in England, yet every creditor was obliged to accept it in payment of debts. The specific significance of money for the pace of economic life is further substantiated by the fact that the crisis that occurs after the excessive issue of paper money retards and paralyses economic life to a corresponding degree. Here too the role of money in the objective development of the economy corresponds to its functions as a mediator in the subjective aspect of that development: for it has been rightly pointed out that exchange is slowed down by the multiplication of the means of exchange beyond what is actually required, just as the increase in the number of brokers eases transactions up to a certain point beyond which, however, it operates as a barrier to transactions. Generally speaking, the more mobile money is, the less secure is its value because everyone tries to get rid of it as quickly as possible. The obvious objection, that trade requires two people and that the ease with which base money is given away is paralysed by the hesitancy to accept it, is not quite valid, because base money is still better than no money at all (and the same cannot always be claimed for poor merchandise). The interest in money as such has to be discounted against the distaste for base money on the part of the seller of merchandise. Hence the interest of the buyer and the reluctance of the seller to exchange commodities for base money do not exactly balance since the latter is weaker and cannot adequately limit the acceleration of circulation through the former. On the other hand, the owner of base money, or money that is valuable only under specific circumstances, has a lively interest in the preservation of the circumstances that give value to his possessions. When in the middle of the sixteenth century the princes' debts had grown to such an extent that there were widespread national bankruptcies, and when in France the sale of annuities was practised to an excessive extent, then it was stated in their defence – since they were very insecure – that in so doing the loyalty of the citizen as an owner of annuities to the king and his interest in saving him would thereby be greatly strengthened. It is significant that the term 'partisan' originally referred to a money-lender who was party to a loan to the Crown, while later, owing to the solidarity of interests between such bankers and the minister of finance under Mazarin and Fouquet, the term acquired the meaning of an 'unconditional supporter' and it has preserved this meaning ever since. This occurred during the period of greatest unreliability in the French finances, whereas during their improvement under Sully the partisans (money-lenders) moved into the background. And later Mirabeau, when introducing the *assignat* (paper currency), emphasized that wherever the currency existed the desire for its reliability ought to exist: 'You consider a defender necessary for the measures taken and a creditor interested in your success.' Thus, such money creates a specific grouping of interests and, on the basis of a new tendency towards inertia, a new animation of contrasts.

However, this assumption that these consequences of an increasing amount of money in circulation make themselves felt to a greater extent in so far as cheaper money affects producers and consumers to the same extent is far too simple. In reality such phenomena are much more complicated and volatile. This may be seen, first of all, in objective terms. The increase in the supply of money at first brings about an increase in the prices of only some commodities and leaves others as they were. It has been assumed that because of the influence of

American precious metals the prices of European goods since the sixteenth century have risen in a definite and slow order of succession. The increase in the supply of money within a country always at first affects only a specific group that takes care of the flood of money. First and foremost, a rise in the prices of those goods will occur for which members of this group compete, whereas other commodities, the price of which is determined by mass consumption, will remain cheap. The gradual influx of larger supplies of money leads to attempts to balance them out, the previous price relationship of commodities is disrupted, and the budget of each household becomes accustomed to disturbances and shifts. In short, the fact that any increase in the supply of money affects the prices of goods *unevenly* necessarily has a disturbing effect upon the process of interpretation of the situation on the part of economically active persons. It leads to widespread experiences of differentiation, to the breakdown of existing parities and to demands for attempts to balance them out. It is certainly true that this influence – partly accelerating, partly retarding – is a result not only of the unevenness of prices but also of the unevenness within money values themselves. That is, it is the result not only of the devaluation of money but, perhaps even more so, of the continuous fluctuation in the value of money. It has been said of the period prior to the great English coinage reform of 1570 that 'if all shillings had been reduced to the value of groats, transactions would have adjusted themselves relatively easily. But the fact that one shilling equalled 6 pence, another 10, and a third one 8, 6 or even 4 pence made every exchange a controversy!'

The unevenness in the prices of commodities results in a situation in which certain persons and occupations profit by a change in money values in a quite specific manner while certain others suffer considerably. In former times this was especially true of the peasantry. Towards the end of the seventeenth century, the English peasant, ignorant and helpless as he was, actually became squeezed between those people who owed him money and paid him its face value, and those to whom he owed money and insisted on payment by weight. Later the same was true in India at every new devaluation of money: if the farmer sold his harvest, he never knew whether the money received would suffice to pay the rent for his mortgage. It has long been known that wages are the last to be adjusted to a general increase in prices. The weaker a social group is, the slower and more sparingly does the increase in the amount of money trickle through to it. Frequently, an increase in income is attained only after an increase in the prices of that strata's consumer goods has long been in force. Out of this process, shocks and agitations of all kinds emerge. The growing differences between the strata require constant alertness because, in view of the new circumstances, conservative and defensive attitudes are no longer sufficient. Instead, positive struggle and conquest are required in order to preserve the *status quo ante* with regard to the relationship between the strata as well as the standard of living of individual strata. This is one of the basic reasons why every increase in the quantity of money has such a disturbing effect upon the pace of social life, since it produces new differences on top of the existing ones and divisions, even in the budget of the individual family, that must constantly accelerate and deepen the level of awareness. It is quite obvious that a considerable decline in the amount of money will bring about similar effects except that they will be in reverse. The close relationship between money and the pace of life is illustrated by the fact that an increase as well as a decrease in the amount of money, as a consequence of its uneven diffusion, brings about those manifestations of differentiation that are mirrored psychologically in break-downs, irritations and the compression of mental processes. This implication of *changes* in the quantity of money is only a phenomenon or an accumulation of the significance of money for the relationship of objects, that is for their psychic equivalents. Money has brought about new equations between objects. We compare them, one with another, according to their utility value, their aesthetic, ethical, eudaemonistic and labour value, with reference to hundreds of relationships of quantity and quality, so that their identity in one of these relationships may coincide with total lack of identity in another. Thus, their money value creates an equation and comparison between them that is in no way a constant function of other values, yet is always the expression of some notions of value that are the origin and combination of others. Every value standpoint that orders and ranks things differently and cuts across the usual mode of ordering things provides, at the same time, a new vitality for their relationship, a suggestion of as-yet unknown combinations and syntheses, of the discovery of their affinities and differences. This is because our minds are constantly endeavouring to counterbalance what is irregular and to force differentiation upon the uniform. In so far as money confers upon things within a given sphere a sameness and differentiation to a greater extent than any other value standpoint, it thereby stimulates innumerable endeavours to combine these with the ranking derived from the other values in the sense of these two tendencies.

The concentration of monetary activity

In addition to the results of changes in the supply of money, which suggest that the pace of life is, as it were, a function of those changes, the compression of the contents of life is evident in another consequence of monetary transactions. It is a peculiar feature of monetary transactions that they tend to concentrate in a relatively few places. As far as local diffusion is concerned, it is possible to establish a scale of economic objects. Here I shall indicate only some of the characteristic levels. The scale commences with agriculture, which by its very nature resists every attempt to concentrate its different areas; agriculture is inevitably bound up with the original dispersal of space. Industrial production can be compressed to some extent: the factory is a spatial condensation compared with artisan production and domestic industry while the modern industrial centre is a manufacturing microcosm, in which every kind of raw material in the world is transformed into objective forms, whose origins are dispersed throughout the world. The most remote link in this scale is money transactions. Owing to the abstractness of its form, money has no definite relationship to space: it can exercise its effects upon the most remote areas. It is even, as it were, at any moment the central point of a circle of potential effects. On the other hand, it also enables the largest amounts of value to be condensed into the most minute form – such as the $10 million cheque that was once signed by Jay Gould. To the possibility of condensing values by means of money and of condensing money by means of its increasingly abstract forms, there corresponds the possibility of condensing monetary transactions. In so far as the economy of a country is increasingly based upon money, financial activities become concentrated in large centres of money transactions. In contrast to the country, the city has always been the seat of money transactions and this relationship also holds for comparisons between small towns and cities. An English historian has stated that in its whole history London, though it never functioned as the heart of England but sometimes as its brain, always operated as its purse. Similarly, it was said that already at the end of the Roman Republic every penny that was spent in Gaul entered the books of financiers in Rome. This centrifugal force that finance possesses supports the interest of both parties: that of the borrowers because they can obtain cheaper money because of the competition of inflowing capital (the interest rate in Rome was 50 per cent lower than the average in ancient times), and that of the creditors because, although money does not have such a high value as in outlying areas, they are sure of chances for investment at any time, which is more important than lending the money at a higher rate in isolated areas. As a result, it has also been pointed out that contractions in the central money market can be more easily overcome than at the various outlying points on the periphery. Through the process of centralization that is inherent in money, the preliminary stage of accumulation in the hands of scattered individuals has been surmounted. The centralization of monetary transactions on the stock exchanges counteracted the superior power that individuals could wield by monetary means. For instance, even though the stock exchanges of Lyons and Antwerp brought enormous gains to individual money magnates during the fifteenth century, they objectified the power of money in a central institution that was superior to the power and rules of even the most powerful individuals, and they prevented the situation from arising in which a single financial house could determine the trend of world history to the extent that the Fuggers had once done.

The more basic reason for the evolution of financial centres is obviously to be found in the relativity of money. This is because, on the one hand, money expresses only value relationships between commodities, while on the other the value of every definite quantity of money cannot be as directly ascertained as can that of any other commodity; it has significance only in comparison with the total amount that is offered. Therefore, the maximum concentration of money at one point, the continuous competition of huge amounts, the balancing of a major part of supply and demand as such, will lead to the more accurate determination of its value and to its greater utilization. A bushel of grain has a particular importance at any one place, no matter how isolated and regardless of its money value. A certain quantity of money, however, is important only in relation to other values. Hence, in order to attain a stable and just valuation, money has to be confronted with as many other values as possible. This is the reason why not only 'everything presses for gold' – men as well as things – but also why money itself presses for 'everything'. It seeks to come together with other money, with all possible kinds of values and their owners. The same interrelationship operates in the opposite direction: the convergence of large numbers of people brings about a particularly strong need for money. In Germany, one of the main demands for money arose out of annual fairs organized by local lords in order to profit from the exchange of currency and the tax on goods. Through this enforced concentration of commercial transactions at a single point in a larger territory, the inclination to buy and sell was greatly increased and the need for money thereby first became a general necessity. Wherever increasingly large numbers of people come together, money becomes relatively that much more in demand. Because of its indifferent nature, money is the most suitable bridge and means of communication between many and diverse people. The more people there are, the fewer are the spheres within which they can base their transactions except through monetary interests.

The mobilization of values

All this illustrates to what great extent money symbolizes acceleration in the pace of life and how it measures itself against the number and diversity of inflowing and alternating impressions and stimuli. The tendency of money to converge and to accumulate, if not in the hands of individuals then in fixed local centres; to bring together the interests of and thereby individuals themselves; to establish contact between them on a common ground and thus, as determined by the form of value that money represents, to concentrate the most diverse elements in the smallest possible space – in short, this tendency and capacity of money has the psychological effect of enhancing the variety and richness of life, that is of increasing the pace of life. It has already been emphasized elsewhere that the modern concept of time – as a value determined by its usefulness and scarcity – first became accepted with the growth of capitalism in Germany when, during the fifteenth century, world trade and financial centres developed together with the quick turnover of cheap money. It was in this period that the church clocks began to strike at every quarter of an hour; and Sebastian Franck, who was the first to recognize the revolutionary significance of money even though in a most pessimistic manner, first called time an expensive commodity. The most characteristic symbol of all these correlations is the stock exchange. Economic values and interests are here completely reduced to their monetary expression. The stock exchange and its representatives have achieved the closest possible local assembly in order to carry out the clearance, distribution and balancing of money in the quickest manner possible. This twofold condensation of values into the money form and of monetary transactions into the form of the stock exchange makes it possible for values to be rushed through the greatest number of hands in the shortest possible time. The New York Stock Exchange, for instance, has a turnover every year that is five times the amount of the cotton harvest through speculation in cotton, and even in 1887 fifty times the total yearly production of oil was sold there. The frequency of the turnover increases with fluctuations in the quoted price of a particular value. Indeed, the fluctuations in the rate of exchange was the reason why regular stock exchange dealings in royal promissory notes [*Königsbriefen*] developed at all in the sixteenth century. For these notes, which reflected the changing credit status of, for instance, the French Crown, provided a completely different inducement to buying and selling than had previously existed with stable values. Changes in valuation are greatly increased and even often brought about by the flexible quality of money to express them directly. And this is the cause as well as the effect of the fact that the stock exchange is the centre of monetary transactions. It is, as it were, the geometrical focal point of all these changes in valuation, and at the same time the place of greatest excitement in economic life. Its sanguine-choleric oscillations between optimism and pessimism, its nervous reaction to ponderable and imponderable matters, the swiftness with which every factor affecting the situation is grasped and forgotten again – all this represents an extreme acceleration in the pace of life, a feverish commotion and compression of its fluctuations, in which the specific influence of money upon the course of psychological life becomes most clearly discernible.

Finally, the relative speed of circulation of money in relation to all other objects must immediately increase the general pace of life wherever money becomes the general centre of interest. The roundness of coins which makes them 'roll' symbolizes the rhythm of the movement that money imparts to transactions. Even where coins originally possessed corners, their constant use must have smoothed the corners and rounded them off; physical necessity has thus provided the most useful form of instrument for the intensity of transactions. For centuries in the countries bordering on the Nile there even existed globular money composed of glass, wood or agate – the differences in the material used suggests that its form was the reason for its popularity. It is no coincidence that the principle of 'rounding off' is applied with reference to large sums of money, since this principle corresponds to the expanding money economy. 'Rounding off' is a relatively modern term. The most primitive form of cheques payable to the English Treasury were tallies for any irregular amount and they frequently circulated as money. Only in the eighteenth century were they replaced by endorsable paper bills which represented rounded-off amounts from £5 upwards. It is surprising how little attention was formerly paid to rounding off, even for large amounts of money. That the Fuggers in 1530 agreed to pay 275,333 florins and 20 crowns to the Emperor Ferdinand, and that Emperor Maximilian II in 1577 owed them 220,674 florins, are not isolated cases. The development of the institution of shares followed a similar course. The joint stock of the East India Company in the Netherlands in the seventeenth century could be split up into any proportions that might be desired. Only the acceleration of transactions finally brought about the situation in which a fixed unit of 500 Flemish pounds became the only possible unit of ownership or 'share' in its trade. Even today in the retail trade, monetary transactions are calculated in rounded off amounts in places with a considerable volume of money transactions, whereas prices in more remote regions would appear to be rarely rounded off.

The above-mentioned development from inconveniently large to smaller coins and money orders clearly has the same significance for the acceleration of the speed of transactions as the rounding off process, which itself suggests a physical analogy. The need to have money in small amounts increases with the speed of transactions. In this context, it is significant that in 1844 an English bank note circulated on average for fifty-seven days before being redeemed, whereas in 1871 it circulated for only thirty-seven days! If one compares the velocity of circulation of landed property with that of money, then this immediately illustrates the difference in the pace of life between periods when the one or the other was the focal point of economic activity. One thinks, for example, of the character of tax payments with reference to external and internal fluctuations depending on the object on which they were levied. In Anglo-Saxon and Norman England taxes were imposed exclusively upon land ownership: during the twelfth century levies were imposed on the possession of cattle; shortly afterwards, certain portions of mobile property (the fourth, seventh and thirteenth parts) became taxable. The objects of taxation became more and more diverse until finally money income was made the proper basis of taxation. In so doing, taxation attains a hitherto-unknown degree of flexibility and adjustability, and the result is a much greater variability and yearly fluctuation in the contribution of individuals, combined with a greater stability of the total revenue produced. The direct significance of and emphasis upon landed property or money for the pace of life may explain the great value that very conservative peoples place upon agriculture. The Chinese are convinced that only agriculture secures the peace and perpetuation of states, and perhaps for this reason they have imposed a huge tax upon the sale of land, so that most sales of land are carried out privately and without official registration. But where the acceleration of economic life that is instigated by money has asserted itself, it seeks to impose its rhythm upon the resistant form of landed property. During the eighteenth century the state of Pennsylvania provided mortgages for private land purchase and permitted the bills to be circulated as paper money. Benjamin Franklin stated that these bills were, in reality, *coined land*. Similarly, in Germany it has been asserted by conservatives that the legislation of recent decades concerning mortages will bring about a liquidation of landed property and will transform it into some kind of paper money that could be given away in bills of any desired amount so that, as Waldeck also puts it, landed property would seem to exist only in order to be sold by auction. Not surprisingly, modern life too mobilizes its contents in the most superficial sense and in several less well known respects. In medieval times and also during the Renaissance, what we today term 'movables' or furnishings in the strict sense were little in demand. Wardrobes, sideboards and benches were built into the panelling; tables and chairs were so heavy that they were often immovable, and small movable fixtures were almost non-existent. Subsequently, furniture, like capital, has become mobile.

Finally, I wish to illustrate by means of a legal regulation the power of the trend in the money economy to subject other contents of life to its own pace. It is an old legal precept that an object that has been taken away from its legal owner has to be returned to him in all circumstances, even if the present owner has acquired it legitimately. Only with reference to money is this precept invalid: according to Roman as well as modern law, money that has been stolen cannot be taken away from a third person who has acquired it in good faith and returned to the original owner. This exception is obviously necessitated by the practice of business transactions which would otherwise be considerably handicapped, disturbed and disrupted. But recently, however, this restitutory dispensation has been extended to cover all other objects that come under rule of the commercial code. This implies that the acceleration in commercial transactions makes every commodity similar to money. It allows them to function only as money value and subjects them to the same regulations that money itself requires for the purpose of facilitating its transactions!

Constancy and flux as categories for comprehending the world

The following consideration may serve to characterize the contribution that money makes to the determination of the pace of life by its specific nature and in addition to its technical consequences that have already been mentioned above. The more precise analysis of the concepts of constancy and change reveals a dual opposition in the form in which they are realized. If we consider the substance of the world, then we easily end up in the idea of an ἐὺ χαὶ πᾶν, of an unchangeable being, that suggests, through the exclusion of any increase or decrease in things, the character of absolute constancy. If, on the other hand, we concentrate upon the formation of this substance, then constancy is completely transcended; one form is incessantly transformed into another and the world takes on the aspect of a *perpetuum mobile*. This is the cosmologically, and often metaphysically interpreted, dual aspect of being. However, if a thoroughgoing empirical method is applied, this contrast between constancy and flux takes on a different aspect. If we observe the image of the world as it immediately presents itself to us, then there are certain forms that do persist through time, whereas the real elements of which they are composed are in continuous motion. Thus, for example, the rainbow persists despite the constantly changing position of the water particles; the organic form persists despite the constant exchange of material of which it is composed. Indeed, in every inorganic object only the relationship and the interaction of the smallest parts persist, whereas the parts themselves, hidden to our eyes, are in constant molecular flux. Thus, reality itself is in a restless flux, and though we are unable to observe this because, as it were, we lack the sharpness of sight, the forms and constellations of movements solidify in the appearance of the enduring object.

As well as these two contrasts in the application of the concepts of constancy and flux to the world as it is perceived, there exists a third. Constancy may have a meaning that goes beyond any extended period of time. The simplest, but in this context a sufficient, instance of this is the law of nature. The validity of the law of nature rests on the fact that a certain constellation of elements necessarily results in a definite effect. This necessity is totally independent of *when* the preconditions present themselves in reality. Whether it be once or a million times, at this moment or in a hundred thousand years hence, the validity of the law is eternal in the sense of timelessness. Its essence and very notion exclude any change or motion. It does not matter, at this point, that we cannot ascribe unconditional validity with unconditional certainty to any single law of nature. This is not only because our comprehension, which cannot distinguish between the recurrent but fortuitous combination of phenomena and actual causal relationships, is necessarily subject to correctibility, but rather, and above all, because each law of nature is valid only for a definite state of mind, whereas for another one the truth would lie in a different formulation of the same factual state of affairs. However, since the human mind is liable to develop no matter how slowly and indiscernibly, there can be no law that is valid at a given moment that is not subject to change in the course of time. Yet this change refers only to the perceptible content of the law of nature and to its meaning and concept. The notion of a law – which exists regardless of any instance of its imperfect realization but which none the less justifies the idea and gives it meaning – rests upon that absence of all motion, upon that validity that is independent of all given conditions because they are changeable. There must be a corresponding phenomenon in the form of motion to this distinctive absolute form of persistence. Just as constancy may extend over any extent of time, no matter how long, until any relationship to a specific moment of time is simply dissolved by the eternal validity of the law of nature or the mathematical formula, so too change and motion may be conceived of as absolutes, as if a specific measurement of time for them did not exist. If all motion proceeds between a 'here' and a 'there', then through this absolute motion – the *species aeternitatis* in reverse – the 'here' completely disappears. Whereas timeless objects are valid in the form of permanency, their opposites are valid in the form of transition, of non-permanency. I am in no doubt that this pair of opposites is comprehensive enough to develop a view of the world out of them. If, on the one hand, one knew all the laws that control reality, then reality would actually be reduced to its absolute contents, to its eternal timeless significance. This would be true even though reality could not yet be constructed on this basis since the law as such, according to its ideal content, is completely indifferent towards any individual instance of its realization. But it is precisely because the content of reality is completely absorbed in these laws, which constantly produce effects out of causes and simultaneously allow these effects to operate as causes, that it is possible, on the other hand, to perceive reality, the concrete, historical, experiential appearance of the world in that absolute flux that is indicated by Heraclitus' symbolic formulation. If one reduces the view of the world to this opposition, then everything of duration, everything that points beyond the immediate moment, is extracted from reality and assembled in the ideal realm of mere laws. In reality itself things do not last for any length of time; through the restlessness with which they offer themselves at any moment to the application of a law, every form becomes immediately dissolved in the very moment when it emerges; it lives, as it were, only by being destroyed; every consolidation of form to lasting objects – no matter how short they last – is an incomplete interpretation that is unable to follow the motion of reality at its own pace. The unity of the whole of being is completely comprehended in the unity of what simply persists and what simply does not persist.

Money as the historical symbol of the relative character of existence

There is no more striking symbol of the completely dynamic character of the world than that of money. The meaning of money lies in the fact that it will be given away. When money stands still, it is no longer money according to its specific value and significance. The effect that it occasionally exerts in a state of repose arises out of an anticipation of its further motion. Money is nothing but the vehicle for a movement in which everything else that is not in motion is completely extinguished. It is, as it were, an *actus purus*; it lives in continuous self-alienation from any given point and thus forms the counterpart and direct negation of all being in itself.

But perhaps it represents, no less as a symbol, the opposite form, that of defining reality. The individual amount of money is, in fact, by its very nature in constant motion. But this is only because its value relates to the individual objects of value, just as the general law relates to the concrete conditions in which it realizes itself. If the law, which itself stands above all motions, none the less represents the form and basis of all motions, then the abstract value of wealth that is not subdivided into individual values and that is represented by money is, as it were, the soul and purpose of economic activities. As a tangible item money is the most ephemeral thing in the external–practical world; yet in its content it is the most stable, since it stands as the point of indifference and balance between all other phenomena in the world. The ideal purpose of money, as well as of the law, is to be a measure of things without being measured itself, a purpose that can be realized fully only by an endless development. Money expresses the relationship that exists between economic goods. Money itself remains stable with reference to the changes in relationships, as does a numerical proportion which reflects the relationship between many and changing objects, and as does the formula of the law of gravity with reference to material masses and their infinitely varying motion. Just as the general concept in its logical validity is independent of the number and modification of its realizations, indicating, as it were, their lawfulness, so too money – that is, the inner rationale by which the single piece of metal or paper becomes money – is the general concept of objects in so far as they are economic. They do not need to be economic; but if they wish to be, they can do so only by adjusting to the law of valuation that is embodied in money.

The observation that this one institution participates equally in the two basic forms of reality may explain the relationship of these two forms. Their significance is actually a relative one; that is, each finds its logical and psychological possibility for interpreting the world in the other. Only because reality is in constant motion is there any sense in asserting its opposite: the ideal system of eternally valid lawfulness. Conversely, it is only because such lawfulness exists that we are able to comprehend and grasp that stream of existence that would otherwise disintegrate into total chaos. The general relativity of the world, at first glance familiar to only one side of this opposition, in reality also engulfs the other side and proves to be its mistress where it only appeared to be a party. In the same way, money transcends its significance as a single economic value in order to represent abstract economic value in general and to entwine both functions in an indissoluble correlation in which neither is the first.

Money, as an institution of the historical world, symbolizes the behaviour of objects and establishes a special relationship between itself and them. The more the life of society becomes dominated by monetary relationships, the more the relativistic character of existence finds its expression in conscious life, since money is nothing other than a special form of the embodied relativity of economic goods that signifies their value. Just as the absolutist view of the world represents a definite stage of intellectual development in correlation with the corresponding practical, economic and emotional conditions of human affairs, so the relativistic view of the world seems to express the momentary relationship of adjustment on the part of our intellect. More accurate, it is confirmed by the opposing images of social and subjective life, in which money has found its real effective embodiment and the reflected symbol of its forms and movements.

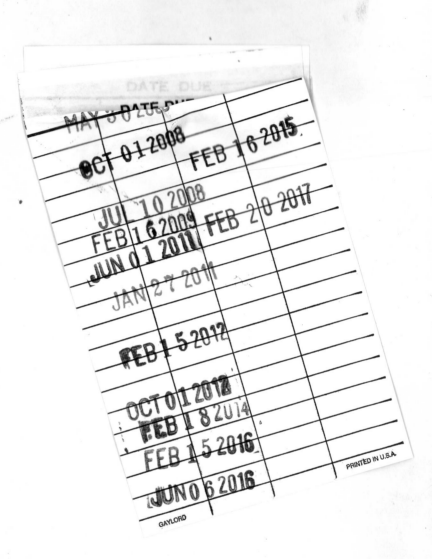